WHAT IS SEXUAL DIFFERENCE?

What Is Sexual Difference?

THINKING WITH IRIGARAY

Edited by Mary C. Rawlinson
and James Sares

FOREWORD BY ELIZABETH GROSZ

Columbia University Press
New York

Columbia University Press
Publishers Since 1893
New York   Chichester, West Sussex
cup.columbia.edu
Copyright © 2023 Columbia University Press
All rights reserved

Library of Congress Cataloging-in-Publication Data
Names: Rawlinson, Mary C., editor. | Sares, James, editor.
Title: What is sexual difference? : thinking with Irigaray /
edited by Mary C. Rawlinson and James Sares.
Description: New York : Columbia University Press, [2023] |
Includes bibliographical references and index.
Identifiers: LCCN 2022054014 (print) | LCCN 2022054015 (ebook) |
ISBN 9780231202725 (hardback) | ISBN 9780231202732 (trade paperback) |
ISBN 9780231554688 (ebook)
Subjects: LCSH: Sex (Psychology) | Sex differences. | Feminist theory
Classification: LCC BF692 .W438 2023 (print) | LCC BF692 (ebook) |
DDC 155.3/3—dc23/eng/20230210
LC record available at https://lccn.loc.gov/2022054014
LC ebook record available at https://lccn.loc.gov/2022054015

Cover design: Milenda Nan Ok Lee
Cover art: Megan Craig, *How We'd Breathe (Swimmer) 2012*, oil on canvas,
80 × 56 inches (private collection).

CONTENTS

FOREWORD
ELIZABETH GROSZ   ix

LIST OF ABBREVIATIONS (WORKS BY IRIGARAY)   xiii

Introduction: Irigaray and the Question of Sexual Difference
JAMES SARES AND MARY C. RAWLINSON   1

PART 1. THE ONTOLOGY OF SEXUAL DIFFERENCE

Chapter One
The Ontological Negativity of Sexual Difference
JAMES SARES   17

Chapter Two
Opening Hegel's Autological Circle: Irigaray and the
Metaphysics of Sexual Difference
MARY C. RAWLINSON   39

Chapter Three
One, Two, Many? Sexual Difference and the Problem of Universals
STEPHEN D. SEELY   59

Chapter Four
Returning to Irigaray's Radical Materialism: Sexuate Difference, Ontology, and Bodies of Water
LAURA ROBERTS   79

PART 2. SEXUAL DIFFERENCE BEYOND SEX/GENDER

Chapter Five
Life Itself and Sexual Difference: Nature and Culture
RUTHANNE CRAPO KIM   103

Chapter Six
Sexuation as a Frame for Human Becoming: Reading a "Plastic" Essence in Irigaray's Philosophy
BELINDA ESLICK   124

Chapter Seven
Looking Back at "This Sex Which Is Not One": Post-deconstructive New Materialisms and Their (Sexual) Difference
PENELOPE DEUTSCHER   143

PART 3. SEXUATE NATURE AND SUBJECTIVITY

Chapter Eight
An Uncontainable Subject: Thinking Feminine Sexuate Subjectivity with Irigaray
JENNIFER CARTER   173

Chapter Nine
Male Re-imaginings: From the Ontology of the Anal Toward a Phenomenology of Fluidity
OVIDIU ANEMȚOAICEI   195

CONTENTS

Chapter Ten
Sexual Difference as Qualitative Becoming: Irigaray Beyond Cissexism?
OLI STEPHANO   211

Chapter Eleven
An Onto-ethics of Transsexual Difference
MITCHELL DAMIAN MURTAGH   227

PART 4. PLACING SEXUAL DIFFERENCE

Chapter Twelve
Sexuate Difference in the Black Atlantic: Reading Irigaray with Hartman
RACHEL JONES   253

Chapter Thirteen
Bloodshed: Kinship as a Site of Violence in Irigaray and Spillers
SABRINA L. HOM   278

Chapter Fourteen
Toward a Sexuate Jurisprudence and on the "Second Rape" of Law
YVETTE RUSSELL   293

Chapter Fifteen
Place Thinking with Irigaray and Neidjie
REBECCA HILL   312

PART 5. BACK TO THE FUTURE OF SEXUAL DIFFERENCE

Chapter Sixteen
Reading *Speculum* Again: Narrative, Optics, Time
EMANUELA BIANCHI   333

Chapter Seventeen
Indebtedness: A Sexuate Malaise
IVÁN HOFMAN   356

CONTENTS

Chapter Eighteen
Mysterics: Extinction and Emptiness
LYNNE HUFFER   372

LIST OF CONTRIBUTORS   427

INDEX   433

FOREWORD

ELIZABETH GROSZ

"What is sexual difference?" is an ontological question, a question about the nature of sexual difference, its consistency, cohesion, and pervasiveness, even within a world of great variations and upheavals, differences of opinion and of definition, regarding what sexual difference is and what it might entail for social, cultural, and political life, let alone for our conceptions of nature. Ontology has received a fresh revitalization in the last decade or two, partly as a result of the overwhelming power and domination of epistemological questions in the recent history of Western thought. What we can know to a large extent depends on the history and limits of human consciousness—knowledges in the sense of truthful and practically useful abstractable knowledges, useful in different contexts and for different thinkers—and, above all, on what there is, both on the side of the knower and on the side of what is known or knowable. The epistemological reliance on the ontological has been hidden or unrecognized. This has in part helped spur a return to the more abstract and difficult—as well as undecidable—questions that constitute various ontologies, that speculate on what is and might be, on what we do not (yet) know and may never fully understand. The limits of our knowledges are not the limits of the beings and becomings that constitute what is, but our own. And these epistemic limits, and the possibilities for their reconstitution, are what enable philosophical speculation, ontological inquiry, the creation of arts, knowledges, and practices that move beyond traditional forms.

If sexual difference is an ontological force, one vigorously at work in the generation of most forms of life on Earth, and one that is particularly productive of more and more other forms difference or variation,[1] it is irreducible, and at present irreplaceable, as the processes by which life is created and regenerated. There may be more than two sexes,[2] but life's proliferation of variation requires at least two, for the increasing intensification of living differences occurs primarily through sexual difference, however this is conceived, and depending on which species one focuses on. Luce Irigaray is, of course, the preeminent philosopher of sexual difference; it has occupied her writings for close to sixty years and over thirty books, and no one has come closer to the intricate understanding of the operations of phallocentrism, the systematic erasure of femininity and its associations with negativity, lack, nature, and the Earth, than Irigaray. From her earliest dissertation work on the languages of male and female schizophrenics to her most recent writings on sexuate difference,[3] Irigaray has unfailingly insisted on the centrality and uniqueness of sexual difference—without ever directly specifying what can be included in this concept, without ever saying what it is but only ever indicating what it may do or accomplish. This insistence on its fundamental openness or indeterminacy, its virtuality, as a concept has both frustrated many of her readers, who would like a clear conception and definition of woman and women beyond patriarchal containment, and inspired others to help in the project of generating a clearer understanding of the role sexual difference plays in class, racial, ethnic, historical, and geographical differences that, taken together, constitute much of the interpersonal and political complexity of human life. Sexual difference does not replace other forms of relation between human beings and with the nonhuman world, yet it helps to constitute them as such. It cannot explain them; but without sexual difference, there can be no other kinds of human differences. Or animal differences. Sexual difference is itself not a universal or universalizing concept, but a concept that insists on heterogeneity, the failure to coincide with oneself or with the social categories under which one is classified, willingly or not. Sexual difference as such does not yet exist, for it remains covered over by the regime of the one or the self-same. But its right to exist, and the social and political necessity of its collective acknowledgment, ensures an insistence on its place still to come. Its place in existence, and in knowledge, is still anticipated, for half of all human activities have not had their chance to exist, to be recognized, to flourish and proliferate.

This volume is an exciting addition to the growing body of literature on Irigaray's conception of sexual difference. Not only are Irigaray's works carefully analyzed, explored, critiqued, debated by three generations of scholars, newer as well as more established scholars, her writings are also expanded, developed, made to ask questions that she herself has not. They are pushed, as epistemic tools, to address new questions and new political crises—race and colonialism, sexualities and sexual identifications in their potentially infinite variations, immigration, globalization, climate change, ecological catastrophes—not fully analyzed by Irigaray but in some ways anticipated by or indicated in her writings. These questions are developed further and with increasing social relevance by generations of her most careful readers. The question of sexual difference—what it is, what it can become, how variable it can be, what its limits are—cannot be definitively answered. But it cannot but be productively asked in as many different political and intellectual contexts as possible.

NOTES

1. Viruses, as we have come to learn painfully and directly in recent years, reproduce themselves, with mutating variations without sexual difference, and their centrality in the creation of life on Earth is attested to through the genetic evidence of the intrusive capacities in RNA in virtually all forms of life; but this capacity for self-generation is both dependent on other living beings, particularly bacteria, and is the condition for the evolutionary emergence of sexually di- or polymorphous reproduction.
2. Many insect species have at least three sexes, and it is possible that mushrooms and other fungi have numerous sexes. Rather than challenging or undermining Irigaray's claims, a multiplicity of sexes confirms her position regarding the "at least two."
3. For example, Irigaray, SF; Irigaray, TBB; and Irigaray, TVB.

ABBREVIATIONS (WORKS BY IRIGARAY)

BOOKS

BEW   *Between East and West: from Singularity to Community.* Translated by Stephen Pluháček. New York: Columbia University Press, 2001. (Originally published as *Entre Orient et Occident: De la singularité à la communauté.* Paris: Grasset, 1999.)

BNW   Luce Irigaray and Michael Marder, eds. *Building a New World. Luce Irigaray: Teaching II.* Basingstoke, UK: Palgrave MacMillan, 2015.

C   *Conversations,* with S. Pluháček and H. Bostic, J. Still, M. Stone, A. Wheeler, G. Howie, M. R. Miles and L. M. Harrington, H. A. Fielding, E. Grosz, M. Worton, B. H. Midttun. London: Continuum 2008.

DB   *Democracy Begins Between Two.* Translated by Kirsteen Anderson. New York: Routledge, 2000. (Originally published as *La democrazia comincia a due.* Turin: Bollati-Boringhieri, 1994.)

EP   *Elemental Passions.* Translated by Joanne Collie and Judith Still. New York: Routledge, 1992. (Originally published as *Passions élémentaires.* Paris: Minuit, 1982.)

ESD   *An Ethics of Sexual Difference.* Translated by Carolyn Burke and Gillian C. Gill. Ithaca: Cornell University Press, 1993.

(Originally published as *Éthique de la différence sexuelle*. Paris: Minuit, 1984.)

FA · *The Forgetting of Air: In Martin Heidegger*. Translated by Mary Beth Mader. Austin: University of Texas Press, 1999. (Originally published as *L'oubli de l'air: Chez Martin Heidegger*. Paris: Minuit, 1983.)

IB · *In the Beginning, She Was*. London: Bloomsbury, 2013.

ILTY · *I Love to You: Sketch of a Possible Felicity in History*. Translated by Alison Martin. New York: Routledge, 1996. (Originally published as *J'aime à toi: Esquisse d'une félicité dans l'Histoire*. Paris: Grasset, 1992.)

IR · *The Irigaray Reader*. Edited by Margaret Whitford. Oxford: Basil Blackwell, 1991.

JTN · *Je, tu, nous: Towards a Culture of Difference*. Translated by Alison Martin. London: Routledge, 1993. (Originally published as *Je, tu, nous: Pour une culture de la différence*. Paris: Grasset, 1990.)

KW · *Luce Irigaray: Key Writings*. London: Continuum, 2004.

ML · *Marine Lover: Of Friedrich Nietzsche*. Translated by Gillian C. Gill. New York: Columbia University Press, 1991. (Originally published as *Amante marine: De Friedrich Nietzsche*. Paris: Editions de Minuit, 1980.)

NCE · *A New Culture of Energy: Beyond East and West*. Translated by Stephen Seely, Stephen Pluháček, and Antonia Pont. New York: Columbia University Press, 2021. (Originally published as *Una nuova cultura dell'energia: Al di là di Oriente e Occidente*. Turin: Bollati-Boringhieri, 2011.)

S · *Speculum: Of the Other Woman*. Translated by Gillian C. Gill. Ithaca: Cornell University Press, 1985. (Originally published as *Speculum: De l'autre femme*. Paris: Editions de Minuit, 1974.)

SF · *Sharing the Fire: Outline of a Dialectics of Sensitivity*. Palgrave Macmillan, 2019.

SG · *Sexes and Genealogies*. Translated by Gillian C. Gill. New York: Columbia University Press, 1993. (Originally published as *Sexes et parentés*. Paris: Editions de Minuit, 1987.)

SN · *To Speak Is Never Neutral*. Translated by Gail Schwab. London: Continuum, 2002. (Originally published as *Parler n'est jamais neutre*. Paris: Editions de Minuit, 1985.)

SW	*Sharing the World*. London: Continuum, 2008.
TBB	*To Be Born: Genesis of a New Human Being*. Palgrave Macmillan, 2017.
TBT	*To Be Two*. Translated by Monique M. Rhodes and Marco F. Cocito-Monoc. 1994; New York: Routledge, 2001. (Originally published as *Être Deux*. Paris: Grasset, 1997.)
TD	*Thinking the Difference: For a Peaceful Revolution*. Translated by Karin Montin, London: Continuum-Routledge, 1994. (Originally published as *Le Temps de la différence: Pour une révolution pacifique*. Paris: Libraire Générale française, Livre de poche, 1989.)
TNH	Luce Irigaray, Mahon O'Brien, and Christos Hadjioannou, eds. *Towards a New Human Being*. London: Palgrave Macmillan, 2019.
TS	*This Sex Which Is Not One*. Translated by Catherine Porter with Carolyn Burke, Ithaca: Cornell University Press, 1985. (Originally published as *Ce sexe qui n'en est pas un*. Paris: Minuit, 1977.)
TVB	*Through Vegetal Being: Two Philosophical Perspectives*, with Luce Irigaray and Michael Marder. New York: Columbia University Press, 2016.
WL	*The Way of Love*. Translated by Heidi Bostic and Stephen Pluháček. London: Continuum, 2002. (Published in French as *La Voie de l'amour*. Sesto San Giovanni: Éditions Mimésis, 2017.)

ARTICLES AND CHAPTERS

AC	"Animal Compassion." In *Animal Philosophy*, edited Matthew Calarco and Peter Atterton, 195–201. London: Continuum, 2004.
BB	"Beginning with Breathing Anew." In *Breathing with Luce Irigaray*, edited by Emily A. Holmes and Lenart Skof, 217–226. London: Bloomsbury, 2013.
LM	"The Language of Man." Translated by Erin G. Carlston. *Cultural Critique* 13 (1989): 191–202.
ODS	"And the One Doesn't Stir Without the Other." Translated by Helene Wenzel, *Signs* 7, no. 1 (1981): 60–67. (Originally published

	as *Et l'une ne bouge pas sans autre*. Paris: Editions de Minuit, 1979.)
PC	"Perhaps Cultivating Touch Can Still Save Us." *Substance* 40, no. 3 (2011): 130–140.
QO	"The Question of the Other." *Yale French Studies* 87 (1995): 7–19.
SFO	"Starting from Ourselves as Living Being." *Journal of the British Society for Phenomenology* 42, no. 2 (2015): 101–108.
WML	"What Does It Mean to Be Living?" With Stephen D. Seely. *Philosophia* 8, no. 2 (2018): 1–12.
WSM	"Women, the Sacred and Money." *Paragraph* 8 (1986): 6–18.

INTRODUCTION

Irigaray and the Question of Sexual Difference

JAMES SARES AND MARY C. RAWLINSON

The very title of this volume may arouse suspicion from the reader. Does asking *what is* sexual difference already make a grave conceptual error? Does the question not already imply a determination of essences, demanding a restrictive delineation of what the sexes must be? Has feminist philosophy not already moved away from this *what* question, from universal and univocal statements about the nature of sexual difference, out of a concern for what is silenced, subjugated, or cast aside when one attempts to answer it? In reaction to this attitude, have others not rejected the question as the casting into doubt, throwing unnecessary skepticism on, a given, empirical matter of biological fact? Is the question today not philosophically nugatory from all sides?

And then there is the subtitle. Do we not find in much of the contemporary reception of Irigaray's philosophy these two oppositional attitudes toward the *what* question, each proclaiming Irigaray as an ally or adversary, located on the one side of the matter or the other? Do we not find in the reception of Irigaray's work the performance of this very opposition? On the one hand, we find Irigaray as the archetypal essentialist proclaiming a biologically determined difference between men and women, and only those two, their bodies determining their subjectivity in a predictable and generic way. On the other hand, we find Irigaray as the great subverter of prior metaphysics whose project of fixing essences is built on the constitutive silencing of sexual difference as what exceeds or subverts that project; we find the figure of the feminine as that which exceeds definition, a rejection of the *what* question as part of that earlier metaphysics.[1]

From both sides of the opposition, the question of this volume is faced with the challenge that it cannot or should not be asked. However, in typically dialectical fashion, opposites reduce to the same: the denial of the question itself and, with it, the neutering of a philosophical analysis of being that Irigaray's work diagnoses as the forgotten substance of metaphysics.[2]

This volume demonstrates not only that the question of sexual difference can be asked with Irigaray against both sides of this opposition but that her project necessitates engaging the question if we are to take seriously Irigaray's diagnosis of sexual difference as "one of the major philosophical issues, if not the issue, of our age."[3] While it might take a new understanding of *whatness* to avoid the traps of prior metaphysics, and while the seemingly simple question unfolds natural and cultural complications that may challenge its formulation in certain senses, we would be unable to speak meaningfully of sexual difference if we were to negate the question abstractly. We would be unable to discern the false paths for thinking sexual difference from the true.

Why, then, think the question of sexual difference *with Irigaray*? Or, to reverse the question, why think Irigaray focusing on the question of sexual difference? The relation between the terms of these questions is by no means arbitrary. Is there another philosopher who has been as dedicated as Irigaray to exploring the ontological and ethical dimensions of sexual difference? We find across Irigaray's oeuvre, in conversation with the figures in the history of philosophy, both a diagnosis of Western culture and metaphysics as a sexual *indifference* eliding the feminine—as some commentators in this volume note, this is a sense in which we might say sexual difference does not (yet) exist—and considerations for developing a culture in which sexually different others may be recognized as autonomous subjects in their own terms. In varied metaphysical, phenomenological, and psychoanalytic registers, Irigaray is the singular philosopher to devote a philosophical corpus to examining how sexual difference structures being and subjectivity, organizes our experience of the world, and affects the images and discourses in knowledge production and practical action. No other philosopher has examined as extensively the significance for conceiving the being of beings as sexually differentiated, refiguring our basic commitments to conceiving being itself.

One complication of positing the question of sexual difference with Irigaray is, however, the typically anatomical and copulative connotations of the word *sexual*. Although these dimensions carry an indelible importance for thinking sexual difference ontologically and ethically, even serving in a sense as the ground of their significance for human and nonhuman life, Irigaray's account moves beyond these registers. Irigaray uses the term *sexual difference* in her earlier works, already beyond such reductionism. Yet, her more recent neologism *sexuate difference*,[4] specifically as it concerns human beings (although extendable in some respects beyond the human), further emphasizes a concern with the significance of this difference in the very formation and expression of subjectivity, through the relations one develops to the world, other subjects, and, through self-affection, oneself.[5] Irigaray's broad concern lends to thinking the various cultural and historical mediations involved in living as a sexuate being, the epistemological regimes in which the body and its sex become intelligible, the relationship between this difference and other human and nonhuman differences, and the dynamism of the body's materiality, including in relation to discourse and technologies. The *what* question thus unfolds a constellation of inquiries and problematics, likewise opening the *so what* question to these expansive concerns.

The terminological shift from sexual to sexuate difference also marks Irigaray's divergence from notions of the sex/gender difference, especially in the Anglo-American context, that have developed in the last several decades, leading to confusions about her work. While she uses both terms, sometimes seemingly interchangeably, Irigaray denies the rigid division between sex as inert biological facticity and gender as an arbitrary cultural system unrelated to bodies. This is not to say, however, that sex predetermines gender identity or performance or that gender creates the material referents of sex, which only preserves the logic of their opposition by collapsing the one into the other at their oppositional extremes. With Irigaray, we may discuss the arbitrariness of various gendered stereotypes and significations without abstractly denying the role of the living body, itself culturally and historically mediated, in structuring subjectivity, hence its gendered expressions. We may discuss the dynamism of the body's materiality without denying its formal consistencies across time and among beings, including those present from birth. Even if Irigaray does not extensively engage in debates about social constructivism, her concept of sexuation can encompass insights about both historically malleable cultural mediations conditioning subjectivity and corporeality, alongside the very intelligibility of sex, and the irreducibility of structured, sexuate materiality to cultural discourse, responsive as it is to that materiality. We thus find resources for addressing the conceptual motivations behind the sex/gender division without adhering to a reductively binary view susceptible to collapse into either one-sided extreme.

Irigaray's concept of sexuation is more dialectically nuanced, we might put it, than these extremes, which would fail to do justice to the experience of the body in its limitations (that is, as active, structured, and adequating only certain possible significations, prompting as they do response from regimes of knowledge production and cultural infrastructures managing life itself), and to the possible sites of discordance between these cultural productions and one's sex in its irreducibility to them, and to the material effects of these mediations on the sexuate body, including how its intelligibility structures how we live and the gendered expressions attributed to it. The good phenomenologist that she is, Irigaray allows for these mediating complexities, refusing an appeal to "natural immediacy,"[6] or to pure bodies unmediated culturally, which can never be experienced for beings already born into culture, and an appeal to the body that would ignore its role, in its sensuousness or materiality, in enabling and resisting cultural production.

While the charges of biological essentialism against Irigaray, meaning that anatomy immediately and statically determines subjective sexuate identity, have been rebutted along these lines for decades,[7] one might nevertheless question whether, for Irigaray, anatomy structures subjectivity to give rise to certain gendered characteristics exclusive and essential to a sex. Indeed, one might criticize Irigaray's account of sexuation as pivoting on stereotypes, deriving from bodily differences distinct forms of masculine and feminine self-affection and differences in how men and women use language. How else could Irigaray's well-trodden contrasts between women's preference for subject-subject relations and men's preference for subject-object relations including in language, between women's greater capacity for self-affection due to her sexuate morphology and men's self-affection with external objects, between the female child's capacity to differentiate from the mother as another subject like her and the male child's anxiety toward and turning against the maternal, and so on be understood?[8] Indeed, these speculations seem to confirm the worst fears that the core of Irigaray's work on sexual difference is nothing but a reproduction of essentializing gender stereotypes.

Irigaray has herself resoundingly rejected the charge that her philosophy is essentialist, at least as critics use the term, denying there to be "immutable values or essences" of humanity as such and of relational sexuate subjects, feminine and masculine, who, "even if specific, [are] each time changing because of the relation(s) with another subject who does not share the same world, the same values."[9] She denies attempting to determine "one single truth or essence" of the feminine and "does not oppose a feminine truth to the masculine truth."[10] She has even denied being a "strategic" essentialist who mimics the stereotypes of women under phallocentric discourse for its internal subversion or who offers new mythical stereotypes for its subversion from the outside.[11] One problem with these strands of essentialist commentary, even of the strategic kind, is that they imply that Irigaray is making universal claims about sexuate identity, when it is not at all clear that she is speaking transhistorically and transculturally when characterizing certain cultural expressions of sex.[12] The second problem is that Irigaray's discussion of these expressions speaks to how they are reflected in the world, or might come to be reflected with the cultivation of new identities, hence as real, yet mutable and contestable, even to the level of our unconscious sexuate investments as the "reservoir of a yet-to-come."[13] Here, again, Irigaray is more dialectical than both her critics and her more sympathetic interpreters have recognized. Irigaray has even dialectically reversed the charge that she reifies stereotypes, claiming that "one might as well say that our body amounts to a stereotype" instead of unleashing its various potentials to become otherwise.[14]

As Margaret Whitford has remarked in the thick of the earlier essentialism debates, Irigaray's call to revolutionize the relations between sexes would be fatalistically nullified if subjectivity were simply predetermined by the body, gendered expressions conflated in how they are with how they must be.[15] Such essentialist readings of Irigaray are not well represented in this volume, failing as they do to recognize the dialectical complexity at work from her earliest to her most recent writings, the repeated emphasis on the dynamism of both the body and identity, and her insistence against closure. This is not to say that, taken individually, certain claims might be plausibly figured as mimicry rather than description or come across as a "real" fixing of qualities, only that, particularly when mobilized to criticize Irigaray, their interpretative weaknesses must be measured against the complexities of her general engagements with real states of affairs, morphological and discursive, in view of futural possibilities. Reading Irigaray's apparent mobilizing of stereotypes thusly, we nevertheless keep open the possibility of critiquing her descriptions of the differences between sexes, including when they figure into a more positive valuation for a sexually differentiated culture, as inaccurate, implausible, narrowly situated, or explanatorily null. We also keep open how and whether Irigaray's emphasis on the sexuate body's significance for structuring subjectivity reflects transhistorical tendencies, including whether they might be known or remain undecidable. The reader must judge whether and when Irigaray's recuperation of the feminine remains tinged with contingencies and stereotypes. In any case, it would be ungenerous to read any such invocation ignoring the dynamism in Irigaray's thought. This volume might be situated as an attempt to push beyond the limits of the earlier essentialism debates as such.

Yet another challenge to Irigaray's project, also opened by the sex/gender distinction, concerns the apparent fixing of the reference of sexual difference to a binary difference between men and women, the first term conflated with maleness and masculinity and the second with femaleness and femininity. Irigaray's rejection of essentialism in the sense given earlier is a different issue than her affirmation of the reality of sexes and that certain corporeal qualities belong to each. Irigaray's more infamous claims about there being only men and women and that these subjects inhabit irreducibly different and untraversable worlds indeed appear to substantiate fears that her account of sexual difference relies on a reductive, unproblematized, and impassable binary that fails to do justice to the lived complexities of trans, intersex, and other gender nonconforming people.[16] In response to Simone de Beauvoir's famous dictum, Irigaray has claimed that "I must still become this woman that I am by nature,"[17] which she has clarified is not meant in the essentialist sense given earlier but reflects how women are appropriated into masculine culture and must cultivate their own sexuate identity, overcoming "the scission between female and feminine identity."[18] Yet, overcoming this scission seems to be precisely the problem for some commentators. While Irigaray deconstructs the significance of the feminine in masculine discourse, one might charge that her project goes only so far in another kind of essentializing move that must be itself deconstructed: the tying of these referents to the male and female bodies of men and women. The concern, in other words, is that Irigaray's philosophy is impervious to thinking beyond a reductively two-sex model and decoupling social from biological referents, with the concept of gender referring immediately to certain subjective expressions of one's sex.

Another motivation for this volume, as we think a future of and for sexual difference, has been to respond to these concerns with nuance. Irigaray has described her own work as progressing in three phases, from a critique of the Western tradition constructed by the logics of a masculine subjectivity to ruminations on the cultivation of an autonomous feminine subjectivity to a thinking through the sharing of worlds between the two.[19] The complex entwining of the critical and the constructive veins in Irigaray's work opens space for divergent interpretations of her use of these sexed and gendered terms, even beyond her intentions. A claim about the feminine in one context might be a description of exclusion from an economy of the same and in another context be a positive giving voice to that difference yet open space for being read otherwise. What might be interpreted as the conflation of the masculine and the feminine with man and woman or male and female might be interpreted instead as distinct modes of relating to self and other often associated with, yet not irreducibly tied to, one gender or the other. At other times, masculine or feminine might be used as mere adjectivals for men and women or male and female without implying anything about their contents or qualities.[20] Irigaray's emphasis on the two might otherwise be put into relief with her mentions of the "at least" two, although Irigaray's emphasis on the two may otherwise be defended in certain respects.[21] By pulling on such threads, some contributors of this volume open readings of sexual difference beyond the perceived limitations of her account through the resources already present in her work, regardless of what her intentions might be.

At the same time, an intellectually honest and hermeneutically generous reader knows that Irigaray cannot, and does not pretend to, say everything at one go. There may indeed be a relatively unproblematized interconnectedness between the terms *male/man/masculine* and *female/woman/feminine* across Irigaray's work. These terminological interconnections might be problematized as we uptake her work for the future: For example, might at least certain stereotypes and practices culturally appropriated by the "masculine" yet exhibited by women be expressed by them as "feminine" or "masculine" without representing a scission between female and feminine identity? Might one's sense of gender identity change how and whether we describe one's sexuate qualities as masculine, feminine, or something else? Might transformations to one's sexuation allow a passage between these terms or a reconfiguration of their very limits? We do not pretend to determine univocally how Irigaray's work might be used to answer these questions. But the starting point might be to recognize how Irigaray uses these terms across her work and how that use might be different for others reading her work, in response to new identities and alternative uses of categories. Such divergences do not imply the falsity of Irigaray's account, only the need to trace how she uses terms and the motivations for doing so, even to defend these motivations against criticisms, as a reflection of differences in the world. One who challenges Irigaray's use of terms based on, for example, the disconnection of gender identity from sex, or who claims that sex is nothing "really" present at birth, might be using terms in a distinct way that can be translated back into Irigarayan terms or might operate on constitutive conceptual gaps exposed by Irigaray, revealing something left unstated or unexplained in such accounts. Exploring these questions would belong to the project of thinking *with*, even when in productive dialogue *against*, Irigaray. The contributors of this volume offer at least some ways of engaging Irigaray thusly.

With such an approach, Irigaray's philosophy reveals the continued urgency of reckoning with sexual difference as "the most basic, universal and irreducible difference,"[22] one that cuts across cultures as a global condition of human being, in a culture currently caught between the undialectical extremes of a reductive essentialism and the denial of the reality of sex itself as anything natural, and at least of its political saliency. If Irigaray considers other culturally constructed human differences as "secondary problems" to sex ontologically speaking,[23] she never labels sexual difference as the "most intense" difference,[24] as if sex matters more than any other difference in a reductive and nonintersectional political hierarchy. Her qualification that race might not be a secondary problem from a "geographical point of view" has been interpreted to indicate that, in the context of colonial parsing of lands, "racial difference, as an instrument of oppression, is not secondary."[25] Still, with this qualification, the challenge for today remains explaining why and how sexual difference has mattered, continues to matter, and will matter in its unique status as the mediator between nature and culture and as it intersects with other differences. The timeliness of reckoning with sexual difference with Irigaray anew, in response to shifting terrains of sexual and gender identity and campaigns for racial and environmental justice, will therefore be made clear: If we are to form a new, positive conception of the human being, indeed of life itself, sexual difference is to be confronted in its actual and possible complexities.

This volume gives voice to a diversity of perspectives on the question of sexual difference in Irigaray's philosophy, opening conversations between philosophers across traditions and disciplines. The reader may trace the interpretative convergences, divergences, and incommensurabilities that arise between authors, in their reckoning with the guiding question of the volume. We do not pretend to exhaust the possibilities of thinking sexual difference with Irigaray, or to cover all the themes and interlocutors engaged by her, only to reveal the continued importance of Irigaray's work, which at times involves moving beyond its limits for rethinking the ontological and political significance of sexual difference. The constellation of chapters provides the reader an opportunity to consider the complex facets of Irigaray's philosophy, how it may be interpreted and interpreted *otherwise*, as a testament to the fecundity of her work and its ability to sustain a readership and be continually reread and renewed. As is the case with Irigaray, none of the authors can say everything at one go. Together, however, these chapters cut across the three periods of Irigaray's work, its critical and constructive strands, and engage the multiple readings of sexual difference that emerge therefrom, in response to the question of this volume.

The first section of this volume, "The Ontology of Sexual Difference," might be contentious for two reasons: first, many, if not most, of the chapters in this volume interrogate the ontological significance of Irigaray's account of sexual difference; and second, they do so by engaging and developing distinct, perhaps at times even conflicting, senses of the ontological. Although imposing sections in a collection of essays might involve a degree of arbitrariness, the chapters in this section clearly consider the significance of sexual difference for conceiving the being of beings, especially the human being—that is, what it means for a being to be a sexuate being, what it means for sexes to exist and structure being. Together, these chapters unfold the importance of Irigaray's interventions into the question of sexual difference as a question of being, both in response to a tradition that understands being as neuter in which the masculine is in fact unmarked and universalized (repressing the ontological significance of sexual difference), and also for imagining futures for sexual difference, confronting in what sense this difference structures one's being and being with others as sexuate, or as (at least) two.

Responding to the complex mediations between nature and culture in Irigaray's philosophy, the second section of this volume, "Sexual Difference Beyond Sex/Gender," develops an analysis of sexual difference in response to the sex/gender binary in contemporary feminist philosophy. These chapters reveal how Irigaray's concept of sexuation problematizes such a rigid binary, refusing both the binarized separation of nature (sex, anatomy) and culture (gender, discourse) and also the symptomatic collapse of the one term into the other extreme in what remains a binarized logic of one-sided determination. These chapters thus offer new ways of conceiving sexuate subjectivity beyond the premises of the earlier essentialism debates about her work. Indeed, as these chapters demonstrate, the concept of sexuation allows instead for a more complex form of mediation between the two terms, implying neither their identity nor their reified difference but a distinction allowing for some reference to the biological body in an understanding of gendered belonging. In turn, these chapters consider more "plastic" readings of these relations.

A discussion of the ontological nature of sexual difference, as a difference between (at least) two, threatens to become abstract if not considered in their morphological determinations—that is, in terms of *how* this difference manifests in the formation of sexuate subjectivity. The third section of this volume, "Sexuate Nature and Subjectivity," more directly thematizes this incarnation of difference as it concerns the mediating relations between nature and culture. It is here that some of the more dangerous work of conceiving the expressions of feminine and masculine subjectivity in Irigaray's philosophy, alongside their future possibilities, takes place. Yet, tarrying with the sexuate limits of the body and their significance for the sexuate expressions of subjectivity does not imply an essentializing move on Irigaray's part. The morphological, rather than a deterministic brute anatomy, concerns for Irigaray a subjective style of being in and through one's bodily limits as they are mediated culturally and discursively. The authors of this section thus see Irigaray as a philosopher of change, of a future open to new expressions of sexual difference. And we also find in this section resources in Irigaray's own accounts of feminine and masculine sexuate subjectivity for thinking with and beyond these categories as cissexual terms.

The fourth section of this volume, "Placing Sexual Difference," understands "placing" in two senses: first, in terms of placing sexual difference in relation to other kinds of differences, particularly in the context of coloniality and technicity; and second, in terms of the place of sexual difference in structuring relations between subjects and their environments. While these chapters less directly engage its ontological significance, they expand the notion of sexual difference to capture aspects of its more general significance in Irigaray's philosophy. This section also allows us to confront the charges that Irigaray leaves whiteness uninterrogated or unmarked in her writings, bringing to question how this absence misses opportunities for examining the intersections of sex with other cultural differences, applying Irigaray's critiques of phallocentrism to other contexts and revealing lacunae in her own work on sexual difference. While this section cannot provide an exhaustive survey of the intersection of sexual difference with other differences and identities, it demonstrates the value of Irigaray's philosophy of sexual difference in these contexts, challenging the notion that an Irigarayan account of sexual difference reduces to any sort of colonial gender project while recognizing Irigaray's limits on these questions.

Although this volume may be generally oriented to the future possibilities of sexual difference, the essays in this final section, "Back to the Future of Sexual Difference," return to Irigaray's *Speculum of the Other Woman* to think this future, underscoring its continued saliency almost fifty years after its publication. Since Irigaray has developed an extensive philosophical corpus on sexual difference since the publication of this magnum opus, we might be tempted to view her later works to be more representative of her mature philosophical position on the matter. The chapters in this section demonstrate instead that returning to Irigaray's early work may provide the most salient insights for thinking Irigaray with the question of sexual difference today and beyond. These essays also close the volume because they reflect, more directly than others, Irigaray's disruptions to phallocentric regimes of representation and, as Lynne Huffer writes in her creative exegesis, "the conditions of the sayable and the seeable" in them. As such, we conclude the volume with this section in part as a warning against getting caught in ossified regimes of representation and against falling into a logic of the same when positing the very *what* question guiding this volume.

Together, the chapters of this volume underscore the continued vitality of Irigaray's thought on sexual difference. They offer routes for future engagement with her work and its promise to think through sexual difference as the issue of our age.

BIBLIOGRAPHY

Hill, Rebecca. "The Multiple Readings of Irigaray's Concept of Sexual Difference." *Philosophy Compass* 11, no. 7 (2016): 390–401.

Whitford, Margaret. "Rereading Irigaray." In *Between Feminism and Psychoanalysis*, edited Teresa Brennan. London: Routledge, 1989.

NOTES

1. "The question 'what is . . .?' is the question—the metaphysical question—to which the feminine does not allow itself to submit." Irigaray, TS, 122.
2. One field in which sexual difference remains a pressing concern is Lacanian psychoanalysis. One of Irigaray's trenchant critiques of Lacan's account of sexual difference is its supposed refusal of the conflation of the penis with the phallus, or the tying of men and women to any anatomical referents, despite those repeated conflations across Lacan's own writings. Irigaray, IR, 86. The best Lacanians today work against these conflations but, in doing so, cut reference to the sexuate body or gender identity.
3. Irigaray, ESD, 5.
4. We will henceforth use the terms *sexual* and *sexuate* interchangeably.
5. Irigaray, SF, 52.
6. Irigaray, ILTY, 107.
7. Margaret Whitford, "Rereading Irigaray," in *Between Feminism and Psychoanalysis*, ed. Teresa Brennan (London: Routledge, 1989), 106–107.
8. For some examples, see Irigaray, DB, 152–153; Irigaray, SW, 101–104; Irigaray, IB, 148–158; Irigaray, JTN, 22–30; Irigaray, TBT, 57.
9. Irigaray, C, 78–79.
10. Irigaray, ML, 84.
11. Irigaray, C, 78–79.
12. For example, "I am not claiming to isolate in any *absolute* way the most important elements in the language spoken by men and by women. I can speak only of what I have observed." Irigaray, SG, 172.

INTRODUCTION

13. Irigaray, IR, 82.
14. Irigaray, SF, 30.
15. Whitford, "Rereading Irigaray," 106–107.
16. See, for example, Irigaray, ILTY, 47; Irigaray, JTN, 122–123.
17. Irigaray, ILTY, 107.
18. Irigaray, C, 78.
19. Irigaray, 124. As Irigaray admits, critical and constructive elements are to be found as early as *Speculum*.
20. Specific examples might be open to contestation. We simply ask: Might concern with the connection between the feminine and its ties to female morphology or womanhood in Irigaray's work not abate when it (at least sometimes) becomes a simple adjective for the one or the other?
21. Irigaray, ILTY, 37.
22. Irigaray, C, 133.
23. Irigaray, ILTY, 47.
24. Irigaray, C, 133.
25. Rebecca Hill, "The Multiple Readings of Irigaray's Concept of Sexual Difference," *Philosophy Compass* 11, no. 7 (2016): 397.

PART I
The Ontology of Sexual Difference

Chapter One

THE ONTOLOGICAL NEGATIVITY OF SEXUAL DIFFERENCE

JAMES SARES

The purpose of this chapter is to defend the ontological character of sexual difference through two senses of negativity in Irigaray's philosophy: a generational negativity by which beings sexually reproduce, giving rise through sexual difference to offspring that are not them; and a negativity characterizing a being's own sexual differentiation, marking its sexuate specificity and relating it to another sex that it is not.[1] While these two senses of negativity may overlap conceptually, they prove to be distinct senses in which sexual difference may be understood ontologically, that is, as an essential determination whereby a being can be that which it is. Indeed, sexual difference determines the being of beings insofar as those beings, in their finitude, involve a negative self-reference or essentially refer in themselves to the difference between sexes. Such beings cannot be themselves except under the condition of sexual difference—to other sexes that they are not.

Despite discussing the ontological significance of sexual difference in terms of negativity, Irigaray does not directly describe sexual difference using the term *negative self-reference*.[2] The term is in fact Hegelian, referring to the idea that a limit not only marks the negation of being but also determines that being through its negation.[3] According to Hegel, finitude is, logically speaking, the kind of existence that depends essentially on its own negation. A finite being exists under the condition of a limit at which it ceases to be and on the other side of which something else exists as equally limited. Therefore, the negativity of a limit is not simply a negation of being but an affirmation of being through the negation, rendering that being determinate in its finitude. The contradiction plaguing finite beings is that they are insofar as they are not; they are something in themselves only insofar as they assert their identity by being negated by otherness.[4] The concept of identity made possible only through difference seems, however, to be at the heart of Irigaray's philosophical project, concerned as it is with a difference unthought in other ontologies.

This chapter provides less a strict exegesis on Irigaray's philosophy than an attempt to develop an account of sexual ontology with it, extending and reformulating aspects of her work in the process. Rather than focus on a particular text, I consider how the question of ontological negativity is a throughline from her earliest to most recent works. I attempt to avoid collapsing her views into mine and mine into hers. But the space between us may draw out the presuppositions and consequences implicit in her work or develop those insights otherwise, albeit with an indelibly Irigarayan ground of possibility for that thought. To this end, I first examine the two forms of ontological negativity in response to Irigaray's account of sexual difference. I then consider the referents of this ontology, exploring challenges with fixing reference to the sexuate nature of its negativity. Finally, I consider the objectivity of this ontology or the reality of sexual difference in response to skeptical challenges. I do not resolve all conceptual problems and ambiguities in these two latter sections, demonstrating instead how the ontology developed in the first section flexibly responds to their concerns. The chapter thus sketches the terrain on which the problems themselves may be confronted for a sexual ontology.

TWO FORMS OF SEXUATE NEGATIVITY

Following Irigaray, sexual difference does not have a hypostatized existence over and against the beings whose existence it structures, as if in a realm separated from life itself. The ontological investigation of sexual difference therefore turns to how individuals incarnate this logic of difference in and through the bounds of their singularity, as the finitude of the living body.

ONTOLOGICAL NEGATIVITY OF SEXUAL DIFFERENCE

We are wont to think abstractly.[5] When determining what something finite is, we think of the qualities or relations it exhibits in the here and now, as it appears before us. The abstractness of such a mode of description lies in how the given immediacy of that appearing is in fact mediated by relations of coexistence and causal dependence. When we are tasked with describing a cup on our table, for example, we might think we do well to describe its color and shape as it appears; when thinking abstractly, we do not think to describe the entire nexus of relations under the condition of which it appears as itself. Yet, upon further consideration, it proves tautologous that anything finite can be what it is only under an entire series of conditions that may not appear in the sensuous immediacy of that being itself.[6] Without the conditions inhering in it as its ground, the being could not arise and persist as itself. Indeed, a finite being is not simply its own immediacy but also, more concretely, the effect of a prior causal series and part of a greater space in which it exists. If we were to give a proper account of what that cup is, we would be tasked with describing its systematic, relational locus in space and time. In turn, while not independently self-subsisting, the finite being is itself something determinate in space and time, unfolding its potentialities as that being and limiting others beyond it as well. It remains something of its own but as mediated.

Where one conceives a limit in a continuous whole may be arbitrary, technically speaking, but follows from its differentiation into delineable individuals, qualities, and kinds.[7] If we explain a finite being in the world, rather than the world in its imagined totality, we may distinguish between causal chains bringing forth that being in its individuality and the coexisting externalities conditioning those delineated causal series. While even those externalities must be involved in the causal process insofar as it determines the series in the whole, one may distinguish between proximate and remote conditions, alongside spatial and material contiguities involved in transformations, as the ground for the distinction and the delineation of particular causal series.

An account of the generational negativity of sexual difference, which operates through causal series in time, may be understood as a modification of the more general logic of temporal finitude. What is time but the form of continuous change negating being into not-being and not-being into being? What exists in time undergoes this negation, being no longer what it was or will be. This negation applies to any worldly being or event whatsoever; even what perdures as "the same" in time is marked by the negativity of no longer being precisely the same insofar as its previous state comes to an end by persisting in its being beyond that state. As such, anything exists temporally by virtue of the negation of its identity into otherness, determined in relation to the rest of time by its constitutive limits as something of its own as well. Because time implies causality, meaning antecedent states serve as the ground for whatever follows from them by transforming into them, prior causes inhere in the finite being following from it, while the being is not those conditions as they were or will be, as if it were nothing of its own in its perduring.

While everything in space and time is related to sexual difference, and while everything generally falls under the logic of finitude, we may refer more specifically with the concept of generational negativity to the particular causal series in the world whereby, through sexual reproduction, sexes give rise to offspring of their kind. Since *Speculum* and even more clearly in her recent work on birth, Irigaray has considered the ontological significance of this generational condition. In *To Be Born*, she characterizes the condition of our sexuate life as a having been "born as one from a union between two," which is a "not appropriable event," meaning an origin of being that is not fully our own and that is dependent on the acts of other living beings.[8] Irigaray's scattered mentions of sexual difference beyond human life lend to the extension of this principle in her work to various kinds of beings existing under this reproductive condition.[9] For such beings, sexually differentiated reproduction is one of the prior conditions to which those beings refer essentially as their ground. As such, those beings refer to the relational structure of sexual difference in their singularity; they are possible in the immediacy of their existence under the condition of a difference that this immediacy does not exhaust. As Irigaray explains, "we have been conceived by two but we are only one, even if we embody something of the two who have conceived us."[10] The one that is here and now cannot have come to be without the union of the past difference as its ground but is not itself that difference in arising and realizing itself as one.

Extending Irigaray's account of generational reproduction, just as we may trace the inherence of prior conditions in what exists presently, so too may we consider the ontological significance of generational effects on prior causes. Assuming the unidirectionality of time, it may be more contestable to argue that the future serves as the ground of past conditions, thus belonging to the description of what it is for them to be themselves as those prior conditions. Yet, by giving rise to future conditions, past conditions implicate the future conditions as what is to be drawn from themselves, out of the potentialities they carry by virtue of being themselves.[11] Indeed, just as a being cannot be what it is without past conditions, it cannot be what it is without giving rise to future effects. Regarding generational negativity, a being is limited not only by the sexual other that it is not yet into which it enters a union but also by those differentiated beings to which it gives rise and will not be. The generational negativity of sexual difference operates immanently through the finitude of that being, marking an essential self-reference to a difference under whose condition it realizes certain sexually differentiated potentialities. Its generational negativity is thus another kind of negative self-reference unfolding effects from itself under the condition of sexual difference. To give an example: my mother had not yet given birth to me before she gave birth to me, but her will have given birth to me was one of her determinations prior to my birth.[12]

Let us consider two complications concerning this form of generational negativity. First, the sexuate nature of this negativity, or the required union of two sexes, may be transformed, even negated, by technological mediations or evolutionary developments.[13] Nevertheless, the reproductive logic of sexual difference might reappear later or, if not, at least serve as a more remote condition. Whether as a proximate or more remote cause, sexual difference serves as part of the prior series of conditions allowing for a being to arise as itself. Second, these aspects of generational negativity may not be at work in the same being. We may imagine a first generation of living beings that does not depend on prior copulative unions, being instead the very origin of sexual difference itself. In that case, only the latter sense of generational negativity would be operative. We may also imagine subsequent generations of beings that arise from prior copulative unions between sexes but that do not themselves engage in them. Only the former sense of generational negativity would be operative in that case. So long as one of these senses is operative, however, a being would refer to the generational significance of sexual difference.

For Irigaray, generational negativity does not exhaust the ontological significance of sexual difference. Despite her concern with birth and generation, Irigaray has repeatedly emphasized that it would be a mistake to conflate the ontological significance of sexual difference with reproduction alone. Such thinking treats sexual difference as a mere "tool" for continuing life rather than as a structure enabling the cultivation of a being's singularity and various kinds of nonreductively reproductive relationships that beings may establish with others and their environments.[14] One may therefore charge that, with a focus on generational reproduction, one illicitly fixes the referent of sexual difference to certain functions, failing to grasp its broader ontological significance.

One may respond to charges of reductionism in two ways. First, the ontological significance of sexual difference does involve the aspect of generational reproduction. Irigaray emphasizes that natural dependencies, particularly the gestation of the mother, have been left unthought in the history of philosophy. Our condition of having been born from a union between two is to be theorized if we are to rectify the false, historical neutering of sexual difference by the ontologies constructed following that history. Second, underscoring the reproductive significance of sexual difference does not exclude the other kinds of ontological significance it holds. While some reference to the qualities and structures associated with generational reproduction may be irreducible for discussing sexual difference, reproduction does not exhaust its significance. Indeed, there is a distinction between discussing the qualities associated with generational reproduction, even labeling them as sexuate, and reducing those qualities to that association. One's sex is irreducible to heterosexual copulation or generational reproduction, indeed need not engage in these activities at all; we know that our sexes can do much more than these functions, which indicates that reducing them to this one function is already an exercise in abstraction. It would require a certain teleological account, for example, one assuming a divine standpoint dictating how the body is supposed to be used, to distinguish the essential from the accidental functions of one's sex. Irigaray's conception of sexual difference warns precisely against this form of teleology.

Following Irigaray's rejection of the reduction of sexual difference to reproduction, another sense of ontological negativity may be marked by the presence of a being's own sexually differentiated body. Most clearly in *I Love To You*, Irigaray writes that sexual difference "inscribes finitude in the natural itself."[15] In the context of human subjectivity, hence with reference to gender,[16] Irigaray presents the negativity of sexual difference as the renunciation of the pretension of being the whole: "I am not the whole: I am man or woman. And I am not simply a subject, I belong to a gender. I am objectively limited by this belonging."[17] One is not "entirely one's self" given the relation to another sex, both genealogical and horizontal, constitutive of the very possibility of one's sex, hence to one's identity as a sexuate being. Irigaray's account of the negativity of sexual difference may be extended in view of the more general logic of finitude as negative self-reference. For any sexuate being, sexual difference marks a condition whereby a being is differentiated according to the shared logic of generational reproduction between sexes for whatever kind of being it is. The one sex is essentially related to the other by virtue of being the not-all of the kind of being it is.

The language of "kinds" may require qualification for interspecies reproduction, evolution, and ostensibly sexuate organisms whose reproductive logics do not neatly follow a model of distinct sexes of its kind. In anticipation of the problem of fixing reference, we may nevertheless preserve the generality of the formulation, allowing for debate over how one might specify or broaden the meaning of kinds to account for or exclude various complications from this ontology.

Despite speaking of the presence of the being's differentiated body, it would be a mistake to characterize the difference between this second sense of ontological negativity and the first sense as a difference between spatial coexistence and temporal difference. Besides the problem that the temporality of worldly finitude is already spatialized, meaning that experience takes the form of a temporalized space, the second sense of ontological negativity may be expansive enough to include reference to sexually differentiated others across time, not simply coexistence in the here and now. Although Irigaray does not discuss such a scenario, one might argue that other sexes need no longer exist, for instance, due to extinction or technological intervention, for a being to relate essentially to them in this second sense. While sexual difference may not be present among many concurrently existing beings as such, the difference would remain operative in determining the presence of the individual itself, determined as it is in relation to differences across time. That being would continue to be sexually differentiated as a member of some kind irreducible to the one sex. As such, that being need not reproduce with others or even maintain active relationships with others of its kind for this second sense of ontological negativity to be inscribed in or as its finitude.

The second sense of ontological negativity may therefore include generational negativity. A sexuate being relates to sexes it is not by virtue of arising from the difference of sexes. The one cannot exhaust the two in its oneness, necessarily relating to different sexuate expressions than its own. Even if the individual were to internalize the structures and qualities of two sexes, it would still not be the all of their sexual difference, differing from the two in their very distinction as two.

Despite the conceptual overlap between these two senses of ontological negativity, thought experiments demonstrate a conceptual distinction between them. We might imagine a case in which the generational negativity of sexual difference is alone operative, for instance if a mutation were to arise allowing non–sexually differentiated beings to arise from sexually differentiated progenitors, or vice versa. It is more difficult to conjure a scenario in which a sexually differentiated being has no relationship whatsoever to a generational negativity, although one might imagine a sexuate being arising from nonsexuate causes and engendering no future generations of its own. Whether such a being would be meaningfully sexuate is another question, one challenge being under what conditions such a being would belong to a kind whose reference is fixed to a structure of generational reproduction, including if we imagine this being as the only individual or sex ever of its kind or in relation to another sex coexisting with it or arising at an entirely different time in the same way. We may leave this question open for further scrutiny.

It does not escape me that these thought experiments are far removed from life as we know it. For good reason, Irigaray's work, phenomenologically invested in how life does appear, does not seriously entertain such scenarios. Still, thinking through the scenarios may provide a buffer against equally contrived attempts to deny the ontological significance of sexual difference.

THE REFERENTS OF SEXUAL DIFFERENCE

Although these accounts provide the framework for understanding the ontological negativity of sexual difference, the question remains to which beings this account extends and to which qualities it may be taken to refer. Must this account of ontological negativity make a definitive judgment of its conceptual extension and intension? Although some determinations must be made for a meaningful sexual ontology, is some analytic vagueness a hindrance or benefit?

ONTOLOGICAL NEGATIVITY OF SEXUAL DIFFERENCE

One difficulty with fixing the reference of sexual difference lies in the Scylla of trivialization. For a sexual ontology, there persists a threat of extending the notion of sexual difference so widely as to reproduce a neuter ontology. When sexual difference and being are identified, sex becomes as abstract as being itself, losing its sexuate specificity. How does one meaningfully say that the inorganic elements or single-celled organisms like bacteria follow the relational logic of sexual difference? What comes of sexual difference if it is broadened to the exchanges between living beings and their environments broadly conceived or, in the Deleuzian-Guattarian vein, to a thousand tiny sexes as rhizomatic exchanges in the body and its milieus? Irigaray herself has spoken at times as if life in general, even the elements themselves, were sexuate: "No world is produced or reproduced without sexed difference. Plants, animals, gods, the elements of the universe, all are sexed."[18] Yet, given Irigaray's later characterization of even plant life as neuter or nonsexuate,[19] and the persistent concern in her philosophical corpus to examine the sexuate specificities of the body, it seems implausible to read such conceptual abstractness into her account of sexual difference. For Irigaray, a rethinking of sexual difference may require a rethinking of space and time, the elements, and life itself against phallocentric accounts; the horizons of experience and the imaginaries by which we conceive being may be sexually differentiated. We do not therefore imply that sexual difference is being *as such*.

Against the trivialization of sexual difference, one might consider our following distinction. In a technical sense, everything in space and time is negatively self-referring to sexual difference by being part of a greater whole with it, hence being limited by it; being as such is sexually differentiated in the technical sense that its identity is constituted through a negative self-reference to sexual difference. However, only certain beings are sexually differentiated in the sense of having their own sex, thus relating to sexuate others from within the relational logic itself.

The other difficulty with fixing the reference of sexual difference lies in the Charybdis of arbitrariness. When restricting the concept of sexual difference to certain sexuate characteristics or expressions, one might be charged with arbitrarily delineating sex when its relational logic may apply more broadly. Although reference to characteristics associated with generational reproduction may be irreducible if we are to avoid the Scylla, one might be expansive or restrictive when fixing reference to sexual difference or the difference between sexes, including which characteristics matter in delineating sexes and which characteristics are designated as sexuate. An account may stake normative claims about how and when qualities must appear or function, or when they must be present in development, for a being to be classified as a sex or sexed at all.[20] Depending on how the reference of sex is fixed to certain characteristics or functions, there may be inclusions or exclusions of some kinds of organisms or individuals in a sexual ontology. Might individuals lacking characteristics that are determined as essential to a sex nevertheless be sexuate by exhibiting other sexually differentiated effects or qualities? How do beings that develop sexuate characteristics from an initially neuter state fall under this ontology? Do fungi mating types fall under the two senses of ontological negativity in this chapter, despite lacking a sex as typically defined? Do these two senses of ontological negativity apply to hermaphroditic organisms who internalize the difference between two as parts of their being one? In what sense might exclusively parthenogenic beings like some lizards be sexuate? How do beings confounding typical notions of selfhood exhibit a negative self-reference as a particular being? An appeal to biological classification as the deciding factor begs the question, as the question is the classification itself.

While I do not pretend to resolve all challenges of fixing reference in this chapter, we might nevertheless consider the problem as a problem. In response to what may be perceived as too expansive or restrictive fixing of reference of sexual difference, competing conceptual schemas may appear, whether in total exclusion or partial agreement. Different conceptual schemas may be mobilized in different contexts as deemed relevant. In contemporary debates, the often-unacknowledged complication with competing schemas is that their exclusion does not imply the truth of one against the other, if truth means staking a claim to objective fulfillment according to whatever conceptual delineations introduced for categorizing worldly being. We need not deny the complications of value-ladenness and perlocutionary force in recognizing that our concepts also correspond to sensuous being irreducible to them and against which their adequacy may be measured. If distinct conceptual schemas stand the common test of adequation with the worldly being they categorize, the conflict between them may be more complicated than a simple difference between truth and falsity. Rather, one might find the fixing of reference, the definitions of concepts, or standards for epistemic adequacy to be too restrictive or expansive. One might otherwise disagree out of a sense of failing to do justice or give voice to phenomena in their nuances or in the ethical or practical demands they make on us. One might exclude certain individuals from their ontology as unintelligible, hence nonsexuate, that others would include. Debates might arise regarding how to categorize individuals in a sex. The disagreement between competing conceptual schemas might then turn from an unreflective adherence to one's own schema as "true" to the self-reflective recognition that the consistency of other schemas lies in their use of concepts or definitions that one might reject.

Let us return to Irigaray. If we find across Irigaray's philosophy descriptions of the sexuate body, we nowhere find attempts at precise definitions or classificatory schemas for delineating sexes or determining which beings incarnate its relational logic. One does not find in Irigaray's philosophy any sustained attempt to delineate or localize the "truth" of one's sex.

One might charge that the lack of such classificatory considerations is symptomatic of an unproblematized account of sex as between two ideal kinds. Irigaray often discusses the relational structure of sexual difference in terms of "the two" and has recently begun using the term *heteros*, which refers to a difference between two of something (eyes, lips, feet, sexes).[21] While the two also has a more general significance in her work, representing an encounter with an other transcendent to me in their sensible presence, it also holds a more specifically sexuate significance in her work, particularly for human beings, reflecting how human life and our cultural infrastructures have been structured around a difference between two sexes. Following our qualifications about fixing reference, challenges based on a lack of specificity, the value-laden and perlocutionary force, or the conceptual extension of this claim do not imply its falsity per se.

Although the language of twoness might be charged with instantiating a reductive binarism that elides the various complexities of sexuate expression,[22] Irigaray's account might be read otherwise in line with her other philosophical commitments. First, Irigaray has also used the phrase "at least two" in the context of sexual difference, bringing forth several lines of inquiry left unexplored in her work.[23] In her discussions of the *heteros*, Irigaray underscores qualitative differences between relations of two and of many. Still, one might emphasize in the concept of the two not its twoness per se but the notion that sexuate being is relational more generally. While Irigaray does not discuss a scenario in which three sexes would be involved in generational reproduction and does not consider possible alternatives for categorizing sexes beyond male and female, the principle that sexuate being is relational, hence negatively self-referring, would hold in these cases as well. Second, although Irigaray might not give enough analytic attention to it, there is a difference between claiming that a reproductive logic is structured according to a difference between two sexes and claiming that there are no possibilities for sexuate embodiment beyond a certain ideal of those two.[24] Intersex phenomena may involve constellations of traits expressing aspects of a sex or recombining qualities associated with different sexes. Trans phenomena may involve the transformation of certain sexuate qualities and an identity of others across time. Beings might lack or express certain sexuate qualities otherwise. Future technologies may transform sexuate expressions in ways not yet realized. Most generally, sexuate life implies a continuous self-differing that may include the development of qualities over time, changes in the constellations of qualities, and their fluctuations and divergences. Given this dynamism, the generational logic of sexuate life may itself be open to formal transformations over time.

While a formal[25] difference between sexes, or positing them as kinds, does not contradict the multiplicity of sexuate expressions in individuals, neither does this multiplicity contradict the determinacy of this difference as it appears among individuals. The categories of sex may then correspond to perceived relevant differences without implying a naivety about the multiplicity of individual sexuate expressions, differentiated as they are in relation to a shared generational logic.

Despite Irigaray's general lack of discussion about these complications, other contributors to this volume underscore how, with the concept of a "frame" or *Gestell*,[26] Irigaray attempts to think both the determinacy and the dynamism of living beings, tracing how sexuation is both delimited relationally and given the space through this very determinacy to potentials for development and transformation into the new. For Irigaray, the determinacy of sexual difference does not collapse into the identification of anatomy with destiny and, concerning the human being more specifically, does not stake claim to a biologistic determinism of subjectivity, as if historical modes of domination were predestined from the composition of bodies themselves.[27] Irigaray's phenomenological concern with the living body, alongside her ethical concern to reconfigure relations between the sexes,[28] would be betrayed if we were to conceive sex as a timeless and inert structure imposed on beings rather than as the structure in which beings develop through their relations to the world and to themselves. As such, Irigaray opens us to examining how sexuate structure opens and forecloses opportunities for development by mediating connections between self and world. We may trace how historical structures have transformed one's experience of and through the body at the same time as recognizing how opportunities for development occur within determinate limits. Following Irigaray, sexuation provides a being with space for becoming.

A critical reader of Irigaray might remain skeptical of this characterization of her work, considering instances of homogenizing stereotypes concerning the differences between men and women, particularly in how they use language, how they use self-affect, and how they relate to others.[29] Where, however, does she proclaim those observations to be universal and inevitable? Where in her work does she proclaim those observations to be historically unmediated by a homogenizing culture? Where does she deny that identity remains to be developed, not assumed as a "natural immediacy"?[30]

Because sexual difference is not statically imposed on beings, it is an abstract exercise to debate whether the formal differentiation of characteristics as kinds or the individual expressions of sex are ontologically prior. A sexuate being cannot exist as meaningfully sexuate without a determinate difference between sexes, at least sexuate characteristics associated with generational reproduction, while its sexuate qualities would not be its own if they were not individually expressed. To deny this, one no longer talks of the sexual difference with whose ontological implications we are concerned or fails to recognize the complexities of sexuate being in its name. We thus find our response against alternative ontologies that might trivialize or erase sexual difference from the perspective of a radical nominalism[31] or another ideological commitment: either they lack a meaningfully sexuate specification or fail to they draw their conclusions without denying the truth that a sexuate ontology unfolds. Yet, challenges to that truth are to be confronted.

THE REALITY OF SEXUAL DIFFERENCE

The conceptual extension of this sexuate ontology would be a matter of indifference if the two senses of negativity described in this chapter refer to nothing in the world. Do our concepts stand the test of experience, proving to be not inadequate impositions on natural objectivity but a reflection of the structure of this objectivity? Is sexual difference objective, a necessary structure of human and nonhuman existence, not a contingent cultural construction we project on ourselves and other beings? Irigaray does not entertain these questions in her philosophical corpus, assuming the view that sexual difference is finitude inscribed in the natural or life itself. Nevertheless, these questions serve to clarify the underlying presuppositions of Irigaray's realism about sexual difference and whether the ontology in this chapter must align with it to stake a claim to reality.

Although Irigaray recently argued that sexuate desire "overcomes the traditional opposition between realism and idealism," by which she means "an objectivity, which is unconcerned about our subjectivity, and the aspirations arising from our internal being alone,"[32] her philosophy assumes a realism in the sense of taking us to be born into a world preexisting us. Such a realism may be, as Alison Stone explains, in line with a branch of the phenomenological tradition taking perceptual experience not to be "a self-contained realm of representations" but to give "us access to things in the world, so that the contours of perceptual experience simultaneously are the structure of the world."[33] Irigaray thus affirms the objectivity of sexual difference in two senses. First, for Irigaray, sexual difference is a real structure of being in the world to which our concepts correspond. Second, Irigaray posits sexual difference as the condition of possibility of various beings and for human subjectivity, as something "given" to and by them as a structure of life itself, even as it is from within the structure of sexual difference that our subjectivity develops.[34] As such, Irigaray's philosophy is directed against abstracting from or eliding the living body in its real dependencies and limitations, particularly in its having become in relation to sexuate others.

The question of the natural givenness of sex, which for our purposes we might understand broadly as its presence as the structure of the living bodily materiality,[35] might be further complicated considering two issues. The first issue concerns a rather obvious yet often overlooked distinction between the historical construction of concepts and the validity of those concepts beyond localization to those historical conditions. Indeed, the historical construction of concepts does not imply their nonuniversality. Following the complications of fixing reference, one need not deny the historical developments in the definition and classification of sexes to allow that the referents to these concepts exist transhistorically as determinations of sexuate beings—that is, that newer definitions or classifications *would have been* evidentially fulfilled. Nor need one deny that expressions of sex might evolve or be negated over time, hence that certain expressions prove non-universal or that sex itself has a history. Depending on our conceptual schemas, new evidence might lead to the refinement, extension, or alteration of categories, particularly if previous proclamations prove unjustified against the test of evidential adequation, or be ignored altogether. The second issue concerns the condition of possibility of cultural (discursive, technological) production. If sexual difference is not a necessary determination of beings, including human beings, how have these productions been possible with the tides of generations? Does sexual difference not serve as the precondition of the life subtending the possibility of denying it as such a precondition? One need not appeal to a pure, culturally unmediated body to affirm this is so.[36]

While the reduction of sexuate nature to contingent cultural construction would be evaded by admitting that such conditions do not *create* their material referents, at least in all relevant respects, it is another question if one affirms the contrary. One need not deny the material reality of sex once it is produced thusly,[37] although a variation of this claim might be to deny its reality beyond our discourse *about* it in another muddied (and probably incoherent) form of idealism.[38]

Yet, even if these positions were to prove incoherent, the general gesture is not so easily dismissed. The most radical recourse for one skeptical about the ontological nature of sexual difference may be to appeal to the illusoriness of the objectivity on which the ontology is grounded. Might sexual difference correspond to nothing outside of its appearing in our experience, whether because there is nothing outside of our conscious experience at all or because our conscious experience is the site of the appearing of this difference, with external reality being otherwise indifferent to it? What if the world does not precede my consciousness but, in an idealist twist, I am the condition of the appearing of the sexually differentiated world itself? Might this world be a hallucination, an extended dream, or a filtering of sensations and images from an external source into my brain or mind? Do these possibilities not challenge both senses of negativity discussed in our sexual ontology, problematizing the claim to the generational power of sexuate beings in the external world and their sexuation as anything with an enduring reality of its own?

Irigaray's philosophy stands in direct repudiation of such speculations. From the perspective of her philosophy, for instance, in view of her criticisms of Descartes,[39] do these speculations not reflect a philosophical tradition of neutering ontology by denying the dependence of the thinker on sexual difference as a having become through the body of another subject, a m/other? Does the reversal of dependence between world and self not emerge out of a masculine fantasy of autoaffection that attempts to reduce the other to the expression of the same? Does this reversal not exemplify a narcissistic drive to reverse my dependence on the world by claiming that *I* have birthed *her*, that *my* consciousness is *her* source of being, that *she* is nothing outside of *my* intending of *her*? In entertaining these questions, do we risk reenacting a primordial matricide?[40]

Such charges do not, however, imply the logical absurdity of these speculations. The epistemological limitation laid bare by this challenge is that one does not have an experience outside of one's own experience, and therefore claiming access to reality as it lies outside of experience is evidentially unfulfilled speculation. One who adheres to such an idealism may respond to the realist that appealing to the natural world and others in it as it preexists our existence begs the question, asserting that which the position challenges given the limits of experience. Indeed, one who adheres to a realism about this external reality makes their arguments only ever from within those limits. Following G. E. Moore's infamous proof, one might hold one's hand in front of oneself and then the other, and conclude there to be these two external objects in the world. Yet, the determination of these objects as external occurs already from within the horizons of experience that cannot be transcended. One would then beg the question.

Without a demonstration of the logical impossibility of such an idealism, the most radical skepticisms remain possibilities to be confronted by our sexuate ontology. Despite ridicule from dogmatists, skepticism reappears as a symptom of a failure to know what lies beyond experience. To risk making a sweeping claim whose defensibility lies beyond the scope of this chapter, the history of philosophy has never produced a definitive proof that the objects of experience correspond to the same objects outside of experience. If one were avoid being charged with begging the question, to lay skepticism about the issue to rest, a proof for one position would require demonstrating not only that the opposite position engenders logical contradictions but also that it is itself free of any contradictions itself. While there may be specific forms of realism and idealism that prove self-consistent or absurd, one would require moving beyond the equipollence between the positions as such. The nature of the problem seems to make this an impossible task.

If it is at least conceivable for the intentional contents of consciousness to represent nothing materially enduring outside of experience, then Irigaray's account of sexual difference might be undergirded by a realist premise that, in the final instance, cannot be accepted as self-evident. What significance might such a challenge have for an ontological account of sexual difference?

If we were to commit to a phenomenological suspension of belief about the nature of being outside of its appearing in experience, the objectivity of this experience would be retained. While it might appear as if we would lose everything by challenging the realist premise of Irigaray's philosophy, we would retain the richness of our experience as it so appears. It is logically inconceivable for conscious experience to be nothing at all since it appears. Although certain claims proclaiming knowledge beyond experience would be suspended, we may turn to an analysis of the constitution of beliefs about the external world and our birth into it through its appearing in experience. With the restriction of an analysis of being to the contents of experience, the two senses of ontological negativity discussed in this chapter may be formulated in terms of the appearing of sexually differentiated phenomena. If one were to carry out a phenomenological reduction to the immanent contents of experience, one might trace the source of our beliefs about sexual difference, including that sexual difference is our own original condition of possibility, in terms of both direct intuitive evidence and indirect or signitive intentions, the latter including what we intend as historical traces and the discourses of other subjects.[41] The ground for a sexual ontology would turn on the description of the constitution of these beliefs and this evidence in their various complexities, through confirmations we experience as our evidential fulfillment. With experience providing access to the being described by our ontology, sexual difference would continue to appear or be signaled as a relational logic reproducing life and differentiating beings.

If one were to adhere most strictly to a phenomenological reduction, the pretension of attaining perfect adequation between numerous commonsensical judgments and worldly being would be renounced. In tracing the immanent constitution of experience, we reflect on the limits of intuitive evidence for our concepts. While we might claim direct access to objects, we constitute objectivity only through the irreducible partiality of perceptual adumbrations. While the temporality of experience must be causal, the after causally dependent on the before, we attribute causality to worldly beings when the problem before us is that their appearance might be the epiphenomenal residue of an underlying cause. While we might claim access to the self-identity of beings over time regardless of our perceiving them, we lack perfect knowledge that particular beings remain what they have been or exist as self-same outside of direct intuitive evidence.

Although one might think these qualifications excessive, and Irigaray would reject this form of phenomenological analysis, they also provide an opportunity to reflect on the concepts concerning sexual difference and to reformulate the two senses of ontological negativity to accommodate evidential limits. One need only to refer to the immanent constitution of conscious experience in the concepts themselves for them to correspond to being understood in terms of directly or indirectly realized evidence. Technically, we might even preserve the adequation of concept with being with these qualifications to our concepts; the concept of a sexuate being might be reformulated, for instance, to correspond to a series of perceptual adumbrations, while various complex temporal phenomena may correspond to other kinds of evidential criteria.

Regardless of whether we transform our concepts as such, however, a critical reflection on the limits of evidential adequacy may allow us to reflect critically with our concepts on the constitution of beliefs about sexual difference, including its temporally extended structures. We also open space for the critique of transhistorical pronouncements about where and how the ontological negativity of sexual difference has been at work, reflecting how beliefs about the past and the future are informed by indirect evidence. We might avoid conflating past evidence with future impossibilities, including our assumptions about our sexuation and that of others. A fecund space for rethinking sexual difference would then open from the pits of our reaction to skepticism.

The two senses of the ontological negativity of sexual difference with which we are concerned may thus be preserved, even if Irigaray would accuse us of neutering at least some of its sexuate significance as a preexisting worldly structure of life into which we our inscribed in our finitude. That accusation may be an irreducible consequence of challenging the realist premise underlying her account of sexual difference. Still, we have not denied the logical coherence of that premise or demanded that one must turn to a phenomenological reduction as the method for analyzing the ontological significance of sexual difference. Rather, we have been considering how a skeptical challenge to the reality of sexual difference implies a critique of all reality and, even then, cannot do away with in its being given or having been given in experience. The point is simply this: to deny sexual difference would be to deny being itself in its very appearing.

Having examined two senses of ontological negativity, their referents, and challenges to the reality of those referents, let us conclude with a final question: Why concern ourselves with the ontology of sexual difference—that is, if the logic of finitude applies to any kind of finite being whatsoever, why consider sexuate being more specifically? Across her writings, Irigaray demonstrates how the eliding of this difference has been a condition at the heart of Western culture and metaphysics. Her work uncovers the ontological significance of sexual difference in structuring life itself, in compelling and structuring our desires and relationships, and in organizing historical divisions of labor. The answer to our question is therefore simple: sexual difference matters and has mattered. It will matter because it will have mattered. If we are to conceive being anew and to build new worlds, as Irigaray puts it, our ontological negativity remains to be thought through.

BIBLIOGRAPHY

Grosz, Elizabeth. *Sexual Subversions: Three French Feminists*. Sydney: Allen and Unwin, 1989.

Jones, Emma. "Finding/Founding Our Place: Thinking Irigaray's Ontology of Sexuate Difference as a Relational Limit." In *Building a New World*, edited by Luce Irigaray and Michael Marder, 15–30. New York: Palgrave Macmillan, 2015.

Hegel, G. W. F. *The Science of Logic*. Translated by G. di Giovanni. Cambridge: Cambridge University Press, 2010.

Sares, James. "Irigarayan Ontology and the Possibilities of Sexual Difference." In *Horizons of Difference: Rethinking Space, Place and Identity with Irigaray*, edited by Ruthanne Crapo, Yvette Russell, and Brenda Sharp, 117–136. Albany: SUNY Press, 2022.

Stone, Alison. *Luce Irigaray and the Philosophy of Sexual Difference*. Cambridge: Cambridge University Press, 2006.

Whitford, Margaret. "Rereading Irigaray." In *Between Feminism and Psychoanalysis*, edited by Teresa Brennan, 106–126. London: Routledge, 1989.

NOTES

1. While these themes are found almost ubiquitously across Irigaray's works, see especially Irigaray, ILTY, 41, for a discussion of sexual difference in both generational and horizontal terms. Other scholars, for example, Emma Jones, have underscored Irigaray's account of sexuate limit as relational. See Emma Jones, "Finding/Founding Our Place: Thinking Irigaray's Ontology of Sexuate Difference as a Relational Limit," in *Building a New World*, ed. Luce Irigaray and Michael Marder (New York: Palgrave Macmillan, 2015), 15–30. Note, however, that my concern with sexual difference in this chapter does not focus on human subjectivity or identity in Irigaray's work; as such, I use the term *sexuate* without any strictly human implications to refer to sexed being. Nevertheless, my aim is to unpack one of the essential ontological questions in her work, which would aid in that analysis.

2. For examples of Irigaray's use of the term *negativity* regarding sexual difference, see Irigaray, ILTY, 105; and Irigaray, SF, 58.

3. G. W. F. Hegel, *The Science of Logic*, trans. G. di Giovanni (Cambridge: Cambridge University Press, 2010), 101.

4. Hegel, 101.

5. This consideration of ground and inherence in space and time is distinctly Hegelian—and, I would venture, something with which Irigaray would agree. For Hegel's analysis of the dialectic between ground and concrete existence, see Hegel, 386–417.

6. For my purposes, sensuous immediacy can be read as something given in the "here and now," even if nothing is purely self-present in time.

7. I avoid discussing paradoxes regarding limits of continuous wholes and will presuppose space and time to be continuous here, although the point works just as well otherwise.

8. Irigaray, TBB, v. See also Irigaray, ILTY, 40, for a similar account of being engendered from two.

9. See, for instance, Irigaray, ILTY, 36; and Irigaray, SG, 107.

10. Irigaray, TBB, 38–39.

11. I will not make further claims about the reality of past and future here.

12. I will bracket questions about the indeterminacy of the future; the example might be reformulated depending on one's stance.

13. See my discussion of technology, which has served as an impetus for the analysis of ontological negativity in this essay but proves too specific for my more mature formulation here, in James Sares, "Irigarayan Ontology and the Possibilities of Sexual Difference," in *Horizons of Difference: Rethinking Space, Place and*

Identity with Irigaray, ed. Ruthanne Crapo, Yvette Russell, and Brenda Sharp (Albany: SUNY Press, 2022), 117–136. I would also add that, in the hypothetical scenario in which technological interventions were to allow members of the "same" sex to reproduce with one another, no longer requiring the "other" sex, sexual difference might even be reformulated in terms of their relations through those intermediaries, although I keep this question open here.

14. See, for instance, Irigaray, SF, 19–22; Irigaray, ILTY, 11. See also Irigaray, SW, xv.
15. Irigaray, ILTY, 35.
16. I will not examine the term *gender* here, although other chapters in this volume engage that question in Irigaray's philosophy.
17. Irigaray, ILTY, 106. See also Irigaray, TBT, 92, for another example of this ubiquitous theme in Irigaray's work. Note also how Irigaray expresses this as a phenomenological difference between "worlds" in such texts as *Sharing the World* (see Mary Rawlinson's chapter in this volume).
18. Irigaray, SG, 178.
19. Irigaray, TVB, 79. One might reject a characterization of plants as nonsexuate.
20. On this point, why would we assume that all members of a sex must share the same quality? Could a sex be defined according to two characteristics, the presence of the one or the other sufficient to label members of the same kind?
21. Irigaray, IB, 146; Irigaray, TBB, 50; Irigaray, SF, 99.
22. Irigaray opens herself to this charge with her infamous claim that there are only men and women and nothing else. Irigaray, ILTY, 47. Her more recent claim that human life operates insofar as "one masculine being and one feminine being . . . gave birth to a boy or to a girl" appears to follow in this vein. Irigaray, TBB, vi. Yet, we might read Irigaray otherwise.
23. Irigaray, ILTY, 37.
24. Note that one might challenge conceptual privileging of sexual difference as between two sexes, including how the two might reappear in our own descriptions of the complications of trans and intersex phenomena. Where one might demand a new category of sex to destabilize the privileging of the discourse of the two, another may interpret differences in terms of the two.
25. Here I am not implying a form separate from matter or eternally unchanging but thinking in terms of consistencies and repetitions.
26. Irigaray, TBB, 3. Irigaray clearly divorces *Gestell* from its Heideggerian implications.
27. Elizabeth Grosz, *Sexual Subversions: Three French Feminists* (Sydney: Allen and Unwin, 1989), 113–119.
28. Margaret Whitford, "Rereading Irigaray," in *Between Feminism and Psychoanalysis*, ed. Teresa Brennan (London: Routledge, 1989), 106–107.
29. See my discussion in the introduction to this volume.
30. Irigaray, ILTY, 107.
31. How could one deny that different beings can fall under the same concept insofar as they exemplify what the concept unfolds? That is all that one needs to claim that our concepts are exemplified in the world.
32. Irigaray, SF, 66.
33. Alison Stone, *Luce Irigaray and the Philosophy of Sexual Difference* (Cambridge: Cambridge University Press, 2006), 111–112. In the secondary literature, there is

some debate over to what extent Irigaray is a "phenomenological" or "post-phenomenological" thinker, although I take Stone's formulation to reflect a central tenant of her work.
34. See, for example, Irigaray, TBB, 3.
35. Others in this volume discuss the complexities of the relationship between "nature" and "culture" in Irigaray's work, a question to which I cannot do justice here.
36. Once there is culture, at least for beings enmeshed in culture, the body *must* be mediated by the larger social whole in which it is embedded, which does not, however, imply that the body is nothing but culture. This is a rather obvious point following the claims about finitude I have made earlier. So is the idea that, assuming that linguistically articulate human subjectivity arises only in intersubjective contexts, sexuate identity is *necessarily* mediated thus, which also does not mean that the sexuate body is not involved in forming subjectivity, albeit perhaps in at times undecidable ways.
37. One complication that I will not explore here is whether it would be coherent, on my account, for a "neuter" or nonsexuate kind of being to become sexuate and remain the same kind of being. Would that neuter being not retroactively be sexually differentiated as not-all in terms of sex vis-à-vis the other sexes? Would it, instead, no longer be considered the same kind of being? The same considerations might be reformulated for imagining a nonsexuate substratum for the mere appearance of sexual difference, as discussed later.
38. This is not the space to engage in an immanent critique of social constructivism, including Judith Butler's nuanced version, which does not claim that discourse fully creates its material referents. It would require examining the limits of discourse, the knowability of what lies outside discourse, and so on, measured against one's premises and metaphysical presuppositions, to engage in such an immanent critique.
39. Irigaray, S, 181–182.
40. I use these pronouns purposefully to reflect Irigaray's emphasis on the forgetting of dependence on the mother in the history of philosophy.
41. Note that the phenomenological attitude to which I am referring is distinctly Husserlian in nature and terminology.

Chapter Two

OPENING HEGEL'S AUTOLOGICAL CIRCLE
Irigaray and the Metaphysics of Sexual Difference

MARY C. RAWLINSON

> Time is the concept itself that *is there* and which presents itself to consciousness as empty intuition: for this reason, spirit necessarily appears in time just so long as it has not *grasped* its pure concept; i.e., has not annulled time. . . . Time, therefore, appears as the destiny and necessity of spirit that is not yet complete within itself.
>
> —G. W. F. HEGEL, *PHENOMENOLOGY OF SPIRIT*, #801

> As soon as I recognize the otherness of the other as irreducible to me or to my own, the world itself becomes irreducible to a single world: there are always at least two worlds. The totality that I project is, at any moment, questioned by the other. The transcendence that the world represents is no longer one, nor unique. . . . [The transcendence of the other] reopens the autological circle of the transcendental horizon of a single subject . . . the transcendental gesture that is fitting to their human existence becomes one of building with the other a relation in which space and time are, at any moment, in-finite and becoming.
>
> —LUCE IRIGARAY, *SHARING THE WORLD*, IX-X

When reading Irigaray on the irreducibility of sexual difference, it is important to remember that she is writing *against* specific philosophical forces in the history of metaphysics. Throughout her career she has engaged with most of the major figures of metaphysics to show how the repression of sexual difference in philosophical thought generates an abusive relation to nature and to human nature, and, more specifically, how it produces the commodification of women's bodies and their reduction to materiality in contrast to man's rational spirit.

Across her writings, from *Speculum of the Other Woman* to *Sharing the Fire*, Irigaray's critique has depended on an undoing of Hegel's "autological circle," his attempt to produce from a phenomenology of consciousness a pure logic, freed from existence.[1] Irigaray clearly has Hegel in mind when she writes in the opening of *Sharing the World*

When the world corresponds to the transcendence projected by a single subject as the horizon of the totality of all that exists, this world converts time into space. Although such a transcendence represents a temporal project on the part of the subject, the fact that this subject ensures, from a unique standpoint, the gathering or closure of the whole of finite things results in the world closing up, even in advance, in a circle.

In Hegel's narrative of human experience in the *Phenomenology of Spirit*, absolute knowing appears as the "circle" that encompasses the whole, to which there is no outside. Absolute knowing is the nonperspective that anticipates each and every determinant perspective. As the thought of all the possible forms of existence, it "annuls" time and turns time into space. In absolute knowing, the difference from the other, sexual difference, has been erased.[2] The production of Hegel's absolute knowing subjects each one to the logic of the same so that the difference of the other is "unfolded" (*aufheben*) as indifferent or philosophically insignificant. From the nonperspective of absolute knowing, each one is substitutable for the other without remainder, and difference, even sexual difference, makes no difference.[3]

Against this Hegelian hegemony of the one and its logic of the same, Irigaray develops a counterconcept of transcendence based on the irreducible two figured in sexual difference. Rather than a transcendence toward the universal that produces and reproduces the same, she invokes a more complicated logic, in which the other is always already inscribed in the arc of my own transcendence *as irreducibly other and not the same.*

While readers, myself included, rightly often read Irigaray as an advocate for justice, for each other and for the rest of nature, her ethics and politics have always been grounded in what I will risk calling the *metaphysics of sexual difference*.[4] Thinking sexual difference not only requires a transformation of human relationships; it requires as well rethinking the philosophical concepts of time and space, identity, existence, and transcendence. Indeed, Irigaray's ethics of "building with the other" toward a more just and "livable" future depends on the revolution she effects in these fundamental metaphysical concepts.

INFINITE BECOMING: RETHINKING TIME AND SPACE

> Spirit is in itself the movement of cognition.... The movement is the circle that returns into itself, the circle that presupposes its beginning and reaches it only at

OPENING HEGEL'S AUTOLOGICAL CIRCLE

> the end.... Spirit is differentiated into its intuited concept, into *time* and into the content or into the *in itself*.... Until spirit has completed itself *in itself*... it cannot reach its consummation as *self-conscious* spirit.
>
> —G. W. F. HEGEL, PHENOMENOLOGY OF SPIRIT, #802

> So long as the other subject remains alive and free with respect to another world, especially to my world, time and space are kept in a dialectical process between us in an always indefinite and open way.
>
> —LUCE IRIGARAY, SHARING THE WORLD, X

> Through the union between two naturally different identities, the absolute itself receives new matter and configuration. It is up to each one to contribute to the qualitative nature of such an absolute, so that it could give rise to both a more accomplished humanity and more responsible relations between all the living beings.
>
> —LUCE IRIGARAY, SHARING THE FIRE, 85

Hegel's project in the *Phenomenology of Spirit* is nothing less than the articulation of all the possible forms of consciousness and all the possible forms of objectivity in the system of their genetic relationships.[5] Beginning where we find ourselves, with the certainty of sensuous immediacy, the method of self-interrogation, in which consciousness attempts to "say what it means" or to articulate the certainty of his experience, will generate a series of shapes, each one more comprehensive than the last.[6] The phenomenological interrogation terminates at that point at which "knowledge need no longer go beyond itself because nothing is other to it." Every domain of experience, every possible object will have been articulated and positioned with respect to other domains and objects in the completed series.

The series, however, forms a circle: "For the self-knowing Spirit, just because it grasps its concept, is the immediate identity with itself which, in its difference, is the *certainty of immediacy or sense-consciousness*—the beginning from which we started."[7] The series of shapes generated one from another through the interrogation will have been implicit in sensuous immediacy all along, just as the oak will always have been the truth of the acorn, or the man, the boy. The necessity of the series is guaranteed by the genetic relationships: the interrogator will not have "imported any of his own bright ideas." The interrogation will have purified immediacy of its opacity and substituted for it the lucidity of the concept.

Absolute knowing appears as an "autological circle"—it is explicitly figured as a circle in Hegel's text—whose closure will put an end to time and open the way for a "pure" logic, detached from sensuous experience. Substance has been transformed into subject, life into the "life of the concept," in which life, the mortal, and the sensuous count *only as concepts*.

Absolute knowing appears as the last and unique shape. It is not a form of life or a mode of cognition, as are the other shapes; rather, it is the thought of the whole system of shapes as whole. In this thinking, thought recognizes itself as pure movement, distinct from the determinate shapes or forms of life that are produced by it. This thought in Hegel's account "annuls" time and releases the "pure 'I'" from its adherence to the substantiality of consciousness and objects. Through the phenomenological interrogation, "Spirit has won the pure element of its existence, the concept." Phenomenology, and Hegel's repeated insistence that the concept is only realized as the infrastructure of life, are left behind for a pure logic and a transcendence that is the same for each and all.

Hegel writes as if consciousness could be freed from the conflict between its experience and its concept of itself. Yet, it is precisely this inadequation that drove the phenomenological analysis. Indeed, on Hegel's account, being is an effect of becoming, and this inadequation of the concept and experience is nothing less than life or desire. Yet, the achievement of absolute knowing, the adequation of the concept and being, Hegel insists, "releases consciousness from the form of its self," and constitutes "the supreme freedom and assurance of its self-knowledge."[8] This form of the self, of experience, from which absolute knowing is exempt is nothing less than time itself: "when [spirit] grasps itself it sets aside its time-form."[9] Absolute knowing does not appear in time as do the shapes of consciousness. Spirit "necessarily appears in time," but "just so long as it has not *grasped* its pure concept, i.e., it has not annulled time." Absolute knowing, then, strictly speaking does not exist. It is not subject to the flux of becoming, nor is it differentiated within itself as to what it is and will be, i.e., it has unfolded the difference between concept and experience that drives forward phenomenology and life itself into the transparency of the concept.

The stillness of absolute knowing, the repose of the pure I of pure thought or logic, is the same for each and all. Absolute knowing, the "pure I," converts substance into the concept and stands nowhere and outside time. It has been produced by working through all the domains of life, discovering the concept as their infrastructure, as the concept of the carpenter is the infrastructure of the table or the concepts of divine and human provide the infrastructure of religious experience. Yet, Hegel would "free" the concept from its immersion in life, from time, from becoming, in order to install a master narrative that anticipates the other in advance, bending becoming back on itself in the autological circle.

After his scathing critiques of the abstract concept and his repeated insistence that the concept is only realized as a form or infrastructure of life, Hegel, nonetheless, extracts from experience a pure I given only in thought and the "aether" of the concept. Certainly, the determinate contents of consciousness in the flux of becoming must be distinguished from the movement of self-consciousness, that negative operation in which consciousness knows itself by distinguishing itself from the other; but Hegel writes as if he could detach the movement of thought from its immersion in life, so as to think the concept *in itself* freed from becoming. Hegel writes as if the book, the *Phenomenology of Spirit*, had no signature, as if it were the autonarrative of spirit itself. There can no longer be a relation to the other *as other*, for here each is the same as the other, and time has been "annulled" in favor of a timeless "pure" logic.[10]

For absolute knowing, space is secondary to time, as the externalization of the subject's world-horizon. As Irigaray remarks, "when the world corresponds to the transcendence projected by a single subject as the horizon of the totality of all that exists, this world converts time into space . . . [which] results in the world closing up, even in advance, in a circle."[11] Hegel's determination of space as the "stable shape" of time or the externalization of becoming closes off the horizon of the other by incorporating it within my own. Time, Hegel argues, as the form of experience expresses itself as shape, "or this subject is just as much substance." On the one hand, the pure I of thought "sacrifices" itself by "externalizing" itself as a "*free contingent happening.*"[12] It yields its purity to a determinate form of life. On the other, as a natural being, consciousness "intuits its pure self as time outside it and equally its being as space." It distinguishes in itself what it *is*—being as space—from the movement of becoming. The "pure self" knows itself "outside" immediacy as the movement of becoming that subtends all the moments or determinate shapes of substance in space. The determinate differences of each one make no difference to the pure I of logic that knows itself to be this movement, not a shape or form of life.

This sacrifice of self-consciousness to pure thought or absolute knowing, in which it recognizes itself as the movement of becoming and sacrifices its attachment to the determinate shapes or forms of life, depends on "knowing one's limit." Not only does pure thought sacrifice itself in its self-externalization as consciousness, as a determinate being, Hegel also calls for each *self-consciousness* to sacrifice itself to the movement of becoming: "Nature, the externalized spirit, is in its existence nothing but this eternal externalization of its *continuing existence* and the movement which reinstates the *subject*."[13] The death of the individual will leave no trace in the "eternal" tides of generations. As in the Bacchanalian revel, when one member drops out another takes his place. The difference of the other is absorbed into the revel without remainder.

Hegel can discount the mortality that singularizes each one only because he assumes the eternality of nature and Earth. As the "eternal individual," Earth provides the transcendental horizon for the mortal individual and the reassurance that the pure I or movement of thought remains unmarked by mortal time. The death of each one, of someone, makes no difference as it will have been surpassed in the tides of generations. Thus would Hegel annul time and erect a horizon of transcendence in which each one is substitutable for the other according to the logic of the same and the hegemony of the one deployed in absolute knowing.

Taking this idea of eternity as the transcendental horizon, Hegel—after so many deaths of so many selves along the way of the phenomenological interrogation, after such a long road of "looking the negative in the face, and tarrying with it," after insisting that "the life of spirit is not the life that shrinks from death and keeps itself untouched by devastation, but rather the life the endures it and maintains itself in it"[14]—renders mortality philosophically meaningless. The mortality that singularizes each must be erased, so that the difference from the other makes no difference. The difference between the pure I and the singularity of consciousness has already been unfolded or surpassed so that it leaves no trace.[15]

In his account of absolute knowing, Hegel decrees the "end of history" and the "end of art." Of course, he does not mean that events will cease to happen or that art will no longer be made; rather, his point is that these realms are at an end *for philosophy*. If the phenomenological interrogation has succeeded in articulating all the possible forms of experience and all the possible forms of objectivity, then philosophy no longer has anything to learn from art or history, as whatever appears in these realms will have been anticipated in those forms.[16] Thinking leaves behind phenomenology for a pure logic of purely conceptual relations. Later, Hegel deploys the concepts of the logic to reclaim all the domains of nature and experience for pure thinking and its forms, laws, and norms.

As Irigaray argues, this philosophical attempt to say the whole in a master narrative inscribes the horizon of one world, however rich and comprehensive, as if it were the only one, the only world-horizon. The gesture is not merely one of epistemological hegemony. The imposition of a world-horizon as absolute, as if the one projecting it were the sun, "determines meaning, appears in terms of requirements, a prioris, laws, ideals, which paralyze the becoming of a different human reality, notably by preventing it from transcending itself towards a world appropriate to it."[17] Irigaray argues throughout her corpus that men have "wanted to give the universe their gender," and that this conceptual gesture is inextricably linked to the imposition of a partial transcendence as if it were absolute, so as to deny to the others their own transcendence.[18] This gesture authorizes all the hegemonies of gender, colonialism, and race.[19]

Irigaray points out toward the end of *Sharing the World* that philosophers from Plato to Hegel have deployed the sun as an image of the horizon of transcendence, a figure of truth and the good. On this analogy, there is but one truth, as there is but one source of light in nature. This literary and conceptual strategy confuses physics with metaphysics, the logic of the natural world with the logic of experience, and in its brightness the image all but obscures the truth that in experience there are multiple sources of light. The world is not projected once and for all in absolute knowing, but irrepressibly and with a difference, over and over again, in every singular experience. A genuinely shared world on Irigaray's account is not given, but the result of collaborative work across a respect for difference. Natural and physical scientists rightly adhere to the norm of one truth in their work, but philosophers or metaphysicians who seek to articulate the truth of experience can never discount the fact of singularity or mortality. To paraphrase Irigaray, "one" does not exist; only *someone* does. The universal always wears a singular face, just as the universal of sexual difference is always appropriated in singular ways. Experience always comes in the first person of the singular being who will die, and the universality of sexual difference teaches us that there will be of necessity more than one narrative of human experience and no pure logic.

Writing always with and against Hegel, Irigaray seizes on his concept of identity in difference, of difference as constitutive of identity, and radicalizes it by acknowledging the difference of the other to be irreducible and by refusing any metaphysical closure of the flux of becoming. The two gestures are linked. By discovering the other as an irreducible feature of my experience, Irigaray opens a lateral transcendence that intersects metaphysics' traditional vertical transcendence from the sensuous toward the idea. Irigaray rethinks space as the lateral transcendence of the other and time as the imbrication of our temporalities. This rethinking reveals an indefinite becoming and holds open, not only the difference *from* the other, but also the difference *within* each and all between concept and experience, subject and substance, consciousness and self-consciousness. This lateral transcendence constantly suspends the closure of the autological circle.

Against Hegel's absolute knowing, a "pure I" or master narrative of pure thinking, the same for each and all, Irigaray advances a transcendence that is "no longer unique, no longer one."[20] This rethinking of transcendence effects a radical transformation in the concept of the absolute and in the very project of philosophy:

> The absolute is no longer to be sought through reaching an adequacy between objectivity and subjectivity.... Rather, the absolute is experienced in an ecstatic relationship between us, as naturally determined subject, an ecstasy in which our origin endeavours to achieve its finality again. In a way such an achievement is unattainable, but we dynamically long for it and this requires a dialectical process which does not implicate only consciousness and speculation but also the body, sensitivity, and flesh as such, in accordance with their different incarnations in the one and the other.[21]

Irigaray's revolutionary thought calls upon each and every one to "renounce projecting in a solitary manner." Transcendence can no longer be figured as the "projection" of the "horizon of a world," nor can the absolute be thought as adequation of the concept and experience in the annulment of time and becoming. The relation to the irreducible other opens up a new space, a lateral transcendence that opens the closure of my world-horizon to the world-horizon of the irreducible other. "And if the gesture of projecting the totality of a world can remain a gesture that has something to do with transcendence, to recognize the partial nature of such a transcendence is even more transcendental.... The transcendental gesture becomes one of building with the other a relation in which space and time are, at any moment, in-finite and becoming."[22] Space is not reducible to time, because the relation to the other always already interrupts and qualifies the horizon of my world. Time cannot be "annulled," because the thought of sexual difference renders pure logic *in principle* impossible.[23] Hegel may pretend that the *Phenomenology* is the autonarrative of spirit itself, but, just as, on his own account, no single act is adequate to realize pure duty, no single narrative can exhaust the movement of becoming. No narrative, however masterful, could produce an absolute knowing, because experience is not one, but "at least" two, and more.

The experience of the transcendence of the other *as other* forecloses the closure of becoming in the autological circle. It forestalls the installation of a logic in which each one is substitutable for the other, in which the other has already been anticipated by the form. The experience of the other as other is erased in absolute knowing, so that a new concept of transcendence is required. After Irigaray, the project of philosophy can no longer be an attempt to articulate the master narrative of absolute knowing; conversely, the task of philosophy is to make the familiar strange by opening the autological circle. This will require a certain cultivation of the self, each one working on himself or herself so as to become capable of holding his or her world-horizon open to the other as other. Philosophy aims at "building with the other" a more just and "livable future" that could sustain the transcendence of each one in his or her singularity.[24]

RETHINKING TRANSCENDENCE: FROM THE SENSIBLE TRANSCENDENTAL TO SELF-AFFECTION

What has been forgotten by the philosopher? What have we forgotten such that we come to be reduced to anonymous individuals on whom a common world is apriori imposed?

—LUCE IRIGARAY, SHARING THE WORLD, 116

Philosophy can open up the horizon of a new logic founded on a relationship between two different subjects.... The difference between these identities is no longer merely constructed and dependent on some or other idea, ideal or ideology, it is also real—and as such it is qualitative and not only quantitative.

—LUCE IRIGARAY, *SHARING THE FIRE*, 84–85

In her essay on Plato's *Symposium* in *An Ethics of Sexual Difference* Irigaray introduces the concept of the *sensible transcendental* as a strategic rethinking of the vertical transcendence that is figured in Plato's account of beauty. The woman Diotima, to whom the discourse on beauty is attributed, does not appear or speak in the dialogue. Socrates speaks in her place. Irigaray notes that the speech has two parts, which are quite different from each other. In the second part of her speech, Diotima prescribes a method of abstraction leading to the transcendence of immediacy in *"one single knowledge."*[25] The method of abstraction—which moves from the contemplation of "beautiful bodies, passes to beautiful occupations, then to beautiful sciences, until one reaches that sublime science which is supernatural beauty alone, which allows the isolated knowledge of the essence of beauty"—mirrors the ascent from sensation to perception and know-how (*praxis*) to mathematics and science and finally to the knowledge of the One in Plato's famous "divided line."[26] For this reason, in the second part of Diotima's speech "her method runs the risk of being reduced to the metaphysics that is getting set up."[27] It seems to serve the method of abstraction to an absolute idea from the singularity of sensuous experience and the reduction of difference in the one.

The first part of Diotima's speech, on the other hand, focused on love as an intermediary between the human and divine, on the sensible and the transcendental, and on beauty as that which causes us to love it, that which provokes the movement of transcendence. In this part of the speech, Diotima engages in a dialectical thinking that Irigaray explicitly contrasts with Hegel's dialectical method of unfolding difference as the same. Diotima describes thought as motivated by love, as a constant movement between the sensible and the "beyond." Love mediates between "knowledge" and "reality," so that the difference between them can never be closed up in a concept. "If we did not, at each moment, have something to learn from the encounter with reality, between reality and already established knowledge, we would not perfect ourselves in wisdom. And not to become more wise is to become more ignorant."[28] Philosophy, as love of wisdom, then, would be the thinking that holds open the distance between the "*four terms*" of her dialectic: the difference between knowledge and reality, the difference between the sensible here and the transcendental beyond. "The mediator is never abolished in an infallible knowledge." Love, and above all love of wisdom or philosophy, is "Never fulfilled, always becoming." And what sets love in motion is beauty. Just as a beautiful body inevitably captures the eye, causing heads to turn, so too a beautiful idea captures thought. Beauty "confounds the opposition between immanence and transcendence," because our experience of beauty reveals how the sensible and the idea belong together in becoming. Thinking, as transcendence in immanence, attends to the beautiful, not merely as a property of objects, which is only a reflection of beauty, but as the "sensible horizon on the basis of which everything would appear."[29] The sensible transcendental is nothing other than beauty or that which causes us to love it and provokes thought, the openness to the other and openness in myself.

By the time of *Sharing the World*, Irigaray has complicated the concept of the sensible transcendental beyond Diotima's fourfold to account for how "the human real is formed by two subjects, each one irreducible to the other." My relation to the real is always already mediated by my relation to the other, who is always already implicated in my movement between the sensible and transcendental and my projection of a world-horizon.[30]

In the history of metaphysics, philosophical accounts of time and temporality always focus on the self-intuition of the thinking subject, on the problem of unity and difference in time, and on temporal intuition as the projection of a world-horizon. Irigaray's thought of sexual difference requires the recognition of a more complex temporality. In the lateral relation to the other, "two temporalities are linked together. The future of each one is then modified, and thus the relations of past and future from which the temporal bridge was built."[31] Beginning from the two, transcendence requires a constant transiting between the sensuous and the world-horizon precisely because of the implication of the other in my experience. Because the irreducible other cannot be anticipated by the logic of the same, the appearance of the other is in principle "each time new and unpredictable."[32] Imbricated in the experience of the other, "what I can foresee of my own being is thus partial. In the accomplishment of myself, a contribution from the other will play a part that I cannot completely anticipate, unless I nullify the existence of the other as other."[33] The lateral transcendence of the relation to the irreducible other "acts as a tear in my temporal weaving."

The other is not present to me but always transcends our meeting; yet our becomings are implicated, one in the other.[34] Thus, it is precisely the relation to the other that "prevents my world from closing up in a totality that includes all beings." The lateral transcendence of the other holds open my own becoming, sustains the love of beauty and wisdom or the transiting between the sensible and the idea, and prevents me from "paralyzing" the movement of transcendence in a figure of absolute knowing.

Irigaray pursues two mutually implicated lines of argument to demonstrate the irreducibility of the other to the same and the implication of the other in my existence, in my transcendence or projection of a world-horizon. First, while I do not wish to pursue here Irigaray's claims about the link between the repression of the maternal bond and male power, it is the case that at the core of the erasure of sexual difference in philosophy lies the erasure of the mother. Philosophy until Irigaray failed to think the philosophical implications of the fact that each one has come forth from the body of another.[35] From the very beginning, my being is received from another and nourished by another. "It is the mother who first brings us into the world. The world she gives to us, and to which she gives us, is necessarily present in our way of experiencing the world and of living in the world. But the philosopher has not yet considered this. He pays no attention and even forgets this original determination of our way of being in the world."[36] This forgetting produces both material and philosophical effects.[37] Philosophically, this forgetting requires that the philosopher perform an "a priori reversal" in his experience, whereby the originary experience of the other as world-horizon gives way to the representation of the other as an object in his experience. His relation with the other will be encompassed by his own world-horizon, rather than the relation of the other inscribing a horizon of transcendence in his experience.

Hegel does not forget maternal love; rather, in his cursory consideration of maternal love in the chapter on ethical life in the *Phenomenology*, he indulges in the grotesque assertion that not only does a mother love all her children in the same way *as her children*, but in her love for them they are also replaceable one for the other: should one die, she can always have another. Contrary to this obtuse objectification of maternal love, the maternal relation requires that each child be loved as that child needs to be loved.[38] And no mother finds compensation for the loss of a child in the birth of another: there will always be the loss of that child, who was *someone*, not a child in general, and for whom there can be no replacement. This misrepresentation of maternal love deprives each one of "an origin and singularity."[39] The forgetting of the specificity of maternal love transforms each one into "a 'whoever' " or an " 'anybody.' " The "real world" of the relation to the mother is transformed into the "anonymous, impersonal, indefinite world: a world of 'one(s),' or 'there is.' " The specificity of maternal love prescribes a new transcendence and a new norm for the relation to the other, one in which the other must be met as a specific other, not as an instance of the logic of the one. Such a meeting with the other indefinitely suspends the closure of becoming, of my world-horizon, in the adequate concept.

Irigaray's brief phenomenology of the nursing mother in *Sharing the World* demonstrates the existential intercalations of mother and child. The child literally imbibes the mother, breathes her air, absorbs her warmth, is lulled by her heartbeat, and first begins to have the sense of a world-horizon by listening to her voice. The child becomes only through the horizon of the mother, even as the mother has herself been transformed by bearing and nursing the child. Two temporalities, inextricably intertwined, each for the other an arc of transcendence.[40]

Irigaray's other line of argument calls into question the priority in the history of metaphysics of sight over touch. A logic that favors sight over touch, whether it is a phenomenology of perception or an "insight" into essences, will always mediate the relation to the other by some third.[41] Famously, Merleau-Ponty in "The Primacy of Perception," demonstrates the intersubjectivity of perception by imagining himself standing on a hill with a companion. He points to a something in the distance, which his friend does not yet see. His companion follows his line of sight, and their gazes converge at the same point on the same object.[42] For Merleau-Ponty, the "third" of the object mediates the relation to the other and establishes intersubjectivity. There is intersubjectivity because all share the same objective world. Here again the philosopher confuses physics with metaphysics, the common sense of the perception of the object with transcendence toward the other and the transit in becoming between the sensible and the idea or world-horizon. What is true for perception and natural science is not true for the relation to oneself or the other or for philosophical thought where there is more than one source of light and there is a complex of world-horizons.

Moreover, the mediation of the relation with the other by the object has produced the story of the war over property that dominates political philosophy, at least from Hobbes to Hegel. In Hegel's narrative of absolute knowing, the encounter with the other is one in which each objectifies the other and experiences himself as objectified. Thus, there must be a "struggle unto death" to prove which is active/thought/master and which is passive/substance/slave. When the relation to the other is mediated by the object of perception, not only is the multiplicity of worlds of experience reduced to the one physical world and thought governed by the norm of one truth, but also the relation to the other is understood in terms of a logic of debt and entitlement governed by the law of property and sexual propriety.

Against this valorization of sight and the one world of perception, Irigaray argues that touch is the "necessary medium" of intersubjectivity, "as light and silence are for seeing and listening." "Metaphysics," Irigaray argues, "seems to have been elaborated in order to allow us to escape an immediate nearness with another living being."[43] Touching and being touched confound the subject/object distinction and the distinction between activity and passivity. In place of the conceptual autoaffection of absolute knowing, in touching and being touched, the subject is at one and the same time both "an affecting and a being affected."[44] This middle-voice between activity and passivity "requires the passage to another space-time" and a "temporal delay."[45] Touching and being touched demonstrate the imbrication of the other in my temporality and the projection of my world-horizon, so that there can be no foreclosure of our becoming. The maternal touch first offers a world-horizon to the child, at the same time that her own becoming in relation to the mother creates an "inward autonomous space-time."[46] The mother opens the world-horizon and makes space for the child's own projecting, and all this is mediated by touch.

In touching and being touched by the other, there is the possibility, by no means sure, of escaping the logic of objectification and the mediation of human relations by the law of property. Substituting the mediation of touch for the mediation of the thing opens up the possibility of collaborating with the other to "build" a truth that nourishes both our solidarity and our singularity.

OPENING HEGEL'S AUTOLOGICAL CIRCLE

BUILDING WITH THE OTHER

> To decide in favor of the human truth that we can be and want to be in relation to and with the other amounts to being faithful to a different truth from the one, dependent on a suprasensible absolute, that has both exiled us from ourselves and separated us from one another.
>
> —LUCE IRIGARAY, *SHARING THE WORLD*, 135

> It is desire which grants us an experience of the infinite which is not merely that of life but which corresponds with our wish to reach the absolute.... Keeping our desire alive amounts to maintaining a passage from a natural absolute to a spiritual absolute. It contributes to preserving our longing for the infinite not only as a driving surge towards becoming ourselves but also as a motion towards uniting with the other in order to become the ones who we are.
>
> —LUCE IRIGARAY, *SHARING THE FIRE*, 99

Irigaray's metaphysics of sexual difference always exerts a political as well as a conceptual force. It provides a counternarrative to the autonarrative of absolute knowing and the regularization of life in laws, norms, and codes, in which the singular human finds himself over and over again as "only an instance." She writes to "overcome nihilism," a nihilism that derives directly from the imposition of the figure of absolute knowing, the reduction of the difference of the other, and the paralyzing of becoming in the annulment of time. Life no longer matters, as the philosopher pursues pure logic. At least not to philosophy.

Like any good phenomenologist, Irigaray lays out the labor required to make the familiar strange. Opening my world-horizon to the horizon of the other requires that I suspend convention, prejudice, bias, habit, norms, and the like, to free myself and the other from a world-horizon that "we inhabit and share only from force of habit and under duress, without having made it ours through perception or creation."[47] Irigaray recognizes as well how the problem of convention afflicts each one in the effort to disclose to the other: "who has already been to the source of one's being, and succeeded in saying something about it to the other?"[48] Even our most intimate and profound experiences, grief, e.g., we are reduced to conventions: "I am so sorry for your loss." "Thank you for your condolences." In this common world, "energy" dissipates and becoming is "paralyzed."

In the endeavor to overcome nihilism in the opening to the other, Irigaray argues, our "multicultural era" offers special opportunity. Against logics of domination and colonization, Irigaray celebrates an encounter with the other that transforms my home-world.[49] "We believed our world to be the only one, but we discover that it is partial and incomplete. A part, until now unrecognized, of our truth can be revealed to us thanks to the other, if we accept to partially open our own horizon in order to perceive and welcome the other as other."[50] The paralysis of becoming in the nihilism of infinite repetition installed by absolute knowing finds relief in the unexpected other, but only if each one suspends the will to dominate and colonize. Only through the "meeting with the other" can I become sufficiently "strange" to myself to be relieved of the problem of novelty and the nihilism of an "annulled" time. I must "distance" myself from my own world, in order to "open myself to the world of another," and to my own world, "I will never return unchanged."[51] Irigaray emphasizes the difficulty of this material and conceptual work, which will require the "cultivation" of new attitudes, habits, and strategies of thought, as well as a constant vigilance against foreclosing the other, and, therefore, myself. "It belongs to the achievement of a human being to want to not want on the other's behalf—to let his or her being be as different."[52] It is all too easy, and often convenient, to substitute my desire for the other's, and, thereby, to dominate the other. Cultivating interiority in relation to the irreducible other might "lead the way towards our becoming universal and convivial beings, capable of coexistence with differences." Only this "art" will produce a "shareable world" and a "livable future" capable of sustaining each and all in singularity and solidarity.

BIBLIOGRAPHY

Hegel, G. W. F. *Phenomenology of Spirit*. Translated by A. V. Miller. New York: Oxford University Press, 1977.

Plato. *Republic*. Translated by Paul Shorey. Cambridge, MA: Harvard University Press, 1958.

Rawlinson, Mary C. *The Betrayal of Substance: Death, Literature and Sexual Difference in Hegel's* Phenomenology of Spirit. New York: Columbia University Press, 2021.

——. "Perspectives and Horizons: Husserl on Seeing the Truth." In *Discursive Vision: The Construction of Vision in the History of Philosophical Thought*, edited by David Michael Levin, 265–292. Cambridge, MA: MIT Press, 1996.

Sares, James. "The Irresolvable Dialectic of Existence and the Antinomies of Time: A Hegelian Argument." PhD diss., Stony Brook University, 2022.

NOTES

1. G. W. F. Hegel, *Phenomenology of Spirit*, trans. A. V. Miller (New York: Oxford University Press, 1977). Translations modified; references are to paragraph numbers.
2. Sexual difference is irreducible in three senses: (1) Humans are not self-reproducing. A human can produce only in relation to another human who is of a different biological sex. (2) The gender division of labor and concepts of man and woman have been constitutive of the history of the humans ubiquitously. (3) Each of us is sexed, and each of us must appropriate that sex in some way. Irigaray's thought of sexual difference opens the way for an exploration of the variety and complexity of gender identities.

    To be fair to Hegel, he is the first philosopher in the West to accord a distinctive philosophical importance to women and women's experience, even as he would preclude their entry into science, politics, and philosophy. In the phenomenology of spirit women are explicitly "left behind" when the brother leaves the immediacy of the family for these public discursive domains, but it is his philosophy of identity in difference that gives Irigaray the key to thinking sexual difference. Hence, she is always writing with and against him, as, indeed, we all must.
3. In the preface Hegel introduces the Bacchanalian revel as an image of appearance or reality, and the image recurs throughout the text. In the revel, it does not matter if a drunk member drops out, as another is always ready to take his place. What endures are not the revelers, but the revel. Or, in philosophical terms, "appearance is the arising and passing away that does not arise or pass away." Hegel, *Phenomenology of Spirit*, #47. The form persists over against and incorporating the passing determinant differences produced by it.
4. By "metaphysics," I do not mean to refer, as is somewhat conventional after Nietzsche, Heidegger, and Derrida, to the "history of metaphysics," to an epoch of philosophy stretching, perhaps, from Plato to Hegel and characterized by a commitment to the hegemony of the one and the logic of the same; nor do I mean to refer to the abstract analyses of modalities, possible worlds, or free will current in analytic metaphysics. In attempting to use the term transgressively and strategically, I mean to invoke the Aristotelian-Husserlian idea of metaphysics as a concern with articulating the formal features of experience—time and space, identity, existence. It comes "after the physics," insofar as it concerns the formal features of experience, rather than claims about the natural world or being. What makes Irigaray's work so philosophically radical is that thinking sexual difference requires a revolution in each and every concept that we inherit from the history of philosophy, from the history of metaphysics. Thus, Irigaray produces against a metaphysics of the one a metaphysics of sexual difference.
5. In the history of metaphysics, "discourse has been constituted with the aim of organizing the world into a significant whole at the disposal of the subject. The world would then double what exists through a gathering that makes it available, in particular by designating, naming and setting into a whole all that exists. Discourse, in some way, amounts to a double of the real that makes it handy for each one who comes into the world. Discourse becomes the world in which the subject

dwells, a world that both ties the subject to and separates the subject from the existing real." Irigaray, SW, 121. Though Irigaray goes on in this passage to focus on Heidegger's idea of language as the "house of Being," his reduction of ekstasis or existence to an internal phenomenon of a solitary subject, and his reduction of existence to the anonymous "da ist," it is Hegel who initiates the project of "transforming substance into subject," into language. For Hegel spirit is language, without which the I would not exist. Hegel, *Phenomenology of Spirit*, #508. Moreover, it his Hegel who undertakes the project of saying the whole in the narrative of absolute knowing.

6. I have argued elsewhere that the subject of Hegel's phenomenological analysis is necessarily male. See Mary C. Rawlinson, *The Betrayal of Substance: Death, Literature and Sexual Difference in Hegel's* Phenomenology of Spirit (New York: Columbia University Press, 2021), xiin2.

7. Hegel, *Phenomenology of Spirit*, #806.

8. Hegel, #806.

9. Hegel, #801.

10. The philosophical project of saying the whole of experience produces a subjectivity "deprived of an origin and singularity—it will correspond to a 'whoever,' a 'someone' or 'anybody' defined by a world that existed before it.... It enters an anonymous, impersonal, indefinite world: a world of 'one(s),' or 'there is.' The relation to the other is imposed by a common belonging to a world that is already there." Irigaray, SW, 125.

11. Irigaray, ix.

12. Hegel, *Phenomenology of Spirit*, #807.

13. Hegel, #807.

14. Hegel, #32.

15. Not only can we no longer assume the eternality of Earth, or the eternality of the tides of generations; Hegel also fails to resolve the problem of thinking absolute knowing as an eternal pure logic in relation to the reality of becoming or time. Either time is unreal, a mere emanation of eternity, which would seem to profoundly contradict the phenomenological evidence, or eternity must somehow be in time, which contradicts the very idea of that which neither comes to be nor passes away. I cannot address this problem here, but see James Sares, "The Irresolvable Dialectic of Existence and the Antinomies of Time: A Hegelian Argument," PhD diss., Stony Brook University, 2022.

    Hegel, always the slyest of metaphysicians, attempts to resolve absolute knowing and becoming, eternity or the concept and time, through the deployment of the future perfect. Absolute knowing appears only at the moment that is "ripe to receive it," as the thought of spirit's self-realization in history in all its possible shapes. Yet, absolute knowing will have been the truth all along. It will always have been the truth of experience, as the oak was always the truth of the acorn.

16. This is why a variety of thinkers from Bataille to Derrida have been concerned with the problem of novelty after Hegel. If there is "nothing new under the sun" in the natural world, as Hegel insists, because nature repeats the same forms, there is novelty in history only until the realization of absolute knowing.

17. Irigaray, SW, xi.

18. Many texts make clear that "man" refers to the white Anglo-European male of the law of property, patriarchy, and colonialism. There are many openings here for thinking critically about racism and colonialism, as well as gender injustice.
19. It has sometimes been claimed that Irigaray's account of the universality of sexual difference foreclosed the narratives of other constitutive differences: nothing could be further from the truth. Thinking the irreducibility of sexual difference as a universal feature of human experience calls for these narratives, opening the logical space for them against the hegemony of the one. Irigaray explicitly links the metaphysics of absolute knowing to racism and colonialism. Her metaphysics of sexual difference, particularly her "new absolute" and her rethinking of transcendence, opens possibilities for philosophical critique of race and colonial power. Irigaray, SW, 134.
20. Irigaray, x.
21. Irigaray, SF, 91.
22. Irigaray, SW, x.
23. "Language, however formal, feeds on blood, on flesh, on material elements. Who and what has nourished language? How is the debt to be repaid?" Irigaray, ESD, 127.
24. Recently individuals who experience themselves as nonbinary have begun to request to be addressed as "they" or "them." While this is a request to be respected in practice, the introduction of this language into the philosophical discussion of sexual difference will need to avoid the reversion to the logic of the same and the idea that each is substitutable for the other. A generic use of "they" would erase again the difference between men and women that still needs to be thought through. The task of transforming relations between men and women remains. The gender division of labor, the identification of women with materiality and the commodification of their bodies, the idea of the one truth and the exclusions it produces—all these remain as infrastructures of life that urgently need to be reworked.

    Moreover, by marking this difference as irreducible, the space is opened for the necessary articulation of other differences. The logic of the same, which the thought of sexual difference disrupts, would erase race, just as it erases sexual difference, with false ideas of equality and "human" rights, instead of thinking through the realities of racism and white supremacy or colonialism that are revealed by holding open to the other as other.
25. Irigaray, ESD, 31.
26. Plato, *Republic*, trans. Paul Shorey (Cambridge, MA: Harvard University Press, 1958), book 6.
27. Irigaray, ESD, 33.
28. Irigaray, 21.
29. Irigaray, 33.
30. See also Irigaray's critique of Hegel's transcendence to the absolute as a failure to think the "fire of desire." "Desire corresponds to a transcendental intuition in search of a truth which has a part of physical reality.... It is no longer a question of an absolute which can definitely reconcile subject with object, subject with predicate, but rather of an absolute which springs from a dynamic mediation between the subjective and the objective both in the self and between the selves." Irigaray, SF, 88.

31. Irigaray, SW, 79.
32. Irigaray, 87. Certainly, I may fail to recognize the other as other, reducing them to some general image or utility, and the other may present in a thoroughly conventionalized way, but each one still presents a singular existence that cannot be anticipated and that always conceals an element of surprise, wonder, or enchantment.
33. Irigaray, 76.
34. Irigaray, 79.
35. Hannah Arendt's concept of "natality" does not capture this relationality; rather, it focuses on the political implications of the fact that new generations regularly appear.
36. Irigaray, SW, 123.
37. Across a variety of texts, Irigaray has diagnosed the relation between the forgetting of the relation to the mother and an abusive relation to nature and human nature that not only produces various forms of injustice but also threatens our health and the sustainability of life on Earth. See, e.g., Irigaray, SG, and Irigaray, JTN.
38. Mothers may and often do fail in what maternal love requires, but that does not render the relation generic or one child substitutable for the other.
39. Irigaray, SW, 123.
40. The phenomenology of the nursing mother does not imply that all children must be nursed, or that it is only in relation to the biological mother that a child comes to be; rather, it supplies a paradigm for the way in which a child comes to be only in relation to others.
41. See Mary C. Rawlinson, "Perspectives and Horizons: Husserl on Seeing the Truth," in *Discursive Vision: The Construction of Vision in the History of Philosophical Thought*, ed. David Michael Levin (Cambridge, MA: MIT Press, 1996), 265–292.
42. Maurice Merleau-Ponty, *The Primacy of Perception*, trans. James M. Edie (Evanston, IL: Northwestern University Press, 1964).
43. Irigaray, SW, 129. No doubt, for Irigaray, it is in particular the nearness to the mother that has been repressed.
44. Irigaray, 128.
45. Irigaray, 128.
46. Irigaray, 129.
47. Irigaray, 125.
48. Irigaray, 127.
49. She explicitly distinguishes this encounter from the sort of tourism in which I might visit the other only to return home unchanged.
50. Irigaray, SW, 132.
51. Irigaray, 89.
52. Irigaray, 91.

Chapter Three

ONE, TWO, MANY?

Sexual Difference and the Problem of Universals

STEPHEN D. SEELY

> Substituting the *two* for the *one* in sexual difference therefore corresponds to a decisive philosophical and political gesture, one which renounces being *one* or *many* in favor of *being-two* as the necessary foundation of a new ontology, a new ethics, and a new politics in which the other is recognized as other and not as the same.
>
> —IRIGARAY, *DB*, 141

In her texts throughout the 1990s—*J'aime à toi* (1990), *Essere Due* (1994), *La democrazia comincia a due* (1994), *Entre Orient et Occident* (1999)—one of Irigaray's central philosophical concerns is to rethink universality on the basis of sexual difference. "The universal has been thought as *one*, thought on the basis of *one*," she writes.[1] "But this *one* does not exist." Starting from the *two* of sexual difference, Irigaray suggests, could facilitate a refounding of philosophy (*To Be Two*), of ethics between the sexes (*I Love to You*), of democratic society (*Democracy Begins Between Two*), and even of the relations between cultures (*Between East and West*) on a difference that is universally shared. As is well remarked, these texts witness a shift in the tone of Irigaray's thinking, from her earlier deconstructions of phallocentrism in the history of Western metaphysics to an affirmative philosophical and political project firmly grounded in notions of "the two," of "man" and "woman," and of sexual difference as "universal," "real," and "natural." Such a shift was poorly received by many readers in Anglophone feminist theory, who saw in Irigaray's later works a betrayal of her own original thinking of the supposed "impossibility" of the feminine, of woman (*la femme*), and of sexual difference.[2]

Although the key interlocutor of Irigaray's thinking of universality is undoubtedly Hegel, this essay will consider this phase of Irigaray's work in light of the medieval problem of universals, particularly with reference to

Duns Scotus. In short, my argument is that Irigaray adopts a realist position on universality and sexual difference that places her at odds with an at least tacit nominalism in Anglophone gender theory. Irigaray's thinking of universality as sexuate, and of sexual difference as universal, is based on a recourse to "nature" that, I suggest, strongly resonates with Scotus's own understanding of "common natures" as an ontological reality that precedes any numerical divisions between the one and the many and any conceptual divisions between the universal and the particular. The fact that Scotus, like other Western male philosophers, continues to imagine common human nature as *one*, while no surprise, only helps to illuminate the radicality of Irigaray's thinking of universality and sexual difference. Scotus's original concept of a "non-numerical unity," I argue, also helps to parse the different registers to "the two" throughout Irigaray's work. Ultimately, I think that the odd pairing of Irigaray and Scotus will not only help to attenuate some of the perceived incompatibilities between Irigaray's earlier and later works; it will also demonstrate what is at stake between a realist versus a nominalist approach to sexual difference. And in so doing, it should also evidence the profundity of Irigaray's intervention of the *two* into Western metaphysics—an intervention that is as simple as it is a complete "game change."[3]

DUNS SCOTUS: REALISM, COMMON NATURES, AND NON-NUMERICAL UNITIES

One of the most pressing problems in medieval philosophy concerned the ontological status of universals. In general, the Scholastics operated with two understandings of what constitutes a universal, which gave rise to two formulations of the problem. The first, and weaker, of the two is Aristotle's well-known definition in the *Categories* of a universal as what is "predicated of many." "Man," for instance, is said of many particular men, while "Socrates" is said of only one. The problem here is whether this "predication" applies only to *terms* or also to extramental entities. The second, and more complicated, sense of "universal" is characterized by Boethius as something that is *common to many things* (a) as a *whole* and not by parts (unlike a pie that is common to everyone who eats a slice), (b) *simultaneously* and not in succession (unlike an apartment that is common to each successive tenant), and (c) in such a way that it belongs to the things *essentially* and not externally or accidentally (unlike a play that is common to each of the spectators).[4] On this account, for "humanity" to be a universal, it would have to not only be *said* of many individual humans but be *some-thing* that is able to be shared by all individual humans in its entirety, at the same time, and constitute the substance of each human. In this case, the question is whether anything could exist that fits such a strong definition, which Boethius denies. The problem here is that within medieval metaphysics, for something to exist it must also have substantial, or "numerical," *unity*.[5] But if "humanity" is in many individual humans at the same time without being divided up between them, then how can it have any *unity*, and therefore existence, of its own? Philosophers who came to be known as "nominalists" responded to this by denying any real existence to universals. A universal such as "humanity" is merely *abstracted* from real individual humans; it exists only as a name or a concept with no extramental entity. While this might seem to be the most ontologically consistent position, it does raise serious epistemological questions. For instance: How is the "humanity" that I abstract from one human the same as that I abstract from another? How do two people both abstract "humanity" from a single human?[6] Or, more significantly, if universals exist only in the mind, then (how) do they tell us anything about the world itself?

As a "moderate realist," John Duns Scotus (c. 1265–1308) accepted that universals are concepts without real existence; however, he also held that there is a *real basis* for universality in things (*in re*) and not only in the mind.[7] Approaching the problem of universals from a different direction than other medieval philosophers, Scotus began with the question of *individuation* as what is most in need of explanation. Thus, rather than taking several individual humans and attempting to define what is common to them all ("Humanity") or beginning with a general concept of "Human" and applying it to individual humans, Scotus would take an individual human, say, Socrates, and ask both what is it that makes Socrates *Socrates* (and not Plato or Aristotle) and what makes Socrates a *human* (and not a horse or a stone). In his *Ordinatio*, Scotus considers and rejects several possible principles of individuation including quantity, accident, and matter.[8] Each of these, he contends, presupposes something else that is itself in need of individuation and is thus, as Paul Spade puts it, "ontologically too late to individuate."[9] Ultimately, Scotus's innovation is to theorize individuation as a "contraction" of a "common nature" (*natura communis*) by what he calls an "individual differentia" or "haecceity" (*haecceitas*). As Scotus defines it, the haecceity is an utterly singular "positive entity" that is *added* to the common nature to produce a unique individual. Socrates, for example, is the result of a haecceity (the Socratizer) that contracts a common nature (humanity) to singularity (humanity-in-Socrates).[10] This means that within each individual being, there are actually *two* ontological principles at play: one that accounts for it being the singular thing—the *this* (*haec*)—that it is, and another that accounts for it being the *kind* of thing—the *what* (*quid*)—that it is. While the first principle makes an entity *really* individual, the second makes it *really* common: if the *haecceitas* is what makes Socrates *Socrates*, then the *natura communis* explains his commonality with Plato and his difference from a horse and a stone. Thus, for Scotus, both commonality and individuality are real (that is, inherent in extramental things, or *in re*). While only individuals exist *as entities*, they do so only insofar as they are *individuations* of a common nature that has existence only through such individuals.

In order to explain how something like humanity can really be in many things at once and in whole, Scotus has to introduce an original notion of a real "less-than-numerical unity." Because of the metaphysical convertibility of unity and being, prior to Scotus's innovation it was assumed that only something that was *numerically one* could have the unity necessary for being.[11] In other words, only if something had numerical unity (as a *this*) could it have quiddity (be a *what*). But, Scotus argues, if this were so, then there would be no way for individuals to share anything because every "what" would correspond to exactly one "this":

> If every real unity is numerical unity, therefore every real diversity is numerical diversity. The consequent is false. For every numerical diversity, insofar as it is numerical, is equal[ly diverse]. And so all things would be equally distinct. In that case, it follows that the intellect could not abstract something common from Socrates and Plato any more than it can from Socrates and a line. Every universal would be a pure figment of the intellect.[12]

For Scotus, common natures (e.g., humanity) must therefore have sufficient unity to be a *what*—i.e., to have quiddative being—although they are irreducible to any singular *this*. A common nature is thus, of itself, neither one nor many, neither universal nor particular, because it does not have the numerical individuality that could allow it to be counted: "[The common nature] is not from itself *one* by numerical unity, or *several* by the plurality opposite that unity. It is neither actually universal—that is, in the way something is universal insofar as it is an object of the intellect—nor is it particular in itself. For although [the nature] is never really *without* some one of these features, yet it is not any of them of itself, but is *naturally prior to all of them*."[13] A nature, then, is not "common" because it is found in many things or acts as a universal concept; rather it is common insofar as it is "*indifferent*" to being in one or many, a universal or a particular.[14] It is only by the addition of haecceities that a common nature is given the numerical unity—the *thisness*—that can be found in one or several things, or correspond to a concept that can be said of one or said of many. Of the two ontological principles that constitute every individual, it is therefore the common nature that defines its *whatness*: while the haecceity gives the individual its thisness, haecceities, by definition, cannot be quiddative because they involve *no common features*. In other words, everything that makes Socrates a *what* (e.g., a human) is common—at least capable of being in other individuals—while everything that makes him a *this* (i.e., distinctly *Socrates*) is radically singular, uncommon, and diverse from all other individuals.

But *how* do haecceities "contract" a common nature to singularity? What is the process of individuation such that it "links" these two ontological principles within an individual entity? In his exegesis of Scotus's dense theory of individuation, Peter King suggests that the "contraction" of which Scotus speaks should be understood as a process of "actualization" wherein an uncontracted common nature is the non-numerical *potentiality* that haecceities actualize as numerical individuals.[15] To explicate this, King helpfully distinguishes actualization from medieval notions of "instantiation" and "differentiation." Derived from Platonic metaphysics, instantiation pertains to the relation between universals and particulars in which a particular merely adds *existence* (*esse*) to the universal, which itself remains unchanged. Because, as Scotus insists, haecceities add real and singular features to common natures that are not contained within the uncontracted natures themselves, an individual is not an "instance" of some ideal form. The notion of differentiation, on the other hand, is associated with the relation between a genus and its species such that a "specific differentia" (e.g., rationality) adds a quality to a genus (e.g., animal) to produce a new species (e.g., human as *animal rationale*). Although Scotus does frequently refer to the haecceity as an "individual differentia," it does not supervene on a preexisting common nature to add an abstract quality (e.g., "thisness"). A haecceity, then, adds neither simply "existence" nor an abstract "thisness" to an otherwise unchanged common nature; rather, it *actualizes the potentiality of a common nature in a radically singular way.* In other words, Socrates is not *human* (whether as ideal form or as species) + *existence* or *thisness*; rather his haecceity, the Socratizer, actualizes—or, more precisely, *Socratizes*—the potentiality of the common human nature in a completely singular way (as *humanity-in-Socrates*). While nothing of the Socratizer is contained within the uncontracted human nature, and while human nature is indifferent to any one haecceity or another, the potentiality of humanity nevertheless *exists* only by being actualized in different individuals by diverse haecceities.

For Scotus, then, every individual *is* its uncontracted nature's *mode of being actual*—that is, its common *what*'s mode of being a singular *this.* Yet although the potentiality (as the common nature) is ontologically prior to being actualized in an individual, it is not exhausted within the individual but remains as a *real potentiality*. In other words, a haecceity like the Socratizer does not actualize (or Socratize) a common nature once and for all such that the individual Socrates is a fully actualized (or Socratized) human; rather, the individual Socrates comprises both singularity *and* a common nature that remains nonsingular.[16] As King points out, Scotus's two ontological principles that make an individual what it is—its *what* and its *this*—thus cross the divide between potentiality and actuality, permitting a coexistence of potentiality and actuality within an individual and putting any metaphysical laws of identity and noncontradiction into serious crisis.[17] As such, there is no metaphysical contradiction between individuality and commonness, numerical and non-numerical unity, existing in the same thing because they apply to *two distinct but simultaneous phases*—actuality and potentiality—within the thing itself. The real potentiality of the common nature that remains in all individuals constitutes a unity that is shared by all individuals of that nature. But this potentiality is only ever *one* by "denomination" insofar as it is only ever found in one individual or another: "Thus I say that the potential, which is contracted by the actual, is 'informed' by the actual, and through this it is informed by the *unity* consequent upon that actuality or that act. Thus [the potential] is one by the unity proper to the actual. However, [the potential] is thus *denominatively* one, but in this way it is not of itself one, nor is it *primo modo* [one], nor [one] through an essential part."[18] While both Socrates and the Socratizer are of themselves singular (*one*), human nature is only "*one*" by *denomination* insofar as it is only ever found in some individual (humanity-in-Socrates). Human nature "itself," on the contrary, always remains a real *less-than-numerical unity*. Thus, a common nature unites its singulars in a very different way than a universal concept unites its particulars. Whereas the universal concept (e.g., "Human") is a *one* that stands over and above its many particulars, a common nature and its (one *or* many) singularities are different *modalities of the same reality*. Unlike a universal (e.g., "Human"), which is a predicate added to already-individuated things without having a reality of its own in any of them, a common (e.g., human nature) is not a predicate that is *said* of many individuals but rather the shared reality *from which* the individuation of singular individuals with diverse predicates proceeds. If, with Scotus, a common nature is therefore in things (*in re*) while a universal is *said of* things, then it is necessary, as Paolo Virno puts it, "to speak of a *realism of the Common* and a *nominalism of the Universal*."[19]

Because the common and the singular are both present in any individual, we are capable of forming two very different types of concepts about them, which Scotus works to distinguish: "[A] distinction is required between (*a*) that from which a common concept is taken, and (*b*) that from which a proper concept is taken—not as a distinction of *reality* and *reality*, but as a distinction of *a reality* and *the intrinsic and proper mode of the same*. This distinction suffices for having a perfect or imperfect concept of the same [thing], of which the imperfect [concept] is *common* and the perfect [concept] *proper*."[20] Here, the "universal" and the "particular" are not two opposed types of realities but two ways of *conceptualizing the same reality*: of Socrates, I can form a "proper" concept of humanity-in-Socrates that is "particular" (predicable only of Socrates) *or* a "common" concept of human nature that is "universal" (predicable of many) because *both* realities are present in him. Because both concepts are rooted in the same reality, the common does not negate the singular, or vice versa. Without a real common nature, however, the only reality would be singular individuals whose radically diverse haecceities permit of no factors by which to characterize them other than the simple fact of their diversity. In this case, all universals would be purely nominal groupings of individuals that *really* have nothing in common: Socrates and Plato would really be as diverse as Socrates and a line, and any commonness between them, such as "Humanity," could only be nominally ascribed to them by intellect or convention. Thus, far from the exclusionary violence of the universal, the common nature is the "elusive ground" of commonality and difference—never existing on its own, never exhausted, always remaining as potentiality in each utterly singular individual. We have, then, on the one hand, Scotus's realist metaphysics in which common natures and singularities are *equally real modalities of the same reality within things* and, on the other, a nominalist metaphysics of the universal and the particular in which only individuals are real and all universals are imposed from outside onto the things themselves. And, as Virno rightly notes, this philosophical difference has everything to do with the politics of building a *commons*.

IRIGARAY: SEXUAL DIFFERENCE, GENDERS, AND THE (NON-NUMERICAL) TWO

As with Scotus, the notion of nature is central in Irigaray's philosophy of universals. Both thinkers make recourse to a *nature* that serves as a real common, both preceding and exceeding any divisions between the one/many and the universal/particular. As far as Irigaray is concerned, this gesture amounts to a necessary step back from the tradition of Western metaphysics, which begins thinking universality on the basis of an originary logos, concept, or transcendent absolute. At the origin of metaphysics, Irigaray suggests, the philosopher (or, generally, man) cuts himself off from nature in order to master it through language and technics, leading Western philosophy, ethics, and politics down a road that takes us further and further from a living and livable commons.[21] Thus, as she insists throughout her later works, we must "return" to nature in order to begin again from a real and "living universal." But for Irigaray, any such return also entails recognizing that nature is not *one*, that there is no such thing as Nature (*la nature*): "The natural is at least two: masculine and feminine. All speculation about overcoming the natural in the universal forgets that nature is not one. In order to go beyond—assuming this is necessary—we should make *reality* the point of departure: it is *two* (a *two* containing in turn secondary differences: smaller/larger, younger/older, for instance)."[22] I think that Irigaray would therefore agree with Scotus that things, at least living things, have within themselves a common nature that gives them their quiddative being (their *whatness*) except that, for her, this nature is never singular. When Irigaray claims that "human nature is *two*,"[23] then, she is thinking this *two* as the common nature *from which* human individuation proceeds and not, as is often assumed, attempting to *distribute* every already-existing human individual (whose individuation would be taken for granted) into two preexisting universal categories. To look at the real origin of every human individuation is thus to recognize that human nature is not, as Scotus understood it, a single nature *created* (i.e., an *ens creatum*) by the one God in his image, but an *engendering from two*. "We do not come from *one*," Irigaray writes, "we are engendered by *two* and Man as a man is born of another. From the time he is born he is thus in relation with another, with an other gender. But in patriarchal mythologies, becoming on the basis of *one* has been inscribed as origin."[24] Each human individual, like nearly all plants and animals, is the result of a distinctive form of individuation in which the common nature from which we come is a *unity of two that are different*. The Western philosopher has never considered the devastating consequences such an engendering from unity-in-difference has for his metaphysics.

If no one human can engender another, then, as Irigaray puts it, "limit is therefore inscribed in nature itself."[25] Indeed, this is precisely what it means to say that human nature is *sexuate*: it is irreducibly *cleaved* by difference. As *engendered* by two, human nature is individuated in *genders* or *genera* (*genres*). Now, it has often been said that whereas there is no notion of "gender" in Irigaray's early work, her later works—beginning with the 1990s texts I am considering in this essay—introduce a problematic slippage between "sex" and "gender." Based on my reading of these texts in terms of Irigaray's project of rethinking universality in Western metaphysics, I would argue that her use of these terms is much more careful than is frequently assumed and should not be assimilated to the Anglophone "sex/gender distinction" (such that "sex" would refer to biology or embodiment and "gender" to psychic, subjective, or sociocultural dimensions). In fact, throughout these later works, Irigaray tends to use "sex" (*le sexe*) when referring to *difference* and *relation* vis-à-vis the sexuate other and "gender" (*le genre*) when referring to *commonality* and *belonging*. In other words, my sex is that dimension of my being that ontologically situates me in relation to an other that is irreducibly different, while my gender is that dimension of my being that gives me a real commonality with others. We might take etymology as a guide here: whereas the root of *sexe* is "to divide" or "to cut," *genre* (which, in French, includes both "gender" and "genus") indexes a grouping or kinship with particular reference to a common genesis. Human nature, then, is *sexuate* insofar as it is cleaved by difference—a difference that is the very condition of possibility of relationality—and is therefore only actualized through the mediation of *genders* (or genera).

Because he understands human nature as *one*, on the model of a created entity in which sexual difference could only ever be derivative (like Eve from Adam), Scotus overlooks these *genders* that must be thought as somehow situated "between" the common nature and its haecceities (although not in such a way that the genders could be said to supervene on an *ungendered* humanity). One would have liked to ask Scotus not only about what explains both Socrates's singularity and his commonness with Plato, but about what explains his difference from, say, *Diotima*? It could be argued that this difference is merely a question of haecceities, such that the Diotimizer simply actualizes a single common human nature differently than the Socratizer or Platonizer. And yet, if haecceities are, as Scotus tells us, *primarily diverse* and *utterly singular* with no quiddative reality whatsoever, then there would be no way of explaining how Diotima and Sappho are *commonly different* from Plato and Socrates. They would all be united by a neuter common nature and their differences would be radically individual and equally different since haecceities are responsible for everything in the individual that is *uncommon* and, by definition, cannot give the individual any commonalities. If, however, we begin by understanding human individuation as engendered by *two*, then *there is no common "humanity" in the singular (neuter)*. Rather, human nature is *bimodal* and is actualized in individuals by haecceities only through the *mediation of genders* that are not modes of predication (as genera are usually understood) but *real and intrinsic modes of a sexuate common nature*. What haecceities actualize, then, is not a neuter human nature, but *one mode* of human nature that is ontologically situated in relation to the other mode. And if the common nature is what gives a thing its quiddative reality, then human nature, as intrinsically sexuate, is a quiddity that includes a *not*. In other words, my individuation as gendered gives me my *what* and as sexuate gives me my *what-I-am-not*: "The reluctance to recognize the importance of sexual difference seems to me to derive from this negative in the self and for the self that it entails. I belong to a gender, which means to a sexuate universal and to a relation between two universals."[26] The common nature of humans (and all sexuate living beings) therefore includes within itself what Irigaray calls a *"nothing in common"* (*rien en commun*)[27] that preserves the irreducibility of one to the other.

Here we arrive at the crux of the most controversial and misunderstood elements of Irigaray's philosophy of universality and sexual difference because it runs directly counter not only to the history of Western metaphysics but to the most popular strands of Anglophone feminist theory (which remains part of that metaphysics). While these debates have most often been understood in terms of "essentialism," I think that reading them in light of the medieval problem of universals (i.e., nominalism versus realism) is illuminative. What I call "gender nominalism" takes the position that individuals are real and they unquestionably exist in their evident multiplicity and diversity, while "genders" are socially or discursively constructed ways of grouping these individuals in whom gender does not really inhere (unless, perhaps, as a form of psychic internalization or "subjectification" that always comes in some sense from *outside* the individual).[28] From this point of view, "gender" is an accidental property of the individual: any recourse to universality with respect to gender is thus inherently arbitrary and violent, and there could (at least theoretically) be as many "genders" as there are individuals. In this sense, gender nominalism belongs to the metaphysics of the one and the many in which the individual is a particular that will always stand against the universal as singular. Irigaray, on the contrary, begins by challenging the *externality* of the universal to the individual: "The individual has been considered as a particular without an adequate interpretation of this universal that is *in* her or him: woman or man."[29] It is precisely this location of the universal within the individual—we could say *in re*—that, to my mind, would place Irigaray on the realist side of the medieval problem of universals. On this reading, "gender" (*genre*) refers to inherent *generic potentialities* that can be actualized within individuals by a diversity of haecceities. From such a perspective, there is no conflict between the universal and the particular because a gender—as one modality of common, sexuate human nature—is that bit of universality that actualized in every singular individual. It is only through this common, gendered potentiality that any human individual has a *what*; but this is only ever present in and through a radically singular *this* or *who*. Each individual thus consists of both a *sexuate and gendered potentiality*—a what that makes the individual really common to their gender and really different from the sexuate other—and a completely *singular actuality* that makes them really *this* unique individual. I quote Irigaray at length, emphasizing as she ties these points together:

> My part of the universal is *within me*, and I do not have to go out of myself or renounce my nature in order to attain it. With *gendered* identity [*identité générique*], there is no longer an opposition between particular and universal in the sense that the universal is already within me and does not have to be *constructed* outside of me. Of course, I am still subject to historical particularity [I would read here: *haecceity*]. But no longer is there any contradiction between the singularity of that history and a neuter (?) universal produced by a culture, a spirit. That tension is resolved within the horizon of belonging to a universal as a gendered identity. . . . I have to realize myself as *what* and *who* I am: a woman. This woman that I am has to realize the *feminine as universal* in the self and for the self as far as possible during the period of History in which she finds herself and given the familiar, cultural, or political contingencies that she has to overcome.[30]

In the 1990s, the gender nominalist position tended to go hand in hand with a particularly strong denial of any notion of "woman." Many of Irigaray's critics have resisted any attempt to define "woman" out of concerns over the inherent essentialism and exclusionary violence of such a gesture, as if the category of "woman" could ever be defined in such a way that it could adequately encompass all individual women. But as Irigaray points out, without a concept of "woman" (*la femme*), we are left with only *man* (*l'homme*) standing in as the universal referent of "humanity," from which women can differ only in a purely individual way:

> Unfortunately, women are the first to say that woman [*la femme*] does not exist and cannot do so. Which means they refuse to accept a generic identity for the feminine. This denial eliminates the possibility of constituting a culture of two sexes, two genders. We remain in the horizon in which man is the model of human kind, and within this human kind, there are empirical women or there are natural entities without an identity of their own. Women's liberation, and indeed the liberation of humanity, depends upon

the definition of a *feminine generic*, that is, a definition of what *Woman* [*la femme*] is, not just *this* or *that* woman.[31]

By denying the reality of what Irigaray calls the feminine generic, "gender" difference can only be thought on the side of individuals: women in their utter diversity *really* have nothing in common apart from their divergence from *man* (in the guise of the neuter "human"). This is why "gender," from the nominalist perspective, is viewed as only one among many types of "diversity," and it leads to a dangerous regression to the empirical where individuals have no option but to assert their individual difference against others through the self-evidency of their radical singularity. However, the presumed incompatibility between defining a generic concept of "woman" and protecting the singularity of each woman, I would contend, is only a problem for the nominalist for whom the one and many, the universal and particular, are fundamentally opposed. As outlined with Scotus earlier, of any individual we can form both a "proper" concept of what they are that includes their common nature plus their haecceity (e.g., the-feminine- or woman-in-Diotima) and a "common" or "universal" concept of the common nature as such (e.g., the feminine or woman) because *both realities really exist in the individual*. In other words, every woman can serve as the basis for the feminine generic—woman—because they *are* "it."[32] The point is not to begin from some abstract concept of "woman" that would unite all empirical women; rather, the feminine (as a gender/genus/*genre*) is always already common to all individual women, and from them it is possible to formulate a common or universal concept of "woman." Properly speaking, such a common concept will always be what Scotus called an *incomplete universal* given that it can only be formed via the singular individuals in which it is actualized, which are always determined by historical, social, and political contingencies. In other words, a universal concept of the feminine generic ("woman") is always open to contestation, to be defined and redefined by the individuals in which it is actualized in any given time and place. As such, "woman" (*la femme*) does not need to be negated, barred, crossed out, or delegated to the "impossible" in order to protect the singularity of each woman or the future anteriority of the feminine. Uncontracted by haecceities, the feminine (as a gendered common nature) *never exists as such*: as potentiality, it cannot exist in actuality apart from the individuals in whom it is actualized, although it is never exhausted by, does not depend on, and is irreducible to any actual individual. While every actualization of the feminine gender within an individual is radically singular, as potentiality it is really common—that is, equally, simultaneously, and wholly present in each individual in whom it is actualized. However, the feminine "itself"—although the non-numerical unity of any common nature troubles any notion of the *it*-self—will always remain *virtual*. This simultaneity of potentiality and actuality that Scotistic metaphysics enables means, to my mind, that there is no inherent incompatibility between Irigaray's early insistence on the future anteriority of the feminine (and of sexual difference) and her later desire to define a concept of the feminine generic ("woman").

Irigaray has done more than any other thinker to alert us to the consistent ways in which the traditional binaries of Western metaphysics—act/potency, form/matter, culture/nature, universal/particular—are mapped onto masculinity and femininity. Not only has this metaphysics systematically devalued the pole in each case associated with the feminine, but it has also bifurcated individuals in themselves. Situating the *two* of sexual difference beyond these divisions, then, amounts to establishing not a dual polarity within a *One*, but a "two times one, which leaves to each person his or her unity, a unity which is limited by his or her incarnation" in a gender.[33] This means that this "two" and this "unity" cannot be understood in any numerical sense. Indeed, since Irigaray's earliest works, she has challenged the metaphysical privilege of numerical unity as a phallomorphic privileging of "the *one* of form, of the individual, of the (male) sexual organ, of the proper name, of the proper meaning."[34] Although Irigaray's early critique of number has, once again, been viewed as being at odds with her later emphasis on "the two," again I think that we might call on Scotus's notion of a non-numerical unity to help push back against this assumption. The sexes or genders are only *two*—i.e., *one* and *one*—in what Scotus would call a "denominative" sense, insofar as they are only ever found in individuals (this *one* or that *one*). As actualized in individuals, the *two* of sexual difference will therefore sit oddly within a representational economy based on a metaphysics of the one/many. This is a point Irigaray makes in *Speculum* when she writes that "in fact, these terms [i.e., man and woman] cannot fittingly be designated by the number 'two' and the adjective 'different,' if only because they are not susceptible to com-parison. To use such terms serves only to . . . speak of the 'other' in a language already systematized by/for the same."[35] But as a sexuate common nature, the *two* must be understood as a *non-numerical unified-duality* that evades enumeration.[36] In this sense, "the two" or "the couple" so frequently invoked throughout Irigaray's 1990s texts is a figuration of a *common nature that is not one* (or *many*). Here, "the two" is not about *two* sexes or genders as *this one* and *that one*; rather, it concerns a *fold* or a *cleaving* in the common nature such that *one* is always situated vis-à-vis *the other*, which both limits it and makes relationality possible. The sexuate other is therefore an *alterity*—from the Latin *alter*, meaning *the* other of *two*, rather than from *allos*, as *an* other of *many*—which ties Irigaray's thinking of sexual difference to the medieval distinction between *difference* (between two that share a common) and *diversity* (between many that have nothing in common). That the genders, as actualized in individuals, are rooted in a sexuate potentiality that is non-numerical means that there is no necessary reason for them to be numerically denominated in binary terms. As non-numerical, the common sexuate nature from which we are each engendered and that we each actualize in our own radically singular way is a unified-duality that does not admit of any possible third. And yet, this sexuate nature only *exists* in and through the actualization of gendered potentiality by singular haecceities. As intersex, trans, and other "nonbinary" individuations attest, this actualization is open-ended in ways that call for denomination beyond any *numerical* two (or, as Irigaray frequently puts it, "*at least* two").

Across her 1990s works, Irigaray's philosophical project of rethinking sexual difference and universality is inseparable from a political and ethical project: the political goal is to build a commons that respects and cultivates the bimodality of human nature, which, for Irigaray, depends on an ethical recognition of alterity that leaves a space for the other as other. As she writes in *I Love to You*:

> With this singular and multiple engagement between subjects of different genders, the impersonality of *one*, and its authority associated with the undifferentiated or with the summoning of a so-called neutral energy, tend to disappear. *Man* is no longer a *one*, a sort of abstract equal-to-all individual whose generic and specific qualities are both concentrated in and abolished by the institution of the family. *Woman* comes out of the anonymity of the *one*, ceases being a potential substitute for another woman, an object of use

and exchange whose properties and functions, both natural and abstract, are determined by the needs of a given society, of a cultural era and its commerce. The *community* ceases to present itself as potentially *one*. It is made up of real persons, women and men, and is organized in terms of and through the economy of their differences.[37]

In *Democracy Begins Between Two*, Irigaray extends this project through concrete proposals seeking to refound the political commons on "the couple." By this she does not mean only to address marital or familial relations, but to move beyond a conceptualization of democracy as a calculus of abstract *ones*, or an undifferentiated multitude of *many*. For Irigaray, realigning civil society and the state on the real alterity that our sexuate common nature engenders would guard against authoritarian efforts to group individuals into purely nominal categories, while facilitating recognition and respect for individual difference given that each person would be attentive to the common limitation that belonging to a gender implies. This is ultimately the point that underlies Irigaray's controversial argument in *Between East and West* that respect for sexual difference could lead to a global and multicultural commons: to build a commons that is capable of cultivating *difference* implies having something real in common, otherwise there is nothing but an agglomeration of radically singular individuals in their *diversity* (as epitomized by neoliberalism) and any universal concepts at work in legal and political institutions (e.g., the "human" in human rights) can only be abstract fictions imposed by those with the power to name. If, as Paolo Virno argues, Scotus's metaphysics of the common-singular helps to rethink political struggles for the democratic commons by recognizing the shared potentiality of our *real common nature* that exists before and beyond any of the state's efforts to transpose this commons into a set of nominal universals of which it is the guarantor, Irigaray's attention to human nature's irreducible sexuation demonstrates the necessary passage of any politics of the commons through an ethics of sexual difference. The common nature from which every human becoming proceeds is engendered by the unity of a *two* that never formed a *one* and will never add up to a *many*. Recognizing this globally common reality means that the universal no longer needs to be understood as the accumulation of all the individual any-*ones*: it is neither the sum total of every-*one* or *One* concept big enough to encompass the many. "The universal is not so immense that it escapes you," as Irigaray writes.[38] "The universal is *within* you and develops out of you as a flower grows from the earth." As gendered, however, the universality that we each carry constitutes only one-half of the potentiality that our common human nature engenders. It is therefore in the interval *between* these two common natures that humanity can be reborn, and where the commons is, now and always, waiting to be built together.

BIBLIOGRAPHY

Bates, Todd. *Duns Scotus and the Problem of Universals*. London: Continuum, 2010.

Boethius. "From His Second Commentary on Porphyry's *Isagoge*." In *Five Texts on the Mediaeval Problem of Universals*, edited and translated by Paul Vincent Spade. Indianapolis: Hackett, 1994.

Butler, Judith. *Gender Trouble: Feminism and the Subversion of Identity*. London: Routledge, 1990.

Cheah, Pheng, and Elizabeth Grosz. "The Future of Sexual Difference: An Interview with Judith Butler and Drucilla Cornell." *Diacritics* 28, no. 1 (1998): 19–42.

Deutscher, Penelope. *A Politics of Impossible Difference: The Later Work of Luce Irigaray*. Ithaca: Cornell University Press, 2002.

Duns Scotus, "Six Questions on Individuation from His *Ordinatio* II d.3 p. 1 qq. 1–6." In *Five Texts on the Mediaeval Problem of Universals*, edited and translated by Paul Vincent Spade. Indianapolis: Hackett, 1994.

Heidegger, Martin. *Introduction to Metaphysics*. Translated by Gregory Fried and Richard Polt. New Haven: Yale University Press, 2014.

King, Peter. "Duns Scotus on the Common Nature." *Philosophical Topics* 20 (1992): 50–76.

Rawlinson, Mary C. "Game Change: Philosophy After Irigaray." In *Engaging the World: Thinking After Irigaray*, edited by Mary C. Rawlinson. Albany: State University of New York Press, 2016.

Riley, Denise. *"Am I That Name?" Feminism and the Category of "Women" in History*. London: Palgrave, 1988.

Spelman, Elizabeth. *Inessential Woman: Problems of Exclusion in Feminist Thought*. Boston: Beacon, 1990.

Virno, Paolo. "Angels and the General Intellect: Individuation in Duns Scotus and Gilbert Simondon," translated by Nick Heron, *Parrhesia* 7 (2009): 58–67.

NOTES

1. Irigaray, ILTY, 35.
2. As a good overview of many of these critiques, see Pheng Cheah and Elizabeth Grosz, "The Future of Sexual Difference: An Interview with Judith Butler and Drucilla Cornell," *Diacritics* 28, no. 1 (1998): 19–42. See also Penelope Deutscher, *A Politics of Impossible Difference: The Later Work of Luce Irigaray* (Ithaca: Cornell University Press, 2002).

3. Mary Rawlinson, "Game Change: Philosophy After Irigaray," in *Engaging the World: Thinking After Irigaray*, ed. Mary Rawlinson (Albany: SUNY Press, 2016), 65–79.
4. Boethius, "From His Second Commentary on Porphyry's *Isagoge*," in *Five Texts on the Mediaeval Problem of Universals*, ed. and trans. Paul Vincent Spade (Indianapolis: Hackett, 1994). 22. See also the editor's introduction.
5. This principle is derived from Aristotle's *Metaphysics* (IV.2 1003b23–24), which equates "being" (τὸ ὄν) with "unity" (τὸ ἕν). In Medieval philosophy, "entity" (from *entitas*, literally "being-ness") therefore implied existence as an *individual unit*.
6. A "strong" Medieval nominalist (e.g., Roscellin) would say that this is only a result of linguistic convention, while a more sophisticated nominalist or "conceptualist" (e.g., William of Ockham) would say that universals are concepts with *mental reality* in the form of "intentional objects" or "qualities" that are inherent in the mind (see Spade, introduction to *Five Texts*).
7. Scotus, like Boethius and Aquinas, is generally called a "moderate" realist because "strong" realism about universals is associated with a Platonist position in which universals have reality *independent* of particular entities.
8. Duns Scotus, "Six Questions on Individuation from His *Ordinatio* II d.3 p. 1 qq. 1–6," in Spade, *Five Texts*.
9. Spade, introduction to *Five Texts*, xiii.
10. Scotus, "Six Questions," 96. Scotus uses the terms *individual, singularity*, and *numerical entity* interchangeably (see "Six Questions," 76). An "individual," for Scotus, is something that is *incapable of further division* into parts that can be characterized by the whole to which they belong (e.g., Socrates's hand is not Socrates). The haecceity, then, adds individual or numerical entity to a common nature in such a way that prevents any further division. See Peter King, "Duns Scotus on the Common Nature," *Philosophical Topics* 20 (1992): 5.
11. Before Scotus, both Avicenna and Aquinas had postulated some version of a real common nature as a sort of intermediary between individual things and universal concepts, but because they accepted the convertibility of unity and being *and* understood unity as *numerical* unity, they rejected that these common natures could have any ontological reality. See Todd Bates, *Duns Scotus and the Problem of Universals* (London: Continuum, 2010), 59–60.
12. Scotus, "Six Questions," 62. For the Scholastics, for two things to *differ*, they must have something in common, while things with nothing in common were said to be *diverse*.
13. Scotus, 63.
14. Scotus, 64. By "indifferent," Scotus means that it is "not incompatible" with the common nature for it "to be found together with some unity of singularity."
15. Peter King, "Duns Scotus," 50–76.
16. As Scotus writes: "in the external thing where the [common] nature is together with singularity, the nature is not *of itself* determined to singularity but is naturally prior to the aspect [i.e., the haecceity] that contracts it to that singularity. And insofar as it is naturally prior to that contracting aspect, it is not incompatible with [the nature] to be *without* that contracting aspect." Scotus, "Six Questions," 64. See also King, "Duns Scotus," 71–72.

17. "From the fact that X is potentially ϕ and potentially ψ, it cannot be inferred that X is *both* ϕ and ψ, or that ϕ and ψ are compossible. Equally, if X is a reality that includes potentiality, and X' is an actuality of X, it does not follow that whatever is attributable to X is attributable to X', nor conversely. The potentialities possessed by X may include features ruled out by the actuality of X', and conversely, something may be X' and *a fortiori* be X as well." King, "Duns Scotus," 70. It is this point that King argues William of Ockham failed to grasp, which therefore "shift[s] the ground" under the feet of the most sophisticated nominalist critique of Scotus.
18. Scotus, *Ordinatio* I d.8 n.214, quoted in King, "Duns Scots," 71.
19. Paolo Virno, "Angels and the General Intellect: Individuation in Duns Scotus and Gilbert Simondon," trans. Nick Heron, *Parrhesia* 7 (2009): 62.
20. Scotus, *Ordinatio* I d.8 p.1 q.3 n.138b-d, quoted in King, "Duns Scotus," 69.
21. The term *metaphysics* literally means "beyond natural or physical things" (μετὰ τὰ φυσικά). The Latin word *natura* is a translation of the Greek φύσις, and the sense in which both Scotus and Irigaray use the word *nature* is close to the Greek φύσις (insofar as each thing "has a nature," or its own way of being and becoming). As Heidegger argues, it was not until the modern physical theory of nature that *natura* became singular ("Nature") as a spatiotemporal realm of objectivity. See Martin Heidegger, *Introduction to Metaphysics*, trans. Gregory Fried and Richard Polt (New Haven: Yale University Press, 2014).
22. Irigaray, ILTY 35, emphasis added.
23. Irigaray, 35.
24. Irigaray, 40.
25. Irigaray, 35.
26. Irigaray, 106.
27. Irigaray, TBT, 52.
28. By "gender nominalism," I am referring to prominent texts from the late 1980s and early 1990s—including Denise Riley, *"Am I That Name?": Feminism and the Category of "Women" in History* (London: Palgrave, 1988); Elizabeth Spelman, *Inessential Woman: Problems of Exclusion in Feminist Thought* (Boston: Beacon, 1990); and Judith Butler, *Gender Trouble: Feminism and the Subversion of Identity* (London: Routledge, 1990)—that have gone on to constitute a sort of *doxa* within Anglophone gender studies (often in excess of what the texts themselves argue) that there is no *extramental reality* to gender. In Medieval terms, I would argue that gender nominalists are *strong* nominalists in the sense that universals (genders) are only products of *normative convention* (i.e., I doubt that any gender theorist would accept a position in which gender has some universal *mental* reality).
29. Irigaray, ILTY, 48.
30. Irigaray, 144–145, translation modified.
31. Irigaray, 65, emphasis modified.
32. It should go without saying that when we formulate concepts of individual humans, we do so through the individual in their entirety, and not some part or other. Thus, neither "proper" nor "universal" concepts of woman (or man) could ever be rooted in some "part" of the individual (e.g., chromosomes or genitals), which we never

encounter as such. As mentioned earlier, a haecceity contracts a common nature in such a way that produces an individual that is incapable of being further divided into parts.
33. Irigaray, TBT, 59.
34. Irigaray, TS, 26.
35. Irigaray, S, 139.
36. In fact, Irigaray has several figures of this *non-numerical two* in her work, including the two lips (Irigaray, TS, 22–33 and 205–218), the intrauterine mother-placenta-fetus relation (Irigaray, JTN, 37–45), and the "couple" (ILTY): a more-than-one that cannot be reduced to a one + one.
37. Irigaray, ILTY, 127, emphasis added.
38. Irigaray, DB, 29.

Chapter Four

RETURNING TO IRIGARAY'S RADICAL MATERIALISM

Sexuate Difference, Ontology, and Bodies of Water

LAURA ROBERTS

Luce Irigaray's philosophy of sexual difference is an ontological project concerned with the erasure of the question of sexual difference in Western traditions and the pursuit of new values and frameworks for a renewed understanding of subjectivity as sexuate. But what does this mean exactly? What does it mean to argue that Irigaray is a philosopher of ontology? How are we to understand Irigaray's claim that "sexuate difference has an ontological status, but not in a traditional sense"?[1] Or when she notes that Being "is split in two, or, rather, is held in two and in the relation between"?[2] What does ontology, ontological status, and Being refer to here? Fixed essences? Static entities? *What* there really is? And, reading Irigaray as a philosopher of ontology, how are we to approach the question: *What is* sexual, or sexuate, difference?[3]

"Sexual difference," Irigaray writes, "would constitute the horizon of worlds more fecund than any known to date—at least in the West—and without reducing fecundity to the reproduction of bodies and flesh. For loving partners this would be a fecundity of birth and regeneration, but also the production of a new age of thought, art, poetry, and language: the creation of a new *poetics*."[4] The problem, for Irigaray, is that Western traditions continue to resist the discovery of these new horizons. Irigaray argues that whether we turn to philosophy or to politics, "no new foundations," "new works," or "new values have been established."[5] And "the scenes of sexuality," she writes, "are a long way from having effected their revolution."[6] Irigaray thus argues that we need a "revolution in thought and ethics ... if the work of sexual difference is to take place."[7] She writes:

> We need to reinterpret everything concerning the relations between the subject and discourse, the subject and the world, the subject and the cosmic, the microcosmic and the macrocosmic. Everything, beginning with the way in which the subject has always been written in the masculine form, as *man*, even when it claimed to be universal or neutral. Despite the fact that *man*—at least in French—rather than being neutral, is sexed.[8]

To pursue this revolution in thought and ethics we must first recognize that the subject is not neutral and that "Man has been the subject of discourse, whether in theory, morality, or politics" and is "the gender of God."[9] Discourses of morality, politics, and religion are realms that produce and maintain the values and frameworks through which we experience and understand the world in micro- and macrocosmic terms, and these have—at least in the West—centered the subjectivity of the masculine upper-class white Man (as Human), reducing the maternal-feminine to a static unchanging matter with no access to autonomous subjectivity. According to Irigaray, in the Western imaginary, the maternal-feminine is the unacknowledged "liquid ground" from where the (masculine) Human subject draws his breath and life. The potential of a horizon of sexuate difference, as Irigaray understands it, is a revolution in thought and ethics, and therefore requires new foundations, new frameworks, and new understandings of subjectivity that situate sexuate subjects in relation with one another and within and in relation to a dynamic sense of nature. These new frameworks, for Irigaray, will enable the recognition of at least two sexuate subjects, existing in nonhierarchical relation, which have the potential to shatter the phallocentric logic that undergirds the Western tradition.[10]

Read in this context, the philosophy of sexual difference, as a revolution and "transition to a new age" that "requires a change in our perception and conception of *space-time* ... and entails a transformation of forms, of the relations of matter and form and of the *interval* between," seems to me nothing less than an attempt to elaborate a new ontology.[11] Elizabeth Grosz observes that Irigaray "is still rarely acknowledged ... in terms of her contributions to and transformations of ontology," meaning "the terms by which we understand our existence as beings in a world larger than ourselves, a world not entirely of our making, whose limits and constraints provide the very limits and constraints of thought itself."[12] Irigaray's account of sexual difference is an attempt to fundamentally refigure the terms by which we understand our existence. An ontology of sexuate difference offers a new frame for understanding our relation with the unacknowledged maternal-feminine through a refiguring of the *interval* between matter and form, nature and culture, masculine and feminine, and the (sexuate) human and more-than-human. Indeed, an ontology of sexuate difference recognizes the originary maternal-feminine required for life and articulates the interdependence of sexuate subjects with one another and with the more-than-human world. This is why we see Irigaray, throughout her work, focus on uncovering and articulating modes of relationality and nonhierarchal relations of sexuate difference, the interval, "the fluid matter,"[13] "the mucous,"[14] and "the liquid ground."[15] Irigaray's project is ontological, articulating new ways to understand being. When Irigaray writes that "sexuate difference has ontological status," we must read these claims in the context of this broader philosophical project.[16]

However, Irigaray's radical refiguring of matter as fluid, dynamic, and always changing and her engagements with the female body, materiality, and biology, have often been mistakenly read as biologically essentialist. Naomi Schor refers to this as Irigaray's "radical materialism" or "*materialism.*"[17] Once we appreciate how Irigaray's sexuate ontology challenges "traditional" Western philosophical conceptions of matter and biology without being biologically essentialist, we can, I suggest, begin to elucidate certain posthuman themes in Irigaray's work. The posthuman themes to which I am referring build upon feminist critiques of humanism and the atomistic (masculine) subject while also challenging anthropocentrism and the idea of the human as the "sole or primary site of embodiment."[18] Feminist posthumanism refuses a self-evident split between nature and culture while recognizing the important critique that any attempt to "move beyond the human" may actually "reintroduce the Eurocentric transcendentalism this movement purports to disrupt."[19] A feminist posthumanism thus challenges a "version of posthumanism that desires *dis*embodiment and the overcoming of worldly bodily difference" as well as technophobic versions.[20] Instead, a feminist posthumanism "strives to connect the many subjects of feminism that were never granted access to the designation of the "human" in the first place."[21] Why is such a posthuman reading of Irigaray important? Following Astrida Neimanis, I suggest that, on the one hand, reading Irigaray in this way will "inflect a genealogy of posthumanism with an important feminist difference" and, on the other hand, a posthuman lens offers "helpful theoretical scaffolds for explaining Irigaray's relation to matter" that does not fall back to the essentialist/antiessentialist debates.[22] Neimanis's queer posthuman reading also positions Irigaray's philosophy of sexual difference as relevant to important themes in contemporary discussions on the environment, offering figurations of the (sexuate) human as always already intimately related with more-than-human worlds.

The first part of this chapter examines some of Irigaray's readers who view sexuate difference as an ontological project and, in doing so, aims to counter misunderstandings of her work, including the criticism of biological essentialism, along with criticisms of heteronormativity, cissexism, and a failure to attend to lived differences among women. I then present Neimanis's reading of Irigaray's work, which positions sexuate difference as ontological and unpacks figurations of fluidity, water, gestationality, and membrane logics to illustrate connections between Irigaray's ontological project and some of the main themes in environmental feminist humanities undergirded by recent posthuman and new materialist feminist approaches.[23] Neimanis's work uncovers and holds in tension Irigaray's descriptions of watery bodies, articulating the relations with our originary watery maternal-feminine and our more general gestational origins. Illustrating this contiguity, Neimanis demonstrates how we ought to read Irigaray's work as challenging the very terms through which we understand the ontological that moves away from reading Irigaray's work as biologically heterosexist and, I claim, toward a posthuman, radical materialism.[24] What I also hope to show through an engagement with Neimanis's work is how this reading illustrates Margaret Whitford's claim that "the important thing for Irigaray is to engage with her *in order to go beyond her.*"[25]

TOWARD A RADICAL MATER-IALISM

Before turning to these important ontological readings of Irigaray's work, specifically those that appear most helpful for developing an account of her radical materialism,[26] let us be clear on what the criticism of biological essentialism entails. Whitford writes:

> The charge of biological essentialism ... assumes that Irigaray posits an unmediated causal relation between biological sex and sexual identity, leaving out completely the imaginary dimension, in which sexual identity may be related in an unstable and shifting way to the anatomical body, or the symbolic, linguistic dimension, in which sexual identity may be constructed. Secondly, biological essentialism (in the form in which it is usually attributed to Irigaray) is a deterministic and often simplistic thesis which makes change impossible to explain, whereas in my view Irigaray is a theorist of change.[27]

Linking the criticism of biological essentialism with Irigaray's "ontological and metaphysical orientation," Whitford continues, emphasizing that Irigaray's project is much more radical, "she is attempting to begin to dismantle from within the foundations of western metaphysics."[28] As Whitford notes, the charge of biological essentialism reduces Irigaray's work to a deterministic framework that fails to recognize how sexual identity is constructed in imaginary and symbolic linguistic dimensions.[29] This charge thus covers over Irigaray's thinking through of this unstable and shifting relation between sexual identity and the anatomical body.[30] It fails to read Irigaray as a theorist of change, which is fundamental to understanding Irigaray's challenges to Western ontology and her refiguring of the relation of sexuate difference.

Schor's 1989 essay "This Essentialism Which Is Not One: Coming to Grips with Irigaray" resonates with Whitford's argument insofar as it directly addresses the criticism of biological essentialism as well as opens spaces for a consideration of biology and materialism in Irigaray's work that does not reduce her ideas to a deterministic framework. Schor notes that "the word essentialism has been endowed within the context of feminism with the power to reduce to silence, to excommunicate, to consign to oblivion. Essentialism in modern day feminism is anathema."[31] Schor's discussion aims to "de-hystericize the debate" and demonstrate how the focus on essentialism and what is "loosely termed the *biological*" in Irigaray's work leads to impoverished readings that do not appreciate Irigaray's "radical materialism."[32] This radical materialism reflects, as in Whitford's account, the unstable and shifting relations between sexual identity and anatomical body, and the dynamism of both terms, while also rethinking the dynamic material conditions of life itself, namely, the maternal-feminine, in a critique of Western metaphysics. Given the focus on biological essentialism, Schor suggests that Irigaray's "*mater*-ialism" and the linking of the female body with notions of elemental fluidity and the feminine are "never really addressed."[33] She notes the "ontological primacy of woman and the fluid are for [Irigaray] one of the represseds of patriarchal metaphysics; the forgetting of fluids participates in the matricide that according to Irigaray's myth of origins founds Western culture: 'He begins to be in and thanks to fluids.' Unquestionably then Irigaray's linking up of the fluid and the feminine rests on a reference to the female body."[34]

Grosz also makes explicit the link between Irigaray's ontological project and criticisms of Irigaray's work, arguing that if we appreciate that "ontology is sexualized," or that human being is sexuate, we can positively understand how lived differences between subjects emerge from the foundational difference between the sexes.[35] Resonating with an interpretation of Irigaray's ontological project as radically materialist, Grosz reads Irigarayan sexuate difference with Darwin's writings on sexual selection and ultimately posits sexual difference as an evolutionarily dynamic that does not ignore the likewise dynamic imaginary/symbolic dimensions of sexuate identity.[36] As such, Grosz points out that Irigaray's project is "not simply the project of restoring female subjectivity or femininity to where it should belong, in the position of an adequate and respected partner of man the subject,"[37] and does not discount the psychical and political significance of sexual difference, but also appreciates sexual difference "primarily as a corporeal and ontological concept that links the human to the natural world as much as to the social world."[38] It is in the context of an ontological priority, unlike other socially constructed differences, that Grosz argues that sexual difference is the condition of possibility of all human life and sociality.[39] Grosz further argues that "race, class, and religion are divisions imposed by cultures on sexed bodies, bodies which are differentiated from each other and in each generation through the implications of sexual reproduction."[40] According to Grosz, the radical implications of this insight have not been tarried with sufficiently due to the fact that the sexual position ontology "possessed has been covered over under the guise of the objective, the one, the neutral, the human."[41]

However, this articulation of sexual difference as ontological has garnered new criticisms about the priority of sexual difference over other differences of, for example, race. Grosz makes clear, in response, that while we must recognize that ontology is sexualized, sexual difference "may not be the most significant thing about other forms of oppression,"[42] and that Irigaray never claimed "that in addressing other forms of oppression we should consider sexual difference the most important, only that we should consider our oppression where it touches us."[43] Ultimately, Grosz argues that no matter how one identifies in terms of gender expression and identity, sexuality, and ethnicity, "sexual difference is still in play," and because of this, "sexual difference is of a different ontological order than other relevant social differences. . . . It is also around which the transition from nature to culture is affected."[44]

Following Grosz's reflections here, James Sares, in his 2019 paper "Irigaray and the 'Priority' of Sexual Difference: A (Qualified) Defense," addresses claims that Irigaray prioritizes sexual difference over other differences with a discussion that carefully articulates the difference between ontological primacy and political primacy in Irigaray's work. Similar to Grosz's claim that sexual difference is always already in play, for Sares, we must appreciate that we as human beings are always in the "frame" of sexual difference—that it is the "precondition of life."[45] Sares is clear that Irigaray's interventions into ontology transform understandings of Western ontology: when reading sexual difference as ontological this does not mean "a timeless structure of being divorced from or preceding life itself" but that "sexual difference is the mode of these beings, their irreducible relationality."[46] To acknowledge the "frame" of sexual difference as the mode of these beings links to Irigaray's call in *An Ethics of Sexual Difference* for new frameworks and new foundations to articulate the revolution in thought and ethics required for a transition to a new age. This point that we are always in the "frame" of sexual difference enables Sares to point out that the priority of sexual difference in Irigaray's work rests in this idea that sexual difference, including the repressed maternal-feminine, is the "ground of our possibility as historical subjects."[47] Sexual difference is ontological for Irigaray as a "necessary condition of the being of the human being"; without it human life would not exist, and it is this difference that creates human life and in doing so makes possible other differences that come to be and are constructed and lived.[48] Sexual difference "cuts across 'geographical' and cultural differences" as it has an ontological, but not necessarily political, priority over other such differences for human existence.[49]

As Sares also points out, Irigaray's claim that ontology is sexuate does not imply "that other kinds of difference do not materialize bodies and subjects," including their sexuate embodiment, or that sexuate materiality is static or deterministic of identity. In response to criticisms of cissexism that are leveled against Irigaray's work, Sares points out that the ontological frame of sexual difference materializes in singular ways among individuals and is dynamically developed and lived through, and mediated by culture, in the limits it provides for becoming.[50] Irigaray, he writes, is "not concerned with delimiting the proper 'bounds' for how one identifies with their sex."[51] This claim provides a crucial opening for an ontology of sexuate difference that takes seriously the ways in which Irigaray understands sexual difference as a frame through which life comes to be and to become—as a frame in which subjectivity and materiality are dynamic and sexuate. Read in this way, sexuate difference as ontological difference does not exclude queer, transgender, or gender-nonconforming identities but perhaps offers a refigured ontological framing that appreciates rather than excludes the various and multiple ways in which sex and gender expression and identity come to be, become, and are lived.

The readings of Irigaray's project as ontological by Whitford, Schor, Grosz, and Sares push back on reading it as biologically essentialist, cissexist, or a simple prioritizing of sex over race and, in doing so, open space for contemporary readers to reengage with it as a radically materialist refiguring of the terms by which we understand our existence, as sexuate subjects intimately related with one another, with the elemental and more-than-human life matter. Moreover, as I hope to show in the next section, reading Irigaray's project as ontological allows us to (re)turn with fresh eyes to read her engagements with matter, biology, and nature as fluid, as dynamic, and as changing in a posthuman context. This (re)turn further enables a (re)consideration and articulation of sexuate difference as an ontological framing that not only refigures matter but also appreciates the *interval* between the material and the semiotic, matter and form, nature and culture in the formation of sexuate subjectivity.

SEXUATE DIFFERENCE AND BODIES OF WATER

In Neimanis's reading, we catch a glimpse of how Irigaray's refiguring of Western ontology as sexuate enables us to appreciate the gestational waters, the liquid ground, from where we all emerge and how these waters connect human bodies as sexuate subjects with the more-than-human bodies of water on our planet. Neimanis opens her 2016 book *Bodies of Water* with the following:

> Blood, bile, intracellular fluid; a small ocean swallowed, a wild wetland in our gut; rivulets forsaken making their way from our insides to out, from watery womb to watery world:
> *we are bodies of water.*
> As such, we are not on the one hand embodied (with all of the cultural and metaphysical investments of this concept) while on the other hand primarily comprising water (with all of the attendant biological, chemical, and ecological implications). We are both of these things, inextricably and at once—made mostly of wet matter, but also aswim in the discursive flocculations of embodiment as an idea. We live at the exponential material meaning where embodiment meets water.[52]

While Neimanis does not refer to Schor's 1989 paper in *Bodies of Water*, her work begins to unpack the links within Irigaray's writings between the "ontological primacy of woman and the fluid" as "the repressed of patriarchal metaphysics."[53] Despite not using the term directly, Neimanis offers a deep engagement and exploration of these entanglements through a consideration of Irigaray's radical *mater*-ialism in a posthuman context. Thus, in her work, Neimanis engages with Irigaray's notion of sexuate difference as ontological, which she expands to the operative concept of the gestational, to help refigure embodiment from the perspective of "our bodies' wet constitution, as inseparable from these pressing ecological questions."[54]

While I begin here with reference to Schor's notion of the fluid, it is important to mark Neimanis's move away from the notion of fluidity to a focus on themes of water in Irigaray's work. Although Neimanis pays careful attention to the figurations of the fluid feminine in Irigaray's work as both figurative (in excess to the masculine paradigm) and literal "in their genital mucosity, their placental interchanges, and their amniotic flows," she ultimately suggests that thinking with *water* offers a broader but more complex and appropriate figuration for her work.[55] For Neimanis, thinking Irigaray with water demands we pay attention to the materiality of bodies as well as "to the ways in which these bodies comprise an elemental-environmental hydrocommons."[56] Neimanis continues noting that water "is a shape-shifter—moving from solid to liquid and gas, and taking up residence in and as bodies of all kinds. Water is undoubtedly related to the fluid, but as the materialization of an abstract property, it allows us to think the mattering of this matter in more specific and situated ways—in terms of the bodies it animates, the operations it makes possible, and the limits it encounters."[57]

These themes of watery embodiment challenge dominant Western understandings of the ontological that figure bodies as individual sovereign subjects, the model of subjectivity that underscores most, if not all, "social, political, economic, and legal frameworks in the Western world."[58] Neimanis challenges this understanding through her articulation of interpermeating yet differentiating bodies of water illustrating that "as bodies of water we leak and seethe, our borders are always vulnerable to rupture and renegotiation."[59] "Discrete individualism," writes Neimanis, "is a rather dry, if convenient myth."[60]

Watery embodiment thus challenges these fundamental and intertwined notions of discrete individualism, anthropocentrism, and phallogocentrism that uphold Western metaphysics.[61] Neimanis writes: "For us humans, the flow and flush of waters sustain our own bodies, but also connect them to other bodies, to other worlds beyond our human selves. . . . The bodies from which we siphon and into which we pour ourselves are certainly other human bodies (a kissable lover, a blood transfused stranger, a nursing infant), but they are just as likely a sea, a cistern, an underground reservoir of once-was-rain."[62] Neimanis describes this watery material relationality as interpermeating and as a "more-than-human hydrocommons," which challenges anthropocentrism and "privileging the human as the primary site of embodiment."[63] Moreover, in her refiguring of Irigaray's sexuate ontology as a watery gestationality, Neimanis challenges the self-sufficient logic of phallogocentrism. The logics of phallogocentrism, as readers of Irigaray know, work to erase "the bodies that have gestated our own, and facilitated their becoming."[64] Countering phallogocentrism, Neimanis's concept of gestationality as sexuate ontology recognizes that we "require other bodies of other waters (that in turn require other bodies and other waters) to bathe us into being."[65] In her queer watery posthuman reading of Irigaray, Neimanis posits that maternal bodies "are but one expression of a more general aqueous facilitative capacity: pond life, sea monkey, primordial soup, amphibious egg, the moist soil that holds and grows the seed."[66]

Astute readers of Irigaray's work might be growing a little weary here, wondering what happens to sexuate difference, and sexuate subjectivity, when we expand the notion to a more general gestational capacity. Crucially, while Neimanis's notion of posthuman gestationality expresses the "facilitative logic of our bodily water for gestating new lives and new forms of life," it does so "without washing away a feminist commitment to think the difference of the maternal, feminine, and otherwise gendered and sexed bodies."[67] On this point, Neimanis reminds us that Western metaphysics erases the debt of life owed to the "maternal, the feminine, the other, the natural" and that we must not forget that Irigaray's project insists on "calling philosophy to task for this 'forgetting.'"[68] It is this work of returning to Irigaray's thinking with matter and unpacking the connections between a planetary gestational capacity and the maternal-feminine in Irigaray's work that I am especially drawn to in Neimanis's writing, which I think provides a novel way of thinking and engaging with the ontological status of sexuate difference in Irigaray's work. Moreover, it expands any answers we might have to the question "What is sexual difference?"

CONTIGUITIES WITH THE ELEMENTAL

In her return to Irigaray's radical *mater*-ialism, Neimanis notes that while Irigaray's focus on the maternal and female morphology has resulted in critiques of biological essentialism, we must remember that the "matter of the body is not a static trap but an opportunity and a generative force."[69] Key to understanding Neimanis's argument is the point she makes about the slippage that occurs in Irigaray's work between the elemental and the feminine morphological body—that this work is "always more than metaphorical" and that in Irigaray's writing we can trace a *contiguity* with the elemental.[70] This slippage allowing a contiguity with the elemental can also be read as posthuman in that the human is figured as contiguous and inseparable from "the environment."[71] We thus find in Irigaray's work that "human embodiment is always more-than-human-too: we are imbricated with elemental and environmental matters in relations of contiguity and belonging, rather than hierarchy."[72]

As readers of Irigaray will appreciate, this contiguity with the elemental is not limited to water. For example, in *Between East and West* Irigaray "suggests that woman engenders with her breath and shares her breath even before she shares the nourishment of her body, this is a true description of some women's bodily experience" and that "the image of mucus . . . can be mapped both according to a female morphology and a mechanics of elemental fluids."[73]

However, in her reading of *Marine Lover*, Neimanis unpacks this contiguity with the elemental with a focus on water and watery matters in order to develop the concept of gestationality. In Neimanis's reading, we see how water marks the qualitative difference of the maternal feminine, a figure familiar to readers of Irigaray: "She is the maternal waters out of which the Overman and the masculine are born," as well as the "fluid woman whom man uses, unacknowledged."[74] Water also marks the masculine sexuate subject as aqueous, as indebted to "the fluid feminine," sustaining him, immersing him, and permeating him as "an incorporated and intimate aspect of his bodily being."[75] Neimanis's reading reminds us that we are all in debt and intimately connected to and (inter)permeated with these primordial maternal waters. Neimanis highlights, however, that, in *Marine Lover*, the figure of the maternal-feminine is *contiguous, touching, connected* with the sea. The operative concept of the gestational is not "simply overlaid upon the maternal-feminine as either perfect coincidence or convenient analogy. These maternal origins are rather *contiguous* with deeper and wider seas."[76] As Neimanis writes,

> If we were to trace a genealogy of our own gestation, it would have no definitive starting point, no clear beginning of beginnings. The waters that gestate one body have come from other bodies, gestated by earlier waters, gestated by waters that precede those. Aqueous origins are diffuse and multiple. As such, gestation cannot be reduced to a single instance in an actualized female womb. Although Irigaray makes clear in *Marine Lover* (and elsewhere) the undeniable relation between the maternal and the gestational, the sea is not simply a metaphor for the female mother or the womb; it has

also provided the womb's very condition of possibility, and continues to leak into our human wombs, in various extended traces.[77]

Neimanis notes here that, throughout her work, Irigaray "insists repeatedly that the fecundity of gestation is not limited simply to the moment of birth, but is rather an ongoing regeneration."[78] Reading sexuate difference as gestational thus enables us to recognize gestationality more broadly as well as an interval or passage between sexuate subjects, "a connecting flow" that "ensures their mutual sustenance and proliferation."[79] For Irigaray, Neimanis writes, "difference begins in the gestational watery elemental."[80] On Neimanis's posthuman reading, an ontology of sexuate difference is "productive of difference"; it "*gestates* difference" (it is necessary for, and frames, life).[81] Feminine and masculine watery bodies are interpermeating, relational, and differentiating, are comprised of water, but "water also comprises the watery gestational element that conditions these sexually different beings in the first place."[82]

This broader sense of gestationality prompts a question: "Could it be, then, that through her descriptions of our bodies of water in *Marine Lover*, Irigaray queers the simple relations between the feminine and the fluid that are too easily extrapolated from her work?"[83] And: "Might Irigaray be asking us to consider our bodies' watery origins as both maternal womb and watery element more generally?"[84]

Neimanis answers these questions affirmatively, framing her responses with what she calls an "onto-logic of amniotics," which describes "[her] way of naming logics that entangle bodily waters in both commonality and difference."[85] These logics are clearly inspired by Irigaray's work on placental and labial logics but further open them. This onto-logic, which indicates a "non-traditional" way (to use Irigaray's descriptor) of understanding ontology, does not "suggest that all bodies of water are the same in terms of their being, but rather that bodies of water share a way of being because they are bodies of water."[86] Using the figure of the amnion, "the inner most membrane that encloses the embryo of a reptile, bird or mammal,"[87] Neimanis articulates a mode of relational being that transits across and between bodies that "also nurtures and facilitates other bodies, while also differentiating them."[88] An onto-logic of amniotics "is at once *of*, *in*, and *between*, while at the same time requiring a force of *becoming*."[89]

Neimanis understands this membrane logic to articulate three modes of embodiment simultaneously: gestational, differentiating, and interpermeating.[90] It is "water," writes Neimanis, that simultaneously "gestates beings, that which is gestated as difference, and that which interpermeates and connects beings."[91] Neimanis thus argues that water can expand our understanding of the ontological. And an onto-logic of amniotics offers an understanding of a "common way of being in the world with all kinds of other bodies of water"[92] or hydrocommons. She notes:

> The point is not just that "we are all 60–90 per cent water"; the brute materiality is not the real take-away here. More importantly, as bodies of water we share a common way of relating to other bodies—and this means that our beings and becomings are bound up in one another's materiality, in specific ways. My second aim (particularly in calling this an onto-logic) is to follow Irigaray in exploding certain understandings of "the ontological." What does it mean to say that the ontological is not just "what is" but what allows another being to be, and that which connects beings to one another?[93]

Central to understanding the power of this onto-logic is Neimanis's operative concept of posthuman gestationality, which enables a reading of Irigaray's figure of the maternal-feminine as contiguous with a more general watery element.[94] Posthuman gestationality enables Neimanis to figure gestationality that is not tethered to the female human, to "read Irigaray beyond humanism and anthropocentrism," and "to suggest a different kind of theory of sexuate difference—one of desirous becoming that cannot be tied to a binaristic logic of two."[95]

Neimanis's posthuman reading brings to light the contiguity of our actual lived existence as watery bodies with this primordial gestational medium and our (inter)permeable relations with all bodies of water on the planet. Neimanis holds in tension a model of a more general gestationality with maternal bodies, emphasizing that, with the concept of planetary hydrocommons and general figurations of gestationality, we must not "enact yet another effacement of the maternal."[96] This is because "the labours of maternal bodies are still undervalued and denigrated, where these bodies are still and increasingly subject to marginalization and technologized colonialism, and where they enact a profound material connection between a present life and a becoming life in an (as of yet) non-substitutable way, there is still reason to attend to the specificity of the maternal bodies within a broader ethics of responsivity to other kinds of life."[97] Ultimately, in her reading of Irigaray's ontological project, Neimanis suggests that Irigaray invites us to think deeply about bodies, their difference, their interconnectedness "and their gestational capacities alongside the obfuscation of any definitive origin or starting point."[98] According to Neimanis, Irigaray's work invites us to further consider the element of water as underpinning these relations, reminding us that "we are created and gestate in an amniotic sac, nutrients are delivered to us by water that enables us to grow. Our waste is removed by similar waterways, and we are protected from external harm by our amniotic waters, waters that are not disembodied or neutral but are themselves in a body of water, a body that is specifically a maternal one."[99] Ultimately, Neimanis's posthuman lens and concept of gestationality offer a refreshing reading through which we can return to Irigaray's elemental thinking and engagements with matter to explore questions of difference and interconnection between the human and more-than-human worlds in ways that do not erase the debt of life owed to the maternal or fall back to the essentialist/antiessentialist debates that frame her earlier work.

There are, however, three concerns that might be raised in relation to Neimanis's reading of Irigaray. First, reflecting on Neimanis's project in *Bodies of Water*, Rebecca Hill suggests that Neimanis's "figuration of ontological amniotics" is "close to Irigaray's thinking on the interval or sensible-transcendental" but that this reading differs from Irigaray in denying any *ideal* aspects to this ontologic.[100] Hill points out that, for Irigaray, "the interval is both material and in excess of materiality, the interval is between," and while she notes Neimanis's onto-logic of amniotics is "radically material," she takes this to mean that any ideal aspects are excluded in this formulation. I am not certain, however, that ideal aspects are excluded by Neimanis, who is always careful to position materiality as always entangled with meaning-making and the symbolic/imaginary realms and, of course, the more-than-human. Nonetheless, it is an important point to make when considering Irigaray's radical materialism, which I have argued is indeed concerned with questions of sexual difference in both the natural and cultural world, and the material and in excess of this.

A second concern relating to Neimanis's posthuman reading of Irigaray is that Irigaray is clearly committed to a form of radical humanism in her rethinking of humanity as sexuate and as at least two. I think this criticism has merit. However, if we recognize, as Rosi Braidotti writes, that posthuman feminism "emerges at the confluence" of posthumanism and post-anthropocentrism and "points to multiple ways out of dominant understandings of the human," then I think Neimanis's posthuman reading does not leave behind the type of radical humanism and post-phallocentric understanding of human being as (at least) two that Irigaray is evoking in her work.[101] Certainly, as both Neimanis and Braidotti suggest, Irigaray's work on sexuate difference ought to be seen as a precursor to a posthuman feminism and fits Braidotti's thinking here when she writes that a "gender-driven cartography enables a posthuman brand of feminism, generated at the intersection of critiques of humanism and of anthropocentrism by subjects who were excluded from full humanity to begin with."[102] Nonetheless, this is another important concern when reading Irigaray's work through a posthuman feminist lens and reminds us that it is important to situate Irigaray's work as a challenge to dominant understandings of the human—no matter how difficult.[103]

Finally, Neimanis's focus in her reading of Irigaray is, clearly, the element of water. It is important to note that Irigaray pays attention to all four elements in her philosophy, and throughout her elemental writing offers a general reconceptualizing of materiality as dynamic and fluid—although all elements are, of course, figured differently. While there is now an emerging literature on Irigaray's work on air and breath, I see Neimanis's work on water as contributing to conversations that will broaden the scope of Irigaray's elemental thinking. While I hope this chapter has offered some reasons why a posthuman lens might find this element most attractive to explore, this focus does not mean that Neimanis disregards the other elements or, as I have mentioned, the transformations of water itself from solid to liquid to gas, or finally that aspects of her onto-logic of amniotics developed in the critiques of Western metaphysics cannot be applied more broadly.

What I hope to have shown in this chapter is that it is important to continue engaging with Irigaray's ontology and elemental thinking more broadly, which allows a reading of her work that opens urgent political discussions on, for example, climate catastrophe as it repositions and refigures human embodiment and subjectivity as an intimate part of a dynamic nature, of life, rather than as transcending (and consuming) a fixed or static nature. I reiterate the point that ontology, as Irigaray understands it, includes the "what is" but reminds us that this "what is" is grounded in a radical understanding of *mater*-ialism as dynamic, sexuate, and intimately connected to natural, cultural, and spiritual realms. Reading Irigaray's work in this way opens an invigorating path for feminist philosophy to think through sexuate subjectivity and its intimate relation with matters of biology and science so urgently required.

BIBLIOGRAPHY

Australian Concise Oxford Dictionary. Melbourne: Oxford University Press, 2004.
Braidotti, Rosi. *Nomadic Subjects: Embodiment and Sexual Difference in Contemporary Feminist Theory*. 2nd ed. New York: Columbia University Press, 2011.
———. "Posthuman Feminism and Gender Methodology." In *Why Gender?*, edited by Jude Brown. Cambridge: Cambridge University Press, 2021.
Grosz, Elizabeth. *Becoming Undone: Darwinian Reflections on Life, Politics and Art*. Durham, NC: Duke University Press, 2011.
———. "Irigaray and the Ontology of Sexual Difference." Luce Irigaray Circle Conference, New York, 2007.
———. *Sexual Subversions: Three French Feminists*. Sydney: Allen and Unwin, 1989.
Hill, Rebecca. "Bodies of Water: Posthuman Feminist Phenomenology by Astrida Neimanis (Review)." *philosSOPHIA* 10, no. 1 (2020): 125–130.
Ince, Kate. *The Body and the Screen: Female Subjectivities in Contemporary Women's Cinema*. New York: Bloomsbury, 2017.
Jones, Emma. "The Future of Sexuate Difference: Irigaray, Heidegger, Ontology, and Ethics." *L'Esprit Createur* 52, no. 3 (2012): 26–39.
———. "Speaking at the Limit: The Ontology of Luce Irigaray's Ethics, in Dialogue with Lacan and Heidegger." PhD diss., University of Oregon, 2011.
Jones, Rachel. *Irigaray: Toward a Sexuate Philosophy*. Cambridge: Polity, 2011.
Mortensen, Ellen. *Touching Thought: Ontology and Sexual Difference*. Lanham, MD: Lexington, 2002.
Neimanis, Astrida. *Bodies of Water: Posthuman Feminist Phenomenology*. London: Bloomsbury, 2016.
Parker, Emily Anne. "Introduction: From Ecology to Elemental Difference." *Journal of the British Society for Phenomenology* 46, no. 2 (2015): 89–100.
Roberts, Laura. "An Alchemy of Radical Love: Luce Irigaray's Ontology of Sexuate Difference." PhD diss., University of Queensland, 2015.
———. "Disrupting Time: Somatechnics and the Opening of the Interval." *Australian Feminist Studies* 34, no. 99 (2019): 60–72.
———. *Irigaray and Politics: A Critical Introduction*. Edinburgh: Edinburgh University Press, 2019.

Sares, James. "Irigaray and the 'Priority' of Sexual Difference: A (Qualified) Defense." Diverse Lineages of Existentialism II: Critical Race, Feminist & Continental Philosophy, George Washington University, 2019.
Schor, Naomi. "This Essentialism Which Is Not One: Coming to Grips with Irigaray." *differences: A Journal of Feminist Cultural Studies* 1, no. 2 (1989): 38–58.
Skof, Lenart. *Breath of Proximity: Intersubjectivity, Ethics and Peace.* New York: Springer, 2015.
Skof, Lenart, and Emily A. Holmes, eds. *Breathing with Irigaray.* London: Bloomsbury, 2013.
Stephens, Elizabeth. "Feminism and New Materialism: The Matter of Fluidity." *A Journal of Queer Studies* 9 (2014): 186–202.
Stone, Alison. *Luce Irigaray and the Philosophy of Sexual Difference.* Cambridge: Cambridge University Press, 2006.
van Leeuwen, Anne. "Irigaray, Heidegger and the Question of Sexual Difference: An Examination of the Phenomenological Stakes of Irigaray's Later Work." PhD diss., New School for Social Research of the New School, 2010.
———. "Sexuate Difference, Ontological Difference: Between Irigaray and Heidegger." *Continental Philosophy Review* 43 (2010): 111–126.
Whitford, Margaret. *Luce Irigaray: Philosophy in the Feminine.* London: Routledge, 1991.
———. "Rereading Irigaray." In *Between Feminism and Psychoanalysis*, edited by Teresa Brennan. London: Routledge, 1989.

NOTES

I would like to thank James Sares for his valuable and helpful feedback on earlier versions of this chapter.

1. Irigaray, C, 133.
2. Irigaray, FA, 313.
3. Following Irigaray, I use *sexual* and *sexuate difference* interchangeably in this essay to indicate a deliberate slippage and challenge to a biological essentialist understanding of sexual in this context. Kate Ince offers an excellent explanation. Ince writes: "If *feminin* is one term in Irigaray's writings that supports her project of sociocultural transformation by blurring the biological and cultural dimensions of sexual identity in this way, another important such term is *sexué*, which French-English dictionaries suggest should be conveyed either by 'sexual' or by 'dimorphic' (a biological term referring to distinct types within a species), but which Irigaray's English translators have rendered by the neologism 'sexuate.' The standard use of *sexué* in French is for plants and animals, so by employing it in relation to human beings as well as culture and cultural projects such as sex-specific rights, Irigaray emphasizes a continuity—one she straightforwardly terms 'life'—between human and non-human life forms. As Jones puts it, 'the 'sexuate' refers neither to a mode of being determined by biological sex nor to a cultural overlay of gendered meanings inscribed on a 'tabula rasa' of passively receptive matter. The 'sexuate' does not separate the becomings that shape our bodily being from the production of social and cultural meanings or behavioural dispositions. Rather, it signals the way that sexual difference is articulated through our different modes of being and

becoming, that is, in bodily, social, linguistic, aesthetic, erotic and political forms." Kate Ince, *The Body and the Screen: Female Subjectivities in Contemporary Women's Cinema* (New York: Bloomsbury, 2017), 13.
4. Irigaray, ESD, 5.
5. Irigaray, 6.
6. Irigaray, 6.
7. Irigaray, 6.
8. Irigaray, 6.
9. Irigaray, 7.
10. "Phallocentrism," as Elizabeth Grosz notes, "is not simply, as Ernest Jones defined it, the primacy of the phallus (or, more precisely, the privilege of the male organ, the penis), but can be identified with a more general process of cultural and representational assimilation. Phallocentrism is the use of one model of subjectivity, the male, by which all others are positively or negatively defined. Others are constructed as variations of this singular type of subject. They are thus reduced to or defined only by terms chosen by and appropriate for masculinity. Irigaray's aim, among other things, is the recategorization of women and femininity so that they are now capable of being autonomously defined according to women's and not men's interests. Phallocentrism is a subtle and not always easily identifiable representational system." Elizabeth Grosz, *Sexual Subversions: Three French Feminists* (Sydney: Allen and Unwin, 1989), 105.
11. Irigaray, ESD, 7–8.
12. Elizabeth Grosz, *Becoming Undone: Darwinian Reflections on Life, Politics and Art* (Durham: Duke University Press, 2011), 99.
13. Irigaray, FA, 310.
14. Irigaray, ESD, 109.
15. Moreover, an ontology of sexuate difference is intimately connected to, but not to be conflated with, the political, as it challenges the phallocentric frameworks upon which the supposedly neutral (masculine) liberal subject of liberal democracy rests.
16. See Laura Roberts, *Irigaray and Politics* (Edinburgh: Edinburgh University Press, 2019), 48–57, for a more detailed reading of Irigaray's ontological project in the chapter "Sexual Difference."
17. Naomi Schor writes on Irigaray's radical "*mater*-ialism" in Naomi Schor, "This Essentialism Which Is Not One: Coming to Grips with Irigaray," *differences: A Journal of Feminist Cultural Studies* 1, no. 2 (1989): 40. For some excellent articles on Irigaray's elemental thinking and ecology, see the special issue edited by Emily Anne Parker, *Luce Irigaray: From Ecology to Elemental Difference*, Journal of the British Society for Phenomenology 46, no. 2 (2015).
18. Astrida Neimanis, *Bodies of Water: Posthuman Feminist Phenomenology* (London: Bloomsbury, 2016), 2, 11.
19. Zakiyyah Jackson cited in Neimanis, 10.
20. Neimanis, 11.
21. Neimanis, 11.
22. Neimanis, 73.
23. Neimanis positions Irigaray's philosophy as an often-unacknowledged influence on feminist new materialism and feminist posthumanism. For more on how both

Irigaray's and Judith Butler's work can be positioned in relation to feminist new materialism, see Elizabeth Stephens "Feminism and New Materialism: The Matter of Fluidity," *Journal of Queer Studies* 9 (2014): 186–202.
24. Neimanis, *Bodies*, 100.
25. Margaret Whitford, *Luce Irigaray: Philosophy in the Feminine* (London: Routledge, 1991), 6.
26. There are other thinkers who read Irigaray's philosophy as ontological, including Rosi Braidotti, Ellen Mortenson, Anne Van Leeuwen, Emma Jones, and Alison Stone. However, while all of these thinkers add important nuance to the conversation, most (except for Braidotti) take up Irigaray's relation to Heidegger's thought, and this is not my focus here. With this in mind, it also seems important to point out that, as Emma Jones writes, "Irigaray's readers are still searching for a way to understand what 'ontology' means for her, and are still in substantial disagreement." Emma Jones, "Speaking at the Limit: The Ontology of Luce Irigaray's Ethics, in Dialogue with Lacan and Heidegger" (PhD diss, University of Oregon 2011), 22.
27. Margaret Whitford, "Rereading Irigaray," in *Between Feminism and Psychoanalysis*, ed. Teresa Brennan (London: Routledge, 1989), 106–107.
28. Whitford, 108.
29. Whitford, 108. See also page 112 in Whitford's "Rereading." Moreover, in Whitford, *Luce Irigaray*, she repeatedly shows that Irigaray is concerned with the ontological, ethical, and social status of woman.
30. Whitford, 108.
31. Schor, "This Essentialism," 40.
32. Schor, 50.
33. Schor, 50.
34. Schor, 49–50.
35. Elizabeth Grosz, "Irigaray and the Ontology of Sexual Difference," Luce Irigaray Circle Conference, New York, 2007. The keynote talk was published in Grosz's 2011 monograph *Becoming Undone*, a book that engages a "philosophy of becoming" through an exploration of the work of Darwin, Nietzsche, Bergson, and Irigaray.
36. Sexual difference, Grosz notes, "is both [the] natural and social condition. . . . not only of subjects but of the human in general and of a living and dynamic nature in its totality." Grosz, *Becoming*, 102.
37. Grosz, 100.
38. Grosz, 6.
39. Grosz, 104.
40. Grosz, 106.
41. Grosz, 104.
42. Grosz, 106.
43. Grosz, 107.
44. Grosz continues, "it is not that all other differences are not significant—on the contrary, they are the very marks of a particular historical and geographical moment and of particular social struggles and concrete power relations—they simply function in a different manner." Grosz, 111.
45. James Sares, "Irigaray and the 'Priority' of Sexual Difference: A (Qualified) Defense," Diverse Lineages of Existentialism II: Critical Race, Feminist & Continental Philosophy (George Washington University, 2019), 3.

46. Sares, 5.
47. Sares, 6.
48. Sares, 7.
49. Sares, 9.
50. Sares, 10.
51. Sares, 10.
52. Neimanis, *Bodies*, 1.
53. Schor, "This Essentialism," 89.
54. Neimanis, *Bodies*, 1. Neimanis engages with Deleuze, Merleau-Ponty, and Stacey Alaimo as well, but for the purposes of this chapter I am focusing on her reading of Irigaray's ontology.
55. Neimanis, 79.
56. Neimanis, 80.
57. Neimanis, 80.
58. Neimanis, 2.
59. Neimanis, 2.
60. Neimanis, 2.
61. Neimanis, 3.
62. Neimanis, 2.
63. Neimanis, 2.
64. Neimanis, 3.
65. Neimanis, 3.
66. Neimanis, 3.
67. Neimanis, 4.
68. Neimanis, 96.
69. Neimanis, 74.
70. Neimanis, 77.
71. Neimanis, 77.
72. Neimanis, 77.
73. Neimanis, 76–77. See Irigaray, BEW, 80.
74. Water, on Neimanis's reading, is also used to situate multiple "feminines" in the text: "women as beings-in-the-present," "woman-in-the-future," and "a maternal primordial feminine who engenders and gestates both the actual and the virtual." Neimanis reads this "multiple-woman" as "diffracted through the multiple ways in which the fluid, water, and the sea figure in *Marine Lover*." Neimanis, *Bodies*, 81.
75. Neimanis, 81.
76. Neimanis, 84.
77. Neimanis, 84.
78. Neimanis, 85. See Irigaray, ESD, 5; Irigaray, SG, 15; Irigaray, ML, 67.
79. Neimanis, *Bodies*, 85.
80. Neimanis, 86.
81. Neimanis, 83.
82. Neimanis, 83.
83. Neimanis, 85.
84. Neimanis, 83, 84.
85. Neimanis, 68.
86. Neimanis, 96–97.

87. *Australian Concise Oxford Dictionary* (Melbourne: Oxford University Press, 2004), 43.
88. Neimanis, *Bodies*, 97.
89. Neimanis, 97.
90. Neimanis, 97.
91. Neimanis, 97.
92. Neimanis, 100.
93. Neimanis, 100.
94. Neimanis, 68, 83.
95. Neimanis, 69.
96. Neimanis, 91.
97. Neimanis, 91.
98. Neimanis, 85–86.
99. Neimanis, 85–86.
100. Rebecca Hill, "Bodies of Water: Posthuman Feminist Phenomenology by Astrida Neimanis (Review)." *philosSOPHIA* 10, no. 1 (2020): 125–130. I thank James Sares for also bringing this criticism of Neimanis's work to my attention.
101. Rosi Braidotti, "Posthuman Feminism and Gender Methodology," in *Why Gender?*, ed. Jude Brown (Cambridge: Cambridge University Press, 2021), 101.
102. Braidotti, 106.
103. While I think this criticism is an important one to raise especially in the broader discussions of posthumanism, it is also important to note that in *Bodies of Water* Neimanis describes her methodology as a "posthuman feminist phenomenology" and spends a chapter engaging with Merleau-Ponty's "embodied phenomenology" in an attempt, I think, to counter these sorts of criticisms. Neimanis, *Bodies*, 6.

PART II
Sexual Difference Beyond Sex/Gender

Chapter Five

LIFE ITSELF AND SEXUAL DIFFERENCE
Nature and Culture

RUTHANNE CRAPO KIM

In this chapter, I propose that the project of sexual difference and Irigaray's overall oeuvre ought to be read as a critical rethinking of the sexes as divisionally procreative and generative. Irigaray's "sexuate,"[1] I argue, expands the conditions of life beyond a phallocentric circumscription to female reproduction, with the notions of sex/gender, nature/culture, and time/temporality serving to clarify her philosophical intervention. While engaging dominant discourses about sex and gender, I recognize Irigaray's sexuate subjectivity as a contribution toward the complexities of human identity. Tracing her critique of the division between nature and culture, I argue that her work offers a socio-politico-ethical stance engaging elemental energy, which allows us to tease out a positive notion of woman as other than lack, unbounded to a narrow essentialism.[2] Coursing through her analysis of nature and culture is also a reorientation toward time/temporality and a retrieval of a matricidal past, necessary to revitalize a living present and futural becoming(s) that are truly (r)evolutionary.[3] As such, her work has the potential to reveal a phallogocentric framing of how Western philosophy perpetuates sameness with issues like labor production/reproduction, racialized capitalism, environmental degradation, and ongoing injustices that insist they too "can't breathe."[4]

Much of Irigaray's oeuvre engages Western male interlocutors, which is a limit of her work that may seem anachronistic and clearly "outdated" with scholars already committed to marginalized voices, body multiplicity, and gender nonconformity. As one considers pressing harms such as disproportionate and ongoing racial violence, trans-targeting policies, ableism, incarceration, global militarism, and environmental injustice, Irigaray's insistence on "feminine being" may sound woefully "out of feminist fashion," a "throw-back Thursday" of second-wave feminism we are forgiven for overlooking in favor of more marginalized or inclusive theories. I suggest that her insistence on not moving toward multiplicity is also a tactic to undermine a masculinist sociopolitical organization of time as progressive and futural. However, sexual difference is not a return to an apolitical or sexually regressive and narrow gender politics. Instead, I situate sex and gender with the implications of the limit or the negative in her work that reframes the morphological and elemental. An analysis of temporality and paradox in relation to her work clarifies the contributions of sexual difference toward an ongoing and evolving gender theory that can have broad and radical sociopolitical outcomes.

SEX, GENDER, AND SEXUATE

I concede that thorny issues plague the reception of Irigaray's work, and I state them clearly so that they do not overly determine my reading of her work. How Irigaray uses the terminology of *sex*, *sexual*, *sexuate*, and *gender* is confusing, even more so for English speakers. She uses the word *sexual* or *sexuate* instead of *sex* (*sexe*) to connote a respect for an ontological difference between living subjects, which includes vegetal, animal, and elemental. She uses *gender* (*genre*) to indicate vertical and horizontal directions for belonging that undermine and remap biological, psychological, linguistic, and social ways we have been cued to belong and relate to ourselves and others. Articulating philosophically the mediation between incalculable and volatile sexual differentiated subjects that engender evolving and shifting relations of belonging, human and otherwise, is a unique contribution to feminist theory.

However, Irigaray's sexual difference theory remains elusive because a sex/gender map dominates the feminist landscape in which Irigaray's work has been read and becomes an almost assumed lens through which a feminist critique rejects her writing as prioritizing sex over gender.[5] Feminist discourse is also critical of sex and gender as *the* or the most salient form of exploitation facing people who identify or are identified as women, omitting other ontologically significant locations of difference.[6] Irigaray's sexual or sexuate is confused with a prioritization of sex whereby men and women are defined according to a supposed biological sex, which implies that women and men have fixed identities, empirically established by reference to their bodies, which serves as a kind of unchanging ground. The assumed correction is to retrieve gender against sex's determinism. Gender is then theorized as deriving from processes such as learning, social expectations, peer pressure, and local and family values. These are all culturally specific and reveal that sex is not free of cultural signification but a malleable process that to some extent can be altered or manipulated.[7] But these assumptions about sex and gender, and their symptomatic corrections, threaten to misread how Irigaray employs the terms.

Irigaray theorizes that the sex/gender map, understood in terms of a nature/culture binary alongside the collapse of one binarized term into the other, itself remains within a polarity of sameness: (1) a somatophobia,[8] or "flesh loathing,"[9] a pitfall for some feminists eager to avoid the biologically determined body in favor of a culturally inscribed sex/gender, and (2) a prediscursive essentialized "woman's" nature or "femininity." Irigaray's work exposes the limited scope for difference when sex is situated as an anatomical fact and gender is situated as malleable identity related to how one comports oneself in the world. Irigaray reveals the implicit feminine rejection of the sexed body and the false assumption that gender thus conceived is rid of masculine domination. Instead, she suggests a dynamic sexed body and a malleable gendered belonging, both responsive to the significations of nature and culture, cultivating a difference that neither collapses nor polarizes sex and gender or nature and culture.

To clarify, I am arguing that Irigaray's work rejects dominant sex/gender discourse in three directions: (1) that gender has nothing to do with sex; (2) that sex is an unchanging ground determining sexual identity; (3) that sex ought to be collapsed into gender, being nothing substantial of its own. I examine all three directions and suggest that Irigaray posits gender belonging rather than gender neutrality to forward a nonbinary formation that radically remaps sex *and* gender.

Regarding the first direction, to hold sex and gender apart is, in a way, to reinscribe the nature/culture divide. Irigaray's project reveals the masculinist logic that forms such a rigid line separating culture from nature and the stasis that tends their construction. From her early reception through today, some Anglo-American feminists have dismissed Irigaray's work as essentialist, heterosexist, and racially blind.[10] During the past three decades, Anglo-American and French materialist feminists have contended that the category of "woman" is a social construction premised upon patriarchal interpretations of the female body.[11] As such, gender as a social construction rejects any assumed brute facts about biological sex, since the hermeneutics of language and value always and already mediate such facts. From this vantage, Irigaray's bodily rich texts, such as *This Sex Which Is Not One* and *Sexes and Genealogies*, sound like hyperbolized, essentialized morphologies of vaginal labia, mucous, breast milk, and gestational seasons—a stasis of feminine meaning and becoming.

To clarify Irigaray's use of sexuate as distinct from an oppositional sex/gender model, I argue her version of sexual or sexuate identity encompasses both biological and morphological schemas of the body often mapped as natural and feminine. At the core of Irigaray's project is a refiguration of the relationship between *logos* (words, rationality) and bodily form (*morphe*) and life (*bio*) itself. Irigaray analyzes these schemas via linguistic and psychoanalytic frameworks that have been mapped as cultural and masculine in order to mobilize a rearticulation of this terrain. Irigaray's move collapses the domination of nature/feminine as typically opposed to culture/masculine by keeping the biological and morphological at play without reducing nature and the feminine to inert matter. She writes, "it would be a matter, for her, of escaping from the simple submission to nature without for all that renouncing it."[12] At the same time, she refuses to reduce the sexed body to solely cultural inscriptions, retaining a material corporeality in her critical analysis of language and sexual relations. Hence, her critique refuses to pit nature versus culture, instead bringing them together in a complex interplay toward an ontological argument about sexuate being.

Irigaray has described the interplay of natural/body and culture/language in terms of "natural language." As she explains:

> Natural language arises above all from a desire which remains rooted in our body, but most generally from a vision of the world, which provides the language of thinking with a specific syntax. Our sexuate body acts as a sort of framework which imprints its structure on our saying. Thus patterns,

especially linguistic patterns, are not merely imposed from an outside, transforming in this way human being into a sort of automaton, they are supplied by our living nature itself. Our sexuate body operates as what enables us to overcome the split between matter and form—it produces matter with form, and form with matter. It acts as a living intermediary which allows us to develop without a frame which is technically conceived and imposed—Heidegger would say a *Gestell*. Perhaps I could also suggest that it is the place which leads us to pass from immanence to transcendence, from an ontical to an ontological level—but also from the one to the other.[13]

In this passage, Irigaray uses natural language to reveal the framework that circumscribes what we experience as bodies in the world. In the same way that death is the ineluctable frame for ontological questions of philosophy, the differences between sexed subjectivities shift the limit of ontology itself from being-toward-death to being-toward-life.[14] In articulating an active ontology of two sexuate subjects, she creates a theoretical framework of relations wherein sexuate structure offers "a finite concreteness"[15] that is "not simply closed or open."[16] Her focus on sexuate structure deploys a refiguration of fluids, previously negatively associated as feminine, actively circulating with desire, energy, and the structuring "of sexuation for the evolution of each human being."[17]

Regarding the second direction in which she rejects the sex/gender map, Irigaray's work undermines sex as the static ground for biological essentialism and gender as that which undoes sex. Biological essentialism signals the idea that my body determines my subjectivity, which is a distinct claim from Irigaray's: that sexes are real. This claim refuses to reduce sexuate subjectivity to a sexuate facticity. To signal this shift in her conception of sex, she reexamines sexual markers and uses the term *sexual* or *sexuate* to differentiate her critique of sex (*sexe*) from the sexuate. She writes, "the whole of my body is sexuate. My sexuality isn't restricted to my sex and to the sexual act."[18] Instead, sexuation brings body and language together to create "a frame capable of shaping our living energy."[19] The frame, or *Gestell*, is a complex nod to Heidegger, amplifying how sexuate identity is interlocked with the question of ontology. My body always has its own sexual specificity, but I am not alienated or determined by it. Instead, sexuation offers a structure to engage in living relations with myself and then with others (elemental, vegetal, and animal beings), and then return anew to myself. It is an oblong cyclical motion where my senses engage with the other, "conjoining" with the other in an expansion of internal and external horizons, reshaping how subjects interpret their past and future as they relate to the other who remains a mystery.

Additionally, Irigaray's use of the word *relation* clarifies the political thrust of her work on the topic of woman, which cannot be defined or closed but does exist. Relation tends to "a subject's history and its impact upon the present encounter with the other, with others."[20] She writes, "in my present body I am already intention towards the other, intention between myself and the other, beginning in genealogy. Although conceived outside of my parents' desire, although raised by them with little love and skill, I am still written in their intentions and animated by my own, whether conscious or unconscious, autonomous or interwoven with theirs. My body is never simple factuality or 'facticity.'"[21] Irigaray keeps at play the inscription of others' intentions and the animus of her own, the interweaving of one's body and the autonomy that is also possible.

The third direction in which Irigaray rejects the sex/gender discourse is in her refusal to collapse sex into gender, as if sex involved no biological substantiality of its own. This means she refuses to relegate sex (polarized or collapsed), as this reifies a rejection of the feminine as biological body. To keep sex neither apart from nor collapsed into gender, Irigaray recasts or reengages language as sexed, revealing a multiplicity of biological and morphological sexual markers. She neither theorizes a totalizing summary of sexual markers nor confers a typical presentation of them. Sexual difference shifts the meaning of sexed bodies as diffuse, multiple, volatile, and capable of pleasure in relation to themselves. These diffuse sexual markers, while not uniform or conforming, still render coherent sexuate subjects. By coherent I mean lucid and intelligible within their body schemas.[22] These bodies are not lacking in the Freudian sense of castrated subjects, but they are finite, such that "the transcendental gesture that is fitting to their human existence becomes one of building with the other a relation in which space and time are, at any moment, in-finite and in becoming."[23] Coherent and limited sexuate subjects make sense or meaning, via an epistemically "sensible" body and the body's multiplicity.

GENDERED BELONGING

Gender, or genus (*genre*), as Irigaray deploys it, includes a sense of collective belonging with other beings that does not alienate or hyperindividualize sexuate subjects. One attempt to create a sense of belonging is to suggest a gender-neutral category, whereby one does not have to subscribe to masculine or feminine identification. But gender neutrality is different than gender nonbinarism in Irigaray's terms, which I suggest challenge the erasure of women in a binary oppositional phallogocentrism as simply negated (not-Man) by thinking their gendered belonging based on differences with men.

In Irigaray's reading, gender neutrality nullifies a charged, animated, and energetic understanding of life that neutralizes sexed bodies and thus implicitly reinscribes a phallogocentric binarism. At the same time, I suggest that Irigaray attempts to rethink sexual difference apart from compulsory heterosexuality, which assumes two stable sexed categories relating antagonistically or complementarily to each other, the couple signifying a union of One. As Judith Butler and other gender theorists argue, the very heterogeneity of women—their racial, class, ethnic, religious, and bodily differences—destabilizes any category of woman as a collective. However, the political category still bears life-altering consequences, and Irigaray's inverted historical and philosophical probe warns of the ongoing and prevailing systemic forces of violence that afflict people who identify and are identified in association with deviancy from phallogocentric masculine-being. Further analysis reveals that this masculine-being is indeed also White, able-bodied, property-owning, and ratio-centric. Thus, the invisible intersectionality of the masculinist logic implies a consequential intersectional analysis of its undoing. To reveal the mechanics of this project, for Irigaray, will imply a necessary intersectional deepening of the invisible/visible that tends to Oneness and limits pleasure and fecundity for those classified negatively, including in terms of race, class, ability, religion, and sexuality. This analysis is not simply a part of a project of identity politics one could call "women's liberation"; it is a project that reveals how sex and gender within an economy of sameness are used to reproduce its own thinking.

To articulate a notion of gendered belonging mediated by sexual difference requires an examination of how a style of discourse subtends our conceptions of life and bodies, invisibly reproducing a phallocentric logic that dialectically sublates he/she (*il/elle*) into a neutered genus, humankind (*genre humain*).²⁴ Irigaray discloses the univocity of this *genre humain* and specifies the latent reproduction of masculine-being in he, she, and humankind:

> *Gender is confused with species.* Gender becomes the human race, human nature, etc., as defined from within patriarchal culture. Gender thus defined corresponds to a race of men (*un peuple d'hommes*).... All that is left is the human race/gender (*le genre humain*) for which the only real value of sex is to reproduce the species. From this point of view, *gender is always subservient to kinship.* Man and woman would not come to a maturity with a thinking and a culture relative to the sexual difference of each. They would be more or less sexed children and adolescents, and then reproductive adults.²⁵

Irigaray distinguishes a Western use of gender that is supposedly neutral, universal, and univocal, collectively categorizing people and denying difference. In the English translation of *The Way of Love* she notes, "it is useless to insist on secondary choices at the level of gender, which runs the risk of attention falling asleep about what is to be accomplished in the present because of linguistic uses which have almost become stereotypes."²⁶ She declares that she will not follow strict rules on gender pronouns but use "he/him," "she/her," and "they/them" in a way that "preserves gender and does not intend to nullify it—that the subject will little by little gain another status."²⁷

I suggest Irigaray's work on gender can advance the spirit of gender plurality and gender nonbinary identities, but her concern is that this disruption does not go far enough if it is mobilized to elide or deny sexuate specificity and belonging in ways that continue to matter for human life and culture. Irigaray's gendered belonging does more than refigure a human bio-morphological schema; it redirects us toward the genus or gendered belonging in relation with the vegetal, animal, and elemental, a move beyond the scope of sex/gender discourse. Belonging also means the body's fullness matters, which is not equivalent to a sex's facticity. The bio-morphological reinscription of how difference is generated (beyond a binary opposition) implicates a body's full sexuation, which may include hair color and texture, bone density, facial bone anatomy, skin pigment, eye shape and color, size, and how a body comports itself in the world. Sexual difference reveals the mapping of the sexed body, which means that cues which trigger racialization, ability, queerness, trans embodiment, sizeism, and ageism are brought out of the realm of abstraction but are also not universally normalized. Irigaray's work specifies a cleavage between a shifting and dynamic sexed body not predicated on feminine erasure (sexual difference) and a collective sense of belonging to share and relate (gender). Her use of gendered terms is meant to specify sexuation, which is to keep the evolution of meaning moving in relation to one's own language-body and other language-bodies and to open the possibility of other worlds corresponding to three reals: the masculine, the feminine, and the relation between. Again, these terms cannot be reduced to any received notion of masculine/feminine, as this already falls prey to the masculine-One. While her own linguistic maneuvers may prove to be less effective in advancing the causes of gender nonbinarism, the ontological scope of her project can be admired.

To recast gender belonging from a standpoint of sexual difference, Irigaray describes her task as carrying out a Nietzschean interrogation of the genealogy of woman, "an inversion of the femininity imposed upon me in order to try to define the female according to my gender. . . . to define the alterity of myself for myself as belonging to the female gender."[28] Rather than only a vertical genealogical retrieval, she coordinately advances a horizontal transcendence that respects alterity. She elaborates, "I am not the whole: I am man or woman. . . . I am objectively limited by this belonging. . . . I belong to a gender which means to a sexed universal and to a relation between two universals."[29] While Irigaray uses the word *universal*, I read her as critiquing a *totalizing* universal, which a sexuate universal erodes. Read with Irigaray, gender signifies sexuate differentiation, the interplay of language-morphology, and the mediation between by which we can rethink bodies, the elemental, and space-time. Gendered belonging is a passive recognition of radical alterity within one's body and then with others, a "particular genealogy and history . . . [and] my particular destiny. . . . a historical community."[30] The generic female sexuate gender is predicated upon a limit of one's own embodied singularity in relation to others and her aim is to create a belonging beyond philosophy's privileging of death as the limit, an obsession toward futural survival by any means.

But the very limit of a body calls into question its cultivation with other singular bodies (or not bodies), which the limit of one's body indicates. A body can only be one instantiation, not the sum of all sexual identities and morphologies. Irigaray, critical of monosexuality, seems attracted to the infinite limit that one can radically reclaim to ensure difference and create a boundary for intersubjectivity, which goes beyond the human species. The gesture of limit, or the dialectic of the negative, becomes a critical method for her theory of intersubjectivity and how subjects can caress, touch, and love without fusion or fissure. She suggests we need "a love remaining in harmony with the natural living universe that serves us a place of existence and of regeneration."[31] Self-limitation is the labor of the negative, whereby we each define our limit in relationship to others, human and more than human. The limit as an ethic for a natural living universe, a place for existence and regenerations, challenges racist-settler capitalism, which consumes to secure only the regeneration of those best able to deploy the logics of Western philosophy—abstraction, property rights, and "neutral" rationality. I concede that the expression "natural living universe" may convey a sense of a prediscursive nature outside of culture's reach, but I argue, by examining Irigaray's use of nature and culture with time, that her work resists such a closure.

NATURE, CULTURE, AND TIME

To investigate sex/gender requires thinking nature/culture since their parallel association implicates both. According to Alison Stone, some of Irigaray's readers,[32] sensitive to Irigaray's resurrection of nature, have problematically theorized nature and culture as intertwined. These feminists, agreeing that Western culture and society pervasively devalue and denigrate nature relative to culture and that women's bodies are linked to nature, conclude that women's situation can be most readily improved through cultural or symbolic change that recognizes culture's dependence upon and continuity with nature: namely, culture has defined nature as matter, a passive substratum. But if nature and culture are continuous, questions Stone, this also implies that there must be some natural basis for current patriarchal culture and that this culture is unchangeable. Not wanting to be pushed into such an undesirable corner, other feminists insist on culture's independence of, or underdetermination by, nature. This affirmation, argues Stone, "threatens to perpetuate the symbolic devaluation of the female, insofar as the female is aligned with nature."[33]

I agree with Stone when she argues that this strategy, while politically advantageous, continues the privileging of culture over nature, simply flip-flopping the present situation instead of calling into question its structural hierarchy. As Stone writes, "If we rethink nature as active and self-changing, then we can recognize (and promote social recognition of) culture's natural roots without implying that women's and men's respective symbolic standings are fixed and cannot be changed for the better."[34] The nature that Stone reads Irigaray's work as positing is active, dynamic, striving for expression, while at the same time not limiting that expression. Rather than abandoning the natural to the overwhelming tide of culture, Irigaray argues, "from the natural we should start over in order to refound reason."[35]

Reading with Stone, I suggest that Irigaray posits what one may reasonably call a quasi-transcendental notion of nature, which poses something without concretizing it, allowing it to be an organic, growing concept. As a universal, the natural is a material actualization that will appear in diverse and multiple incarnations. The natural is not a universal pregiven matter, but it is what she identifies as a *rhythm* that has bodily expression in different sexuate experiences and whose meaning is fluid and unfolding.[36] Stone exhaustively examines Irigaray's assertion that each sex has its own rhythm, universal nature, and transcendent shape.[37] While Stone investigates rhythm or syncopation to expound Irigaray's challenge of the nature/culture binary, I fear that even sympathetic readers of Irigaray struggle with a lurking essentialism in her examples,[38] and I suggest that a temporal and paradoxical analysis clarifies the slippage between her radical and mundane uses of these tropes. I explore the productiveness of an Irigarayan incompleteness and the failure of language to yield a knowable sexed signifier and yet posit sexual difference.

True to her commitment in *An Ethics of Sexual Difference*, Irigaray seeks to rethink both space *and* time. I suggest that scholars often misread her when they miss the temporal character of Irigaray's work, the reversal and transversal movements she deploys as she veers vertically into the past and horizontally toward alterity, both of which resituate her futural directions. Typically, scholars note two temporal paradigms, linear and cyclical, and Irigaray's work reveals a masculinist association with linear time and a feminine association with cyclical time.[39] But this rendering, I suggest, is descriptive rather than prescriptive, and concluding that her sexual difference elaborates a supposed "feminine" cyclical time as the thrust of her work misses the doubled tension always at play within her methodology. Additionally, such a singular conclusion assumes a stability of time to represent a singular unfolding of change and evolution. While an exhaustive reading of Irigaray's complex engagement with time and temporality are beyond the scope of this chapter,[40] I note a common theme of "renewal" and "return" as signatory to Irigaray's oeuvre.

Penelope Deutscher describes this temporal return as a "far-flung elasticity" whereby Irigaray lets loose a revolution that she promises will exceed even the Copernican revolution, one that "counters and displaces historical formulations of sexual difference that have been nourished by their inevitable excesses, their enfolded exclusions. At the extreme, a rethinking of the spatiality of envelopment is certainly an ethics of sexual difference, but thought at that extreme, it can also be unrecognizable."[41] Deutscher traces how Irigaray's anticipation of a wholly unrecognizable revolution also "snaps back" using the terms *man* and *woman*, which are now transformed from their bivocal meaning.[42] However, this revolutionary couple appears traditionally mundane. Herein is the continuum, tension, or paradox between what is and what is not that Irigaray intentionally leaves intact, refusing to sacrifice one for the other. Deutscher elaborates that Irigaray flings wide the doors of sexual difference, revolutionizing the couple, the family, gender, religion, culture, and politics, making much of what is not (excluded) by revealing what these systems strategically occlude—true difference. To do so, Irigaray returns to phrases like *man and woman*, signaling there are man and woman but that the revolution gives us a doubled vision. Man and woman exist yet sexual difference means that their differentiation remains at stake (man and woman do not yet exist, nor are these subjects meant to be foreclosed). Irigaray doubles these paradoxical assertions so one may not conclude or foreclose the work of sexual difference. Man and woman are both there and not there, as the revolution ought not cement their meanings or evolving differences. Few theorists redomesticate the language they just took pains to deconstruct, and it is a peculiarly Irigarayan move, submits Deutscher.

The snap back is, as Lynne Huffer notes, a doubled metaphysics of both *what is* and *what is not*, and as such, Irigaray's maneuver offers a

LIFE ITSELF AND SEXUAL DIFFERENCE

quintessentially queer methodology "that includes but goes beyond antisocial queer theory."[43] Huffer's point is that the Irigarayan snap back offers an effective antireading of the feminine and what gender theorists seek to dismantle—traditional feminine gender. It also offers a positive reading of feminine being or gender but one that is constantly unraveling the signifiers we normally use to determine what feminine is. Such a move, Huffer notes, includes what Jane Gallop observes as a "poiesis—the lips articulate an ethics of relation that differentiates them from the pure negativity of queer antisociality."[44] I observe in Irigaray's work a return always to oneself, to an interiority that she signals as a seat of authenticity necessary for relations between.[45] Irigaray's doubled use of sexual difference, there is and there is not man and woman, reveals the failure of a substance or the present system of signification to articulate what sex is. Given this paradox that she does not close, the singularity of the subject is critical for sex's misfire to be productive. Thinking with Huffer, Irigaray positively leverages a Lacanian *méconnaissance*, a misrecognition of the self in the mirror stage. The dissonance of what is lacking, what is not present, becomes the birth of a positive self-affection, turning negativity toward a positive ethics of the negative.

The doubled methodology of Irigaray makes present and absent a feminine being, revealing the underbelly of not-One within the Symbolic and imaginary system of codification and consciousness. Sexual difference reinscribes bodies no longer as lack. Irigaray's sexual difference refuses to render feminine-being as teleological essence or undecideable sex/gender; both are calculable maneuvers. Instead, by thinking sexual difference via both what is and what is not, the outcome of sex remains truly incalculable, as these variables change with the dynamics of nonabstract living beings.

Irigaray also points toward the necessity of the other as *other* for subjects to be in the present and not haunted by the past: "You are the one who helps me to remain in myself, to stay in myself, to contain or keep me in myself, to remain present and not paralyzed by the past or in flight towards the future.... This pause in front of the other returns me to the present, to presence."[46] She posits a transcendental immanence, offering an "in-stasy"[47] and "ex-stasy" of difference toward sensible life. The limit "delineates a horizon of interiority," a self-affection where one's own schema is reoriented. This interval limits, mediating the self from others and returning one back to oneself anew, an (in)carnation of renaissance.

> In order to avoid the interval, the irreducible separation between-us, in most cases we produce children and create familial sentiments from desire. Others ... build intellectual constructions which claim to overcome the sensible.... We have not yet cultivated our attraction toward each other, above all together, between two. From *I Love to You* onwards, I have attempted to perform such a task. Within my intentions there is a desire to overcome the immediate inclination between us, thus preserving both the energy and the between-two.[48]

In this passage, Irigaray shifts from substance or *esse* to energy and her later works[49] develop this turn that rethinks sex and desire, away from the confines of a metaphysics of presence and linguistic signs, toward energy—a return to natural physics. Acknowledging Karen Burke's insight that Irigaray's French phrase "la culture de la nature" could be translated in two ways—"the cultivation of nature" and "the culture of nature"—and that both are correct,[50] Lucia Del Gatto explains Irigaray's sense of physis:

> In fact, "culture" derives from the Latin verb *colere* ("to cultivate"), while "nature" derives from *nascor* ("to be born," "to start," "to begin"): grammatically, the word *natura* coincides with the future participle of a middle voice, periphrastic form which means a process that contains in the present the possibility of a real future. Only that of which maturation we take care of can come to birth, and Irigaray proposes restoring a relation between *logos* and *physis* according to a non-hierarchical dialectic, in order not to prevent the blossoming of the human, but instead of freeing its generative potentialities.[51]

This turn toward energy also coincides with Irigaray's turn toward birth, generation, and the meaning of physis—growing, being. Sexuation is her demand because her task is to grow our very sense of being from one world to worlds that can be shared.[52] Again, for Irigaray, difference, especially sexual difference, is a nontotalizing universal, a phenomenon that does not reject bodies (somatophobia) and respects that bodies are not blank or neutered canvases for culture's strokes. To deny sexual difference, urges Irigaray, is "to deny the material, materialistic, social, and cultural reality of difference."[53] Her reading of sexual difference anticipates the horizon of both nature and culture as active, changing, and dynamic. Bodies can take on many incarnations, notions, forms, and what some might call deformities, abnormalities, augments, and variances.

Rather than a masculinist push toward linear release, fullness, and a metaphysics of presence, Irigaray's work is most powerful in its autoerotic moments of pleasure that re-read historicity via forgotten genealogies, both vertical and horizonal. Her work offers a becoming that does not invoke a final eschaton of fullness or leave it empty, paradoxically advancing sexual difference as it cannot be joined to a definitive signifier. Her touching of the other and her touching of herself shift from substance to proximity, the space between and within. Sexual difference recasts the othered pasts, presents, and futural becoming(s), undoing a singular location or temporal rhythm by which we make sense of reality. This doubled sense of time (what is and what is not) undermines a static notion of sexuate being.

I have examined Irigaray's insistence on sexuate difference as an unfolding structure that does not foreclose differentiation as humanly dimorphic. Irigaray explains, "the natural, aside from the diversity of its incarnations or ways of appearing, is at least *two*: male and female."[54] It is not just two, but at *least* two. The diversity of differentiations bears the naturalness of a changing, moving, nontotalizing universal. The question of sexual difference, as I read Irigaray, has an inextricable bearing and unrealized contribution to the sociopolitical critiques of racism, colonialism, ableism, sizeism, heternormativity, and transphobia, which readers may overlook.

Irigaray has infamously stated that "sexual difference is one of the major philosophical issues, if not the issue, of our age,"[55] performing the doubled task of feminism: to uncover what a certain training in Western philosophy forces her to see, while uncovering what this posture represses, oppresses, and claims is invisible, namely, that there is nothing to see.[56] I have suggested that she adds an active third position: to rally for this invisible, repressed difference, or alterity (female subjectivity) to come into its own being. I have argued that a narrowly essentialized version of two sexuate subjects misses the aim of the task. Her sexuate difference is inextricably connected to space-time and the question of being. Therefore, the differences between sexed subjects will yield differences in how subjects temporally shift, occupy, or offer space, become, and belong to a gender. The rhythm that Irigaray postulates is different than a concrete positivity of a fixed identity or a reduction to an essential biological or romantic view of nature. An Irigarayan definition of the female gender must yield an ideal that accords with how we have repressed the elemental, denying the diffuse, multiple, and voluminous to rewrite language.[57] I suggest that her images of sexuate identity are not meant to reify identity into a static normative identity but are intended to be new modes of being and thinking.

Time and temporality expand our understanding of Irigaray's claims, which concern a limit of time: our age. For Irigaray, sexual difference is the issue for the age in which she participates because it conditions the possibility of epochal change with a troubling of time whose wide ellipses refigures present, future, and past. Sexual difference is necessary to interrupt the inscription of meaning in the notion of epoch or age.[58] I suggest that she does not think that sexual difference will fix or repair all other forms of repression, but within her time, sexual difference morphologically, linguistically, and psychoanalytically reveals the structures that eradicate being-toward-life. Sexual difference is capable of interpolating difference beyond the confines of sameness, which does not pit differences against one another but arrests temporal progress toward a linear or singular utopia. This ontology is not reducible to a simple essentialism that identifies body with being but is radically informed by the elemental experienced through one's language-body, temporal ellipses, and proximities—the complexities of living. She is not willing to undo the entanglements of nature or culture as they inform sexuate difference and becoming.

Irigaray's work challenges us to offer space and place and give time to consider intimacy with different economies. By using the "undecidable," "excess," or "silent invisible" of the phallocratic economy, she can contend with patriarchy while philosophically theorizing a transvaluation of a different economy. The morpho-logic of the female body informs a new mode of approaching difference via an inscription of the body in time. This will invite a cultivation of the senses, bodily and temporal, preserving a lived body with a cultural orientation to the world and the constant mediation between. Irigaray's work offers a horizon or turn that inspires a scope beyond the self-confessed limits of her lived experience.[59] To shift our thinking and being, or the metaphysical project, away from the ec(h)onomy of sameness is her first gesture toward that definition.

BIBLIOGRAPHY

Baker, Mike, Jennifer Valentino-DeVries, Manny Fernandez, and Michael LaForgi. "Three Words. 70 Cases. The Tragic History of 'I Can't Breathe.'" *New York Times*, June 29, 2020. www.nytimes.com/interactive/2020/06/28/us/i-cant-breathe-police-arrest.html.

Baruch, Elaine Hoffman, and Lucienne J. Serrano. *Women Analyze Women: In France, England, and the United States*. New York: New York University Press, 1988.

Beauvoir, Simone de. *The Second Sex*. Translated by H. M. Parshley. 1949; New York: Vintage, 1989.

Bornstein, Kate. *Gender Outlaw: On Men, Women and the Rest of Us*. New York: Routledge, 1994.

Braidotti, Rosi. *Nomadic Subjects: Embodiment and Sexual Difference in Contemporary Feminist Theory*. New York: Columbia University Press, 1994.

Burke, Carolyn, Naomi Schor, Margaret Whitford, eds. *Engaging with Irigaray: Feminist Philosophy and Modern European Thought*. New York: Columbia University Press, 1994.

Burke, Karen I. "Masculine and Feminine Approaches to Nature." In *Teaching*, edited by Luce Irigaray and Mary Green, 189–200. London: Continuum, 2008.

Butler, Judith. *Gender Trouble: Feminism and the Subversion of Identity*. New York: Routledge, 1990.

Canters, Hannecke, and Grace M. Jantzen. *Forever Fluid: A Reading of Luce Irigaray's Elemental Passions*. Manchester: Manchester University Press, 2005.

Chanter, Tina. *Ethics of Eros: Irigaray's Rewriting of the Philosophers*. London: Routledge, 1995.

Crenshaw, Kimberly. *On Intersectionality: Essential Writings*. New York: New Press, 2017.

Del Gatto, Lucia. "A Philosophy Faithful to Happiness." In *Building a New World*, edited by Luce Irigaray and Michael Marder, 3–14. Basingstoke, UK: Palgrave MacMillan, 2015.

Deutscher, Penelope. "Conditionalities, Exclusions, Occlusions." In *Rewriting Difference: Luce Irigaray and the "Greeks,"* edited by Elena Tzelepis and Athena Athnansiou, 247–258. Albany: SUNY Press, 2010.

Fuss, Diana. *Essentially Speaking: Feminism, Nature, and Difference*. New York: Routledge, 1989.

Kelly, Joan. "Some Methodological Implications of the Relations Between the Sexes." In *Women, History and Theory: The Essays of Joan Kelly*, 1–18. Chicago: University of Chicago Press, 1984.

Grosz, Elizabeth. *Becoming Undone: Darwinian Reflections on Life, Politics, and Art*. Durham, NC: Duke University Press, 2011.

Guillaumin, Collette. *Racism, Sexism, Power and Ideology*. London: Routledge, 1995.

Holland, Sharon Patricia. *The Erotic Life of Racism*. Durham, NC: Duke University Press, 2012.

hooks, bell. *Feminist Theory: From Margin to Center*. Boston: South End, 1984.

Huffer, Lynn. *Are the Lips a Grave: A Queer Feminist on the Ethics of Sex*. New York: Columbia University Press, 2013.

Jones, Rachel. *Irigaray: Towards a Sexuate Philosophy*. Cambridge: Polity, 2011.

Kim, Ruthanne Crapo. "Artificial Life, Autopoiesis, and Breath: Irigaray with Ecological Feminism and Deep Ecology." In *Horizons of Difference: Rethinking Space, Place, and Identity with Irigaray*, edited by Ruthanne Crapo Kim, Yvette Russell, and Brenda Sharp. Albany: SUNY Press, 2022.
Lee, Jonathan Scott. "The Impossible Real." In *Jacques Lacan*, 133–170. Boston, MA: Twayne, 1990.
Rich, Adrienne. *Of Woman Born: Motherhood as Experience and Institution*. New York: Norton, 1988.
Söderbäck, Fanny. *Revolutionary Time: On Time and Difference in Kristeva and Irigaray*. Albany: SUNY Press, 2019.
Spelman, Elizabeth V. *Inessential Woman: Problems of Exclusion in Feminist Thought*. Boston: Beacon, 1988.
Stone, Alison. *Luce Irigaray and the Philosophy of Sexual Difference*. New York: Cambridge University Press, 2006.
———. "The Sex of Nature: A Reinterpretation of Irigaray's Metaphysics and Political Thought." *Hypatia* 18, no. 3 (2003): 60–84.
Wittig, Monique. "One is Not Born a Woman." *Feminist Issues* 1, no. 2 (1981): 47–54.

NOTES

1. Rachel Jones, *Irigaray: Towards a Sexuate Philosophy* (Cambridge: Polity, 2011), 161, 183–184, 187–189, 194–195, 198. Throughout this essay I use *sexual difference* to express how most readers understand Irigaray's work and "sexuate" to indicate her clarifications of the expression. See Jones to situate and contextualize Irigaray's move from sexual to sexuate difference. Throughout this essay I will use both terms interchangeably.
2. See Diana Fuss, *Essentially Speaking: Feminism, Nature, and Difference* (New York: Routledge, 1989). Gender or sex essentialism is itself a multifaceted concept, and I am signaling a departure from a reductive essentialism. Other contributors in this volume will suggest a more capacious notion of essentialism that exceeds a static categorization of woman.
3. See Elizabeth Grosz, *Becoming Undone: Darwinian Reflections on Life, Politics, and Art* (Durham, NC: Duke University Press, 2011); Fanny Söderbäck, *Revolutionary Time: On Time and Difference in Kristeva and Irigaray* (Albany: SUNY Press, 2019). I parenthetically note the (r) to bring together the arguments of two notable defenders of Irigaray's work. Grosz argues that Irigaray's ethics of sexual difference is an evolutionary project; hence, there is an undoing implicit in becoming human. This Darwinian undoing, I suggest, can be paired with the thesis of a revolutionary turn in Irigaray's work given its turn toward renewal and return. Her (r)evolutionary ethics is a project of Darwinian undoing, capable of undoing the vice-grip of phallogocentrism, not in yielding a full or positive new category of woman, but in a retrieval of the past as integral with futural becomings, which are inherently unfixed as they are contingent upon coevolving relations with other humans and situated in material ecologies.
4. See Mike Baker et al., "Three Words. 70 Cases. The Tragic History of 'I Can't Breathe,'" *New York Times*, June 29, 2020, www.nytimes.com/interactive/2020/06

/28/us/i-cant-breathe-police-arrest.html. This refrain reverberates most closely with the Black Lives Matter movement's attention to the use of deadly force against Black people in the United States. Global political pitch with these three words increased after the murder of Eric Garner (2014) and George Floyd (2020), but the three words capture the pleas of countless numbers deprived of the fundament right to breathe and be free of racialized harassment and violence in the guise of law and order. Irigaray's work on breath (e.g., *Forgetting the Air*) and the invisible element of air, which constitutes a living ethics, remains an underanalyzed connection with this expression rejoindering breath, life, and body morphology together with an invisible system that seeks to stifle racialized beings through a project of white masculine Being.

5. Tina Chanter, *Ethics of Eros: Irigaray's Rewriting of the Philosophers* (London: Routledge, 1995), 26. Chanter specifies, "The sex/gender distinction has been so influential that it is almost taken for granted, with the result that it sometimes acts as a silent center."

6. See bell hooks, *Feminist Theory: From Margin to Center* (Boston: South End, 1984); Sharon Patricia Holland, *The Erotic Life of Racism* (Durham, NC: Duke University Press, 2012); Kimberly Crenshaw, *On Intersectionality: Essential Writings* (New York: New Press, 2017). There are sufficient and justified reasons that ought to pause feminist theorists from prioritizing sex/gender over and against other categories such as race, dis/ability, orientation, religion, citizenship, and colonial status. While it is beyond the scope of this chapter to argue this point, persuasive and historic accounts warn against such a move.

7. Chanter, *Ethics of Eros*, 25.

8. Elizabeth V. Spelman, *Inessential Woman: Problems of Exclusion in Feminist Thought* (Boston: Beacon, 1988), 120–131.

9. Adrienne Rich, *Of Woman Born: Motherhood as Experience and Institution* (New York: Norton, 1988), 107–108.

10. Carolyn Burke, Naomi Schor, Margaret Whitford, eds., *Engaging with Irigaray* (New York: Columbia University Press, 1994), 3–14, 15–33; Sabrina L. Hom, "White Supremacist Miscegenation: Irigaray at the Intersection of Race, Sexuality, and Patriarchy," in *Horizons of Difference: Rethinking Space, Place, and Identity with Irigaray*, ed. Ruthanne Crapo Kim, Yvette Russell, and Brenda Sharp (Albany: SUNY Press), 191–214. In *Engaging with Irigaray*, Schor and Whitford provide context for Irigaray's early reception and challenge a reading of her as narrowly essentialist. Hom acknowledges the inadequacy of Irigaray's racial analysis, but also forwards how Irigaray's work discloses the multivalent sexual threat of miscegenation, which seeks to control white women's reproduction while white men retain access to nonwhite women's bodies.

11. Simone de Beauvoir, *The Second Sex*, trans. H. M. Parshley (1949; New York: Vintage, 1989); Monique Wittig, "One is Not Born a Woman," *Feminist Issues* 1, no. 2 (1981): 47–54; Judith Butler, *Gender Trouble: Feminism and the Subversion of Identity* (New York: Routledge, 1990); Kate Bornstein, *Gender Outlaw: On Men, Women and the Rest of Us* (New York: Routledge, 1994); Collette Guillaumin, *Racism, Sexism, Power and Ideology* (London: Routledge, 1995). A myriad of thinkers has written on the development of gender as a social construction and this list only scratches the surface.

12. Irigaray, BEW, 114.
13. Irigaray, SF, 10.
14. Rosi Braidotti, *Nomadic Subjects: Embodiment and Sexual Difference in Contemporary Feminist Theory* (New York: Columbia University Press, 1994), 131.
15. Irigaray, TBB, 3.
16. Irigaray, 4.
17. Irigaray, 4.
18. Irigaray, JTN, 53.
19. Irigaray, TBB, 85.
20. Irigaray, TBT, 30.
21. Irigaray, TBT, 32.
22. See Athena V. Colman, "Tarrying with Sexual Difference: Toward a Morphological Ontology of Trans Subjectivity," in *Horizons of Difference*, ed. Ruthanne Crapo Kim, Yvette Russell, and Brenda Sharp (Albany: SUNY Press), 17–40. By coherent body schema I am thinking with Colman's analysis of trans embodiment that sexual difference ensures that trans embodiment does not remain an abstraction or posit a universal trans subject that "negates the phenomenological and feminist work that has led us to attend to experience in its location, history, and specificity in the first place" (21).
23. Irigaray, SW, x.
24. See Irigaray, JTN, 31, translator's note 3.
25. Irigaray, SG, 3, 4.
26. Irigaray, WL, xvii.
27. Irigaray, xviii.
28. Irigaray, ILTY, 66, 63.
29. Irigaray, 106.
30. Irigaray, 39, 145.
31. Irigaray, BEW, 55.
32. Alison Stone, *Luce Irigaray and the Philosophy of Sexual Difference* (New York: Cambridge University Press, 2006), 130–31. Stone cites both Elizabeth Grosz and Moira Gatens as feminists seeking to avoid the split between nature and culture by intertwining nature with culture. This intertwining, while more genuinely attempting to reconcile these concepts, still leaves many questions for Stone, such as, how can culture be modified through natural tendencies that direct this change?
33. Stone, *Luce Irigaray*, 130.
34. Stone, 131.
35. Irigaray, ILTY, 37.
36. This is Stone's analysis of Irigaray's position on nature. She argues that it is not so much a thing as it is a rhythm of life.
37. Alison Stone, "The Sex of Nature: A Reinterpretation of Irigaray's Metaphysics and Political Thought," *Hypatia* 18, 3 (2003): 60–84; Stone, *Luce Irigaray*, 87–126.
38. Stone proposes a realist essentialism as indicated by rhythm that she reads with Irigaray's work. My theorization considers rhythm as an indicator of difference that presses against an ocular ratiocentric discourse, and I resist a rhythm of nature that reduces or closes that expression into an unchanging material ground or specific cultural expression.

39. See Söderbäck, *Revolutionary Time*, 7n14. Stephen J. Gould, *Time's Arrow, Time's Cycle: Myth and Metaphor in the Discovery of Geological Time* (Cambridge, MA: Harvard University Press, 1988).
40. See Söderbäck, *Revolutionary Time*. Söderbäck offers a compelling and carefully researched analysis of historicity, temporarily, and time as unique variants and the relation to these terms in the thinking of both Kristeva and Irigaray.
41. Penelope Deutscher, "Conditionalities, Exclusions, Occlusions," in *Rewriting Difference: Luce Irigaray and the "Greeks,"* ed. Elena Tzelepis and Athena Athnansiou (Albany: SUNY Press, 2010), 250–251.
42. Deutscher, 250–251.
43. Lynne Huffer, *Are the Lips a Grave: A Queer Feminist on the Ethics of Sex* (New York: Columbia University Press, 2013), 43. To clarify an antisocial queer theory Huffer points to Leo Bersani's diagnosis of a social imaginary "that homophobically and misogynistically links both women and gay men with death. . . . what has become known as the antisocial thesis of a nonredemptive sexuality" (35).
44. Huffer, 43.
45. Ruthanne Crapo Kim, "Artificial Life, Autopoiesis, and Breath: Irigaray with Ecological Feminism and Deep Ecology," in *Horizons of Difference*, ed. Ruthanne Crapo Kim, Yvette Russell, and Brenda Sharp (Albany: SUNY Press, 2022), 241–263.
46. Irigaray, TBT, 37.
47. Irigaray, DB, 116.
48. Irigaray, TBT, 37.
49. See Irigaray, NCE.
50. Karen I. Burke, "Masculine and Feminine Approaches to Nature," in *Teaching*, ed. Luce Irigaray and Mary Green (London: Continuum, 2008), 195.
51. Lucia Del Gatto, "A Philosophy Faithful to Happiness," in *Building a New World*, ed. Luce Irigaray and Michael Marder (Basingstoke, UK: Palgrave MacMillan, 2015), 5.
52. See Irigaray, TBB and SW.
53. Elaine Hoffman Baruch and Lucienne J. Serrano, *Women Analyze Women: In France, England, and the United States* (New York: New York University Press, 1988), 155.
54. Irigaray, ILTY, 37.
55. Irigaray, ESD, 5, 13.
56. Joan Kelly, "Some Methodological Implications of the Relations Between the Sexes," in *Women, History and Theory: The Essays of Joan Kelly* (Chicago: University of Chicago Press, 1984), 1ff.
57. See Hannecke Canters and Grace M. Jantzen, *Forever Fluid: A Reading of Luce Irigaray's* Elemental Passions (Manchester: Manchester University Press, 2005).
58. I understand her to be saying that within her bodily existence, her task has been to limit strategically her work in order to open up other areas of justice and distribution, not to close or render the work complete.
59. Irigaray, BEW, 115. She attests to this theorization beyond any solipsistic reference back to her.

Chapter Six

SEXUATION AS A FRAME FOR HUMAN BECOMING

Reading a "Plastic" Essence in Irigaray's Philosophy

BELINDA ESLICK

> That "woman" is now emptied of her essence only serves to emphasize the fact that she does not define herself and cannot define herself except through the violence done to her. . . . She's nothing but an ontological amputation, formed by that which negates her.
>
> —CATHERINE MALABOU, *CHANGING DIFFERENCE*

> Our sexuation represents a limited structure that life itself gives in order for us to develop according to our singularity.
>
> —LUCE IRIGARAY, *TO BE BORN*

Luce Irigaray's claim that women must cultivate subjectivities that are representative of women's sexuate[1] specificity is a central tenet of her feminism and her philosophy more broadly. Aiming to adopt—or be recognized as *equal to*—the already-existing philosophical and political Subject position is ultimately conservative, she claims, because it assumes the dominant subject (which is conceptually male and has been cultivated by men) to be normative or ideal. This position is based in her critique of the phallocentrism of Western philosophy, which, she claims, has failed to properly think sexuate difference. Women have been conceptualized in Western thought only ever *in relation to* men rather than as subjects in our own right, and arguments for equality only reinforce this logic. It is therefore necessary, Irigaray argues, that women make claims for subjectivity and selfhood based on our difference, not sameness, to men and necessary to reimagine subjectivity to allow for the possibility of at least two subjects that are irreducible to each other "while sharing equivalent dignity."[2] In addition, Irigaray argues that sexuation is constitutive of subjectivity and that, as a consequence, there is an irreducible difference between differently sexuate human beings. Because of this emphasis on sexuate specificity, she has been criticized for being—and is often dismissed as—an *essentialist*.[3] I argue that claims of essentialism in Irigaray's philosophy and feminist politics are misplaced, however, and that they overlook important aspects of her philosophical project. A number of scholars have previously defended Irigaray's work against criticisms that it is essentialist by suggesting that any apparent essentialism is a kind of "strategic" or "political" essentialism aimed at linguistic subversion.[4] While these perspectives are based in more sympathetic readings of Irigaray's work, I argue that such readings also misrepresent her thought and obscure the radical intervention into Western philosophy that her work offers.

In a seminar that I attended with Irigaray in 2018, she defended herself against claims of essentialism by saying that they are based in an *old metaphysics*. Her work, importantly, seeks to bring about a new metaphysics, or a new world—one that would make it possible for sexuate difference to be properly conceptualized and represented, and thus for women to be acknowledged as subjects. Indeed, Irigaray claims that it is not possible to properly think sexuate difference—or difference generally—within a current (or "old") Western metaphysics.[5] I argue that readings of Irigaray's notions of sexuation and sexuate difference, which inevitably encounter questions of essentialism and essence, must take this crucial aspect of her project into account. This is because a "new metaphysics" would arguably presume a "new" way of thinking essence. I argue that there is a kind of "essence" operating in Irigaray's thought but that it is not the *fixed* essence rejected by antiessentialists, nor is it one that assumes a predetermined ideal or end point. This is particularly evident, I suggest, in Irigaray's recent works, including *Through Vegetal Being*, *To Be Born*, and *Sharing the Fire*, where she articulates her notion of sexuation as a "framework,"[6] a "structure,"[7] or a "frame"[8] that gives a kind of originary "structure"[9] to our becoming, while simultaneously emphasizing the importance of our continual becoming and growth. Our sexuation, Irigaray claims, represents a "limited structure," given to us by life for us to "develop according to our singularity."[10] However, such developing or becoming *necessitates* repeated transformation—what she describes as a process of continually giving birth to oneself anew.[11] I think that such an ontology acknowledges, and even foregrounds, the significance of a kind of "originary structure" (for her, a sexuate "frame") while not denying the possibility (indeed, the necessity) for continual growth and repeated transformation. It is this dual commitment to acknowledging sexuation as a frame or originary structure as well as emphasizing the need for continual becoming through repeated transformation that I suggest signals the novel ways that "essence" operates in Irigaray's work. It is also, significantly, this aspect of Irigaray's recent works where I find parallels between her thinking on sexuation as a frame and Catherine Malabou's thinking on the *plasticity* of essence, which she develops through her critique of the antiessentialist position.

In this essay, I offer an overview of some previous readings of "essence" and "essentialism" in Irigaray's work before offering my own reading through engaging with Irigaray's recent claims and discussing Malabou's argument against antiessentialism. I consider how Malabou's thinking on plasticity offers a way of conceptualizing Irigaray's thinking on sexuate difference that moves beyond simplistic and reactionary charges of essentialism. In doing so, I suggest that we can find a kind of "plastic" essence in Irigaray's notion of sexuation as a frame.

TENSIONS BETWEEN "ESSENTIALIST" AND "ANTIESSENTIALIST" FEMINIST PERSPECTIVES

There has been significant ongoing debate about questions of essentialism (as well as universalism and biological determinism) within feminist thought and politics broadly.[12] Feminists, importantly, continue to challenge patriarchal and phallocentric claims of women's identity (or notions of an "essence of woman") that work to justify women's subordinate position in patriarchal thought and culture. As Elizabeth Grosz writes, patriarchal claims of the identity of "woman" work to "rationalize and neutralize the prevailing sexual division of social roles by assuming that these roles are the only, or the best, possibilities, given the confines of the nature, essence or biology of the two sexes."[13] It is therefore not surprising, as Grosz notes, "that these terms have become labels of danger zones or theoretical pitfalls in feminist assessments of patriarchal theory."[14] Suspicions of such terms are evident in readings of Irigaray's thought, and debates about apparent essentialism in her work are significant. Because Irigaray affirms that women's subjectivity is *particular*, engagements with her work inevitably encounter questions about what this particularity or difference is and where it originates—and critics claim that Irigaray mobilizes a restrictive kind of essentialism that feminism should in fact seek to overcome. For example, the ways that Irigaray symbolizes female bodies in her writing (including the vaginal lips,[15] the placenta,[16] and lactating breasts) are necessary,[17] she claims, in her project of transforming Western culture because it, significantly, brings female corporeality and bodily experiences (which have been, in a psychoanalytic sense, repressed in patriarchal culture and phallocentric philosophy) into symbolic representation. However, some—including, perhaps most notably, Toril Moi[18]—criticized these aspects of her work as an attempt to reduce women and feminine subjectivity to bodily features or phenomena that are not shared by all women.[19] Such perspectives risk, Moi and others claim, reinvigorating a kind of restrictive biological determinism. Irigaray has avoided offering a definition of "woman" or the feminine,[20] but she does attribute women's specificity to sexuation and (it appears) sexuation to the morphology of the body. While she has previously been opaque about what she considers to be the nature or origin of women's specificity, in her recent works she does describe, with more clarity, (sexuate) subjectivity as emerging from or through the sexuate body.[21] Further, Irigaray's assertion that, to be truly emancipated, women must cultivate our own subjectivities, rather than transcending the feminine (Object) position to join the masculine (Subject) position, has led some to criticize her for mobilizing a universal category of "woman" that denies the plurality of women's identities and experiences. As such, assessments of Irigaray's work as essentialist or universalist have, as Rebecca Hill notes, "marked Irigaray's thought as a no-go zone for many feminist philosophers and feminist theorists for several years."[22]

Feminists have good reason to be suspicious of essentialist or universalizing notions of "woman," or even a collective category of "women," and these arguments are well understood. Attempts to define women's subjectivity risk reaffirming the restrictive ontologies that limit our capacity for personal flourishing and transcendence. Further, the idea that the body predetermines subjectivity and one's possibilities of transcendence has been rejected by many feminists, often because women's bodies have been conceptualized and characterized, in patriarchal culture, in terms of deficiency and subordination and because women's identities have been cultivated, and limited, in men's terms.[23] Those who challenge or reject Irigaray's claim that sexuation is constitutive of subjectivity by suggesting that she is an essentialist typically argue that such a position risks reinscribing such restrictive views of women's being, and thus enables a kind of ontological violence. However, Grosz points out that alongside the dangers in defining (and thereby limiting) women, a category of "women" remains politically necessary.[24] To be able to make feminist claims on behalf of women, and to point out the systemic oppression of women, Grosz claims that it is necessary to understand women as constituting some kind of unifiable group. Without a category or concept of "women," Grosz asks, how can feminism be taken seriously?[25] She describes this tension between the need to avoid defining women and the need to affirm women's specificity as a "double bind" between essentialist and antiessentialist theoretical positions on sexual difference. On the one hand, perspectives that seek to define the category of "women" should be challenged because they restrict—as well as misrepresent—women's identities. On the other, denying women's particularity fails to recognize the *specific* nature of women's oppression—as well as the ways that patriarchal thought and culture exclude and silence women and deny women subjectivity and voice. Alison Stone similarly describes debates between essentialist and antiessentialist feminist positions, which have questioned "whether there are any properties common to all women in virtue of which women belong together as a group."[26] She says that, "if there are any such properties (e.g. shared biological features, or shared suffering from gender oppression), then women are a unified group and can act together politically."[27] However, "if there are no such properties, then it seems that nothing really unites women, which throws the possibility of feminist politics into question."[28] In addition to being considered politically necessary, Irigaray claims that acknowledging the specificity of "woman" is necessary in articulating a subject position for women that departs from patriarchal and phallocentric characterizations of women's identity (that is, as understood only in relation to the masculine position). Further, in her more recent work, she claims that the failure to recognize one's sexuation limits a human being's capacity to flourish and move "towards a human blooming which corresponds to them."[29]

PRIOR READINGS OF "ESSENTIALISM" IN IRIGARAY'S WORK

Numerous scholars have offered analyses of the ways that a notion of essence might operate in Irigaray's thought. Virpi Lehtinen, for example, offers a careful consideration of the ways that essentialism has been read in Irigaray's work and suggests that it is typically read in one of four ways: as "metaphysical" (Platonic or Aristotelian), "strategic" (or political), "deconstructive," or "realist." As she describes, readings of Irigaray as a metaphysical essentialist interpret her conception of woman as promoting "the idea that essences are non-temporal and unchanging ontological and/or conceptual structures," which "does not allow cultural or political variations and transformation."[30] Following early critiques that suggest Irigaray mobilizes a metaphysical essence, later readers (including, as Hill notes,[31] Tina Chanter, Elizabeth Grosz, Naomi Schor, and Margaret Whitford) have offered more considered and sympathetic interpretations of her thinking on sexuate difference. Among these was the argument that the apparent essentialism in Irigaray's work was representative not of a metaphysical notion of (a fixed and unchanging) essence but of a "strategic" essentialism aligned with Irigaray's strategy of *mimesis* and aimed at political or discursive subversion and disruption.[32] As Lehtinen writes, the reading of strategic essentialism "understands Irigaray's idea of mimesis as a textual and discursive strategy . . . and claims that this is her principal method." In her earlier work, Irigaray calls for women to adopt the "feminine" position mimetically (and not entirely faithfully) as a way of illuminating and problematizing patriarchal definitions and representations of femininity.[33] Some, Lehtinen describes, use this as evidence to defend Irigaray against claims of essentialism, suggesting that Irigaray's calls for the representation of women's specificity are only in order for her to point out its construction, or fabrication, within patriarchal discourse—not to suggest that there is some kind of "natural" feminine position. Likewise, others have read the apparent essentialism in Irigaray's work in deconstructive terms, arguing that sexuate difference and, specifically, "the feminine" operate in Irigaray's work to designate the space of what has not been or cannot be represented in discourse.[34] Lehtenin notes that, in such a reading, "woman and the feminine form the constitutive 'outside' of discourse."[35]

However, as with Lehtinen, Stone argues that readings of Irigaray as a nonrealist essentialist are "unhelpful" given Irigaray's apparent, and seemingly increasing, commitment to what Stone describes as a "realist" kind of essentialism.[36] Stone suggests that debates about apparent essentialism in feminist thought and Irigaray's work specifically "have inspired a now-widespread assumption that no realist form of essentialism is acceptable."[37] As a result, she claims, "Irigaray can only be read as an essentialist in some distinctively non-realist sense."[38] But she criticizes readings of Irigaray as a political or strategic essentialist as "internally unstable."[39] This is partly because this position pursues, she says, "the revaluation of femaleness and the body only as culturally imagined and symbolized, thereby reinforcing the very valorization of symbolic over corporeal, cultural over natural, which it seeks to contest."[40] In other words, such interpretations remain within a worldview that conceives of matter and "nature" largely as inert or passive—as capable of receiving *but not giving* form. As Stone suggests, Irigaray's philosophical project seeks to overcome these hierarchical dichotomies. Rachel Jones also argues that charges of essentialism against Irigaray are misplaced and challenges readings that describe her as a strategic essentialist.[41] Jones argues, importantly, that positioning Irigaray in such a way can "obscure the ways in which the transformation she seeks would *undo traditional models of essence*, insofar as these rely on a constitutive opposition between form and matter."[42] Stone claims that there is indeed a "sophisticated" realist essentialism in Irigaray's work that has radical, transformative potential in terms of its capacity to challenge a traditional dualism between "nature" and "culture."[43] I agree with Stone that Irigaray maintains some notion of a "natural" sexuate duality but argue that it is important to recognize that she considers the categories that this supposes as *open*,[44] which Lehtinen's own reading of a "dynamic essence" acknowledges.

Lehtinen notes that some readings of the apparent essentialism in Irigaray's work—including the reading of Irigaray as a strategic essentialist and Stone's reading of Irigaray as a realist essentialist—are more sympathetic than those that dismiss her as a metaphysical essentialist but questions whether they accurately represent Irigaray's position. She argues that debates over apparent essentialism (and, in addition, an apparent heterosexism) in Irigaray's work have obscured interpretations of her thought,[45] which she describes as "an exemplification and catalyst of the dynamic forces of change and transformation."[46] Offering an alternative reading of Irigaray's apparent essentialism, she proposes that essence operates in Irigaray's work as a "dynamic essence" or, drawing on Husserl and Merleau-Ponty, as "existential style."[47] In reading essence in Irigaray's work as *style*, Lehtinen draws on phenomenology of the body—a perspective from which "experience is never fully given, but always open, partial and perspectival."[48] In this sense, Lehtinen argues that Irigaray's work, rather than proposing a restrictive definition of women's essence, indeed attempts to "*open* and *elaborate* the sense and significance of feminine being" and to "liberate feminine being from the fixed and biased notions of femininity."[49] The emphasis on generativity and growth in Irigaray's work is significant to Lehtinen and she argues that it must be seriously considered when understanding notions of essence in Irigaray's work. Reading sexuation in terms of *style* acknowledges the dynamism of becoming, Lehtinen suggests, and shifts the focus away from an end point, ideal, or telos. "Style as an existential, perceptual unity," she writes, "is an open and dynamic form, and as such has no pre-determined end-point or perfection."[50] Lehtinen argues convincingly that, in contrast to Aristotelian and Platonic notions of a metaphysical essence, which see essence as either "a potency striving for its actualization" or "non-temporal and static," Irigaray's work promotes an ontology of continual becoming and transformation that has no predetermined end point. Significantly, as is particularly evident in her recent work, Irigaray seeks to shift focus away from death and instead orient toward birth: she claims that we can continually give birth to ourselves anew, and transformation is thus conceived of as a *series of beginnings*. Recognizing this focus on birth and beginnings is, I argue, crucial for understanding how essence might operate in Irigaray's ontology.

"A LIMITED STRUCTURE THAT LIFE ITSELF GIVES": SEXUATION AS A "FRAME" IN IRIGARAY'S RECENT WORKS

In Irigaray's most recent works, she continues her project of writing a book dedicated to each of the "main elements which constitute the matter of the world and of all the living beings,"[51] which she began with her earlier works *Marine Lover of Friedrich Nietzsche* and *The Forgetting of Air in Martin Heidegger*. Her four most recently published English titles are each—in various ways—concerned with the failure of much of Western[52] philosophy and culture to attend to "the cultivation of our sensitive and sensuous life."[53] As with her earlier works, she is concerned with bringing about the conditions under which women could be recognized as subjects, and this task requires us, she claims, to consider how we might address the limitations and failings of Western culture. Such a reimagining of Western thought and culture would also allow us, as she suggests, to emerge from the significant crises facing humanity—and all planetary life—in the twenty-first century.

Her recent works are characterized by a sense of urgency to address these current crises. In opening *Sharing the Fire*, for example, she asks: "Is humanity coming to an end or merely reaching a stage which calls for a radical cultural evolution?"[54] She suggests that such an evolution is possible but requires that we "question our way of conceiving of human being itself."[55] A major theme of Irigaray's recent works is her argument that significant aspects of Western culture encourage our alienation from the natural world, our breath, our bodies, and thus what she describes as our "sexuate belonging."[56] She also calls on us to return to our breath and our "natural belonging," specifically describing, in *A New Culture of Energy*, her experiences of yogic practice. In *Through Vegetal Being*, she also describes how the natural, or vegetal, world has nourished and supported her through her life, and she draws on these experiences in arguing that the West must reconfigure its relationship to "nature." This would involve a rethinking of our conception of subjectivity, she claims, "in order to become able to give birth to a new way of being and existing, especially with regard to the whole living world."[57] It also requires a "more radical refoundation of our culture starting from the determination, especially the sexuate determination, of our subjectivity, which allows respect for life and its development."[58] Irigaray argues that Western culture fails to prioritize birth and life or a "living energy," instead orienting around death as the horizon that gives structure to human becoming.[59] This is a mistake, she claims, and encourages an alienation from our natural belonging, thus thwarting our capacity for flourishing. She claims that, rather than death, it is indeed our *breath* and our *sexuation*, both originary gestures in the life of the human being, that structure human becoming—and that Western thought and culture must reorient to acknowledge this.

I suggest that we can observe the ways that essence operates in Irigaray's work in part through paying attention to the way that she addresses the themes of birth, breath, and desire. The theme of birth, as well as the breath, is central to Irigaray's recent work, particularly *To Be Born*. Her major claim in *To Be Born* is that the human baby *gives birth to itself* through its first breathing after leaving the mother's body.[60] Without denying the significance of the baby's reliance on the maternal body—or the activity of the mother's birthing—the breath comes to represent our will to live, leading her to suggest that, through cultivating our breath, we can (and must) repeatedly give birth to ourselves anew throughout our lives. However, she argues that, as the human child develops, it is discouraged, through many customs and institutions, from cultivating a desire for life. Rather than considering human becoming as emerging from within, she argues, Western culture positions it as an "idea" outside of oneself to which the child is supposed to strive.[61] Such a metaphysical view of one's becoming, she suggests, encourages a process where, rather than a kind of natural flourishing or blossoming, the human being becomes a "manufactured product."[62] She claims that it is through returning to and cultivating the breath that we can reignite this desire to live and thus continue to give birth to ourselves again and again. In this sense, our developing or becoming necessarily involves a process of repeatedly forgoing whom we have been. In *To Be Born*, for example, she writes:

> Our way of behaving attempts to grasp and fix the mystery of our origin into a face, whereas we ought always to abandon any face that has already appeared so that we can develop. We can remain living only at the price of a continuous becoming, which means relinquishing what is already flowered, which falls into appearance as soon as it has appeared. Faithfulness to itself of a human being cannot content itself with one presence, one reproduction or representation. Life cannot settle in one form only, it ceaselessly grows in different forms on pain of being already, at least in part, death.[63]

The breath is significant in Irigaray's ontology, and specifically to her notion of sexuation, because through breathing, she claims, we encounter the threshold of our being and the bodily structure that contains our breath. She suggests that this allows us to acknowledge the morphology, and thus particularity, of our corporeal structure—as well as our natural belonging and origin. "Our sexuation supplies us," she says, "with a setting . . . for the organization of the living," and it acts as a structure that allows us to "internalize air—thus the breath, and the soul and even the spirit which were born of it—in a singular manner."[64] Importantly, acknowledging our particularity through the process of returning to our breathing also cultivates desire: it is in encountering the threshold of our own world that we are called to move beyond it to that of another.[65] The cultivation of sexuate desire (which is, she emphasizes, not always *sexual*), as Irigaray conceptualizes it, therefore requires that we give attention to our origins or birth while remaining future-focused and open to growth that has no foreseeable end.

"While being faithful to that which is in the beginning," she writes, "desire endlessly aims at its fulfillment because the absolute after which it aspires can never be completely reached."[66] Irigaray claims, however, that the Western tradition has "underestimated, and even ignored, the importance of desire for our human accomplishment."[67]

Acknowledging ourselves as sexuate also "solves the question of its finiteness without necessarily having to resort to death."[68] Instead of an end or ideal, the point of focus for Irigaray is at the *multiple* and continual births that she claims enable a human being's becoming or flourishing. It is in this sense that, I suggest, the idea of sexuation as a frame offers a significant break from typical ways of conceptualizing essence in Western metaphysics. In viewing essence as an Irigarayan frame provided at birth rather than as an immutable, metaphysical *form*, Irigaray's ontology appears to suggest that a human subject can become endless "versions" of itself but cannot become an other; it cannot uproot itself from its origins or from the originary movement that acted as a precondition for subsequent "rebirths." Further, and significantly, acknowledging our sexuation and living as sexuate allow us to recognize our singularity, Irigaray claims, and are thus a precondition for her ethic of *intersubjectivity*: sexuation, she argues, "makes us capable of building a volume from the void that is opened in each of us, and also between us, by acknowledging that we are not the other, that we are not, and never will be, the whole of human being."[69]

While Irigaray's recent works offer a particularly clear view of her thinking on sexuation and how sexuation relates to her philosophy more generally, they also, as I have claimed, allow us to consider the ways that "essence" operates in her work. Careful readings of these works (and the ways that notions of essence present in them) therefore make it possible, I suggest, to respond to critiques of Irigaray's apparent essentialism with greater nuance. Here, I offer a reading of a "plastic" essence, informed by Malabou.

MALABOU, PLASTICITY, AND THE "VIOLENCE" OF ANTIESSENTIALISM

Malabou is perhaps best known for her work on bridging neuroscience and philosophy and for her thinking on the concept of plasticity, which, in simple terms, designates the capacity of matter to be altered or to change form irreversibly. The term is widely used in the arts (to refer to the "plastic arts," such as ceramics or sculpture), engineering, and neuroscience (i.e., neuro-, brain, or cerebral plasticity). Importantly, the plastic transformation of matter is shaped, and thus limited, by the matter itself and so, as Malabou notes, the term also signifies "an equilibrium between the receiving and giving of form."[70] In *Ontology of the Accident,* Malabou uses the concept of plasticity to examine the potential for human transformation (or metamorphosis) following negation or trauma. Here, Malabou draws partly from studies in neuroscience (including relating to cerebral plasticity and brain trauma) to conceptualize metamorphosis and her notion of "destructive plasticity."[71] She situates her discussion with particular interest at the point of destruction or negation, which she says allows for subsequent transformation. Key to Malabou's thinking on transformation and the notion of destructive plasticity is her claim that the transformation that occurs after trauma or negation is total: the process amounts to "well and truly the fabrication of a new person, a novel form of life, without anything in common with a preceding form."[72] "The fact that all creation can only occur at the price of a destructive counterpart is a fundamental law of life," Malabou claims.[73] Plasticity, she says, "refers precisely to this power of modification of the identity in proportions that exceed the simple detour or hiccup."[74]

Importantly, Malabou's notion of plasticity emphasizes the significance of an originary model or movement, which precedes any subsequent negation and transformation. While Malabou is concerned with the potential for continual and total transformation and rejects any notion of a fixed and unchanging essence, she challenges a "purely" antiessentialist perspective and the rejection of any notion of essence. While the anti-essentialist position disputes the possibility of an essence, Malabou positions a kind of (plastic) essence as the *precondition* for subsequent transformation. In *Changing Difference,* Malabou addresses the theme of essence specifically and considers the tensions between essentialist and anti-essentialist perspectives in feminist, gender, and queer thought. She describes a shift in feminist thinking from a kind of essentialist perspective (according to which women are defined as subjects, even if this subjectivity is limited by an "essence of woman" that is understood as fixed and universally shared), to the "erasure of all ontological specificity" of women in the antiessentialist, linguistic turn in some feminist, gender, and queer theory.[75] Malabou criticizes the antiessentialist position, arguing that it is a *violent* gesture[76] and that, through denying any essence to women, antiessentialism enacts a theoretical violence against women.[77] This serves to "empty woman of herself, to disembowel her."[78] Such violence equates to physical violence against women, she claims, and maintains women's status as nonsubjects. In an introductory note to the book, she writes:

> That "woman" finds herself now in the age of post-feminism deprived of her "essence" only confirms, paradoxically, a very ancient state of affairs: "woman" has never been able to define herself other than through the violence done to her. Violence alone confers her being—whether it is domestic and social violence or theoretical violence. The critique of "essentialism" (i.e. there is no specifically feminine essence) by gender theory and deconstruction is but one more twist in the ontological negation of the feminine.[79]

Crucially, Malabou's critique of the antiessentialist position is based on her argument that antiessentialists, in rejecting the essentialist position, have in fact *misunderstood* essence. She frames this argument in plastic, dialectical terms: in her critique of antiessentialism, she suggests that the antiessentialist position negates essentialism but has not yet transformed into something new. In this sense, the antiessentialist position is considered not only theoretically violent toward women but theoretically unsound. The antiessentialist rejection of essence is thus too simplistic, and is "based on *a current, ordinary conception of essence*."[80] Malabou therefore calls for a "third moment"—for essence to be transformed beyond its mere negation. Rather than being rejected, the notion of essence must be *reexamined* to acknowledge what Malabou considers the plasticity of essence and of being (claiming that essence is not being itself but something "behind" being),[81] which she says the antiessentialist position denies. She does this herself "not through heavy ontological enquiry," but "by asking whether this term has been correctly understood by those who malign it."[82] Essence, she writes, has "only ever designated . . . the transformability of beings, never their substantial stability," and "does not say presence; it says *entry into presence*, in other words, an originary movement that, again, is the movement of change or exchange."[83] In this sense, accusations of essentialism mean something only, Malabou claims, "at the price of a total philosophical ignorance of the meaning of the word 'essentialism.'"[84] Essence, she argues, is neither concrete (completely fixed) nor fluid (without form), but *plastic*.[85]

Malabou then asks how we might move toward some kind of "essence of Woman"[86] and recognize a certain feminine space (something that she says seems "impossible" yet "also very dangerous to try to deny") without reinscribing the violence of essentialism as conventionally understood and deployed under patriarchy to oppress women.[87] Her own proposal is offered through her notion of destructive plasticity. While Malabou says that "woman" is now nothing but an "ontological amputation," she sees the point of amputation (that is, negation) as powerful. Through the continual denial of women's being, it has become *resistant* and "explosive," she claims.[88] Malabou posits a "minimal concept of Woman" and a "negative" subjectivity for women, suggesting that, following the deconstruction of the feminine, there remains not debris but a "kernel of resistance, a kernel with the strength of a new beginning."[89] By describing women as negative subjects, Malabou is not suggesting that "woman" is a passive "non-subject" but that a woman's capacity to "negate the negation of her essence" *is our essence.*[90] This means, she claims, that women have the capacity to continually transform our being despite the repeated material and theoretical violence that we experience. Malabou's concept of negative subjectivity is a way of positively reconceptualizing this negation.

Stone questions whether Malabou's suggestion that women's essence is to be found in our constantly being negated is "unduly negative," however, and asks: "Has patriarchy really violated women's being so totally that nothing more positive than violation is left to define them?"[91] Malabou's claim that woman's essence *is* the constant negation of her essence (from which emerges an explosive locus of power) is reminiscent of claims, in deconstructive readings of essence in Irigaray's work, that the feminine represents that which cannot be symbolized. Malabou does not directly consider the role of the material, sensuous body in subject formation or symbolization—something that Irigaray's work does. However, Malabou's call for a "third moment" beyond essentialism and antiessentialism—along with her argument that antiessentialism has failed to acknowledge the plasticity of being—is significant. As Stone suggests, Malabou's work on plasticity "has considerable potential to advance our thinking about gender and essentialism."[92] Further, Malabou's claim that antiessentialists have misunderstood essence is also reminiscent of Irigaray's suggestion that those who dismiss her as an essentialist are working within an old metaphysics. While it seems obvious that we must reject any notion of a fixed, ahistorical essence, Malabou calls on us to consider the ramifications of a "pure" antiessentialist position for women's subjectivity—but also, importantly, for the ways in which such a position seems to reinscribe a problematic dualism between form and matter or "culture" and "nature," where form and culture shape matter and nature but not vice versa. Irigaray's description of sexuation as a frame for human becoming seriously problematizes antiessentialist readings of her work because it suggests, we could say, a plastic—not fixed—essence.

A "THIRD MOMENT": SEXUATE FRAME AS PLASTIC ESSENCE?

Irigaray's thought remains subject to criticism for mobilizing an essentialist perspective. While Irigaray does claim that sexuation shapes, and limits, our human becoming, I argue that it is simplistic to dismiss this as naive essentialism, biological determinism, or universalism. Malabou's call to reexamine essence—that is, to imagine what essence is to become beyond its mere negation—can act as an invitation to readers of Irigaray's work to consider the presence of plasticity in her ontology. Irigaray's notion of sexuation corresponds to a way of conceptualizing being and becoming neither as fixed by essence nor as completely emergent and devoid of essence. If the sexuate body is understood as the "essence" of sexuate subjectivity in Irigaray's notion of sexuation and sexuate difference, I argue that it must be understood, in Malabou's terms, as a *plastic* essence. This formulation, I suggest, acknowledges the possibility of transformation and becoming without denying sexuate specificity, and vice versa. In Malabou's terms, acknowledging the plasticity of Irigaray's notion of sexuation shows how the sexuate body can be considered a "kernel"—an originary movement on which all subsequent transformations depend and where the sexuate body designates entry into presence, not presence itself. In this sense, I suggest that Irigaray's ontology could represent the "third moment" that Malabou calls for—beyond the mere "negation of essentialism" that she claims grounds the antiessentialist position.[93] Indeed, Malabou has described Irigaray as "one of the only people to think explicitly together ontology and gender differences"[94] and claims that Irigaray is "by far the most convincing and daring 'feminist' woman philosopher."[95]

BIBLIOGRAPHY

Butler, Judith, Drucilla Cornell, Pheng Cheah, and E. A. Grosz. "The Future of Sexual Difference: An Interview with Judith Butler and Drucilla Cornell." *Diacritics* 28, no. 1 (1998): 19–42.
Fuss, Diana. *Essentially Speaking: Feminism, Nature and Difference.* New York: Routledge, 1989.
Grosz, Elizabeth. *Space, Time, and Perversion: Essays on the Politics of Bodies.* New York: Routledge, 1995.
Hill, Rebecca. "The Multiple Readings of Irigaray's Concept of Sexual Difference." *Philosophy Compass* 11, no. 7 (2016): 390–401.
Jones, Rachel. *Irigaray: Towards a Sexuate Philosophy.* Cambridge: Polity. 2011.
Lehtinen, Virpi. *Luce Irigaray's Phenomenology of Feminine Being.* Albany: SUNY Press, 2014.
Malabou, Catherine. *Changing Difference: The Feminine and the Question of Philosophy.* Translated by Carolyn Shread. Cambridge: Polity, 2011.
———. *Ontology of the Accident: An Essay on Destructive Plasticity.* Cambridge: Polity, 2012.
———. "Post-Gender Theory and the Feminine." Filmed May 2014 at International Conference, 7th Subversive Festival: Power and Freedom in the Time of Control. Video, 1:31:11.
Moi, Toril. *Sexual-Textual Politics: Feminist Literary Theory.* London: Methuen, 1985.
Ping Xu. "Irigaray's Mimicry and the Problem of Essentialism." *Hypatia* 10, no. 4 (1995): 76–89.
Stone, Alison. "Book Review: Changing Difference by Catherine Malabou." Review of *Changing Difference* by Catherine Malabou. *London School of Economics*, May 15, 2012.
———. "From Political to Realist Essentialism." *Feminist Theory* 5, no. 1 (2004): 5–23.
———. *Luce Irigaray and the Philosophy of Sexual Difference.* Cambridge: Cambridge University Press, 2006.

NOTES

1. Irigaray privileges the terms *sexuate* and *sexuation* over terms like *sex* and *gender*.

    As Rachel Jones has noted, the term *sexuate* was first used in English translations of *Speculum of the Other Woman* (1985), for the French *sexué*, and, as Rebecca Hill notes, Irigaray has herself, since *Key Writings* (2008), used the term when speaking and writing in English. Jones writes that "'the 'sexuate' refers neither to a mode of being determined by biological sex nor to a cultural overlay of gendered meanings inscribed on a 'tabula rasa' of passively receptive matter" (Rachel Jones, *Irigaray: Towards a Sexuate Philosophy* [Cambridge: Polity, 2011], 14). I adopt the term *sexuate* in this essay in line with Irigaray's use.

2. Irigaray, QO, 8.

3. Alison Stone, *Luce Irigaray and the Philosophy of Sexual Difference* (Cambridge: Cambridge University Press, 2006), 18; Virpi Lehtinen, *Luce Irigaray's Phenomenology of Feminine Being* (Albany: SUNY Press, 2014), 1.
4. See, for example, Diana Fuss, *Essentially Speaking: Feminism, Nature and Difference* (New York: Routledge, 1989); Ping Xu, "Irigaray's Mimicry and the Problem of Essentialism," *Hypatia* 10, no. 4 (1995): 76–89. For an overview of the multiple readings of Irigaray's notion of sexuate difference, see also Rebecca Hill, "The Multiple Readings of Irigaray's Concept of Sexual Difference," *Philosophy Compass* 11, no. 7 (2016): 390–401.
5. Importantly, Irigaray's challenge to Western philosophy is significantly influenced by her engagement with Eastern philosophies and practices—most significantly, the yogic tradition—and her relations with the natural world and nonhuman living beings, which she describes in detail in *Between East and West* and *Through Vegetal Being*, respectively. While I do not address these aspects of her work explicitly in this essay, they are, for me, always front of mind when engaging with her philosophy, and I argue that it is necessary to consider the significance of these perspectives when reading her work.
6. Irigaray, TVB, 99; Irigaray, SF, 10.
7. Irigaray, TBB, 3.
8. Irigaray, SF, 20.
9. Such an "originary structure" is, of course, always already mediated by and situated in the conditions of one's birth (including those who enable one's birth as well as the historical, cultural, social, and ecological [etc.] context of one's birth). Irigaray does not, I think, suggest that sexuate structure exists in any kind of presocial or pure, unmediated conditions.
10. Irigaray, TBB, 3.
11. Irigaray, 3; Irigaray, SF.
12. For example, scholars have challenged universalizing tendencies in feminism that privilege white and largely middle-class women's perspectives, and queer critiques of feminist thought and politics have highlighted tendencies to universalize heterosexual and cisgender women as the privileged or singular subject of feminism.
13. Elizabeth Grosz, "Sexual Difference and the Problem of Essentialism," in *Space, Time, and Perversion: Essays on the Politics of Bodies* (New York: Routledge, 1995), 49.
14. Grosz, 49.
15. Irigaray, TS.
16. Irigaray, "The Maternal Order," in JTN.
17. Irigaray, ODS.
18. Toril Moi, *Sexual-Textual Politics: Feminist Literary Theory* (London: Methuen, 1985), 139.
19. Rebecca Hill, "The Multiple Readings of Irigaray's Concept of Sexual Difference," *Philosophy Compass* 11, no. 7 (2016): 390–401, 391.
20. Irigaray, TS, 78.
21. See chapter 5 of TBB.
22. Hill, "The Multiple Readings of Irigaray's Concept of Sexual Difference," 391.
23. Irigaray, TS, 69.
24. Grosz, *Space, Time and Perversion*, 55.

25. Grosz, 55.
26. Alison Stone, "Book Review: Changing Difference by Catherine Malabou," London School of Economics, May 15, 2012.
27. Stone, "Book Review."
28. Stone, "Book Review."
29. Irigaray, TBB, 10.
30. Lehtenin, *Luce Irigaray's Phenomenology of Feminine Being*, 7.
31. Hill, "The Multiple Readings of Irigaray's Concept of Sexual Difference," 393.
32. Irigaray, TS, 76.
33. Irigaray, 76.
34. See also Drucilla Cornell's discussion in Judith Butler, Drucilla Cornell, Pheng Cheah, and E. A. Grosz, "The Future of Sexual Difference: An Interview with Judith Butler and Drucilla Cornell," Diacritics 28, no. 1 (1998): 19–42, https://doi.org/10.1353/dia.1998.0002.
35. Lehtenin, *Luce Irigaray's Phenomenology of Feminine Being*, 9.
36. Stone, *Luce Irigaray and the Philosophy of Sexual Difference*, 18.
37. Stone, 18.
38. Stone, 18.
39. Stone, 19.
40. Stone, 19.
41. Jones, *Irigaray: Towards a Sexuate Philosophy*, 148.
42. Jones, 148, my italics.
43. Alison Stone, "From Political to Realist Essentialism," *Feminist Theory* 5, 1 (2004): 5–23, 19.
44. Stone, *Luce Irigaray and the Philosophy of Sexual Difference*, 49.
45. Lehtenin, *Luce Irigaray's Phenomenology of Feminine Being*, 1.
46. Lehtenin, ix.
47. Lehtenin, 4.
48. Lehtenin, 1.
49. Lehtenin, 1, my italics.
50. Lehtenin, 5.
51. Irigaray, SF, 5.
52. Irigaray uses the terms *Western* and *the West* to describe philosophy, cultures, and customs emerging from Euro-centric perspectives of the West or Global North. While acknowledging the limitations of these terms (in that they tend to homogenize what are wide-ranging perspectives as well as establish a binary between West/East and Global North/Global South), I use them here in the way that Irigaray does—namely, to signify perspectives that have become dominant in the Euro-centric perspectives of the West or Global North.
53. Irigaray, SF, 2.
54. Irigaray, 1.
55. Irigaray, 1.
56. Irigaray, TBB, 3
57. Irigaray, TVB, x.
58. Irigaray, x.
59. Irigaray, TBB, 29.
60. Irigaray, 5.

61. Irigaray, 16.
62. Irigaray, 16.
63. Irigaray, 41.
64. Irigaray, 3.
65. Irigaray, 69.
66. Irigaray, SF, 3.
67. Irigaray, 5.
68. Irigaray, TBB, 3.
69. Irigaray, SF, 11.
70. Catherine Malabou, *Ontology of the Accident: an Essay on Destructive Plasticity* (Cambridge: Polity, 2012), 3.
71. Malabou, vii.
72. Malabou, 17–18.
73. Malabou, 4.
74. Malabou, 36.
75. Catherine Malabou, "Post-Gender Theory and the Feminine," filmed May 2014 at International Conference, 7th Subversive Festival: "Power and Freedom in the time of Control," video, www.youtube.com/watch?v=0MOlisKRO5M.
76. Malabou, "Post-Gender Theory and the Feminine."
77. Catherine Malabou, *Changing Difference: The Feminine and the Question of Philosophy*, trans. Carolyn Shread (Cambridge: Polity, 2011), 95.
78. Malabou, 139.
79. Malabou, 139.
80. Malabou, 136, my italics.
81. Malabou, "Post-Gender Theory and the Feminine."
82. Malabou, *Changing Difference*, 95.
83. Malabou, 136.
84. Malabou, 136
85. Malabou, 136.
86. Malabou, "Post-Gender Theory and the Feminine."
87. Malabou, *Changing Difference*, 2.
88. Malabou, 93.
89. Malabou, 93.
90. Malabou, "Post-Gender Theory and the Feminine."
91. Stone, "Book Review: Changing Difference by Catherine Malabou."
92. Stone, "Book Review: Changing Difference by Catherine Malabou."
93. Malabou, "Post-Gender Theory and the Feminine."
94. Malabou, *Changing Difference*, 10.
95. Malabou, 122.

Chapter Seven

LOOKING BACK AT "THIS SEX WHICH IS NOT ONE"

Post-deconstructive New Materialisms and Their (Sexual) Difference

PENELOPE DEUTSCHER

In 1984, Irigaray speculated that sexual difference might be the issue of our age.[1] Just one of the many questions[2] provoked by the declaration has been engaged by theorists including Jacques Derrida, Catherine Malabou, and Eve Kosofsky Sedgwick among others: How should we understand the time of a theory?[3] In this chapter, I will consider the time of Irigarayan sexual difference with a focus on recent developments in the interpretation of materiality, nature, biology, and embodiment by a number of Irigaray commentators. I will consider some of the conducts and conventions of commentary, such as seeking to defend a body of theory, to correct, preserve, or protect it, to avert theory fatigue or putative conceptual blunders. I will give the closest attention to the pursuit of potential for transformation within Irigaray's work, and within materiality, and in relation to several interpretations of the concept of plasticity.

VICKI KIRBY AND THE PINCH

In an early essay interrogating the status of Irigarayan embodiment, Vicky Kirby offered an acute diagnosis of an effort within secondary commentary to preserve Irigaray's work from a projected misinterpretation. Kirby also attributed this effort to those who saw Irigaray as elaborating the significance of women's "two lips" morphology as a "decidedly literary"[4] gesture. Insofar as she was developing a *poétique du corps*, Irigaray had been grouped with several other contemporaneous French feminist writers, among them Hélène Cixous, as collectively developing an *écriture feminine*. The feminine "two lips" to which Irigaray referred was deemed a "figurative strategy, a metaphor through which the significance of women's embodiment could be reinterpreted as morphology."[5] The term *morphology* was used to differentiate this from a project whose primary point of reference would be female anatomy[6] or biology. In this context, the latter had been considered by feminism the more conceptually impoverished term. One should not, it was argued, overlook the specific resources with which she undertakes to reinvent female embodiment by means of figurative innovations or fail to appreciate her project of reimagining and transforming, rather than merely correcting, habits of reference to the female body. From the perspective of the conduct of commentary there was a potential misunderstanding against which to defend Irigaray. In this milieu of interpretation, the term *biology* encapsulated that possible misunderstanding. As those who came to be associated with new feminist materialisms would point out, this was a period within feminism in which the term *biology* often bore the status of a blunder.[7]

According to Kirby, and some other theorists associated with new materialist feminisms, such arguments frequently lead to a cul-de-sac. They tend to explain the conceptually figurative and transformative dimensions of Irigarayan embodiment through a contrast with an alternative—biology—that is projected as nonfigurative and nontransformative. Yet biology is not without figurative and transformative capacities. Kirby explained the cul-de-sac when she described a feminist explanation of terms such as *poétique du corps*, *écriture feminine*, and *morphology* as pinching skin to indicate the putatively biological body to which feminism (in this case, Irigaray) would not be referring. This pinch's intent was to indicate what was being conceptually excluded.[8]

Referring to Kirby's discussion, Elizabeth Wilson describes the same pinching maneuver as "stress[ing] the figurative, libidinal, and evocative nature of Irigarayan embodiment over and above any naïve anatomical or biological concerns."[9] Her point is not, of course, that anatomical or biological concerns are naive. Instead, like Kirby, Sedgwick, and others, Wilson is characterizing the long-standing, earlier tendency in feminism to *deem* references to anatomy or biology precritical and naive.[10] Accordingly, Kirby questions the theoretical trajectory that—in defense of the putatively proper interpretation of Irigaray's work—reinstalls what it repudiates to indicate the importance of avoiding it.

Kirby offers further examples, and perhaps they too, more generally, could be seen as effecting such a "pinch" within feminist theory. For example, she suggests there is a proximate gesture in the work of Jane Gallop. Gallop may not have pinched herself in front of an audience to indicate what she did not mean. But Kirby focuses on Gallop's point that Irigaray's *poétique du corps* aims to transform female embodiment and not "just" to represent it imaginatively.[11] Kirby asks the following question about that distinction: Doesn't it still demarcate a *poétique du corps* from a prior body assumed to be "inert"? The latter would make itself available for interpretation, figuration, imagination, and transformation, and would be animated by the former. Isn't there a lingering distinction between matter, body, or flesh on the one hand (if understood as what it is passively available) and its inscription, reinscription, or transformation by culture, activist refiguration, and feminist politics on the other hand?[12]

Feminism's "not that" would now have taken on the qualities of a phantom materiality that is concertedly *not* referred to. Kirby has interpreted the early work of Judith Butler in similar terms. In *Gender Trouble*, Butler argues that the "prior" natural or physiological body is the retroactive effect that results from the projection of anteriority or originality behind the gender construction that is supposed to be the "secondary" expression of the sexed body.[13] Kirby does not claim that this account makes an identical "pinch" to those she has attributed to some Irigaray commentators. And yet, in conversation with Judith Butler, Kirby does make a related point: "Don't we recuperate the . . . nature/culture split and its conservative legacies all over again if we argue that culture is radically incommensurable with whatever precedes it?"[14] In other words, Butler resituates both nature and culture, both gender and sex, within the category of cultural construction. But, on Kirby's interpretation, this still projects a radically incommensurable domain of materiality, now anterior both to what is understood as "gender" and to what is understood as "sex."

Different as they are, Kirby diagnoses each of these projects as situating fabrication, construction, meaning, innovation, transformation, and politics on the side of culture, however radically nature, anatomy, physiology, morphology, or sex are understood as cultural productions. In different ways, a more bedrock materiality remains projected, as if it is prior to or beyond these registers of cultural significance and effect.

This phantom effect is also common in the wake of Anglophone feminism's watershed sex/gender distinction. According to this distinction, gender is the domain of social construction, of malleability, of transformability, and of transformable futures, as opposed to the more static, fixed, and determined status attributed to sex, biology, and nature. Butler herself has conceded that *Gender Trouble* tended to "overemphasiz[e] the priority of culture over nature." One reason she gives for this tendency in her own work is the *cultural* "use of 'natural' arguments to provide legitimacy for so-called natural genders or natural heterosexuality."[15]

So, though their resulting projects are very different, both Kirby and Butler attribute a broad significance to developing alternatives for such modeling. Kirby also discusses that alternative as a means of questioning the defensive stress on the poetic, or else the performative, dimensions of Irigarayan morphology. In this case, her alternative is to attribute an "intelligent performativity"[16] to nature, to matter, and in *that* sense to bodies. She proposes a renewed attention to this disavowed category "biology," to which feminism has generally *not* been referring.[17]

IRIGARAYAN SEXUAL DIFFERENCE

Both Michel Foucault and Luce Irigaray have offered accounts of how human intelligibility is established through the "imaginary point" of sex. But, as Butler observes, of the two of them, only Irigaray stresses the importance of sexual differentiation to that intelligibility.[18] In doing so, Irigaray both reconstructs and revises her understanding of the concept, through several steps.

Irigaray distinguishes, first, a sanctioned, binarized version of sex difference. She characterizes what has emerged from a long-standing tradition of situating femininity as a pole of otherness that serves as the negative reflection of the masculine.[19] The resulting relations of sexual difference are those of nonreciprocal alterity. In consequence, Irigaray argues that femininity has only ever been rendered in terms of opposition, complementarity, or equality to male sovereign subjects.[20] None of these allows for a truly reciprocal form of alterity. So, as a second step, Irigaray annexes for her own purposes the term *sexual difference*, about which history seems to have said so much. According to her alternative, recoined usage of the term, sexual difference never has been established. In this sense, a genealogy of sexual difference can also be understood, third, as the genealogy of how it has been repeatedly averted. Looking back at some of the historical archives of references to women and femininity, Irigaray argues that we are confronted with a constant reiteration of the avoidance of the possibility of sexual difference. In this sense, Butler characterizes her as having offered "a quite brilliant rendition of a certain economy in which there are not two sexes, there is the sex that is one and then the feminine which is necessary for the reproduction of that masculinity but is always figured as its outside."[21] Irigaray refers to the latter as the "sex which is not one," giving it the status of an excluded possibility. Fourth, and in consequence, a hypothetical sexual difference not dominated by relationality to a masculine reference point acquires the status of "impossible"[22] in the sense that it exceeds the historical parameters of representation and social existence. In the final section, I turn to a more recent consideration of metaphysical impossibility—and also of plasticity—in light of a parallel with Irigaray's strategy that has been briefly suggested by Calvin Warren.

Moving toward that argument, we have first seen a further reason why many Irigaray commentators do not see her as describing history's exclusion of a truer but inadequately recognized sexual difference. To the contrary, Irigaray is describing conditions under which a hypothetical, reconfigured sexual difference (a term she has co-opted for her own purposes, to indicate an alternative conceptual possibility) could *not* have emerged. Her intellectual innovation is to hollow out within the archive of historical depictions, and their repeated forms of opposition, sameness, or complementarity, an account of what could not be tolerated, what is "not," without that account relying for its legitimacy on a reference to an excluded truth or denied reality. On this account, she might aspire to new and creative ways with which to refer to female morphology. But she is not referring to more accurate accounts of female bodies in her alternative poetics for feminine morphology.

And this is why an Irigaray commentator might have suggested that the reference point for the latter is not the body one can pinch. But this line of interpretation must contend with a complication. Irigaray's work does also refer to the specificity of female corporeality and also to physiological differences between men and women. For this reason, an early and influential argument was that such gestures were best understood as the mimetic performances of a "strategic essentialism."[23]

IRIGARAY AND WHAT THEORY KNOWS "TODAY"

Some two decades later Janet Halley included feminism's preoccupation with sexual difference[24] (even where the latter is understood as failed or impossible) within a group of theories from which, she argued, it might be salutary to take a break. Philosophies of sexual difference had also been associated with a problematic heteronormativity. Irigaray's work included a pejorative reference to the "homme-osexuality" of the exclusion of sexual difference.[25] True, Irigaray did not use the expression to refer to homosexuality but to a conceptual field dominated by the male sex. But Halley and Sedgwick were also associating sexual difference with the phenomenon of theory fatigue. In 1995, Sedgwick had already extended a (differently motivated) invitation to take a break from some of the "things theory knows today."[26] The expression communicates a form of saturation, or exhaustion of ideas, a type of overuse:

> Here are a few things theory knows today . . . theory after Foucault, after Greenblatt, after Freud and Lacan, after Lévi-Strauss, after Derrida, after feminism) when it offers any account of human beings or cultures. . . . The distance of any such account from a biological basis is assumed to correlate near-precisely with its potential for doing justice to difference (individual, historical, cross-cultural), to contingency, to performative force, and to the possibility of change.[27]

What are some of the forms of feminism that might have seemed fatigued in this context? Halley importantly pinpointed governmental forms. Sedgwick included feminism's criticism of biological determinism, along with feminism's supposition that theories of social and gender construction were more feminist-friendly and the promising resource for rejecting the inevitability of binarized sex. Catherine Malabou speaks to this conceptual association in *Changing Difference*: "to say that gender is constructed is to question difference understood as binary. There are not just two genders; there is a multiplicity of genders."[28]

Such comments shed light on the novel character of several interpretations of Irigaray discussed later. Each of these represents a significant break with what, as Sedgwick put this, theory has come to "know"—in other words, a significant break with habits of theory that become overly reiterated, including within feminism. There are, of course, diverse reasons to take breaks from the habitual patterns of thought within theory, and a number will be discussed here.

A first example is Alison Stone's *Luce Irigaray and the Philosophy of Sexual Difference*. It belongs to a broader group of feminist refutations of the view that "culture" or "social construction" is the privileged realm of transformative possibility as against a materiality erroneously seen as more static, determined, or determining. It rings a change by not straining to demonstrate the strategic or mimetic status of Irigarayan terms, or straining to avert Irigaray's references to nature or the physical. Rather, Stone declares her intention to "defend an understanding of sexual difference as natural," and to "challenge the prevailing consensus within feminist theory that sexual difference is a culturally constructed and symbolically articulated phenomenon,"[29] for all that (as she observed) this was likely to jolt many feminist readers.

When Stone reads Irigaray with Friedrich Schelling, just as when Elizabeth Grosz reads Irigaray with Charles Darwin,[30] she extends an invitation to conceive nature as thoroughly open to its own transformation. They challenge the polarized nature/culture and sex/gender prisms through which Irigaray's work has often been interpreted, particularly by Anglophone readers for whom these latter distinctions have been so consequential. Most of all, Stone finds in Irigaray's work the means for reconsidering the binary oppositions in terms of which nature, biology, and physiology are typically understood by feminist thought. And this possibility has given rise to an "afterlife" for conceptualizing sexual difference. Further variations are seen in interpretations of Irigaray by Gayle Salamon, Ewa Ziarek, and Catherine Malabou.

CORPOREAL UNDECIDABILITY AND SEXUAL DIFFERENCE: SALAMON ON IRIGARAY

In *Assuming a Body: Transgender and Rhetorics of Materiality*, Gayle Salamon finds alternative resources within Irigaray's own work to grapple, critically, with the claim presented in *I Love To You* that "without doubt the most appropriate content for the universal is sexual difference.... Sexual difference is an immediate natural given and it is a real and irreducible component of the universal. The whole of human kind is composed of women and men and of nothing else."[31]

On the one hand, Salamon shares the widespread consternation at the heteronormative connotations of sexual difference in Irigaray's work, including the insinuation that queer sexuality could amount to a flight from difference with which one might contrast a politics of sexual difference.[32] On the other hand, Salamon finds an alternative that does not only reduce Irigaray to her most off-putting or questionable moments. To that end, Salamon differentiates certain of Irigaray's actual statements from the broader capacities of her philosophical outlook. In other words, Salamon identifies a conceptual potential she sees as diverging at points from Irigaray's actual statements. This allows her to ask whether it is "possible that Irigaray's notion of sexual difference and her insights into the ways in which sexual difference is crucially generative might be of use in an account of sexual difference that aims to challenge gender and sexual heteronormativity."[33]

One example is the resources Salamon finds within Irigaray's work for conceptualizing the body in terms of the play of self-difference otherwise than in Irigaray's own account. Here, bodily undecidability would not concern how sexual difference is represented, or its symbolic or poetic dimensions.[34] Rather, Salamon affirms an account of being sexed as being inhabited by a primary autodifferentiation, whether one is male, female, or nonbinary. Salamon sees in autodifferentiation a means of rethinking Irigaray's projected depiction of "man and woman as the most mysterious ... most creative couple."[35]

An understanding of all bodies as in a constant negotiation with difference *and* sexual difference would apply, she points out, to the relation between a gay man and a trans man, and to masculinities in relation to themselves and one another. One is always mediated by such relationality, such that being sexed is never a self-present, stable identity. In consequence, rationality and self-differentiation do mediate the sexes, but not in a privileged way. Making this point, Salamon reroutes Irigaray's work toward a pluralization of sexual difference.

Salamon also reconsiders Irigaray's interest in the historical association of masculinity with form and of femininity with matter and corporeality.

The view that we are all mediated by sexual difference relies, Salamon points out, on a more general understanding of identity as mediated by embodiment. So Salamon suggests we revise Irigaray's resources to theorize that mediation by building on and modulating the "two lips" toward a transformative understanding of skin that is consistent with the former but more capacious. This would be to see each individual as enfolded by the simultaneously inside and outside relationship of our skin. Our skin gives us a concurrent relationality with the other and with the self. It delineates us not only from others but also from ourselves.[36] It is a means of seeing ourselves as "place" for ourselves, as self-relational and self-differentiating, rather than self-identical or self-present. Salamon also sees an alternative to the traditional association of femininity with matter and place.[37] Rather, the universality of skin means that each of us is mediated by a relationality to matter and place (and so with what traditionally has been *associated* with femininity). This mutates the resources of Irigaray's view away from the focus on mediation by "sexual difference." A further term used by Salamon in this context is plasticity. Salamon suggests we can identify within Irigaray's work an understanding of the plasticity of embodiment with which to reconceptualize sexual difference.[38]

But Salamon's reconfiguration of Irigaray's resources also presupposes they possess a conceptual availability for change and are sufficiently flexible for this project. Can elements of Irigaray's work be viably amplified by commentators and propelled toward the theme of plasticity of interest to Salamon, and also to two further theorists discussed later: Ewa Ziarek and Catherine Malabou? Salamon seeks within the resources of Irigaray's work an alternative to her affirmation of sexual difference as a universal principle of embodiment or existence. Salamon does not thematize the methodological or textual presuppositions of this project of conversion. Yet an important quality implicitly attributed to Irigaray's work by Salamon's and similar readings (as further seen later) is its potential for such rerouting, its thinkability in terms of its own further capacities, and very availability or hospitality, even if partial, to Salamon's (and similar) projects.

This could be contrasted with the potential Irigaray herself has previously located in the work of historical figures such as Plato and Aristotle, Freud, Hegel, and Merleau-Ponty. She was able to draw on their failures and ellipses in support of her argument that sexual difference was repeatedly being excluded in their work.[39] We will see Salamon's argument that

(Irigarayan) sexual difference presupposes an undertheorized corporeal plasticity cited to further ends by Malabou and Ziarek when they, too, transform Irigaray's declarations that "sexual difference is an immediate natural given."[40] While they confront these with a different countering strategy, they affirm "a plastic notion of nature" in the sense that it is "open to retrospective cultural and political elaborations." They too propose that this is theorizable using the resources of Irigaray's work.

ZIAREK AND MALABOU ON SEXUAL DIFFERENCE AS PLASTICITY

Ewa Ziarek is among the commentators who have interpreted Irigarayan sexual difference as lacking specific content. Instead, the concept is "performed" by Irigaray so as to draw philosophical attention to its own impossibility.[41] In an essay on Irigaray jointly written by Ziarek and Catherine Malabou, this dual understanding of sexual difference as excluded, and as never having taken place, is also associated with a self-disappropriating, corporeal transformability. On this point they cite Salamon's work as a reference. The term *plasticity* (understood most broadly as that which both receives and gives form)[42] is here applied to an interpretation of Irigaray's work as "contest[ing] any unmediated natural identity."[43] In this case, nature is understood as "always already cultural," in the sense of already bearing those properties one might otherwise ascribe only to "culture": that which is form-giving and gives rise to its own self-transformation. The term is used to emphasize an Irigarayan understanding of nature in terms of its "dynamic metamorphosis"[44] in addition to its receptivity to change.

Similarly, birth would be seen neither as a natural beginning on the basis of which culture establishes itself, nor as "a fixed determination . . . [that is] dissolved in culture."[45] As an *always already* plastic condition, being born could instead be understood as a constant movement of concurrently "both giving form to oneself and receiving it from the other."[46] Irigarayan nature would encompass a concept of the plasticity of birth and a revision of the sex/gender distinction. For "being born is a natural aspect of gender, but it is always already cultural."[47] This is what also prompts Ziarek to ask,

> Can we say that such a plastic understanding of "being born" is open to transgender becomings and transformations? Such becomings might resonate

with Gayle Salamon's critique and extension of Irigaray towards the undecidability of genders: "[G]enders that find no easy home within the binary system are still animated by difference. Sexual undecidability does not condemn the subject to placelessness, but . . . locates difference at the heart of both subjectivity and relation."[48]

Ziarek agrees with Salamon that Irigaray "misunderstand[s] the place of sexual difference, locating it always *over there*"[49] as if the other is impossibly mysterious to me *as* another sex. But Ziarek also shares Salamon's project of locating a "nonheteronormative reading of body and relation . . . within the logic of Irigaray's work."[50] Attributed to the latter, this conceptual potential concerns sexual identities and relationships that "cannot be understood as strictly male or female" and that "fall outside the scope of the strictly heterosexual."[51] This means that, for Salamon, as for Malabou and Ziarek, to think sexual difference "*with*" Irigaray is also to be (as Ziarek puts this) "moving now in a different direction than Irigaray."[52]

In short, we could direct the same question to Malabou and Ziarek as to Salamon: What is presupposed by a methodology that follows an Irigarayan form of thought *as* a means of concurrently departing from it?

MALABOU AND THE PLASTICITY OF SEXUAL DIFFERENCE

One of Malabou's embarkation points in this regard is Butler's earliest reading of Irigaray. In *Gender Trouble*, Butler had outlined her concern that a putative female biology (whether literal or strategic) persists as the reference for an Irigarayan "two lips" morphology as feminine.[53] When Malabou aligns herself with this objection, she does not turn immediately to the creative responses to Irigaray that have emerged within the field of feminist new materialisms. These have, by following a post-deconstructive trajectory, emphasized a view of nature, matter, or embodiment as active and autotransformative, as capable of "un-writing" themselves, or as capable of change in their programming.[54]

Instead, Malabou provisionally attributes to Irigaray's work the nature/culture distinction challenged by the theorists considered here.[55] Doing so prompts her to ask how femininity relates to the female body.[56] This could be understood in a number of ways, for example, as a question of meaning: "indeed the 'feminist' discourse which tends to oppose the feminine—understood as femininity *of woman*—to masculine domination, simultaneously restricts the meaning of the feminine, understood as openness and plurality."[57] Malabou argues that, sometimes, Irigaray does refer to femininity as a property of women and as one pole in a binary opposition with masculinity.[58] Therefore, she concludes, there is in Irigaray's work an intermittent "harden[ing] of the distinction between masculine and feminine."[59] She uses the term *hardening* because "to think [difference] from the feminine would always amount to limiting it, to restricting the primordial opening of the originary welcome or gift."[60] And, she continues, "if we reduce 'the feminine' to woman and lips to 'feminine' sexuality, then we produce the very exclusion we were trying to avoid."[61] Malabou reiterates the point made by other commentators mentioned here: to some extent, Irigaray does associate the self-touching of women's two lips with a female physiology, as a figure of women's being otherwise. This limits the extent to which the Irigarayan feminine is open to a more radically transformative potential.

But it is also Malabou's view that more plastic readings of Irigaray can be generated that reconfigure the status of "gender."[62] Put most simply, these conditions include an ambivalence within Irigaray's work.[63] The most promising dimension of her corporeal "self-touching" (and, on this point, Malabou agrees with Salamon) lies in there being "no real conflict between a feminine and a masculine self-touching."[64] At the most radical point, "femininity" would no longer be intelligible as such. The term would be a placeholder, a "hospitality" toward an alternative, radical difference that is also understandable as femininity's plasticity. At that point, the term *femininity* is understood differently from the more rigid version Malabou criticizes. Instead, femininity would be a radical contesting of its own form and meaning, as—for example—"lips or vulva . . . turning back against themselves, that is, against the feminine."[65] Malabou therefore identifies the relevant plasticity of Irigaray's work in an aporia that consists in the necessarily hovering relationship between rigidity and radical unintelligibility.

On the point that femininity ought not be "tied back to women," Malabou agrees that there is no privileged relationship between them. But that, she argues, does not mean there is no correspondence between them. As she puts this, "if we name [this anonymity] . . . the feminine . . . we do run the risk of fixing this fragility, assigning it a residence. . . . If we resist it . . . it becomes anything at all under the pretext of referring to anyone."[66]

In this context, plasticity is situated between the implausibility of projecting the radical future of a femininity unrelated to women's bodies and the inadequacy of doing so absent any such reference. In other words, Malabou adds herself to those commentators for whom Irigarayan femininity bears the status of impossibility for this further reason: "I seek recognition for a certain feminine space that seems impossible yet is also very dangerous to try to deny."[67] Here, to identify this ambivalence as plastic is to characterize it as *transformability*. The term refers to the necessary hovering between a radically open feminine-to-come, which could only as catachresis be named feminine, and a feminine tied back (more rigidly, to recall Malabou's metaphorics) to women.[68]

In short, to the extent that femininity's capacity for radical transformation is a problem "tied back to women" it would be, for Malabou, insufficiently plastic. Because the feminine can only be so named in the mode of its own impossibility, it has a constantly ambivalent status. Malabou also names this aporia through which an impossibility presents as an identity, the former's "transvestism" or "going in drag."[69]

A reference to a "female biology" (figured in this context as "rigid") would short-circuit (*but importantly also requires*) the "salutary" betrayal of the feminine that amounts to its more radical transformation of meaning. For this reason, Malabou refers to this relationship in three ways: the transformability of the feminine, the resistance of the feminine to its own deconstruction,[70] and an oscillation between these two that she also associates with the term *plasticity*.

THE SCOPE OF PLASTICITY

Since we can also turn to Malabou's work for rich accounts of organic and neural capacity for self-transformation, we could have expected her emphasis of sexual difference's self-transformative capacities to avail itself of these resources. Instead, she focuses on the extent to which Irigaray refers the feminine back to women, and so to a "rigid" relationship between women and a female physiology, and a "hardened" distinction between femininity and masculinity. In lieu, Malabou proposes an alternative formulation: "let us then think of this name 'woman' as an empty but resistant essence, an essence that is resistant because it is empty, a resistance that strikes out the impossibility of its own disappearance once and for all."[71]

Does Malabou's maneuver diverge from her own reflections on biology, in which plasticity is ascribed to the excitement of synaptic connections or to the self-transformative potential of the stem cell, including its capacity for unwriting, for auto-deprogramming? Could her own reading of Irigaray more fully avail itself of these resources? In Malabou's interpretation of Irigarayan sexual difference, plasticity is reserved for the hinge between the necessary radical openness to the future (femininity's radical hospitality to becoming otherwise) and a female corporeality, to which that becoming otherwise both should *not* refer and should *not not* refer. By contrast to its plasticity, the rigidity of sexual difference would manifest insofar as the feminine is tied back to women in modes other than affirmative impossibility, aporia, or oscillation.

For her part, Vicki Kirby, it will be recalled, proposes two alternative routes in relation to this "not." One is a recognizably deconstructive maneuver: instead of disavowing reference to biology or nature, Kirby reassigns the generalized attributes of what is more commonly associated with culture to a broader category that can also include matter, the organic, the physiological, and the bodily. These attributes include animation, agency, relationality, social constructionism, difference, poetics, meaning, expression, excitability, the capacity for transformation, mutability, and writing. For surely, Kirby declares, it must "be in the nature of biology to interpret, to theorize, to read and write."[72] In that sense, Kirby's "Corpus Delecti" argues for understanding the biological body in terms of its changing differential script.[73] The second route would "cast the net wider" toward the promise, as she puts it, of a "generalized geo-graphy (as the body of the world)."[74] This direction has since been adopted in a wide range of contemporary work, including Bennett's *Vibrant Matter*.[75] It is more broadly understood as the capacity for initiation, spontaneity, transformation, as that which changes us as we change it, and as the capacity to rewrite itself. As such, this capacity can be considered "an attribute of man *and* animal *and* plant *and* stone."[76]

Kirby's earliest interpretation of Irigaray followed the contours of this argument. Instead of a *poétique du corps*, Irigaray's work would (by way of Kirby's reading) speak to "biology's capacity to rewrite itself."[77] Thus, she suggests different terms through which to consider Irigaray as realizing a "virtuoso rewriting" (of) the body" in which biology emerges as enfolding its own textual adventure, disturbing the status within feminism of body-as-surface and of matter as available for inscription or cultural construction. To this end, Kirby attributes to an Irigarayan body (whose capacities have been rethought and expanded) not just the two lips, or the other forms of self-touching and self-relationality considered so far (such as Salamon's revision of skin), but also the "the peristaltic movements of the viscera, the mitosis of cells, the electrical activity that plays across a synapse, the itinerary of a virus, and so on.... All the oozings and pulsings that literally and figuratively make up the differential stuff of the body's extra-ordinary circuitry."[78] At this point, the *potential* of Irigaray's work to offer this account—or to mutate toward it—becomes the most consequential factor for an affirmative interpretation of her work.[79] But in her dialogue with Kirby, Butler asks whether this is to privilege a biology understood as "multiple, contrary, disseminated, undecidable."[80]

ANTIBLACKNESS, SEXUAL DIFFERENCE, PLASTICITY

In light of her alternative terms in which she has construed new and feminist materialisms, sexual difference, and the plasticity of matter, we could imagine Zakiyyah Iman Jackson sympathizing with Judith Butler's query. Butler asks Kirby, warily: What of biology's capacity for "fixation, recurrence, monotony, negativity and fatality"?[81] Jackson's *Becoming Human* makes a case for theorizing "plasticity" in terms that are acutely alert to that capacity. She proposes another meaning for "plasticity" to that developed by Malabou,[82] showing how it bears on the intertwining of sexual difference with the history of racial domination.

Thus, for all that Jackson is not one of Irigaray's interlocutors, I conclude with Jackson's response to Malabou and her innovations within the field of new materialism. This closing section is framed by a remark made in passing by Calvin Warren: that Irigaray's account in *Ethics of Sexual Difference* of woman's placelessness is similar—as an argument—to the account he discusses in *Ontological Terror*, of black being's metaphysical nothingness.[83] Rather than engage this fleeting suggestion directly, I turn to the reasons why Jackson suggests that sexual difference should be understood in terms of plasticity (not a term used by Warren). Her elaboration of this argument prompts the meanings of plasticity to augment, and also to take some leave, from those elaborated by Catherine Malabou. My concluding suggestion is that the meanings of Irigaray's sexual difference—notwithstanding their impossibility, openness, and à-venir status—are also called upon to reformulate themselves.

JACKSON, PLASTICITY, AND SEXUAL DIFFERENCE

This is also to return to the grounds for querying her view of sexual difference as the question of the age. What alternatives might lay a claim to that status? For example, what if another possibility was the emergence within and beyond feminism, of intersectionality? What might be the impact of its claims on Warren's fleeting proposal that there is a similarity between Irigaray's argument concerning the dependency of women's place-lessness on man's "existential unfolding" and arguments discussed in *Ontological Terror* concerning the dependency on the place-lessness of black being of the unfolding of whiteness.

It may be coincidental that Warren is discussing Hortense Spillers's contributions to this argument at the point where he suggests in a footnote the parallel with Irigaray. But what would be productive intersections between these bodies of thought? I think the question can be asked in three ways. First, we could expect intersectionality theorists' long-standing wariness of analogies between sex and race to apply not only to subordination, experience, standpoint, identity, discrimination, and rights-deprivation but also to arguments concerning impossibility of being. Second, the suggestion of affinities tends to presuppose greater access to (or reestablishment of) the identity of that with which an affinity is being suggested—this would be a further reason for some wariness of this conduct of critique. And third, we could expect an intersectional critique[84] of Irigaray's own references to "woman" to be alert to its silent exclusions of Black being and Black women. For example, where Irigaray describes the association of femininity with lack, Jackson points out that gendering is also a technique of European humanization in contrast to the animalization of Black alterity. In its relation to white sovereign masculinity, Irigaray depicts femininity, generally, as occupying the role of lack. Yet does that account render invisible "the perpetual specter of black female lack in the realm of culturally and historically produced femininity, at the register of both performativity and morphology"?[85] Jackson's point concerns the inseparability of sexual differentiation from racialization, with the result that sexual difference (in the phallocentric sense described by Irigaray) presupposes that some women are humanized at once by gender and whiteness at the expense of those who are dehumanized in relation to whiteness, just as they are excluded from the white norms of gender. In consequence "ontologizing racial characterization not only divides and stratifies gender but also calls into question the very meaning of sexual difference."[86] This is the point missed by Irigaray and toward which her work must be modulated.

For all that Jackson is not in direct dialogue with Warren or Irigaray, her work orients critical inspection of the latter's development of sexual difference in terms of impossibility. It is not just that Irigaray fails to differentiate the women (and the exclusion of women and femininity) to which she refers. She also overlooks the impossibility's raced and sexed relationality. The alternative that emerges through Jackson's engagement with new materialism also bears on a difference between her and Warren's interpretations of Spillers. For Warren seems to refer to flesh (as conceptually developed by Spillers) as a prior materiality presupposed by the capturing production of enslaved women and enslaved embodiment. According to Warren's commentary:

> Flesh ... is the primordial relation that antiblackness works tirelessly to destroy, ... what is wiped out during the metaphysical holocaust that we can call the "transatlantic slavetrade." The body, however, emerges from the ashes of this holocaust. It is not strictly corporeality (or physicality), but the signification of nothing that the black body comes to mark in an antiblack symbolic (or, as Spillers describes it, a "category of otherness").[87]

On this version, Spillers's reference to flesh is best understood in terms of a primordial materiality anterior to and presupposed in the reduction by antiblackness to the fungible bodies of slavery and its aftermath. But Jackson presents Spiller's argument with a different emphasis that accords with her own contributions to new feminist materialist analysis: "Spillers's 'before' is often interpreted as affirming the notion that the biological matter of the flesh can and does exist prior to cultural inscription, but this is precisely what I am arguing against."[88] Along with other theorists considered here, Jackson concertedly avoids the separation of nature and culture, matter and power's inscription, here insofar as it would give Black materiality a passive status and assign agency and activity only to the constructions and destructions of racial domination and insurgent resistance.

As an alternative, Jackson conceptualizes a materiality that can be understood simultaneously in the following ways. It arises from and in the context of racial domination. But it is also a milieu of material agency. If we compare with the relatively vital, animate connotations of new materialism (we could think again of the synaptic activity and peristaltic viscera with which Kirby broadens the domain of an expressive, articulate, and diacritical materiality), Jackson might respond that matter's agency and self-differentiation are, of course, not necessarily that of a "flourishing" embodiment. In the conclusion of *Becoming Human*, she explores the agency of racial domination's toxic bodies. On the one hand, she reiterates accounts given by writers from Dorothy Roberts to Audre Lorde, and contemporary accounts of differential maternal, natal, and Black health in the United States. The result of the geographically and economically differential impact of racial capitalism within populations is higher rates of cancer, diabetes, pregnancy complications, death in childbirth, miscarriage, curtailed life expectancy.[89] But for Jackson, this is to understand Black maternal bodies as more than the passive effects of the environments created by racial domination. The resulting materiality is an environment of racial domination, and not just an effect of the latter. There is a marked difference between the electrical synaptic connections, cellular mitosis, and peristaltic movements of the viscera emphasized by Kirby in her response to Irigaray and the molecular environments emphasized by Jackson in her analysis of antiblackness and of black(ened) bodies:

> In the contrasting framework elaborated here, the black(ened) maternal body's endocrine system, organ systems, neuropsychological pathways, and cellular functioning are essential agencies in antiblack necropower, such that the distinction between the body and war's weapon no longer rests on a solid boundary between human subjectivity and external environment, nor that of subject and object.[90]

In other words, when Jackson emphasizes that the effects and environments of antiblackness are not just cultural but biocultural, this supposes—as she points out—a meaning for plasticity that she differentiates from others developed within new feminist materialisms. Two senses of plasticity are particularly operative at this point. According to one of these, material, corporeal plasticity is presupposed by slavery and racial domination, but also its product. Slavery relies on techniques that are preoccupied with the adaptability of Black embodiment for the purposes of enslavement's transport, sale, work, psychic and physical forms of violence, and with a constant testing the limits of that assigned adaptability. This plasticity is both a strategically produced representation and a materially produced effect of slavery. Insofar as it is presupposed, it is retroactively projected as prior to those techniques, as if it were an original property of Black bodies. Thus, as Jackson defines the term: "plasticity is a praxis that seeks to define the essence of a black(ened) thing as infinitely mutable, in antiblack, often paradoxical... terms."[91] Moreover, Jackson reminds that an (impossible) sexual difference is never far from the scene, for the terms of this paradoxical praxis also produce the association of whiteness with a humanizing sex and gender in conjunction with the historical denial of humanity (and of white norms for sex and gender) to Black bodies.[92] Thus, these arguments already give two senses in which plasticity (and its complex temporality) must be understood in conjunction with antiblack racialization. The third sense may be found in Jackson's account of molecular bodily environments that become not only the effects but also the agents of racial domination's material toxicity.[93] But a fourth belongs to the potential for further transformation Jackson attributes to the bodily plasticity that is both the condition and effect of racial domination. It is true that she situates this potential with the poetic and aesthetic strategies of artists and writers for whom this conflicted materiality becomes the occasion for artistic and literary forms of reconfiguration.[94] But in *Becoming Human* she also attributes this potential to forms of embodiment and biological life that even, in their very toxicity, contradictions, or chaos, can also be understood as expressive, material, corporeal forms of critique of racial domination.[95]

This chapter first outlined expansions of Irigarayan resources by theorists associated with feminist phenomenology, new materialist, post-Foucauldian, and post-deconstructive thought. These readings and interventions assume the further capacities, flexibility of form, and potential of Irigaray's philosophical work in ways that call for further analysis and the development of new terminologies. This is to look back at the "sex which is not one," with the aim of locating its own capacities for self-departure, in at least two senses. One—apparent in the approaches of Salamon, Kirby, Stone, Ziarek, Malabou, and (without commenting specifically on Irigaray) Jackson—concerns the self-departure and capacity for transformation of morphology, embodiment, biology, nature, sex, sexual difference. The second understands Irigaray's own body of work and concepts as always already departing from themselves in terms of their potential for further transformation. Since the latter is not necessarily best characterized as critique, as counter-reading, as symptomatic, or as deconstructive, Malabou's work has suggested the applicability of the philosopheme *plasticity* to Irigaray's writing in this sense also.[96] Also used, though not extensively, by Salamon, Kirby, and Ziarek, the term *plasticity* takes on different meanings for each. But it could be said that for all these theorists, the materiality and bodies theorized by Irigaray's work (and in some cases the work itself) are deemed capable of unwriting, of reprogramming, and of the change characterized by Ziarek as a "movement in another direction."

Since these redirections of Irigarayan capacities arise within affirmative readings seeking to give them further propulsion, they could be distinguished in intent from symptomatic, unveiling, hostile, corrective, recuperative, or reparative strategies of reading. The potential resources of textual and corporeal plasticity are being doubly attributed: at once to nature, matter, environment, bodies, corporeality, and to Irigaray's concepts, frameworks, texts, and textual limits. These readings move at once "with" her work, and diverge from it, re-forming the form, meaning, and outcome of her terms. Additional forms and senses are generated in terms of which plasticity becomes attributable to Irigaray and her texts, in the broadest of the senses suggested for the term by Malabou: the concurrent giving and reception of form.

BIBLIOGRAPHY

Bennett, Jane. *Vibrant Matter: A Political Ecology of Things*. Durham, NC: Duke University Press, 2010.

Butler, Judith. *Gender Trouble: Feminism and the Subversion of Identity*. New York: Routledge, 1990.

———. "Sexual Inversions." In *Foucault and the Critique of Institutions*, edited by J. Caputo and M. Yount, 81–98. University Park: Pennsylvania State University Press, 1993.

Cheah, Pheng, Elizabeth Grosz, Judith Butler, and Drucilla Cornell. "The Future of Sexual Difference: An Interview with Judith Butler and Drucilla Cornell." *Diacritics: Irigaray and the Political Future of Sexual Difference* 28, no. 1 (1998): 19–42.
de Beauvoir, Simone. *The Second Sex*. Translated by Constance Borde and Sheila Malovany-Chevallier. New York: Alfred A. Knopf, 2010.
Derrida, Jacques. *Of Grammatology*. Trans. G. C. Spivak. Baltimore: Johns Hopkins University Press, 1997.
Deutscher, Penelope. *A Politics of Impossible Difference: The Later Work of Luce Irigaray*. Ithaca: Cornell University Press, 2002.
Gallop, Jane. "Quand nos lèvres s'écrivent: Irigaray's Body Politic." *Romanic Review* 74, no. 1 (1983): 77–83.
Grosz, Elizabeth. "The Nature of Sexual Difference: Irigaray and Darwin." *Angelaki: Journal of the Theoretical Humanities* 17, no. 2 (2012): 69–93.
———. *Sexual Subversions: Three French Feminists*. Sydney: Allen and Unwin, 1989.
Halley, Janet. *Split Decisions: How and Why to Take a Break from Feminism*. Princeton: Princeton University Press, 2006.
Jackson, Zakiyyah Iman. *Becoming Human: Matter and Meaning in An Antiblack World*. New York: New York University Press, 2020.
Kirby, Vicki. *Judith Butler Live Theory*. London: Continuum, 2006.
———. *Telling Flesh: The Substance of the Corporeal*. New York: Routledge, 1997.
Lorde, Audre. *A Burst of Light: Essays*. Ann Arbor: Firebrand, 1988.
———. *The Cancer Journals*. Aunt Lute: San Francisco, 1997.
Malabou, Catherine. *Changing Difference*. Translated by Carolyn Shread. Cambridge: Polity, 2011.
———. *The Future of Hegel: Plasticity, Temporality and Dialectic*. Translated by Lisabeth During. London: Routledge, 2004.
———. *The Heidegger Change: On the Fantastic in Philosophy*. Edited by Peter Skafish. Albany: SUNY Press, 2011.
Malabou, Catherine, and Ewa Ziarek. "Negativity, Unhappiness or Felicity: On Irigaray's Dialectical Culture of Sexual Difference." *L'Esprit créateur* 52, no. 3 (2012): 11–25.
Miller, Ruth A. *The Biopolitics of Embryos and Alphabets: A Reproductive History of the Nonhuman*. Oxford: Oxford University Press, 2017.
Roberts, Dorothy. *Killing the Black Body: Race, Reproduction and the Meaning of Liberty*. New York: Vintage, 2017.
Salamon, Gayle. *Assuming a Body: Transgender and Rhetorics of Materiality*. New York: Columbia University Press, 2010.
Schor, Naomi. "This Essentialism Which Is Not One: Coming to Grips with Irigaray." In *Engaging with Irigaray: Feminist Philosophy and Modern European Thought*, edited by C. Burke, N. Schor, and M. Whitford, 57–78. New York: Columbia University Press, 1994.
Sedgwick, Eve Kosoksky. *Epistemology of the Closet*. Berkeley: University of California Press, 1990.
Sedgwick, Eve, and Adam Frank. *Shame in the Cybernetic Fold: Reading Silvan Tomkins*. Durham, NC: Duke University Press, 1995.
Stone, Alison. *Luce Irigaray and the Philosophy of Sexual Difference*. Cambridge: Cambridge University Press, 2006.

Warren, Calvin. *Ontological Terror: Blackness, Nihilism, and Emancipation*. Durham, NC: Duke University Press, 2018.
Wilson, Elizabeth. *Neural Geographies: Feminism and the Microstructure of Cognition*. London: Routledge, 1998.
———. *Psychosomatic: Feminism and the Neurological Body*. Durham, NC: Duke University Press, 2004.

NOTES

1. Irigaray, ESD, 5.
2. This chapter concludes with further questions that arise from theories foregrounding antiblackness's assignment of nonbeing to Blackness.
3. See the references to the epoch of writing in Jacques Derrida, *Of Grammatology*, trans. G. C. Spivak (Baltimore: Johns Hopkins University Press, 1997), 4, 6–7, 9; and Catherine Malabou's critical scrutiny of (in this sense) the timeliness of Derridean writing, and the conditions for its being more, or less, in the air, Malabou, *Changing Difference*, trans. Carolyn Shread (Cambridge: Polity, 2011), 50. Sedgwick's reflections on the time of theory are discussed further later. See also Ruth A. Miller, *The Biopolitics of Embryos and Alphabets: A Reproductive History of the Nonhuman* (Oxford: Oxford University Press, 2017), 3–4, 10, for her accounts of velocity and nostalgia in the field of biopolitics.
4. Vicki Kirby, *Telling Flesh: The Substance of the Corporeal* (New York: Routledge, 1997), 70.
5. Kirby, 70.
6. Kirby recalls Jane Gallop's account of Irigaray as referring not to "genital anatomy but [to] the symbolic interpretation of that anatomy—the ways in which a phallomorphic morphology reconstructs anatomy in its own image," Kirby, 74.
7. For her rich reflections on the avoidant, if not repudiating, relationship between feminism and biology, see Elizabeth Wilson, *Psychosomatic: Feminism and the Neurological Body* (Durham, NC: Duke University Press, 2004), 7–8 and 13–14.
8. See Kirby's account of the "pinch" as at once denying and preserving a reference to a bedrock biology: Kirby, *Telling Flesh*, 70.
9. Wilson, *Psychosomatic*, 7. For her own discussion of the "pinch," see Elizabeth Wilson, *Neural Geographies: Feminism and the Microstructure of Cognition* (London: Routledge, 1998), 15.
10. Wilson, *Psychosomatic*, 8.
11. Further reflecting on the importance of the term *morphology* for Gallop's interpretation of Irigaray, Kirby recalls how, for Gallop, "Irigaray's *poétique du corps* [was] not an expression of the body but a poiesis, a creating of the body," citing Jane Gallop, "Quand nos lèvres s'écrivent: Irigaray's Body Politic," *Romanic Review* 74, no. 1 (1983): 77–83, 79. For Gallop, anatomy would be "just another moment in culture's refiguring of itself": Kirby, *Telling Flesh*, 75. On this reading, then, the status of anatomy for Irigaray would be somewhat like the status of body, nature, biology, and matter for Butler. Thus, the discussion is linked to Kirby's reservations concerning the status of matter in Butler's work, discussed in chapter 4 of *Telling Flesh* (101–128).

12. Kirby, *Telling Flesh*, 75.
13. Judith Butler, *Gender Trouble: Feminism and the Subversion of Identity* (New York: Routledge, 1990), 7.
14. Judith Butler with Vicki Kirby, "Butler Live," in *Judith Butler Live Theory*, by Vicki Kirby (London: Continuum, 2006), 144–158, 144. In other words, when Butler describes a (retroactively projected) original nature that is in fact culture, nature is assumed by Butler to be that which "does not think." It bears the qualities of culture because in Butler's work (according to Kirby's argument) it is given the status of a cultural production. Butler's argument is obviously not intended to preserve the categories of biology and nature, but Kirby argues that it can have this effect, nonetheless.
15. Butler with Kirby, "Butler Live," 145.
16. Kirby, *Telling Flesh*, 78.
17. So, to reiterate Kirby's intervention, Butler accounts for "sex," no less than "gender," as a fabrication of culture (according to Kirby's gloss, "a sign we've interpreted"): Butler with Kirby, "Butler Live," 144. But that account would still retain a conventional notion of biology *as what is disavowed*, even when sex is deemed a cultural sign of the prior. For Butler, the natural remains a cultural artifact. In response, in conversation with Kirby, Butler clarifies that nature and culture might be better understood in terms of a "chiasmatic relationship." This, she suggests, would situate nature "beyond the nature/culture divide" (145).
18. For Butler's account of Irigaray on the intelligibility of sex and its reliance on erasure and effacement, see Judith Butler, "Sexual Inversions," in *Foucault and the Critique of Institutions*, ed. J. Caputo and M. Yount (University Park: Pennsylvania State University Press, 1993), 81–98, 90; and for her reference to Foucault's "indifference to sexual difference," see Butler, *Gender Trouble*, xii.
19. This characterization sounds like Simone de Beauvoir's famous declaration that "The relation of the two sexes is not that of two electrical poles: the man represents both the positive and the neut[ral], . . . woman is the negative, the Other." But for Beauvoir, this characterization problematizes the failure of sexual reciprocity and equality. For Irigaray it describes the *failure* of sexual difference. See Simone de Beauvoir, *The Second Sex*, trans. Constance Borde and Sheila Malovany-Chevallier (New York: Knopf, 2010), 5–6.
20. See Elizabeth Grosz's path-breaking introduction to Irigaray in *Sexual Subversions: Three French Feminists* (Sydney: Allen and Unwin, 1989).
21. Judith Butler and Drucilla Cornell, with Pheng Cheah and Elizabeth Grosz, "The Future of Sexual Difference: An Interview with Judith Butler and Drucilla Cornell," *Diacritics: A Review of Contemporary Criticism* 28, no. 1 (1998): 19–42, 27.
22. For further discussion of this point, and of commentators who particularly emphasize the theme of sexual difference in terms of a paradoxical impossibility (including Ewa Ziarek and Elizabeth Grosz), see Penelope Deutscher, *A Politics of Impossible Difference: The Later Work of Luce Irigaray* (Ithaca: Cornell University Press, 2002).
23. As Naomi Schor put this, an "essentialism which is not one": see Naomi Schor, "This Essentialism Which Is Not One: Coming to Grips with Irigaray," in *Engaging with Irigaray: Feminist Philosophy and Modern European Thought*, ed. C. Burke, N. Schor, and M. Whitford (New York: Columbia University Press, 1994), 57–78.

24. Halley identifies feminism's fantasy that women are the "ethically good" sex: see Janet Halley, *Split Decisions: How and Why to Take a Break from Feminism* (Princeton: Princeton University Press, 2006), 66.
25. Irigaray, TS, 170–191. In *Epistemology of the Closet*, Sedgwick refers to the heteronormativity of Irigaray's association of the *à-venir* with "sexual difference" Eve Kosoksky Sedgwick, *Epistemology of the Closet* (Berkeley: University of California Press, 1990), 154n36. Irigaray was among those to whom Sedgwick attributed the viewpoint that "male homosexuality was . . . the practice for which male supremacy was the theory" (36).
26. Also discussed in Wilson, *Neural Geographies*, 3.
27. Some of the propositions included by Sedgwick and Frank in the introduction to their anthology of the work of Tomkins include (1) "Human language is assumed to offer the most productive, if not the only possible, models for understanding representation" and (2) "The biopolar, transitive relations of subject to object, self to other, and active to passive . . . are dominant organizing tropes to the extent that their dismantling as such is framed as both an urgent and an interminable task." Eve Sedgwick and Adam Frank, *Shame in the Cybernetic Fold: Reading Silvan Tomkins* (Durham, NC: Duke University Press, 1995), 1–29, 1.
28. Malabou, *Changing Difference*, 6. According to Malabou's rejoinder, "to speak of the feminine as a 'philosopher' requires a revisiting of ontology and biology" (4). She adds, "we now know that to speak of 'genders' is no longer to speak of 'sexes.' . . . This situation also impacts the supposed integrity of the concept of 'sexual difference'" (5–6).
29. Alison Stone, *Luce Irigaray and the Philosophy of Sexual Difference* (Cambridge: Cambridge University Press, 2006), 1.
30. See Elizabeth Grosz, "The Nature of Sexual Difference: Irigaray and Darwin," *Angelaki: Journal of the Theoretical Humanities* 17, no. 2 (2012): 69–93.
31. Irigaray, ILTY, 47. Salamon also characterizes the tendency to consider language and culture as domains of transformability and to deem nature, matter, and body as more inert. As she points out, the latter are deemed available for inscription and interpretation, as if they only receive form from language and culture.
32. Speaking to criticisms of Irigaray's account of sexual difference as being "located at various points on the spectrum between heteronormative and homophobic," she comments, "Irigaray has responded to charges of this kind by affirming the primacy of sexual difference, suggesting homosexuality is a matter of sexual *choice* rather than sexual *difference* and that the problem of sexual difference is as primary for homosexuals as it for heterosexuals." Salamon points to the absurdity of seeing homosexuality as a flight from, rather than a renegotiation of, sexual difference. But she responds, "and yet, even as she appears to be dismissing homosexuality as a flat and frictionless nonrelation, her own theory of relation offers the tools for describing its possibilities otherwise." Gayle Salamon, *Assuming a Body: Transgender and Rhetorics of Materiality* (New York: Columbia University Press, 2010), 142.
33. Salamon, 133.
34. In this regard, Salamon emphasizes Irigaray's use of the term *morphology* as breaking with an opposition between embodiment and language. Thus, morphology is

neither "physiology" nor "meaning about physiology." This can be compared to Gallop and Kirby's interpretations of the use of the term "morphology," given earlier.
35. Irigaray, ESD, 199.
36. Salamon, *Assuming a Body*, 136.
37. See, for example, the chapter "Place, Interval" in ESD, and Irigaray's affirmation that "each of us (male or female) has a place—this place that envelops only his or her body, the first envelope of our bodies" (ESD 36), discussed in Salamon, *Assuming a Body*, 132, 141.
38. For Salamon's use of the term *plasticity* in this context, see Salamon, *Assuming a Body*, 7 and 146, and this work's chapter 5 for Salamon's critical reading of sexual difference in the work of Elizabeth Grosz. For Ziarek and Malabou's interest in a plastic notion of nature in Irigaray's work, see Catherine Malabou and Ewa Ziarek, "Negativity, Unhappiness or Felicity: On Irigaray's Dialectical Culture of Sexual Difference," *L'Esprit créateur* 52, no. 3 (2012): 11–25.
39. In Irigaray's hands, the history of philosophy is reconfigured as the scene for symptomatic or deconstructive readings of that repetition. See in particular S and ESD. Irigaray's more deconstructive readings of historical philosophical texts could also indicate there is further potential for more deconstructive (or more plastic) readings of her own work. But, and as further discussed later, Salamon's argument is also that (Irigarayan) sexual difference presupposes an undertheorized corporeal plasticity that is neither symptomatic nor deconstructive.
40. Irigaray, ILTY, 47. For example, Malabou and Ziarek cite Salamon to bolster their account of Irigaray offering an account of sexual difference (or the differently sexed) as autotransformative, a conduit of social change: Malabou and Ziarek, "Negativity," 18. (See also Salamon, *Assuming a Body*, 131.) Malabou and Ziarek emphasize that Salamon's counterreading of Irigaray also contributes to an alternative understanding of the relevance of the term *transgender* in an Irigarayan context: Malabou and Ziarek, "Negativity," 18.
41. "Impossible" in the sense that sexual difference has, historically, always implied a relationality to the masculine. Responding to the most common characterizations of Irigaray as a philosopher of sexual difference, Ewa Ziarek has affirmed of her work "it is the disappropriating character of sexual difference [which] is the most promising aspect." She is referring to an argument presented in her book *Ethics of Dissensus*, cited Malabou and Ziarek, "Negativity," 24n12.
42. Malabou and Ziarek, "Negativity," 18, discussing Malabou, *The Future of Hegel: Plasticity, Temporality and Dialectic*, trans Lisabeth During (London: Routledge, 2005), 8–12.
43. Malabou and Ziarek, "Negativity," 17.
44. They interpret this as the location of an "implicit negative in nature itself": Malabou and Ziarek, 17. In this regard, they give attention to Irigaray's "I am sexed" as meaning "I am not everything" (see also Irigaray, ILTY, 51–52). Alison Stone offers a further account of the role of negativity and nature in Irigaray's work. Note also that Ziarek, Malabou, Stone, and Salamon all value Irigaray's thought as a contemporary feminist theory in which sexual difference is autodifferentiating, self-referential, autoaffective, and autotransformative in conjunction with a parallel

understanding of nature. This is preferred (as further discussed later) to a social constructionism for which autodifferentiation, self-referentiality, autoaffectivity, and transformation would belong to the side of "culture."

45. Malabou and Ziarek, "Negativity," 18.
46. Malabou and Ziarek, 18. The definition is ascribed to Malabou on plasticity as discussed in Catherine Malabou, *The Future of Hegel: Plasticity, Temporality and Dialectic*, trans Lisabeth During (London: Routledge, 2004). See also Malabou on the plasticity of the brain in *What Shall We Do With Our Brain* (for example, her discussion at 71); and Malabou, *Changing Difference*, 41–66, in which Malabou reformulates Derridean *differánce* as presupposing plasticity.
47. Malabou and Ziarek, "Negativity," 18.
48. Malabou and Ziarek, 18, citing Salamon, *Assuming a Body*, 144.
49. Salamon, *Assuming A Body*, 143.
50. Salamon, 131.
51. Salamon, 131. This repudiates characterizations of homosexuality as flat, frictionless, or a flight from difference.
52. Malabou and Ziarek, "Negativity," 18.
53. Malabou, *Changing Difference*, 28, citing Butler, *Gender Trouble*, 41.
54. See Malabou's application of the term *plasticity* to stem cell biology.
55. Accordingly, gender and sex would be considered two categories, only one of which bears a privileged potential for difference and multiplicity: Malabou, *Changing Difference*, 14.
56. Malabou does ask whether this potential can be expanded to comprise transgender and transsexuality. She also asks what it is for femininity to be attributed to a man. But when she turns to a discussion of sexual violence, she also makes the remark, "we have to admit that 'femininity' does *owe* something to women!": Malabou, *Changing Difference*, 14.
57. Malabou, 27.
58. Malabou, 27.
59. Malabou, 27.
60. Malabou, 31.
61. She continues, "The lips or the vulva then change their meaning, turning back against themselves, that is, against the feminine." However, it is not made clear exactly which exclusion we are trying to avoid, or exactly in what sense it is nonetheless produced: Malabou, *Changing Difference*, 29.
62. When Malabou describes a transformational feminine in terms of radical openness to the plurality of its *à-venir*, she also names this the openness of *gender*, referring to the "space of play of genders," the "empty and multiple space of between-genders," and the "proliferation of gender" in a sense not reducible to the feminine: Malabou, *Changing Difference*, 28–29.
63. Malabou, 28.
64. Malabou, 28. To return to the issue that is also salient to Salamon's project, an affirmative framework for understanding Irigaray emphasizes her work's capacity for being read otherwise. This can be contrasted with criticizing her work for ambivalent, contradictory, or autoresistant content.
65. Malabou, 29.
66. Malabou, 35.

67. Malabou, 2.
68. Malabou uses the terminology when she seeks to expand an understanding of the transformability, or radical futurity, of difference: Malabou, *Changing Difference*, 14, 133. In *The Heidegger Change* she had already described a "necessary" relationship in which the ontological has to go "in drag" as the ontic: Catherine Malabou, *The Heidegger Change: On the Fantastic in Philosophy*, trans. and ed. Peter Skafish (Albany: SUNY Press, 2011), 17, 145, 314.
69. Malabou, *Changing Difference*, 14, 133.
70. Malabou, 4.
71. Malabou, v.
72. Butler with Kirby, "Butler Live," 144.
73. In Kirby, *Telling Flesh*, 56; and see 158.
74. Kirby, 158.
75. See Vicki Kirby, "Corpus Delecti," in *Telling Flesh*, 51–81; and Jane Bennett, *Vibrant Matter: A Political Ecology of Things* (Durham, NC: Duke University Press, 2010).
76. Kirby, *Telling Flesh*, 158.
77. Kirby, 158. This raises the question of how deconstructibilty could be compared with plasticity as means of reorienting or converting Irigaray's resources.
78. Kirby, 76. Butler offers a circumspect response in Butler with Kirby, "Butler Live," 149, discussed next.
79. Bearing in this in mind, one could usefully think here of Butler's response to Elizabeth Grosz's proposal that Irigarayan sexual difference offers the potential for a more transformative notion of negativity, a more positive access to the other, and a more positive recognition of the irreducibility of the other. This potential, she argues, pertains as much to relations between women as between women and men. Butler offers a comical response: "you are the one to provide that supplement, and God bless you for doing that, but then let's claim it as the Liz Grosz-Pheng Cheah supplement to Irigaray": Butler and Cornell, with Cheah and Grosz, "The Future of Sexual Difference," 29.
80. Butler with Kirby, "Butler Live," 149.
81. Butler with Kirby, 149.
82. Zakiyyah Iman Jackson, *Becoming Human: Matter and Meaning in An Antiblack World* (New York: New York University Press, 2020), 71–72.
83. Calvin Warren, *Ontological Terror: Blackness, Nihilism, and Emancipation* (Durham, NC: Duke University Press, 2018), 187n23.
84. For her discussion of this term, see Jackson, *Becoming Human*, 5, 10, and 251n65.
85. Jackson, 8.
86. Jackson, 8.
87. Warren, *Ontological Terror*, 44, citing Spillers.
88. Jackson, *Becoming Human*, 194.
89. See Dorothy Roberts, *Killing the Black Body: Race, Reproduction and the Meaning of Liberty*, 20th anniversary ed. (New York: Vintage, 2017), and Jackson's discussion of Lorde, *The Cancer Journals* (Aunt Lute: San Francisco, 1997); and Lorde, *A Burst of Light: Essays* (Ann Arbor: Firebrand, 1988).
90. Jackson, *Becoming Human*, 205.
91. Jackson, 11.
92. Jackson, 11.

93. Jackson, 210–211. For example, with this distinction in mind, Jackson draws attention to the frequent eclipsing of concern for the conditions of Black woman's lives (in relation to maternity and more broadly), in favor of the relentlessly professed (anti-Black) concern for "fetal life" (210).
94. See, in particular, *Becoming Human*'s discussion of the innovative reimaginings of reproduction, sexual difference, birth, and embodiment in Octavia Butler's *Bloodchild* (in chapter 3), and of the aesthetic strategies concerning mutation of reproductive organs in the artwork of Wangechi Mutu (in chapter 4).
95. See, in particular, *Becoming Human*, 10, 194–198, 202–213.
96. For Malabou, the term *plasticity* has certainly offered an alternative means of understanding the brain, and genetic inheritance, but, particularly in her early work, it has also offered an alternative means of reading texts. She refers also to the plasticity of a term within a text. The term can also apply to the innovation of her projects on Hegel and Heidegger. It can refer to a mode of invention, as when one as reveals "an unimagined force through the old text," and, by that means, text's absolute singularity": Malabou, *Changing Difference*, 68. Jackson emphasizes these various aspects of plasticity in Malabou's thought: see Jackson, *Becoming Human*, 71–72, 226.

PART III
Sexuate Nature and Subjectivity

Chapter Eight

AN UNCONTAINABLE SUBJECT
Thinking Feminine Sexuate Subjectivity with Irigaray

JENNIFER CARTER

Luce Irigaray's extensive work on subjectivity reveals that the morphological organization of bodies provides a background for the development and evolution of subjectivity. For Irigaray, bodies offer not only physical but symbolic contours that shape modes of exchange between subjects and form semantic networks through which subjects make meaning. Irigaray offers a truly distinctive way of understanding subjectivity not only in terms of the symbolic meaning of reproduction and its relation to bodily morphology; she also articulates an understanding of the implications of bodily morphology itself as a condition of affective self-relation. The folds, contours, and openings of bodies are not generic centers of affect, sensation, pleasure, or discomfort; rather each bodily site has its own specific quality and character that it expresses in addition to its functional significance, a meaning that is related to its very form and sensory qualities. Irigaray has paid particular attention to feminine specificity in the bodily morphological context, an antidote to the often-unacknowledged preoccupation with masculine bodies that seeps into psychoanalytic and philosophic discourse. Irigaray's work on sexuate subjectivity, in particular feminine subjectivity, subverts classical psychoanalytic and philosophical models that center male bodies and psyches and that establish a hierarchy between male and female modalities of affection.

In discussing sexuate subjectivity, and subjective development more broadly, this chapter gives an account of the lips in Irigaray's philosophy, tracing their recurring place in her work from *Speculum of the Other Woman* (1974) to her recent *Sharing the Fire* (2019). More specifically, I am interested in how Irigaray engages the figure of the lips in terms of their open-closed nature, their uncircumscribability, their tactile and sensible qualities, and their valence between duality and unity. In thinking the lips, Irigaray considers how they "open up" both literally and figuratively a caesura in a culture of sameness, both interrupting its totality and instantiating a different subject in a language within a culture that has not recognized it, that has treated it as hostile, foreign, or inferior, a subject that subverts traditional logics of static or complete self-identity. I suggest in dialogue with Irigaray's oeuvre that it is possible to articulate other subject positions besides the masculine, and one of the first and most important tasks of that project is to make a place in language for speaking differently about identity, sex, and subjectivity. While Irigaray gives many examples of how this sort of articulation could unfold, the lips prove a particularly generative figure for such a project and suggest that there is a necessity of using language in new ways that may not follow familiar logics.

Lips are among a multiplicity of aspects of subjectivity that contribute to a full picture of subjective development, including relational, bodily, social, cultural, and historical factors. Irigaray treats lips in various and developing ways throughout her oeuvre and lips connect different domains, in particular those of sexual difference, sexuate subjectivity, and tactility, that help to further elucidate the relation between self- and hetero-affection and subjectivity, prominent themes especially in Irigaray's recent works. In this chapter, I hope to address the fundamental open-endedness that Irigaray's account of subjectivity of the lips "opens," one that does not side with biological reductiveness, in particular an exclusively genital model of sexual difference, or alternatively with an exclusively figurative understanding of the meaning of lips. Finally, I intend to explore how thinking about lips and subjectivity could contribute to building a culture that is more hospitable to femininity as well as more welcoming of difference more generally.

MEDIATING BETWEEN THE BODILY AND SEMANTIC

Recently, Emily Anne Parker has suggested that Irigaray's work presupposes a genitally reductive point of view of sexual difference. Parker writes, "I worry that Irigaray's oeuvre . . . presupposes 'genital difference,' the very idea of which is synonymous with the two-sex model."[1] I would like to respond to Parker's concern by affirming that the lips, whether or not they are "genital" in the reproductive or scientific senses, should continue to be understood both bodily and figuratively, yet they need not be understood in reductively genital terms. In particular, while it may appear that two understandings of lips, the bodily on the one hand and the figurative on the other, are at odds, it is a virtue of Irigaray's work that these two levels can be understood to be operating together. Affirming or even presupposing "genital difference" in thinking sexual difference is consistent with, and perhaps even fundamental to, her project, even if "genital difference," assuming we understand what it means, does not fully encompass sexual difference. I offer that grounding or cogrounding sexual difference in bodily differences does not entail adherence to any theoretical, scientific, or political model of sexuation. To differ sexuately does not require that there be two and only two biological terms pregiven or established in advance. Differing can happen among two *or more*. Thus emphasizing difference as opposed to identity alleviates the need to establish in advance a theory or model of sexes and, in particular, of sex identities. It might be argued that there remains a covert presupposition of a classical "two sex model" in thinking sexual difference as connected to "genital difference," a model that is rightly criticized as devolving into indifference, but this need not be the case if "difference" is not taken to refer to a scientific model of sex. On the contrary, it is possible to emphasize bodily differing without taking a scientific stance toward bodies. Rather, focusing on particular bodily forms and ways that bodies differ frees up the possibility of nonreductive understandings of relations between the bodily and the sexuate, that bodies may be widely various while still conferring the possibilities of identity as well as sexuation. Introducing a figure such as the lips as an articulable and livable bodily form realizes in language a possibility of a positive contour of the body that does not conform to the classical logics of scientific and philosophical understandings of bodies. As I understand Irigaray, there is a middle ground that operates in "betweens" of sexual difference that allows the lips to mediate between the discursive and the material, between masculine and feminine, between the one and the two, between literal and figurative. Irigaray is often read to be siding with either a figurative or a carnal valance of lips, but readings that attempt to reduce her point to either side of that apparent divide miss the radical, ontological dimension of her discussion of the lips. Lips as forms of bodily expression and alternatives to the phallic model of meaning and symbolics are polyvalent figures that move between discursive and material domains and between bodies.

In contrast with the anatomically reductive perspective on Irigaray's thinking of the lips, some commentators, notably Jane Gallop and Vicky Kirby, have taken Irigaray to be articulating a primarily symbolic, literary, or linguistic model of feminine being and/or lipped being.[2] Such a reading of Irigaray's texts contemplates an important facet of Irigaray's thinking of lips, since Irigaray does intend to reimagine lips as enabling an opening in discourse and providing an alternative form of symbolization, a form that has been, at times, associated with the movement surrounding feminine writing. Kirby emphasizes the distinction between biology and morphology, articulating that morphology sets up a literary figure that finds its symbolic root in the figure of the lips, a reading that is consistent with Irigaray's articulation of lips though incomplete.[3] I would like to stress, however, that while lippedness and lips, mucous, and other bodily figures have important discursive and even linguistic valences, their physical, and most importantly tactile, reality as bodily forms plays a role that is irreducible to the metaphoric or symbolic, though nevertheless interwoven with it. The semantic aspects of lips are connected to their tangibility and tactility as well as their significant shape(s), contiguity, and position/condition of being both interior and exterior, skin and mucous, visibility and invisibility. They are not merely functional but affectively integrated into the semantic as well as tactile field of the subject's (bodily) experience and provide an important backdrop to the evolution of subjectivity that conditions its emergence in language. Bound up with subjects and symbols emerging discursively, the tactile and semantic field of subjects' experience is arrayed as/through sensory awareness. To assign lips to the semantic without reference to the first-personal subjective and intersubjective experience of lipped touching and exchange, including birth, speech, and breath, is to forget the importance of touch in language, thinking, and relating, as well as the importance of language and thinking in touch. To eschew the tactile/sensory/physical in favor of a primarily linguistic interpretation of lips is to reinscribe a binary between embodiment and language that the figure and existence of lips help get beyond.

While Irigaray often draws our attention to the formation of subjectivity based on the figures of sexual characteristics—genitals and other bodily organs—her extended meditation on feminine embodiment breaks with pasts of both psychoanalysis and philosophy in that it centers an existence other than the exclusively masculine and is a positive discussion of the subject that does not focus on a disembodied subjective ideal. When Irigaray writes about the two lips, she is suggesting that the figure of the lips functions on an imaginative level as well as a physical one. A subject for whom a central (sexual) motif is lips takes on characteristics of/as their morphology in ways both literal and figurative, felt and imagined. Irigaray writes, "woman 'touches herself' all the time, and moreover no one can forbid her to do so, for her genitals are formed of two lips in continuous contact. Thus within herself, she is already two—but not divisible into one(s)—that caress each other."[4] Irigaray thus portrays how psychic development and intersubjective relations transform not only how subjects relate to themselves and meet together but also their relationship to meaning. Irigaray intends to articulate gender-relative styles of bodily affection as part of an effort to create an opening in the closed system of a culture that erases affection of both self and other as well as neutralizes difference beginning with sexual difference. From the beginning, emphasizing lips acknowledges relatedness between bodies/subjects and themselves, and from bodies/subjects to others. Lips thus figure a relational gesture-form between one and oneself, between one and another, and between sexes.

Empirically speaking, it may be the case that lips have a variety of natural "expressions," counterparts, and appear on continuums of bodily forms that may or may not fit the ideal of the "perfect" or even "imperfect" expression of ("feminine") lips. Such realities are not counterexamples to the figures of lippedness as forms of bodily expression, as alternatives to the phallic model of meaning and symbol. Nor do they contradict lips' inclusion as a feature of identities that are truly different, and that defy the logic of sameness implicit in the discourses of subjectivity in philosophy and psychoanalysis. It is important to discuss the degree to which lipped bodily expression(s) are "feminine." While it is not feasible here to elucidate the extensive debate on this subject, I suggest that it is possible to maintain an association between lippedness and femininity without reducing either to the other, or excluding the possibility of masculine lippedness, or thinking of femininity in other ways besides the lips. Noting sexually differentiated styles of self-affection invoking lippedness and acknowledging lips' complex association with femininity indeed offer another point from which to approach sexual difference that does not demarcate an artificial boundary between "masculine" and "feminine" body types, since lippedness is not exclusive to a single sex. In short, lips are polyvalent figure(s) that move between domains. They do not represent a static biological or subjective ideal, and in fact subvert the very logic that posits such an ideal. Rather, Irigaray's accounts of feminine subjectivity resist being tied to a finite organ or set of organs and suggest that any theory of subjectivity that tends toward anatomical reductivity should be questioned. Lips, as one figure of feminine subjectivity, are both sensible, real physical forms and symbolic, semantic figures conditioning language, thought, and culture. They bridge as well as maintain a separation between these domains.

It is crucial to note that Irigaray often associates "lips" with woman and femininity but not exclusively so. For instance, when referring to teaching children of differing sexes to be aware of self-affection, she writes, "to succeed in this, I suggest focussing, at least in the first instance, one's attention on the perception of one's lips, one's hands and one's eyelids touching one another. Such a gesture—that I call 're-touch'—contributes to realizing what our limits are and the thresholds between the inside and the outside of the space that is ours, something which favors a repose in ourselves."[5] It is clear that she intends for self-affection and lippedness to be a universal possibility among embodied human subjects. Nevertheless, she also affirms a consistent association between femininity and lips. For instance, she writes, "I suggested that the morphology of the two lips could be a privileged place for woman to maintain a process of self-affection."[6] Yet such an association does not entail a reductive or exclusive relation between lips and women or femininity.

Irigaray maintains an at least terminologically straightforward differentiation between "man" and "woman," and correspondingly "masculine" and "feminine" styles of self-affection. For instance, in the chapter "The Return" of her 2013 book *In the Beginning, She Was*, she writes, "the modalities of self-affection are not the same for man and woman, and nor are their lack or perversion the same."[7] There is widespread founded concern that invoking sexually specific universals such as "woman" and "man" and associating them exclusively with "femininity" and "masculinity" as their "counterparts" unproblematically or in certain contexts lead to confusion and harm. This is the case in part because of the historic use of the universal "man" to refer to all humankind, but also because of the problematic and reductive use of "man" and "woman" and "masculine" and "feminine" in specifying typologies of bodies that may or may not correspond to real embodied subjects, in particular to the lived reality of self-identified trans, intersex, and gender nonconforming persons. Even if in some cases they are unproblematized, Irigaray's uses of the terms *man/masculine* and *woman/feminine*, at least in terms of their consistent associations with each other, provide a guide to tracing her claims about bodily morphology and the subjects who bear/express that morphology. Because she avoids pigeonholing subjects into biological frameworks, her texts are often immanently readable as consistent with possibilities of gender nonconformity. Irigaray relies on familiarity with bodies, in particular, provided that each one of us has first-person experience with bodies, both self and other, to guide understandings of morphology, sexual difference, and subjectivity. Noting this does not do away with the need to mediate between the complex issues of first-person and second-/third-person experience of the meaning of morphology for given subjects, or the complexities and multiplications that arise amid myriad expressions of subjectivity and morphology and their social meaning and interpretation. Nevertheless, even as social norms must evolve to better address the lived reality of subjects, Irigaray's articulations of the important and close associations between morphology and subjectivity are even more helpful and crucial to provide not only tangibility and articulability to emerging subject positions, but also ways to talk about morphology and subjectivity that do not repeat the historical patriarchal repression and erasure of sexuate differentiation and of femininity.

The discussion of lips does not resolve the tension between the concrete singular reality of (individual) human being and universals of sexual difference, but it helps to bridge discussions of the body with those of subjectivity in a way that allows the rebuilding of a language and culture that connects subjectivity and sexuation in ways that both acknowledge masculinity, traditionally associated with the phallic model, and introduce a positive feminine style and reality of affection. It is important to guard against reproducing the harm, violence, and exclusivity of the patriarchal milieu and its tendency toward artificially cutting through necessarily complex connections and adjacencies between styles and bodies that do not neatly fit presupposed associations between bodily shapes and genders, and other categories of identity and difference such as race and ability. This sort of consideration requires sensitivity, since articulating a relation between femininity and lippedness is also crucial for being able to think through subjectivity and sexual difference in the context of Irigaray's oeuvre. In light of Irigaray's carefully constructed but oftentimes challenging language, it is helpful to note that our diverse but also shared experiences with bodies, both our own and the bodies of others, form the basis of her/our inquiry and can serve as a guide to keep from being led into excessive abstraction or naturalizing, and instead to maintain links between our thinking and living reality.

LIPS AND TACTILITY

How, then, might we move beyond reductive biologism or reductive semanticism and toward an articulation of the ontological significance of the lips between materiality and discourse? How might we understand the particular intervention Irigaray uses with the lips not to once and for all define the feminine but to think subjectivity in a new way? We might approach these questions by reintroducing the role of touch in mediating between the materiality of bodily forms and their qualitative shaping of and by subjects. According to Irigaray, bodily forms exist not only as material facts that are represented to and by subjects in language, but as qualitative sensible realities, notably ones experienced tactilely, that profoundly condition the emergence of subjectivity. At the same time Irigaray does not suggest that the tactile experience of lippedness is unmediated by thought. She conceives sexuate subjectivity to be nonteleological and nondeterministic: each subject develops amid a specialized organization of factors, among them linguistic and bodily, that come into play and correspond to concrete realities that are distinct for each one and that condition but do not define their evolution. These factors do not create totalities that enclose subjects in a fixed web of possibilities or dictate insurmountable absolutes. Irigaray, in exploring the constitution of subjectivities, decries a lack of comprehension, recognition, and nuance concerning a culture of differing subjects, particularly feminine ones. Most importantly, she points out that historically subjectivity has been conceived as "one." The subject itself has been presupposed to be self-enclosed, self-sufficient, nonporous, nonfluid, and nonrelational. This already suggests an exclusion of femininity. It has been customary to posit that there is a single (masculine) subject that stands for or amounts to all subjects, which are assumed to be fundamentally similar, if not the same.[8] On the contrary, Irigaray proposes that sexual differentiation demands an understanding of subjectivity that appreciates radical difference and that makes room for at least two radically different "subjects" grounded in sexual difference. Irigaray reimagines subjectivity itself to be radically sexuate and radically differentiated vis-à-vis sexuation, differentiation that is necessarily complex because sexuation is not reducible to any single event, process, domain, or outcome. Vital subjective sources of differentiation arise from a background of bodily differences and their influence on touch of which the lips are a privileged site, according to Irigaray.

Her focus on how sexual morphology specifies modalities of touching shows ways understanding touch can help to complicate as well as more clearly articulate the relationship between sex and subjectivity.[9] Touch is a sensory modality that also provides access to the form, volume, and texture of materiality. Subjective self-sensing combines these two. There is a reduplication of sensing: the affective or sensory quality of tactility on the body, as well as a perception of that which the body touches. This and other mediating aspects of touch play an important role in subjectivity, especially in relation to the lips, because touch allows the lips both to sense and to be sensed from both lips at the same time. This has important implications for the potential to develop a relation to the self that is both objective, in the sense of being an object for oneself, and subjective, in the sense of sensing (oneself), and sensing sensing oneself. This series of doublings of sensed-and-sensing is highly significant to the development of subjectivity and finds an important figure and expression in lips.

It is important, then, to clarify how lips provide a different way of cultivating self-affection and developing subjectivity. In particular, the polyvalent nature of lips allows for subjectivity and its concrete relation to the sensible to find a privileged site of cultivation. The forms of the lips themselves are what enable these special modes of self-touch, but also compose symbolizations of form itself. Especially in light of her earliest discussions of lips, Irigaray has at times been read as taking feminine subjectivity to be so radically fluid that there is no morphological concreteness to it. But Irigaray has imagined the lips as somewhere between structure and fluidity. Irigaray connects self-affection to the figure of lips as a positive conception resisting the idea that the feminine has no shape.

To better understand Irigaray's radical approach the lips' role in sexual difference and sexuate subjectivity, her remarks in her 1974 "Volume Without Contours" (also "Volume-Fluidity") in *Speculum of the Other Woman* add some clarification.[10] Irigaray reflects on the paradoxes that have arisen in the context of some comments she makes regarding lips and feminine subjectivity, including the following:

> Now woman is neither closed nor open. Indefinite, unfinished/in-finite, *form is never complete in her*. She is not infinite, but nor is she *one* unit: a letter, a figure, a number in a series, a proper name, single object (of a) sensible world, and the simple ideality of an intelligible whole, the entity of a foundation, etc. This incompleteness of her form, of her morphology, allows her to become something else at any moment, which is not to say that she is (n) ever unambiguously anything.[11]

In particular, Irigaray rejects interpretations that take her to mean that feminine embodiment and feminine subjectivity, and in particular lips, offer no contours whatsoever. This misreading introduces the perplexing claim that woman is formless, contour-less, and even perhaps intangible, but, at the same time, carnal subjects, including feminine ones, are sites of definite limits and exchanges between themselves and concretely living others. Even the term *fluidity* in the context of the lips may be an overstatement of the mutable quality of informal/formal, open-closed touching of lips. Irigaray does not mean that lips are chaotic, abyssal, or in absolute flux.[12] They are situated within a continuum of dynamism and repose, form and fluidity, and offer the possibility of being in relation to the self without collapsing into oneself, nor being completely closed off from the outside or the other. Commenting on what the differences in translation reveal, Irigaray writes,

> Errors of translation may come from the fact that I am opening a new field of thought.... By 'l'incontournable volume' I simply meant a volume that

can't be circumscribed because it's open. Thus, it didn't mean either 'volume fluidity' or 'volume without contours' [two different translations of title, "L'incontournable Volume"]. It's an allusion to the morphology of the female body and I say that this morphology is an open volume, one that can't be circumscribed. A closed volume can be circumscribed; an open volume can't be circumscribed.[13]

It is important, then, to recognize that what Irigaray means by feminine embodiment does not imply a total lack of structure or form, which would repeat in a certain sense the psychoanalytic inscription of woman as lack. While Irigaray does associate woman with fluidity, her discussions of the lips stress the not-closed/not-open nature of feminine embodiment, which is figured in/as lips, rather than a bare incompleteness or formlessness. Notions Irigaray develops in relation to lips such as threshold, interval, and continuous touching illustrate the radical, even metaphysical difference that lips instantiate with respect to traditionally masculine bodily/(meta)physical forms or objects that are presupposed to be solid and impenetrable—forms thought to be destroyed if they are open(ed), or porous, with such openings being characterized as ruptures or fissures that "disrupt" or "wound" the "solidity" of the form/body. With her emphasis on the lips, Irigaray elaborates a genuinely different bodily sense of form that does not reinscribe the milieu of sameness, self-enclosedness, solitariness, and inhospitability of the traditional subject/body of Western philosophy and psychoanalysis. Irigaray instead foregrounds how a subject's own body relates to its particular style of self-relating, or as she terms it, *self-affection*.[14] Bodies, especially lips, condition how subjective development accrues in styles of affection, both *self-affection* and *hetero-affection*, relating with others. Bases for differing styles of affection include differences in the ways bodies are composed, and how bodies are enabled to touch themselves and to touch others, particularly relative sexuation and generation.[15] It is in this way that lips are important morphological site(s) for thinking self-affection for both masculinity and femininity.

First and foremost, lips are an important morphological site for thinking feminine self-affection. Especially in earlier formulations of the concept of self-affection, Irigaray refers to self-affection as "retouch." In "Volume Without Contours" / "Volume Fluidity," for instance, she writes,

> (The/A) woman does not obey the principle of self-identity ... Which implies an excess of any identification with/of self. But that excess is (not) nothing: the abeyance of form, the fissure in form, the reference to another edge where she re-touches herself without anything/thanks to nothing. Lips of the same form—yet never simply defined—overlap by retouching one another, referring one (to) the other for a perimeter that nothing arrests in *one* configuration.[16]

Irigaray also explains, for instance, in "This Sex Which Is Not One,"[17] how the shape of lips allows a body to touch itself in ways that are topologically complex and take on wide-ranging significance for them, from the symbolic to the social. Such self-touching that is sexually differentiated but nevertheless experienced in some ways by everyone, Irigaray suggests, could bring subjects to qualitative awareness of their own relationship to internality and externality, their relationship to their own self-sensing/feeling/relating, and make them more consciously aware of their relation to others. In some of her more recent works, she outlines how that awareness of difference both within oneself and in relation to others could influence subjects to relate more easily with one another in horizontal, that is, less hierarchical, ways. Such metonymical links as those between the shapes of the lips and horizontality are given to subjects by bodily contours and, Irigaray argues, profoundly influence subjects' lives and social relatedness.[18]

To pay attention to bodies is not to put limitations on what it means to be feminine or masculine but to expand the understanding of the role form and relation play. It is not only the form itself that matters to the subject but also the tactile relations that form and formlessness represent along the continuum of bodily contours. This is in contrast to sketches that Freud, Lacan, and others have presented of how the phallus or "masculine" body supersedes or stands in for any other form, and of how we only make sense of that form as self-consistent, and singular, as having or not having (it). Irigaray is developing a subjective understanding of what the feeling and shape of the body do in the psyche, inviting us to consider symbolic subjective forms that occur as first-person experiences of the body and other subjects. Irigaray suggests that those whose bodies accentuate lips experience self-touching in a special or emphasized way, and through this touching form a subjectivity, particular to their own bodily formation, that takes on qualities of lippedness, for instance, being especially sensitive to subject-to-subject relations. Such formative experiences take place through the relations that one has with one's own body, a tactile economy that exists for oneself as self-affection, and through one's relations with other bodies, that may or may not share a similar tactile style.[19]

This economy has historically been subject to disruptions in cultural or political climates that do not favor the cultivation and development of tactile economies with the self and with others, for instance, patriarchal cultures that do not value relations between mothers and daughters.[20] Those disruptions and their relation to sensations may themselves become inflected by language but also inform language. Irigaray characterizes the in/form of feminine bodily morphology and its relation to language:

> She does not set herself up as *one*, as a (single) female unit. She is not closed up or around one single truth or essence. The essence of a truth remains foreign to her. She neither has nor is a being. And she does not oppose a feminine truth to the masculine truth. Because this would once again amount to playing the—man's—game of castration. If the female sex takes place by embracing itself, by endlessly sharing and exchanging its lips, its edges, its borders, and their "content," as it ceaselessly becomes other, no stability of essence is proper to her. She has a place in the openness of a relation to the other whom she does not take into herself, like a whore, but to whom she continuously gives birth.[21]

As Irigaray discusses, for instance, in "This Sex Which Is Not One,"[22] the psychoanalytic theorization of subjectivity has focused on the phallus, or on the shadows of the phallus/penis. Because women's experiences have not traditionally informed the foundations of psychoanalysis, some in the discipline emphasize women's psychological subordination and ultimate reducibility to men. Correspondingly the role of maternity and motherhood, and masculine subjectivity itself, has structured the discourse and expectation of the psychology of women.

Yet it is important to refocus on the notion that subjectivity is also formed through a self-to-self relation—not just mental self-awareness, but the experience of the topology, texture, openings, enfoldings, gestures, and speaking of the body. To emphasize, this is difficult for anything but a radically new form of thinking to do since the traditions of both psychoanalysis and philosophy have tended to privilege sight over touch and rationality over sensing, and therefore incline not to notice the profound conditions of touch that influence subjective development through awareness of bodily contours, volume, tactility, consistency, moisture, etc. Irigaray suggests that alternative figures like the lips can both structure language and symbolize desire, and help to reorient ourselves with respect to touch as opposed to sight.[23] To understand how such systems of meaning and desire might be elaborated, a culture of speaking and listening to experience that embodies or foregrounds lippedness is vital. Emphasizing touch is a path toward freeing incarnation from exclusive relation to the visual and improving the possibility of deemphasizing visual characteristics associated with race, gender, and ability that have traditionally been a central element in oppressive regimes of colonization. Touch itself can provide openings toward different values that on multiple levels subvert patriarchal projects and styles.[24] Moreover, the significance of lippedness as a general human experience has been overlooked precisely because the masculine historically has come to stand for all symbolization and all desire. To overcome this history demands the articulation of the experiences of others, women and "other" others who have been excluded from/by the discourse around subjectivity and sex.

DIFFERENCE AS A CONDITION OF SUBJECTIVITY

For each relation between two (subjects, sexes, bodies, lips, and the like), according to Irigaray, sexual difference provides a context for the relation.[25] This sort of qualitatively influenced relation with an other is one aspect of what Irigaray calls *hetero-affection*—generally, the affective relation between oneself and another.[26] How these relations between and within sexes operate is complex: human beings do express/embody sexuate morphology, and to be human is to live as a corporeal being with skin, limbs, and senses, even if we do not go so far as defining which are sexual characteristics in a fixed way. Bodily characteristics that present themselves anatomically in a morphological shape—organs, cells, systems, folds, lips—deeply influence our subjective possibilities and experience. A crucial step in understanding human subjectivity is to acknowledge that some organs are uncontainable:

> Now, the/a woman who does not have one sex [*sexe*]—which will usually have been interpreted as no sex—cannot subsume it/herself under *one* term, generic or specific. Body, breath, pubis, clitoris, labia, vulva, vagina, neck of

the uterus, woman . . . and this nothing which already makes them take pleasure in/from their apartness [*jouir dan/de leur écart*] thwarts their reduction to any proper name, any specific meaning, any concept.[27]

But we cannot imagine human consciousness without a body, without being able to touch itself and others, or without being sexed. Similarly, to deny that the form of the body is influential to subjectivity would be to suppress how the body both opens possibilities for and gives limits to the subject. According to Irigaray, in contrast to the open-endedness she attributes to feminine subjectivity, the traditional masculine imaginary articulates a single subject that relates primarily with objects. Irigaray writes,

> For man needs an instrument to touch himself: a hand, a woman, or some substitute. The replacement of that apparatus is effected in and through language [*langage*]. Man produces language for self-affection. And various forms of discourse, can be analyzed as various modes of the auto-affect(at)ion of the "subject." The most ideal being the philosophical discourse that privileges "self-representation." A mode of auto affect(a)tion that reduces the need for an instrument to *almost* nothing: to the thought (of) the soul. An introjected, internalized micro, in which the "subject" ensures, in the most subtle most secret manner possible, the immortal preservation of his autoerotism.[28]

Irigaray suggests that a more interestingly and less unconsciously elaborated philosophy of masculine subjectivity could be possible, especially if its relationship with self-affection and hetero-affection were made more explicit. It is not that masculine subjectivity and masculine embodiment are restricted from the possibility of self-affection; rather, as Irigaray puts it, a culture in the (exclusively) masculine has preempted the articulation of such relations. A rearticulation of lipped being as a step toward the elaboration of a culture of feminine being can help to restore the possibility of a culture of sexual difference that would support masculine self-affection. Thus elaborating lipped subjectivity is beneficial to subjects of differing genders.

Unlike Lacan, who theorizes that subjectivity emerges only after a period of latency prior to visual self-recognition in a mirror,[29] Irigaray offers the position that conditions of subjectivity are already emerging as the subject begins to touch themselves and others. Irigaray highlights these moments of subjective recognition as electrifying in their tactile modality, whereas Lacan assigns them to an external visual source. These moments of subjective self-recognition take place when touching one's own body, either through external contact between areas of the skin, through the internal sensation of inner bodily touching, from a combination of interior and exterior sensation, as that which occurs at lips, or through touching/being touched by the body of another. An understanding of subjectivization informed by Irigaray's thought acknowledges that subjective development is conditioned by these relations and processes even in early life. It recognizes touch as an important influence on subjective development, including the touch of the body with itself, the touch of the other in the womb, and the touch of others. To trace such an understanding introduces an important language for thinking about subjective development beyond the boundaries of patriarchal dividing lines that categorize by a logic of existence and lack. To develop an understanding of affectivity as it relates to bodily style, especially the figure of the two lips, could allow a more inclusive understanding of subjectivity while remaining connected to the body. An understanding of sexual difference can be developed that does not rely heavily on a radically dualistic rendition of sex, which risks devolving into the past patriarchal hierarchy of male and not-male. To cultivate an ethos that is nonhierarchical, it is necessary to overcome defaulting to singularity in the patriarchal mode.

NEWLY SUBJECTIVE

In Irigaray's texts, there are multiple ways that the style of body can self-relate or relate to others so that certain aspects of a subject's awareness or self-touching are emphasized.[30] A bodily style expressive of lips not only could encourage subjects to develop awareness of their body as being shaped in particular ways, but also could actualize their capacity to relate to the self and others more readily because of their "natural" self-touching. Thus what Irigaray describes as being particularly emphasized in the subjectivity of women does not necessarily need to be read as applying to cis women alone. Irigaray has argued that each of us has a world, a specific existence that we encounter on the basis of who we are and what the world has presented us with.[31] The world is that context that we find ourselves in, and one of the first, and most important contexts is bodily, both our own and the bodies of others. Without implying that one's social or psychical existence is in perfect harmony with bodily experience, Irigaray suggests that the body forms a background condition of who we are that persistently gives rise to the climate of the subject, even if, as the body grows, changes, and develops, that climate is changing. Even when we are able to transcend our bodily limitations through means beyond them, enhancing or restoring our bodily capacities, we do so in light of our living bodies. Finally, the signs that we use to think and communicate with are related to our carnal existence. Irigaray suggests that the two lips are a figure that emerges from a different ethos that we can try to understand and develop. The two lips are not a "master" signifier, an exclusive universal, like Lacan's phallus, which not only dominates but signifies domination. The lips embody a way of relating that makes meaning and generates thought through their very relatedness and difference, providing a place and a figure of reciprocity.

When we think of bodily forms, we can understand them as having a physical manifestation that, through experiential processes, make up the world of the subject. Bodies differ radically for the subjects who live them, and subjects are radically influenced by living through their distinct bodily compositions. Irigaray writes, "In order to touch himself, man needs an instrument: his hand, a woman's body, language. . . . And this self-caressing needs at least a minimum of activity. As for woman, she touches herself in herself without any need for mediation, and before there is any way to distinguish activity from passivity."[32] In this sharply drawn contrast, two figures of subjectivity emerge based on not only social difference but morphological difference. This means for Irigaray that the process of self-touching is very different for different subjects based on bodily composition because of both their relation with their own bodies and their complex relations with the bodies of others, including the one who bore them. Nevertheless, bodily composition may be juxtaposed in different ways with gender presentation and social perception for each subject, thus adding to differentiation and individuation.

Irigaray has expanded on this in her analyses of hetero-affection and self-affection in recent years to think through a positive project of affective cultivation as part of articulating a truly sexually differentiated notion of subjectivity. She often contrasts masculine subjectivity with feminine in an effort to communicate the perils of remaining within an exclusively masculine paradigm without the elaboration of the feminine as an independent sexuate identity. She writes, "Another motive for explaining masculine behavior is that the male sex is in some way outside of his body and internal self-affection thus cannot exist for the masculine subject, as is possible for a woman thanks to the self-touching of lips. The ways of being in the world are thus rather different for man and woman."[33] She provides an explanation here of the positions of two sexually different subjective identities and how they contrastingly engage with self-affection. In addition to articulating challenges in developing a culture of masculine self-affection, Irigaray makes such delineations among differing subjects in order to preserve the possibility for the emergence of femininity without it being subsumed within the masculine and to articulate challenges to the emergence of feminine subjectivity within a patriarchal context. For feminine subjectivity to situate itself with respect to the masculine as well as for the masculine to establish a place for itself without appropriating the feminine as its projection demands a positive articulation of their difference.

Irigaray has suggested that her comments regarding masculine self-affection are not posed from the point of view of a masculine subject, but rather are commentary on "a culture in the masculine." She writes, "As I am not a male person, it is difficult for me to define what self-affection could be for a man; it would amount to substituting myself for him. I can only question a culture in the masculine. I note, then, that masculine subjectivity did not become differentiated enough from the maternal world. . . . This has entailed several consequences."[34] Thus it is possible to read her as not drawing a sharp line excluding men from self-touching "without instrument." Instead, her point can be understood as articulating the most pronounced aspects of masculine subjectivity as lived in a patriarchal culture, in contrast to the qualities of a feminine subjectivity that is not at home in such a culture. We may speculate that men, whether cis, trans, gender-conforming, or not, may be capable of internal self-affection of various kinds. Thus the possibilities of internal self-affection for men are important and necessary to explore, as a way not of appropriating the feminine but of becoming more consciously aware of self-affection and hetero-affection, and of making the cultivation of affection a positive and conscious project for masculine subjectivity in dialogue with feminine subjectivity.

Such articulations form bases for intersectional solidarity and for connecting subjective differences to social relationships and identifications.

They offer a context for discussing the role of the forms of lips, penis, and other bodily contours that comprise, differently, the background of each of our subjective worlds. These crucially influence each of our affective styles even when our lived identities and genders do not fall neatly along the lines expected in a patriarchal culture, as is the case for trans, intersex, and gender-nonconforming persons as well as feminine subjects. The specifics of the lived experience and affective styles that emerge based on particular bodily compositions require a great deal of thoughtfulness to articulate. Irigaray has presented extensive starting points for the discussion that can be unpacked and built upon. Such building includes the recognition of others as radically different yet crucially related. As Irigaray articulates, "The other sex—as the other hand, the other foot, the other lip, the other eye—signifies an other of two, whose individuation and relationship involves a really specific economy. The same as and different from the other, each element of the pair has an autonomy that is granted it notably through its relation to the other. Entering into relation with one another takes place through a finite structure which appears, is cleared, thanks to the space that, then, exists between the two."[35] It is thus possible to think of compositions of self and other as cultures of difference without presuming that every relation in difference will be the same. There can be different relations of difference between others, even as sexually different others, thus contributing both to singularity and community.

There will continue to be different stories to tell from different bodies and, significantly, from differently sexuate bodies. We learn from Irigaray's project that differentiated bodies grow into differentiated psyches, and that there will be different subjectivities, in particular, sexuately different ones. None will embody the ideal of the rational universal subject who can speak from all positions at once. Rather, concrete subjects speak to one another through the medium of bodies that are sexuately differentiated. The elaboration of affective styles as influenced on both individual and collective levels can be a crucial step in dismantling cultures that organize to suppress the voices and lives of some in favor of the single subjective narrative. To acknowledge and work to understand the existential bodily conditions that combine to influence subjectivity is an integral part of relating to ourselves, each other, and understanding the kind of world that we should build with one another to suit living together as radically different.

BIBLIOGRAPHY

Carter, Jennifer. "How to Lead a Child to Flower: Luce Irigaray's Philosophy of the Growth of Children." In *Towards a New Human Being*, edited by Luce Irigaray, Mahon O'Brien, and Christos Hadjioannou, 3–16. London: Palgrave Macmillan, 2019.

———. "Touch and Caress in the Work of Luce Irigaray." PhD diss., Stony Brook University, 2018. ProQuest (10932831).

Deutscher, Penelope. *A Politics of Impossible Difference: The Later Work of Luce Irigaray*. Ithaca: Cornell University Press, 2002.

Gallop, Jane. *Thinking Through the Body*. New York: Columbia University Press, 1988.

Hirsch, Elizabeth, Gary Olson, and Gaëton Brulotte. "Je—Luce Irigaray: An Interview with Luce Irigaray." *Hypatia* 10, no. 2 (1995): 93–114.

Kirby, Vicki. *Telling Flesh: The Substance of the Corporeal*. New York: Routledge, 1997.

Lacan, Jacques. *Écrits: The First Complete Edition in English*. Translated by Bruce Fink, with Héoïse Fink and Russell Grigg. New York: Norton, 2006.

Lehtinen, Virpi. *Luce Irigaray's Phenomenology of Feminine Being*. Albany: SUNY Press, 2014.

Malabou, Catherine. *Changing Difference: The Feminine and the Question of Philosophy*. Malden, MA: Polity, 2016.

Mitchel, Elspeth. "To Be Born a Girl? Irigaray, Sexual Identity and the Girl." In *Towards a New Human Being*, edited by Luce Irigaray, Mahon O'Brien, and Christos Hadjioannou, 35–50. London: Palgrave Macmillan, 2019.

Mulder, Anne-Claire. "Divine Flesh, Embodied Word: 'Incarnation' as a Hermeneutical Key to a Feminist Theologian's Reading of Luce Irigaray's Work." PhD diss., Universiteit van Amsterdam, published by Amsterdam University Press, 2006.

Parker, Emily Anne. *Elemental Difference and the Climate of the Body*. New York: Oxford University Press, 2021.

NOTES

1. Emily Anne Parker, *Elemental Difference and the Climate of the Body* (New York: Oxford University Press, 2021), 67.
2. See, for instance, Kirby's description of Irigaray's lips as a "figurative strategy." Vicki Kirby, *Telling Flesh: The Substance of the Corporeal* (New York: Routledge, 1997), 70. See Gallop's chapter "Lip Service" in her 1988 book *Thinking Through the Body* for a reading of Irigaray's philosophy of female sexuality, particularly lippedness in *This Sex Which Is Not One*, in terms of literary textuality, symbolic and poetic referentiality. Jane Gallop, *Thinking Through the Body* (New York: Columbia University Press, 1988), 92ff.
3. "If we keep on speaking the same language together, we're going to reproduce the same history. Begin the same old stories all over again. Don't you think so? Listen: all round us, men and women sound just the same. The same discussions, the same arguments, the same scenes. The same attractions and separations. The same difficulties, the same impossibility of making connections. The same . . . Same . . . Always the same." Irigaray, TS, 205.

4. Irigaray, 24.
5. Irigaray, TBB, 17.
6. Irigaray, IB, 156.
7. Irigaray, 148.
8. There is an important discussion to be had concerning the status of the transcendental in Irigaray's philosophy, which she often modifies into a different form, the sensible transcendental (see Irigaray, FA, 94). As to the status of "the" transcendental subject, this issue is best left for a more specialized discussion of the status of transcendental subjectivity and sexual difference. Here I will concentrate on the existential and psychoanalytic aspects of subjectivity, and leave a focused discussion of transcendental subjectivity, which is nevertheless implicated here, for another time.
9. See, for instance, Irigaray, BNW, 251–296; and Irigaray, IB, 239–262.
10. Irigaray, IR, 53–76; and Irigaray, S, 227–240.
11. Irigaray, IR, 55. I quote from David Macey's translation of *"L'incontournable volume"* in *The Irigaray Reader* (IR, 53–67), edited by Margaret Whitford. There is another English translation of this essay in *Speculum of the Other Woman* (S, 227–240), translated by Gillian C. Gill. Comparing the two translations brings attention to the general problematic and different possibilities of translation, as well as highlights Irigaray's intended meaning. These issues are acutely revealed in the difference of the titles: "Volume-Fluidity" (Gill) and "Volume Without Contours" (Macey). See also Elizabeth Hirsch, Gary Olson, and Gaëton Brulotte, "Je—Luce Irigaray: An Interview with Luce Irigaray," *Hypatia* 10, no. 2 (1995): 93–114, 98n5.
12. Cf. Irigaray, TS, 213.
13. In an interview published as "Je—Luce Irigaray: A Meeting with Luce Irigaray" (Hirsch, Je—Luce Irigaray, 98). See also Whitford's introduction to David Macey's translation of *"L'Incontournable volume"* (IR, 27–29), and also Mulder's discussion of mucous: Anne-Claire Mulder, "Divine Flesh, Embodied Word: 'Incarnation' as a Hermeneutical Key to a Feminist Theologian's Reading of Luce Irigaray's Work" (PhD diss., Universiteit van Amsterdam, published by Amsterdam University Press, 2006), 110–113.
14. See for instance, Irigaray, TBB, 17; Irigaray, "Ethical Gestures Towards the Other," in BNW, 253–271; and Irigaray, "The Return," in IB, 139–162.
15. See "The Return," in IB, 139–162.
16. Irigaray, IR, 56.
17. Irigaray, TS, 23–33.
18. See, for instance, Irigaray, BNW, DB, IB, TBB, SW, SF, TNH, etc.
19. See, for instance, Irigaray, "Ethical Gestures Towards the Other," in BNW, 253–271.
20. Irigaray, IB, 154–158; Elspeth Mitchel, "To Be Born a Girl?: Irigaray, Sexual Identity and the Girl," in *Towards a New Human Being*, 35–50. See also Jennifer Carter, "How to Lead a Child to Flower: Luce Irigaray's Philosophy of the Growth of Children," in *Towards a New Human Being*, 3–16.
21. Irigaray, ML, 86.
22. Irigaray, TS, 23–33.
23. Irigaray, "This Sex Which Is Not One," in TS, 23–33; Irigaray, LM, 191–202.

24. Jennifer Carter, "Touch and Caress in the Work of Luce Irigaray" (PhD diss., Stony Brook University, 2018). ProQuest (10932831).
25. For discussions of these relations, see, for instance, Irigaray, "Body Against Body: In Relation to the Mother," in SG, 9–21.
26. For a discussion of hetero-affection, see also Irigaray, TBB, 50; Andrew Bevan's discussion of *heteros* in his chapter in *Towards a New Human Being*, "Re-Founding Philosophy with Self-Affection," 181; and Irigaray, SF, 63.
27. Irigaray, IR, 59, ellipsis in the original.
28. Irigaray, 58.
29. Jacques Lacan, "The Mirror Stage as Formative of the *I* Function as Revealed in Psychoanalytic Experience," in *Écrits: The First Complete Edition in English*, trans. Bruce Fink, with Héoïse Fink and Russell Grigg (New York: Norton, 2006), 75–81.
30. For some discussion of these, see Irigaray, TBB; Irigaray, "Body Against Body" in SG, 7–22.
31. See, for instance, Irigaray "To Inhabit the World," in TBB, 19–24; and Irigaray, "Dwelling in Oneself," in TBB, 25–30.
32. Irigaray, TS, 24.
33. Irigaray, SW, 102.
34. Irigaray, IB, 148.
35. Irigaray, SF, 99–100.

Chapter Nine

MALE RE-IMAGININGS

From the Ontology of the Anal Toward a Phenomenology of Fluidity

OVIDIU ANEMȚOAICEI

Irigaray's philosophical project focuses largely on rethinking the relationships between women and men within a culture of sexuate difference, meaning as subjects lived, defined, and expressed in their own terms. Her critique reveals that the so-called sexual difference within Western cultures does not support an equally valorized presence of feminine sexuate specificities within the symbolic or cultural realms, as they are dominated by a certain (male) imaginary and structured according to specific masculine norms.[1]

According to Irigaray, this patriarchal logic perpetuates itself through a startling trick: masculine sexed morphology is projected into the symbolic as universal and, therefore, sexually unspecific, while presenting itself as irrelevant on the path toward transcendence as a hierarchical and oppositional mode of relating between the self and the other, subject and object. At the same time, feminine sexuate subjectivity is negated or excluded from this form of transcendence and simultaneously instrumentalized for specular male self-affection and autorepresentation.[2] Irigaray's project opens a journey for a feminine sexuate subjectivity, never predefined, within a culture of sexual difference, whereby "we must constitute a possible place for each sex, body and flesh to inhabit."[3] As Margaret Whitford explains, *"while men need to take back and own their body,* women need to accede to a symbolic representation of their own."[4] Such a project implies a nonhierarchical relational identification, a "horizontal transcendence," which is another aim of Irigaray's work: the exploration of a "new model of possible relations between man and woman, without the submission of either one or the other."[5] Irigaray's philosophy of sexual difference calls for, therefore, a difference in thought and practice, an interval between a masculine that retreats from monopolized symbolic and material spaces and assumes its own limits, and a feminine that is culturally articulable as an explicit affirmation of different female bodily expressions.

By compelling us to look at men and their bodies through a different conceptual lens that would not consume, devalue, or define the feminine and female bodies in masculine terms,[6] it seems that Irigaray's account of sexual difference would provide a fruitful framework for engaging with and reconceiving the relationship between masculinities and male bodies.[7] It could certainly contribute to the growing academic subfield of critical studies on men and masculinities, where male bodies have been often presupposed unproblematically when thinking about masculine subjective formations. Following Irigaray, this reconceiving would involve a critical interrogation and a novel reimagining of the modalities of male subjective and intersubjective constitutions. While Irigaray herself does not focus on this project, we can do so, I claim, by starting from Irigaray's critique of the "ontology of the anal" as a grounding imaginary of Western thinking. We can then offer a more positive articulation of this novel reimagining by bringing in other bodily morphological locations and fluidity as alternative figurations for the restructuring of masculine subjectivities in relation to male bodies.

IRIGARAY AND THE ONTOLOGY OF THE ANAL

According to Irigaray, the dominant Western imaginary has been not just an expression of phallomorphic projections in relation to the male bodily activities and experiences resulting in a colonization of thought but also an *anal imaginary* or an *ontology of the anal* to which phallocentrism belongs. The "anal," in Irigaray's critique of the love of sameness characterizing the masculine subject, masks the dispossession of the maternal-feminine or the phantasmatic appropriation of its reproductive life force, as an appropriative logic whereby otherness is absorbed into the self: "The love of sameness among men often means a love within sameness, which cannot posit itself as such without the maternal-natural-material. It represents the love of a production by assimilation and mediation of the female or females. It often constitutes a kind of *ontology of the anal* or else a triumph of the absorption of the other into the self in the intestine."[8]

Irigaray develops an account of anality in *Speculum: Of the Other Woman* and *An Ethics of Sexual Difference*, specifically in response to Freud's account of anal erotism. Given that, according to Freud, children are ignorant of the vagina and rarely witness childbirth, the Freudian "cloacal theory of childbirth" refers to the supposed belief of children that a mother obtains a child by eating something special and gives birth through the anus, since for the child the only possible way to imagine the material leaving the body is through the anus.[9] In Freud's account, the phantasy of being born through the anus, correlated with that of losing objects through the anus, expresses an anxiety that leads to the repression of the phantasmatic figure of an active maternal as representative of death and castration.

However, for Irigaray, the anal imaginary does not just characterize individual phantasies pertaining to the psychoanalytical domain but is projected as a larger social imaginary made explicit by Freud. Noting that "it does not seem to be a problem for Freud that the *mouth* and *anus* are 'neutral' from the standpoint of sexual difference,"[10] Irigaray claims that this theory negates female bodily specificities, reflecting a more general reduction of women to the logic of "the same," on the one hand, and the consequent unmasking of the Freudian psychoanalytical discourse as expressing a certain logic of desire that defines "sexual difference as a function of the a priori of the same," on the other hand.[11] Still, while rejecting the Freudian etiology and its sexual neutrality,[12] Irigaray considers how the repression of the active maternal origin operates in the masculine imaginary, throwing male sexuality in a *fort-da*, with the mother as a manipulable object that can be thrown away and retrieved. Irigaray speculates that, failing to recognize the mother as an autonomous subject like themselves, and therefore failing to relate to the maternal in such a way as to preserve the subjective interval with her, men are subsequently torn between the desire to merge with the unity of the maternal world representing the whole of nature, on the one hand, and the desire for emerging from an undifferentiation with nature through an ideal masculine shape, a dream of ideal beauty, on the other hand, allowing them to control it as object. According to Irigaray, this ambiguous relation to the mother and the failure to healthily differentiate from her as another autonomous subject generates a tension in male sexuality.[13]

But the appropriative and violent nature of the relation to the mother/feminine extends male sexuality in terms of power also in relation to other men, thus marking the absorption of the maternal into the logic of the same (among men) and the erasure of sexual difference.[14] By denying her autonomous subjectivity, the ontology of the anal reduces the mother/feminine to a passive receptacle for birthing for men and the general perpetuation and circulation of power recognized and shared by them: "As for woman, she will be the receptacle for the sperm (gift) injected by the penis (stool) and she forces the child (feces) out through the vagina (rectum). Thus she is apparently party to anal erotism."[15] Ultimately, to summarize her extended account, Irigaray theorizes that the male struggle with the desire for the maternal "origin" finds its "peace" through creating "an(other) economy of desire."[16] Irigaray calls this new order of desire the "hom(m)osexual monopoly," that is, the "exclusive valorization of men's needs/desires, of exchanges among men," not as "an 'immediate' practice, but in its 'social' mediation,"[17] as compared to the female relationship to the mother, and other nonphallocentric relations between women (and men and women), which do not find themselves expressed or expressible in it except as perpetuating it. Women are thus absorbed into the intestines of this anal ontology.

In the context of showing how the (male) order circulates women, signs, and commodities from one man to another and requires hom(m)osexuality for the very possibility of this order, Irigaray puts the following question: "Why is masculine homosexuality considered exceptional, then, when in fact the economy as a whole is based upon it? Why are homosexuals ostracized, when society postulates homosexuality? Unless it is because *the 'incest' involved in homosexuality has to remain in the realm of pretense.*"[18] Here, Irigaray operates with two understandings of homosexuality (while word-playing with *homme* as "man" or "human") and suggests that we should not confuse the ideological and cultural, that is, patriarchal, hom(m)osexuality with the practice of homosexuality.[19] The first sense pertains to the general male-male relations in this anal imaginary (i.e., there exists one sex, one desire expressed and shared between and among men) exemplified, for instance, by "*father-son relationships*, which guarantee the transmission of patriarchal power and its laws, its discourse, its social structures."[20] However, in the second sense, homosexuality, as erotic relations between men, "*openly interpret[s] the law according to which society operates.*"[21] And precisely this very double meaning, this sliding of the male desire for the same, in both its cultural and sexual expressions, threatens to unmask the mechanism of transactions among men, an unveiling that would affect the symbolic structure: "Once the penis itself becomes merely a means to pleasure, pleasure among men, the phallus loses its power," that is, the power over women, as well as other men.[22]

I am interested in how, by implication, male eroticism and pleasure beyond the phallus, including anal eroticism, might serve to disrupt this economy as well, revealing the pretensions of the anal imaginary underlying it. Not accidently, "anality," posited as a possible subversive element for dephallicizing or queering the hegemonic images of straight male bodies, has become a recurrent theme in the work of several scholars working on sexualities, masculinities, and male bodies. The position that sees the anus and the anal eroticism as an answer to the phallic straight male body becomes particularly intriguing when considered in light of Irigaray's comments on the ontology of the anal and its disruption.

Perhaps most notably, Calvin Thomas "explores, on the one hand, anxieties about the *ways* male bodies *are* produced, visibly rendered, *caused* to appear, both physically and in representation, and, on the other, anxieties about the matters that male bodies themselves *do* produce, render visible, *cause* to appear, both physically and in representation."[23] The analysis of the "production of men's bodies" leads Calvin Thomas to several related "corporeo-discursive fields," including most importantly in conversation with Irigaray's critiques of the ontology of the anal, "*the physical production of male bodies in, by, and through female bodies.*"[24] Like Irigaray, Thomas also speculates on the consequences of the particular phantasy about how male bodies are produced by female bodies addressed by Freud's cloacal theory. The argument that anal anxiety effects a repression or a suppression of the "fantasmatic figure of the *actively* cloacal mother, the abject*ing* mother that is prior to any abject*ed* or castrated maternal object" leads Thomas to conclude that "the subject's 'anxiety of production' with respect to the abjecting mother is *prior* to any 'castration anxiety,' and indeed ... the latter *normatively* functions as the former's symbolic remedy."[25] However, employing the idea that there is another anxiety close to the castration complex, namely, that "certainly we've all lost objects from the anus," Thomas argues that this anxiety, mixed up with "the not completely abandoned cloacal theory of birth," might help expose the anxieties about gender or sexual difference, "as displaced scatontological anxieties about primordial symbolization."[26] As such, "what falls out of the anus," the anus itself, and anal eroticism could become sites of significant refigurations of straight male bodies and straight sexual rituals.

In a similar move, for Leo Bersani, in "Is the Rectum a Grave?," written in the context of homosexuality and AIDS crisis in the 1980s, the anus and the receptive male anal eroticism become the loci of radical desubjectivization or self-debasement, since phallocentrism is "not primarily the denial of power to women (although it has obviously also led to that, everywhere and at all times), but above all the denial of the *value* of powerlessness in both men and women. I don't mean the value of gentleness, or nonaggressiveness, or even passivity, but rather of a more radical disintegration and humiliation of the self."[27] Thinking with Bersani, the desubjectivization or self-debasement of the masculine, through the disquieting rectum-grave, may be connected with an "initial" maternal horror that reminds of both possibilities of life and death (expulsion as life, or engulfment as castration) but that ultimately gets appropriated as just another "anus." In other words, receptive anal eroticism may have a function in destabilizing the "oneness" of the (heterosexual male) subject because it relates to the acceptance that death is inevitable. The desire to become "objectified" and "instrumentalized," to be passed through, or to value powerlessness, is one of accepting dissolution and death.

Others have taken up Bersani's idea that the phallicized ego experiences sexuality only as power. As Catherine Waldby argues, since specific images of hegemonic masculinity are intertwined with the understanding of the male body as phallic and impenetrable, the anus and anal eroticism become possible sources of male disturbances, nonphallic expressions, or masculine desubjectivization.[28] The denial (repression or elision) of receptive anal eroticism in heterosexual men is, for Waldby, a homophobic and misogynist response to the heterosexual male bodily anxieties of *permeability* and *penetrability*. Brian Pronger makes the same point: "Masculine desire protects its own phallic production by closing orifices, both anus and mouth, to the phallic expansion of others. Rendered impenetrable, the masculine body differentiates itself as distinct and unconnected."[29] Waldby and

Pronger thus present images of possible refigurations of heterosexual male bodies through opening literally or metaphorically erotic spaces and reshaping male desires.

Is the "anal," as understood by Bersani, Thomas, Waldby, and Pronger, the same as the one posited by Irigaray in her critique of the male imaginary? Can "anality" be both the grounding feature (phantasy, anxiety) of a male imaginary and masculine symbolic with disastrous effects on female sexualities and feminine sexuate subjectivity and, at the same time, the subversion of the phallic expressions of straight male bodies? Where Irigaray stops in her critique of anality these other thinkers propose alternative resignifications of the male body via anality. That is, they propose "anality" as part of a new imaginary by imploding the *oneness* of the male phallic body and *multiplying* it, offering other sites of pleasures beyond the "one" phallus, while bringing in various minoritarian male lived experiences and practices. Indeed, anality represents a possible site for unmasking the hom(m)osexual economy of exchange and desire and for contesting the heteronormative order. On the other hand, however, following Irigaray, a single focus on anality's subversiveness might repeat the "danger" of forgetting to account for sexual difference if blocked in a solipsistic turn toward the (straight) male body. Although these researchers on male bodies and masculinities are not necessarily reproducing an ontology of the anal through their understanding of anality, looking only at anality as a site of restructuring male sexuality and male imaginaries may run the risk of preserving the masculine self-representation of the male body as the negation of the maternal and the female on the basis of the anxiety related to the production of life.[30]

WITH AND BEYOND ANALITY: MALE BODILY REIMAGININGS

Despite refusing to prescribe how men might come to be outside of phallocentrism, claiming that she is not in the position to do so and that it is not her project to follow this through,[31] Irigaray offers us further morphological locations helpful for a revaluation of male bodily specificities that would situate us on the path of reimagining male morphologies and, consequently, of refiguring masculine subjectivities that would avoid these risks.

In *Sexes and Genealogies* and in *I Love to You*, Irigaray considers both the male imaginary and its symbolic expressions as masking, covering, inverting, or negating (1) the mother's body and reproductive power, (2) the mother's primary nurturing space and relationship to the child, and (3) the appropriation of female puissance, sexuality, and desire through language. The phallus symbolically takes the place of the umbilical cord, thus presenting the castration complex as primary instead of the original cut from the mother, and the womb and the placenta are forgotten, erased, or negated through a specific language defined in the terms of the male (iso)phallomorphic imaginary/phantasies in relation to men's bodily activities and experiences. In response, Irigaray invokes two important morphological locations for rethinking the male imaginary: (1) the *navel* as the tribute place/scar memory for the primary bond/home (the umbilical cord, the placenta, and the womb with the mother) and (2) the phallic erection radically reinterpreted as a masculine version of the umbilical cord, not as the all-powerful appropriating signifier but more of a repetition of the "living bond to the mother" out of respect for "the life of the mother."[32]

Irigaray's rethinking of man's bodily relation with the mother's body is taken further by Britt-Marie Schiller, who develops three gestures that would prepare the space for rethinking masculinity. The first gesture rethinks *nursing/breastfeeding* as "the experience of being penetrated [that] can open a male to a different sense of interiority and vulnerability."[33] As Schiller writes, "there is an irreducible interval between two bodies: between his lips, a nipple; a breast not his; her milk flowing into his cavity, from her body into his body. The little boy's mouth is penetrated in this carnal act."[34] The second gesture would rethink masculine subject formation not in terms of renunciation, mastery, or subjugation in relation to the mother but in terms of a safeguarded proximity with her. The third gesture, through a kind of "improvisation," would open men to new forms of intersubjective relations. In doing so, Schiller claims, he can "begin to speak with others in a non-assimilating, non-dominating dialogue, a play space wherein two subjectivities can unfold, be recognized and recognize each other without subjugation."[35] Schiller builds from Irigaray's concept of the *negative* of sexual difference to rethink the masculine as a limited and incomplete subject in his own terms and within another type of relationship with his, thus recognized, other(s).[36]

Following these suggestions, one might develop several routes for reimagining men's relations to their own sexuate bodies. In addition to a sexually differentiated anality,[37] *testicularity*[38] and *male bodily fluids/orifices* might become figurations of a radically different male imaginary against the dominating phallic heteronormative representations of male bodies. The impetus for investigating both the fluids and orifices of the male bodies more specifically is the role they have in men's anxieties and phantasies in the conception of their own masculinities and how they project these onto their bodies and women's bodies. Moreover, since male fluids and orifices tend not to be thematized, as Elizabeth Grosz puts it, there is a mystery about them as "unspoken and generally unrepresented particularities of the male body."[39]

A phenomenological ontology, "as the thematizing of the character and being of our experience, which speaks to the nature of our being generally,"[40] may reveal mediations between male morphologies and the various masculine subjective and intersubjective representations, like those mentioned earlier. Following Whitford, such a phenomenological account of male bodily experiences would explore the relations between lived experiences, on the one hand, the imaginary, on the other hand, and the discursive construction of both.[41] This exploration might reveal various interplays in the constitution of male masculine subjectivity between (1) the ways male bodies experience their "fluid" (blood, saliva, urine, semen,[42] mucus, tears, sweat, vomit, faeces, and the like), "solid" thresholds (skin, hair, even eyes), and orifices (mouth, lips, anus, nostrils); (2) the imaginary projection of the "limits" of their bodies onto other bodies; and (3), implicitly, the constitution of their own subjectivities. In turn, we might explore how bodies are "materialized" within shared sexual and cultural events they enter and other axes of signification and power relations.[43] Thinking through these specific interplays would contribute to a *carnal knowledge* responsive to Irigaray's suggestion that "it is this sameness that constitutes the subject as a living being but that man has not begun to *think*: his body."[44]

Besides offering suggestions for reimagining various bodily locations, Irigaray has also developed an analysis of *self-affection* relevant for rethinking masculine forms of subject formation. Expressed in linguistic terms, self-affection presupposes a return to the *middle voice* as a way of internalizing the *middle-passive* and not the hierarchical and oppositional dichotomies of active and passive (to affect and to be affected). Self-affection, understood as a way of relating to oneself, of returning to one's interiority as at once both affecting and affected, has implications for relating to others as a hetero-affection: "Self-affection today needs a return to our own body, our own breath, a care about our life in order not to become subjected to technologies, to money, to power, to neutralization in a universal 'someone,' to assimilation into an anonymous world, to the solitude of individualism."[45] Irigaray thus advocates for the elaboration of a carnal knowledge that would take into account the importance of life in the constitution of the self in relation with oneself and other(s), that is, the construction of an ethical relationship based not on extraneous rules cut off from our embodiments but on the respect for the otherness and on the very limits of our own bodies.[46]

Irigaray admits that it is difficult for her to define self-affection for men, since she is not one, but she can at least question the cultural logics preventing its cultivation.[47] In the article "Perhaps Cultivating Touch Can Still Save Us," echoing Heidegger's "Only a God Can Save Us," Irigaray argues that the artificial neutrality of our world of communication is cut off from the natural singular energies and differences of both women and men who remain caught between instinctive, uncultivated intensities (sublimated through domination or submission) and formal rules and standards. According to Irigaray, men's supposedly neutral modes of individuation, organized "through a logic of representation that institutes an artificial permanent reality that is separated from the present and an embodied presence,"[48] allows them to escape from a merging with a universal nature yet leaves unsolved the problem of their own sexually differentiated, oscillating energies, their flows of life and those of others. As Irigaray claims, for men, "self-affection has been confused with a dependence on the surrounding world, through which man believes he touches himself again"[49] using technologies, fabricated environments, and the like. This only apparent autonomy is fed by the domination of otherness.

In response to this, Irigaray urges a revival of eros, irreducible to sexual desire, which could guide us on the path of the journey toward sexually differentiated human individuation, taking into account the importance of touch and breath in the subjective and intersubjective constitution of oneself in relation with other(s), that is, in the construction of an ethical relationship based on the respect for the otherness and on the very limits of our own bodies.[50] As Irigaray writes, "to recover this humanity requires us to start again from our singular embodiment and cultivate it with respect for its difference(s)."[51] One's path and the return to one's self, as the condition of possibility for that path, for both men and women, become the fundamental aspects of laboring together for a culture of "real" sexuate difference that recognizes breathing and touching as dimensions of a carnal knowledge.

As Irigaray argues, touch and breath have been poorly recognized and lived in our culture for entering into relation with ourselves and with others, including with both the visible and the invisible parts of our embodiments like skin and mucous membranes.[52] Mutual desire between others, as a desire for intimacy, can be cultivated through self-affection, that is, in a bordered manner through which the other is not objectified, fragmented in bodily parts, or violently consumed for libidinal fulfillment. For Irigaray, cultivating a certain kind of touch, including but not limited to sexual touching, would offer a way of approaching the other while respecting its embodied presence as otherness. Likewise, the cultivation of or attentiveness to breathing and the sharing of breath with others can "render our body and our bodily exchanges spiritual" in the sense of a continuous dialogue and communion between the body and the mind/thought.[53] Because of its mediating role between the two, both elemental and expressing thought, acknowledging air and cultivating breathing would be a step toward a male/masculine union beyond mind-body dichotomy. It is also through the cultivation of air, of breathing, thus through the acknowledgment of that which is the first to give autonomous existence to man, that Irigaray claims men can acknowledge the gift of being born, the debt of life, especially from the mother.

Finally, for Irigaray, the cultivation of new forms of masculine self-affection and sharing of breath would involve changes in how we *hear* and *listen* to the other so that we could authentically speak with the others while respecting our differences. But in order to hear so as to listen to the other, one needs to cultivate *silence*, as a space outside of ourselves where the others can come and express themselves. Silence and listening would thus open our world and welcome the other's world not in predefined terms or according to a language and thought already stratified with established or coded meanings. Rather, silence would allow a listening to the other's words as something unique, not totally reducible to the meanings to which I have access through the language in which I already dwell. This might facilitate a renewal in meaningful exchanges, with language not considered abstracted from embodied participations but recognized as allowing us to enter into relation between at least two subjects with respect for their embodied differences. Recognized in this way, we can reflect on the connection of language with the energy of the one's body, of the other's body, and of the surrounding world.

The question of what it means to rethink "male bodies" and "masculinities" within the feminist paradigm of sexual difference through a feminist phenomenological account is both challenging and fruitful. The assemblage between sexual difference, as a feminist philosophical matriceal position, and phenomenology's view on the relation between body and language, materiality and representation, privileges the body as the meaningful horizon of our existence and leaves a space for agential interventions in subjective and representational constitutions. A feminist phenomenological approach toward the ways men experience the world with their bodies and perceptions of their bodily fluids/orifices, on the one hand, and the ways the minoritarian male experiences can be reimagined as male bodily specificities, on the other hand, might help us in finding exit points for facilitating novel masculine representational articulations faithful to their own male bodily realities. A world grounded in sexual difference and understood as "at least two" would rest on a radically different conception of bodies, identities, and subjectivities with the aim of refiguring different coalitions and generating various ways of making and sustaining political claims. Male lived experiences provide starting points for deconstructing dominant masculine imaginaries and for enriching feminist thought for further political engagement.

BIBLIOGRAPHY

Aydemir, Murat. *Images of Bliss: Ejaculation, Masculinity, Meaning*. Minneapolis: University of Minnesota Press, 2007.

Bersani, Leo. "Is the Rectum a Grave?" *October* 43 (1987): 197–222.

Fisher, Linda. "The Character of Sexual Difference." In *Wissen Macht Geschlecht/ Knowledge Power Gender: Philosophie und die Zukunft der "condition feminine,"* edited by B. Christensen et al., 687–695. Zürich: Chronos, 2002.

Flannigan-Saint-Aubin, Arthur. "The Male Body and Literary Metaphors for Masculinity." In *Theorizing Masculinities*, edited by H. Brod and M. Kaufman, 239–258. Thousand Oaks, CA: Sage, 1994.

Grosz, Elizabeth. *Volatile Bodies: Toward a Corporeal Feminism*. Bloomington: Indiana University Press, 1994.

Hirsh, Elizabeth, Gary A. Olson, and Gaëton Brulotte. "'Je—Luce Irigaray': A Meeting with Luce Irigaray." *Hypatia* 10, no. 2 (1995): 93–114.
Pronger, Brian. "On Your Knees: Carnal Knowledge, Masculine Dissolution, Doing Feminism." In *Men Doing Feminism*, edited by T. Digby, 69–79. New York: Routledge, 1998.
Schiller, Britt-Marie. "The Incomplete Masculine. Engendering the Masculine of Sexual Difference." In *Thinking with Irigaray*, edited by Mary C. Rawlinson, Sabrina L. Hom, and Serene J. Khader, 131–152. Albany: SUNY Press, 2011.
Thomas, Calvin. *Masculinity, Psychoanalysis, Straight Queer Theory: Essays on Abjection in Literature, Mass Culture, and Film*. New York: Palgrave Macmillan, 2008.
Waldby, Catherine. "Destruction: Boundary Erotics and the Refigurations of the Heterosexual Male Body." In *Sexy Bodies: The Strange Carnalities of Feminism*, edited by Elizabeth Grosz and Elspeth Probyn, 266–277. New York: Routledge, 1995.
Whitford, Margaret. *Luce Irigaray: Philosophy in the Feminine*. London: Routledge, 1991.

NOTES

1. When employing the notion of "imaginary," Irigaray has in mind primarily the psychoanalytical understanding, which was developed by Lacan in his interpretation of Freud's texts. However, for her, the concept of imaginary has fluctuating meanings. Whitford explains this by giving an account of the history of the term and its sources in Irigaray's work: phenomenology—imaginary as the conscious, imagining and imaging mind; Bachelard—imaginary as a function of the imagination; Castoriadis—imaginary both as the primordial creative source or magma, and as a social formation. Margaret Whitford, *Luce Irigaray: Philosophy in the Feminine* (London: Routledge, 1991), 53–57. In this essay, when discussing mainly the relationship between men, male bodies, and masculinities, I employ the psychoanalytical understanding of the relation between Imaginary/Symbolic and identity/subjectivity. While subjectivity (masculinity) as a position of enunciation belongs to Symbolic (the Lacanian order of meaning, of language and discourse), identity (man) is imaginary (bodily fantasies for example) and is structured or takes a representational form within the Symbolic.
2. Irigaray, TS, 24.
3. Irigaray, ESD, 18.
4. Whitford, *Luce Irigaray*, 156, italics mine.
5. Elizabeth Hirsh, Gary A. Olson, and Gaëton Brulotte, "'Je—Luce Irigaray': A Meeting with Luce Irigaray," *Hypatia* 10, no. 2 (1995): 96.
6. Irigaray, ESD, 98.
7. In this essay, my discussion focuses only on the relationship between masculinities, men, and male bodies and not in relation to other masculine subjectivities such as female masculinities.
8. Irigaray, ESD, 100–101, italics mine.
9. Irigaray, S, 74.
10. Irigaray, TS, 35, italics in original.
11. Irigaray, S, 28.

12. Irigaray claims that, as compared to boys, girl's relationality to the mother's sexuate identity facilitates a different response to the mother's absence-presence, whereby she reconstructs a subject-subject relation precisely because they share the same subjective identity. In *Sexes and Genealogies*, for example, when discussing Freud's account of the child's neutral sexual identity, Irigaray argues: "In Freud's text, then, the child is a boy. And Freud never wrote that it might have been a girl. My hypothesis is that it couldn't have been a girl. Why? A girl does not do the same things when her mother goes away. She does not play with a string and a reel that symbolize her mother, because her mother is of the same sex as she is and cannot have the object status of a reel. The mother is of the same subjective identity as she is." SG 97. See the editors' introduction to this volume for critical commentary on how one might read such claims beyond essentialism and the analysis in this chapter later for reimagining boys' relations to the mother.
13. Irigaray, TS, 24–25.
14. Irigaray, S, 26–27.
15. Irigaray, 75.
16. Irigaray, 40–41, italics in original.
17. Irigaray, TS, 171.
18. Irigaray, TS, 192, italics in original.
19. Hirsh, Olson, and Brulotte, "Je—Luce Irigaray," 112.
20. Irigaray, TS, 193, italics in original.
21. Irigaray, 193, italics in original.
22. Irigaray, 193.
23. Calvin Thomas, *Masculinity, Psychoanalysis, Straight Queer Theory: Essays on Abjection in Literature, Mass Culture, and Film* (New York: Palgrave Macmillan, 2008), 1.
24. Thomas, 2; italics in original.
25. Thomas, 3–4.
26. Thomas, 47.
27. Leo Bersani, "Is the Rectum a Grave?" *October* 43 (1987): 217, italics in original.
28. Catherine Waldby, "Destruction: Boundary Erotics and the Refigurations of the Heterosexual Male Body," in *Sexy Bodies: The Strange Carnalities of Feminism*, ed. E. Grosz and E. Probyn (New York: Routledge, 1995), 272.
29. Brian Pronger, "On Your Knees: Carnal Knowledge, Masculine Dissolution, Doing Feminism," in *Men Doing Feminism*, ed. T. Digby (New York: Routledge, 1998), 69–79.
30. In Irigaray's account, for the masculine order, the most radical ontological other or the paradigmatic otherness is the maternal and the feminine. This does not mean that the feminine is reduced to the maternal in my discussion about masculinities and male bodies, but rather the argument is that, following Irigaray's diagnosis, a restructuring of the relationship with both the maternal and the feminine is a necessary step in the refiguring of male masculine subject formation.
31. Irigaray has refused to hypothesize about the "new" being and saying of the "other" man: "But is it up to me, I wonder, to speak of the other 'man?' It's curious, because it's a question that I am constantly being asked. I find it quite amusing. . . . I am constantly being asked what that 'other' man will be. Why should I appropriate for myself what that 'other' man would have to say? What I want and what I am

waiting to see is what men will do and say if their sexuality releases its hold on the empire of phallocratism. But this is not for a woman to anticipate, or foresee, or prescribe." Irigaray, TS, 135–136.
32. Irigaray, SG, 17.
33. Britt-Marie Schiller, "The Incomplete Masculine. Engendering the Masculine of Sexual Difference," in *Thinking with Irigaray*, ed. Mary C. Rawlinson, Sabrina L. Hom, and Serene J. Khader (Albany: SUNY Press, 2011), 133.
34. Schiller, 135.
35. Schiller, 143.
36. Schiller, 147.
37. I thank James Sares for his suggestion concerning the prostate as a powerful male morphological location that might help refiguring male subjectivities against heteronormative and phallic imaginaries.
38. Arthur Flannigan-Saint-Aubin provides a more detailed proposal whereby testicularity/testerity can become a source of destructuring the monopoly of the phallus/penis: "the male issue is to accept and to experience fully the biosexual, the body, the genitals the way that they are most of the time: nonerect but 'hanging in there.' Men, who have often reduced women to their biologic sexuality, must indeed acknowledge the truth of their own bodies, of their own sexuality. Men must indeed dare to remove the steel fig leaf." Arthur Flannigan-Saint-Aubin, "The Male Body and Literary metaphors for masculinity," in *Theorizing Masculinities*, ed. H. Brod and M. Kaufman (Thousand Oaks, CA: Sage, 1994), 239–258, 250–251.
39. Elizabeth Grosz, *Volatile Bodies: Toward a Corporeal Feminism* (Bloomington: Indiana University Press, 1994), 198.
40. Linda Fisher, "The Character of Sexual Difference," in *Wissen Macht Geschlecht/ Knowledge Power Gender: Philosophie und die Zukunft der "condition feminine,"* ed. B. Christensen et al. (Zürich: Chronos, 2002), 689.
41. Whitford, *Luce Irigaray*, 152.
42. In *Images of Bliss: Ejaculation, Masculinity, Meaning*, Murat Aydemir picks up Irigaray's suggestion "that the consideration of semen qua liquid, its treatment as material object, can promisingly intervene in the economy of meaning and gender historically set in place," as both the phallus and the castration anxiety are posited against "an even greater apparential specter: the visibility of the quintessential male substance of sperm in its fluidity" (xvi–xvii). As both presence and absence of solid, semen escapes the economy of solidification and threatens the masculine imaginary: "Indeed, as a liquid, sperm shares that crucial characteristic with the uterine, environmental, and cultural 'sea' that envelops and threatens masculine form. Semen, then, is somehow both central and excessive to the phallic economy, potentially as deforming as it is formative" (xvii).
43. For example, heterosexual bodies will express quite different morphologies from those of gay, queer, trans, and nonbinary bodies, not only of a "biological" kind, but also of an experiential one.
44. Irigaray, ESD, 98, italics in original.
45. Irigaray, IB, 161.
46. Irigaray, PC, 139.
47. Irigaray, IB, 148.
48. Irigaray, PC, 133.

49. Irigaray, IB, 151.
50. Irigaray, PC, 139.
51. Irigaray, 136.
52. Irigaray, 138.
53. Irigaray, BB, 224.

Chapter Ten

SEXUAL DIFFERENCE AS QUALITATIVE BECOMING

Irigaray Beyond Cissexism?

OLI STEPHANO

Luce Irigaray's intervention into sexual difference indicates that extant schemas of sexuate subjectivity foreclose rather than develop the differentiating force of what she takes to be the primary ontological difference: sex. "Sexuation is not only an empirical and secondary thing with regard to our being," she notes, "it is what brings to it a specific morphology and individuation."[1] Sexual difference differentiates beings, and, simultaneously, sexual difference itself calls to be lived and taken up otherwise.

Sexual difference is thus a force of becoming that itself needs to become other. For Irigaray, this means positive difference between sexuate subjects rather than sexual (in)difference, where there is only one sexuate subject (Man) with attendant patriarchal forms of social organization and culture.[2] My question, in line with a body of scholarship inquiring into the limits of Irigaray's focus on cisgender forms of sexual difference with attendant heterosexual schemas of desire,[3] is whether Irigaray's work provides conceptual resources for reconceiving sexual difference as itself capable of changing in kind, of differentiating bodies and subjectivities in a multiplicity of ways alongside cissexually differentiated morphologies and identities. In response, I argue that Irigaray's early formulation of "the/a woman" as a subject in becoming outlines a model of becoming to which her own concept of sexual difference is itself susceptible. In elaborating her conception of "the/a woman" as a processual, qualitative multiplicity, Irigaray provides a fecund model for thinking the transformation of sexual difference itself. Sexual difference emerges as a site of transformation, where sexual in/difference is supplanted by multiple forms of sexual difference—rather than the exclusively cissexual forms of individuation given voice in Irigaray's own account.

Since much of Irigaray's thinking on sexuate becoming works through an attention to sexuality and the erotic, I enter this question of becoming through an engagement with Irigaray's treatment of place and self-touching in sexuality. My inquiry follows two main threads: First, I outline Henri Bergson's distinction between two types of multiplicity, framing the inquiry into the model of becoming opened up by Irigaray's concept of "the/a woman." I trace "the/a woman" as a figuration of fluidity and a particular kind of auto-affection that reconceives the relation between place and the feminine. Second, I explore Irigaray's notion of the interval as a productive *space between* the terms of dualistic sexual difference that allows for porosity and touch between them. Twining the two threads together, I consider how Irigaray's tactile and erotic theorization of sexuate becoming yields a conception of sexual difference as itself a qualitative multiplicity, generating a variety of sexuate differences that do not reduce to only two kinds. My claim is not that Irigaray herself espouses this view of sexual difference but that there are generative resources in her work for conceiving of sexual difference as qualitative becoming not limited solely to cisgender kinds.

BERGSON, QUALITATIVE MULTIPLICITY, AND SEXUAL DIFFERENCE

Throughout her work, Irigaray insists that dominant, masculinist logics of quantifiable identity have little to do with the female bodies and pleasures they seek to define and circumscribe. Within prevailing economies of sexual (in)difference, she argues, "woman" is denied a place of her own in order to serve as/secure the ground of the masculine subject. This subjection is accomplished in part through the imposition of discursive regimes of calculation, numericity, and solid form. As long as this imperative of proper form stands, Irigaray suggests, true sexual difference is impossible "since what is excess with respect to form—for example the feminine sex—is necessarily rejected as beneath or beyond the system currently in force."[4]

Against this foreclosure of sexual difference, Irigaray articulates female corporeality and sexuality in terms of incalculability, fluidity, and a self-touching that confounds numericity. This, in turn, leads her to posit the possibility of sex as an activity with the potential to reconfigure the ways in which sexed subjects place and touch one another. "This place, the production of intimacy," she writes, "is in some manner a transmutation of earth into heaven, here and now. . . . Always working to produce a place of transcendence for the sensible."[5] Sex can only serve this alchemical function, however, when sexual difference is itself swept up in this transvaluation.

Irigaray unpacks this model of self-touching via her concept of "the/a woman," that is, woman understood as both internally multiple and divergent from masculinist projections of "the feminine." Accordingly, her project pays special attention to the ways in which the materiality of female-assigned women's bodies exceeds and confounds the discursive limits of solidity and identity through which sexed bodies are compelled to cohere. Irigaray proposes a specifically feminine kind of auto-affection that yields not immunized identity but rather an open-ended series of transformations.

Turning to Henri Bergson's distinction between quantitative and qualitative multiplicities, I suggest that Irigaray gives us an understanding of becoming as the (self- and intersubjective) induction of qualitative transformations. For Bergson, qualitative multiplicity involves difference in kind (rather than comparative degree) and becomings that cannot be fully determined in advance. While Irigaray herself makes no explicit reference to Bergson, his theorization of multiplicity and becoming helps unpack the distinct contributions Irigaray makes in those realms. Clearly, for Irigaray, "the/a woman" is herself an internally different, constantly self-differentiating multiplicity, different in kind (rather than degree) from masculine subjects.

In this, Irigaray's account of "the/a woman" shares important conceptual characteristics with Bergson's theorization of qualitative multiplicity. A multiplicity can be understood as a manifold field or differentiating structure, delineated by the points at which it divides, changes, and connects to other multiplicities.[6] Bergson distinguishes qualitative multiplicity, a flux of intensive states that cannot change without changing in kind, from quantitative multiplicity, an ordered series of discrete units in extensive sequence. With his distinction between the two multiplicities, Bergson demonstrates that quantitative models cannot do justice to the kind of difference at play in qualitative flows. The model of becoming Bergson offers with his theory of qualitative multiplicity elucidates the nuances of Irigaray's "the/a woman," providing a useful conceptual framework for exploring how Irigarayan difference might transform sexual difference from a hierarchical binary into a virtual multiplicity: that is, a field of sexuate differences in kind that actualize according to their own emergent tendencies.[7]

At its heart as a tool for thinking difference, Bergson's distinction between the two multiplicities is introduced in the context of his discussion of temporality. He argues that time is not a homogenous medium comprising enumerable instants but rather a differentiating force, a flow of duration that becomes "clock-time" only by being thought along the spatial logic of countable, discrete moments arrayed in a linear sequence. Duration, he argues, "has no moments which are identical or external to one another, being essentially heterogeneous, continuous, and with no analogy to number."[8]

This basic distinction subtends his elaboration of the two types of multiplicity. While quantitative multiplicity deals with numerical relations between homogenous terms, qualitative multiplicity concerns intensive relations between heterogeneous terms. Quantitative multiplicity pertains to identical, interchangeable units, which are countable precisely because of this substitutability "in which the inmost nature of each of them counts for nothing."[9] The terms composing a quantitative multiplicity are taken to be fully present at any given instant, devoid of any internal difference that might inhere in them; they are thus delineated from one another as discrete units that vary from one another only by degree. Accordingly, quantitative multiplicity can only produce difference in degree and magnitude, since its numerical terms can be divided and compared without any sort of qualitative change occurring.

Qualitative multiplicity, by contrast, deals with difference in kind and intensity. Qualitative multiplicity is composed of internally different terms that cannot be parsed and compared to one another according to a common measure; the imposition of quantitative form induces change in the multiplicity itself. Bergson suggests that pure quality confounds the logic of number. A state of qualitative multiplicity is neither one nor many, and thinking it along those numerical terms immediately alters it. Bergson uses the example of emotion to illustrate this continuous, intensive quality.

Subjects seized by intense emotion, Bergson argues, "feel a thousand different elements which dissolve into and permeate one another without any precise outlines, without the least tendency to externalize themselves in relation to one another; hence their originality. We distort them as soon as we distinguish a numerical multiplicity in their confused mass."[10] When a qualitative multiplicity changes, its elements are not simply arranged in a different sequence; it is not a matter of adding or subtracting interchangeable units from a whole that remains essentially the same. Rather, any alteration of a qualitative multiplicity induces transformations in its very components and composition, changing it in kind.

ON THE/A WOMAN

What Irigaray names "the work of sexual difference" is the task of transforming sexual difference from a hierarchical, quantitative comparison between two terms that are really only One (Man and his other) into truly qualitative difference. This is the perspective from which Irigaray launches her exploration into place, touching, and sexuality. "The transition to a new age requires a change in our perception and conception of *space-time*, the *inhabiting of places*, and of *containers*, or *envelopes of identity*," she writes. "It assumes and entails an evolution or a transformation of forms, of the relations of *matter* and *form* and of the interval *between*."[11] My animating question, then, is whether and how Irigaray's conception of "the/a woman" as herself a qualitative multiplicity opens sexual difference itself to transformation. How does Irigaray help us think what it might mean for sexual difference itself to change in kind, to become a multivectored force of differentiation rather than a hierarchical dualism?

To broach this question, it is first necessary to dig into Irigaray's diagnostic of the current situation of hierarchical sexual difference, which she derides as "sexual (in)difference" for its inability to conceive of autonomous, sexually differentiated subjects rather than just Man and his negative inverse or silent ground.[12] Within this schematic, she argues, the feminine simply serves to secure a place for the masculine subject. Granted no specificity of her own, the feminine has served as the disavowed condition of possibility of masculinist subjectivity.[13] This is the central point of Irigaray's argument about place and sexual difference. It is not only that the feminine is consigned to immanence, a nourishing well or fertile ground from which masculine transcendence can feed and flee. Rather, the specific ways in which this plays out foreclose both (a) self-determination on the part of the feminine term and (b) positive difference between at least two autonomous, sexually differentiated positions within the matrix of sexual difference.

Irigaray argues that this economy of sexual (in)difference produces woman as a thing delimited and designed by man's demands. This is a profoundly nonreciprocal constitution of one pole of sexual difference as pure object in order to substantiate the other pole's pretense to pure subjectivity.[14] To the extent that woman figures as maternal, domestic, and sexual place for man, she serves as both useful object and containing envelope, "the starting point from which man limits his things." So constituted, Irigaray argues, "she remains inseparable from the work or act of man, notably insofar as he defines her and creates *his* identity with her as his starting point or, correlatively, with this determination of her being."[15]

Serving as place for the masculinist subject, the feminine is divested of her own place. Within the hierarchical dualism that masquerades as sexual difference, the feminine does not have her own orbit or ambit except as delimited by the masculine. Irigaray argues that in "taking from the feminine the tissue or texture of spatiality," the masculinist subject "contains or envelops her with walls while enveloping himself and his things with her flesh."[16] Framed in this way, the epochal (read: temporal) question of sexual difference becomes a problem of spatiality and placing. Hence Irigaray's insistence that the transition to a new age of sexual difference requires entirely different conceptions of spatiality, place, and inhabitation.

In lieu of a conception of the feminine as the enveloping container or fertile field for Man, Irigaray posits a different relation between place and sexual difference. Her approach roughly adheres to the two prongs I mentioned earlier: first, opening an autonomous place for the feminine's own self-constitution and unfolding—that is, reconceiving the relation between place and the feminine—and, second, opening a *space between* the terms of binary sexual difference that allows them to reach and touch each other in love and difference—that is, reconceiving the relation between place and sexual difference as spacing. I would like to address each of these in turn, before twining them together to see how Irigaray's tactile and erotic theorization of sexed becoming might contribute to the transformation of sexual difference itself.

SEXUAL DIFFERENCE AS QUALITATIVE BECOMING

Irigaray begins her essay "Volume-Fluidity" with the assertion "So woman has not yet taken (a) place."[17] This refers both to the feminine's dispossession within economies of sexual difference (where woman has not yet taken a place) and the fact that "woman" as a singularity with positive, not merely comparative or negative, difference is still to come (that woman as such has not yet taken place). The feminine is precisely that which is still to-come, that which has not counted within the hierarchical dualism of sexual difference. In fact, so-called sexual difference as it has been known so far can really only count to One: Man. Woman is simply defined as not-One.

Seizing on this exile from the realm of countability and numericity, Irigaray flips the quantificational logic of sexual (in)difference on its head. In sexual (in)difference, the feminine serves as place for the masculine and has no proper place of her own; the feminine lacks the solid borders and self-same identity attributed to the masculine. Mimetically, Irigaray takes these specular projections of the feminine and transvaluates them. Rather than marks of feminine lack, these figurations of impropriety, mobility, and plasticity become the very features allowing for a positive articulation of "the/a woman" as a feminine subject in process.

This positive articulation of "the/a woman" should not be mistaken for a definition specifying a necessary and sufficient set of conditions or contents for the category "woman." This, in fact, is precisely what Irigaray's locution of "the/a woman" is meant to disrupt. Irigaray's conceptual figuration of "the/a woman" is positive in the sense that it provides a way of thinking the feminine in its singularity, that is, in its specificity apart from any comparative or denigrated difference from Man. It is emphatically *not* a specification of a set of qualities proper to or definitive of the feminine as such. By articulating "the/a woman" in terms of her transgression of the logic of static form, Irigaray reveals the impossibility of any such categorical coagulation of sexuate essence. Perhaps more importantly, by underlining the "the/a woman's" disjuncture with seamless self-identity or solid form, Irigaray offers a potent conception of the feminine as a site of qualitative becoming.

This model of becoming unfolds primarily through a logic of tactility or, more specifically, self-touching. Self-touching, or auto-affection, refers to the looping movement of the embodied self upon itself; it can be most broadly construed as the recursive movement by which embodied self shapes and fashions itself. Masculinist models of auto-affection, Irigaray argues, hinge on the illusion of a cohesive body-self that remains the same each time it returns upon itself. The circular return of the self upon itself is here sealed up in a closed circle.[18] Auto-affection here functions in a mode of ipseity, securing the masculinist subject's illusory self-image of immutable, impenetrable form. Irigaray's critique of this masculinist model of auto-affection, far from reifying a view of masculine and/or male embodiment as closed and static in contrast to feminine fluidity, may actually have implications for a range of sexuate embodiments: no embodiment is in fact static in the ways putatively secured by masculinist fantasies of ipseity.

However, Irigaray explores the possibility of auto-affection operating otherwise through her elaboration of what could be called a feminine auto-affection. Rather than secure fixed form, the touch of this feminine auto-affection opens up the embodied self to transformation. This kind of self-touching, Irigaray suggests, is in fact only possible because "the/a woman" is not constituted according to a logic of homogenous form or immutable solidity. "When the/a woman touches herself," she writes,

> a whole touches itself because it is in-finite, because it has neither the knowledge nor the power to close up or to swell definitively to the extension of the infinite. This self-touching gives woman a form that is in(de)finitely transformed without closing over her appropriation. Metamorphoses occur in which there is no complete set, where no set theory of the One is established. Transmutations occur, always unexpectedly, since they do not conspire to accomplish any telos.[19]

The/a woman is not a discretely bounded unit and, consequently, her form is never entirely settled or stable. Because of this, Irigaray indicates, feminine auto-affection results not in a closed circle or feedback loop, but in a self-touching that springs from and generates plasticity.

Furthermore, the locution of "the/a woman" is meant to underscore the point that the logic of fixed form and countability simply does not apply to woman in either the singular or the plural. Neither "woman" nor women as a group are anything like a delimitable, definable being or entity, Irigaray argues. "One woman and one woman and one woman will never add up to some generic entity: women," she insists. "(The/a) woman refers to what cannot be defined, enumerated, formulated, or formalized."[20] Thus "the/a woman" reiterates a characteristic "gap in form" on multiple levels,[21] making it difficult to disentangle Irigaray's claims about corporeal and conceptual configurations. Perhaps that is part of Irigaray's point. To wit, she claims that "Woman is neither open nor closed. She is infinite, in-finite, *form is never complete in her.* She is not infinite but neither is she *a* unit(y), such as letter, number, figure in a series, proper noun, unique object (in a) world of the senses, simple ideality in an intelligible form, entity of a foundation, etc. This incompleteness in her form, her morphology, allows her continually to become something else."[22] So Irigaray elaborates a conception of "the/a woman" that exceeds fixed or proper form, consistent identity over time, and a homogenizing spatial logic of discrete, countable entities. Instead, "the/a woman" models a dilated conceptual/corporeal form, opening her to a self-touching that results in particular kinds of transformations.

In contradistinction to the logic of solid forms, "the/a woman" is explicitly aligned with the tactile properties of fluids. Fluids cannot be analyzed or quantified according to the same measures as solids, nor do their movements or transformations from one state to another correspond to those proper to solids. Fluid dynamics are qualitatively different from those of solids: that is, different not in degree but in kind.

The unique properties of fluids are primarily tactile, having to do with the way flows touch and pass into one another. Fluidity can be distinguished by the fact that it is "continuous, compressible, dilatable, viscous, conductible, diffusible; . . . that it is unending, potent and impotent owing to its resistance to the countable; that it enjoys and suffers from a greater sensitivity to pressures; that it is, in its physical reality, determined by friction between two infinitely neighboring entities—*dynamics of the near and not of the proper.*"[23] Just as fluids flow, compress, and dilate in excess of the logic of bounded solids, Irigaray suggests, so too does the feminine. This fluid dynamics of nearness, of porosity, contact, and touching, underpins Irigaray's conception of feminine self-touching.

The types of transformation opened by the auto-affection of this fluid feminine subject have a particular character. They do not assemble into a complete set, nor do they aim toward a telos that may be determined in advance. As a consequence, the quality and course of these transformations themselves remain unpredictable. The body-subject formed and swept up by these metamorphoses is, in turn, never quite reducible to a solidly defined entity or a simple unity—remember Irigaray's assertion that "(The/a) woman refers to what cannot be defined, enumerated, formulated, or formalized."[24] This conception of "the/a woman" as a subject-in-becoming emphasizes a fluidity that is only ever provisionally captured by quantitative measures.[25]

Not only does "the/a woman" partake of the fluid properties of qualitative multiplicity; on Irigaray's account, sexual difference itself emerges as a qualitative, rather than quantitative, difference in Bergson's sense: sexual difference differentiates not by comparative degree but rather produces sexuate differences in kind. Recasting sexual difference such that "the/a woman" can constitute a place for herself necessarily opens up the masculine to transformation as well— and, I would argue, for gender kinds that do not resolve into Irigaray's own framework of the feminine and the masculine.

Rather than a comparative difference between preestablished, internally homogenous terms, Irigaray situates sexual difference as a field of differentiation between qualitatively distinct terms that are still to come. In other words, while sexual (in)difference describes a hierarchical binary between Man and not-Man, sexual difference refers to the spacing between autonomous sexuate singularities. Irigaray elaborates this conception of sexual difference through the figure of the interval.

THE INTERVAL(S) OF SEXUAL DIFFERENCE

The interval is a polyvocal concept in Irigaray's work. In the opening essay of *An Ethics of Sexual Difference*, it figures as a limit that separates and thus opens the possibility of relation between matter and form, between humans and the divine, and between sexuate subjects. Irigaray links the interval to desire, claiming that desire "designates the place of the *interval*"[26] and thus cannot be defined without freezing its characteristic dynamism. Desire marks the interval because it concerns attraction, which implies the spacing relations of proximity or distance. In this formulation, Irigaray means to untether desire from pregiven fixed scenarios, and instead describe it as "a changing dynamic whose outlines can be described in the past, sometimes in the present, but never definitively predicted."[27] Desire, in other words, might be described retroactively or touched in its unfolding, but its movements cannot be prescriptively predicted in advance.

Irigaray thus describes the interval as something other than a fixed space anchoring economies of sexual (in)difference. "Our age will have failed to

SEXUAL DIFFERENCE AS QUALITATIVE BECOMING

realize the full dynamic reserve signified by desire if it is referred back to the economy of the *interval*," she writes.[28] The key word here is "economy"; it is not the differential spacing of the interval that is the problem but rather its quantitative formalization in terms of an economic system of fixed units and circuits of exchange.

The interval is a limit, however shifting, that secures the possibility of each term's relation to itself and the other terms. As indicated by its alignment with a desire that cannot be described in advance, the interval is less a fixed border between delimited territories than a dynamic aperture allowing for the differentiation of the forces it produces through this very spacing. It is not a fixed measure or space between terms delimited in advance but rather the dynamic, generative condition of their unpredictable emergence.

For Irigaray, the interval enables sexual difference: it is what allows for different sexes to have their own places, crossing into and touching one another without being subsumed therein. Irigaray articulates the interval as the condition by which the masculine and feminine poles she sees as constitutive of sexual difference might come into their own and so touch without simply displacing, expropriating, or swallowing each other. "One sex is not entirely consumable by the other," she writes. "There is always a *remainder*."[29] This remainder is the qualitative difference generated by the interval. The interval thus not only produces sexual difference, but dilates it, holding it open as a space of wonder and unsubstitutability. Unlike the economy of sexual (in)difference where only one term, Man, counts and holds its own place, the kind of sexual difference opened by the interval allows for mutual autonomy and amazement on the part of differently sexed subjects. "Wonder maintains their autonomy within their statutory difference," Irigaray writes, "keeping a space of freedom and attraction between them, a possibility of separation and alliance."[30] The interval is what produces this noncomplementarity, the joint possibility of autonomy and affinity between differently sexed subjects.

While Irigaray claims that the masculine and feminine poles of sexual difference are irreducible to each other, she insists that this interval of difference is also the very possibility of their touch and interpenetration. The interval enables each sex to articulate and inhabit a place of its own; in so doing, it enables the generative power of porosity *between* these sexuate places. The interval is the generative spacing of sexual difference that allows for touching between and across this difference, maintaining it not as an impermeable solid but as a stretchable and porous membrane: "There are times when that relation of places in the sexual act gives rise to a transgression of the envelope, to a porousness, a perception of the other, a fluidity. And so it becomes possible to imagine that generation of a certain kind might occur by crossing membranes and sharing humors with the other."[31] This vision of sex as fluid bonding hinges on what Irigaray names "the fecundity of the porous,"[32] which locates the porosity between irreducibly different sexed body-subjects as a site of creativity.

This is not the procreative generativity possible in some sexual encounters but rather the intersubjective creation of new modes of inhabiting body, world, and cosmos. "Pleasure is engendering in us and between us," Irigaray writes, "an engendering associated with the world and with the universe, with which the work of the flesh is never unconnected. Either pleasure is a mere expenditure of fire, of water, of seed, of body and of spirit . . . or else it is a unique and definite creation."[33] As long as each sexuate subject involved in a sexual encounter is "reborn and touched anew by inner communion,"[34] there is the potential for each to touch the other transformatively. The fluid self-touching exemplified by the feminine subject, Irigaray suggests, can spill over and affect intersubjective encounters too. Only when each participant is grounded in their own autonomous place can sex become "the act whereby the other gives new form, birth, incarnation to the self" without this becoming an act of dispossession or appropriation.[35]

Through this reworked conception of tactility and place, Irigaray elaborates a model of becoming as sensate, qualitative transformation that is never given in advance. Sexual difference is thus not a difference of degree between essentially equivalent terms, but rather an ongoing, productive differentiation between emergent terms that do not share a common measure. As evidenced by the concept of the interval, sexual difference is not a quantitative comparison between two solid, self-same entities, but rather a qualitative spacing, a differentiation that produces the possibility of contact and touch. As Rebecca Hill suggests, "The masculine and feminine poles of life should be reconceived as autonomous thresholds of becoming. . . . These sexed poles of life would not be given as static concepts; they would be constituted through the differentiating movement of the interval."[36] Thus the interval, Hill clarifies, might be best understood as a "threshold for the becoming of sexed forces."[37]

SEXUAL DIFFERENCE AS QUALITATIVE MULTIPLICITY: BESIDE THE CISSEXUAL TWO

It seems, then, that Irigaray provides a way to reconceive sexual difference not as a hierarchical binary but as a qualitative multiplicity, changing in kind each time it emerges in and through an interval. Sexual difference is a threshold of becoming, a relation between sexually differentiated subjects—and sexual difference *itself* is subject to becoming. Sexual difference becomes otherwise—not only through the epochal task of overcoming sexual (in)difference in favor of positive difference between cisgender women and men, but also through the articulation of diverse sexuate positions, forces, and kinds.

Sexual difference thus does not denote a fixed matched set of sexuate beings adhering to prescriptive forms. Rather, it names the production and emergence of sexuate difference that is simply *different*: not comparatively evaluated on one kind's terms. Irigaray's analysis of sexual difference strongly indicts the paucity of comparative models of sexual (in)difference based on only one sexuate term. My claim here is that it is similarly inadequate to circumscribe the forms that human sexuate becoming may take by reducing all forms of sexuate subjectivity and embodiment to only two cisgender terms. The reduction of sexual difference to the cisgender two fails to attend adequately to the plurality of sexuate kinds already extant and to-come, and risks denigrating trans and nonbinary people in ways that perpetuate both moral and bodily harms.[38]

In outlining an irreverently Irigarayan model of sexual difference as qualitative becoming, I suggest that Irigaray's focus on cissexual difference may be more a matter of her own theoretical scope rather than an ontological limit internal to sexual difference. Understanding sexual difference in terms of qualitative becoming, in fact, yields a fecund account of how all sorts of gender kinds emerge and touch through intervals of sexuate difference. Irigaray's corpus, in other words, may yet provide tools for overcoming the cisnormativity (exclusive valuing of cissexual identities and embodiment) it seemingly enacts.

The Irigarayan account of sexual difference as qualitative becoming I offer here demonstrates that sexual difference is by no means exclusively captured by dualistic categories of sexual difference that map solely onto cisgender kinds of embodiment and subjectivity. Even if we follow Irigaray in articulating two primary poles of sexual difference, masculine and feminine, it need not follow that sexual difference is therefore limited to a dualistic relation, however nonhierarchical, between cisgender men and cisgender women. Far from it: for sexual difference as a tendency of sexuate becoming unfolds via qualitatively different forms of sexuate corporeality and subjectivity that are not circumscribed by pregiven categories of comparative difference. If sexual difference is not, as we have seen, an immutable relation between already-given terms, then surely it can proliferate sexuate difference beyond the primary categories within which it has been circumscribed, however inadequately, thus far.

Insofar as Irigaray's own account of sexual difference prioritizes this capacity for creativity and the engendering of new forms, a creative reading and uptake of her work could produce an understanding of sexual difference that is not limited to the congruently sexed, heterosexually oriented subjects privileged in her own exposition. Irigaray's work reconceives sexual difference as a creative interval rather than a static structure. Considered as a multivectored force of differentiation rather than a hierarchical dualism, sexual difference emerges as a productive interval with innumerable locations. A mobile threshold, it produces many places of sexuate difference across which touch might pass.

BIBLIOGRAPHY

Bergson, Henri. *Key Writings*. Edited by Keith Ansell Pearson and John Mullarkey. Translated by Melissa McMahon. London: Continuum, 2005.
Bettcher, Talia Mae. "Evil Deceivers and Make-Believers: On Transphobic Violence and the Politics of Illusion." *Hypatia* 22, no. 3 (2007): 43–65.
Braidotti, Rosi. *Nomadic Subjects*. New York: Columbia University Press, 1994.
Deleuze, Gilles, and Félix Guattari. *A Thousand Plateaus: Capitalism and Schizophrenia*. Translated by Brian Massumi. Minneapolis: University of Minnesota Press, 1987.
Hill, Rebecca, "At Least Two: The Tendencies of Sexual Difference." *Australian Feminist Law Journal* 43, no. 1 (2017): 25–40.
———. *The Interval: Relation and Becoming in Irigaray, Aristotle, and Bergson*. New York: Fordham University Press, 2012.
———. "The Multiple Readings of Irigaray's Concept of Sexual Difference." *Philosophy Compass* 11, no. 7 (2016): 390–401.
Lennon, Erica, and Brian J. Mistler. "Cisgenderism." *TSQ* 1, nos. 1–2 (2014): 63–64.

Lorraine, Tamsin. *Irigaray and Deleuze: Experiments in Visceral Philosophy*. Ithaca: Cornell University Press, 1999.
Stephano, Oli. "Irreducibility and (Trans) Sexual Difference." *Hypatia* 34, no. 1 (2019): 141–154.

NOTES

1. Irigaray, TVB, 54.
2. Irigaray, ILTY 35, 47. In this essay, Irigaray uses the Aristotelian language of "at least two" sexes, while a few pages later insisting that "sexual difference probably represents the most universal question we can address. Our era is faced with the task of dealing with sexual difference because, across the whole world, there are, there are only, men and women."
3. For a comprehensive overview of this literature, see Rebecca Hill, "The Multiple Readings of Irigaray's Concept of Sexual Difference," *Philosophy Compass* 11, no. 7 (2016): 390–401. For a critique of how claims about the irreducibility of sexual difference can prioritize cissexual difference while invalidating trans modes of embodiment and identification, see Oli Stephano, "Irreducibility and (Trans) Sexual Difference," *Hypatia* 34, no. 1 (2019): 141–154.
4. Irigaray, S, 111.
5. Irigaray, ESD, 53.
6. Cf. Gilles Deleuze and Félix Guattari, *A Thousand Plateaus: Capitalism and Schizophrenia*, trans. Brian Massumi (Minneapolis: University of Minnesota Press, 1987), 8.
7. For more on sexual difference as the actualization of divergent tendencies, see Rebecca Hill, "At Least Two: The Tendencies of Sexual Difference," *Australian Feminist Law Journal* 43, no. 1 (2017): 25–40.
8. Henri Bergson, *Key Writings*, ed. Keith Ansell Pearson and John Mullarkey, trans. Melissa McMahon (London: Continuum, 2005), 68.
9. Bergson, 76.
10. Bergson, 74.
11. Irigaray, ESD, 7.
12. I capitalize "Man" here to illustrate both the mythic proportions and the purportedly universal status of the unmarked masculinist subject.
13. A word on terms: While Irigaray pivots between woman, man, female, male, feminine, and masculine in the texts I will consider, I am sympathetic to Tamsin Lorraine's point that "feminine" and "masculine" have the benefit of emphasizing discursive positioning rather than fixing those positions by reading them back through bodily attributes. Lorraine uses these terms "in order to indicate that in a masculinist specular economy it is the masculine subject who functions as the 'active' subject at the expense of the subjectivity of his feminine counterpart." These two positions, she notes, are easily parsed if this specular economy is working perfectly. However, as Lorraine argues, "fortunately no actual economy ever works so perfectly; it is unlikely that an embodied human being will ever fully manifest either position without complication or 'excess.'" Tamsin Lorraine,

Irigaray and Deleuze: Experiments in Visceral Philosophy (Ithaca: Cornell University Press, 1999), 22.
14. Borrowing Irigaray's language of polarity, I do not mean to imply that there are only two poles to sexual difference: normatively presenting cisgender men and cisgender women respectively. In fact, this is something I contest in my reading of her work here. I simply mean to invoke her atomic metaphor of positive and negative charges. The problem, within the hierarchical binary of sexual (in)difference, is the ascription of exclusively negative (receptive) flows to the feminized pole and positive (active) ones to the masculine. These capacities need to circulate within and between each term in order for actual sexual difference to occur. Cf. Irigaray, ESD, 9.
15. Irigaray, 10.
16. Irigaray, 11.
17. Irigaray, S, 227.
18. Irigaray, ESD, 233.
19. Irigaray, 233.
20. Irigaray, 230.
21. Irigaray, 230.
22. Irigaray, 229.
23. Irigaray, TS, 111, emphasis added.
24. Irigaray, ESD, 230.
25. I borrow this terminology from Rosi Braidotti, *Nomadic Subjects* (New York: Columbia University Press, 1994).
26. Irigaray, ESD, 8.
27. Irigaray, 8.
28. Irigaray, 8.
29. Irigaray, 14.
30. Irigaray, 14.
31. Irigaray, 46.
32. Irigaray, 18.
33. Irigaray, IR, 181.
34. Irigaray, ESD, 50.
35. Irigaray, 51.
36. Rebecca Hill, *The Interval: Relation and Becoming in Irigaray, Aristotle, and Bergson* (New York: Fordham University Press, 2012), 114.
37. Hill, 2.
38. There is a robust and growing body of literature on cissexism—the valuing of only cisgender identities and embodiment and the corresponding denigrating of trans and nonbinary subjects—and its harms. A full review is beyond the scope of the present work, but an introduction to the literature might include Erica Lennon and Brian J. Mistler, "Cisgenderism," *TSQ* 1, nos. 1–2 (2014): 63–64; and Talia Mae Bettcher, "Evil Deceivers and Make-Believers: On Transphobic Violence and the Politics of Illusion," *Hypatia* 22, no. 3 (2007): 43–65.

Chapter Eleven

AN ONTO-ETHICS OF TRANSSEXUAL DIFFERENCE

MITCHELL DAMIAN MURTAGH

> Nietzsche used to say that we would continue to believe in God as long as we believed in grammar. Yet even, or perhaps particularly after the fall of a certain God, discourse still defends its untouchable status. To say that discourse has a *sex*, especially in its syntax, is to question the last bastion of semantic order. It amounts to taking issue with the God of men in his most traditional form. Even if language is emptied of meaning—or perhaps the more it is emptied of meaning?—respect for its technical architecture must remain intact. Discourse would be the erection of the *totem* and the *taboo* of the world of man.
>
> —LUCE IRIGARAY, *AN ETHICS OF SEXUAL DIFFERENCE*

Irigaray calls on Nietzsche in *An Ethics of Sexual Difference* to draw out that, even after "the God of men" is pronounced dead in his most traditional form, he continues to live on so long as the grammar that produced him remains intact, even as his contents are emptied out of it. For Irigaray, it is not "the God of men" alone that is at issue but the technical architecture out of which his form is erected. As long as the underlying structure remains the same, discourses that arise out of it, even those that are critical of "the God of men," replicate the grammar that erected him in the first place.

In this chapter, I challenge rejections of Irigaray's philosophy of sexual difference and Elizabeth Grosz's uptake of it from two schools of feminist thought—social constructivism and new materialism—for failing to think it from its own logic or underlying grammar structure. I argue that these rejections operate from within a binary grammar when conceiving the relation between the material and social, or nature and culture, and its significance for sex and gender. Consequently, contemporary queer and trans critiques that pick up from social constructivist and new materialist lineages inherit and continue to assume such relations in binary terms. However, Irigaray's philosophy of sexual difference is an attempt to revolutionize such relations or to think them otherwise. In her grammar of sexual difference, one term acknowledges—rather than disavows—the other. Most importantly, one term functions as the very condition of possibility for the other, while the two remain irreducible to each other by an interval, preventing their unification or collapse into one. Hence, part of the project of sexual difference is to rethink the underlying relation between the material and the social, or nature and culture, beyond a binary. Moving beyond such binaries undergirds how the material and social mediate one another in the expression of sexuate materiality and subjectivity. Rather than opposites, the material is the condition of possibility for the social; the social is an elaboration of the material but not reducible to it.

My main objective is to demonstrate that accusations of transphobia against such a philosophy of sexual difference are not only a misreading but transphobic in their own way. Most arguments against sexual difference purport it to mean a reductive ontology of male and female sexes, and turn to gender, or gender performativity as a more inclusive and self-determining alternative. However, when sexual difference is relegated to the ontological and gender to the epistemological while rejecting one and affirming the other, this not only assumes a binary relation between the ontological and the epistemological but leaves a transphobic conception of ontology intact rather than considering the possibility that ontology itself can be conceived otherwise. Instead, I argue that, while allowing for the general bimodality of human sexes, sexual difference does not assume that sexuate ontology is reducible to static and untraversable categories of "male" and "female," making it "unpreferable" to transsexuality or trans modes of being.

Starting from the claim that sexual difference cannot be jammed within the sex/gender binary, I aim to show how some new feminist materialists do reduce it to an anthropocentric concept of sex, or something akin to "gender," where gender is a specifically human concept, while social constructivists critique it on grounds that whatever presumes to be prediscursive is essentialist and therefore potentially transphobic. But turning to gender, or gender performativity (as many social constructivists do as though a "choice" to be made between the two), I assert, still operates *within* a binary grammar. Subsequently, critiques of Irigaray and Grosz via the Grosz Paradox, called on by new materialists and social constructivists alike, argue that the two senses of the "irreducibility" of sexual difference cannot be squared. This, too, I think, is symptomatic of remaining within a binary "one or the other" mode of thinking. I propose a way out of this "Paradox,"

AN ONTO-ETHICS OF TRANSSEXUAL DIFFERENCE

used to dismiss Grosz and by extension the claims she's made about transsexuality, by reconsidering sexual difference through the grammar of sexual difference, rather than through a binary logic or binarized critiques of it. I conclude by proposing an onto-ethics of transsexuality instead. Grosz, working *with* rather than *on* Irigaray, connects ontology to ethics in a relation of sexual difference—an ethics understood as practices of living, living "one's fate" as the Stoics or Nietzsche conceive it. Working from Irigaray in a new direction, Grosz connects the art of living *with* the limits reality imposes on life to arrive at a Stoic definition of onto-ethics:

> We are not capable of controlling what is not within our power—what we are as bodies, how others perceive us, what nature has given us or bestowed upon us, fate, necessity. Ethics is the organization and understanding of what, in our power, we can do to expand our nature and that of other humans, living beings, and things themselves. It thus addresses humans in their relations to each other and to every component of the cosmos.[1]

To reiterate Grosz, an onto-ethics reconceives the ontological as the condition of possibility for the ethical and the ethical as an elaboration of the ontological. This acquiesces being itself as neither completely determined *nor* completely willed but as an effect produced by the constant struggle, or tension, between the two. Sexual difference is precisely this striving or struggling with the problem of sexed being, a problem we must contend with by *living with*. In this way, sexual difference actually affirms transsexuality, both ontologically and ethically. Transsexuality is one way of living with the problem of sexual difference, a way of life, an *ethics*. And at the same time, the way that one lives their transsexuality, their ethics, produces ontological effects on the very sexedness of their being. Far from being transphobic, then, an onto-ethics of sexual difference opens the possibility of thinking transsexuality as a way of *being* rather than merely a way of identifying and may be the most affirming philosophy of transsexuality there is.

THE BEYOND-BINARY GRAMMAR OF SEXUAL DIFFERENCE

Feminist, queer, and trans studies scholars who critique, reject, and dismiss sexual difference today tend to rely on "translations" of sexual difference that reduce it to one or the other term of the Anglophone sex/gender binary. Some of the most robust arguments *against* sexual difference are built on the premise that it is inherently essentialist, meaning that it assumes anatomical sex determines gender identity, and is transphobic on these grounds. By contrast, Rachel Jones insists that "the sexes" in Irigaray's work are never merely biological *or* cultural:

> The "sexuate" refers neither to a mode of being determined by biological sex nor to a cultural overlay of gendered meanings inscribed on a "tabula rasa" of passively receptive matter. The "sexuate" does not separate the becomings that shape our bodily being from the production of social and cultural meanings or behavioural dispositions. Rather, it signals the way that sexual difference is articulated through our different modes of being and becoming, that is, in bodily, social, linguistic, aesthetic, erotic and political forms.[2]

Those who argue against sexual difference presuppose either the sex/gender or biological/cultural binary themselves or that sexual difference implies it. In neither case is sexual difference contended with beyond a binary grammar. Rejections of sexual difference on these grounds are made by both social constructivists and new materialists, but each orientation makes it differently.

While social constructivists do not deny the reality of sex, they often take issue with a definition of sexual difference that is "ontological," at least assuming that the ontological refers to a body's prediscursive givenness. For social constructivists, it is not possible to know or experience the sexedness of a body prediscursively because the sexed body is inextricably tied to the discursive structures of a particular sociocultural matrix. In other words, social constructivists accept the reality of sex as a product of gender. They deny sex as the basis for an ontology insofar as ontology itself, for them, is always already culturally produced and only apprehended *through* the cultural. Social constructivists who reject an ontology of sexual difference simultaneously tend instead to affirm Judith Butler's concept of "gender performativity." In *Gender Trouble*, Butler describes gender performativity as "an expectation that ends up producing the very phenomenon that it anticipates."[3] Gender is produced not in a singular act, but in "a repetition and a ritual, which achieves its effects through its naturalization in the context of a body, understood, in part, as a culturally sustained temporal duration."⁴ Gender performativity thus refers to iterations of acts that congeal social, psychic, corporeal, and temporal dimensions into gendered identity. According to Butler, this destabilizes "the naturalizing narratives of compulsory heterosexuality" and their central protagonists, "man" and "woman." For them, the fact that gender requires repetition exposes the illusion that gender identity has some kind of intractable depth, or inner substance. As a series of "acts," gender performativity reveals the fundamentally phantasmatic status of what is otherwise thought to be "natural."⁵ As such, Butler claims, sexed bodies are indissociable from these repetitions and the regulatory norms that govern the signification of their material effects.⁶

While some new materialists write positively on Irigaray and sexual difference broadly, others such as Luciana Parisi, Myra J. Hird, and Jami Weinstein reject sexual difference, and on other grounds than social constructivists do. For them, it is too anthropocentric a theory, too focused on human "gender." In the strange and prolific worlds of plant and animal species—the worlds of sea horses, bacteria, viruses, and amoebas—species can self-replicate, they can reproduce sexually or asexually, males can become pregnant and carry offspring to term, species may be entirely intersex, members within a species may have multiple sexes, change sexes, or sexually modulate depending on the external temperature or social environment. Whereas humans tend to think of "sex" itself in terms of the two-sex model, new materialists argue that this is too narrow or restrictive. Sex, they insist, is much more capacious and multiplicitious than the culturally constructed idea of a discursive ontology of sex being limited to "male" and "female." Hence, they reject sexual difference when that concept is understood to mean two human sexes. Thinking about bacteria, microbes, molecules, and inorganic life, Myra J. Hird posits that "human imagination may be limited to a narrow understanding of 'sexual' reproduction."⁷ Similarly for Luciana Parisi, sex and sexual difference are dynamic, not because they are linked to historical or epistemological contingencies, but because, through a lens of evolutionary theory, matter demonstrates itself as having infinite potentialities to become anew, beyond transformations incited by discourse. Put another way, if sexual difference = Man/Woman, then the new materialists argue that it simply is not enough to account for the innumerable variations of sex in both human and non-human species.

But how do we use this new materialist radical empiricism to live our human lives differently, or in different terms when it comes to human sexed subjectivity? While observations of sex in species that exceed the two-sex model are exciting, what do we do with this? New materialists' claims of the infinite multiplicity of sex seem to ignore, or at least cast to the side, the statistical "bimodality" of human sexes.

So while social constructivists, according to new materialists, may not have a complicated enough concept of morphological differences, new materialists, according to social constructivists, do not have a way of linking sexed human beings back to the radical empiricism of their observations of the multiplicities of sexes in species that exceed the two-sex model. Each side of the debate implicitly critiques the other in its rejection of sexual difference as a certain sex/gender binary is retained. Either "sex" is outside the scope of what is constructible by human subjects and should be rejected according to the social constructivists on those grounds or "gender" cuts off sexed human subjects from the rest of the world via human exceptionalism and should be rejected by the new materialists on those ground. In both cases, the definition of sexual difference presented falls under a binary logic. And in both cases, the definition of sexual difference can be rendered transphobic. Each side, in turn, charges Irigaray *and* Grosz with allegations of transphobia because of their respective defenses of sexual difference. However, a certain irony seems lost: the feminists calling for "the death of sexual difference"[8] divide themselves and their critiques in this way. This irony is part of the case I want to build here: that binarized rejections of Irigaray's concept of sexual difference do not engage with sexual difference in its own grammar.

IS SEXUAL DIFFERENCE TRANSPHOBIC?

There are a few places in Irigaray's writings often cited to justify the charge of transphobia against her. In *I Love to You,* for example, she writes, "some of our naive contemporaries, women and men, would like to wipe out this difference by resorting to monosexuality, to the unisex and to what is called identification: even if I am bodily a man or woman, I can identify with, and so be, the other sex. This new opium of the people annihilates the other in the illusion of a reduction to identity, equality, and sameness, especially between man and woman, the ultimate anchorage of real alterity."[9] It is worth noting there is some scholarship that provides a positive valuation of sexual difference for trans narratives.[10] Further, Irigaray has not really discussed trans issues much in her written work despite these passing mentions. As an Irigarayan, Grosz has inherited critiques that sexual difference is transphobic. Not only does Grosz speak in a more direct and pronounced way about transsexuality in her work than Irigaray, but her emphasis on the onto-ethical heightens concerns for those who link ontology with essentialism, or think of ontology in terms of two static and immutable sexes. For this reason, I will now turn to two infamous passages where Grosz discusses transsexuality in relation to sexual difference in order to think through these issues.

The first of these passages can be found in *Volatile Bodies* (1994) in the chapter "Sexed Bodies," where Grosz makes an argument for the irreducible specificity of the sexes:

> There will always remain a kind of outsideness or alienness of the experiences and lived reality of each sex for the other. Men, contrary to the fantasy of the transsexual, can never, even with surgical intervention, feel or experience what it is like to be, to live, as women. At best the transsexual can live out his fantasy of femininity—a fantasy that in itself is usually disappointed with the rather crude transformations effected by surgical and chemical intervention. The transsexual may *look* like a woman but can never feel like or *be* a woman. The one sex, whether male or female or some other term, can only experience, live, according to (and hopefully in excess of) the *cultural significations* of the sexually specific body. The problematic of sexual difference entails a certain failure of knowledge to bridge the gap, the interval, between the sexes. There remains something ungraspable, something outside, unpredictable, and uncontainable, about the other sex for each sex.[11]

What could be read as intentionally incorrect pronoun usage—"his fantasy of femininity"—may be enough to warrant an automatic disqualification of whatever larger point Grosz is trying to make here. However, if we are willing to linger with the passage, there are other curious phrases that seem to open the possibility for a more nuanced reading. For starters, sexual difference is not reducible to genital dimorphism for Grosz. In the sentence that begins "The one sex ..." Grosz specifies "male" and "female" and importantly adds, "or some other term." This "some other term" leaves open a consideration that "male" and "female" are not the only ways for human subjects to be sexed, just that, whatever sex one is, they cannot become other to themselves. It is not at all clear that Grosz's claim about sexual difference conflicts with or discounts one's sexed or sexual *identity*.[12] She is nowhere claiming, in other words, that what validates a person's identity as a man or a woman is their genitalia or any other particular anatomical fact.[13] She is instead refusing that any person can occupy a different sexed specificity than the specificity of their own sex. Being sex, sexed being, is being that is split, partial, that which requires an other in order for sex itself to be coherent.

Understood in these terms, Grosz's Irigarayan account of sexual difference need not gatekeep the binary cisgender categories of male and female. Rather, it simply acknowledges that any one being has a limit, which is their sexedness. This is not to say that the limit cannot be transformed or expanded in interesting ways. It is to say that a cisgender female body can never become a cisgender male body and vice versa. It acknowledges sex as a constraint, perhaps a creative constraint, but one that demonstrates we are not infinitely malleable or limitless in our capacities to become otherwise because we desire to become otherwise. Our sex reminds us we do not have full mastery to determine ourselves completely at our own wills. As Grosz says in an interview with Esther Wolfe, "I know that my work, especially in *Volatile Bodies*, has been quite heavily criticized in certain trans circles. But the point I made is something that I still believe. I'll say this nervously: we're born into a body, like it or not. The body is not made by us, but given to us: partly through nature, partly through environment."[14] While Grosz does not deny that all sexed bodies have the potential to become otherwise, these potentials have origins that produce thresholds, which orient their becoming. These thresholds remind us that there is always some other that we cannot be. In order for there to be sex at all, there must be an irreducible other. If I can become you, then I can become my other. Otherness itself dissolves. Sex becomes something I can master and determine in accordance with my identity. On the contrary, sexual difference is not determined by the desire or will of the subject's agency. It is an ethics of the subject's profound yielding to this limit, contending with this irreducibility of the other, and living threshold as part of one's fate.

AN ONTO-ETHICS OF TRANSSEXUAL DIFFERENCE

The second passage raising concern about transphobia comes out of *Becoming Undone* (2011), where Grosz amplifies her earlier position from *Volatile Bodies*, explaining transsexuality as a disavowal of one's bodily specificity combined with a desire to become the opposite sex. As Grosz summarizes in the chapter "Irigaray and Sexual Difference,"

> However queer, transgendered, and ethnically identified one might be, one comes from a man and a woman, and one remains a man or a woman, even in the case of gender-reassignment or the chemical and surgical transformation of one sex into the appearance of another. Sexual difference is still in play even to the extent that one identifies with or actively seeks the sexual organs and apparatus of the "opposite" sex: at most one can change the appearance and social meaning of the body, but the sexually specific body that is altered remains a sexually specific, if altered, body. Sexual difference has no one location, no one organ or condition. This is why surgical or hormonal alterations do not actually give one the body of the other sex, instead providing an alteration of only some of the key social markers of gender.[15]

Grosz's main point here seems to be that medical interventions augmenting or altering sexually specific bodies, while introducing the possibility for radical transformation that may alleviate the psychic pain of gender dysphoria, can never transform a sexually specific body into an "opposite" sexually specific body. In defense of Grosz's claim, one reason might be because there is no "opposite sex" according to the grammar of sexual difference. All bodies, according to this interpretation, *tend* in two diverging directions, to varying degrees.[16] The categories "male" and "female," as opposites, group individual differences by approximation. Another reason might be because individual bodies develop over time, and development is irreversible, foreclosing certain virtualities as others actualize. Over time, equipotentiality diminishes. This does not mean one cannot reorient their development from any given starting point but that whatever has already been determined in a body cannot be undetermined. It can only be determined differently from the present. To "become the opposite sex" would require time-reversibility to undo whatever determinations have been determined, and would require determining them "oppositely," whatever that would mean, and assuming such an "opposition" is even possible to conceive.

These passages in Grosz's writings are difficult to confront, yet there is something deeply indisputable here, two indisputable points, in fact. One is that a sexually specific body that is altered does remain a sexually specific, if altered, body. The other is that *however* a person identifies, "one comes from a man and a woman." Simply put, there are no identities without living subjects that are the effects of one kind of sexual difference, a sexual difference that orients generational reproduction. Although the language of "man" and "woman" is overdetermined with identity, Grosz's point is to invoke this principle of life. Regardless of the words being used, we understand that certain human bodies have the capacity to reproduce with other bodies, and certain bodies do not. However one identifies, one also knows that when it comes to issues of sexual intercourse, reproductive health, and reproductive justice, sexually specific bodies are effected differently. Trans folks know this. We live with this. There are trans men who need access to birth control and pap smears. There are trans women who need access to prostate exams and vasectomies. Family planning can be complicated. There are pregnant trans fathers and trans mothers who cannot birth, or carry their babies to term. These examples speak to Grosz's point that no "surgical or chemical intervention" is available, at least not of this writing, with the capacity to change the sexed specificity of a transsexual body to "actually give one the body of the other sex." One's sex need not be defined by reproductive capacity. Still, one's being is possible because of reproduction, which, in the human species, requires a certain form of sexual differentiation. Rather than delegitimating or invalidating transsexuality, reckoning with these limits that sexual difference imposes on *all* sexed bodies actually opens a way for acknowledging some really difficult parts of trans experience, parts that theories rejecting sexual difference erase, mute, or render invisible.

Let me be clear: I am not suggesting gender-affirming interventions do not make significant and necessary contributions to making trans lives more liveable. Gender-confirmation surgery and hormone replacement therapy have revolutionized my own life in affirming ways. Still, there are issues—medically, sexually, and otherwise—that I must contend with because of the sexually specific body I was born with, and still others I will never contend with because of the body I was not. To dismiss the *problem of sexual difference* simply because it is *problematic* is to dismiss the complicated, embodied experiences of transsexual being. In the passages I just gave, Grosz does not deny subjects the ability to identify and express their gender identify at the expense of sexual difference. Sex and gender are not mutually exclusive but co-constitutive. Sexual difference is part of what must be navigated in gender performativity. Grosz, therefore, recalibrates the relation, insisting, rightly, I think, that we live our identities within sexually specific bodies, and that identities cannot wholly determine the sexedness of our being (even though we can modulate the sexedness of our bodies, partially, in ways that do align with our identities). To imagine that identities can wholly determine our being risks what Jasbir Puar calls "trans exceptionalism," the idea that bodies are infinitely malleable and endlessly available for hormonal and surgical manipulation.[17] Affirming "trans exceptionalism" by theorizing transsexuality as "limitless," as capable of self-overcoming the limits of sexual difference, without giving way to the realities of sex determination that Grosz brings to the fore, is unrealistic and irresponsible and conceals the very real struggles of some transsexuals, which are often incited precisely by these limits to the changeability of their sex. The rejection of sexual difference implicit in trans exceptionalist accounts is also a rejection of that which makes transsexuality possible in the first place. Sexual difference, however violent it may appear, does give all sexed subjects a theoretical starting point for contending with, and sometimes confronting, the limits of our individually sexed bodies. It is a philosophy for how to live with, in, and at odds with them.

THE GROSZ PARADOX

Some scholars argue the alleged transphobia in Irigaray's *and* Grosz's writings is enough to reject sexual difference full stop. Others attempt to undo Grosz's philosophical position by suggesting that her thinking about sexual difference contradicts itself. In "A Requiem to Sexual Difference," Jami Weinstein refers to this "internal conflict" as "The Grosz Paradox":

> This claim to an enduring binary of sexual difference stands in conflict with her own assertions regarding the infinite possibility of matter for unpredictable change and self-overcoming.... By leaving the binary form of sex

concrete and stable, we are still left with the conclusion that, with regard to sexual difference, change rests only in the socially constructed, sociocultural, and fluid notions of the epistemological realm, even if we derive this realm, as Grosz suggests, from the natural and material.[18]

Some new materialists, including Weinstein, worry that sexual difference is a reductive cultural reification of male/female sexes, understood in terms of the gamete egg/sperm difference, without accounting for complexities of organic materiality that cannot be determined in advance. Weinstein, in drawing out the Grosz Paradox, compels us to relinquish sexual difference ontologically if we accept the reality of sex in excess of biological forms that rely on the irreducibility of twoness.

Some social constructivist arguments have also picked up on or anticipated this paradox and used it to render Grosz's defense of an ontology of sexual difference not only transphobic but unsound. In *Assuming a Body: Transgender and Rhetorics of Materiality*, Gayle Salamon lays out a thorough critique of Irigaray and Grosz, opposing them to Butler. Salamon defends Butler's social constructionist theory of the morphological imaginary as images and discourses that produce anatomy against an ontology of sexual difference. Sexual difference, she asserts, "pretends to deliver a certain 'truth' of identity at the level of anatomy, [while] this 'truth' arrives *only at the level of the imaginary*, which both governs the production of that anatomy and makes it available to the psyche."[19] Tim Johnston and Oli Stephano call on Salamon's social constructivist scaffolding in their own critiques of Grosz in the context of readings of Irigaray.

In "Questioning the Threshold of Sexual Difference," Johnston argues that insisting sexual difference is *the* essential difference requires denying ontological irreducibility to transgender, intersex, and gender-nonconforming (TIGNC) people.[20] Describing Grosz as "one of Irigaray's staunchest defenders,"[21] he characterizes her defense of sexual difference as follows: everyone is born into one of two sexes and will always identify in some way with those two sexes. His concern is that "this echoes the incredibly damaging belief that trans people are not 'really' their lived gender."[22] If sexual difference requires denying the ability to move from one sex to the other, then this would imply all TIGNC people are really just members of either the male or female sex, and "this is a form of violence."[23] Johnston points out that there are many queer and feminist theorists who resist this, fighting for everyone's right to gender self-determination (Butler is named in his footnote 2). However, he still thinks it is worth confronting that some feminist theory is at odds with respecting the very possibility of gender self-determination.[24] Obviously, he has Irigaray and Grosz in mind.

According to Johnston, Irigaray and Grosz are just too ambiguous about what sexual difference actually is and are "unwilling" to describe exactly what is being differentiated.[25] They do not give concrete, positive definitions of the sexes. Still, on their account, Johnston says, the conceptual coherence of sexual difference rests solely on the asserted "irreducibility" of one sex to the other: the interval that cannot be crossed. While he applauds the application of this interval to relations between men and women because it stopgaps phallocentrism, he is concerned about how it divides cis- and noncispeople: "Irigarayan sexual difference is made coherent through the disavowal of TIGNC experience."[26] At the same time that he admits not understanding it—"How are we to understand sexual difference if the only thing we know about it is that it is the irreducible difference?"[27]—he claims that it is made coherent through the disavowal of TIGNC experience. This disavowal is the driving force of his argument against ontologizing sexual difference as irreducible difference. For Johnston, "irreducibility" does not provide satisfying answers to either the *epistemological* question (i.e., how do I know that I am a man or a woman?) *or* to the *ontological* question (i.e., what is the exact difference between men and women?). Interestingly, though, he explicitly refuses to answers these questions himself: "I am not attempting to offer an alternative epistemological or ontological account of how we adopt or embody a sex."[28] While acknowledging how sexual difference undoes the binary that phallocentrism posits between men and women, he ends up reifying another binary in his critique, between cis and TIGNC people, which relies on staging an opposition. He also binarizes ontology and epistemology. In fact, his argument requires upholding the binary between them since he rejects ontology and embraces epistemology, while avoiding providing an alternative way to think their relation. Johnston's rejection of ontology almost makes way for turning epistemology into *theology*.

Citing Weinstein's Grosz Paradox directly in "Irreducibility and (Trans) Sexual Difference," Oli Stephano reframes it as a question: "Sexual Difference: Generative Yet Fixed?" Stephano's article seeks to illuminate "a tension internal to Elizabeth Grosz's theory of the irreducibility of sexual difference."²⁹ While Grosz establishes sexual difference as an ontological force of differentiation, according to Stephano, she, like Irigaray, delimits the forms it can take as fixed and uncrossable. Transsexuality becomes a limit case in Grosz's ontology because it is where "generativity" narrows down to unchangeable dimorphic sexes in discrete bodies. Unlike Johnston, who completely rejects an ontology of sexual difference as transphobic, Stephano proposes a revision. To do this, he demonstrates Grosz's use of "irreducibility" in two distinct senses that appear to be at odds with each other:

> (1) as an insuperable ontological force and (2) as indelible morphological difference yoked to a given anatomical sex—come together to curious effect in Grosz's account (Footnote 2, The Grosz Paradox). For while Grosz affirms sexual difference as a generative ontological force of differentiation, she simultaneously insists that this generativity engenders only fixed and dimorphic categories of sex. Endorsing the Irigarayan definition of sexual difference... Grosz stakes a claim for the ultimate unchangeability of the body's sexed specificity, while insisting simultaneously that sexual difference itself has no fixed, static, or predetermined vectors of manifestation. She sees sexual difference as open to "potentially infinite" expressions, but argues that its intractability means that the sexually specific body will always be specified as male or female in accordance with its interpellation at birth.... Sex is in Grosz's view more properly understood as a simple biological given.³⁰

Stephano asks: How can Grosz affirm sexual difference as ontologically generative, while insisting on its fixed determination in individually sexed bodies? It seems Stephano hopes that by showing a contradiction between the two senses of "irreducibility," he can make a case for discarding the second sense, which is transphobic on his account, in order to replace it with something less transphobic, something more Butlerian. He asks rhetorically, "Isn't sex itself materialized through the productive imperatives of *regimes* of sexual difference, where it could be understood as a *discursively mediated and mediating system* by which bodies emerge as intelligibly sexed?" For him, Grosz's second sense of "irreducibility" contests this consideration, which he points out is "articulated most strongly by Judith Butler."³¹ Grosz, he adds, views trans identification as a "category mistake," whereby trans subjects attempt an impossible passage across an interval of

AN ONTO-ETHICS OF TRANSSEXUAL DIFFERENCE

sexual difference anchored by cissexual positions.[32] His essay, therefore, aims to offer an experimental negotiation of a definition of sexual difference that holds onto Grosz's first sense of irreducibility (ontologically generative) while replacing the second sense (fixed bodies) with something discursively shaped and mediated. For Stephano, this conceptual cherry-picking "yields preferable ethical implications" for trans embodiment.[33] Preferable to what though? What does it mean for ethics to be based on what is preferable? Are ethics about preference?

It almost seems that a choice *between* sexual difference and gender performativity is implied for some scholars. Those who resist Irigaray and Grosz's uptake of an Irigarayan sexual difference have called on Butler's gender performativity to serve as a complete replacement, as Johnston does, or partial replacement, as Stephano does. In *Elemental Difference and the Climate of the Body*, Emily Anne Parker proposes a "revised Irigarayan study" without sexual difference. She critiques what she takes to be the biocentrism and, following Salamon, the supposedly reductive genital dimorphism of Irigaray's philosophy vis-à-vis the binaristic two-sex model that Thomas Lacquer historicizes in the book *Making Sex*.[34] She reflects on how the invention of the concept of gender-as-malleable is what made it possible for someone like Butler to wonder whether the concept of "sex" is not also malleable. Parker argues that the trouble with the social constructionist concept of gender is that its emergence actually hinges on a binaristic contrast to the materiality of sex, even as gender has something of agency attached to it. Butler's concept of gender performativity is not entirely voluntaristic, Parker notes, but retains something of this flavor given its contrast with sex. Even though Butler ultimately rejects this contrast, and Parker notes that she does too, Parker still admits that her "own sympathies, too, are squarely on the side of gender, if the choice is between these two concepts."[35] As Parker concludes, "and so of course if the choice is between sex and gender, I give respect to the latter, what a person can appreciate about themselves, herself, himself."[36] Hence, the basis of Parker's rejection of Irigaray's account of sexual difference is that it is equivalent to the two-sex model, which she claims relies on a prediscursive materiality of bodies rather than what a person may appreciate about themselves, their lived sense of embodied identity. Self-determination is the more important choice, if a choice is to be made. But does prediscursive materiality necessarily imply a two-sex model? Can prediscursive materiality not be more than that effect?

To summate, proponents of gender performativity that reject sexual difference understand and define it as the reductive binary opposition between man and woman, or male and female. They subsequently dismiss the concept because, according to this definition, it is biologically or ontologically essentialist, and therefore transphobic. They motion to replace sexual difference with gender under the assumption that an ontology of sexual difference contests transsexuality, or trans being, while an epistemology of gender is more inclusive and trans-affirming. The logic at play here is that ontology itself is binaristic—reductive to male and female sexes—so we should reject the ontological and stick to the epistemological domain of gender. This, however, does *not* affirm trans being. It simply dismisses questions of being altogether. It does not invite the possibility of conceiving a different ontology, conducive to trans being, because it positions itself against the ontological. Even more crucially, "choosing" gender over sexual difference does not open a way for thinking the relation *between* the epistemological and the ontological because it perpetuates staging them in this opposition, where the ontological is necessarily transphobic and the epistemological is not. While an emphasis on gender or gender performativity, on the surface, may appear more trans-affirming, it does not produce an *ethics* that affirms transsexuality if it cannot conceive an *ontology* that affirms transsexuality, too, and conceptually bridge the two.

PRIMARY AND SECONDARY SEXUAL DIFFERENCE

Starting in the 1990s, an opposition between Grosz and Butler has been staged in Anglo-American feminism where Grosz has been staged as the primary defender and inheritor of Irigaray's sexual difference and Butler its main critic from a concern that it implies essentializing not only genital dimorphism but compulsory heterosexuality. The contrast between the two is instructive for defending Irigaray and Grosz against charges of transphobia. As we have seen, Butler and their defenders *start* from a subject, whose relation to the world is always already mediated by language, discourse, grammar, or the human mind more generally. Questions of ontology are already always epistemological because reality only exists vis-à-vis its mediation by the subject. Yet, as a counterpoint to this starting point, are we not living subjects because of a prediscursive reality that produced us, which we can only engage with discursively now as subjects who use discourse?

What about other species who are sexed but do not engage in discourse? Does the fact that we can only engage with reality discursively, as subjects, preclude that our sexed subjectivity itself is not predicated on a prediscursive reality? Grosz responds to the subjectivitism of Butler's account by thinking these questions, not to deny the incorporeality or ideality of the world but to consider how "it is the world itself that generates idea(l)s and indeed generates consciousness of many different kinds."[37] While Grosz would not deny that sexual difference is subject to cultural norms, her starting point is that sex ontologically precedes and exceeds its mediation by the subject and the subject's epistemological representations via discourse. She begins from an ontology that is sexuate, and of which individually sexed human subjects can be reconceived as one expression.

Following Grosz's explanation of Raymond Ruyer's primary and secondary consciousness in *The Incorporeal*, I propose reconceiving sexual difference through primary and secondary orders as a development of Grosz's view. Primary sexual difference would refer to the ontological sexual difference, the "sexuateness" of being itself, or the sexual difference that "the world itself generates," to use Grosz's language. This ontology exceeds but subtends each individual sexed being because it is out of which all such beings are produced. Secondary sexual difference, then, would refer to precisely those sexed individuations, human or otherwise, as various effects of primary sexual difference. Hence, human sexed subjects may construct epistemologies to describe their sexed being, but sexual difference itself is not limited to human instantiations or discourse. Those who conceive a philosophical "choice" between gender performativity and sexual difference, and dismiss sexual difference through the Grosz Paradox, operate in terms of a binary grammar, in terms of a choice between the epistemological and the ontological. However, reducing transsexuality to the epistemological forecloses considerations of trans *being*, in the literal sense that ontology is the philosophy of being itself. The relation of primary and secondary orders offers a way out of the Grosz Paradox where the two senses of sexual difference—a generative force and a fixed discretization—can now make sense by reconceiving the relation between the ontological and the epistemological as a continuity rather than a choice between one or the other. This opens a way of reconceiving sexual difference that is not transphobic and does not require resorting to gender performativity as an alternative.

Moreover, sexual difference, as an onto-ethics, reveals that such a "choice" is not entirely ours to make. We may modulate our sexedness from within the limits of our bodies, but we cannot master the ontological force of sexual difference entirely or simply deny its reality, since it remains the very condition of our existence. We exist, as sexed bodies, as an effect of sexual difference. All sexed beings live *with* the relation, live *as* the relation, between primary *ontological* sexual difference and the discursive knowledges that human sexed subjects, as secondary effects of this difference, produce to represent sexed being. From this framework, the Groszian Paradox between the "two senses" of the irreducibility of sexual difference are no longer really paradoxical or oppositional.

This way of thinking sexual difference by starting from the ontological as "primary" and arriving at the epistemological as "secondary" is also crucial for reconceiving "sex" beyond the male-female binary. In "At Least Two: The Tendencies of Sexual Difference," Rebecca Hill challenges the assumption that a prediscursive sexual difference refers to a two-sex model that essentializes male and female. She argues that various forms of human sexedness are each their own effect of the expression of the ontological force of sexual difference, although these generally tend in two directions. Following Grosz's project of linking Irigaray's sexual difference with Charles Darwin's sexual selection, Hill takes up Henri Bergson's concept of evolution in *Creative Evolution* as tendencies of differentiation, and proposes a Bergsonian approach to sexual difference. She argues that while the actualization of sexual difference is real, it is not universal law. Tendencies in the evolution of life are open-ended and do not preexist the bodies they produce. Hence, there is no proper form of man, woman, or intersex person.[38] This has important implications for feminist and queer theory's thinking sexual difference in human beings:

> At the level of virtual tendencies, both the female tendency and the male tendency can be defined by specific aspects that differ from one another without one tendency being seen as better than the other sexed tendency and without one tendency serving as the yardstick against which the other sex is defined. Here, the two of sexual difference are two different tendencies. They are not binaries—binary sexual difference is not based on a relation between two but on a logic of the privileged one and its negation, a violent hierarchy in which the male (A) possesses a cluster of valued

attributes such as activity and rationality and the female is seen as the opposite (Not A).[39]

Hill asserts here that sexual differentiation, as the actualizations of tendencies, qua Bergson, occurs not only at the *species* level but also at the level of *individuals*. Within individuals, "we can say that the female tendency is actualised in embodied women along with the male tendency in a de-emphasized state. And in men the male tendency is actualised along with the female tendency in a de-emphasized state. In some subjects, the actualised tendencies of sexual specificity are intermingled such that a determination of femaleness or maleness in that human being is reductive."[40] By Hill's Bergsonian account, we may be able to reconceive transsexuality *ontologically* as the active reemphasizing of tendencies by the individual that were initially deemphasized by the ontological force of sexual difference. Actualizing such tendencies vis-à-vis HRT, surgical intervention, voice training, exercise training style, and so on can lead to different configurations, or accentuations, of one's sexed tendencies. The Bergsonian idea of the sexes as actualized tendencies resonates with Vernon Rosario's definition of human sexes not as *binary* but as *bimodal*, "with two curves corresponding to two typical functional outcomes, male and female."[41] Hill affirms diverging actualizations of sexual difference and embraces the tremendous variety of articulations of female, male, and intersexuality within the human species *and within individuals*, as the capacity to modulate one's own sexed tendencies *is* virtually possible. This addresses the new materialist concern with the dynamism of materiality. At the same time, it makes space for the consideration that discourse and culture more broadly are involved in the actualizations of human beings already encultured. In short, we are a product of sexual difference but also that through which sexual difference continues to develop. This mediating of the cultural and natural in the expression of sexuate bodies points back to thinking sexual difference in its own grammar.

CODA: TRANSSEXUALITY AS A NIETZSCHEAN, OR STOIC ONTO-ETHICS

In *The Gay Science*, Nietzsche exclaims that philosophy *is* the art of transfiguration. "We philosophers," he says, "are not thinking frogs, nor registering mechanisms with their innards removed. Constantly, we have to give birth to our thoughts out of our pain and, like mothers, endow them with all we have of blood."[42] Life, for Nietzsche, is the means for constantly transforming all that we are: "We simply can do no other!" It is only great pain, he insists, that is our ultimate liberator. Pain "compels us philosophers to descend into our ultimate depths." Although he doubts that such pain makes us "better," he contends that it makes us more "profound." From pain, we emerge *as* philosophers, we ask questions differently: deeper, further, more intensely than before. Life itself, Nietzsche concludes, becomes a question, a philosophical *problem*.[43] In the spirit of Nietzsche, then, I call myself a transsexual philosopher.

Also in the spirit of Nietzsche, I put forth that there is no denying sexual difference as a philosophical problem. Here, I am not referring to the problem of "essentialism" or "transphobia," which must be replaced with gender or gender performativity. Rather, sexual difference is a philosophical problem in the sense that it calls for an ethics, or a "how to live," rather than a "how to resolve." For transsexuals, but really for everyone, it requires inventing new techniques for living and relating to oneself and others. All sexed subjects live with the problem of sexual difference whether they identify as transsexual or not. It is a problem in the way that *death* is a problem, or *gravity* is a problem. There is no "solution." We live our lives in relation to it. As devout readers of Nietzsche, both Irigaray and Grosz would likely agree that we live with the problem of sexual difference even when we fail to acknowledge, or consciously reckon with, it.

As a problem, sexual difference does not prohibit our will to identify in whatever way we choose. Following Grosz, if onto-ethics is about making the most of one's situation—affirming one's fate—then it is an ongoing practice, a way of living one's life, ethically, by living it well and in relation to the ontological, to a reality that exceeds the individual subject's self-determination or will but simultaneously responds to some of its provocations. In this way, Grosz's onto-ethics is as Stoic as it is Nietzschean:

> The Stoics created a beautiful conception of ethics as a kind of culmination of existence rather than a set of rules or principles by which to regulate life from the outside. Ethics, for them, is the capacity to live up to one's impersonal fate, to bear it, to live it. In this sense, it is immanent in life itself, not just human life, but in all forms of life. Some people, perhaps a majority, have

considered this the realm of religious thought; but for the Stoics, this is not an order separate from the world for it is inherent to it. I wanted to create a perhaps paradoxical non-normative ethics, an ethics unrelated to (Kantian) judgment, one related to the ways in which one directs one's life. The incorporeal is thus a name for the direction immanent in our actions, the direction to the future in which we may overcome ourselves, become more than ourselves.[44]

An onto-ethics of sexual difference acknowledges and respects that sexed bodies have limits to the ranges within which we can determine our own sexed trajectories, or tendencies. We affirm sexual difference ontologically, sometimes even in spite of ourselves, whenever we, as transsexuals, engage in practices of self-transformation that confront the limits sexual difference imposes on our being by pushing back, struggling against, striving to overcome. Whether it is weekly testosterone injections, practicing post-vaginoplasty dilation, or voice lessons, these rituals or practices of care and self-constitution are part of living *with* the problem of sexual difference, which all sexed subjects do differently. Simultaneously, this onto-ethics acknowledges and respects that there *are* trajectories or tendencies that have ranges and that sex cannot be completely or statically determined in advance or reductively in accordance with a binaristic two-sex model. Even though our sexually specific, irreducible bodies can never be completely undone and remade according to our subjective wills, trajectories can diverge in unexpected ways if we will them to. Sexual difference, in this way, is more of an anchor than a cage—a creative constraint that our ways of living begin from, but of course, can differ, be novel or experimental, as many queer, trans, and nonbinary modes of being demonstrate.

Recuperating an affirmative way of thinking transsexuality in relation to a Stoic ontology or onto-ethics of sexual difference through the work of Irigaray and Grosz is possible when sexual difference is dehiscenced from an underlying binary grammar. And it is here that we return to Irigaray's words on the grammar of Nietzsche's dead "God of men." In a later passage, she claims creation must go beyond the circularity of discourse to form a line that goes "from the humblest detail of everyday life to the 'grandest,' of which *we would be* the mediators and bridges."[45] Rather than mourning the dead God of Nietzsche, Irigaray calls for us to conjure God up "among us, within us, as resurrection and transfiguration of blood, of flesh, through a language and an ethics that is ours."[46] An onto-ethics of sexual difference is such a conjuring. It is more than just a subject's gender identity, or another epistemological discourse of transsexuality. Far from being transphobic, it reorients transsexuality from the small place of gendered pronouns *within* grammar to a transfiguration of blood and flesh in a language and ethics that are ours. If Nietzsche himself wasn't transsexual, conceiving transsexuality as a way of life that reckons with and confronts the problem of sexed being is as Nietzschean or Stoic as ethics gets; theirs is an onto-ethics of transsexual difference.

BIBLIOGRAPHY

Bell, Vikki. "An Interview with Elizabeth Grosz: 'The Incorporeal.'" *Theory, Culture and Society* 34, nos. 7–8 (2017): 237–243.

Butler, Judith. *Gender Trouble: Feminism and the Subversion of Identity*. New York: Routledge, 1999.

Coleman, Athena. "Tarrying with the Sexual: Toward a Morphological Ontology of Trans Subjectivity." In *Horizons of Difference: Rethinking Space, Place, and Identity with Irigaray*, edited by Ruthanne Crapo Kim, Yvette Russell, and Brenda Sharp, 17–39. Albany: SUNY Press, 2022.

Grosz, Elizabeth. *Becoming Undone: Darwinian Reflections on Life, Politics, and Art*. Durham, NC: Duke University Press, 2011.

———. *The Incorporeal: Ontology, Ethics, and the Limits of Materialism*. New York: Columbia University Press, 2017.

———. *Volatile Bodies: Toward a Corporeal Feminism*. Bloomington: Indiana University Press, 1994.

Hill, Rebecca. "At Least Two: The Tendencies of Sexual Difference." *Australian Feminist Law Journal* 43, no. 1 (2017): 25–40.

Hird, Myra J. "Re(pro)ducing Sexual Difference." *Parallax* 8, no. 4 (2002): 94–107.

Johnston, Tim R. "Questioning the Threshold of Sexual Difference: Irigarayan Ontology and Transgender, Intersex, and Gender-Nonconforming Being." *GLQ: A Journal of Lesbian and Gay Studies* 21, no. 4 (2015): 617–633.

Jones, Rachel. *Irigaray: Towards a Sexuate Philosophy*. Cambridge: Polity, 2011.

Nietzsche, Friedrich Wilhelm. *The Gay Science: With a Prelude in Rhymes and an Appendix of Songs*. Translated by Walter Kaufmann. New York: Random House, 1974.

Parisi, Luciana. "Event and Evolution." *Southern Journal of Philosophy* 48, no. 1 (2010): 147–164.

Parker, Emily Anne. *Elemental Difference and the Climate of the Body*. New York: Oxford University Press, 2021.

Poe, Danielle. "Can Luce Irigaray's Notion of Sexual Difference Be Applied to Transsexual and Transgender Narratives?" In *Thinking with Irigaray*, edited by Mary C. Rawlinson, Sabrina L. Hom, and Serene J. Khader, 111–128. Albany: SUNY Press, 2011.

Puar, Jasbir K. "Bodies with New Organs: Becoming Trans, Becoming Disabled." *Social Text* 33, no. 3 (2015): 45–73.

Salamon, Gayle. *Assuming a Body: Transgender and Rhetorics of Materiality*. New York: Columbia University Press, 2010.
Stephano, Oli. "Irreducibility and (Trans) Sexual Difference." *Hypatia* 34, no. 1 (2019): 141–154.
Weinstein, Jami. "A Requiem to Sexual Difference: A Response to Luciana Parisi's 'Event and Evolution.'" *Southern Journal of Philosophy* 48, no. 1 (2010): 165–187.
Wolfe, Esther. "Bodies of Philosophy: An Interview with Elizabeth Grosz." *Stance: An International Undergraduate Philosophy Journal* 7, no. 1 (2014): 115–126.

NOTES

1. Elizabeth Grosz, *The Incorporeal: Ontology, Ethics, and the Limits of Materialism* (New York: Columbia University Press, 2017), 48.
2. Rachel Jones, *Irigaray: Toward a Sexuate Philosophy* (Cambridge: Polity, 2011), 9.
3. Judith Butler, *Gender Trouble* (New York: Routledge, 1999), xiv.
4. Butler, xv.
5. Butler, 187.
6. This clarification of "sex" vis-à-vis social constructivism is owed to James Sares.
7. Myra J. Hird, "Re(pro)ducing Sexual Difference," *Parallax* 8, no. 4 (2002): 94.
8. Jami Weinstein, "A Requiem to Sexual Difference," *Southern Journal of Philosophy* 48 (2010): 177. "My response is that even if we want to pronounce the death of sexual difference so figured by Irigarayan-inspired feminist theorists as an enduring form, sexual difference ontology nonetheless deserves a proper eulogy before laying it to its final resting place in the genetic virtuality of our conceptual history."
9. Irigaray, ILTY, 61–62.
10. See Danielle Poe, "Can Luce Irigaray's Notion of Sexual Difference Be Applied to Transsexual and Transgender Narratives?," in *Thinking with Irigaray*, ed. Mary Rawlinson, Sabrina Hom, and Serene Khader (Albany: SUNY Press, 2011), 111–128; Athena Coleman, "Tarrying with the Sexual: Toward a Morphological Ontology of Trans Subjectivity," in *Horizons of Difference: Rethinking Space, Place, and Identity with Irigaray*, ed. Ruthanne Crapo Kim, Yvette Russell, and Brenda Sharp (Albany: SUNY Press, 2021), 17–39.
11. Elizabeth Grosz, *Volatile Bodies: Towards a Corporeal Feminism* (Bloomington: Indiana University Press, 1994), 207–208.
12. Esther Wolfe, "Bodies of Philosophy: An Interview with Elizabeth Grosz," *Stance: An International Undergraduate Philosophy Journal* 7, no. 1 (2014): 120. "I'm not denying there's a social and psychical dimension, but I'm also not denying that there's a biological dimension to this. I have no problem with the surgical transformation of your body or the chemical transformation of your body. I've no problem at all with it. But I think it's a category mistake to believe that by transforming the body you have you acquire the body of the opposite sex. . . . Look, I think that what identifications are is an absolutely interesting and open possibility. If we identify as women, if we identify as men, if we identify as neither, that's a very interesting question of the art of how to live one's life. But, honestly—I'll say it again, and I'll get in trouble again—I think many people are making a category

mistake when they think that by altering their body chemically or surgically they're getting the body of another sex."
13. According to Irigaray, sex is not restricted to genitals. In JTN, 53: "The whole of my body is sexuate. My sexuality isn't restricted to my sex and to the sexual act."
14. Wolfe, *Bodies*, 120.
15. Elizabeth Grosz, *Becoming Undone: Darwinian Reflections on Life, Politics, and Art* (Durham: Duke University Press, 2011), 109.
16. Rebecca Hill, "At Least Two: The Tendencies of Sexual Difference," *Australian Feminist Law Journal* 43, no. 1 (2017): 25–40.
17. Jasbir K. Puar, "Bodies with New Organs: Becoming Trans, Becoming Disabled," *Social Text* 124, vol. 33, no. 3 (2015): 45–73.
18. Weinstein, "A Requiem to Sexual Difference," 48.
19. Gayle Salamon, *Assuming a Body: Transgender and Rhetorics of Materiality* (New York: Columbia University Press, 2010), 35.
20. Tim Johnston, "Questioning the Threshold of Sexual Difference: Irigarayan Ontology and Transgender, Intersex, and Gender-Nonconforming Being," *GLQ: A Journal of Lesbian and Gay Studies* 21, no. 4 (2015): 618.
21. Johnston, 626.
22. Johnston, 627.
23. Johnston, 618.
24. Johnston, 619.
25. Johnston, 627.
26. Johnston, 629.
27. Johnston, 628.
28. Johnston, 628.
29. Oli Stephano, "Irreducibility and (Trans) Sexual Difference," *Hypatia* 34, no. 1 (2019): 141.
30. Stephano, 142.
31. Stephano, 143.
32. Stephano, 143.
33. Stephano, 143.
34. Emily Anne Parker, *Elemental Difference and the Climate of the Body* (New York: Oxford University Press, 2021), 66–68.
35. Parker, 62.
36. Parker, 62–63.
37. Grosz, *The Incorporeal*, 210.
38. Hill, "At Least Two," 27.
39. Hill, 39.
40. Hill, 39.
41. Vernon Rosario quoted in Hill, "At Least Two," 40.
42. Friedrich Nietzsche, *The Gay Science: With a Prelude in Rhymes and an Appendix of Songs*, trans. Walter Kaufmann (New York: Random House, 1974), 35–36.
43. Nietzsche, 35–36.
44. Vikki Bell, "An Interview with Elizabeth Grosz: 'The Incorporeal,'" *Theory, Culture and Society* 34, nos. 7–8 (2017): 242–243.
45. Irigaray, ESD, 129.
46. Irigaray, 129.

PART IV
Placing Sexual Difference

Chapter Twelve

SEXUATE DIFFERENCE IN THE BLACK ATLANTIC

Reading Irigaray with Hartman

RACHEL JONES

In Saidiya Hartman's unflinching reckoning with the afterlives of slavery, she notes that "it is only when you *lose your mother* that she becomes a myth."[1] Hartman's insight echoes Irigaray's analysis of the symbolic matricide that subtends Western thought and culture and that leads to the myth of the mother as an originary plenitude, feeding phallic phantasies of threatening engulfment or lost wholeness. Just as Fanon reinscribes Hegel's lordship and bondage dialectic in the material existence of white master and Black slave,[2] so Hartman's work reinscribes Irigaray's symbolic matricide in the flesh:[3] in the violent appropriation and disfiguring of maternal generative power that fed the transatlantic slave trade.

Lose Your Mother resists the temptation to attempt to heal the resulting genealogical rupture and "natal alienation"[4] by returning to Africa as to a motherland that could restore a once whole identity. Instead, Hartman claims a legacy rooted in the break constituted by the slave hold and in the diasporic commons "created by fugitives and rebels," by "the ongoing struggle to escape, stand down, and defeat slavery in all of its myriad forms." The book concludes with "the dream of an elsewhere, with all its promises and dangers, where the stateless might, at last, thrive."[5] Similarly, Hartman's subsequent work, *Wayward Lives*, begins and ends with "dreams of the otherwise," of "what has yet to come into view . . . the time and place better than here; a glimpse of the earth not owned by anyone." Hartman suggests that this "otherwise" and "elsewhere" not only is a "resolute, stubborn desire" but surges up *within* the confines of captivity, in the "ceaseless practice of black radicalism and refusal"[6] and, more specifically, in the fugitive resistance of Black women and girls who find ways of living, loving, and making kin that refuse the grip of an anti-Black world.

Like the labors of Black women that Hartman details in "The Belly of the World," the "experiments with freedom"[7] explored in *Wayward Lives* fall "outside of the heroic account of the black worker and the general strike" and remain "marginal or neglected in the narratives of black insurgency, resistance, and refusal."[8] Noting that the Greek roots of "chorus" (*khoros*) refer to *dancing "within an enclosure*,"[9] Hartman attends to the chorus of Black women whose lives simultaneously endure and defy capture, both by enslavement and in the diasporic afterlives of slavery, and whose significance as "social visionaries" and political revolutionaries "has not only been overlooked, but is nearly unimaginable."[10] If the mastery of the White gaze as it emerged in the transatlantic world was dependent on Blackness as a mode of nonbeing produced in the slave hold,[11] Hartman shows how this racializing logic both captures and loses its grip in the lives of Black women and girls. Slipping away while apparently held in place, "she eludes the law and transforms the terms of the possible."[12]

Hartman's invocation of an "elsewhere" and "otherwise" that emerges in the midst of a saturating anti-Blackness parallels the *"elsewhere of 'matter'"* that Irigaray allies with the repressed feminine-female-maternal ground that subtends a totalizing phallogocentrism while nonetheless refusing to be fully captured by its terms.[13] This resistant remainder retains its potential to erupt *"as divergencies*, otherwise and elsewhere than ... expected," in ways that "deconstruct the logical grid" of the subject, troubling the orderly reproduction of the Law of the Father and "driv[ing] him out of his mind."[14] As Emanuela Bianchi suggests in her elaboration of this "aleatory" elsewhere of matter (both inspired by and generatively unfaithful to Irigaray), its interruptive force lends itself to an antipatriarchal feminist politics even as it refuses identification with "a long-buried site of essential feminine sexual difference" (the lost mother).[15] On Bianchi's approach, Irigaray's "elsewhere" is allied with a "conception of matter as inappropriable and excessive—not merely a placeholder for negation or privation but as *the very possibility of otherwiseness*."[16] Bianchi thereby draws out a point that is critical to both Irigaray's and Hartman's work: that which is nothing in the master's eyes, registering as merely an absence of being or a disorderly lack of form, refuses containment by such operations of negation and "cannot be reduced to transgression or to nothing at all,"[17] harboring instead possibilities for articulating human being otherwise.

Despite such evocative resonances, this parallel between Irigaray's "elsewhere of matter" and Hartman's "dream of an elsewhere" is too swiftly drawn. In her invocation of the "wayward lives" of young Black women "who tirelessly imagined other ways to live and never failed to consider how the world might be otherwise,"[18] Hartman reminds us that, in the context of the racializing logic that structures the transatlantic world, anti-Black racism overcodes the dereliction of sexual difference, violently rearticulating the relations between human-mat(t)er-flesh. In particular, the making-malleable of female flesh that Irigaray diagnoses as symptomatic of the Western philosophical tradition is redistributed along racial lines, while her diagnosis of symbolic matricide needs to be rethought in relation to the "Mother-dispossessed [who] defined what it meant to be a slave."[19] Thus, before we can disinter the aspects of Irigaray's thinking that might be allied with the modes of fugitive resistance to which Hartman attends, we need to allow an Irigarayan analysis of sexual difference to be overwritten by the history and afterlives of the transatlantic slave trade and transposed through the critical lens of race. Inspired in part by Sabrina Hom's juxtapositional reading of Irigaray and Cherríe Morega, the first two sections of this chapter will attempt such a transposition, exploring how sexual difference is "marked and transformed through racialization"[20] in the context of the Black Atlantic, so as to return in the third section to the possibilities for a generative alliance between Irigaray's and Hartman's work.

SEXUATE DIFFERENCE AND ANTI-BLACKNESS IN THE TRANSATLANTIC WORLD

As others have explored,[21] issues of race and racialization can themselves be seen as a constitutive absence in Irigaray's work, in ways that occlude the colonial context of her project and displace the struggles of women of color, as Françoise Vergès argues is typical of late twentieth-century French feminism.[22] To the extent that the effects of anti-Black racism on the dereliction of sexual difference remain un(re)marked, sexual difference too remains "a category of Whiteness"[23] that repeats the colonizing logic of Sameness that Irigaray so astutely exposes. My claim here is not that there is anything inherently "white" about sexuate difference,[24] nor am I invoking Whiteness as an empirical given, but as a historically emergent category with ontological force, insofar as it constitutes Western modernity by redistributing relations of being and nonbeing according to what Fanon calls the "epidermal racial schema."[25] If the White gaze sees Blackness as absence and lack—of rationality, civilization, development, humanity—Whiteness becomes the unseen and "seemingly unraced" mark of the human.[26] By anchoring what Hortense Spillers calls "the politics of melanin" that shapes the transatlantic world,[27] the White/Black couplet acts as a reorganizing "cut" making possible a plethora of new racial schemas that overcode existing social structures and obscure alternative social imaginaries.[28]

In the context of philosophy, as Charles Mills notes, this reschematization results in a double disappearance: the racial markers of Whiteness "vanish into the apparent universality of the colorless normative," while the lived experience of Black folks is absented from the canonical texts of the modern Western tradition in ways that demand a critical "taxonomy" of "silences and invisibility."[29] If an anti-Black, racializing logic overcodes and reschematizes the forgetting of sexual difference in Western colonial modernity, then a lack of attention to its disfiguring force would perpetuate an invisibly structuring Whiteness, in ways that are suggested by both Mills's analysis and Irigaray's own unsurpassed methodology of reading for constitutive silences. My concern is thus less with what *is* said about race in Irigaray's texts and more with what is *not* said or attended to: with a metaphorics of blackness that is invoked without critical reflection on its racialized connotations;[30] or a call to *parler femme* that retains a universality apparently unmarked by race;[31] or the positioning of sexual difference as "one of the major philosophical issues, if not the issue, of our age" that critiques the sexual indifference of the West without sufficiently thematizing its colonial, racializing history, which problematizes this "*our*" from the start.[32]

As Tina Chanter suggests, it is Irigaray's own insistence on "thinking difference without relapsing into another version of the same"[33] that calls on us to grapple with the difference that race and colonialism make to the question of sexuate difference and the ways in which it is asked. This chapter is intended as a contribution to that collective "grappling," focusing in particular on the difference that anti-Blackness makes to the question of sexual difference in the transatlantic world. This, of course, is by no means the only axis along which the intersections of race and sexual difference can be explored, given the manifold racial geographies and diverse diasporas that span Atlantic, Pacific, and Indian Ocean worlds, and that mean that women of color (including within the Americas) occupy multiple nonidentical positionings. Vergès's work is particularly pertinent here. Given her critique of French feminists' neglect of the entanglements of race and (post) colonialism, and her focus on the exploitation of "the wombs of women" by racial capitalism, it is Vergès's analysis of the reproductive injustice perpetrated against women of color in Reunion Island that perhaps most urgently invites critical juxtaposition with Irigaray's work.[34] Nonetheless, as my aim here is to find a way to approach the potentially generative resonances between Irigaray and Hartman, my focus will be on transposing Irigaray's insights via the Black Atlantic. To do so, I will foreground the insights of a range of work, predominantly by Black feminist thinkers, that situates Black women "at the crux of unprecedented individual and systemic violence" while at the same time, as Jennifer Morgan insists, refusing their reduction to mere "indexes of suffering."[35] Together, these thinkers provide a lexicon for the disfigurement of gender and kinship in the transatlantic world while making captive maternity central to a resistant Black radicalism.[36]

Thus transposed, I will suggest, Irigaray's work provides resources with which to amplify the affirmation of Black maternity as a site of resistance in ways that avoid reinscribing heteropatriarchal, colonizing myths of the mother. That Irigaray's texts lend themselves to such transposition is both indicative of their generativity and symptomatic of the structuring absence I wish to interrogate, as in her incisive analysis of woman as an object of exchange that never quite confronts the way that some women were bought and sold on the basis of the color of their skin. Reading Irigaray in a transatlantic context asks us to consider the asymmetries of "reproductive unfreedom"[37] between those who, as Hazel Carby notes, gave birth to heirs of property and enslaved Black mothers whose children inherited their status *as* property,[38] in the paradox that Morgan names "reproducible kinlessness."[39] At the same time, rather than simply voiding Irigaray's project, transposing it via Black feminist thought serves to clarify and intensify the significance of her insistence on sexuate difference as *ontological* difference. The dereliction of sexual difference and birth that, on Irigaray's analysis, was *already* constitutive of the Western tradition, prior to the invention of race, preconditions their utter disfigurement in the racialized ontology of the transatlantic world, where, as Spillers notes, captive bodies are turned into flesh such that "we lose at least *gender* difference *in the outcome*," and as Christina Sharpe observes, "the birth canal [is turned] into another domestic Middle Passage with Black mothers ... still ushering their children into their condition; their non/status, their non/being-ness."[40] Thus we might ask: What might Irigaray's reclaiming of the ontological significance of sexuate difference and birth have to offer, when reinscribed in the Black Atlantic? How might her retrieval of the insurgent and (I will suggest) decidedly queer spatio-temporalities of gestation amplify Hartman's endeavors to counter the natal dispossession of slavery *without* reinstating a myth of the mother?

My suggestion is that three aspects of Irigaray's project are particularly significant when transposed into this context: (1) The insight that the modern western categories of sex/gender constitute a *forgetting* of sexual difference—though as we will see, this requires recalling the ways in which sex/gender are also produced through captive Black flesh. (2) Irigaray's insistence on sexuate difference as ontological difference, that is, as that mode of differing on which human beings depend for their *coming-to-be*;[41] though again, the full import of this insight emerges only when the ontological (or, as Calvin Warren more aptly puts it, onticidal) significance of the invention of Blackness is restored to the question of sexual difference.[42] And (3) the figure of a "placental economy" that harbors resources for a relational ontology that resists and displaces the colonizing, racializing logic of the "self-same of Western man."[43] Thus transposed, my wager is that Irigaray's philosophical lexicon might be more fully allied with the "otherwise" and "elsewhere" that Hartman locates in the wayward lives of Black women and girls, providing us with figures for the relational ontology that materializes in (and as) their gestures of fugitive resistance and radical care. At the same time, I will suggest, reading Irigaray in the context of the Black Atlantic aids the recovery of that which is most generatively wayward in her thinking, refusing both the master's fetishization of Sameness and the insistence on *two* (sexes) that reinserts itself in her own work.

According to the slave code formalized in 1662 in Virginia, the status of being free or enslaved follows "according to the condition of the mother—*Partus Sequitur Ventrem*."[44] When read together, via a juxtaposition that allows their differences to make themselves felt, Hartman and Irigaray call on us to pause with this thought and ask, with Spillers,[45] "what *is* the 'condition' of the mother?" *while also* making it clear that there can be no single answer. The difference that the invention of race makes to sexual difference means that the condition of the mother is not one, in ways that undo and disperse the universality implicit in the question. Likewise, if Irigaray, like Spillers (and Hartman), is "less interested in joining the ranks of gendered femaleness than gaining the *insurgent* ground as female social subject,"[46] the route to that insurgent subject position cannot be universal, given the asymmetries of racialized (un)gendering. Thus we might ask not what is *the* condition of *the* mother, but how might Irigaray's figure of a "placental economy" be reinflected not to "justify" but to "amplify"[47] Hartman's work on captive Black maternity and the ways in which, under these conditions, gestational relations not only are the site of systemic violence but also manifest resistance, both to the forgetting of sexuate difference and to captivity and enclosure within an anti-Black world.

SEX/GENDER AS THE RACIALIZED FORGETTING OF SEXUATE DIFFERENCE

Reading Irigaray with Hartman and other Black feminist thinkers allows the question of sexual difference to be resituated in relation to the political ontology of race in the transatlantic world. While intended to avoid a disavowal of racial difference, this interpretative gesture nonetheless risks reinforcing a racial discourse centered in the United States that, as Tiffany Lethabo King notes, "tends to be organized by a White-Black paradigmatic frame that often erases Indigenous peoples."[48] To counter this while decentering settler colonial epistemes, King entwines Black diasporic studies and Indigenous thought. Her work both confronts the ways in which the anti-Black histories and presents of the Americas (including the land on which I currently work and write) are inextricably bound up with the genocidal violence of settler colonialism and shows how Black and Indigenous resistance (past and present, singularly and together) generates possibilities for "articulating world-altering mode[s] of existence."[49] As King notes, a helpful voice in this context is Sylvia Wynter, whose work provides "a crucial pivot point" enabling "the emergence of a shared critique . . . between Black and Native Studies."[50] For this reason, Wynter's work is also a helpful starting point for reading Irigaray in a transatlantic context. While this chapter insufficiently counters the erasure of which King writes, Wynter's analysis of the "overrepresentation of Man"[51] allows Irigaray's critique of "the self-same of Western man" to be transposed in ways that at least register the devastating entanglement of anti-Black racism and settler colonial violence against Indigenous peoples in the establishment of the transatlantic world.

On Wynter's account, a specific sociogenic type—the white, European, heterosexual, middle-class, able-bodied male—becomes conflated with the human per se, "*as if* it were the universal of the human species."[52] This "cultural-relative" conception emerges in the form of Man1 around the sixteenth century as the image of "a rational being and a political subject." The peoples that European explorers categorized as "*indios/indias*" and "*negros/negras*" are Man1's (still human) "Others" because they are deemed irrational and uncivilized.[53] It is only with the emergence of the "scientific" concept of race in the eighteenth and nineteenth centuries, Wynter argues, and its inscription into a Darwinian register of evolved/unevolved, selected/dysselected, that Blackness becomes the mark of the "not *quite* human," the "*subhuman*,"[54] and the native becomes Other *because* of their nonwhiteness, captured by the totalizing effects of the color line and pulled in to the "production and nullification" of Black(ened) (non)being.[55] Henceforth, Man2 defines himself not against "a negative degree of rationality," but "a negative degree of being human,"[56] produced by "the epidermal racial schema" but represented as biological fact. Race transforms what European colonizers had previously seen as convertible inadequacies into supposedly ineliminable variations at the level of the species, and makes skin color the mark of racial variation such that Whiteness becomes the "seemingly unraced" sign of the human.

Wynter shows that what Irigaray's analysis of the logic of the Same misses is the *non-homogeneity* of the Other that results from racialization. If "woman" in her sexuate specificity is consigned to nothingness and non-being, as Irigaray suggests,[57] within the racializing logic of colonial modernity, Whiteness still *confers* being and *makes human*. This means that, even as the sexuate specificity of white women is foreclosed, and their positioning across multiple axes including sexuality, class, dis/ability, and age renders them open to objectification and exploitation, their Whiteness nonetheless gives them a provisional foothold—variable, precarious, and always erasable—on the side of the human. As Lugones notes, in the "modern colonial gender system," gender and race are co-constitutive such that "race [is] gendered and gender [is] raced in particularly differential ways for Europeans/'whites' and colonized/'non-white' peoples."[58] The ideals of (bourgeois, patriarchal) womanhood aligned with Whiteness are defined against the "unfeminine" strength, "excessive" sexuality, and supposed "animality" of women of color.[59] In the context of the transatlantic slave trade, as Spillers suggests, gender becomes irrelevant to bodies reduced to "captive flesh" and "taken into 'account' [only] as *quantities*."[60] Yet it was also the case, as Hartman observes, that Black women "defined the norms of gender and the meaning of womanhood" via their very exclusion from its terms.[61] Thus Wynter notes, "at the beginning of the modern world, the only *women* were white and Western."[62]

The point here is not of course that white, bourgeois women were not also oppressed by patriarchal norms, but that the terms of both their gendered oppression and their degree of racial privilege were predicated on the racial-sexual-gendered oppression of women of color. In the Black Atlantic, it is not an unraced "woman" who is consigned to nonbeing and social death but Black women and girls, even as they found ways to reinvent the very terms of womanhood and sustain "a practice of possibility" that refused disposability and enclosure.[63] As Wynter suggests, the racialized redistribution of gendered humanity in the transatlantic world unsettles Irigaray's quasi-universal figure of a repressed feminine-female-maternal ground via the "doubly silenced 'ground' "[64] of those oppressed along the co-constituting axes of both gender and race and rendered (as Hartman puts it, riffing on Wynter) "neither subject nor object, but a mute silenced thing."[65] It is this doubled silencing (whose refusal) we might hear in Sojourner Truth's "Ain't I a Woman?" and its implication of an incompossible "no" (in the eyes of the master—and the mistress who inherited enslaved people as property) and "yes" (as a reclaiming of the category "woman" that reopens its possible meanings). In Truth's words, as Haraway puts it, "the identity of 'woman' is both claimed and deconstructed simultaneously."[66]

In parallel fashion, Wynter argues that in its constitutive exclusion, this "doubly-silenced 'ground'" of racialized (un)gendering both is the condition of "our present governing system of meaning, or theory/ontology" *and* remains outside its terms, sustaining possibilities for "being/feeling/knowing" otherwise.[67] Building on Wynter, Zakiyyah Iman Jackson emphasizes that "The black *mater*(nal), as *mater*, as matter . . . gestures toward the foreclosed, enabling condition of the grammar of the Human" *and* harbors the potential to disrupt and reinvent this grammar.[68] In noting that "the term *sexual difference* evokes *racial difference*, even as it symptomatically represses the conditioning function of the 'ontological absence' to which Wynter refers,"[69] Jackson's work provides an alternative entry point to Irigaray's project. Following Wynter and Jackson, and in the specific context of the Black Atlantic, we might reread the disclosure of the forgetting of sexual difference as itself covering over a forgetting of "the black *mater*(nal)" as long as this disclosure does not attend to the redistribution of humanity along the axis of race. Irigaray's own method of reading for constitutive absences—the "white spaces [*blancs*] that subtend the scene's structuration"[70]—might thus be folded back on itself to attend to the ways in which sexual difference theorizing can itself replicate an "unmarked" Whiteness.

To amplify the silenced ground of the Black(ened) *mater*(nal), we might recall, with Petra Kuppers and C. Riley Snorton,[71] the twelve or more enslaved Black women sent to physician James Sims in Montgomery, Alabama, in the 1840s, who were subjected to the extensive medical experiments that led to Sims's development of the modern speculum. Only three are named in Sims's autobiography—Betsey, Lucy, and Anarcha—but their bodies are the absented material condition for one of the organizing figures of Irigaray's work. As Snorton shows, the Blackening that "ungendered" enslaved women also made them available as malleable flesh for experiments that helped to constitute both the field of gynecology and its object, the female sex, understood through the already racialized lens of modern biology. It is this anatomical-reproductive figure of "the female sex" that will operate as the supposed ground of the gendered category of "woman," even as this social designation is withheld from those who were "a condition of possibility for the science and symbolics of modern sex" but whose "nonreproductive, inverted, unfeminine" flesh was an index of their supposedly subhuman status.[72] If, as Spillers suggests, "the entire captive

SEXUATE DIFFERENCE IN THE BLACK ATLANTIC

community becomes a living laboratory,"[73] Snorton's unflinching attentiveness to Betsey, Lucy, and Anarcha shows how the Black(ened) maternal served as the silenced ground and material condition "for mediating and remaking sex and gender as matters of human categorization" and "producing a field of sex/gender knowledge."[74]

It is here that it seems crucial to insist on Irigaray's concept of sexuate difference *as distinct from either (biological) sex or (socially constructed) gender*. If captive Black flesh becomes the experimental site where the sex/gender distinction[75] solidifies, in those "sexually marked as female" but judged to be lacking the proper "characteristics of femininity,"[76] this wrong cannot be redressed by (re)humanizing Black bodies via a set of gender norms that are constitutively anti-Black. Rather, it is the whole sex/gender schema that is the problem, insofar as it is symptomatic of *both* anti-Blackness *and* the forgetting of sexual difference. As Irigaray suggests, this forgetting is enacted not only by the specular conceptualization of sex and gender within a phallocentric system, but also by the hylomorphic relation that the sex/gender distinction perpetuates between (biological) matter and the (cultural) forms that give it meaning; equally, as Snorton and Spillers suggest, this distinction both enabled and was supported by the positing of Black female flesh that was deemed not just analytically but materially and ontologically separable from gender's humanizing effects. As Hartman notes, "The failure to comply with or achieve gender norms would define black life; and this 'ungendering' inevitably marked black women (and men) as less than human," while simultaneously allowing for the capture of ungendered-but-still-sexed female flesh as "an instrument for social and physical reproduction."[77] Thus Hartman confronts the danger of living in "the lexical gap between black female and woman"—and gives voice to those who, rather than seeking entry into the gendered "grammar of the human," ventured the refusal of its categories as openings toward "a radically different scheme of being."[78]

It is to amplify this opening that I wish to emphasize what I take to be a key implication of Irigaray's work, namely, that insofar as it analytically separates biologically "given" bodies from their socially ascribed meanings, the sex/gender distinction constitutes a *forgetting* of sexuate difference as an ontological difference that is a condition of our being in the world. This forgetting is not a falsification: sexuate difference is not an object or entity that can be mis-represented, that is, we are not in the realm of truth as correctness here.⁷⁹ Rather, the sex/gender distinction conceals sexuate specificity's significance as that mode of morphological differing that is the condition both of our coming-to-be and of our relations to others, acting as an ontological limit that means no-one is "the One." If for Irigaray, as indicated by her consistent refusal of nature/culture, matter/form binaries, sexuate being is irreducible to the solely biological and encompasses what has (in Western modernity) been parsed as the social, cultural, political, material, and sensible aspects of our being, neither is sexuate difference reducible to anatomical or biological "sex difference." To reflect this crucial aspect of her thought, I use "morphological" to refer not to a sequestered biological/anatomical form but to the (relationally constituted) differences that individuate bodily beings; shape (and are shaped by) their relations to others and the world, in emergent processes of co-constitution; and are the condition of generation and birth. In other words, to borrow from Spillers, I intend the "morphological" as an Irigarayan refusal to sever bodily flesh from relationally meaningful embodiment. On Irigaray's approach, the very conception of "the biological" depends on an artificial separation of the fleshy materiality of our bodies from the lived (sociocultural, political, and spiritual) forms through which we cultivate our being.⁸⁰ It is this separation, on which the sex/gender divide depends, that Snorton suggests is violently enacted by Sims's experiments, among others.

I thus think it is worth holding on to the thought of sexuate difference as irreducible to a difference between "the sexes," and not only because of the ways in which, as Irigaray so compellingly shows, Western thought and culture has taken one sex as norm and ideal such that sexuate difference has been masked by the variously threatening, enticing, or instrumentalized projections-reflections-inversions of his "Other." Hence the risk of "a femininity that conforms and corresponds too exactly to an idea—Idea [*Idée*]—of woman, that is too obedient to a sex—to an Idea of sex—or to a fetish sex [that] has already frozen into phallomorphism."⁸¹ As Irigaray suggests, what is at stake in this "phallomorphism" is not only the reification of (what is already abstracted as) "the male body," but a metaphysics of Sameness that figures difference as *difference from*, where there is only ever One standard of comparison: the governing "Idea of sex" as phallic wholeness that is isomorphic with a phantasy of perfectly self-sufficient, unified identity and that functions as both Platonic *eidos* and regulative ideal. If this reign of "the same as One"[82] forecloses the possibility of manifold morphologies of sexuate specificity "without telos or arche,"[83] in refusing "the model of the *one*," Irigaray also refuses "woman" as the name of a generic identity, insisting that "no woman has the morphology of another."[84]

I want to put pressure on Irigaray's concern about a femininity that is "too obedient to a sex—to an Idea of sex" to insist that it is crucial not only that sexuate difference is not modeled on the One, but that it is not reduced to the "Idea of sex" at all, phallic or otherwise. This is particularly important given the racialized history of this "Idea" as a phantasmatic abstraction that not only exerts but is produced by regulative force, as Snorton discusses. Refusing the Idea of sex (as a supposedly biological given that operates as a metaphysical essence) holds open a space for attending to the sexuate specificity of captive Black bodies and of the Black(ened) maternal without subjecting them to the racialized violence of the sex/gender schema. At the same time, foregrounding the irreducibility of *sexuate* difference to (biological) *sex* difference pushes back on the figuring of sexual difference as a difference *between two* that increasingly comes to the fore in Irigaray's later work.[85] As others have noted,[86] constraining sexuate difference to two (modes of being or sexuate subjects), particularly when this is written in at an ontological level, repeats an exclusionary gesture that harms those who do not conform to dimorphic categories and forecloses nondimorphic possibilities—whether these are as-yet-unimagined or already lived, in existing forms of social life or in resistance to dominant norms.[87]

Enframing human existence as a natural duality at the ontological level (which Irigaray sometimes figures as "the real as such")[88] is no longer phallocentric or hylomorphic: that is, it does not treat a feminized matter as passive receiver-resource awaiting determination by masculine forms,[89] but allows that sexuate difference can express itself in open-ended morphologies that cannot be fully determined in advance: "matter and form each engender the other, without the end prescribed by the domination of the one—the One—over the other."[90] Nonetheless, inserting the "two" back into sexuate difference as ontological difference remains hylo-eidetic, insofar as it constrains human morphological becomings via the Idea that (human) being is necessarily structured as two, mapping onto two sexuate subjects, even if each of these materializes in infinitely variable ways. Given that the modern colonial gender system was predicated on the concept of biological dimorphism, as Lugones notes,[91] in the hylo-eidetic Idea of the two, a trace of that system remains, haunting the recovery of sexuate difference and constraining the more subversive "at least two" onto which Irigaray's work repeatedly opens.[92]

To hold on to the indeterminacy of the "at least two" in the thought of sexuate difference as ontological difference, we might understand this in terms of the manifold morphological differences on which human beings depend for their *coming-to-be*—that is, as indicated earlier, the morphological differences and specificities that allow for generation and birth—*without*, however, deciding that, in accordance with the historical a priori of "sex," these differences correspond to "the real" of the two. Released from both the "reign of the One" and the hylomorphic metaphysics that secures its reproduction, and the still hylo-eidetic constraint of the "two," "the potency of the maternal" ceases to be led "back into the same—to Sameness—in itself and for itself"[93] and is restored as an open-ended, non-teleological generative power, which, as Adriana Cavarero reminds us, is a power to generate *or not to generate*.[94] This call to recognize the ontological significance of birth and the generative powers of maternal bodies in ways that refuse their reduction to a merely reproductive function seems particularly crucial given both the "theft, regulation and destruction of black women's sexual and reproductive capacities"[95] in the transatlantic world *and* the diverse forms of agency that Black women have persisted in exerting over their power to birth even in the midst of captivity.[96]

If sexuate difference is ontological difference in the sense that it constitutes that mode of morphological differing on which human beings depend for their coming-to-be, it is violently disfigured via the political ontology of race, where birth is deformed into the reproduction of social death and kinlessness and captive Black maternity is codified as the hinge "between the human and the non-human world."[97] Yet at the same time, it is also attested to in the work of Hartman and others who attend to Black maternity not only as a site of rupture and wounding, but in its generative potency for relational sense-making that refuses to be fully captured by either racial capitalism or the reproductive logic of Man. In this context, Irigaray's conception of sexuate difference might be taken up to help dislodge the violent legacies of the racialized sex/gender schema and allied with antiracist feminist endeavors to articulate "world-altering modes of existence."

PLACENTAL ECONOMIES OF FUGITIVE RESISTANCE

Here we might return to the question raised earlier: What *is* the condition of the mother as it is "indexed by race"[98] in the Black Atlantic? According to Irigaray, the condition of maternal generative power is a "placental economy" that allows the pregnant body to bear otherness within in ways that are more akin to "continuous negotiation" than undifferentiated fusion. Irigaray draws on embryologist Hélène Rouch, who suggests that the placenta constitutes a "mediating space between mother and fetus" that operates as "a system regulating exchanges between the two."[99] In ways that echo Maggie Nelson's suggestion that there is "something inherently queer about pregnancy,"[100] Irigaray reclaims pregnancy as resistantly nonconforming even as it is enclosed by the heteronormative, reproductive logic of the One, whose bounded identity depends on a cut from the m/Other.[101] Refusing this oppositional logic, Irigaray (with Rouch) figures maternal-materiality as a fluidly self-regulating process that allows for differentiation *without separation*, in ways that depend on that which passes between singular-relational beings who come to be constituted as distinct without either being severed from or becoming wholly "Other" to one another.[102]

In keeping with Nelson, who questions the "presumed opposition" of queerness and maternity and its status as "the mark of some ontological truth,"[103] Irigaray's "placental economy" provides a figure for the decidedly queer maternal-material condition of human beings' coming-to-be: a dissident sensible transcendental[104] for a relational ontology in which the in-between is ontologically primary, as a space-time shared between one and another even as it is the condition of the relations that differentiate and co-constitute them. My suggestion is that this affords an ontological register for the insurgent maternity of Black and enslaved women to which Hartman attends, whose generative powers are expropriated by anti-Black violence yet who persist in "insist[ing] Black being" into existence[105] and sustain fugitive modes of being-living-relating "otherwise" that refuse the deathly forms of the master. The opaque generativity of gestational relations that resist speculative capture rematerializes in the emergence of forms-of-living from Black women's "brilliant and formidable labor of care" that "enable those 'who were never meant to survive' to sometimes do just that."[106] In Hartman's insistence that these "forms of care, intimacy, and sustenance exploited by racial capitalism, most importantly, are not reducible to or exhausted by it," Irigaray's insistence on an "*elsewhere*" of maternal-matter is rewritten so as to center Black women's labors of survival where consent is not possible, but resistance is.[107]

Reading Irigaray with Hartman attunes us to the way that the French word for "pregnant" (*enceinte*) also means enclosure. Irigaray's efforts to release the maternal body from a metaphysics of containment and refigure it as a fluid generativity that is always open to passage—between one and another, past and future—might thus be transposed and reread via Hartman's exploration of the fugitive intimacies and relational care of Black women and girls that create "possibilit[ies] in the space of enclosure".[108] "Neither permanently fixed, nor shifting and fickle. Nothing solid survives, yet that thickness [of flesh] responding to its own rhythms is not nothing. Quickening in movements both expected and unexpected. . . . The force unleashed has an intensity which can neither be measured nor contained. Does not submit to nullification, unless by pouring itself out in mortal ecstasy."[109] The opaque fluidity of this maternal-material—or erotic— "quickening" generates the differences and relations that foster an insurgent life and becoming, in rhythms that not only escape the master's gaze but confound the bounded forms of quantifiable units on which the violence of his accounting depends. The "anamorphosis"[110] of these rhythms that, for Man, register only as threatening disturbance—or as nothing at all—amplifies the "*anagrammatical blackness*" to which Sharpe attests and that "exists as an index of violability *and also potentiality*."[111] If Blackness is invented to bear the weight of nothingness and nonbeing, as Warren suggests,[112] the gestational rhythms that generate and sustain Black lives and that are extended through Black women's labors of care are nonetheless "not nothing." Their opaque hapticity is shared between bodies in ways that refuse the codification of birth via the grammar of property and generate "indefinite possibilities" continually on the way to "becom[ing] something else."[113]

The figure of a placental economy allows Irigaray to reclaim the ontological significance of maternal generative power without reinstituting a myth of the mother: it is the generative passage *between* gestating/gestated bodies that Irigaray seeks to recover, not a hypostatized figure of "the mother" as lost origin. In keeping with Hartman's refusal of a lost motherland, this displacement of mythic plenitude seems particularly important given the risk of idealizing Black motherhood, making it bear the weight of the future as "a placeholder for freedom."[114] In place of such mythologies, Irigaray's critique of the appropriation of the maternal body (as container, resource, and "store of substance"),[115] coupled with her insistence on its resistant gestational agency, might be read as reinforcing Hartman's emphasis on the *antinomies* of Black maternity, according to which "the material relations of sexuality and reproduction defined black women's historical experiences as laborers *and* shaped the character of their refusal of and resistance to slavery."[116]

Transposed through the lens of Black feminism, Irigaray's critique of "the self-same of Western man" that is threatened by "life that lives without him, life that reproduces itself, that orders itself without his governance"[117] can be read as diagnosing a white, colonizing master who is unsettled by "the refusal to be governed"[118] and who disavows his dependence on the *non-human*, elemental materialities that give life to sexuate, human beings. A fuller account of placental relations would need to reckon with both the toxicity of anti-Blackness and settler colonial violence, and the effects of environmental racism on what flows between bodies in prenatal exposure,[119] as well as with the microchimerism that results from fetal cells passing into gestating bodies and maternal cells being carried over into those who are born, as Marjolein Oele explores.[120] This, too, is "an index of violability and also potentiality" that structures the nonlinear, transgenerational afterlives of slavery. The an-archic in-between of placental relations attests to beginnings that are always impure and entangled, allowing for the elemental to be carried within the human and otherness to be borne within the self in ways that refuse the grammar of racial purity as well as the logic of One versus Other. If Hartman seeks a "we" whose plurality is open to contested identities and no longer defined in terms of nationhood, perhaps it begins in the fugitive gestational relations that are the condition for "*we who become together.*"[121]

Irigaray's insistence on a relational ontology and a lexicon of incalculable difference, in which "two does not divide into ones" and "relations defy being cut into units,"[122] might thus be repurposed and allied with Katherine McKittrick's resistance to the deathly arithmetic of the slave ledgers—what Spillers calls "the mighty debris of the itemized account."[123] The incalculable entanglements and opaque fluidities that gestate new bodily beings and that, as Hartman describes, are transgenerationally extended through Black women's labors of care testify to the possibility of "count[ing] it out differently": honoring "the ways in which blackness is archived as a violent beginning" while "reading the mathematics of these violences as possibilities that are iterations of black life that cannot be contained by black death."[124] As McKittrick attests, even if "the numbers set the stage" for "stories of survival—what is not there is *living*."[125] And as Irigaray allows us to add, in this fugitive living that persists as an elsewhere in the midst of violence, "the accounts overflow, calculation is lost."[126]

To counter the forgetting of sexuate difference as ontological difference while registering the ways in which that forgetting is overcoded by the ontocidal production of (anti-)Blackness in the transatlantic world means attending—with Hartman, McKittrick, and others—to Black maternity as a site of both rupturing loss *and* fugitive resistance that recorporealizes commodified flesh as social and singular bodies and natal-relational beings. As Wynter and Jackson suggest, in the wake of the invention of race and the context of the Black Atlantic, it is not simply a neutral "remainder" of feminine-female-maternal matter but more specifically the Black(ened) mater(nal) that operates as the doubly "silenced ground" of "the dialectics of the Subject" and that carries the "latent symbolic-material capacities of black *mater*, as mater, as matter, to destabilize or even rupture the reigning order of representation."[127] Yet as Hartman notes, these insurgent capacities have remained "marginal or neglected" in narratives of resistance, even as "gestational language has been key to describing the world-making and world-breaking capacities of racial slavery."[128] Perhaps, then, once rerouted through Hartman and other Black feminist work, Irigaray's "placental economies" might contribute to a gestational counterlanguage that disrupts the terms of the trade that (still) reduces some bodies to numbers in a ledger: an ontological register that lends itself to the incalculable, an-archic possibilities for refiguring the human that are harbored by the fugitive resistance of Black(ened) maternity and Black women's labors of radical care. With Hartman, then, we might transpose Irigaray's "elsewhere of mat(t)er" and relational ontology of sexuate difference to attest to a resistantly aleatory Black(ened) *mater*(nal) that undoes the colonizing grip of Sameness and "transforms the terms of the possible" in a fugitive living and insurgent dance that persists even in the midst of enclosure.

BIBLIOGRAPHY

Bianchi, Emanuela. *The Feminine Symptom: Aleatory Matter in the Aristotelian Cosmos*. New York: Fordham University Press, 2014.
Carby, Hazel V. *Reconstructing Womanhood: The Emergence of the Afro-American Woman Novelist*. Oxford: Oxford University Press, 1987.
Cavarero, Adriana. *In Spite of Plato: A Feminist Rewriting of Ancient Philosophy*. Translated by S. Anderlini-D'Onofrio and Á. O'Healy. Cambridge: Polity, 1995.
Chanter, Tina. *Ethics of Eros*. London: Routledge, 1995.
Fannin, Marie. "Placental Relations." *Feminist Theory* 15, no. 3 (2014): 289–306.
Fanon, Frantz. *Black Skin, White Masks*. Translated by R. Philcox. New York: Grove, 2008.
Haraway, Donna. *Simians, Cyborgs and Women*. New York: Routledge, 1991.
Hartman, Saidiya. "The Belly of the World: A Note on Black Women's Labors." *Souls* 18, no. 1 (2016): 166–173.
———. *Lose Your Mother: A Journey Along the Atlantic Slave Route*. New York: Farrar, Straus and Giroux, 2007.
———. *Wayward Lives, Beautiful Experiments*. New York: Norton, 2019.
Heidegger, Martin. *The Essence of Truth*. Translated by T. Sadler. New York: Continuum, 2002.
Hom, Sabrina. "Between Races and Generations: Materializing Race and Kinship in Moraga and Irigaray." *Hypatia* 28, no. 3 (2013): 419–435.
Jackson, Zakiyyah Iman. *Becoming Human: Matter and Meaning in an Antiblack World*. New York: New York University Press, 2020.
———. "'Theorizing in a Void': Sublimity, Matter, and Physics in Black Feminist Poetics." *South Atlantic Quarterly* 117, no. 13 (2018): 617–648.
Jones, Rachel. *Irigaray: Towards a Sexuate Philosophy*. Cambridge: Polity, 2011.
King, Tiffany Lethabo. *The Black Shoals: Offshore Formations of Black and Native Studies*. Durham, NC: Duke University Press, 2019.
Kuppers, Petra. "The Anarcha Project: Performing in the Medical Plantation." In *Sustainable Feminisms*, edited by S. Sarker, 127–141. Bingley: Emerald, 2007.
Lugones, Maria. "The Coloniality of Gender." *Worlds and Knowledges Otherwise* 2, no. 2 (2008): 1–17.
McKittrick, Katherine. "Mathematics Black Life." *The Black Scholar: Journal of Black Studies and Research* 44, no. 2 (2014): 16–28.
Mills, Charles. *Blackness Visible: Essays on Philosophy and Race*. Ithaca: Cornell University Press, 1998.
Morgan, Jennifer. "*Partus Sequitur Ventrem*: Law, Race and Reproduction in Colonial Slavery." *Small Axe* 55, no. 3 (2018): 1–17.
Nelson, Maggie. *The Argonauts*. Minneapolis: Greywolf, 2015.
Oele, Marjolein. *E-Co-Affectivity*. Albany: SUNY Press, 2020.
Parker, Emily. *Elemental Difference and the Climate of the Body*. Oxford: Oxford University Press, 2021.
Patterson, Orlando. *Slavery and Social Death*. Cambridge, MA: Harvard University Press, 1982.
Sharpe, Christina. *In the Wake: On Blackness and Being*. Durham, NC: Duke University Press, 2016.

Snorton, C. Riley. *Black on Both Sides: A Racial History of Trans Identity*. Minneapolis: University of Minnesota Press, 2017.
Spillers, Hortense. "Mama's Baby, Papa's Maybe: An American Grammar Book." *Diacritics* 17, no. 2 (1987): 64–81.
Stone, Alison. *Feminism, Psychoanalysis, and Maternal Subjectivity*. London: Routledge, 2011.
———. *Luce Irigaray and the Philosophy of Sexuate Difference*. Cambridge: Cambridge University Press, 2006.
———. "Matter and Form: Hegel, Organicism and the Difference Between Women and Men." In *Hegel's Philosophy and Feminist Thought*, edited by K. Hutchings and T. Pulkkinen. New York: Palgrave MacMillan, 2010.
Tzelepis, Elena, and Athena Athanasiou, eds. *Rewriting Difference: Luce Irigaray and "the Greeks."* Albany: SUNY Press, 2010.
van Leeuwen, Anne. "Sexuate Difference, Ontological Difference: Irigaray and Heidegger." *Continental Philosophy Review* 43, no. 1 (2010): 111–126.
Vergès, Françoise. *The Wombs of Women: Race, Capital, Feminism*. Translated by K. L. Glover. Durham, NC: Duke University Press, 2020.
Warren, Calvin. *Ontological Terror: Blackness, Nihilism and Emancipation*. Durham, NC: Duke University Press, 2018.
Wynter, Sylvia. "1492: A New World View." In *Race, Discourse and the Origin of the Americas*, edited by V. Hyatt and R. Nettleford. Washington, DC: Smithsonian Institution Press, 1995.
———. "Beyond Miranda's Meanings." In *Out of the Kumbla: Caribbean Women and Literature*, edited by C. Davies and E. Fido. Trenton, NJ: Africana World, 1990.
———"Unsettling the Coloniality of Being/Power/Truth/Freedom." *New Centennial Review* 3, no. 3 (2003): 257–337.
Wynter, Sylvia, and David Scott. "The Re-Enchantment of Humanism: An Interview." *Small Axe* 8 (2000): 119–207.

NOTES

1. Saidiya Hartman, *Lose Your Mother: A Journey Along the Atlantic Slave Route* (New York: Farrar, Straus and Giroux, 2007), 98.
2. Frantz Fanon, *Black Skin, White Masks*, trans. R. Philcox (New York: Grove, 2008), 191.
3. See Hortense Spillers on the transatlantic slave trade as a *"theft of the body"* that strips it to flesh; the flesh/body distinction thus denotes the difference between "captive and liberated subject-positions." Spillers, "Mama's Baby, Papa's Maybe: An American Grammar Book," *Diacritics* 17, no. 2 (1987): 67.
4. Orlando Patterson, *Slavery and Social Death* (Cambridge, MA: Harvard University Press, 1982).
5. Hartman, *Lose Your Mother*, 234.
6. Hartman, *Wayward Lives, Beautiful Experiments* (New York: Norton, 2019), 348–349, 46, 348. Henceforth WLBE.
7. WLBE, xv.

8. Hartman, "The Belly of the World: A Note on Black Women's Labors," *Souls* 18, no. 1 (2016): 166, 171.
9. WLBE, 347.
10. WLBE, xvi–xv.
11. On "the zone of nonbeing," see Fanon, *Black Skin, White Masks*, xii; and Calvin Warren, *Ontological Terror: Blackness, Nihilism and Emancipation* (Durham, NC: Duke University Press, 2018).
12. WLBE, 349.
13. Irigaray, TS, 76.
14. Irigaray, S, 142.
15. Bianchi, *The Feminine Symptom: Aleatory Matter in the Aristotelian Cosmos* (New York: Fordham University Press, 2014), 241, 224. For an important elaboration of the "elsewhere of matter" as elemental difference, see Emily Parker, *Elemental Difference and the Climate of the Body* (Oxford: Oxford University Press, 2021).
16. Bianchi, *The Feminine Symptom*, 240, emphasis added.
17. WLBE, 62.
18. WLBE, xv.
19. WLBE, 67.
20. Hom, "Between Races and Generations: Materializing Race and Kinship in Moraga and Irigaray," *Hypatia* 28, no. 3 (2013): 425.
21. In addition to Hom, see especially Tina Chanter, "Irigaray's Challenge to the Fetishistic Hegemony of the Platonic One and Many," Penelope Deutscher, "Conditionalities, Exclusions, Occlusions," and Ewa Ziarek, "'Women on the Market': On Sex, Race and Commodification," in *Rewriting Difference*, ed. E. Tzelepis and A. Athanasiou (Albany: SUNY Press, 2010), 217–229, 247–258, 203–216, respectively.
22. Vergès, *The Wombs of Women: Race, Capital, Feminism*, trans. K. L. Glover (Durham, NC: Duke University Press, 2020).
23. Tiffany Lethabo King, *The Black Shoals: Offshore Formations of Black and Native Studies* (Durham, NC: Duke University Press, 2019), 20.
24. This chapter shifts between *sexual* and *sexuate* difference fairly fluidly, reflecting the increased use of the latter in Irigaray's more recent work; broadly, I understand sexual difference as that which the Western philosophical tradition has constitutively foreclosed by mapping all human beings with reference to the One masculine-male subject, and sexuate difference as that which Irigaray calls on us to cultivate via genres of being that refuse this phallocentric logic of the Same.
25. Fanon, *Black Skin, White Masks*, 92.
26. Mills, *Blackness Visible: Essays on Philosophy and Race* (Ithaca: Cornell University Press, 1998), 12.
27. Spillers, "Mama's Baby," 71.
28. See Lugones, "The Coloniality of Gender," *Worlds and Knowledges Otherwise*, no. 2 (2008): 1–17; Sylvia Wynter, "1492: A New World View," in *Race, Discourse and the Origin of the Americas*, ed. V. Hyatt and R. Nettleford (Washington, DC: Smithsonian Institution Press, 1995); Sylvia Wynter and David Scott, "The Re-Enchantment of Humanism: An Interview," *Small Axe* 8 (2000): 119–207.
29. Mills, *Blackness Visible*, 12, 3.

30. As Ruthanne Crápo Kim drew to my attention, the section of *Speculum* that discusses the hysteric is subtitled "*Une sexualité bien noire?*," referencing the premodern association of melancholia and blackness in the theory of the humors. *Speculum* reinflects this but without taking account of the invention of Blackness that intervenes between this premodern tradition and Freud.
31. On Irigaray's "purely Western assumption of a universal category, 'woman,' whose 'silenced' ground is the condition of what she defines as an equally universally applicable, 'patriarchal discourse,'" see Wynter, "Beyond Miranda's Meanings," in *Out of the Kumbla: Caribbean Women and Literature*, ed. C. Davies and E. Fido (Trenton, NJ: Africana World, 1990), 355.
32. Irigaray, ESD, 5.
33. Chanter, "Irigaray's Challenge," 220.
34. Vergès, *The Wombs of Women*.
35. Morgan, "*Partus Sequitur Ventrem*: Law, Race and Reproduction in Colonial Slavery," *Small Axe* 55, no. 3 (2018): 16.
36. In addition to Hartman, King, Lugones, Morgan, Spillers, Vergès, and Wynter, cited earlier, other thinkers on whom I draw here—whose texts represent only a small selection of the extensive work in this field—include Hazel V. Carby, *Reconstructing Womanhood: The Emergence of the Afro-American Woman Novelist* (Oxford: Oxford University Press, 1987); Zakiyyah Iman Jackson, *Becoming Human: Matter and Meaning in an Antiblack World* (New York: New York University Press, 2020); Katherine McKittrick, "Mathematics Black Life," *The Black Scholar: Journal of Black Studies and Research* 44, no. 2 (2014); Christina Sharpe, *In the Wake: On Blackness and Being* (Durham, NC: Duke University Press, 2016); and C. Riley Snorton, *Black on Both Sides: A Racial History of Trans Identity* (Minneapolis: University of Minnesota Press, 2017).
37. Donna Haraway, "'Gender' for a Marxist Dictionary: The Sexual Politics of a Word," in *Simians, Cyborgs and Women* (New York: Routledge, 1991), 146; see also the helpful discussion on pages 144–148.
38. Carby, *Reconstructing Womanhood*, 24–25, 54.
39. Morgan, "*Partus Sequitur Ventrem*," 14.
40. Spillers, "Mama's Baby," 67: for reasons I will explain later, I do not understand "gender difference" to be equivalent to sexuate difference; Sharpe, *In the Wake*, 74.
41. Here I follow readers who situate Irigaray in a Heideggerian tradition where the ontological concerns the meaning of being, for example: Tina Chanter, *Ethics of Eros* (New York: Routledge, 1995); Alison Stone, *Luce Irigaray and the Philosophy of Sexuate Difference* (Cambridge: Cambridge University Press, 2006); Anne van Leeuwen, "Sexuate Difference, Ontological Difference: Irigaray and Heidegger," *Continental Philosophy Review* 43, no. 1 (2010): 111–126. Whereas Heidegger situates ontological difference between Being and beings, Irigaray resituates it in that mode of morphological differing she calls sexuate difference that allows human beings to come-to-be (where being is understood as an in-finite becoming; ESD 20–33). This reading pulls away from that aspect of Irigaray's thought where the ontological concerns (or, from a Heideggerian perspective, is covered over by) the question of *what* is (or that which makes something *what* it is, rather than that which allows beings to be), such that sexual difference is allied with "the real"

understood as the forces and structures that determine an empirical reality of two sexuate subjects (see Irigaray, WL, 108–117). It is in this strand of Irigaray's thinking, I suggest, that the two which is partly inherited from colonial modernity is retrojected back into the ontological. In contrast, I wish to hold the morphological differing that is the condition of our coming-to-be open to the indeterminacy of the "at least two" that also appears in Irigaray's texts, providing this is understood as an asymmetrical pluralization that is irreducible to a multiplicity of "Ones."

42. Warren, *Ontological Terror.*
43. Irigaray, JTN, 41; Irigaray TBT, 71.
44. See Morgan, "*Partus Sequitur Ventrem,*" 1.
45. Spillers, "Mama's Baby," 79.
46. Spillers, 80. See also WLBE, xiv.
47. WLBE, 287: though Hubert Harrison's socialist lectures "amplified the radical breadth" of the actions of Black women, they did not need him "to justify anything."
48. King, *Black Shoals*, 13.
49. King, 22.
50. King, 15.
51. Wynter, "Unsettling the Coloniality of Being/Power/Truth/Freedom," *New Centennial Review* 3, no. 3 (2003): 257–337.
52. Wynter, "1492," 43.
53. Wynter and Scott, "The Re-Enchantment of Humanism," 176.
54. Wynter and Scott, 182.
55. Zakiyyah Iman Jackson, "'Theorizing in a Void:' Sublimity, Matter, and Physics in Black Feminist Poetics," *South Atlantic Quarterly* 117, no. 13 (2018): 621. My discussion here generally, and the figure of the black(ened) mater(nal) in particular, is indebted to Jackson's work: see Jackson's extended elaboration of this figure in *Becoming Human.*
56. Wynter and Scott, "The Re-Enchantment of Humanism," 182.
57. See Irigaray, EP, 50: "In the place where my being should take place there is at present nothingness."
58. Lugones, "The Coloniality of Gender," 12.
59. Lugones, 12–16; see also WLBE, 184–186; Carby, *Reconstructing Womanhood,* 20–39.
60. Spillers, "Mama's Baby," 72.
61. WLBE, 53; see also Carby, *Reconstructing Womanhood,* 30.
62. Wynter and Scott, "The Re-Enchantment of Humanism," 174.
63. WLBE, 228; see also Carby, *Reconstructing Womanhood.*
64. Wynter, "Beyond Miranda's Meanings," 365.
65. WLBE, 259.
66. Haraway, "'Gender,'" 148. See also WLBE, 275. For an exemplary account of such deconstruction/claiming, see Carby, *Reconstructing Womanhood,* 45–61.
67. Wynter, "Beyond Miranda's Meanings," 356, 364.
68. Jackson, "'Theorizing in a Void,'" 631; Jackson, *Becoming Human,* 39.
69. Jackson, "'Theorizing in a Void,'" 620.
70. Irigaray, S, 138.

71. Kuppers, "The Anarcha Project: Performing in the Medical Plantation," in *Sustainable Feminisms*, ed. S. Sarker (Bingley: Emerald, 2007), 127–141; Snorton, *Black on Both Sides*.
72. Snorton, *Black on Both Sides*, 24, 20.
73. Spillers, "Mama's Baby," 68.
74. Snorton, *Black on Both Sides*, 20, 33.
75. On this model, "sex" is understood as a matter of biology and maps onto bodies typically categorized (in Western modernity) as male or female (though it can also encompass intersexed bodies); "gender" concerns the sociocultural meanings, roles, and expectations attached to those bodies and is typically framed in terms of masculinity and femininity. My concern here is less with the relation between sex and gender and more with the way the entire sex/gender couplet depends on a racializing hylomorphism, which, I argue, constitutes a forgetting of sexuate difference.
76. Lugones, "The Coloniality of Gender," 13.
77. WLBE, 186; Hartman, "Belly of the World," 168.
78. WLBE, 184, 274–275.
79. See Heidegger, *The Essence of Truth*, trans. T. Sadler (New York: Continuum, 2002).
80. Thus, while Irigaray does refer to the difference/relations between the sexes throughout her work, I would argue that part of her point is to reinscribe "the sexes" as never merely biological.
81. Irigaray, S, 229.
82. Irigaray, SN, 230.
83. Irigaray, S, 229.
84. Irigaray, SN, 231, 243; Irigaray, S, 229–230.
85. See, for example, WL, 108–117; ILTY, 47. My point here is not that biological sex difference, in human or nonhuman life, has to be figured as two, but that Irigaray's work bears the trace of its having been thus confined in the Western colonial imagination.
86. See Parker, *Elemental Difference*.
87. In contrast to Irigaray's "The whole of humankind is composed of women and men and of nothing else" (ILTY 47) Hartman asks about a "way beyond this language of being a man and being a woman" (WLBE, 274).
88. Irigaray, WL, 111.
89. For an exemplary analysis of gendered hylomorphism, see Alison Stone, "Matter and Form: Hegel, Organicism and the Difference Between Women and Men," in *Hegel's Philosophy and Feminist Thought*, ed. K. Hutchings and T. Pulkkinen (New York: Palgrave MacMillan, 2010). On hylomorphism in the context of Irigaray's work, see Jones, *Irigaray: Towards a Sexuate Philosophy* (Cambridge: Polity, 2011), 173–177.
90. Irigaray, SN, 232.
91. Lugones, "The Coloniality of Gender," 12.
92. See Irigaray, SN, 231; Irigaray, TS, 26; or Irigaray, ILTY, 35–42, which wavers between two and at least two.
93. Irigaray, S, 229.
94. Cavarero, *In Spite of Plato: A Feminist Rewriting of Ancient Philosophy*, trans. S. Anderlini-D'Onofrio and Á. O'Healy (Cambridge: Polity, 1995), 64.

95. Hartman, "Belly of the World," 166.
96. See Hartman, "Belly of the World," and Morgan, "*Partus Sequitur Ventrem*."
97. Spillers, cited in Sharpe, *In the Wake*, 78.
98. Hom, "Between Races and Generations," 419, 432.
99. Irigaray, JTN, 39–41. For rich discussions that inform my own, see Marie Fannin, "Placental Relations," *Feminist Theory* 15, no. 3 (2014): 289–306; and Marjolein Oele, *E-Co-Affectivity* (Albany: SUNY Press, 2020), 79–105.
100. Nelson, *The Argonauts* (Minneapolis: Greywolf, 2015), 13.
101. If "queer" is not to be reduced to a synonym of nonconforming and emptied of its specific relation to non-hetero sexualities, further work would be required to tighten the link between pregnancy's disruption of self-contained identity and the regulative force of the heterosexual matrix.
102. Irigaray, JTN, 42. I borrow the figure of differentiation without separation from Alison Stone, *Feminism, Psychoanalysis, and Maternal Subjectivity* (London: Routledge, 2011).
103. Nelson, *Argonauts*, 13.
104. Irigaray, ESD, 32.
105. Sharpe, *In the Wake*, 11.
106. Hartman, "Belly of the World," 171, referencing Audre Lorde's poem, "A Litany for Survival."
107. Hartman, "Belly of the World," 171, where Hartman also notes that "you cannot choose what you cannot refuse."
108. WLBE, 33.
109. Irigaray, EP, 13, translation modified.
110. Irigaray, S, 230.
111. Sharpe, *In the Wake*, 75, second emphasis added.
112. Warren, *Ontological Terror*.
113. Irigaray, S, 229–231.
114. Sharpe, cited in Hartman, "Belly of the World," 171.
115. Irigaray, S, 224.
116. Hartman, "Belly of the World," 166, emphasis added.
117. Irigaray, TBT, 70.
118. WLBE, xv.
119. See, for example, http://blackrj.org/wp-content/uploads/2020/04/6217-IOOV_EnviroJustice.pdf; www.iitc.org/wp-content/uploads/2013/08/DECLARATIONFORHEALTHREV1eng.pdf.
120. Oele, *E-Co-Affectivity*, 101–105.
121. Hartman, *Lose Your Mother*, 131, 134.
122. Irigaray, S, 236.
123. Spillers, "Mama's Baby," 69.
124. McKittrick, "Mathematics Black Life," 22–23, 24, 20.
125. McKittrick, 23.
126. Irigaray, EP, 58–59.
127. Jackson, "'Theorizing in a Void,'" 621; Jackson, *Becoming Human*, 39.
128. Hartman, "Belly of the World," 166.

Chapter Thirteen

BLOODSHED

Kinship as a Site of Violence in Irigaray and Spillers

SABRINA L. HOM

In 2017 and 2018, the U.S. government "cracked down" on illegal immigration and asylum seekers at the southern border; asylum seekers who would previously have been released to await immigration hearings were incarcerated and forcibly separated from their children. While many Americans decried this action with slogans like "this is not America," the fact is that family separation policies have a long history in the United States and other white settler states. Significantly, the recent policy of migrant family separation is far from an aberration in the history of the United States and other settler states: state violence targeting the kin relations of indigenous people and racialized groups recurs characteristically as a strategy of racial and colonial domination. From the erasure of kinships under American slavery, to the forcible removal of indigenous children in the residential school system, kinships have been systematically denigrated and attacked in the United States and other white settler states. As Stephen Lee points out,[1] the U.S. immigration system systematically causes the "slow violence" of family separations by delaying and refusing to reunite family members. Dorothy Roberts argues that the interconnected systems of child welfare and mass incarceration in the United States separate families at a large scale.[2] Such practices, then, are common, ongoing, and often taken for granted.

The profound harms produced by family separations are of great political and moral significance. As many feminist theorists have pointed out, relationships are central to the development and sustenance of autonomy and subjectivity.[3] I thematize those caring and intimate relationships that are most generative to subjectivity as *kinships*. These relationships are not only prior to and fundamental to the autonomous self; they are also—as the places at which we both exceed and become ourselves—a profound point of vulnerability. Furthermore, as kinships are by definition points of connection and affective flow, harms to them flow outward, through further and subsequent relationships: hence the intergenerational trauma that is well documented as a result of family separations and other harms to kinship.[4] Given an understanding of relational autonomy, it is clear that the harms of family separation are not only harms to individuals, but harms that undermine the very conditions of selfhood, across multiple subjects and generations—a profound and insidious form of violence and trauma.

Despite these evident harms, defenders of family separation have both precedent and tradition on their side. Their focus on the atomic individual as the locus of rights, freedom, and moral considerability is characteristic of modern Western philosophy. It is widely accepted that punishments such as incarceration, which of course impact entire families and communities, are justified solely on the basis of an individual's action. The narrow focus on individual rights and deserts generates a political and moral perspective from which systematic and severe harms to relationships are justified and erased.

A concept to describe this sort of violence is necessary and overdue. In the sort of institutionalized and deliberate ignorance that Charles Mills describes as central to the "racial contract" underlying colonization, this violence has been rendered nameless and untheorized by philosophical and legal approaches concerned with the rights and status of atomic individuals. In this chapter, I will explore how the principle of kinship that Luce Irigaray calls *blood* helps to illuminate a form of violence that is used extensively by colonial and white supremacist regimes: violence that targets bonds of kinship. I argue that we may read Irigaray's work alongside that of race theorists to gain insight into the specific ways in which kinship and sexual difference are erased as a part of racial and colonial violence and to gain insight into how to assert rights of kinship that will not reinscribe patriarchal and racist violence.

THINKING KINSHIP: BLOOD IN IRIGARAY AND SPILLERS

In this chapter, I argue for the importance of kinship or "blood" and for political and moral values that respect this importance. I do not wish, however, to idealize kinship or blood relations uncritically. Both the political rhetoric around families and the dynamics of real families are frequently oppressive. The language of "family values" is used to marshal a defense of semimythical two-parent families that epitomize the gender roles, sexual politics, and middle-class morality of the mid-twentieth century, while at the same time demonizing nonnormative families and kinships such as single-parent households. Feminist and queer theorists have emphasized that kinship comprises both natal and chosen families, normative and nonnormative configurations. Feminists have also pointed out the potential for abuse and domination within caring relationships and have fought for greater protections against intimate-partner abuse and child abuse. Political and moral engagements with kinship must take a critical, contextual, and nonessentialist perspective toward kinship to avoid reiterating these harms and exclusions.

My interpretation of kinship as the embodied relations that generate and sustain subjectivity is formed through a reading of *blood* in Irigaray. While "blood" is often used as a metaphor for biological kinship, this is reductive of the richness of blood and its flows. From the ancient concept of "blood brothers" to contemporary blood donation practices, blood flows generate kinships in all sorts of nonessentialist ways. As Kath Weston's example of interracial blood donation shows, blood is a principle of material connection that does not simply reduce to the biological/natural, though it is rooted in embodied life.[5] I will take blood as a figure that is material and embodied, but not necessarily tied to genetic or gestational ties.

Irigaray argues that the relationship between the natal mother and the child is characterized, first of all, by a meaningful and nondominating placental exchange of blood.[6] Like other feminist theorists, Irigaray emphasizes that this exchange forms the basis for individual autonomy—a version of selfhood that is intersubjective as opposed to atomic and agonistic. The relationship of the mother to the child is always appropriated, in patriarchal culture, since her gestational labor is necessary to reproduction but is erased as the child is attributed to the paternal "line" and placed under paternal control. In her analysis of the story of Antigone in "The Eternal

Irony of the Community,"[7] Irigaray describes the resurgence of this suppressed law as the logic of *blood*—that is, Antigone's responsibility to her co-uterine brother resists and ultimately defeats the human law or "law of the father" represented by her uncle, the king. Irigaray argues that the red blood of maternal kinship, exemplified by Antigone's relationship to her co-uterine brother, is "bleached" into a clear, lymphatic fluid: the reproductive and care labor underlying the state is made invisible, and irreducibly specific blood relations are reduced to fungible legal concepts. Irigaray's figuration of fluid blood emphasizes that kinship serves as the necessary nourishment of the political sphere, producing and sustaining the individual subjects of the polis, while its flows cannot be localized to any one subject. She describes repressed flows of blood underlying the patriarchal state as both the ontological precondition of human life and the necessarily unspoken element repressed by patriarchy. The erasure of this flow of blood is also an erasure of sexual difference and denial of the specificity of the maternal relation (indeed, by erasing the natural irreducibility of blood types, it erases not only sexual difference per se, but the variety and diversity of nonfungible ways of being that proliferate as a result of sexual difference).[8]

Irigaray argues for a "divine law" of blood that competes against and potentially undermines the patriarchal law of the state. Here, blood is distinguished from other concepts of familiality such as lineage, which are intrinsically bound up with questions of power, control, and property. For Creon, the king of Thebes and Antigone's uncle, kinship is the means by which he inherits power over Thebes (albeit in a circuitous manner, since he has inherited the throne from his brother-in-law and again from his nephew) and over Antigone—including power over her marriage and her life—not only as king but as her senior male relative. For Irigaray, this is characteristic of how blood, bleached of its specificity and embodiment, is reduced and transformed into the matter of patriarchal and civic power. But Antigone's (and her sister Ismene's) conception of blood is not one of control or inheritance. Instead, Antigone sees her blood relationship to her brother as an ongoing connection, surpassing even death, that generates a responsibility to care. In Irigaray's analysis, Antigone's irreducible connection to her dead and traitorous brother—a kinship that exceeds the laws of the state, which forbids his burial—has the power to undermine the state itself, which is parasitically founded on these principles of care and connection but constitutively breaches them.

While Irigaray's exclusive situation of blood in the context of biological mother-child relationships risks a reductive essentialism, it also provides an important critique of the patriarchal conceptions of "parental rights" that are in general circulation in the United States. Khader has analyzed father's rights rhetoric as characteristically reducing both maternal and paternal roles to a financial obligation.[9] A constitutional amendment proposed by a right-wing parents' rights group defines parental rights as "the liberty of parents to direct the upbringing, education, and care of their children."[10] In other words, the parental role is conceived of as a matter of control over the child—for example, the "right" to deny children access to vaccines and sexual health education, to public education and abortion. These conceptions of parental rights, rooted in control over the child, in financial obligations, and in the power to disperse familial wealth, are merely reiterations of traditional patriarchal power. Rather than assenting to such a reductive account of kinship as patriarchal power, Irigaray's focus on a maternal logic of blood and her critique of control-oriented father-right open the possibility of another aspect of kinship—one in which central value is placed on continued care and connection, on the capacity to nurture and the ability to transmit rhythms, language, culture, and affects through kin relations.[11]

Irigaray's figure of blood is foundational for me in several ways. By emphasizing the ways in which kinship preexists and exceeds social norms, as well as the ways in which kinships are strategically breached by systems of domination, Irigaray allows for a critical account of kinship—one that does not simply accept the status quo of hegemonically defined kin relations within a given culture but emphasizes that the historical product of the family generally appears as the result of patriarchal, heteronormative, and racial breaches. By asserting what she calls a "divine law" of blood that exceeds and precedes human law, Irigaray sketches the basis for moral and political claims on the basis of these breached and suppressed kinships, while critiquing the power- and property-based form that political claims of kinship often take in a patriarchal context. And by emphasizing that the bleaching/breaching of kinships is a constitutive and continuous act of the state, she highlights the centrality of kinship violence to the political sphere.

While Irigaray's work on the "bleaching" and breaching of kinships gestures toward the centrality of kinship violence in the patriarchal state, it fails to theorize the intensifications of kinship violence characteristic of colonial and slaveholding states and the ways in which this "bleaching" is used to erase not only maternal kinships but black personhood itself. Emphasizing the importance of thinking kinships as a site of colonial and racial violence, Hortense Spillers accounts for American slavery as process of systematic unkinning.[12] Strategies of unkinning in American slavery were means to dehumanize, to control, and to render human beings into fungible products and property. This kinlessness is emphasized both in the legal denial of any kin relations to the enslaved person, who can be separated from parent or child, lover or sibling, at the owner's whim, and in the systematic denial of paternity by white men who fathered children with enslaved women. By shedding, breaching, bleaching away kin relations, the very relations that define unique persons and legal subjects is erased, leaving only the legal construct of the "slave."

For Spillers, the maternal bond—"unique and unambiguous"[13]—persists, even in the absence of either social/legal recognition or the usual gendered norms around maternity (and these are norms that do not apply to enslaved persons, who are, for Spillers, explicitly ungendered), while paternal bonds are more successfully obviated. Like Irigaray, Spillers claims that a bond to the mother is a site of potential (particularly, for her, as a space for the development of innovative male subjectivities), but her account emphasizes the inadequacy of Irigaray's approach of analyzing the appropriation of kinship through a deracialized lens of gender. Instead, she situates breaches of kinship as a central strategy of racial violence and explains the function of kinship violence as a means of dehumanization and control.

It is important to note that, for Spillers, the attempted erasure of the kinships and maternal lines of enslaved people is of a piece with strategies of ungendering and dehumanization. Enslavers divide their spoils, she points out, with no regard to family relations, "as fathers are separated from sons, husbands from wives, brothers from sisters and brothers, mothers from children—male and female,"[14] reducing their captives from unique and valued relations to fungible tokens of capitalist exchange. Within this system of dehumanization, not only relation but gender and, in large part, sex are erased: there is no "distinct female space" or allowance for sexual difference, with minor exceptions. Within the horrifying spatial accounting of the Middle Passage, a female prisoner was allotted rather less space than males, Spillers points out, but remains "quantifiable by the same rules of accounting as her male counterpart."[15] Spillers's work emphasizes that unkinning is intrinsically an erasure of sexual difference, insofar as it deracinates the specific and sexed relations that distinguish unique persons from objects of exchange. At the same time, this hyperbolic erasure of sexual difference and relation cannot be theorized adequately through the lens of phallologocentrism but instead within a specific framework of colonialism and antiblackness.

Spillers's work is also significant for emphasizing that kinship is both embodied and, at least in the case of a mother-child bond, shaped by nature, and also that it is enabled or erased by the social. She points out that, while feelings of kinship are described as "natural," they "must be cultivated under actual material conditions"[16] that must entail the material means—proximity, ability, some minimal resources—to care. It is important to denaturalize kinship not only because discourses of "natural" kinship are patriarchal, heteronormative, and exclusive, but also in order to emphasize that all kinships are possible only under the material condition that allow for their cultivation. For Spillers, there is indeed something irreducible to maternal kinship, but the history of transatlantic slavery illustrates how thoroughly such "natural" kinships can be effaced and erased given a lack of legal recognition or material support. Far from a natural given, the sustenance and repair of kinship are a pressing political, moral, and economic issue.

Both Spiller's and Irigaray's work dramatizes the ways that kinships, in the white supremacist and patriarchal framework, are already marked by a set of systematic breaches and denials. In both her emphasis on an undifferentiated relation between mother and daughter and the patriarchal line from father to son, Irigaray, like many other psychoanalytic theorists, ignores the ways in which race strategically breaches kinships.[17] When Achille Mbembe describes colonization as a "phallic gesture" acted out through literal and figurative rape, "making horror and pleasure coincide,"[18] I am called to remember that the formative power of the phallus is to demarcate kinships, lines of descent, and inheritance. In the context of colonization and slavery, the power of disinheritance and unkinning is emphasized. As Abdul JanMohamed says, responding to Foucault, "power 'introduces discontinuities, separates what is joined, and marks off boundaries.' This is the central principle around which slavery and racism consolidate themselves, in my view. Power is used in this context to institute a radical demarcation and denial of kinship between two groups while one of them intimately and brutally exploits the other."[19] JanMohamed refers here to the example of white families systematically repressing and forgetting their kinship to the black children, siblings, and cousins born of privileged white men's sexual relations with black women. The control of kinship is also central to gender norms, not only, as Irigaray describes, as the means to establish patriarchal control and father-right, but also insofar as racial norms for sexuality and kinship shape the norms around gendered sexuality. The extreme and cruel examples of kinship violence that I have emphasized thus far—the unkinning of slavery, family separations perpetrated as part of mass incarceration or immigration detention—are intensifications of pervasive systems of kinship regulation and breaching such as the forgotten cousins in JanMohamed's example. These strategic breaches of kinship, which Irigaray calls the appropriation of blood, should be recognized as a central apparatus of racialization and patriarchy.

RESISTING KINSHIP VIOLENCE

While Irigaray argues that women must demand sexed rights of their own, including special rights for mothers, I argue that such rights cannot be conceived of through the traditional lens of parental right as the freedom *to* control children and the freedom *from* interruptions of kin relation. The work of feminist and race theorists does not just lay bare the workings of kinship violence but also cautions against the tempting but doomed path of attempting to combat it through a discourse of individual rights that is intrinsically inadequate to valuing kinships and protecting against kinship violence. The language of kinship rights also threatens to protect the very acts of interpersonal violence and abuse against which feminists have demanded state protection. Irigaray's conception of a mother's right to her child, I suggest, may be best thought through Spillers's focus on the necessity of material cultivation of kinships.

Classical rights discourse is ill suited to protect kinships, first, because its individualized focus threatens to cast the parties of a relationship as rivals, erasing their shared interests and constitutive connection. The legal setting of family court sets the stage of kin relations as a struggle over individual rights and control of the dependent child. To dramatize the conflict, the United States is the only country in the world that has not ratified the UN Convention on the Rights of the Child, on the justification that it threatens the rights of parents: frequently cited "parental rights" include the right to corporal punishment, to prevent children from accessing information regarding sexuality, gender identity, and sexual health, and to withhold access to mental health care.[20] Struggles that pit the interests of parents and children against one another are at times necessary, of course, but this conception of children's and parents' rights, rather than valuing a kin relation, reduces them to a scene of conflict over power and control.

Furthermore, in the orientation of parental rights toward control—rather than toward the principles of vulnerability, connection, and mutual care emphasized by Spillers's *flesh* and Irigaray's *blood*—is a discourse of paternal power. It is no surprise that the rights discourse that for centuries established women, children, and enslaved persons as varieties of chattel do not offer a robust defense of kinship, since erasing the maternal bloodline and erasing the kinships of the enslaved are central to the workings of both patriarchy and slavery. As Mary Rawlinson points out, "the discourse of rights still reflects its origin in the right of property and norms of sexual propriety,"[21] and its abstraction serves to cover over actual differences and inequalities. The idea of a rights-bearing individual was formulated as a way to preserve bodies and kinships as property; indeed, the rights of fathers and husbands have historically often functioned as property rights. Such a rights discourse threatens to redouble relations of domination and abuse within families.

If a rights discourse is more suited to protect property than kinships—threatening to reduce kinships *to* property—it is also in practice unsuited to protecting the kinship interests of nonwhite and otherwise marginalized people. Charles Mills has described a system of rights and liberties in which "conceptions of rights, duties, and government responsibilities have all been racialized,"[22] such that the rights and privileges of white citizens are systematically and carefully protected, while the rights of nonwhites are systematically flouted. We can look to the removal of Native American children to residential schools as an example: while the right to parent their own children was taken for granted for white citizens of the middle class, such a right was openly disregarded for Native Americans. Removals were justified as a means of assimilation, and through recourse to a nascent discourse of children's rights: it was claimed that "savage" Native American parents would not bring up their children properly.[23] Similarly, the discourse of individual rights and responsibilities is used to justify family separations by way of mass incarceration, immigration enforcement, and child protective services.[24]

Given the genealogical relationship between rights discourse and oppressive power, it is no surprise that claims to familial and parental right are often used to bolster abusive or dominating relationships. The limitations of individualistic rights to kinship are laid bare when we remember that no one has a right to be in kinship to anyone else against the other's will or interest. While the discourse of child protection often functions in racist and destructive ways, it is tragically the case that some parents are abusive and neglectful. While parental and children's rights need not and do not conflict in all instances, there are instances where children must be protected from their own kin. Furthermore, it is a common experience for one partner within a couple to choose to terminate their relationship unilaterally, or for adult family members to "cut off" other family members when they judge the relationship to be irreparably toxic. By asserting that kinships are worthy of moral and political consideration, I do not mean to limit the rights of individuals to remove themselves—or, in the case of minors and others who are unable to act on their own behalf, to be removed—from kinships that are abusive and dominating. I fear that articulating classical "rights" of kinship would reiterate a patriarchal conception of kinship as a means of control, or rights over the other.[25]

A political and moral commitment to the significance of kinship necessarily entails support for the material conditions of kinship. I conceive of the rights of kinship, then, in terms of positive rights to the supports required to maintain kin relationships in which members can care for one another freely and well.[26] These would include paid parental leave and high-quality, affordable childcare; access to respite care and home health care; housing and food assistance; a so-called "family wage"; and universal access to health care, including a full range of reproductive care, gender-affirming care, and culturally appropriate mental health and addiction care. Of course, a material commitment to sustaining dignified and livable kin relations also necessitates the right to determine when, how, and whether to enter into a kin relations (Irigaray calls this the "right to virginity," emphasizing that it includes not only reproductive self-determination, but the right to an "autonomous identity" free of sexual coercion of all kinds).[27]

Dorothy Roberts, in her scathing critique of the American child welfare system, describes such supports as "abolitionist" in the sense of contributing to the progressive decentering of social workers and foster care in favor of practices that support the welfare of children within their communities and kin networks.[28]

In Irigarayan terms, we can think of sexed rights, for mothers in particular, through a reproductive justice framework, in which the necessities for dignified and thriving kinships have already been thoughtfully enumerated.[29] Kinships thrive when mothering persons have the right to livable futures for themselves and their children;[30] to have their kinships and ways of being respected and protected by due process; to have choices to and not to enter into romantic, sexual, and parental relations. There is no guarantee that, under such conditions, kin relations will never be abusive or dominating, or that individuals will never find it necessary to diminish or breach these relations. Only then, however, could the decision to generate kin relations and to breach them be made without economic or moral coercion.

Blood is a metonym for violence and for kinship. Here I have argued that these concepts are intimately related: kinship is frequently and constitutively the site of state violence. Shedding "blood" by breaching/bleaching inconvenient kinships is the means by which the raw material of bodies are processed into the substance of the state: for example, into pure-white citizens, neatly pared of their kinships to nonwhite children, siblings, and cousins; into enslaved people, marked legally by their unkinning; into asylum seekers, rejected by the state and separated from their families to deter them from further "infecting" the bloodstream. This violence is both foundational and largely invisible—systematically erased with the help of a political/philosophical framework that reduces subjects to atomic individuals. While it is omnipresent, kinship violence is also profoundly harmful, undermining its victims at the most fundamental level. As Irigaray argues, the trace of placental blood also functions as an enduring reminder that we might relate to one another in sustaining and nondominating ways. Such sustaining and nondominating kinships can be cultivated by asserting the right to the material supports needed for enduring and thriving relations.

BIBLIOGRAPHY

Attiah, Karen. "Why Won't the U.S. Ratify the U.N.'s Child Rights Treaty?" *Washington Post*, November 21, 2014. www.washingtonpost.com/blogs/post-partisan/wp/2014/11/21/why-wont-the-u-s-ratify-the-u-n-s-child-rights-treaty/.

Brave Heart, Maria Yellow Horse. "The Historical Trauma Response Among Natives and Its Relationship with Substance Abuse: A Lakota Illustration." *Journal of Psychoactive Drugs* 35, no. 1 (2003): 7–13.

Collins, Patricia Hill. *Black Feminist Thought: Knowledge, Consciousness, and the Politics of Empowerment.* New York: Routledge, 2002.

Graff, Gilda. "The Intergenerational Trauma of Slavery and Its Aftermath." *Journal of Psychohistory* 41, no. 3 (2014): 181–197.

Hartman, Saidiya. *Lose Your Mother: A Journey Along the Atlantic Slave Route.* New York: Macmillan, 2008.

Held, Virginia. *The Ethics of Care: Personal, Political, and Global.* New York: Oxford University Press, 2006.

Hom, Sabrina L. "Between Races and Generations: Materializing Race and Kinship in Moraga and Irigaray." *Hypatia* 28, no. 3 (2013): 419–435.

JanMohamed, Abdul R. "Sexuality on/of the Racial Border: Foucault, Wright, and the Articulation of Racialized Sexuality." In *Discourses of Sexuality: From Aristotle to AIDS*, edited by Domna Stanton. Ann Arbor: University of Michigan Press, 1992.

Jones, Rachel. "Vital Matters and Generative Materiality: Between Bennett and Irigaray." *Journal of the British Society for Phenomenology* 46, no. 2 (2015): 156–172.

Khader, Serene J. "When Equality Justifies Women's Subjection: Luce Irigaray's Critique of Equality and the Fathers' Rights Movement." *Hypatia* 23, no. 4 (2008): 48–74.

Kittay, Eva Feder. *Love's Labor: Essays on Women, Equality and Dependency.* New York: Routledge, 2013.

Laurence, Robert. "Indian Education: Federal Compulsory School Attendance Law Applicable to American Indians: The Treaty-Making Period: 1857–1871." *American Indian Law Review* 5, no. 2 (1977): 393–413.

Lee, Stephen. "Family Separation as Slow Death." *Columbia Law Review* 119, no. 8 (2019): 2319–2384.

Mackenzie, Catriona, and Natalie Stoljar, eds. *Relational Autonomy: Feminist Perspectives on Autonomy, Agency, and the Social Self.* New York: Oxford University Press, 2000.

Mbembe, Achille. *On the Postcolony.* Berkeley: University of California Press, 2001.

Mills, Charles W. *Black Rights/White Wrongs: The Critique of Racial Liberalism.* New York: Oxford University Press, 2017.

———. "Racial Liberalism." *PMLA/Publications of the Modern Language Association of America* 123, no. 5 (2008): 1380–1397.

———. "White Ignorance." In *Race and Epistemologies of Ignorance*, edited by Shannon Sullivan and Nancy Tuana, 11–38. Albany: SUNY Press, 2007.

Parentalrights.org. "The Parental Rights Amendment." https://parentalrights.org/amendment/.

Patterson, Orlando. *Slavery and Social Death: A Comparative Study, with a New Preface.* Cambridge, MA: Harvard University Press, 2018.

Rawlinson, Mary C. *Just Life: Bioethics and the Future of Sexual Difference*. New York: Columbia University Press, 2016.

Roberts, Dorothy E. "Prison, Foster Care, and the Systemic Punishment of Black Mothers." *UCLA Law Review* 59 (2011): 1474.

———. "The Social and Moral Cost of Mass Incarceration in African American Communities." *Stanford Law Review* 56 (2003): 1271–1305.

———. *Torn Apart: How the Child Welfare System Destroys Black Families—and How Abolition Can Build a Safer World*. New York: Basic, 2022.

Robertson, Lloyd Hawkeye. "The Residential School Experience: Syndrome or Historic Trauma." *Pimatisiwin: A Journal of Aboriginal and Indigenous Community Health* 4, no. 1 (2006).

Ross, Loretta, Erika Derkas, Whitney Peoples, Lynn Roberts, and Pamela Bridgewater, eds. *Radical Reproductive Justice: Foundation, Theory, Practice, Critique*. New York: Feminist Press at CUNY, 2017.

Schwab, Gail. "Women and the Law in Irigarayan Theory." *Metaphilosophy* 27, no. 1–2 (1996): 146–177.

Sholchet, Catherine. "Inside the Search for the Parents of 545 Children Separated at the Border." *CNN.com*, October 22, 2021. www.cnn.com/2020/10/22/us/family-separations-search/index.html.

Spillers, Hortense. "Mama's Baby, Papa's Maybe: An American Grammar Book." *diacritics* 17, no. 2 (1987): 65–81.

Stack, Carol B. *All Our Kin: Strategies for Survival in a Black Community*. New York: Basic, 1975.

Weston, Kath. *Families We Choose: Lesbians, Gays, Kinship*. New York: Columbia University Press, 1997.

———. "Kinship, Controversy, and the Sharing of Substance: The Race/Class Politics of Blood Transfusion." In *Relative Values*, edited by Sarah Franklin and Susan McKinnon, 147–174. Durham, NC: Duke University Press, 2002.

NOTES

1. Stephen Lee, "Family Separation as Slow Death," *Columbia Law Review* 119, no. 8 (2019): 2319–2384.
2. Dorothy E. Roberts, "Prison, Foster Care, and the Systemic Punishment of Black Mothers," *UCLA Law Review* 59 (2011): 1474.
3. Catriona Mackenzie and Natalie Stoljar, eds., *Relational Autonomy: Feminist Perspectives on Autonomy, Agency, and the Social Self* (Oxford: Oxford University Press, 2000); Patricia Hill Collins, *Black Feminist Thought: Knowledge, Consciousness, and the Politics of Empowerment* (New York: Routledge, 2002).
4. Maria Yellow Horse Brave Heart, "The Historical Trauma Response Among Natives and Its Relationship with Substance Abuse: A Lakota Illustration," *Journal of Psychoactive Drugs* 35, no. 1 (2003): 7–13; Lloyd Hawkeye Robertson, "The Residential School Experience: Syndrome or Historic Trauma," *Pimatisiwin: A Journal of Aboriginal and Indigenous Community Health* 4, no. 1 (2006); Gilda Graff, "The Intergenerational Trauma of Slavery and Its Aftermath," *Journal of Psychohistory* 41, no. 3 (2014): 181.

5. Kath Weston, "Kinship, Controversy, and the Sharing of Substance: The Race/Class Politics of Blood Transfusion," in *Relative Values: Reconfiguring Kinship Studies*, ed. Sarah Franklin and Susan McKinnon (Durham, NC: Duke University Press 2001), 147–174.
6. Irigaray, JTN, 38ff.
7. Irigaray, S, 214ff.
8. See Elizabeth Grosz, *Becoming Undone: Darwinian Reflections on Life, Politics, and Art* (Durham, NC: Duke University Press, 2011).
9. Serene J. Khader, "When Equality Justifies Women's Subjection: Luce Irigaray's Critique of Equality and the Fathers' Rights Movement," *Hypatia* 23, no. 4 (2008): 48–74.
10. Parentalrights.org, "The Parental Rights Amendment." https://parentalrights.org/amendment/.
11. For elaboration on a critical "ethic of care" as distinguished from dominating and controlling practices, see Virginia Held, *The Ethics of Care: Personal, Political, and Global* (Oxford: Oxford University Press, 2006).
12. Hortense Spillers, "Mama's Baby, Papa's Maybe: An American Grammar Book," *diacritics* 17, no. 2 (1987): 65–81.
13. Spillers, 76.
14. Spillers, 70.
15. Spillers, 72.
16. Spillers, 76.
17. Sabrina L. Hom, "Between Races and Generations: Materializing Race and Kinship in Moraga and Irigaray," *Hypatia* 28, no. 3 (2013): 419–435.
18. Achille Mbembe, *On the Postcolony* (Berkeley: University of California Press, 2001), 139.
19. Abdul R. JanMohamed, "Sexuality on/of the Racial Border: Foucault, Wright, and the Articulation of Racialized Sexuality," in *Discourses of Sexuality: From Aristotle to AIDS*, ed. Domna Stanton (Ann Arbor: University of Michigan Press, 1992), 101.
20. See Karen Attiah, "Why Won't the U.S. Ratify the U.N.'s Child Rights Treaty?," *Washington Post*, November 21, 2014.
21. Mary C. Rawlinson, *Just Life: Bioethics and the Future of Sexual Difference* (New York: Columbia University Press, 2016), 13.
22. Charles W. Mills, "Racial Liberalism," *PMLA/Publications of the Modern Language Association of America* 123, no. 5:1381.
23. The disingenuousness of this argument is clearer when we consider that the legal means to remove white children from their parents, even when the parents were flagrantly abusive, did not exist at the time these schools began: in 1874, the American Society for the Prevention of Cruelty to Animals brought suit to protect a severely abused white girl from her parents, because no laws existed to prevent a parent's cruelty toward her children, and the first child protective agency in the United States was founded the same year. At this point, mission schools for the purpose of assimilating Native American children had existed for hundreds of years, and the US government had already begun efforts to make such education compulsory. See Robert Laurence, "Indian Education: Federal Compulsory School Attendance Law Applicable to American Indians: The Treaty-Making Period: 1857–1871," *American Indian Law Review* 5, no. 2 (1977): 393–413.

24. Dorothy E. Roberts, "The Social and Moral Cost of Mass Incarceration in African American Communities," *Stanford Law Review* 56 (2003): 1271; Dorothy E. Roberts, "Prison, Foster Care, and the Systemic Punishment of Black Mothers," *UCLA Law Review* 59 (2011): 1474.
25. Gail Schwab raises similar concerns about the potential for Irigaray's "sexed rights" to protect abusive mothers. Gail Schwab, "Women and the Law in Irigarayan Theory," *Metaphilosophy* 27, nos. 1–2 (1996): 146–177.
26. For further discussion of a public "ethic of care" in support of both caregivers and dependents, see Eva Feder Kittay, *Love's Labor: Essays on Women, Equality and Dependency* (New York: Routledge, 2013).
27. Irigaray, TD, 61.
28. Dorothy Roberts, *Torn Apart: How the Child Welfare System Destroys Black Families—and How Abolition Can Build a Safer World* (New York: Basic, 2022), 296.
29. Loretta Ross, Erika Derkas, Whitney Peoples, Lynn Roberts, and Pamela Bridgewater, eds., *Radical Reproductive Justice: Foundation, Theory, Practice, Critique* (New York: Feminist Press at CUNY, 2017).
30. Irigaray's own work focuses on the relation of mothers to daughters and, particularly, on gestational mothers. While such a focus may serve as a necessary corrective to the erasure of such relations, a discussion of the rights and needs of kinship focused only on such relations would be reductive and exclusionary. Here, I make use of Ruddick's language or "mothering persons" to describe all people engaged in nurturing labor. See Sara Ruddick, *Maternal Thinking: Toward a Politics of Peace* (Boston: Beacon, 1995).

Chapter Fourteen

TOWARD A SEXUATE JURISPRUDENCE AND ON THE "SECOND RAPE" OF LAW

YVETTE RUSSELL

That there is some violence in the word of law, to use Robert Cover's phrase,[1] is not a new way to think about law in critical legal studies, at least, but work that traces the ontological force of law is less common. That latter inquiry is of interest to me here in the context of the ongoing discussion generated by the authors in this volume, and in the course of my work trying to understand what the law "does" to complainants of sexual violence. In this chapter I interrogate what survivors of sexual violence and the criminal justice system refer to as the "second rape" of the courtroom. What does it mean to claim that one has been raped by the law after giving evidence in a trial to seek justice in the aftermath of sexual violence? I argue that the ontological force of law is profoundly nihilistic and that if we are to understand the "second rape" of law in cases of sexual violence, we need to interrogate law's investment in the simultaneous expulsion and invocation of sexual difference, and its role in engendering the material becoming of the subjects in the rape trial.

Irigaray's work has been central in formulating my critique of the rape trial process and the conscious and unconscious violence of law. Irigaray's project works sequentially through three stages: first, she diagnoses the pathology of Western metaphysics; second, she imagines a feminine subjectivity; and third, she renders practicable an intersubjective culture.[2] This approach provides a useful template against which we can map the steps for change that are necessary for the law adequately to respond to crimes of sexual violence. In the latter part of this essay, I consider the conditions under which we might move toward a sexuate jurisprudence in which the law is orientated toward life and intersubjectivity and through which it might be possible to express the harm of sexual violence without such grave consequences for those naming it.

FORCE OF LAW

In 2016, the Crown Court in Liverpool in the North of England heard a historic rape case that was prosecuted in the aftermath of the Operation Yewtree investigation in the United Kingdom.[3] This case would probably have gone unreported in the mainstream media had the complainant, a forty-three-year-old white woman named Anna Black, not committed suicide shortly after she gave her evidence in court and before the jury's verdict was given.[4] Black had been a talented ballet dancer in her youth and had moved into a residential program for ballet training in Liverpool when she was twelve years old. The defendant, David Kennedy, was the director of the ballet academy Black attended, and a well-known choreographer. Black's complaint alleged multiple sexual offenses against her by Kennedy in the late-1980s, when Black was aged thirteen or fourteen years old.

I was drawn to Black's story at the time because of its tragic consequences, and because she was reported to have been so distressed after giving evidence in Court that she described the experience to a cousin as being like "a second rape." It is not unusual for victims of sexual violence to describe the criminal justice process in this way,[5] but there is very little analysis in critical rape studies that tries to understand what such a claim means. In the course of my broader work on rape and the rape trial, I became interested in trying to trace and account for the second rape of law. Black's case provided the impetus for that inquiry.

A coronial inquest into the circumstances of Black's death found that in the year leading up to the trial, she had taken a series of overdoses, which coincided with key dates in the criminal process (the case being listed for trial, and being reported in the national press, for example).[6] It would be unwise to infer causation between participation in the rape trial and Black's suicide—indeed the coroner's report makes no such conclusion—but there is certainly a correlation. This is evidenced by the timeline of events (Black committed suicide five days after giving her evidence and before the trial was concluded), statements of her family and others attesting to her distress in the lead-up to the trial and after giving evidence, and the coroner's recommendations for changes to criminal justice practice in similar cases.

In seeking to further understand this correlation, I obtained a transcript of Black's evidence at trial.[7] I approached reading the transcript with some apprehension. There is a distinctly voyeuristic and ethically oblique quality to seeking out and bearing witness to an intimate account of trauma of a woman who only days after making it was deceased. I, the reader, experienced the law in those pages as an intangible, but malignant, force—a force whose role in generating and producing the material becoming of its participants remains underthought in legal studies.

The metaphor or description of law as force is one that has been called up before by critical legal scholars trying to think about how the law manifests itself as violent not just in its prohibitive function but also discursively and symbolically. In Derrida's well-known 1989 lecture on the subject, the law is force in its punitive function but also because, in being backed by sanction, it wields the possibility of enduring violence or force at all times.[8] Because law does not address the legal subject in the singular, there is a generalizing violence involved in its acts and pronouncements, which Derrida likens to the violence inherent in language where the application of arbitrary rules misses the singularity of a situation, or of an address.[9] The reference to violence in law's constitution is present from its origin, as by presupposing its own legitimacy it necessarily refers to an extralegal act, which is simultaneously unnamable, but constantly referenced to justify its authority. The historically equivocal nature of law's origin functions as an opaque foundational secret that reappears in the performative character of legal speech and that Derrida calls "mystical."[10] In Drucilla Cornell's words, "what is 'rotten' in a legal system is precisely the erasure of its own mystical foundation of authority so that the system can dress itself up as justice."[11]

Tracing that mystical foundation of authority has been a concern of several critical legal scholars who remain unconvinced by the benign social contract story of law's origin, whereby a sovereign wields law's force by rational consensus. In the alternative story, law's constitution and continuing operation require some level of violence that is inevitably written on the bodies of its subjects. In Nietzsche's reading of the origin of responsibility, memory is the key to "making man to a certain extent, necessitated, uniform, like among his like, regular, and consequently calculable."[12] The process of deeply fixing law to the consciousness of the "man-animal" such that it will be permanently present will not be by gentle means but inscribed on the body by a system of mnemonics: "Something is burnt in so as to remain in his memory: only that which never stops *hurting* remains in his memory."[13] It is via this mnemonics of pain that man is said to attain reason and to be constituted as a responsible or juridic subject.[14] For Cover too, the world of norms around which law is constituted is never merely subjective: "A legal world is built only to the extent that there are commitments that place bodies on the line. . . . The interpretive commitments of officials are realized . . . in the flesh."[15] The fact that law is written on and about the flesh of its subjects binds the very essence of human being to law's rationality and to the dogma of legal reason.[16]

For Alain Pottage, law supplies the answer to the question "What is human being?": "Law's aesthetic captures and institutionalizes the vital energy of human life, securing the raw material which sustains the social order."[17] Subjectivity is constructed and communicated through the language of law and the subject itself is brought into being by the juridically infused aesthetic of Reason.[18] In this way, law can be understood as both a cause and an effect of contingent social relations that "inscribe the body and generate a rational force that will in turn legitimate these configurations in rational-teleological terms."[19] That this violence is performative is a consequence of the tenuous contingency between shifting social relations and the rational force of law; the painful memory of law has to be continuously reinscribed on the bodies of its subjects. We should thus conceive of law generally, argue Pheng Cheah and Elizabeth Grosz, "as an originary and inhuman violence operative in embodiment and which is subsequently appropriated into human action and explained in terms of social causes."[20] Violence then is not just a simple consequence of an instrumental force wielded by a human agent. It is instead "a founding violence at the level of the body [that] stands at the origin and limit of the law."[21]

The themes of sacrifice, of the violent inscription and co-option of bodies in the service of maintaining the mystical origin of law's authority and the alibi of justice, are thus written through the critical histories of law.

What this scholarship does not capture, however, are the ways in which this found violence at the level of the body is a *sexuate violence*.

LAW, ONTOLOGY, AND SEXUAL VIOLENCE

In Derrida's formulation, the founding violence of any truth system always involves some necessary repression or exclusion. Irigaray would insist that it is the maternal or the feminine that takes that excluded place. Excavating the other subject of law, or what Derrida and Ronell refer to as law's "feminine silhouette,"[22] reveals the extent to which the rational force of law for its coherence relies on the simultaneous expulsion and invocation of difference and, in particular, sexual difference. The maternal figure is a problem for the hierarchy of laws in that she represents a plural or fluid form of being, which is a threat to the rational unity of legal logic.[23] In many of law's origin stories we can see the foregrounding of legal discourse as a conceptual and technical apparatus with symbolic matricide at its heart.[24] Peter Goodrich contends that the dissociation of the feminine or maternal from the divine, and thus from the mystical origin of law and laws in God alone, is necessary for the law to continue to support the fantasy of itself as a unitary discourse.[25] Law's coherence thus requires it to be cut off from living nature and the feminine such that it comes, in Irigaray's terms, to mirror masculine morphology. That is, law and legal discourse are phallomorphic systems of thought and expression in that they are underpinned by the masculine imaginary that privileges the phallus as the principal symbolic representation of masculine being. However, there always exists a remainder, or a "feminine silhouette," supplying the matter both to ensure the functioning of the discourse and to act as the mirror reflecting man back to himself as the universal subject with mastery over the whole.

In the context of sexual violence, the consequences of the exclusion of the feminine in law are acute. Because sexual violence inflicts a gendered harm—it is directed to and strikes at the sexuate subjectivity of the victim/complainant[26]—the law has trouble comprehending the harm of rape in many situations. As I have argued elsewhere, inured in law's very logic is the expulsion of sexual difference, or the means by which the sexuate identity of the legal subject might emerge and express the nature of the harm of sexual violence to law.[27] Testifying to sexual violence in court often involves a fragmentation of the sexuate self. In other words, "success" in the courtroom is often highly contingent on a complainant's ability to "mimic" the masculine logos and to speak through the language of law, or to represent or themselves only in fragments, cut off from their singular sexuate identity. Irigaray observes the tendency to read women's unmediated voices as incoherent throughout history, which manifests most starkly in psychoanalysis in the figure of the female hysteric.[28] I have observed a similar pattern emerging from women who testify to sexual violence in the courtroom, many of whom experience that process as a "second rape."[29] The feminine is invoked in the rape trial as the materiality sustaining legal discourse, while at the same time it is expelled as a threat to the story law tells about itself as a neutral and unified system of thought and expression accessible via the application of the tools of rationality and Reason. Rape complainants' experience this disorientating paradox in real time when testifying to their trauma in court.

Irigaray is clear about the ontological implications for Western metaphysics of its being cut off from the living cosmos and from sexual difference: without relation to oneself or with the other as a limiting horizon, Being can only be orientated toward death.[30] Stephen Seely's reading of Irigaray in conversation with Heidegger in the context of a discussion of planetary technicity and climate crisis is instructive in helping to explain the implications of the Western ontological comportment.[31] In the modern age, technicity is characterized by a general ontological comportment by which all being is reduced to equivalency with itself and each other, or to a "standing reserve" for its ready appropriation and manipulation.[32] Under such conditions nothing has any value in itself, because everything (including human being) is stripped of its own natural ends and principles, so technics relate only to themselves.[33] "Being" becomes merely the process of ordering the standing reserve for its most efficacious accumulation. Technicity is therefore fundamentally nihilistic because it "works to denature life and death by converting them into objects of technical-scientific representation, production, management, and administration."[34]

Seely highlights in Irigaray's dialogue with Heidegger the importance of seeing this process first and foremost as sexuate; the "global death project" of technicity is an expression of masculine Being in that it is stripped of any living relation to the feminine or to sexual difference:[35]

Irigaray's point is not (or not only) that the death project is the product of an arbitrary *historical* exclusion and subordination of women that enables men to control technology on a planetary scale, but rather that the relationship between technicity and masculinity is *ontological*, that is, that technicity is, in its essence a "phallomorphic" determination of Being.... Western metaphysics is therefore a death project from the start because it begins with the ontological annihilation of birth and the living sexuate body; it is only on the basis of this ontological annihilation of life—this Being-towards-death—that the global death project of technicity, and that of European Man's technical domination of the rest of the planet can proceed.... Irigaray understands the project of technicity as a *sexuate project* that is grounded in the desexuation and devitalisation of the *cosmos*, which conflates a phallocentric understanding of Being with Being "as such."[36]

Reading Anna Black's testimony and reflecting on her experience of the trial and her untimely death, I was drawn back to Irigaray's warning of the ontological consequences of planetary technicity in which Being is alienated from nature, the cosmos, and sexual difference. Death features in the margins of the existing scholarship on the force of law,[37] and legal method is often thought of as a tool or technics of governance over the contours of life and death.[38] There is, however, a will to power at the heart of legal rationality profoundly contingent upon the material destruction of any opposing force, the violence of which is covered over by the aesthetic of Reason. In the following section I argue that we can see that deathly logic reveal itself through the text of the rape trial transcript.

THE "SECOND RAPE" OF LAW

Reading the transcript of the trial of David Kennedy for the historic sexual abuse of Anna Black, one experiences a mix of the tedium of the legal procedure, with the focus on minute detail and process, with the infrequent shock of salacious revelation, attempted outpouring of emotion, or infliction of cruelty. I came across the excerpt I reproduce nestled inconspicuously in among a procedural recess. At this juncture in the case, Black had been giving evidence on direct examination (by the prosecution) for several hours. She had become distracted during this process because Kennedy had been smiling or smirking at her, which had caused the judge to halt the proceedings and to send the jury, defendant, and witnesses (including the complainant) out of the Court so he could speak to the attorneys about how to manage the defendant's behavior and the complainant's reaction. In England and Wales sexual offense complainants are classified as "vulnerable witnesses" and can elect to trigger what is known as "special measures" when giving their evidence in court. This can involve giving evidence outside the courtroom via video-link, or having a curtain drawn across the witness box so that the complainant does not have to see the defendant in the dock and the defendant cannot see the complainant as they give evidence (though he can hear her). Black had several times declined special measures while giving her evidence. The following exchange took place in the absence of the jury but after the complainant and defendant had been called back into court:

JUDGE: Come forward please, [Ms. Black] and resume your place in the witness box.
    [...] [To the complainant]: The anxiety that you entertain, legitimately, is one which I have raised with counsel, and [the defendant's attorney] has discussed the matter with Mr [Kennedy]. It does seem that effectively his default position, as she puts it, and it is as good a way of expressing it as any, is that he smiles. He is one of life's smilers. I'm not inviting you to comment on this yourself. It seems to be something that he does. Indeed, during the administrative hearings that I have conducted in relation to this trial when you were not here, his demeanour was very similar. And he understands the anxiety that that is causing you. So of course the ultimate remedy, and of course that is a matter of law, but it is available to us, is for, as they are called, "special measures" to be adopted[....] Now, you have just indicated to me that you do not want that to happen, that you want to carry on delivering your evidence in the way that you have been doing thus far; is that right?

THE COMPLAINANT: If it doesn't make me so angry seeing him, which is a reaction that I'm not used to having, and therefore I feel as if I'm not being able to be—think clearly, then I will have the curtain drawn. But at the moment I would rather—

JUDGE: Carry on as we are?

THE COMPLAINANT: Carry on as we are.

JUDGE: The remedy, if remedy it is, that we are proposing at the moment is that he effectively doesn't look at you, he simply looks at the floor and listens to what you are saying, and that you keep well and truly focused on the jury so far as your sight line is concerned. [. . .]

THE COMPLAINANT: But I'm actually—I'm finding his reactions very interesting.

JUDGE: Well, that's—

THE COMPLAINANT: Which is wrong. But I—

JUDGE: Well, it's the jury that matter, and—

THE COMPLAINANT: I know, but he's driving me insane, and it's good for me to feel so goddamn angry with him.

JUDGE: Well, forgive me. The process in which we are engaged is not designed as a—it is not designed for those purposes. We are here for the jury to hear the evidence that you give.

THE COMPLAINANT: Yes.

JUDGE: And in the end for the evidence he gives and any other witnesses in the case, and for them to evaluate—

THE COMPLAINANT: Yes.

JUDGE:—the charges that have been brought.

THE COMPLAINANT: I understand.

JUDGE: Its function is not—

THE COMPLAINANT: I understand.

JUDGE:—to be a cathartic exercise for you.

THE COMPLAINANT: No, I understand that.

JUDGE: In the end, that may be for you what it is. But my role is to ensure that this trial is conducted in accordance with the rules of evidence.

THE COMPLAINANT: Yes.[39]

What this excerpt portrays is an interaction that, on its face (to lawyers in any case), is an entirely appropriate application of the relevant legal rules of criminal evidence. The judge must keep the witness focused on what is relevant to enable the jury to adjudicate on the charges as they have been brought. How the witness experiences that process is largely irrelevant and her narration of that experience, left unchecked, risks tainting the integrity of the whole process. When we strip away the mask of Reason, however, what the passage actually describes is an incidence of profound violence.

The violence is hidden or covered over by the rational force of law, and the judge is enabled or empowered as the purveyor of that violence by his role.[40]

What I argue we can see in this brief passage is the law revealing itself as a powerful ontological force by which Black and her affect, her interaction with her body in its becoming in the space, are expelled and where she is returned or rendered as a tool, an object in the service of the broader goal: the performance of the "correct" legal procedure and a "just" outcome. In this moment we see the complainant neutered, deprived of her living and sexuate breath, a mere technic with no value independent of her function as grist for the mill of the legal process. As Cheah and Grosz point out, "the bonds that hold together a shared normative universe or *nomos* are necessarily violent because they are established by a projective imposition of ideality onto materiality."[41] What is left when the inconvenience of her call for her own becoming is cast out is an (sexuately) undifferentiated mass of matter, a being through which the law speaks and by which justice is arrived at.

The moment at which the judge wields the ontological force of law is simultaneously productive and destructive. The law is produced by and produces the consciousness of the legal subject through its iterability in determinate bodies before it.[42] The "cut" of judgment in this instance also requires the ontological destruction of the legal subject or, in other words, the orientation of Being-toward-death.[43] The excerpt provides a good example of the simultaneous erasure and invocation of the maternal or feminine body Irigaray reminds us takes place constantly to sustain the current symbolic order,[44] whereby Black's body serves as the matter upon which the law maintains its fiction of itself, its groundless ground. One can imagine that to be constituted in this way in the courtroom—to be reminded of your status as instrument, to undergo the "second rape"—might be a deathly experience.

It is worth noting too the characterization of Kennedy's affect in the courtroom in contrast to that of Black. According to the judge he is "one of life's smilers." He is not purposefully tormenting her by smiling at her while she gives evidence of his alleged sexual crimes against her when she was a child; rather, his "default position . . . is that he smiles." Kennedy's body is allowed to behave how it will in the courtroom ("it seems to be something that he does") and it is she that will have to avoid his gaze, should he raise it from the floor. If she is unable to manage herself, it is she that will have to draw the veil or the curtain over herself to shield herself from him, to become the disembodied voice from beyond the curtain providing the evidence upon which the system proceeds. The passage is perhaps more poignant still when we realize that Black died soon after this interaction took place; her body was literally erased or sacrificed after performing its function in the courtroom.

TOWARD A SEXUATE JURISPRUDENCE

If the ontological force of law in the rape trial is orientated toward death, is it possible to fathom a juridical space that engenders a Being-toward-life? What are the elements necessary for a return to Being prior to its annihilation in masculine laws and technicity? In other words, upon what metaphysical basis might we conceive of a sexuate jurisprudence that is capable of comprehending the harm of sexual violence, and that does not necessitate the destruction or the "second rape" of those who dare name it? What seems clear in answering these questions is that law itself would have to be profoundly rethought, and its relationship to the feminine reconstituted.

Sophocles's Antigone has fascinated historians and philosophers alike for centuries, and she has been a constant presence in Irigaray's work.[45] She is important to us here because her story is very much one of law and sexual difference. In Irigaray's work Antigone's story usually performs two clear functions: she provides the example par excellence of what a culture in the feminine means; and she serves as a historical touchstone from which Irigaray discerns the environmental, legal, ethical, and cultural requirements for a life in intersubjectivity.[46] For Irigaray, Antigone's story indicates the ethical necessity of access to a singular concrete sexuate identity for establishing humanity in intersubjectivity. Such identity is said to have existed in Antigone's time before masculine law rendered the universal neuter and supplanted the cultivation of desire with natural immediacy.[47]

Antigone is important for thinking through the implications of Irigaray's schema of sexuate rights for law because she represents a historical figure who, "at the dawn of our culture, was struggling to maintain feminine laws against an imperialist masculine power."[48] Sexuate rights are envisioned by Irigaray in the second phase of her project as a schema of rights that attach to each sexuate subject and guarantee and protect the expression of each in their unique difference.⁴⁹ Antigone's story occurs, argues Irigaray, at the cusp of the descent of modern culture into phallocracy, from which we have still to free ourselves. Antigone "demanded rights to be respected and the order of the city to be maintained."⁵⁰ For these reasons, she represents a historical figure whose ethics embody the rights and responsibilities associated with sexual difference and her legacy, says Irigaray, demands that we "[enter] another time of History, [revive her] message . . . and [pursue] its embodiment in our culture."⁵¹

Irigaray's analysis of the world in which Antigone's story plays out assumes Hegel's critique of the state as a body that demands as part of the social contract that citizens cede their individuality, nurtured within the family, to the needs of human law. Irigaray reveals the way in which Antigone overturns that rationality "by rejecting the expectation that her role should be circumscribed by the needs of the state."⁵² In trying to understand Antigone's actions in refusing to accept the legitimacy or rationality of the state and human law by which Creon would deny her the ability to fulfill her duty to provide her brother a burial, Irigaray reads the existence of sexual difference in nature as informing Antigone's desire to fulfill her duty to three important laws: those of the cosmos, generational order, and sexuate differentiation. These are laws that are no longer recognised by Creon's administration, but that are valued by Antigone as of paramount importance in maintaining justice and balance.

In respect of the cosmic order, yet to be reduced to a "fabricated human world" that no longer respects a natural equilibrium between nature, gods, and humans,⁵³ Antigone understands that a failure to provide her brother, Polynices, with the appropriate ritual of burial would harm the living world that surrounds it.⁵⁴ Antigone's respect for this order, for the cosmos, and for her duty to respect life, preserves, says Irigaray, her "autonomy and her feminine world, and prevents her from becoming a mere function or role in the patriarchal world."⁵⁵ In respect of generational order, Antigone, says Irigaray, "embodies in her actions a faithfulness to a maternal order which Creon is attempting to destroy through his use of arbitrary law. Polynices is her mother's son and in carrying out his burial she is respecting generational conditions."⁵⁶ Finally, regarding sexuate differentiation, Antigone's story reflects for Irigaray a respect for the duality present in nature itself and in which horizontal transcendence first appeared. This is not between the fecund couple or between mother and son, but between sister and brother between whom "genealogy becomes the generation of two different horizontal identities."[57]

The law Antigone recognizes, therefore, accords with her identity as a singular sexuate being. Antigone is compelled, we might say, by the force of a sexuate jurisprudence. The origin of law that Antigone observes is not based in the violent erasure of the self/other; in fact, she explicitly rejects the alienation human law requires of her from the cosmos, her genealogy, and her rights and responsibilities as a sexuate being.

Is the ontological force of Antigone's sexuate jurisprudence, then, orientated toward life? This is clearly a crucial question, given we know that the specter of death haunts Antigone's story and she herself accepts death as a necessary corollary of her actions. While death does ultimately mark her story, as Costas Douzinas and Ronnie Warrington point out, Antigone herself belongs to a different temporality; her measure of Being is not a mortal lifetime:

> It is a gain to die before her time she says to Creon. . . . Always, forever, eternity: these are the temporal markers of her existence. The sequential time of law and institutions that bind generations through calculations of gain and the totalizing time of history have intruded upon Antigone's timelessness and have upset the cyclical rhythm of earth and blood that pre-exist and survives the writing of the law. But Antigone's infinite temporality does not appeal just to the time of nature (*physis*) but to a timelessness of *dike* [justice]. It is the laws presided over by *dike*, unwritten and everlasting, the laws of Hades that Antigone gladly follows.[58]

Irigaray saw too in Antigone a possibility of return to the original clearing of Being before its alienation in the logos and technicity.[59] The unity of Being here encompasses the full "constellation within which human life is organized, including its relationship to primordial Being and ethos."[60]

There is, therefore, an ontological orientation toward life in Antigone's story that embraces a plurality of concepts, lineages, and knowledges. We can immediately see that Antigone invokes a radically different legal world than the one Anna Black found herself in while testifying to sexual violence. The possibility of "feminine justice," as Peter Goodrich calls it, forces law into an encounter with another site of knowledge and challenges "the law of masters, the genre and categories of the established institution of doctrine and its artificial and paper rules."[61] In so doing, we are open to the possibility of new modes of adjudication in which the sexuate Being of the parties before the law, rather than being violently erased, is the driving force of justice: "The difference of such a justice resides in a fluidity or contingency that can only judge according to the sudden and future orientated acts of a subjectivity created between two subjects, a mixing of subjectivities or 'interpenetration,' a space between, a space—touch, caress, body or bond— that is not of itself but rather for the other."[62]

The essence of the argument I make here is that the existence of a sexuate jurisprudence in which the law is concerned with the regulation of intersubjectivity in its cosmic, genealogical, and ethical context raises the specter of an entirely new legal hermeneutics: one through which it might be possible to express the harm of sexual violence and one capable of comprehending the nature of that harm without inflicting a "second rape," being based on an ontological orientation toward life and to sexual difference. The legal system to which Black was subject before she died required she suppress any trace of her sexuate identity in order for her to serve the ritual and process of the law. In such a juridic space the possibility of another subjectivity is erased, and with it the capacity to comprehend the nature of a harm like sexual violence and the impact that it might have on Being and becoming. These aspects of the system in turn engender a nihilistic ontological comportment, a Being-toward-death, by which justice requires the subject to submit themselves for sacrifice as the matter upon which the discourse proceeds. "Feminine justice," or the legal world Antigone invokes, asks a different question of law and, in so doing, opens up different avenues for becoming. An adjudicative space in which the sexuate rights and responsibilities of the subject are the driving force of justice leaves open the possibility for a new kind of relationship to self and other. The mechanics or precise functions of such an adjudicative space remain to be thought, but the ethos upon which such a notion of justice might proceed places life at its center, provides a space for the continued becoming of the bodies within it, and calls on holistic precedent to determine what is owed as justice.

Law provides the framework through which we understand our lives; it determines the literal the boundaries of life and death. As Alain Supiot reminds us, it is an important duty of legal scholarship to trace and account for the anthropological functions of positivist law—"that is, to recognize the role it plays in constructing collective and individual identities and in providing each new life with a humanly created social 'given.'"[63] I am regularly reminded of Supiot's exhortation in my own research into rape law and into the experience of rape complainants in the courtroom. Rape complainants often, and strikingly, refer to their interactions with the criminal justice system using visceral and violent language and imagery. It is common to hear complainants refer to participating in a trial, for example, as a "second rape." What precisely does it mean to assert that one has been raped by the law while testifying in court? I propose that we need to see the force of law in the context of the rape trial as a profoundly self-making and self-effacing ontology. As Irigaray has so convincingly argued in her critique of Western metaphysics, the annihilation of the sexuate body in the universal neutral subject engenders a Being-toward-death upon which Man's domination of the world proceeds. Law is a key component of technicity of governance strategies that are mobilized to ensure and perpetuate that domination of the planet and its people, and the devitalization and desexuation of nature and the cosmos. I argue we can see the ontological force of law reveal itself in the rape trial, the place in which law must confront the incoherence of sexual difference stripped of its necessary relationship to life. The possibilities for a new legal hermeneutics lie in our capacity to reimagine law as sexuate jurisprudence, in which there is a return to Being prior to its alienation in masculine law and technicity, and through which we might better name and account for a gendered harm like sexual violence.

BIBLIOGRAPHY

Anemtoaicei, Ovidiu, and Yvette Russell. "Luce Irigaray: Back to the Beginning." *International Journal of Philosophical Studies* 21 (2013): 773–786.

Campbell, Rebecca, Sharon M. Wasco, Courtney E. Ahrens, Tracy Sefl, and Holly E. Barnes, "Preventing the 'Second Rape': Rape Survivors' Experiences with Community Service Providers." *Journal of Interpersonal Violence* 16 (2001): 1239–1259.

Chanter, Tina. *Ethics of Eros*. New York: Routledge, 1995.

Cheah, Pheng, and Elizabeth Grosz. "The Body of the Law: Notes Towards a Theory of Corporeal Justice." In *Thinking Through the Body of the Law*, edited by Pheng Cheah, David Fraser, and Judith Grbich, 3–25. New York: NYU Press, 1996.

Conaghan, Joanne, and Yvette Russell. "Rape Myths, Law, and Feminist Research: 'Myths about myths?'" *Feminist Legal Studies* 22 (2014): 25–48.

Cornell, Drucilla. "The Violence of The Masquerade: Law Dressed Up as Justice." *Cardozo Law Review* 11 (1990): 1047–1078.
Cover, Robert. "Violence and the Word." *Yale Law Journal* 95 (1986): 1601–1629.
Derrida, Jacques. "Force of Law: The 'Mystical Foundation of Authority.'" *Cardozo Law Review* 11 (1990): 919–1045.
Derrida, Jacques, and Avital Ronell. "The Law of Genre." *Critical Inquiry* 7 (1980): 55–81.
Douzinas, Costas, and Ronnie Warrington. "Antigone's Law: A Genealogy of Jurisprudence." In *Politics, Postmodernity and Critical Legal Studies*, edited by Costas Douzinas, Peter Goodrich, and Yifat Hachamovitch, 187–225. London: Routledge, 1994.
Drakopoulou, Maria. "Of the Founding of Law's Jurisdiction and the Politics of Sexual Difference: The Case of Roman Law." In *Jurisprudence of Jurisdiction*, edited by Shaun McVeigh, 33–60. London: Routledge, 2007.
Du Toit, Louise. *A Philosophical Investigation of Rape: The Making and Unmaking of the Feminine Self*. London: Routledge, 2009.
Gehring, Petra. "Force and the Mystical Foundation of Law: How Jacques Derrida Addresses Legal Discourse." *German Law Journal* 6 (2005): 151–169.
Goodrich, Peter. *Languages of Law: Logics of Memory to Nomadic Masks*. London: Weidenfeld and Nicolson, 1990.
———. *Law in the Courts of Love*. London: Routledge, 1996.
———. *Oedipus Lex: Psychoanalysis, History, Law*. Berkeley: University of California Press, 1995.
Hengehold, Laura. "An Immodest Proposal: Foucault, Hysterization, and the 'Second Rape.'" *Hypatia* 9 (1994): 88–107.
Legendre, Pierre. *Leçons II: L'empire de la vérité*. Paris: Fayard, 1983.
Madigan, Lee, and Nancy Gamble. *The Second Rape: Society's Continued Betrayal of the Victim*. Toronto: Macmillan, 1991.
Nietzsche, Friedrich. *The Genealogy of Morals*. Translated by Horace B. Samuel. New York: Dover, 2003.
Pottage, Alain. "The Paternity of Law." In *Politics, Postmodernity and Critical Legal Studies*, edited by Costas Douzinas, Peter Goodrich and Yifat Hachamovitch, 147–186. London: Routledge, 1994.
Russell, Yvette. "Theorizing Feminist Antirape Praxis and the Problem of Resistance." *Signs: Journal of Women in Culture and Society* 46 (2021): 465–488.
———. "Thinking Sexual Difference Through the Law of Rape." *Law and Critique* 24 (2013): 255–275.
———. "Woman's Voice/Law's Logos: The Rape Trial and the Limits of Liberal Reform." *Australian Feminist Law Journal* 42 (2016): 273–296.
Seely, Stephen D. "Irigaray Between God and the Indians: Sexuate Difference, Decoloniality, and the Politics of Ontology." *Australian Feminist Law Journal* 43 (2017): 41–65.
Supiot, Alain. *Homo Juridicus: On the Anthropological Function of Law*. Translated by Saskia Brown. London: Verso, 2007.
———. "Ontologies of law." *New Left Review* 13 (2002): 107–124.
Valverde, Mariana. "Pain, Memory, and the Creation of the Liberal Legal Subject: Nietzsche on the Criminal Law." In *Nietzsche and Legal Theory: Half-Written Laws*, edited by Peter Goodrich and Mariana Valverde, 67–88. Oxford: Routledge, 2005.

NOTES

My thanks to Kimberley Brayson, Peter Goodrich, Catherine Kelly, Nick Piška, and the editors for thoughtful feedback on earlier drafts of this essay. I am grateful to the Leverhulme Trust for the funding that supported this research (RF-2021-433).

1. Robert Cover, "Violence and the Word," *Yale Law Journal* 95 (1986): 1601–1629.
2. Irigaray, C, 124.
3. Operation Yewtree was an investigation led by the London Metropolitan Police into allegations of historic sexual abuse of children against the English media personality Jimmy Savile and several others. The investigation started in 2012 and lasted several years. Over the period of Yewtree, the focus on historic sex offenses led to the increased visibility and reporting of such crimes throughout the United Kingdom.
4. The names of the parties and several details of this case have been changed to protect the anonymity of the complainant.
5. On the "second rape," see further Lee Madigan and Nancy Gamble, *The Second Rape: Society's Continued Betrayal of the Victim* (Toronto: Macmillan, 1991); Laura Hengehold, "An Immodest Proposal: Foucault, Hysterization, and the 'Second Rape,'" *Hypatia* 9 (1994): 88–107; Rebecca Campbell, Sharon M. Wasco, Courtney E. Ahrens, Tracy Sefl, and Holly E. Barnes, "Preventing the 'Second Rape': Rape Survivors' Experiences with Community Service Providers," *Journal of Interpersonal Violence* 16 (2001): 1239–1259.
6. Coronial report on file with the author.
7. In England and Wales trial transcripts can only be obtained by seeking permission from the Court that heard the case, and then commissioning and paying a private transcriber to provide the transcript.
8. Jacques Derrida, "Force of Law: The 'Mystical Foundation of Authority,'" *Cardozo Law Review* 11 (1990): 919–1045.
9. Petra Gehring, "Force and the Mystical Foundation of Law: How Jacques Derrida Addresses Legal Discourse," *German Law Journal* 6 (2005): 155.
10. Gehring, 156.
11. Drucilla Cornell, "The Violence of The Masquerade: Law Dressed Up as Justice," *Cardozo Law Review* 11 (1990): 1061.
12. Friedrich Nietzsche, *The Genealogy of Morals*, trans. Horace B. Samuel (New York: Dover, 2003), 35.
13. Nietzsche, 37, emphasis in original.
14. Nietzsche, 38. See also Mariana Valverde, "Pain, Memory, and the Creation of the Liberal Legal Subject: Nietzsche on the Criminal Law," in *Nietzsche and Legal Theory: Half-Written Laws*, ed. Peter Goodrich and Mariana Valverde (Oxford: Routledge, 2005), 67–88.
15. Cover, "Violence," 1605.
16. See further Pierre Legendre, *Leçons II: L'empire de la verité* (Paris: Fayard, 1983), 25–33; Alain Pottage, "The Paternity of Law," in *Politics, Postmodernity and Critical Legal Studies*, ed. Costas Douzinas, Peter Goodrich and Yifat Hachamovitch (London: Routledge, 1994), 147–186, 149; Alain Supiot, *Homo Juridicus: On the Anthropological Function of Law*, trans. Saskia Brown (London: Verso, 2007).
17. Pottage, "Paternity of Law," 151.

18. Pottage, 151.
19. Pheng Cheah and Elizabeth Grosz, "The Body of the Law: Notes Towards a Theory of Corporeal Justice," in *Thinking Through the Body of the Law*, ed. Pheng Cheah, David Fraser, and Judith Grbich (New York: NYU Press, 1996), 3–25, 7.
20. Cheah and Grosz, 10.
21. Cheah and Grosz, 10.
22. Jacques Derrida and Avital Ronell, "The Law of Genre," *Critical Inquiry* 7 (1980): 79.
23. See further Peter Goodrich, *Languages of Law: Logics of Memory to Nomadic Masks* (London: Weidenfeld and Nicolson, 1990).
24. Maria Drakopoulou, "Of the Founding of Law's Jurisdiction and the Politics of Sexual Difference: The Case of Roman Law," in *Jurisprudence of Jurisdiction*, ed. Shaun McVeigh (London: Routledge 2007), 33–60; Yvette Russell, "Woman's Voice/Law's *Logos*: The Rape Trial and the Limits of Liberal Reform," *Australian Feminist Law Journal* 42 (2016): 273–296.
25. Peter Goodrich, *Oedipus Lex: Psychoanalysis, History, Law* (Berkeley: University of California Press, 1995).
26. Louise du Toit, *A Philosophical Investigation of Rape: The Making and Unmaking of the Feminine Self* (London: Routledge, 2009); Joanne Conaghan and Yvette Russell, "Rape Myths, Law, and Feminist Research: 'Myths About Myths?,'" *Feminist Legal Studies* 22 (2014): 37–38; Yvette Russell, "Theorizing Feminist Antirape Praxis and the Problem of Resistance," *Signs: Journal of Women in Culture and Society* 46 (2021): 471–473.
27. Russell, "Women's Voice."
28. Irigaray, S, 11–133.
29. Russell, "Women's Voice," 294–296.
30. See Irigaray, SG, 186–187.
31. Stephen D. Seely, "Irigaray Between God and the Indians: Sexuate Difference, Decoloniality, and the Politics of Ontology," *Australian Feminist Law Journal* 43 (2017): 41–65; See also Pottage, "Paternity of Law," 154.
32. Seely, 45.
33. Seely, 46.
34. Seely, 47.
35. Seely, 47.
36. Seely, 48, emphasis in original.
37. Costas Douzinas and Ronnie Warrington, "Antigone's Law: A Genealogy of Jurisprudence," in *Politics, Postmodernity and Critical Legal Studies*, ed. Costas Douzinas, Peter Goodrich, and Yifat Hachamovitch (London: Routledge, 1994), 187–225, 222; Drakopoulou, "Founding of Law's Jurisdiction."
38. See Pottage, "Paternity of Law," 151; Supiot, *Homo Juridicus*, viii.
39. Transcript on file with the author.
40. See Cover, "Violence," 1617.
41. Cheah and Grosz, "Body of the Law," 9.
42. Cheah and Grosz, 16.
43. Derrida, "Force of Law," 963.
44. Irigaray, SN, 228.
45. See Irigaray, S, 214–226; Irigaray, IB, 113–139.

46. Ovidiu Anemtoaicei and Yvette Russell, "Luce Irigaray: Back to the Beginning," *International Journal of Philosophical Studies* 21 (2013): 780–781.
47. Anemtoaicei and Russell, 782–783.
48. Irigaray, KW, 198.
49. See Irigaray, JTN, 86–89; Irigaray, TD, 60–62; Irigaray, ILTY, 132.
50. Irigaray, KW, 198.
51. Irigaray, IB, 116.
52. Tina Chanter, *Ethics of Eros* (New York: Routledge, 1995), 81.
53. Irigaray, IB, 119.
54. Irigaray, 123.
55. Irigaray, 124.
56. Anemtoaicei and Russell, "Luce Irigaray," 783.
57. Irigaray, IB, 133. On horizontal transcendence, see further Irigaray, ILTY, 103–108; Irigaray, TBT, 85–93; Irigaray, IB, 113–137.
58. Douzinas and Warrington, "Antigone's Law," 210.
59. Irigaray, IB, 139–160.
60. Douzinas and Warrington, "Antigone's Law," 218.
61. Peter Goodrich, *Law in the Courts of Love* (London: Routledge, 1996), 2.
62. Goodrich, 64.
63. Alain Supiot, "Ontologies of Law," *New Left Review* 13 (2002): 123.

Chapter Fifteen

PLACE THINKING WITH IRIGARAY AND NEIDJIE

REBECCA HILL

Luce Irigaray's philosophy of sexuate difference is articulated in relation to the Western traditions of continental philosophy, psychoanalysis, and linguistics. On her diagnosis, these traditions, and the French culture in which Irigaray lives, are alienated from the Earth and from what it means to be living.[1] Her philosophy of sexuate difference is a sustained criticism of the disconnection at the heart of Western culture and the global formation of modernity-coloniality. But her project is much more than a critique of this profound alienation and its fundamental implication in the nihilistic destruction of life on Earth; she strives to transform the norms of Western thinking and relations to life through the elaboration of a philosophy that is attentive to and respectful of the natural rhythms of life and the cosmos.[2]

Irigaray's diagnosis of the failure of the Western tradition to respect and think life is continuous with her critical description of Western metaphysics as phallocentric. Through brilliant readings of the Western philosophical canon over many years, she has demonstrated repeatedly that what is rendered as materiality, as nature, as object, as standing reserve is denigrated as feminine (passive and/or chaotic). The phallocentric gestures of rendering and striving to contain woman-nature represent her-it as other to the subject, but woman-nature is not a real other; she-it is the projection or mirror of the subject. On Irigaray's argument, subjectivity is isomorphic with the form of Western man. The failure to allow for the possibility of a different kind of subjective relation to the world than that of Western man is a failure to give woman a subjective life. It is also a failure to acknowledge that there are different ways of being human that articulate different relations and engender different worlds. Even though the conceptual architecture of Western metaphysics fails to thematize different ways of relating to the self and the world than that of Western man, Irigaray finds that traces of different relations murmur within the discourse of Western philosophy. These traces betray the living on of other orders of relation, the orders of the natural rhythms of the cosmos and sexuate difference. Irigaray builds on these traces to elaborate a philosophy of sexuate difference in a nonhierarchical sense.

While close engagement with the Western philosophical canon and psychoanalysis is central to Irigaray's elaboration of sexuate difference, this chapter argues that affective intuition is the fundamental ground of her thought and ethics. The sources of Irigaray's affective intuition are rhythms of the cosmos, which Irigaray participates in, bears witness to, and speaks in relation to, without claiming to say what the rhythms are.[3] A claim to say what they are would in any case miss the mark, for the temporal and spatial becoming in which Irigaray thinks radically overflows her finite knowing and becoming.

In Irigaray's philosophy all of life is sacred, and nature is permeated with nontotalizable alterity.[4] For her, the interval of sexuate difference is the most important alterity to live and think. The interval is the threshold from which woman and man must begin to relate if they are to find ways to relate to the cosmos or any aspect of the milieus in which they are that are not naive projection of their sexuate selves onto the world.[5] Thinking and living the interval are not the same for a woman as they are for a man thinking and living his relation to the interval of sexuate difference. These two sexuate subjects constitute different ways of relating to the rhythms of the whole cosmos.[6] Since the nineties, Irigaray has complicated her argument for two sexes and affirmed that there are at least two sexes and at least two modes of relating to the cosmos.[7] This affirmation is profoundly important because it gives space for more than two modes of relation, and this enables a thinking of sexuate difference that respects the living becoming of trans people—women and men and nonbinary folk.[8] All of these sexually specific relations to the interval must be thought in their distinctness and they must be thought together in their relations to one another as irreducible sexuate subjectivities that constitute human being.

In an article for a special issue on her philosophy in relation to ecological thought in this age of environmental devastation, Irigaray contends that the first biodiversity a Western thinker must account for is their own sexuate being.[9] This is necessary because the frame of subjectivity that Western philosophers and activists presuppose in their thinking and acting is a frame of projective mastery that renders the world as an object. For Irigaray, attending to my sexuate specificity involves an acknowledgment of my finitude in relation to sexed others, who remain transcendent to me. Respecting the alterity of a sexuate human other is a path toward learning that the whole cosmos is open and permeated with otherness that I cannot master.[10] This chapter affirms sexuate difference as a crucial approach for learning to think and live situated relations to a nontotalizable world. This is especially important for people who have become subjects through the disciplinary and normalizing procedures of coloniality-globality. I also believe that that the task of decolonization is a fundamental imperative of life and thought. Indigenous peoples and decolonial theorists have long argued that there are other ways of being human and of relating to the cosmos than the Western mode of projective mastery. Thinkers and activists seeking ways out of this rootless and nihilistic mode should learn to relate to these other ontologies, as well as learning an ethics of sexuate difference.

This chapter situates Irigaray's thinking of sexuate difference in relation with the teaching of the Bunitj clan elder, Bill Neidjie. His book *Story About Feeling* is a work of Indigenous thought based on transcriptions by Keith Taylor of audio recordings that Taylor made with Neidjie in 1982 on Bunitj clan lands in the Northern Territory in Australia.[11] Neidjie referred to the narratives recorded by Taylor as "story about feeling," and a monograph with this title was published by an Aboriginal managed press in 1989. Neidjie's teaching of story about feeling offers a way of relating to world that is grounded in respect and love for the entire cosmos. I argue that his thinking has important resonances with Irigaray's, which is not to suggest that their work is reducible. Both writers offer teachings in which "nature" participates in thinking, to constitute forms of what I call place thinking. Place is not understood here as an empty and static container that is filled with bodies; on the contrary, place designates a relational threshold that is generative of bodies and the very spatiotemporal arrangements in which they exist.

Story About Feeling and Irigaray's writings on sexual difference are markedly different bodies of work created in different situations by thinkers from profoundly different cultures. A crucial difference between Neidjie and Irigaray and their respective corpuses resides in the fundamentally different relationship of each of author and their work to the places in which their projects have come to be thought and articulated. Neidjie is a senior law man of the Bunitj clan. His education includes knowledge of the language, laws, ecology, philosophy, ceremony, and songlines not only of his own clan but also of neighboring Aboriginal clans.[12] His teaching about listening to feeling on and with his Bunitj clan country is grounded in this deep knowledge, knowledge in which the Earth speaks. Irigaray is not an elder of a culture in which laws emanate from a direct relation to the land. Her philosophy constitutes a sustained effort to get beyond the alienation hegemonic to the Western tradition and to situate herself in nonappropriative relationships to other humans and nonhumans. This effort involves a respectful attentiveness to the living places in which she thinks and lives. At times, rhythms of place speak in her thought—for instance, the speaking of immemorial waters of *Marine Lover of Friedrich Nietzsche* are a speaking of the sea.[13]

Another important difference between the thought of Neidjie and Irigaray resides in the status of sexuate difference. For Irigaray, writing in relation to Western culture, sexuate difference is the primary difference to be lived and thought.[14] In the narratives of Neidjie's *Story About Feeling*, sexuate difference is not a central concern. Nonetheless, and in marked contrast to the monosexual culture of the Eurocentric traditions, Neidjie's culture is a sexuate culture. He speaks at length of a woman creator, Warramurraungi, as well as male creators, and of sexuate laws in his society. Neidjie's teaching emanates from his knowledge of Bunitj men's law, and he specifies that Bunitj women have different sacred laws and knowledge and places to which he does not have access.[15]

There is an interval between the thinking elaborated in this chapter and the philosophy of Neidjie; there is also an interval between my thinking and Irigaray's philosophy; these intervals are irreducible and cannot be suppressed. This is to acknowledge that the configuration of ideas drawn from Irigaray's body of work and from Neidjie's corpus is motivated redeployments that diverge from the respective ways of thinking of these two great thinkers. Acknowledging the interval is especially important to my approach to Neidjie's teaching because he is an Indigenous thinker who needs to be listened to in a context that is dominated by the logic and regimes of settler colonialism. As Patrick Wolfe argues, settler colonialism is primarily about land, and it elaborates a logic of elimination.[16] Settler colonialists grabbed the lands of First Nations peoples, and, in order to seize Indigenous lands, the settlers sought to destroy Indigenous societies, Indigenous conceptual worlds, and Indigenous systems of sovereignty. The colonists strove to replace Indigenous worlds with their world, with Western practices, regimes of governance, and ethics.[17] As Wolfe and others emphasize, settler colonialism is not confined to the historical past; it is the fundamental structure that orders settler societies to this day.[18] Despite the tremendously destructive regimes of settler colonialism, Indigenous peoples and their worlds live on and resist.[19] This essay's reading of Neidjie with Irigaray does not seek to incorporate Neidjie's teaching of *Story About Feeling* within the framework of Western metaphysics. This would be just another gesture of destructive appropriation. This essay is an effort to make space for a relationship between the affective intuition of Irigaray, a thought at the limits of Western philosophy, and story about feeling, which grounds another conceptual world that is irreducible to Western metaphysics. This essay seeks to be open to the teaching of story about feeling that Neidjie offers without claiming to contain this offering. In this context, the interval marks a distance between my reading of Neidjie and the authority of his text, a text and authority that always remain beyond appropriation.

PLACE IS AN INTERVAL

Irigaray's postulation of the interval is articulated in her well-known transvaluation of Aristotle's theory of place (*topos*) in *Physics IV*.[20] Where Aristotle conceives of place as an immobile limit surrounding a body while remaining distinct from that body, Irigaray suggests that place is an interval.[21] For Irigaray, place is mobile and overflows presence. Yet place is a sensible relation between at least two bodies that remain irreducible. To say that place is a sensible relation is to acknowledge that place is permeated with other dimensions of time and other places that remain necessarily open. In her chapter on Aristotle, Irigaray focuses on thinking nonhierarchical sexual difference as the place of heterosexual lovers, engendering an open whole together, through their respect for the double dissymmetry between them as embodied beings-in-relation.[22] But her argument for the interval has implications that radically exceed a rethinking of heterosexual carnality. The interval of sexuate difference is a differentiating movement that grounds and propels the *poeisis* of life.[23]

The interval can be partly sensed by a thinker as she thinks to herself but is not something that a thinker can really know, for the interval flows through her and beyond her. This mysterious alterity constitutes her as an other in relation to her flowing through time, her being in place, and her sexuate nature, which is traced with the alterity of sexuate difference.

The interval is also called the sensible-transcendental, which as Margaret Whitford emphasizes is one the ways that Irigaray speaks of the divine.[24] Divine intuition guides Irigaray's thought. She makes this explicit in recalling her intentions while composing the renowned cycle of elemental works, *Marine Lover*, *Elemental Passions*, and *The Forgetting of Air*. Irigaray writes: "I wanted to return to those natural matters which constitute the origin of our bodies, of our life, of our environment, the flesh of our passions. I was obeying a profound intuition, necessary and obscure, even when it was shared with other thoughts."[25] Irigaray's obedience is obedience to the natural rhythms of the cosmos, which are the rhythms of sexual difference.

In a recent interview Irigaray describes the cosmic rhythms as "the *logos* that nature is."[26] This is not an ordering that proceeds from the a priori framework of transcendental subjectivity, or an ordering imposed by a philosophy of transcendence in Plato's sense.[27] The logos that nature is are the rhythms of life. The logos that nature is designates living matter that makes and remakes itself, in a *poeisis* without ceasing, a *poesis* of in-finite relations to other dimensions.[28] Her thinking of the interval of sexuate difference is a thinking of the myriad becomings of life. These becomings are both corporeal and incorporeal, both extensive and intensive.[29]

Place thinking is thinking in which a writer is not sovereign. Writers attain visions that are not their own; place thinks. This is thinking which is not merely that of a woman open to the forces of the Earth; place thinking, when it happens, is thinking in which the forces of place and the very cosmos "speak." In this labor, a writer is both active and passive to forces of place of which she is an aspect; the writer herself is made up of forces.

LEARNING TO LISTEN TO STORY WITH SPIRIT

Neidjie's *Story About Feeling* is a complex work operating at manifold levels of reality and speaking to multiple interlocutors. The fact that Neidjie elaborates his narratives in Kriol rather than his first language, Gagadju, indicates that he wants his thinking to be widely accessible to both Aboriginal and non-Aboriginal people. His discourse is not merely addressed to human beings. Neidjie's ancestral country participates in his narrative and listens to him speak story about feeling. This is place thinking.

Philip Morrissey cautions against a romanticizing framing of Neidjie's philosophy as an impersonal and primordial wisdom.[30] On Morrissey's argument, the technology of the book is taken up by Neidjie to reach a broader audience than he could through oral teaching. His book is a direct engagement with the "challenge of modernity."[31] I agree with Morrissey, though I also wish to say that the authority of *Story About Feeling* as a teaching of "story with spirit" is primordial and comes from the land, which is the source of the law in Indigenous philosophy.[32] This authority is more than human and never changes.[33] In Neidjie's language, Gagadju, it is called *Djang*. *Djang* is the law, the cosmic force ordering the world. For the Bunitj and many Aboriginal people, *Djang* is under the Earth.[34]

Neidjie's authority to speak of *Djang* comes from his status as a senior law man with direct experience of ceremony of the King Brown Snake Dreaming relating to *Djang*.[35] While he cannot share fundamental aspects of these ceremonies—to do so is against Bunitj men's law—he offers a teaching of aspects the sacred power of *Djang*. The awesome power of this sacred power is the "biggest one."[36] Neidjie emphasizes that there is much that he does not know about *Djang*; *Djang* is beyond comprehension. For a long time, he says, Indigenous people did not speak to non-Indigenous people about *Djang* because it is sacred knowledge.[37] He relates aspects of the law about *Djang* to people all over Australia and the world because of the immense danger and ongoing devastation to the environment through heavy industrial production, land clearing, and extractive mining.[38] His teaching is particularly directed toward warning about and objecting to the operation of the Ranger Uranium Mine, which is built on an especially sacred law place on Mirrar clan lands, which are also sacred to the Bunitj and to many other Aboriginal people.

We sitting on top that Djang.
You sitting on this earth but something under,
Under this ground here.
We don't know. You don't know yourself.
I don't know myself but that story.

Because that Djang we sitting on under,
e watching, that Djang, what you want to do.
If you touch it you might get heavy cyclone,
heavy rain, flood or e kill in another place . . .
other country e might kill im.

That why we fright little bit we can stop im mining.
Oh some mining might be alright . . . this Ranger mine
but we said . . .
"You try. E might be alright."[39]

A careless reader could take "E might be alright" at face value; this would be a mistake. As Black says, Neidjie's speech is heavy with irony.[40] Damaging a sacred law place and disrespecting *Djang* have immense consequences not only on Mirrar lands but also elsewhere in the world. In a 2011 documentary, Yvonne Margarula, senior traditional owner of the Mirrar people and antimining activist, offers the same teaching as Neidjie, though her teaching is no longer speaking about virtual outcomes. Margarula says that the Fukushima disaster has come from the violation of *Djang* at the Ranger uranium mine. "That's why that place Fukushima is destroyed."[41]

In the face of the climate catastrophe and the myriad of violations of Earth by corporate and government industries, Neidjie's and Margarula's calls to obey the laws of the *Djang* are pertinent to people not just in Australia but around the world. For Neidjie, respecting the sacred power of *Djang* is foundational to a way of living that is irreducible to the framing of the Earth as standing reserve. He argues that a relationship with *Djang* can be learned by Aboriginal and non-Aboriginal people, "by anyone" who is able to "listen carefully."[42]

Well I'll tell you about this story,
About story where you feel . . . laying down.

Tree, grass, star...
because star and tree working with you.
We got blood pressure
but same thing... spirit on your body,
but e working with you.
Even nice wind e blow... having a sleep...
because that spirit e with you.

Listen carefully this, you can hear me.
I'm telling you because earth just like mother
and father or brother of you.
That tree same thing.
Your body, my body I suppose,
I'm same as you... anyone.
Tree working when you sleeping and dream.

This story e can listen carefully, e can listen slow.
If you in city well I suppose lot of houses,
you can't hardly look this star
but might be one night you look.
Have a look star because that's the feeling.
String, blood... through your body.[43]

Kinship between the Earth and people is a central teaching of this passage. In Neidjie's terms, "Earth" includes people, animals, plants, the air, wind, the sky, waterways, the cosmos as such. Relations of feeling—string and blood—extend through the entire cosmos. The fundamental importance of these relations of feeling is underlined in Neidjie's repeated use of the pronoun "e." As Tristen Harwood explains, in Kriol and in Aboriginal English, "e" is an ambiguously gendered pronoun. Harwood suggests that "e" is open to and contingent on everything in the cosmos.[44]

Feeling is a knowing of spirit connecting, for instance, a star and a person. In this form of knowledge, a person participates in feeling with a star; a person participates in feeling with grass; a person participates in feeling with a tree. This is not a form of knowledge of individual subjective mastery. Far from it, the person who feels as she is laying down is a being in a multiverse of relationships with other beings who also feel that person, as she feels them. The source of story about feeling is *Djang*, the cosmic force ordering the world. To hear or feel story is to experience an emanation of this ordering law.

Feeling is not seen with eyes or heard as sound, but it can be felt while looking at a tree as it moves with the wind. "Have a look while e blow, tree / and you feeling with your body / because tree just about like your brother or father / and tree watching you."[45] Feeling is invisible and inaudible participation in the spiraling energy between beings that has its ultimate source in the cosmic force of *Djang*. An open and attentive reader accesses feeling as she reads Neidjie's "story where you feel." This feeling guides the reader as she reads his text. It is also an invitation to engage in practices of feeling in relation with other living beings. As Neidjie says, it is best to be outside and engaged with beings such as trees or the stars in the night sky.

Neidjie acknowledges that some people will struggle to access story about feeling; they "must listen hard."[46] Some people are not capable of tuning in at this level, and I think it is especially hard among those of us raised in the anaesthetized cultures of calculative rationality. Morrissey suggests that such people will be "impervious" to Neidjie's teaching.[47] Then there is the "no good man" who cannot listen. She, he, or they can be Indigenous or Non-Indigenous. This person feels something else, something destructive.[48]

In Neidjie's philosophy, participation in feeling is a fundamentally ethical or, more precisely, a lawful basis for all living beings. Feeling situates beings in relationship to one another and the source of life, *Djang*. To listen to feeling and to learn respect for this energy are necessary "because you love it, this world." For Neidjie, love includes deep respect and is not limited to humans. For instance, trees are kin to humans and actively care for people.[49] Neidjie's statement can be taken both as a reading of his addressees as people who love the world and as an injunction to love the world.

LOVE THAT ALLOWS EACH THEIR OWN LIVING BECOMING

The concept of love is also central to Irigaray, and she articulates this concept in many texts. What does Irigaray mean by love? In *Elemental Passions* she distinguishes between two forms of love.

Love can be the becoming which appropriates the other for itself by consuming it, introjecting it into the self, to the point where the other disappears. Or love can be the becoming, allowing both the one and the other to grow. For such a love, each must keep their body autonomous. The one should not be the source of the other nor the other of the one. Two lives should embrace and fertilise each other, without either being a fixed goal for the other.[50]

Appropriative love is a relation in which a subject does not respect the integrity of the other. This is an essentially phallocentric dynamic in which the appropriator is masculine and the other is feminine in a denigrated sense. The other is not respected as another subject and is consumed in this form of love. Strictly speaking in this phallocentric encounter, the lover strives to consume the beloved and often believes that he succeeds in his appropriation. While the lover may not recognize it, the other is never entirely consumable, even in extreme situations in which the very life is taken from the other who is appropriated. There is always a remainder that exceeds his horizon. In a situation where the other's vitality is stolen, the remainder is a corpse at the material level; in spiritual terms, the remainder sings her otherness in time, though this song is beyond the ears and feelings of those who think they have mastered the feminine. Appropriative love is inherently violating and destructive. While it does not always or even usually result in death, it allows no space for alterity between the one and the other. This is love that is not worthy of its name.

In the passage under discussion, Irigaray posits another kind of love in which the one and the other keep their bodies autonomous from one another. Growth happens between the lovers and both lovers are active and passive in this relationship. Their trajectories of passivity-activity are not the same. In chapter 5 of *Elemental Passions*, the two lovers are masculine and feminine, and the figuration of sexuate difference is manifested as carnal love between them. The threshold between them is an abyss and the very condition of their being.[51] It is the fluid and dynamic ground from which each subject grows. Love is another name for the interval, which makes place.

In *I Love to You*, Irigaray sketches a felicity between woman and man that is not necessarily carnal. She invents the speech act, "I love to you" (*j'aime à toi*), as a way for a woman to announce to a man or for a man to announce to a woman a feeling of love, in which the one who is addressed remains a subject and cannot be appropriated by the speaker.[52] The preposition "to" (*à*) marks a space, leaving the other subject, the one who is addressed by the statement, a right to her or to his own other, to her or his own desire, a desire that is dissymmetrical from the subject who declares their love.[53] For Irigaray, "I love to you" is a way of enunciating sexual difference in an actual relationship.

While there are shifts in emphasis in Irigaray's extensive oeuvre, there is consistency in her figuration of love that respects sexuate alterity as the fluid ground of sexual difference. For her, this threshold is the place of the divine; love is a figuration of the interval.[54] In *To Be Born*, the figuration of desire and love between woman and man understood as different sexuate subjects is offered as an image of the rebirth of the world into a new age beyond the nihilism of modernity-coloniality.[55]

In contrast to the pervasive valorization of relationality in current posthuman theory, most of Irigaray's postulations of sexuate difference as love are anthropocentric and heterosocial. Her thinking privileges sexuate difference as the first interval to be thought and lived. Irigaray's concept of love or interval can be drawn upon in the elaboration of different kinds of relationships, not only in respecting the irreducibility of alterity in the thresholds of other encounters between human beings who are different, but also in relations with nonhuman animals and different living species. Her postulations of relation are original and rigorous articulations of non-appropriating relations of respect. Such thinking is sorely needed in our age, including in posthuman thought, which sometimes slides into what Michael Marder calls clichés of relationality.[56]

In "Animal Compassion" Irigaray suggests that in a number of significant encounters in her life she interacted with nonhuman animals who showed her compassion (birds, a rabbit, a cat, and a butterfly).[57] She emphasizes an interval between herself and each of these animals. She cautions that she does know what these encounters meant for the animals that she remembers but that she experienced these encounters as compassionate.[58] I have argued previously that her reading of these nonhuman animal gestures as manifestations of compassion slides into anthropomorphic projection.[59] This was an ungenerous response to her essay. I am in no position to know if Irigaray was projecting, and regardless, she is getting at something important, something that is foreign to the hegemonic formation of Western thought, especially in its Cartesian iteration. Irigaray is describing some of her lived experience of sharing of affect and thinking in a milieu with nonhuman animals. I have also had encounters with nonhuman animals, including birds, in which I believe I shared affects with these animals. Like Irigaray, I do not know what it is like to inhabit the relational worlds of birds; nor do I know what it is like to be a bat; nor do I know what it is like to be a mob of kangaroos. And I don't know what these animals felt in relation to me. Nonetheless in these encounters with nonhuman animals with whom I have shared time and space, I have received their companionship as wonderful, as joyful, as spiritual moments of connection.

WITH THE TREES

In *Through Vegetal Being*, her epistolary collaboration with Michael Marder, Irigaray makes explicit that the vegetal has long been a participant in her thought.[60] She is also influenced by Patanjali's *Yoga Sutras*. In reading Patanjali, she learned to cultivate all of her senses in relation to other living beings. She says that in the cultivation of her senses she learns to share energy with other life forms, and she suggests that contemplation of and with living beings through all the senses can lead to a state of ecstasy. According to Irigaray, Patanjali teaches a process of mental internalization that can lead to a state in which the subject-and-object distinction is abolished, such that, for instance, a tree and a woman merge. In contrast to Patanjali, for her, the beings do not merge; there is instead an ecstasy in which the tree and the woman remain in a state of duality. There is sharing and participation by remaining different. This mode of relation goes beyond the senses of touch, taste, smell, sound, and sight, though it arises from a silent letting be through these senses. It is a sensing that is invisible.[61]

For Neidjie, trees are kin to humans. Trees are "just like mother, father, brother or grandma."[62] When trees are cut down people become sick. "Because you pull it up from that earth this tree, / You feel it. / Not myself but everyone, anybody, no-matter who. / We all feel it."[63] Palyku elder and mother Gladys Idjirrimoonya Milroy and her daughter Jean argue against the "genocide" of trees in Australia and speak of trees as agential beings and of forests as multigenerational communities.[64] The Milroys say that their essay is a response to a call from the trees to Gladys to tell their story.[65] Ancient forests in Australia are being logged, and it must stop. In the face of this destruction, the trees speak through Indigenous writers, elders, and activists.[66] The trees have also made "deep friendships" with non-Indigenous people who also fight for the forests.[67] In stark contrast to the crusader complex rhetoric and tactics deployed by many environmentalists (what Irigaray calls the frame of Western mastery), Milroy and Milroy argue not that the trees need "saving" but that we need to care for ourselves. Campaigns for the forests, campaigns to defend Country, should be collaborations between trees and people; there must be respect and care between us, as related beings who share life on Earth.[68]

Relationality designates our porous being in the world with others—it is the locus of struggle, disease, and destruction, and it is also a threshold where we can care for our shared life. In the networks of colonial-global capitalism, Earth is relentlessly gouged for profit without acknowledgment or respect for the natural limits of relational life. This means that pollutants such as micro-plastics, radioactive waste, and poisonous gases are expelled into waste dumps only to find these "wastes" seep into the soils, the oceans, and the air and into our bodies (even into the rich humans who live in fantasies in which they fly above life).[69]

In opposition to the suicidal framework of coloniality-globality, I have argued that both Irigaray and Neidjie, in different ways, elaborate relationality as practices of place thinking. For Neidjie, place thinking is learned through participating in feeling. The feeling that Neidjie describes between a tree "watching" me and me "watching" a tree is not an intersubjective relation between me and another distinct being. Listening to feeling designates a preindividual interpenetrating feeling of the cosmic force of *Djang* in which the tree and I participate. To listen to feeling is a presubjective way of being-knowing, the basis of love for the world and of the world. For Neidjie, to listen to feeling is an injunction to care for the world, for other living beings, for ourselves.

For Irigaray, place thinking is an attentiveness to our participation in the rhythms of the cosmos through the interval of sexual difference. When this happens, there is a silent and invisible letting be. In contrast to Neidjie, Irigaray emphasizes a remainder between a woman and the beings sharing in place thinking. For her, there are shared life, respect, and love in cultivating and respecting alterity between beings.

In different ways, Neidjie and Irigaray offer methods of place thinking, thinking that may allow people in this age of crisis to learn how to come back to Earth, to ways of connecting with the milieus in which we live, the milieus that we are. These methods of place thinking should not be mistaken for postulations of nonviolence—whatever that might be. But they are methods for thinking and living that are far less destructive and alienated from the Earth than the modes of living and thinking that issue from the all-too-pervasive framework of coloniality-globality.

BIBLIOGRAPHY

Aristotle. *Aristotle's Physics*. Text and Commentary by W. D. Ross. Oxford: Clarendon, 1936.

Black, C. F. *The Land Is the Source of the Law: A Dialogic Encounter with Indigenous Jurisprudence*. London: Routledge, 2011.

Gill-Peterson, Jules. "The Miseducation of a French Feminist." *E-flux Journal*, no.117 (2021), www.e-flux.com/journal/117/382426/the-miseducation-of-a-french-feminist/.

Grieves-Williams, Victoria. "A New Sovereign Republic." *Griffith Review*, no. 60 (2018): 82–96.

Grosz, Elizabeth. *The Incorporeal: Ontology, Ethics, and the Limits of Materialism*. New York: Columbia University Press, 2017.

Gundjeihmi Aboriginal Corporation and Environment Centre Northern Territory. *Dirt Cheap, 30 Years on . . . the Story of Uranium Mining in Kakadu*. 2011. https://vimeo.com/73373709.

Gundjeihmi Aboriginal Corporation and Environment Centre Website. www.mirarr.net/pages/uranium-mining.

Harwood, Tristan. "The Forgetting—of That Forgetting, Memory of the Future." Paper Presented as Part of the Online Seminar, *From Here; For Now—Spaces That Can Be Occupied, Where Some Things Can Be Done*. www.youtube.com/watch?v=FXLoEUSjscM.

Hill, Rebecca. *The Interval: Relation and Becoming in Irigaray, Aristotle and Bergson*. New York: Fordham University Press, 2012.

——. "Milieus and Sexual Difference." *Journal of the British Society of Phenomenology* 46, no. 2 (2015): 101–108.

Irigaray, Luce. "Animal Compassion." Translated by Marilyn Gaddis Rose. In *Animal Philosophy: Essential Readings in Continental Thought*, edited by Mathew Calarco and P. Atterton. London: Continuum, 2004.

Jones, Rachel. *Irigaray: Towards a Sexuate Philosophy*. Cambridge, MA: Polity, 2011.

Marder, Michael. *Dump Philosophy*. London: Bloomsbury, 2020.

Milroy, Gladys Idjirrimoonya, and Jill Milroy. "Different Ways of Knowing: Trees Are Our Family Too." In *Heartsick for Country: Stories of Love, Spirit and Creation*, edited by Sally Morgan, Tjalaminu Mia, and Blaze Kwaymullina. Perth: Freemantle Press, 2008.

Moreton-Robinson, Aileen. "Toward an Australian Indigenous Women's Standpoint Theory." *Australian Feminist Studies* 28, no. 78 (2013): 331–347.
——. *The White Possessive: Property, Power and Indigenous Sovereignty*. Minneapolis: University of Minnesota Press, 2015.
Morrisey, Philip. "Bill Neidjie's Story About Feeling: Notes on Its Themes and Philosophy." *Journal of the Association for the Study of Australian Literature* 15, no. 2 (2015): 1–11.
Neidjie, Bill. *Story About Feeling*. Edited by Keith Taylor. Broome: Magabala, 1989.
Turner, Margaret Kemarre. *Iwenhe Tyerrtye: What It Means to Be an Aboriginal Person* as Told to Barry McDonald Perrurle with Translations by Veronica Perrurle. Alice Springs: IAD Press, 2010.
Ward, Nura. *Ninu: Grandmother's Law: The Autobiography of Nura Nungalka Ward*. Broome: Magabala, 2018.
Watson, Irene. *Aboriginal Peoples, Colonialism and International Law: Raw Law*. Routledge: New York, 2015.
Whitford, Margaret. *Luce Irigaray: Philosophy in the Feminine*. London: Routledge, 1991.
Wolfe, Patrick. "Nation and MiscegeNation: Discursive Continuity in the Post-Mabo Era." *Social Analysis* October 36 (1994): 93–152.
——. "Settler Colonialism and the Elimination of the Native." *Journal of Genocide Research* 8, no. 4 (2006): 387–409.
——. *Traces of History: Elementary Structures of Race*. London: Verso, 2016.
Wright, Alexis. *The Swan Book*. Sydney: Giramondo, 2013.
——. "What Happens When You Tell Someone Else's Story? A History of Aboriginal Disempowerment." *Meanjin* 75, no. 4 (2016): 58–76.

NOTES

1. Irigaray, SG, 76–77; Irigaray, SFO, 101; Irigaray, TVB, 16–17.
2. Irigaray, SG, 77.
3. Irigaray, 57; Irigaray, TVB, 7.
4. Irigaray, SG, 108.
5. Irigaray, EP, 74–75; Irigaray, SFO, 103.
6. Irigaray, SW, 102.
7. Irigaray, ILTY, 37; and Jules Gill-Peterson "The Miseducation of a French Feminist," *e-flux journal*, no. 117 (2021), www.e-flux.com/journal/117/382426/the-miseducation-of-a-french-feminist/ 2021).
8. Irigaray is widely read as transphobic, or at least as unfriendly to trans subjectivities, especially in the wake of some notorious comments in ILTY, 61–62. Paradoxically, this is the same book in which, to my knowledge, she first makes use of the open formulation "at least two" (37). In an essay that advocates for a trans feminism of difference, Jules Gill-Peterson gives a moving account of being a student at Irigaray's graduate seminar in Bristol and of corresponding with Irigaray in letters for a year after taking the seminar. Gill-Peterson emphasizes that Irigaray genuinely respected the interval of difference between herself and Gill-Peterson

as she struggled with her identity and as she moved toward becoming a transwoman. The essay also relates a conversation between Gill-Peterson, another student, and Irigaray at the Bristol seminar, in which Irigaray was asked her position on trans subjectivities. In response, Irigaray affirmed more than two sexes and trans becoming. Gill-Petersen recalls Irigaray saying, "I never meant that there can only be two sexes," she offered, turning to look at us with what I had to interpret as feeling. "I would be unhappy if those who have read my work use it for such ends. We can say that there may be 'at least two' sexes. My point is that we have only a single sex at this time." Gill-Peterson also suggests that Irigaray's philosophy is limited insofar as it omits to engage "thoughtfully and expansively" with "Western Europe's colonial relation to the rest of the world." Gill-Peterson says that Irigaray "never saw" Gill-Peterson's brown skin. Gill-Peterson, "The Miseducation."

9. Irigaray, SFO, 103.
10. Irigaray, 101–103.
11. Bill Neidjie, *Story About Feeling*, ed. Keith Taylor (Broome: Magabala, 1989).
12. C. F. Black, *The Land Is the Source of the Law: A Dialogic Encounter with Indigenous Jurisprudence* (London: Routledge, 2011), 17. In this chapter, I deploy the terms *Aboriginal* and *Indigenous* to designate collectively the First Nations peoples of Australia. In doing so, I am following the protocols of many authoritative Indigenous writers, including Goenpul/Nunukul scholar Aileen Moreton-Robinson of the Quandamooka Nation, in Moreton-Robinson, "Toward an Australian Indigenous Women's Standpoint Theory," *Australian Feminist Studies* 28, no.78 (2013): 331–347; and Moreton-Robinson, *The White Possessive: Property, Power and Indigenous Sovereignty* (Minneapolis: University of Minnesota Press, 2015); the Warraimaay historian Victoria Grieves-Williams, "A New Sovereign Republic," *Griffith Review*, no. 60 (2018): 82–96; Meintangk and Tanganekald legal theorist Irene Watson, *Aboriginal Peoples, Colonialism and International Law: Raw Law* (New York: Routledge, 2015); and the Waanyi novelist Alexis Wright, *The Swan Book* (Sydney: Giramondo, 2013); and Wright, "What Happens When You Tell Someone Else's Story?—a History of Aboriginal Disempowerment," *Meanjin* 75, no. 4 (2016): 58–76.
13. Irigaray, ML, 1–69.
14. Irigaray, SG, 108 and Irigaray, TVB, 99–100.
15. Neidjie, *Story About Feeling*, 94, 102. I am not claiming that Neidjie's culture is a nonhierarchical culture of sexuate difference; I am in no position to make such a judgment. Sexually specific and differentiated laws are found throughout in Indigenous societies in Australia. See Watson, *Aboriginal Peoples*; Nura Ward, *Ninu: Grandmother's Law: The Autobiography of Nura Nungalka Ward* (Broome: Magabala, 2018); Margaret Kemarre Turner, *Iwenhe Tyerrtye: What It Means to Be an Aboriginal Person*, as told to Barry McDonald Perrurle with translations by Veronica Perrurle (Alice Springs: IAD, 2010).
16. Patrick Wolfe, "Settler Colonialism and the Elimination of the Native," *Journal of Genocide Research* 8, no. 4 (2006): 388.
17. Wolfe, 388.
18. Wolfe, "Nation and MiscegeNation: Discursive Continuity in the Post-Mabo Era," *Social Analysis* 36 (October 1994): 93; Wolfe, *Traces of History: Elementary*

Structures of Race (London: Verso, 2016), 34; Watson, *Aboriginal Peoples*, 1–10; Wright, "What Happens."

19. Watson, *Aboriginal Peoples*; Wright, "What Happens."
20. Irigaray, ESD; Aristotle, *Aristotle's Physics*, text and commentary by W. D. Ross (Oxford: Clarendon, 1936).
21. Aristotle, *Physics*, 212a20–21; Irigaray, ESD, 48.
22. Irigaray, ESD, 43–44, 53–54.
23. Irigaray's transvaluation of Aristotle is also centrally concerned with the status of the maternal and the elaboration of woman's subjectivity as a place for herself. For a sustained elaboration of this argument, see Rebecca Hill, *The Interval* (New York: Fordham University Press, 2012), 11–88.
24. Margaret Whitford, *Luce Irigaray: Philosophy in the Feminine* (London: Routledge, 1991), 47.
25. Irigaray, SG, 57, translation modified. "Je voulais retourner à ces matières naturelles qui constituent l'origine de notre corps, de notre view, de notre environment, la chair de nos passions. J'obéissais à une intuition profonde, nécessaire, obscure même si elle est partagée par d'autre pensées." Irigaray, *Sexes et Parentés* (Paris: Minuit, 1987), 69.
26. Irigaray, WML, 2.
27. For a reading of Irigaray's philosophy as post-Kantian, see Rachel Jones, *Irigaray: Towards a Sexuate Philosophy* (Cambridge: Polity, 2011), 114–129.
28. Irigaray, EP, 89; Irigaray, ESD, 37. I read Irigaray's deployment of logos in this interview as congruent with her conceptualization of the matter-interval-form relation in *An Ethics of Sexuate Difference*. As I have written previously: "For Irigaray, matter and form are brought together by the interval, the place of desire. Matter is shaped by form, but matter is by no means subordinate in this formation. What impels the form is not a lack in matter but the generative interval between form and matter. And the interval always remains in play, ceaselessly inducing new formations and reformations. Matter and form entwine with each other in attractions, tensions, and acts that are never accomplished." Hill, *The Interval*, 87.
29. For an elaboration of the incorporeal, see Elizabeth Grosz, *The Incorporeal: Ontology, Ethics, and the Limits of Materialism* (New York: Columbia University Press, 2017).
30. Philip Morrisey, "Bill Neidjie's Story About Feeling: Notes on its Themes and Philosophy," *Journal of the Association for the Study of Australian Literature* 15, no. 2 (2015): 1.
31. Morrissey, 1.
32. Black, *The Land*, 25.
33. Neidjie, *Story About Feeling*, 19.
34. Black, *The Land*, 25; Neidjie, *Story About Feeling*, 80–81.
35. Neidjie, *Story About Feeling*, 103; Morrissey, "Bill Neidjie's," 4.
36. Neidjie, *Story About Feeling*, 81.
37. Neidjie, 81, 78, 82.
38. Neidjie, 78, 81–83.
39. Neidjie, 81.
40. Black, *The Land*, 31.

41. Gundjeihmi Aboriginal Corporation and Environment Centre Northern Territory, "Dirt Cheap, 30 Years on . . . the Story of Uranium Mining in Kakadu" (2011), https://vimeo.com/73373709.

    Ranger Uranium Mine was closed in January 2021. The Mirrar people have expressed grave concerns about the willingness and commitment of ERA, the mining company, to fulfill their contractual obligations to remediate Mirrar land from the immense damage of the mine and heavily contaminated soil and water: Gundjeihmi Aboriginal Corporation and Environment Centre website, www.mirarr.net/pages/uranium-mining.
42. Neidjie, *Story About Feeling*, 3.
43. Neidjie, 2–3.
44. Tristen Harwood, "The Forgetting—of That Forgetting, Memory of the Future," paper presented as part of the online seminar "From Here; for Now—Spaces That Can Be Occupied, Where Some Things Can Be Done," June 24, 2020. www.youtube.com/watch?v=FXL0EUSjscM.
45. Neidjie, *Story About Feeling*, 168.
46. Neidjie, 168.
47. Neidjie, 121; Morrissey, "Bill Neidjie's," 1.
48. Neidjie, Story About Feeling, 102; Morrissey, "Bill Neidjie's," 5.
49. Neidjie, *Story About Feeling*, 35–36.
50. Irigaray, EP, 27.
51. Irigaray, 28.
52. Irigaray, ILTY, 109–113.
53. Irigaray, ILTY. See the translator's note on 102n3.
54. Irigaray, ESD, 128–129; Irigaray, TVB, 54.
55. Irigaray, TBB, 99.
56. Michael Marder, *Dump Philosophy* (London: Bloomsbury, 2020), xii.
57. Irigaray, AC, 195–200.
58. Irigaray, 195, 199.
59. Hill, "Milieus and Sexual Difference," *Journal of the British Society of Phenomenology* 46, no. 2 (2015): 136–137.
60. Irigaray, TVB, 7, 12.
61. Irigaray, 47–49.
62. Neidjie, *Story About Feeling*, 30.
63. Neidjie, 33.
64. Gladys Idjirrimoonya Milroy and Jill Milroy, "Different Ways of Knowing: Trees Are Our Family Too," in *Heartsick for Country: Stories of Love, Spirit and Creation*, ed. Sally Morgan, Tjalaminu Mia, and Blaze Kwaymullina (Perth: Freemantle, 2008), 38.
65. Milroy and Milroy, 25.
66. Milroy and Milroy, "Different Ways"; Neidjie, *Story About Feeling*; Wright, *The Swan*, 78–99.
67. Milroy and Milroy, "Different Ways," 34.
68. Milroy and Milroy, 36–37, 42.
69. Marder, *Dump*, 3.

PART V
Back to the Future of Sexual Difference

Chapter Sixteen

READING *SPECULUM* AGAIN
Narrative, Optics, Time

EMANUELA BIANCHI

Luce Irigaray's early, magisterial engagement with the history of Western philosophy, *Speculum of the Other Woman* (1974), begins, as is well known, with an extended engagement with Freud on femininity, "The Blind Spot of an Old Dream of Symmetry," and ends with a long meditation on Plato's cave, "Plato's *Hystera*." In the center of the book lies the section called "Speculum," a series of ten essays that return to an almost orthodox chronology of the Western philosophical tradition from Greek antiquity through Neoplatonism to the modern era, bookended by two critical meditations. In a 1975 interview, "The Power of Discourse and the Subordination of the Feminine," published in *This Sex Which Is Not One*, perhaps the clearest guide to *Speculum* we have, Irigaray gives an account of this narrative strategy:

> Strictly speaking, *Speculum* has no beginning or end. The architectonics of the text, or texts, confounds the linearity of an outline, the teleology of discourse, within which there is no possible place for the "feminine," except the traditional place of the repressed, the censured.
>
> Furthermore by "beginning" with Freud and "ending" with Plato we are already going at history "backwards." But it is still a reversal "within" which the question of the woman still cannot be articulated, so this reversal alone does not suffice. That is why, in the book's "middle" texts—*Speculum*, once

again—the reversal seemingly disappears. For what is important is to disconcert the staging of representation according to *exclusively* "masculine" parameters, that is, according to a phallocratic order. It is not a matter of toppling that order so as to replace it—that amounts to the same thing in the end—but of disrupting and modifying it, starting from an "outside" that is exempt, in part, from phallocratic law.[1]

In what follows I attempt a belated return to the question of this reversed and disrupted discourse with "no beginning or end," seeking to shed new light—if I may be permitted this most naïve of optical metaphors—on the operations and, as I hope to show, the quite radical effects of *Speculum*'s extraordinary narrative strategy as it pushes toward a possible articulation of the feminine within sexual difference at the level of temporality.[2] This articulation of "the feminine within sexual difference" or "feminine sexual difference," while it represents the ongoing, poetic, narrative work and force of the text, nonetheless will never *arrive* at a stable location or congeal into an essence. *Speculum* is, rather, a work of opening, of experimentation, of *poiesis* in the senses both of an ongoing productive activity and of poetic language, and the task of this essay is thus both to limn its shape and to demonstrate something of the extraordinary nature of its philosophical achievement.[3] It will perhaps not be quite possible to adequately tease apart the different layers at which this disruption of the masculine discourses of philosophy takes place, but we will have to bear the following in mind as we proceed: mimesis, mirroring, optics, image, matter, dramaturgy, narrative, teleology, and temporality. *Speculum* effects its work on all these registers at once, simultaneously inhabiting and undermining the classical Lacanian distinctions between Imaginary, Symbolic, and Real. Narrative strategy is, on the face of it, an intervention at the level of the symbolic order, that of language, but Irigaray immerses us in discourses about images, their production and their staging, and therefore continually engages the register of the imaginary, reflectively, refractively, and diffractively. In so doing she also radically undermines their separation from the registers of the bodily sensorium, the carnal, the divine, the material, and the maternal— one way of understanding her incursion upon domain of the real.[4] The figure of the female mystic: her discourse, her *jouissance* (which for Lacan resides in the terrain of the Real), her abyssal carnality, and her transcendent sublimity will be found nestled in the center of the text, disrespecting and undoing any clear analytic separation between these registers.[5]

Attending to layers of sexed bodily morphology, to feminine carnal and spiritual experience, to questions of bodily integrity, to the optical dynamics and properties of mirrors and lenses, to the mimetic and poetic potentialities of language and the limits of sense and reference, as well as to the expectations within Western philosophical narrative, Irigaray undermines the masculine, phallic assumptions of psychical and subjective unity at the level of the imaginary, and of a phallic dynamic of desire framed by lack and telic satisfaction at the level of the symbolic. The conceit of the *miroir ardent*, or "burning glass," as I will show, permits an immersion in the real (here carnality, divinity, materiality, *jouissance*) through an engagement with the discourse of the female mystics that mines its potentials for bringing the feminine within sexual difference to light, which for Lacan would remain strictly impossible or indeed even psychotic. Her mode of "bringing to light," however, will never again be separable from other sensory or carnal modalities on the one hand, or from the disclosures afforded by logos on the other.[6]

As Margaret Whitford put it in her 1991, and in many ways unsurpassed, study of the early Irigaray, "these two principles: to look for the specular relationship, to uncover the buried mother, underlie all her analyses of the philosophers."[7] As we learn in Irigaray's essay "The Power of Discourse," the path of the feminist philosopher must attend to the conditions of systematicity of masculine discourse, to the "elsewhere" of matter, to the scenography by which the traditional philosophical inquiry is staged, and to the "elsewhere" of women's *jouissance* or sexual ecstasy. Initially, she must proceed via mimicry (*le mimétisme*) and by "jamming the theoretical machinery," seeking a "disruptive excess" to a philosophical optics in which feminine being is reduced to a mirror that reflects and functions to render whole the masculine subject of philosophical discourse, apparently without remainder.[8]

Speculum's intervention at the level of the philosophical imaginary thus takes place quite literally by way of the speculum. Speculum is the Latin word for mirror, but in French and English, it also refers to a refractive mirror or lens within a telescope that aids and intensifies vision, and specifically to the instrument which is used to dilate and investigate the interior of bodily cavities, in particular and most familiarly the vagina. *Speculum* points, then, to the operation of what Linda Williams, in her in-part Irigaray-inspired analysis of hard-core pornography, calls "the frenzy of the visible"—an avid desire, well attested throughout modernity, to penetrate with one's vision, and especially to penetrate the mysterious depths of women's bodies, to see and thus to know; to see, to possess, and to enjoy formerly hidden secrets especially through the power of appropriation granted by visual technologies.[9] Irigaray thus actively takes up the speculum, which originally promised full disclosure of the objects of interest to the (male) viewer, and demonstrates how woman functions *as* mirror and ground for the masculine subject, her multidimensionality and motility frozen into a reflective surface that nourishes his speculative desire. More than this, as mimic, she puts the speculum to work, as concave mirror or elliptical lens, to incessantly refract, diffract, ironize, distort, hystericize, throw into question, resituate, reverse, and overthrow (these are two meanings of the French *renverser*) the terms of the philosopher's texts, in a way that seeks to bring into being, however dimly or dazzlingly, the woman on the other side of the mirror. This will include her bodily morphology in its own specificity and multiplicity rather than as reflection (recall, for instance, that "vagina" means literally "sheath," in its very signification nothing more than a teleological mirror of phallic desire), as well as her desire, her pleasure or *jouissance*, and her language. As Irigaray engages with the texts of Western philosophy we observe this strategy of mimesis at work. She quotes, she comments, she questions, she meditates, she reflects, she refracts, she critiques, she poetizes. In some chapters, "On the Index of Plato's Works: Woman" and "*Une mère de glace*," she simply reproduces the philosophers' words and allows them to resonate and refract in their new specular context. In a sense her approach is a model of what we might call "close reading": intimate, creative, and critical. As she indicates in *This Sex*, she is attentive, perhaps hyperattentive, to the optical tropes at work in the text—what they are able to reveal and how, stretching and hystericizing the images she explores into sometimes extreme anamorphoses.

The "two lips" undoubtedly constitute Irigaray's most vivid and celebrated contribution to the imaginary of the feminine within sexual difference. As elaborated in *This Sex Which Is Not One*, in their embodied, plural indeterminacy as both the lips of the mouth and the lips of the vulva, neither/both open and/or closed as they frame the possibility of passage from interior to exterior and back again, they directly counter the unitary logic of the phallus and are implicated in both speech and bodily pleasure ("Woman 'touches herself' all the time").[10] However, the motif of the lips does not appear with any real insistence in *Speculum*.[11] What we do see as a recurrent image is rather the *miroir ardent*, or "burning glass," a concave mirror or lens, a *speculum*, in fact, that concentrates light in order to convert it into heat and fire. The significance of the figure of the *miroir ardent* for *Speculum* has been explored at some length by Philippa Berry,[12] and this present analysis relies necessarily and heavily on her brilliant reading while considerably extending the conceit, showing that it bears a striking relation to the lips in its specifically textual and narrative function.

The *miroir ardent* makes its appearance in the first of the essays in the "Speculum" section, in the immediate wake of Irigaray's own meditation upon the formal necessities of her discursive procedure, which I quote at length:

> Turn everything upside down, inside out, back to front.... Insist also and deliberately upon those *blanks* in discourse which, ... by their *silent plasticity*, ensure the cohesion ... of established forms. Reinscribe them hither and thither *as divergencies* ... in *ellipses* and *eclipses* that deconstruct the logical grid of the reader-writer.... *Overthrow syntax* by suspending its eternally teleological order.... Not by means of a growing complexity of the same, of course, but by the irruption of other circuits ... short-circuits that will disperse, diffract, deflect endlessly making energy explode sometimes, with no possibility of returning to one single origin.[13]

She then moves toward introducing "a scintillating and incandescent concavity, of language also, that threatens to set fire to fetish-objects and gilded eyes."[14] The concave mirror, the very instrument that is used for the "exploration of internal cavities,"[15] is thus also disclosed as a *miroir ardent*, which, in its "incandescent hearth," transforms light into heat.[16] A masculine logic of visuality and distance is transformed into fire, into the tactile, sensory, material dimensions of transcendence that will come to the fore in the discourse of the mystics, occasioning a loss of boundary of the self as it merges with the other/God, a *jouissance* at once spiritual and carnal. This first half of "Speculum," as well as disconcerting philosophy's optics via the refractions of mimesis, performs a kind of downgoing or *katabasis* that prefigures or echoes the journey into Plato's cave, or womb (*hystera*) at the end of the text, in which woman is thereafter encrypted and the identification of the feminine with "matter" consolidated. Toril Moi, one of the few commentators to consider the structure of *Speculum* in any detail, argues that the text is itself shaped like a speculum, with a series of successive framing devices that deepen the discourse or rather cause it to "sink in," with the chapter on Descartes lying at the center: "Descartes sinks into the innermost cavity of the book."[17] Commentators seem to be roughly divided as to whether the Descartes chapter or "*La Mystérique*," the next chapter, constitutes the "true" center.[18] As I hope to show, the question of the "true center" is not quite the correct one to be asking, although, because of its "arrival" at feminine sexual difference in its engagement with the spiritual and bodily dimensions of feminine *jouissance*, "*La Mystérique*" necessarily forms a kind of culmination of the text, and its central position is not at all accidental on this account.[19]

"*La Mystérique*" investigates the figure of the female mystic who is also a "hysteric"—no doubt pathological in the frame of patriarchal psychoanalysis—whose psychical and somatic organization is inherently unstable and therefore subject to all sorts of conversions among and between psyche and soma, disordered or otherwise reordering. In her the channels between psyche and soma are open and productive. In her the transformation of matter/body/spirit through fire will take place, a refractive turn to upward motion or *anabasis*, once again via the operation of the burning glass.[20] Before we arrive there, the chapters on Plato and Aristotle take us from the dazzlement of the sun as figure of the Good (as well as its capacity to burn) to a consideration of matter in which the origin of life in the body of the mother is radically eclipsed and effaced. In Aristotle, woman or the feminine represents a privation or deformation of form, and a physics and metaphysics are thereby established in which the function of matter is to simply receive form, where form itself represents the masculine telos of Being. This rendering of matter as progressively evacuated of Being *as such* reaches its depths in the Neoplatonic discourse of Plotinus, in which Matter becomes a "bare seeming" with no reality in itself: "Its every utterance, therefore, is a lie; it pretends to be great and it is little, to be more and it is less; and the Existence with which it masks itself is no Existence, but a passing trick making trickery of all that seems to be present in it, phantasms within a phantasm; it is like a mirror showing things as in itself when they are really elsewhere, filled in appearance but actually empty, containing nothing, pretending everything."[21] Plotinus's discourse, itself a reflection or rendering of Plato's *Timaeus*, is reproduced verbatim by Irigaray, who renders herself invisible in the process, letting Plotinus himself make her point quite plainly. Tellingly (and at the exact mathematical center of *Speculum*), Plotinus also uses the image of a burning glass, a "reflecting vessel" full of water that produces fire in the sunlight, to illustrate the mysterious process of how matter, a "ground that repels," might find its way to reflecting Reality while having no being in itself, thereby becoming "the cause of the generated realm; the combinations within it hold together only after some such reflective mode."[22] This transformative power of the Neoplatonic burning mirror, giving rise to sensible beings while having precisely no being in itself, exemplifies for Irigaray the fate of the feminine within sexual difference. The burning glass, with its mysterious capacity of transmogrification or sublimation, its conversion of light into heat and fire, will turn out to be exactly the instrument that is needed for transforming the mysterious, hysterical, hitherto-unspeakable being of the woman into discourse, tactility, and visibility.

What is at issue, I contend, in the very narrative structure of *Speculum* is a scene of reversals, refractions, ellipses, and displacements in which the *miroir ardent*, or rather *miroirs ardents* in the plural, is the operative "metaphysical conceit," to take a term applied to metaphysical poets such as John Donne, contemporary of Descartes (Donne, strangely enough, appears surprisingly Irigarayan in some of his themes).[23] It is somewhat mysterious, after all, that the Descartes chapter *precedes* the chapter on the late medieval mystics—yet another chronological reversal or break. The Descartes chapter deals mainly with the classic transformation of the body, nature, the body of the mother into *res extensa* and the ontological severing of the "I," the thinking thing or *res cogitans*, from this order, but it also broaches the issue of optics and what optics owes to the body in its very title, ". . . And If, Taking the Eye of a Man Recently Dead, . . ." The chapter title is taken from the Fifth Discourse of Descartes's *Dioptrique* or *Optics*, and it requires us to consider the carnal foundation of vision, even if now in the form of a corpse. It is not without its ironies, then, that we also find a commentary on the burning glass, that instrument capable of transforming light into heat, or perhaps even *res cogitans* back into *res extensa*, in the *Optics*'s Eighth Discourse: "those mirrors with which, it is said, Archimedes burned far-off ships must have been extremely large—or rather, they are fabulous."[24] The Eighth Discourse also begins with a consideration of the figure of the ellipse, that figure that bears the significations of defect, deficiency, omission, falling short, wanting, or lacking (from the Greek *elleipsis*), and that, significantly, also stands as a motif and instrument throughout the text of *Speculum* (Elizabeth D. Harvey, for example, notes that the "disembodied eye" of the Descartes chapter title is itself placed between two ellipses).[25]

The ellipse, as recounted by Descartes, is most easily inscribed if, in the manner of a gardener, one places two pickets in the earth and ties a length of string between them that is longer than the distance between them. If one puts a finger against the string and pulls it taut, away from the pickets, and then inscribes a figure in the earth around the two pickets as if one were using a compass, the resulting figure will be an ellipse. In figure 16.1, the ellipse is inscribed at point B by a string connected at H and I.[26] And indeed if one moves the pickets close together, so close that they finally coincide, one will have arrived at a circle. An ellipse is thus in a sense a circle with two centers, a defective and deficient circle that, so to speak, is *not one*. As

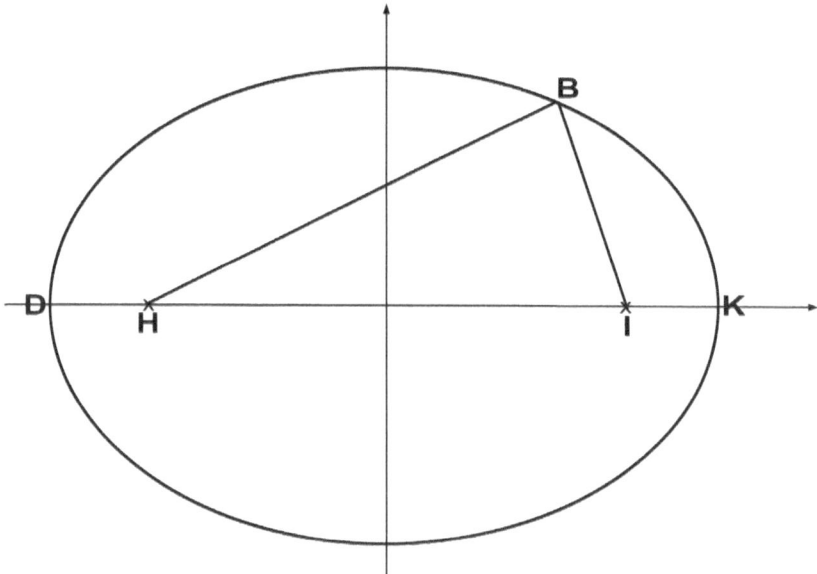

FIGURE 16.1 Based on fig. 33, Eighth Discourse, Descartes's *Optics*, 167.

READING *SPECULUM* AGAIN

Descartes mentions, these two centers, H and I, are known as the "burning points." In English they are called the foci, so named by Kepler, meaning "hearths" or "fireplaces," and this nomenclature is due to the fact that the ellipse has the following extraordinary property: if a mirror is inscribed upon the inner surface of the ellipse, and a lamp is lit at one of its burning points, light and heat will immediately appear at the other focus.

It is this astonishing action at a distance, at once geometrical, optical, physical, and sensible, that is exploited by the experimental device subsequently developed in the eighteenth century called the "conjugated mirrors"—two mirrors facing each other, at the burning point of one of which is placed a light and heat source, and at the other burning point of which is placed some kindling (figure 16.2). Experiments show that sound is also transmitted in this way. It is this configuration of the *miroirs ardents*,

Fig. 300 (h = 1ᵐ,50).

FIGURE 16.2 Adolphe Ganot, *Traité élémentaire de physique expérimentale et appliquée: et de météorologie suivi d'un recueil de 103 problèmes avec solutions* (Paris: Auteur, 1868). Hagley Museum and Library, Wilmington, DE 19807. Courtesy of the Hagley Museum and Library.

ellipses and parabolic, the conjugated mirrors and their *points ardents*, that I want to suggest forms the metaphysical conceit of *Speculum of the Other Woman*. It is through the conjugated mirrors that we might begin to discern the anamorphic logic, the transformative, synaesthetic action at a distance, that structures this ateleological, reversed, interrupted, specular text.

The narrative structure of *Speculum* has of course been remarked upon by numerous commentators over the years, most recently by Anne van Leeuwen, who convincingly associates Irigaray's strategy of "disconcertion" with Derridean deconstruction and Lacanian defiguration.[27] *Speculum*, I am contending, does more than simply effect a *de*-structuration, *dis*-ruption, or *dis*-concerting of traditional philosophical discourse, but rather a discernable *refiguration* is set in motion via the ellipse, the conjugated mirrors, and their *burning points*. Something novel and constructive is effected at the level of narrative, and at the levels of figuration and optics, which pushes toward a positive conception of a feminine imaginary and symbolic with its own morphology and its own temporality. In this way we might begin to account for the ending of the text that is not an ending, in which the male subject seeking truth from within the darkness of Plato's cave seems to literally run aground in the figure of the death of the mother who stands, shadow-like, behind the death of Socrates. The final section of the Plato section, "Plato's *Hystera*," is, after all, titled "'Woman's' *Jouissance*." But the pleasure to come, the pleasure or *jouissance* that burns with spiritual fire is not found here at all, as perhaps indicated by the quotation marks placed around "Woman." Rather, these raptures may be discovered at the center, or one of the centers of the book, in "*La Mystérique*," whose epigraph from the fourteenth-century mystic Ruysbroeck the Admirable describes the burning glass with fine concision: "Take a concave mirror and put it next to a dry and inflammable material; then expose the mirror to the rays of the sun; the dry material will catch fire and burn because of the heat of the sun and the concavity of the mirror."[28] In this central chapter, the cave of mimetic *doxa* gives way to bottomless abyss and is transfigured or sublimed into ecstasy in a blaze of light and heat: "A burning glass is the soul who in her cave joins with the source of light to set everything ablaze that approaches her hearth. Leaving only ashes there, only a hole: fathomless in her incendiary blaze."[29] And further: "In her and/or outside her, as in her jouissance, she loses all sense of corporeal boundary. Her distance from herself is all the greater because the fire was more deeply 'inward.' Because the deepest summit of her cave has been touched. Her remoteness in ecstasy, the flights of her soul, are all the greater because they reach further into that absence of soul that she is."[30] The "hole" is in a sense the hole at the center of the text where the im/possible woman's voice starts to speak, but that hole, the absence or lack, the falling short signified by the ellipse, has its counterpart in an equally indistinguishable conflagration that never stops burning.

Not only, then, does the ellipse or the figure of the conjugated mirrors redirect a presumptively teleological philosophical narrative away from the *end* of the text and to its center, but it also endlessly divides that center, which is also endlessly displaced. Woman's sex, after all, as Irigaray repeatedly expresses, is not simply a hole, a lack, a "horror of nothing to see," but a multiplicity that explodes outward, that scintillates, as well as permitting an endlessly downward fall, a concentric vortex: "Body, breasts, pubis, clitoris, labia, vulva, vagina, neck of the uterus, womb, . . . and this nothing that already gives pleasure by setting them apart from each other: all these foil any attempt at reducing sexual multiplicity to some proper noun, to some proper meaning, to some concept."[31] The "conceit" of the conjugated burning mirrors that endlessly reflect back and forth light and heat, in mutually intensifying involutions, and of the ellipse and its burning points (which, if set on its side, may also remind us of a vulva), may also be metonymically connected to the two lips, that corporeal, multiple, restless signifier of feminine sexual difference. The two lips, after all, famously signify not simply the lips of the vulva but also the lips of the mouth and thus the speaking subject and her capacities for signification, as well as the non-self-same-ness and multiplicity of women's sexual organs and sexual capacities, beyond the unitary ordering and teleological logic of the phallus. Read this way, the entire text works to reconfigure imaginary, symbolic, and real in the form of the vulva: an elliptical, labial, invaginated image effected by narrative structure.

At the limits of the entire text, then, the conjugated burning mirrors, reflecting and intensifying each other: Freud and Plato. As Rachel Jones explains, "in the echo-chamber *Speculum* becomes, psychoanalysis informs Irigaray's reading of Plato while her reading of Plato retroactively inflects the sections on Freud, making the implicit metaphysical commitments of psychoanalytic theory more readily discernable."[32] At the outer limits of the central section called "Speculum," the burning points: Irigaray's meditations, diagnoses, analyses—"Any Theory of the Subject . . ." and "Volume-Fluidity." At the center of the center of the text, indeterminately displacing one another, *les miroirs ardents*: Plotinus's freezing, burning mirror in which the feminine is locked; Descartes's deathbound yet polysemic optics; the open channels and *jouissance* of the mystics.

In this way, the text that is *Speculum* makes a radical intervention into traditional philosophical narrative that goes beyond mere reversal or "disconcertion" and pushes toward a transformation that is at once imaginary, symbolic, ontological, and temporal, in the name of sexual difference. This is not an easy claim to make, since the question of narrativity, which has been explored at length with regard to fictional and historical narratives, for example, in the work of Gérard Genette, Mieke Bal, and Paul Ricoeur, has received scant attention in relation to the texts of philosophy. Nonetheless, if we consider the traditional "monumental" Western philosophical treatise, for instance, Aristotle's *Metaphysics* or Hegel's *Phenomenology of Spirit*, we can discern how the philosophical narrative builds, slowly moving forward according to a teleological schema arguably inaugurated and consolidated by Aristotle. In the *Metaphysics*, Aristotle proceeds first by considering what others have said (and foreshadows his own conclusions), in the spirit of getting inadequate accounts out of the way, and subsequently in the central books by considering the many ways that being is said (according to accident, according to the true and false, according to substance, and according to potentiality and actuality), and by thinking through each of these avenues in turn.[33] Each successive line of inquiry seems more promising than the last, bringing us ever closer to a true account of being as substance, while inadequate solutions are considered and discarded. The *Metaphysics* reaches its teleological culmination in book 12, with the account of the divine prime mover as the best and most perfect form of life and the being in movement of the whole cosmos to which it gives rise qua telos. Telos functions here in all of its senses as goal, completion, and perfection, both in content and in the form of the unfolding of the text as narrative. In Hegel's *Phenomenology*, "spirit is indeed never at rest but always engaged in moving forward," and the text likewise moves through successive shapes of spirit toward Absolute Knowing, which encompasses all possible shapes.[34] While the question of genre in philosophy is no doubt a complex one (philosophy is after all found in forms as varied as the poem, dialogue, essay, aphorism, confession, meditation, deduction, and so on), and few texts achieve the level of internal coherence and completeness as these two, it is at this level of scale, ambition, and achievement that we ought to consider *Speculum*. In closing, then, let us, all too briefly, consider the possible significance of Irigaray's specular narrative as an in(ter)vention at the level of temporality, taken in Heideggerian spirit as an ontological terrain through which to think through the meaning of sexual difference.

At work, as we have seen, are the functions of mimesis as mirroring and, via the burning glass, as an operation of transformation/sublimation that traffics between the sensible and the intelligible, by way of the abject and the sublime, confounding their originary separation in the Western tradition since at least Plato. In Lacanian psychoanalytic terms, one might say that via this operation at the level of the imaginary, that of the mirror, one approaches the jouissance of the impossible real: the conflagration. And yet at the level of the symbolic, which is never a completed unfolding of language but an endless sliding of the signifier animated by a desire structured by lack and a fantasy of fullness, driven by the object, something else entirely seems to be at work. By beginning with the critique of Freud, Irigaray undoes the enshrinement in sexual difference of this dynamic of desire as lack and satisfaction, disabusing us from the start of the essentially phallic idea that there is a punctual moment of fullness, or of knowledge, or of wisdom, or of completion, at which the discourse will arrive. Instead, as we learn from Irigaray's oeuvre as a whole, she seeks to bring into being an ontology of the two, of two sexually different forms of life and of being that are not in any case substitutable for each other (for to seek substitution or substitutability would be for her once again to reduce the other to the same).[35] And yet, at the level of narrative strategy, what we have is not a modernist atelic wandering, nor do we have a traditional teleological narrative. What, then, are the consequences for a temporal and ontological consideration of sexuate being of a consideration of narrative as such?

As Gérard Genette tells us in *Narrative Discourse: An Essay in Method*, published contemporaneously with *Speculum*, first quoting Christian Metz: "One of the functions of narrative is to invent one time scheme in terms of another time scheme."[36] He continues further: "written narrative exists in space and as space, and the time needed for 'consuming' it is the time needed for *crossing* or *traversing* it, like a road or a field. The narrative text, like every other text, has no other temporality than what it borrows, metonymically, from its own reading."[37] He famously supplies the terms *prolepsis* and *analepsis* to designate flash-forwards and flashbacks, and reserves the term *anachrony* "to designate all forms of discordance between the two temporal orders of story and narrative."[38] Irigaray certainly deploys all of these in her disconcerting of philosophical history, which might itself be thought in turn as a history of attempts to pull embodied, sexuate beings outside of the ordinary time of coming to be and passing away, especially in their efforts to cover over our temporal origins in the body of the mother. Paul Ricoeur, in the three volumes of *Time and Narrative*, will make the case that time itself, the experience of time in the phenomenological sense, cannot be thought apart from narrative, in that it is always experienced in a dialectical relation with and implicated in a kind of narrativity, which involves three different moments of mimesis: $Mimesis_1$, $Mimesis_2$, and $Mimesis_3$. $Mimesis_1$ for Ricoeur is our unreflective involvement in a world of signification, presented as obvious and self-evident but constituted by a system of cultural symbolism—here we might simply think of the patriarchal architecture of the Western philosophical tradition that Irigaray is seeking to disconcert. At this level it is simply self-evident that one thing happens because of another and that what is sought is wholeness, completion, and satisfaction—so a nonreflective notion of causation is at work. The configuring act of narration begins with "a preunderstanding of the world of action, its meaningful structures, its symbolic resources, and its temporal character"[39] (the echoes of Aristotle's notion of plot, or *muthos*, as "imitation of an action" from the *Poetics* are strongly present). The second stage of mimesis, $Mimesis_2$ involves the introduction of the *as if*. In fiction, this counterfactual operation is self-evident, but here, in the genre of philosophy, something else takes place. In fiction, $Mimesis_2$ draws us into the fictive plane where, in a sense, "anything may happen" as long as the author is able to sustain credibility, whereas in the philosophical narrative we are arguably being drawn into a story, allegory, dialogue, meditation, confession, or argument in which where we are being led is presumed to be *more* real rather than *less* real (although let us recall Aristotle's claim in the *Poetics* that poetry "is more philosophical and more serious than history: in fact poetry speaks more of universals, whereas history of particulars").[40] Plotting and narrative at the level of $Mimesis_2$ Ricoeur tells us, enable us to grasp a manifold of chronological events as a whole; as he says "the act of emplotment . . . extracts a configuration from a succession."[41] Here, we see the significance of Aristotle's "universal," or *katholou*, of which poetry speaks more than history, a word that is more accurately rendered as "in relation to the whole." *Speculum* disabuses us of the fantasy of the kind of whole that is granted by the traditional philosophical plot or narrative, and via its elliptical conceit of the burning mirrors provides us with a glimpse of an entirely different notion of emplotment altogether, as we travel backward and downward from Freud, forward through the philosophers from Plato to Hegel, via the burning points of her two specular meditations, and through the fiery crucible of *La Mystérique*, only to arrive at a second *katabasis* of the cave, where we might glimpse the possibility of a rebirth from the womb, only to find that this is never granted. We are thrown backward, or forward again, to Freud, and thence to a ricochet through the text, into a resonant vortex that displaces, *heats up*, and certainly grants a kind of *jouissance*, a pleasure far removed from any teleology, any model of desire predicated upon the proleptic or anticipatory filling of a lack. Here, then, we are in the territory of Ricoeur's Mimesis$_3$, where the text intersects with the world and with the reader and where, according to Ricoeur, time itself must be understood as conditioned by and capable of refiguration by narrativity. The radicality of Irigaray's thinking, here, inhabits and transforms Aristotle's insistence upon the philosophical power of *poetry*, of emplotment, reversal, recognition, denouement, catharsis, insofar as poetry is itself understood to involve a relation to a *whole*.

This is not the place to broach the complexities of Ricoeur's understanding of temporality as such, which includes the phenomenological analysis of memory, direct perception of the present, and anticipation, a sense of what is to come; an analysis rooted in Augustine but that also passes through Husserlian retention and protention as well as Heideggerian ecstatic temporality; and finally a sense of time as a "collective singular," a common and agreed-upon sense that we draw on when we say something like "time passed." Ricoeur ultimately understands time as a dialectic between an aporetics of temporality (the aporia being between time as experienced and time understood as shared and collective), on the one hand, and a poetics, a narrativity that is always a "discordant concordance" at the level of temporality insofar as it broaches both totalization and heterogeneity, on the other. In a later essay, "The Female Gender," Irigaray contrasts the repetitive, machinic, patriarchal time of "the same" with the unfolding and never self-same temporality of nature, which may be cyclical but is never self-same or truly repetitive.[42] *Speculum*'s experimentation with temporality through narrative, however, could by no means be described as miming that of nature; something else entirely is going on here as Irigaray forges her intervention.

Let us note, as Ricoeur does, that for Aristotle the *denouement* of a plot, as well as its reversals (*peripeteiai*) and moments of recognition (*anagnōriseis*), effects something like a hysterical conversion, in that it produce a *purgation* (*catharsis*) via the effects of pity and fear that may be easily understood in a somatic register. No doubt for Aristotle, and the subsequent tradition, these effects are produced as a result of proleptic, teleological expectations embedded in emplotment in which wholes may be momentarily grasped. But in her efforts to not simply state but also show or experientially demonstrate the being of sexual difference at multiple levels, Irigaray engages in a poetic, narrative practice that, via the procedure outlined by Ricoeur, undertakes a refiguration or rearrangement of lived temporality, one in which a preunderstanding of a causal, temporal order governed by the expectation of a whole, perfect, and complete emplotment gives way to a disconcerting movement that is at once deficient and overfull, that at once disappoints and undermines our expectations, but also seduces us back around, at once proleptically, analeptically, and anachronically, through a kind of specular *mise-en-abyme*, to a forgotten or lost *decentered center*. *Speculum*, in this way, draws our attention to a certain dimension of lived, sexuate, temporal experience, namely, an *invaginated* temporality: temporal abyss, temporal intensification, or temporal ablation, perhaps, secreted or involuted within ordinary time.

Understanding Irigaray's philosophical text as poetic text, via the conceit of the burning mirrors and their specular, sensory *mise-en-abyme*, demonstrates not simply that mimesis leads to the reproduction of degraded copies, but rather that conversion at the level of soma, the hysterical conversion that may be understood in classical terms as a downgoing or *katabasis*, may also, under certain conditions of intensification, necessarily involve an *anabasis*, or upward movement (this foreshadows Irigaray's later notion of the "sensible transcendental" in *An Ethics of Sexual Difference*). As her mimetic narrative crosses and traverses time and space, we find our telic expectations interrupted, reversed, restarted, disconcerted, decentered, and finally refigured, in such a way that we are led to an embodied and sexuate sense of temporality, a feminine temporality that is less cyclical or monumental, as Kristeva would have it, than both incomplete and overfull, riddled with something like *interruptivity*. Interruptivity, I have argued elsewhere, names a capacity to interrupt and be interrupted, a temporal mode of being primarily associated with women's bodily, social, affective, and political experiences (Irigaray would, no doubt, add spiritual experience).[43] Since *Speculum* remains poetic, experimental, proleptic, and critical, any such claim about a nascent feminine temporality within its pages must remain at the level of suggestion. Indeed, my own argument and understanding of "interruptive" temporality on the side of the feminine result from an analysis in which the feminine as symptomatic aleatory matter, so designated within a specifically Aristotelian Western philosophical frame, is transvalued and appropriated as a temporal capacity for feminist interruption and overthrow, rather than making any positive claim about sexual difference at the level of ontology. In considering both abject downgoing and the ecstasy of *jouissance* at the site of the feminine as *mystérique*, and the restless turnings, overturnings, openings, and conversions among and between the corporeal, the sensible, the imaginary, the symbolic, and the divine effected by the burning mirrors, Irigaray, in her poietic practice, pushes toward a temporal understanding of feminine sexual difference in which an expansive and liberatory carnal/spiritual temporality is enfolded and secreted within ordinary, everyday temporality. This is quite unlike any Platonic/Christian aspiration to eternal time that involves the transcendence of everyday temporality. That is, any further elaboration of feminine sexual difference may need to consider a kind of temporal expansion and depth, an *invaginated* temporality, that is available at every moment to those willing and able to access mystical experience but nonetheless by no means obvious or self-evident under the presumptively undiffracted glare of the traditional philosophical gaze. Such experience may yet, or not yet, provide something like a groundless ground for an ontological understanding of sexual difference.

BIBLIOGRAPHY

Aristotle. *Metaphysics I–IX*. Translated by Hugh Tredennick. Cambridge, MA: Harvard University Press, 1989.
——. *Metaphysics X–XIV, Oeconomica. Magna Moralia*. Translated by Hugh Tredennick. Cambridge, MA: Harvard University Press, 1977.

———. *Poetics*. Translated by S. Halliwell. In Aristotle, *Poetics. Longinus, On the Sublime. Demetrius, On Style*, 27–141. Cambridge, MA: Harvard University Press, 2005.
Berry, Philippa. "The Burning Glass: Paradoxes of Feminist Revelation." In *Engaging with Irigaray: Feminist Philosophy and Modern European Thought*, edited by Carolyn Burke, Naomi Schor, and Margaret Whitford, 229–246. New York: Columbia University Press, 1994.
Bianchi, Emanuela. "The Interruptive Feminine: Aleatory Time and Feminist Politics." In *Undutiful Daughters: New Directions in Feminist Thought and Practice*, edited by Henriette Gunkel, Chrysanthi Nigianni, and Fanny Söderbäck, 35–47. New York: Palgrave Macmillan, 2012.
Cheah, Pheng, Elizabeth Grosz, Judith Butler, and Drucilla Cornell. "The Future of Sexual Difference: An Interview with Judith Butler and Drucilla Cornell." *Diacritics: Irigaray and the Political Future of Sexual Difference* 28, no. 1 (1998): 19–42.
Descartes, René. "Optics." In *Discourse on Method, Optics, Geometry and Meteorology*, translated by Paul J. Olscamp, 65–175. Indianapolis: Bobbs-Merrill, 1965.
Genette, Gérard. *Narrative Discourse: An Essay in Method*. Translated by Jane E. Lewin. 1972; Ithaca: Cornell University Press, 1980.
Greenstadt, Eliza A. "Irigaray's Speculum Conceit." Unpublished paper on file with the author.
Grosz, Elizabeth. *Sexual Subversions: Three French Feminists*. Sydney: Allen and Unwin, 1989.
Haraway, Donna. "Situated Knowledges: The Science Question in Feminism and the Privilege of Partial Perspective." *Feminist Studies* 14, no. 3 (1988): 575–599.
Harvey, Elizabeth D. "'Mutuall Elements': Irigaray's Donne." In *Luce Irigaray and Premodern Culture*, edited by Elizabeth D. Harvey and Theresa Krier, 66–87. New York: Routledge, 2004.
Hegel, G. W. F. *Phenomenology of Spirit*. Translated by A. V. Miller. Oxford: Oxford University Press, 1977.
Hollywood, Amy. "'That Glorious Slit': Irigaray and the Medieval Devotion to Christ's Side Wound." In *Luce Irigaray and Premodern Culture*, edited by Elizabeth D. Harvey and Theresa Krier, 105–125. New York: Routledge, 2004.
Irigaray, Luce. *Sharing the Fire: Outline of a Dialectics of Sensitivity*. New York: Palgrave Macmillan, 2019.
Jones, Rachel. *Irigaray: Towards a Sexuate Philosophy*. Cambridge: Polity, 2011.
Knowles Middleton, W. E. "Archimedes, Kircher, Buffon, and the Burning-Mirrors." *Isis* 52, 4 (1961): 533–543.
Kristeva, Julia. "Women's Time." In *The Portable Kristeva*, edited by Kelly Oliver, 351–370. New York: Columbia University Press, 2002.
Lacan, Jacques. *Écrits*. Translated by Bruce Fink. New York: Norton, 2006.
———. "Seminar XXII, R.S.I." Translated by Cormac Gallagher. www.lacaninireland.com/web/wp-content/uploads/2010/06/RSI-Complete-With-Diagrams.pdf.
———. *The Seminar of Jacques Lacan, Book XX/ On Feminine Sexuality: The Limits of Love and Knowledge: Encore, 1972–1972*. Translated by Bruce Fink. New York: Norton, 1999.
Moi, Toril. *Sexual/Textual Politics*. London: Methuen, 1985.
Plantzos, Dimitris. "Crystals and Lenses in the Graeco-Roman World." *American Journal of Archaeology* 101, no. 3 (1997): 451–464.

Poe, Danielle. "Can Luce Irigaray's Notion of Sexual Difference Be Applied to Transsexual and Transgender Narratives?" In *Thinking with Irigaray*, edited by Mary C. Rawlinson, Sabrina L. Hom, and Serene J. Khader, 111–128. Albany: SUNY Press, 2011.

Ricoeur, Paul. *Time and Narrative*. Vol. 1. Translated by Kathleen McLaughlin and David Pellauer. Chicago: University of Chicago Press, 1984.

Söderback, Fanny. *Revolutionary Time: On Time and Difference in Kristeva and* Irigaray. Albany: SUNY Press, 2019.

Vade, Dylan. "Expanding Gender and Expanding the Law: Toward a Social and Legal Conceptualization of Gender That Is More Inclusive of Transgender People." *Michigan Journal of Gender and Law* 11, no. 2 (2005): 253–316.

van Leeuwen, Anne. "Deconstruction, Defiguration, Disconcertion: On Reading *Speculum de l'Autre Femme* with Derrida and Lacan." In *Thinking Life with Luce Irigaray*, edited by Gail M. Schwab, 257–267. Albany: SUNY Press, 2020.

Whitford, Margaret. *Luce Irigaray: Philosophy in the Feminine*. New York: Routledge, 2003.

Williams, Linda. *Hard Core: Power, Pleasure, and the Frenzy of the Visible*. London: Pandora, 1990.

NOTES

1. Irigaray, TS, 68.
2. These reflections (the optical metaphors may be unavoidable) grew out of a graduate seminar on *Speculum* I taught at NYU in spring 2020 and were in particular inspired by Rachel Jones (also in this volume), who graciously visited our class (which had "gone remote" in the wake of the Covid-19 pandemic) on two occasions. The ideas in this piece would not have emerged were it not for Rachel's key insights, and for the collaborative reading of *Speculum* undertaken with graduate students Tuhin Bhattacharjee, Darja Filippova, Iván Hofman (see this volume), and Colin Stragar-Rice. I thank them all for their attentive, patient, and productive engagements with the text in an often-traumatic semester. I also thank A. Eliza Greenstadt for her wonderful undergraduate paper "Irigaray's Speculum Conceit," written at Wesleyan College for a feminist theory class taught by the late Christina Crosby in the 1980s (on file with the author), and for illuminating discussions by phone and email about Irigaray, John Donne, and the "metaphysical conceit." Last, my heartfelt thanks to our editors, to Mary Rawlinson first of all for encouraging me to put these speculations into writing, and to James Sares for his careful editorial interventions, which, among other things, pushed me to clarify the work of *Speculum* in relation to the Lacanian schema of imaginary-symbolic-real.
3. The question of Irigaray's possible essentialism was treated thoroughly by a variety of thinkers in the years following the 1985 translations into English of *Speculum* and *This Sex Which Is Not One*. See, for example, Carolyn Burke, Naomi Schor, and Margaret Whitford, eds., *Engaging with Irigaray: Feminist Philosophy and Modern European Thought* (New York: Columbia University Press, 1994); and Pheng Cheah, Elizabeth Grosz, Judith Butler, and Drucilla Cornell, "The Future

of Sexual Difference: An Interview with Judith Butler and Drucilla Cornell," *Diacritics: Irigaray and the Political Future of Sexual Difference* 28, no. 1 (1998): 19–42.

4. This is not the place to rigorously describe the various definitions and transformations undergone by the concepts of Imaginary, Symbolic, and Real and their interrelationships in the thought of Jacques Lacan over the course of many decades. Irigaray does not adhere to either Lacan's implicit Kantianism, or his association of the real with Freud's death instinct or compulsion to repeat, or the sanctity of the bar that defends against the real, but rather approaches and undoes this terrain on her own terms. For the Imaginary and Symbolic respectively, see Jacques Lacan, "The Mirror Stage as Formative of the I Function as Revealed in Psychoanalytic Experience" and "The Function and Field of Speech and Language in Psychoanalysis," in *Écrits*, trans. Bruce Fink (New York: Norton, 2006), 75–81, 197–288; for the Real, see Lacan, *The Seminar of Jacques Lacan: Book XX, On Feminine Sexuality: The Limits of Love and Knowledge: Encore, 1972–1972*, trans. Bruce Fink (New York: Norton, 1999).

5. Three weeks after the publication of *Speculum* in France in the fall of 1974, Irigaray was fired from her teaching position at *L'Ecole freudienne* at the University of Paris (Vincennes) by Jacques Lacan for "deviance," and never again held a university position. That very season, Lacan delivered his seminar XXII, R.S.I. (Real, Symbolic, Imaginary), where he attempted to limn the intrication of the three registers. At the time of writing the only available English translation of this seminar, by Cormac Gallagher from unedited French manuscripts, is available online at http://www.lacaninireland.com.

6. There is a mimetic echo of Lacan in this engagement with the mystics insofar as he cites Bernini's statue of St. Teresa in Rome as evidence of feminine *jouissance*, knowledge of which is barred from the woman experiencing it (Lacan, *Seminar XX*, 76), a gesture that is roundly mocked by Irigaray at TS, 91. Her engagement with the writings of the mystics in *Speculum* takes place, rather, in a decidedly experimental, avant-garde, and antiessentialist feminist mode of "writing the body," tending toward the breakdown and disruption of Lacanian analytic categories, in which the aim seems to be to open up the possibilities inherent in speaking as or from the positionality and bodily situation of a woman, *parler femme*, beyond the discourse of the phallus, rather than locking women or the feminine into any particular specificity. In this poetic practice of *écriture féminine*, Irigaray is aligned with other French feminist writers of the period such as Hélène Cixous and Marguerite Duras, and the strategy is to be distinguished from the more programmatic, ontologically secure, and politically oriented descriptions of sexual difference that may be found in many of her later works.

7. Margaret Whitford, *Luce Irigaray: Philosophy in the Feminine* (New York: Routledge, 2003), 34.

8. Irigaray, TS, 74–80.

9. Linda Williams, *Hard Core: Power, Pleasure, and the Frenzy of the Visible*, (London: Pandora Press, 1990). For another key feminist critique of the technological fantasy of full visual knowledge, see Donna Haraway, "Situated Knowledges: The Science Question in Feminism and the Privilege of Partial Perspective," *Feminist Studies* 14, no. 3 (1988): 575–599.

10. Irigaray, TS, 24.

11. In "Blind Spot," for example, she refers to the "lips, any of the lips," in the context of Freud's insistence in the "Femininity" essay that the little girl's initial genital drive is purely clitoral, understood on the masculine model (S, 29); otherwise the references are desultory, and include several references to the violent imagery of lips sealed over or sewn up (S, 188, 200, 230, 240).
12. Philippa Berry, "The Burning Glass: Paradoxes of Feminist Revelation," in *Engaging with Irigaray: Feminist Philosophy and Modern European Thought*, ed. Carolyn Burke, Naomi Schor, and Margaret Whitford (New York: Columbia University Press, 1994).
13. Irigaray, S, 142, emphasis in original.
14. Irigaray, 143.
15. Irigaray, 146.
16. The *miroir ardent* was legendarily put to use by Archimedes, who was said to have burned the attacking fleet of Marcellus with a parabolic *speculum* that focused the sun's rays (Irigaray, S, 148). The story is referenced as the earliest occurrence of "speculum" as a scientific instrument in the *Oxford English Dictionary*, 2nd ed. (1989), s.v. "speculum." Descartes famously argued that it would have not been possible to set ships on fire at a distance with a mirror because of the limitations of the sun's diameter, a claim that effectively rendered the Archimedes story a fable. This military use of the *miroir ardent* was the subject of repeated experiments by Kircher and then Georges Buffon in eighteenth-century Paris, who proved that at a smaller and more realistic distance the feat would have indeed been possible. See W. E. Knowles Middleton, "Archimedes, Kircher, Buffon, and the Burning-Mirrors," *Isis* 52, no. 4 (1961): 533–543.
17. Toril Moi, *Sexual/Textual Politics* (London: Methuen, 1985), 131.
18. Moi, *Sexual/Textual Politics*: and Elizabeth D. Harvey, "'Mutuall Elements': Irigaray's Donne," in *Luce Irigaray and Premodern Culture*, ed. Elizabeth D. Harvey and Theresa Krier (New York: Routledge, 2004), claim it is the Descartes chapter, while Elizabeth Grosz, *Sexual Subversions: Three French Feminists* (Sydney: Allen and Unwin, 1989); and Berry, "Burning Glass," contend it is "*La Mystérique*."
19. This "central" insight I owe to Rachel Jones, offered during her visit to my spring 2020 graduate seminar on *Speculum*.
20. Berry, "Burning Glass," 231, argued that *Speculum* was Irigaray's "unwritten" fire book, anticipating her tetralogy devoted to the four elements of antiquity: *Marine Lover of Friedrich Nietzsche*, *The Forgetting of Air in Martin Heidegger*, and *Elemental Passions*. In 2019, Irigaray published *Sharing the Fire: Outline of a Dialectics of Sensitivity*, in which she reads desire as a kind of inner fire.
21. Irigaray, S, 168–169. Irigaray here cites Plotinus's Sixth Tractate, "The Impassivity of the Unembodied," from his *Enneads*.
22. Irigaray, S, 176. The words are still those of Plotinus. The "burning glass," including the glass filled with water that produces fire, was known throughout antiquity, and attested in Theophrastus, Pliny, Lactantius, and Titus Bostentris. See Dimitris Plantzos, "Crystals and Lenses in the Graeco-Roman World," *American Journal of Archaeology* 101, no. 3 (1997): 451–464, 459.
23. Compare, for example, the conceit of the pair of compasses, another contemporary geometrical device, in Donne's "A Valediction: Forbidding Mourning," and his sensuous invocation of the "two lips" in "Sappho to Philaenis." I thank Eliza

Greenstadt for alerting me to these poems, themes, and connections, as well as to the conceit of the "conceit," developed in her essay "Irigaray's Speculum Conceit." For a different approach to the connection between Donne and Irigaray, see Harvey, "Mutuall Elements."

24. René Descartes, "Optics," in *Discourse on Method, Optics, Geometry and Meteorology*, trans. Paul J. Olscamp (Indianapolis: Bobbs-Merrill, 1965), 147. That the burning glass appears here as weapon of war, a corpse-making machine, perhaps has a deironizing force, and reinscribes the Cartesian rendering of body as machine or corpse.

25. Harvey, "Mutuall Elements," 69.

26. Descartes, "Optics," 127–128.

27. Anne van Leeuwen, "Deconstruction, Defiguration, Disconcertion: On Reading *Speculum de l'autre femme* with Derrida and Lacan," in *Thinking Life with Luce Irigaray*, ed. Gail M. Schwab (Albany: SUNY Press, 2020).

28. Irigaray, S, 191.

29. Irigaray, 199.

30. Irigaray, 201. Berry, "Burning Glass," shows in detail how the discourse follows that of the late medieval mystics Angela of Foligno, Catherine of Siena, Teresa of Avila, and Marguerite Porete. See also Amy Hollywood, "'That Glorious Slit': Irigaray and the Medieval Devotion to Christ's Side Wound," in *Luce Irigaray and Premodern Culture*, ed. Elizabeth D. Harvey and Theresa Krier, (New York: Routledge, 2004).

31. Irigaray, S, 233.

32. Rachel Jones, *Irigaray: Towards a Sexuate Philosophy* (Cambridge: Polity, 2011), 41.

33. Aristotle, *Metaphysics*, books I–IX, trans. Hugh Tredennick, (Cambridge, MA: Harvard University Press, 1989); and Aristotle, *Metaphysics*, Books X–XIV, in Aristotle, *Metaphysics X–XIV; Oeconomica: Magna Moralia*, trans. Hugh Tredennick, (Cambridge, MA: Harvard University Press, 1977). He lays out these different ways of saying being, and thus the analysis to come, at *Metaphysics* VI, ii 1026a33f—and though he lists the third as "according to the categories," it is the only the first category of the ten of the *Organon*, that of substance, that is afforded serious consideration in the discourse of the *Metaphysics*.

34. G. W. F. Hegel, *Phenomenology of Spirit*, trans. A. V. Miller (Oxford: Oxford University Press, 1977), 6.

35. To briefly address a complex issue, while Irigaray herself has been accused of transphobic positions (see Danielle Poe, "Can Luce Irigaray's Notion of Sexual Difference Be Applied to Transsexual and Transgender Narratives?," in *Thinking with Irigaray*, eds. Mary C. Rawlinson, Sabrina L. Hom, and Serene J. Khader [Albany: SUNY Press, 2011], 111–128, for a survey of these critiques and subsequent defense of Irigaray), this claim as stated is in no way aligned with any form of transphobia. In fact, on many conceptions of trans*-ness it is taken for granted, and while it avers that sexual difference is a phenomenal and natural facticity structured as two mutually unsubstitutable modes of being, this does not in any way obviate the fact that each one of us negotiates this "regime of two" in our own fashion and according to our own understanding and experience of our sexuate selves, giving rise to a galaxy of possible lived and embodied sexuate positions deserving protection and dignity under the law and in everyday life. In fact, imagining the

sexuate possibilities of the feminine imaginary, as proposed by Irigaray, expands the possible palate of identities and expressions of sexuate being since it does not assume one sex as the original standard unmarked "nonsexuate" term against which sexuateness itself appears as "feminine." For the concept of the "gender galaxy," see Dylan Vade, "Expanding Gender and Expanding the Law: Toward a Social and Legal Conceptualization of Gender That Is More Inclusive of Transgender People," *Michigan Journal of Gender and Law* 11, no. 2 (2005): 253–316.
36. Christian Metz, cited in Gérard Genette, *Narrative Discourse: An Essay in Method*, trans. Jane E. Lewin (1972; Ithaca: Cornell University Press, 1980), 33.
37. Genette, *Narrative Discourse*, 34.
38. Genette, 40.
39. Paul Ricoeur, *Time and Narrative*, vol. 1, trans. Kathleen McLaughlin and David Pellauer (Chicago: University of Chicago Press, 1984), 54.
40. Aristotle, *Poetics*, 9, 1451b5–7.
41. Ricoeur, *Time and Narrative*, 1:66.
42. Luce Irigaray, "The Female Gender," a lecture given in 1985 and published in SG, 107–108. See also the reflections on Irigarayan time in Fanny Söderback, *Revolutionary Time: On Time and Difference in Kristeva and Irigaray* (Albany: SUNY Press, 2019).
43. For accounts of feminine temporality as cyclical and monumental, as opposed to linear, see Julia Kristeva, "Women's Time," in *The Portable Kristeva*, ed. Kelly Oliver (New York: Columbia University Press, 2002). For interruptivity, see Emanuela Bianchi, "The Interruptive Feminine: Aleatory Time and Feminist Politics," in *Undutiful Daughters: New Directions in Feminist Thought and Practice*, ed. Henriette Gunkel, Chrysanthi Nigianni, and Fanny Söderbäck (New York: Palgrave Macmillan, 2012), 35–47.

Chapter Seventeen

INDEBTEDNESS
A Sexuate Malaise

IVÁN HOFMAN

It has long been recognized, though rather obliquely, that indebtedness is a structural trait of sexual difference. Both Plato and Aristotle, for example, drawing on the polysemy of the Greek word *tokos*, which means both "offspring" and "interest," punningly blend the concept of interest with the problem of reproduction and sexuation.[1] Yet, while there has recently been increased interest in the concept of indebtedness,[2] little has been said about the question of sexual difference being itself inscribed within an economy of indebtedness.[3] Luce Irigaray, however, shows how the ontological significance of sexual difference can be better grasped when understood as a problem involving indebtedness. Irigaray claims that the objectivization of women in philosophical discourse "provides the financial backing [or guaranteeing mortgage, *l'hypothèque garante*] for every irreducible constitution as an object: of representation, of discourse, of desire."[4] The subjectivity denied to women during the process of construction of the object of representation ("Woman") not only is appropriated by the masculine but also provides, she asserts, the *financial infrastructure* that enables man's representation of the feminine in the first place.

Beginning with *Speculum of the Other Woman*, Irigaray performs a reading of "Western philosophy" as a great system of exchange, a huge financial system of indebtedness. She sees Western philosophy as producing a "specular economy" whose techniques and tactics are those of indebtedness:

since men are indebted to women insofar as birth condemns them to a condition of originary ontological dependence, it is the repression of the latter that constitutes the fiction on which the *sexuate* foundations of Western philosophy, themselves embedded within a masculine imaginary and symbolic, are built. Irigaray sees philosophy and psychoanalysis as reversing men's originary dependence and construing women as one-sidedly indebted to men. For the category of women to appear in that specular economy, it must be only in perpetual debt to men, as property or progeny of his seed, or insofar as women's sexuality is construed in the image of his own.

Other thinkers have used debt metaphors to describe philosophical systems. Theodor W. Adorno, for instance, often uses debt metaphors and has compared Hegelian idealism and Heideggerian ontology to a "gigantic" or "highly developed" credit system."[5] This economic metaphor explicitly construes a relation of analogy or isomorphism between capitalist techniques and tactics such as indebtedness, on the one hand, and philosophical systems, on the other. Catherine Malabou has argued that it is possible to read Heidegger's philosophy as a system of exchange if we consider the privileged place held by economic metaphors in the discourse of metaphysics.[6] David Graeber clarifies how the historical emergence of philosophy can be read in terms of moral concerns about debt. For Graeber, to tell the history of debt is an attempt to "reconstruct how the language of the marketplace has come to pervade every aspect of human life."[7] Philosophy being no exception, the intrusion of the economic language of indebtedness into philosophy has to be reconstructed if we are to grasp the full significance of what Irigaray claimed to be "one of the major philosophical issues, if not the issue, of our age":[8] sexual difference.

Irigaray has most clearly articulated how Western philosophy, understood as a structural system of exchange whose general equivalent is the phallus and whose commodities—women—are exchanged in the marketplace, has relied not only on economic metaphors but also on a structural condition of originary indebtedness to the mother, repressed and reversed by men.[9] In the first section of this chapter, I discuss how Irigaray constructs sexual difference as being originally produced and fabricated within the framework of ontological indebtedness. Despite its manifest presence in the etymology of the Greek word *tokos*, the financial problem at the heart of ontology—that is, the problem of the gift of being and its debts—has been analyzed without sufficient attention to sexual difference. As Irigaray claims, the latter is the real "forgetting" involved in ontological discourse or what has been erased from it. To counter this, she shows the long-lasting and all-pervasive effects of the category of debt in philosophical discourse and insists on the necessity of disclosing it to understand sexual difference and its philosophical, political, and economic implications. The second section of this chapter discusses Irigaray's construction of an ethics of sexual difference concerned with reversing the phallocratic erasure of the indebtedness to the mother. By revealing yet destabilizing the financial tactics of philosophy, her "ethics of sexual difference" turns to women's writing as one ground for a possible "feminine transcendency."[10] For Irigaray, it is within the matrical domain of feminine transcendence that it is possible to envision a reversal of the phallocratic economy of indebtedness.

THE STRUCTURE OF ONTOLOGICAL INDEBTEDNESS: REREADING *SPECULUM*

In *Speculum of the Other Woman*, Irigaray foregrounds the "optical considerations" in the representation of the category of "Woman" in Western philosophy by problematizing the politics of the gaze over the feminine. For Irigaray, the history of Western philosophy, which she explores achronologically from Freud to Plato, is a continuous monologue whereby men speak among themselves about the "riddle, the logograph," or the "enigma" of Woman.[11] As a closed discourse, which is kept cleansed from the actual presence of women and yet is invariably interested in defining her, the ontometaphysical and psychoanalytic discussions about femininity have always been a reflection of the masculine self: as much as men have tried to understand women as the "mysterious" other, all they have managed to say is a reflection of the desires of the self. Within the specular economy of discourse construed by men, otherness is canceled out into identity. But, Irigaray claims, the representation of women in philosophical discourse, their circulation for the consumption of men, provides the symbolic infrastructure of the social system itself.[12] The specular economy of philosophy is thus intimately dependent on modes of appropriation: what she calls the phallocentric economy of discourse and phallocratic power itself gain their force, sustenance, and capacities from nothing else than the representation—that is, the exchange, substitution, and equivalence—of women in the economy of the same.

The language of political economy is textually inscribed in Irigaray's *Speculum*. But her analysis of the specular dimensions of representation is not just economical in the general sense, as she heavily relies on the specificity of the financial language of indebtedness.[13] Irigaray formulates debt as one of the conditions of our being. More specifically, she argues that the fundamental trait that structures our being from its very beginning is a dependence on the body and gestation of the mother—what she frames as an originary indebtedness to her who has given birth to us. According to Irigaray, the forgetting of the originary indebtedness to the mother and to her gestation is the basis of a whole patriarchal economy of indebtedness. She describes the condition of man's ontological indebtedness in tandem with the "feminine transcendency" of the mother whose otherness is inappropriable but who is nonetheless erased or turned by patriarchy into an instrument that needs to be inseminated and cultivated for it to bear the fruit of its seed.[14] Irigaray traces the structure of this transformation within the history of Western philosophy[15] while disclosing the ways in which philosophical discourse constructs ontology as *sexuate*.[16]

Irigaray lays bare how patriarchal thought reverses the originary indebtedness to the body of the mother by crafting a notion of the subject either as autonomous and autarkic vis-à-vis the mother or as dependent on women as passive receptacles for men's reproduction of their seed, name, and property. Aristotle is one representative of the latter form of reversal and Descartes of the former. On the one hand, Irigaray traces how Aristotle's idea that "human life takes its form only from its father, or more specifically from the male sperm,"[17] has structured ontological thinking up to modern times. Irigaray claims that Aristotle's notion of "first matter," *prōtē hylē*, by which he called the "menstrual fluid" that he saw as the basis for the *generation of animals*, is endowed with an "ontological privilege." Yet this privilege is fleeting and inconsequential, Irigaray tells us, as he saw this "matter" as "radically lacking in all power of logos."[18] If Aristotle saw "matter" as being provided by the female, he nonetheless attributed the needed "form" and "principle of movement" to the male's seed. The female, he thought, only provides the "material," the receptacle where shape is given by the soul and principle of motion originating in the male.[19] Yet, on the other hand, the "ontological privilege" both endowed to and withdrawn from the *prōtē hylē* is more radically denied, or forgotten, by modern thinkers like Descartes, for whom the subject's "condition of being results from self-reflection." This "self-reflection" operates, Irigaray tells us, "like the backing of a mirror that has been introjected, 'incorporated,' and is thus beyond perception."[20] The Cartesian subject incorporates the mirror of knowledge into his self to "perceive itself as the *matrix* of everything that is thought (within it)."[21] Irigaray claims that this privileging of self-certainty, as well as its implication of self-sufficiency, is tantamount to a rejection of the very idea of the subject's primordial dependence on an other human subject, particularly of the fact of having been originated, gestated, by a woman.

The dream for a "reproduction (of self) without matter, or mother" would enable men, Irigaray writes later in her analysis of Plato, to "never need to pay off the debt [*échéance*], either in the past or in the future, if one can only attain the ideal of sameness."[22] This dream for self-creation, she continues, is a "mirage in the gold of the Father's speculation, which would do away with the 'death' that at the outset is credited to him [*se fie à son crédit*]."[23] The male subject either claims self-sufficiency or else, against the originary *Schuld* to the mother, desires to "be indebted [*redevable*] only to the father's law"—including the laws of the city or of God.[24]

If the patriarchal system cannot tolerate indebtedness to women, it is because the relation between the creditor and the debtor is fundamentally a power relation based on an understanding of debt as the promise of repayment. The patriarchal anxiety about the originary ontological indebtedness to women, what it sees as the submission involved in becoming a debtor, is what causes men, if they are to sustain their phallocratic power, to turn upside down the condition of ontological indebtedness. This is what Irigaray sees as a great work of reversal that converts man's condition of dependence not only into a condition of autonomy but also into one of mastery. As Nietzsche writes, by punishing "the debtor, the creditor partakes of a *master's* right."[25] Irigaray is aware of this Nietzschean insight as she discusses how philosophy is a great financial system, which, by reversing roles, dispossesses woman from her pleasure and bestows profit and pleasure to the newly established creditor, who is now eligible for "repayment and compensation."[26]

As Irigaray argues, "woman will support that [newly erected] economy, without ever really being a party to it, without her sexuality ever being accounted for. She is reduced to a function and a functioning whose historic causes must be reconsidered: property systems, philosophical, mythological, or religious systems."[27] The father's main concern in this economy is the preservation of his seed, which he cannot reproduce and whose continuity cannot be ensured on his own. He is dependent on the womb of the female if he is to secure the continuity of his progeny, name, and property. In fact, she supports this economy without taking an active part in it. "In this economy," Irigaray writes, "woman's job is to tend the seed man 'gives' her, to watch over the interests of this 'gift' deposited with her and to return it to its owner in due course."[28] She is a mere instrument for the continuation of the father's law, his usury. The father, in his "exorbitant empire," requires the mother to be "a mere receptacle for his germinating seed, the matter needed to give birth to his deeds of credit [*titres de créance*], charged with the maieutics of making them appear 'as such.'"[29] After the financial reversal, women become the mere receptacles for the continuity of the father's seed, a mere passive container enabling men to reap the fruits of their investment.

The speculum, the concave mirror with which men explore nature's internal cavities, the mysteries of women's sex, is not only an instrument of specularization, of reflection and distortion, but also itself an apparatus of *speculation* in the financial sense. Irigaray plays with the semantic richness of this word. Men's representation of women is not only a distorted mirroring of its referent but also a speculative undertaking in the economy of the self-same. Man's eye, as a substitute for his phallus, seeks to "explore the mine" of women; it "seek[s] there new sources of profit."[30] Such profit is retrieved not only in the act of reversal that relieves man of his dependency on his mother but by a generalized projection of men's anxieties and fears unto women. By so doing, men can redeem their "guilt" (or "debt"), once more, and displace it on their other. The alleged "penis-envy" that Freud claimed women felt might be the best example of this specular and speculative strategy, which denies the irreducible singularity of women's sexuality and the nonteleological excess of her "*jouissance.*"[31] It rather construes her sexuality in the image of his own. Such a "penis-envy," Irigaray suggests, is in fact the "remedy for man's fear of losing" it.[32] It is because of his own obsession with his phallus and the "castration anxiety" arising out of noticing there is "nothing to see" in the female's sex that man transfers his fixation unto women. And it is only after being transferred that it can acquire its status and force. The phallus, as a signifier not only of the male reproductive organ but more importantly of power itself, as "the very standard of value," is dependent on its fetishization as an "indispensable support of its price on the sexual market."[33]

REVERSING THE REVERSAL? DEBT BEYOND *SPECULUM*

Irigaray does not content herself merely with revealing the ways in which financialization is at play in the patriarchal appropriation of philosophy. She does not only expose the persistence of *financial* or *speculative* thinking in philosophical discussion around sexual difference. She does not simply uncover the reversal of the originary dependency on the mother resulting in the foundation either of a fully autonomous self-generating subject or of a subject who only relies on women as passive receptacles for the reproduction of his seed. Along its work of critique and exposure, Irigaray's project has another dimension, what she characterizes as an *ethical* one that seeks to dismantle the patriarchal foundations of Western philosophy as it formulates an understanding of being that is no longer neuter but rather sexuate. It is within this part of her philosophical project that she finds the grounds for reversing the reversal of the indebted man.

In *An Ethics of Sexual Difference*, Irigaray characterizes the entrenched unpayable debt of men to the mother who gave him birth as "a debt contracted toward the one who gave and still gives man life, in language as well," since not only life but language too "feeds on blood, on flesh, on material elements."[34] Just like Nietzsche, who, by noticing the philological relation between debt and guilt, formulates the moral problem of punishment and guilt in its materialist foundations—namely, as the contractual relation between the debtor and the creditor—so too does Irigaray frame the question of *sexuate* indebtedness as an ethical question. However, their answers differ fundamentally. An answer to this ethical question of indebtedness, she writes, must first recognize what was forgotten through the patriarchal reversal of indebtedness: the "unpaid debt to the maternal, the natural, the matrical, the nourishing."[35] Irigaray rewrites the narrative about the foundational forgetting of Western philosophy: what Heidegger saw as *the* forgotten ontological difference is no longer that between Being and beings but sexual difference itself.[36] She no longer construes the history of Western philosophy as a narrative about the question of the meaning of

Being in the abstract, as Heidegger would have it, but rather as one about the forgetting of the indebtedness to the body of the mother: if having to pay one's debts functions as the moral foundation of credit, the fact that indebtedness to the mother remains forever unpaid constitutes the ethical foundation of sexual difference. She writes: "*To forget being is to forget the air*, this first fluid given us gratis and free of interest in the mother's blood, given us again when we are born, like a natural profusion that raises a cry of pain: the pain of a being who comes into the world and is abandoned, forced henceforth to live without the immediate assistance of another body."[37]

Following this idea, in *The Forgetting of Air in Martin Heidegger*, published around the same time as *An Ethics of Sexual Difference*, Irigaray shows how, although the metaphysician is a "trafficker in airs," it has been precisely air, one of the most fundamental material conditions of being's existence, that has been unthought by philosophy.[38] This is the case not only because air, in its transparency, does not appear and does not show itself, but also because it is the mother's first gift to her child in her womb. *The Forgetting of Air* thus clearly outlines how the problem of debt ought to be understood ontologically as a structural trait of sexual difference. Air is her first gift (*son premier don*): "She gives—first—air." Air, the very possibility of man's beginning is given, she writes, "with no possibility of a return. He cannot pay her back in kind." He can only take: "This debt of life seems natural and like it must remain unpaid. Unpayable."[39] Man's ontological condition is framed by Irigaray as originating from a dependence on a never fully appropriable otherness to whom man owes his life and growth. This material dwelling and the breathing that is first gratuitously bestowed by the mother, Irigaray tells us, are essential not only for the formation of being but also to "form the essence of his maleness: language."[40] Irigaray sees language and speech, despite their ephemeral and formal nature, as indebted to "material elements." "Who and what has nourished language? How is this debt to be repaid?" Irigaray asks.[41] The "mother tongue," the language first learned, "feeds on blood, on flesh," she says. It feeds on the blood of the mother. Yet, like the ontological indebtedness to her, language as the mother's gift is also forgotten and is instead construed as the "essence" of masculinity, as the foundation of his logos. Irigaray thus traces the way in which man forgets "Her" not only as his material origin and foundation but as the source of his speech, which he subverts and reappropriates.

This question continues to be of concern for Irigaray in her later works. Most notably, *In the Beginning, She Was* constructs a cosmogonical account of the originary forgetting of "Her"—"nature, woman, Goddess"—the mysterious source of both knowledge and life. For Irigaray, "she" is the source of knowledge and speech appropriated by men: "He begins to teach the true when he begins his instruction with: I say. He does not begin his discourse with: she said, even though it is she, Goddess or nature, who inspired him. In fact, he repeats or transposes the meaning that she, or they, transmit. But he appropriates it and presents himself as the master of the message received in secret from her."[42] He creates the illusion of his mastery, an illusion of a world from which "women and the gods have withdrawn"; their inspiring speech is subverted and "displaced into a speaking between men."[43] Men, no longer inspired by her speech, form a discourse among themselves and inaugurate a logos concerned with fully erasing her trace and their indebtedness to her, a logos of mastery over nature that takes the hierarchical structure of the master teaching his pupil.[44] Just as "she" is actively forgotten as the source of knowledge and life by the patriarchal structure of knowledge transmission, so too is her role in the generation of man diminished or even erased. He excludes her not only from his becoming but even from his origin and language.[45]

Given that for Irigaray the anxiety regarding the indebtedness of man to "Her" is most apparent in her erasure from his language, the contestation of the phallocentric anxiety about his dependency, one that he cannot even recognize as not requiring repayment, should take place in language itself. As a retrieval of "Her" speech, it does not confirm the very condition of financial indebtedness by reversal. Irigaray, through her play with language, rather seeks to perform an immanent critique of masculinist discourse but in a way that takes seriously the concave baroque nature of the mirror: the latter is always to reflect in a distorted manner.[46] It is by pointing to the distortions of representation, its inability to maintain a close economy of the same, that the self-sameness of the phallocratic system begins to crack, its fissures become apparent; its language withers away and the financialization of men's discourse can begin to be dissolved:

> The (male) subject collects up and stitches together the scattered pieces of female merchandise (scattered in silence, in inconsequential chatter, or in

madness) and turns them into coins that have an established value in the marketplace. What needs to be done instead, of course, if she is to begin to speak and be understood, and understand and express herself, is to suspend and melt down all systems of credit [*suspendre pour leur refonte les systèmes de crédits*].[47]

If woman is to begin to speak again, if she rebels against the silencing imposed upon her by the monologue of patriarchal philosophy, another economy is to be instituted through her discourse. In "Commodities Among Themselves" Irigaray asks: "*But what if these 'commodities' [women] refused to go to the 'market?'* What if they maintained another kind of commerce, among themselves?"[48] A different economy could be born, one whereby women's speech inaugurates an economy of ecstatic expenditure. This economy, by "suspend[ing] and melt[ing] down all systems of credit," is one in which exchanges are carried out "without identifiable terms, without accounts, without end. . . . Without additions and accumulations, one plus one, woman after woman. . . . Without sequence or number." This is an economy, Irigaray continues, in which "Nature's resources would be expended without depletion, exchanged without labor, freely given, exempt from masculine transactions: enjoyment without a fee, well-being without pain, pleasure without possession."[49]

Irigaray frames the reversal of the economy of indebtedness, which she sees as a structural trait of sexual difference as well as the source of the anxieties associated with it, as the key toward constructing an ethics of sexual difference, which she claims involves "the creation of a new *poetics*."[50] This new poetics mimics mystical speech and, by so doing, approaches what Hélène Cixous calls "feminine writing."[51] For Irigaray, mystic speech has been a female discourse. It is, in fact, "the only place in the history of the West in which woman speaks and acts so publicly."[52] Irigaray presents it as a heteronomous reach for the other—as the "place where consciousness is no longer master" or where consciousness is not equated to mastery.[53] It is the place where a mystic embrace for otherness inaugurates the possibility of a feminine subjectivity. Such a subjectivity would only be possible, she argues in *Elemental Passions*, if a "feminine transcendency" is established, for which the very paradigm of masculine transcendence needs to be amended.[54] She sees feminine transcendence as dismantling masculinist discourse and its turn to women's mystic speech as foregrounding that which is irreducible to the self, inappropriable; it is transcendent in the particular sense that it posits an irreducible difference that cannot ever be sublated into identity. That is to say that her notion of "mysticism" is not concerned with losing the self in a divine beyond this world, with the annihilation of individuality in the wholly other, or with an undifferentiated unity with the divine in its expansiveness. Rather, her emphasis on the divine is strictly speaking concerned with the establishment of difference. The feminine other would then be seen as a transcendent sexuate other in her sensible presence, setting boundaries between beings.

By descending into the dark night of mystic speech, where the burning power of love touches the deepest regions of the soul—what Jacques Lacan called "a *jouissance* that is beyond"[55]—"the poorest in science and the most ignorant" prove to be the "most eloquent."[56] It is precisely in this domain, Irigaray argues in *Speculum*, that the dismantling of the financialization of thought can finally take place, that systems of credit can at last be "suspended" or melted down:

> Nothing has a price in this divine consummation and consumption. Nothing has value, not even the soul herself, set apart from standardization, outside the *labor* market. The soul spends and is spent in the margins of capital. In a strictly non-negotiable currency, an expenditure without accountability [*une dépense incomptable*], in the resources of its loss. . . . At the final reckoning, the richest person will certainly be the one who has most depleted the stores. But even saying that is being too calculating, too logical even in this reversal of all known economics [*ce* renversement *de toute économie connue*].[57]

If Irigaray's methodology involves an immanent critique of the masculine discourse on femininity that disturbs the specular economy of representation in *Speculum*, it is by turning to the mystical domain that she conceives of the "*reversal* of all known economics" in "La Mystérique." This is a "reversal" that, while acknowledging the originary ontological indebtedness to women, can construe the latter not as a relation of debt—that is, as involving the contractual power relation between creditor and debtor—but as a relation of originary gratuitousness through which the mother brings us to the world. This is what is a stake in her notion of an "ethics of sexual difference": remembering the "first fluid given us gratis and free of interest in the mother's blood" and building a whole notion of ethics on the basis of such a *sexuate alternative economy*.

As Irigaray has herself demonstrated in her reading of Plato's allegory of the cave, metaphors are not innocuous. They often reveal, as Hans Blumenberg has taught us, what is most profound and true not only in the world but also in language.[58] The imbrication of the language of political economy in Irigaray's reading of Western philosophy reveals an entrenched complicity between financial metaphors and the specular dispositive that philosophy shows itself to be when analyzed obliquely. If other philosophers and thinkers have turned to economic and specifically financial metaphors, Irigaray's thinking does not only disclose relations of isomorphism or of analogy between economic techniques and philosophical systems but also shows how a notion such as debt is itself *sexuate*. Debt, the power relation between creditor and debtor, proves to be not only the paradigm of social relations, as Nietzsche maintained,[59] but that of sexual relations themselves. The circulation of women, their exchange for the consumption of men, and the hypostatization of the phallus as general equivalent are not only to be read as the infrastructure of metaphysical discourse; Irigaray also shows how the speculum of Western philosophy itself is structured by the repression and forgetting of the originary dependency of men on the body of the mother, the erection of a notion of the subject as autonomous and self-generating, and the reversal of his indebtedness to the mother into her own dependence. She is now to be fully and perpetually indebted to him and to his sexuality. It is to counter this reversal that Irigaray construes a vision of ethics as that which is to reverse *his* reversal without concomitantly restituting the very structure of terms that made it possible in the first place. Her ethics of sexual difference dislocates the very foundations of the structure of masculinist discourse and its economy. If men's philosophy relied on women as a mere receptacle enabling the (re)production of his seed, a means for sowing his profit, and if men saw women and the mother's womb/cave as a site of exploration or mining, as a field to plow or as a piece of earth waiting to be tilled, Irigaray instead suggests that the cultivation of a feminine transcendency can become the foundation for a *"reversal* of all known economics."

BIBLIOGRAPHY

Adorno, Theodor W. *Against Epistemology: A Metacritique; Studies in Husserl and the Phenomenological Antinomies.* Translated by Willis Domingo. Cambridge, MA: MIT Press, 1983.

——. *Negative Dialectics.* Translated by E. B. Ashton. New York: Continuum, 1973.

——. "Skoteinos, or How to Read Hegel." In *Three Studies on Hegel*, translated by Shierry Weber Nicholson. Cambridge, MA: MIT Press, 1999.

Aristotle. *Generation of Animals.* Translated by A. L. Peck. Loeb Classical Library. Cambridge, MA: Harvard University Press, 1943.

——. *Politics.* Translated by C. D. C. Reeve. Indianapolis: Hackett, 1998.

Blumenberg, Hans. *Paradigms for a Metaphorology.* Ithaca: Cornell University Press, 2010.

Buci-Glucksmann, Christine. *La folie du voir: de l'esthétique baroque.* Paris: Galilée, 1986.

Cixous, Hélène. "The Laugh of the Medusa." *Signs* 1, no. 4 (1976): 875–893.

Freud, Sigmund. "Femininity." In *New Introductory Lectures on Psycho-Analysis*, edited by James Strachey. Standard Edition of the Complete Psychological Works of Sigmund Freud 22. London: Hogarth, 1964.

Goux, Jean-Joseph. *Symbolic Economies: After Marx and Freud.* Translated by Jennifer Curtis Cage. Ithaca: Cornell University Press, 1990.

Graeber, David. *Debt: The First 5,000 Years.* New York: Melville House, 2011.

Holland, Nancy J. "'Everything Comes Back to It': Woman as the Gift in Derrida." In *Women and the Gift: Beyond the Given and All-Giving*, edited by Morny Joy, 92–100. Bloomington: Indiana University Press, 2013.

Hollywood, Amy. *Sensible Ecstasy: Mysticism, Sexual Difference, and the Demands of History.* Chicago: University of Chicago Press, 2002.

Jones, Rachel. *Irigaray. Towards a Sexuate Philosophy.* Cambridge: Polity, 2011.

Kaminski, Phyllis H. "Daughters, Difference, and Irigaray's Economy of Desire." In *Thinking Life with Luce Irigaray: Language, Origin, Art, Love*, edited by Gail M. Schwab, 195–207. Albany: SUNY Press, 2020.

Lacan, Jacques. *The Seminar of Jacques Lacan: On Feminine Sexuality: The Limits of Love and Knowledge, Book XX, Encore 1972–1973.* New York: Norton, 1998.

Lazzarato, Maurizio. *The Making of the Indebted Man: An Essay on the Neoliberal Condition.* Los Angeles: Semioxt(e), 2012.

Malabou, Catherine. *The Heidegger Change: On the Fantastic in Philosophy.* Albany: SUNY Press, 2011.

——. "Heidegger critique du capitalisme ou le destin de la métaphore économique." *Po&sie* 114 (2005/4): 104–110.

Nietzsche, Friedrich. *Beyond Good and Evil/On the Genealogy of Morality.* Translated by Carol Diethe. Stanford: Stanford University Press, 2014.

Plato. *Republic.* Translated by G. M. A. Grube. Indianapolis: Hackett, 1992.

Sandford, Stella. "Feminism Against 'the Feminine.'" *Radical Philosophy* 105 (2001): 6–14.

Szendy, Peter, ed. "Narratives of Debt." *differences* 31, no. 3 (2020).

NOTES

I am grateful to Emanuela Bianchi, James Sares, and Mary Rawlinson for their comments on this essay. The writing of this article was supported by the Fondo Nacional para la Cultura y las Artes and by the CONACYT.

1. Plato, *Republic*, trans. G. M. A. Grube (Indianapolis: Hackett, 1992), 507a; Aristotle, *Politics*, trans. C. D. C. Reeve (Indianapolis: Hackett, 1998), 1258b.
2. Most recently, see the special issue of *differences*, "Narratives of Debt," ed. Peter Szendy 31, no. 3 (December 2020).
3. Jacques Derrida is perhaps an exception as he explicitly relates the question of the "gift" (but not explicitly that of indebtedness) to sexual difference. In a 1981 interview, he said, for example, "one wonders whether this extremely difficult, perhaps impossible idea of the gift can still maintain an essential relationship to sexual difference. One wonders whether sexual difference, femininity for example—however irreducible it may be—does not remain derived from and subordinated to either the question of destination, or the thought of the gift." Quoted in Nancy J. Holland, "'Everything Comes Back to It': Woman as the Gift in Derrida," in *Women and the Gift: Beyond the Given and All-Giving*, ed. Morny Joy (Bloomington: Indiana University Press, 2013), 94.
4. Irigaray, S, 133; Luce Irigaray, *Speculum de l'autre femme* (Paris: Éditions de Minuit, 1974), 165.
5. Theodor W. Adorno, "Skoteinos, or How to Read Hegel," in *Three Studies on Hegel*, trans. Shierry Weber Nicholson (Cambridge, MA: MIT Press, 1999), 147. Theodor W. Adorno, *Negative Dialectics*, trans. E. B. Ashton (New York: Continuum, 1973), 76. In *Against Epistemology*, Adorno also refers to Husserl's epistemology as being "roped into a debit structure." "Its system resembles," Adorno says, "in modern terms, a credit system." Theodor W. Adorno, *Against Epistemology: A Metacritique, Studies in Husserl and the Phenomenological Antinomies*, trans. Willis Domingo (Cambridge, MA: MIT Press, 1983), 26.
6. Catherine Malabou, "Heidegger critique du capitalisme ou le destin de la métaphore économique," *Po&sie*, no. 114 (2005/4): 104–105, 107. See also Malabou, *The Heidegger Change: On the Fantastic in Philosophy* (Albany: SUNY Press, 2011); Jean-Joseph Goux, *Symbolic Economies: After Marx and Freud*, trans. Jennifer Curtis Cage (Ithaca: Cornell University Press, 1990), 9–63, 112–121.
7. David Graeber, *Debt: The First 5,000 Years* (New York: Melville House, 2011), 89.
8. Irigaray, ESD, 5.
9. As Irigaray reminds us, the phallus ought to be considered, fundamentally, as a privileged signifier of power. See Luce Irigaray, "Women on the Market" and "Commodities among Themselves," in TS, 170–197.
10. Irigaray, EP, 4.
11. Irigaray, S, 13.
12. Luce Irigaray, "Women on the Market," in TS, 170–191.
13. Phyllis H. Kaminski analyzes Irigaray's ethics of sexual difference as involving "a new economy of relations," but does not discuss the problem of indebtedness. Kaminski, "Daughters, Difference, and Irigaray's Economy of Desire," in *Thinking Life with Luce Irigaray: Language, Origin, Art, Love*, ed. Gail M. Schwab (Albany: SUNY Press, 2020), 195–207.

14. Irigaray, EP, 4.
15. See, for instance, Irigaray, S, 181.
16. Rachel Jones, *Irigaray: Towards a Sexuate Philosophy* (Cambridge: Polity, 2011), 1–15.
17. Irigaray, S, 167.
18. Irigaray, 162.
19. Aristotle, *Generation of Animals*, trans. A. L. Peck, Loeb Classical Library (Cambridge, MA: Harvard University Press, 1943), 109, 185.
20. Irigaray, S, 181.
21. Irigaray, 181.
22. Irigaray, S, 351; *Speculum de l'autre femme*, 440.
23. Irigaray, S, 351; *Speculum de l'autre femme*, 440.
24. Irigaray, S, 306; *Speculum de l'autre femme*, 382.
25. Friedrich Nietzsche, *Beyond Good and Evil/On the Genealogy of Morality*, trans. Carol Diethe (Stanford: Stanford University Press, 2014), 253.
26. Nietzsche, 253.
27. Irigaray, S, 129.
28. Irigaray, 75.
29. Irigaray, S, 301; *Speculum de l'autre femme*, 375–376.
30. Irigaray, S, 145.
31. Despite saying that "the economy of *jouissance* is something we can't yet put our fingertips on," Lacan understood it in economic terms, as Irigaray would also do. Lacan discusses *jouissance*'s relationship to "usufruct"—what can be enjoyed without being wasted. As noninstrumental enjoyment, *jouissance* is what "serves no purpose." Jacques Lacan, *The Seminar of Jacques Lacan: On Feminine Sexuality: The Limits of Love and Knowledge, Book XX, Encore, 1972–1973* (New York: Norton, 1998), 116, 3.
32. Irigaray, S, 53.
33. Irigaray, 55–61, quote in S, 53; See also Sigmund Freud, "Femininity," in *New Introductory Lectures on Psycho-Analysis*, ed. James Strachey, in *The Standard Edition of the Complete Psychological Works of Sigmund Freud*, vol. 22 (London: Hogarth, 1964), 112–135.
34. Irigaray, ESD, 127.
35. Irigaray, 127.
36. Stella Sandford, "Feminism Against 'the Feminine,'" *Radical Philosophy* 105 (2001): 10–11.
37. Irigaray, ESD, 127.
38. Irigaray, FA, 6.
39. Irigaray, 28. I am grateful to James Sares for bringing these passages to my attention.
40. Irigaray, ESD, 127.
41. Irigaray, 127.
42. Irigaray, IB, 35.
43. Irigaray, 42.
44. Irigaray, 42.
45. Irigaray, 84, 90.

46. On Irigaray's mimicry following a baroque aesthetic style causing a "maddening of vision" that disorients the paradigm and hierarchies of Western philosophy, see Irigaray, S, 138, 142, 144, 230, where Irigaray's motif of the concave mirror foregrounds a baroque "revolution in the ways of seeing." Cf. Christine Buci-Glucksmann, *La folie du voir: de l'esthétique baroque* (Paris: Galilée, 1986).
47. Irigaray, S, 234; *Speculum de l'autre femme*, 290.
48. Irigaray, TS, 196.
49. Irigaray, 197.
50. Irigaray, ESD, 5.
51. Hélène Cixous, "The Laugh of the Medusa," *Signs* 1, no. 4 (1976): 875–893. On the role that mysticism plays in Irigaray's thought, see, for instance, Amy Hollywood, *Sensible Ecstasy: Mysticism, Sexual Difference, and the Demands of History* (Chicago: University of Chicago Press, 2002), 187–210.
52. Irigaray, S, 191.
53. Irigaray, 191.
54. Irigaray, EP, 4. In "Women, the sacred and money," she further lays out how modifying the patriarchal model would involve instituting a "new form of sociality" differing from the "sacrificial, technological, technocratic society set up and managed by men alone." Irigaray, WSM, 10.
55. Lacan, *On Feminine Sexuality*, 76.
56. Irigaray, S, 192.
57. Irigaray, 195; *Speculum de l'autre femme*, 243. "Renversement" is in italics in the original.
58. Hans Blumenberg, *Paradigms for a Metaphorology* (Ithaca: Cornell University Press, 2010).
59. Maurizio Lazzarato, *The Making of the Indebted Man: An Essay on the Neoliberal Condition* (Los Angeles: Semioxt[e], 2012), 39.

Chapter Eighteen

MYSTERICS

Extinction and Emptiness

LYNNE HUFFER

"God" will prove to have been her best lover.
—KATHRYN BOND STOCKTON[1]

Ecstasy is there in that glorious slit where she curls up in her nest, where she rests as if she had found her home.

—LUCE IRIGARAY[2]

Lynne Huffer, *La Mystérique I*, collage, 2021

MYSTERICS

1.

Ceci n'est pas une

This is not a
pussy, vagina, vajayjay, vag, cunt, beaver, poon-
ani, muff, snatch, twat, hoo ha, pootang, coochie,
squeeze box, cha cha,
or
honey pot.
Treachery of images.
This is not Magritte's pipe inverted.

This is not Irigaray's Other of the Same: castrated speculum of Magritte's famous painting, The Treachery of Images (1929).

This treachery is apophatic.

2.

]

]

It's a cut. A caesura perhaps. But not the cut of castration. Not a psychosexual space, not an Other built to receive the Same.

The cut is an empty bracket. Could be a caesura, or could be the cut at the end of a line. The bracket migrated from Anne Carson's translation of Sappho, *If Not, Winter*. Brackets mark those places where the papyrus dissolved or burned.

]   led her astray[143]

]

Brackets cut into pages, slicing open their bright white surface. Cuts form fragments and columns, arranged here for experiments in thinking: thought collage.

"I make incisions into the skin of culture."[144]

3.

For Hannah Arendt, "thinking resembles tracking, a kind of place 'beaten by the activity of thought,' which turns to ploddingly follow a course towards a pause."³ Michel Foucault's genealogical method is a way to think in this Arendtian sense. The genealogist tracks lacunary events, events that "did not take place."⁴ To say that something did not take place is not to say that something didn't occur. There is eventialization—the happening of an event—but it is "empty form, without content or value."⁵ It did not take place because it had no place in history. It is "both empty and peopled,"⁶ "a lacunary reserve."⁷

to hold open "those blanks in discourse," "their silent plasticity."¹⁴⁵

That which is empty is a verb: to empty. The movement of that verb is not the same as nothingness. A verbal composition that decomposes, this collage think-tracks the movement of emptying.

"Emptiness . . . should not be seen as nothingness."¹⁴⁶

"the muscle of a poem is in the verbs. . . . muscles give shape, hold it up"¹⁴⁷

Brackets are a reminder that to fill the emptiness is a storyteller's trick. Filling the emptiness only masks it. Emptiness happens, whether the gaps in the archive are filled or not.

Of course, the bracket is also a something: a kind of "filling in." It may not be a word, but it is a writing or, rather, an overwriting: a marking over, in the mode of Lacan's writing over woman, *la femme*, as la femme.⁸ But the overwriting bracket signals the paradox of emptying. The bracket fills a gap by leaving it open. By emptying it. Like "the uncertain furrow of the wake."⁹

4.

Fragments float in a sea of unreason.

d

é

MYSTERICS

raison

"a great unreason . . .
dragged everyone along
in its wake."[148]

Reason inhabited by its own undoing. The activity
of thought is a "bark tossed on [that] sea."[10]
To think in fragments is to willingly enter
unreason's murmur. This willing "twists . . . into
a stance of nilling":[11] "an empty form . . . where
all that figures is the imprint of a reason that
has fled."[12]

*"The will is split within
itself, not between
carnal and spiritual
considerations, but
between willing and
nilling."*[149]

5.

Will exerts itself here in this writing. The will
of the thought collage is in the numbering
of fragments, 1–49. Numbers give thinking
something to track. Moments of respite, ports
of call, they are there to steady the reading.

But the will to read, like the will to write, will
be torn: between following the numbers and
wandering off into the right-hand column. How
to navigate this columnar disturbance, this errant
nilling on the edges of *déraison*? Top to bottom
or back and forth? Forward or sideways, from
number to number or pier to pier? Where's
the shore?

To read and write emptying is to flirt with
déraison, to surrender to the tension between
errancy and order. The split between willing and
nilling is a ship of fools: "both rigorous division
and absolute Passage."[13]

To think is to track this emptying: "the uncertain
furrow of the wake,"[14] this watermark of a fugitive

reason. "Despite these crossovers" between reason and unreason, "the division is nonetheless made."¹⁵ The ship of fools doubles. *Déraison*, inhabited by a split or is it a slit? Always doubled, at least 2 ships. Errancy will recede in the wake of fools, inverted and eclipsed by capture.

"*there are always at least 2 poems*"¹⁵⁰

> 26 PART ONE
>
> paint them as they are within,' said Joseph de Sigüença.⁸⁰ And it was that unsettling irony, that desire of wisdom to denounce all folly, that the same early seventeenth-century commentator saw in almost all of Bosch's paintings, in the clear symbolism of the burning torch (the never-sleeping vigil of contemplative thought) and the owl, whose strange, fixed stare 'keeps watch in the calm and the silence of the night, consuming oil, not wine'.⁸¹
>
> Despite these crossovers, the division is nonetheless made, and from now on the gap between these two radically different visions of madness will not cease to widen. The paths taken by the figure of the cosmic vision and the incisive movement that is moral reflection, between the tragic and the critical elements, now constantly diverge, creating a gap in the fabric of the experience of madness that will never be repaired. On the one side is the ship of fools, where mad faces slowly slip away into the night of the world, in landscapes that speak of strange alchemies of knowledge, of the dark menace of bestiality, and the end of time. On the other is the ship of fools that is merely there for the instruction of the wise, an exemplary, didactic odyssey whose purpose is to highlight faults in the human character.
>
> Bosch, Brueghel, Thierry Bouts and Dürer line up beside their silent images. For madness unleashes its fury in the space of pure vision. Fantasies and threats, the fleeting fragments of dreams and the secret destiny of the world where madness has a primitive, prophetic force, revealing that th... ...surface of illusion opens onto bottomle...

Other ships will follow, silhouettes of conquest on a New World horizon. The Santa Maria.¹⁶ The White Lion.¹⁷ The Zong.¹⁸ The Whitby and the Hesperus.¹⁹ The list goes on, crisscrossing our present, an abyssal archive beneath our modern *mappa mundi*.

"*Zong! is the Song of the untold story; it cannot be told yet must be told, but only through its untelling.*"¹⁵¹

And yet as ships "berth at the quay . . . a great forgetting falls on the world."²⁰ Ships are verbs that hold; "modernity is sutured by this hold."²¹ In the looping wake of shipping-holding is the carceral archipelago of the prison form: Hospital, Colony, Plantation, Asylum, Panopticon, Facebook, Control Society.

The descendants of the ships' hold listen for the fugitive sounds of "the *undercommons of enlightenment*."²² Sounds "resound and echo underwater. In the bone beds of the sea."²³

Poets call: listen and keep watch, "creatures of the word."²⁴ Practice "care in the wake as a problem for thinking."²⁵

Brackets, cuts, and columns open gaps among numbers, reordering them willy-nilly. Willing nilling thoughts. To empty among fragments is to gape like a wake: to make a "track," a "disturbance," "a region of disturbed flow."²⁶ To think is to make another wake. To be awake to that "mental geography" that takes place on the "threshold" between this and that fragment, in the sulcus, in the "uncertainty that surrounds all things."²⁷ These "crossroads" of thought are "on the inside of the outside and vice versa."²⁸ "Never present" and "always present."²⁹ Epistemic rupture in a crisscrossed world. Tracking fissures to form an X. Genealogy as crossings, in the wake.

*"I mean wake work to be a mode of inhabiting and rupturing this episteme."*¹⁵²

6.

The opening collage, *Mystérique I*, starts with a cut. Without cutting or tearing there would be no collage. But the image is treacherous: *Speculum*'s caesura, "*La Mystérique*," is not what it seems.

—Could a sore be *holy*?³⁰
—But of course.

7.

The *arma Christi* that surround the crimson-edged slit identify the opening as Christ's side wound. The Passion's last ignominy. Post-mortem mortification. Death's exclamation point. Not castration but a bracket, empty like the tomb.

In medieval Christendom, a fourteenth-century French noblewoman, Bonne de Luxembourg, contemplates this wound in her luxury prayer book. Attributed to the artist Jean le Noir, the stunning tempera, grisaille, and gold-leaf miniature illuminates her daily psalter's final devotional poem.

European medieval theology invented this image as a mother figure. Christ, like Bonne, is maternal. "Explicitly female images of Jesus in the Middle Ages stress gestation, birthing, and lactating, not sexual union," Carolyn Bynum says, contra queer medievalists like Karma Lochrie who understandably read such images through an erotic lens.[31] For Christians like Bonne, the side wound means redemption will come to her: a mother returning to an original virginity. The blood of childbirth is the same fluid as Christ's blood on the cross. Such birthing is virginal because "paradoxically, [it] precedes conception."[32]

The wound offers comfort, milk and blood, respite from war, sickness, the death of dear ones. Catherine, Bonne's second child, barely born. Suddenly limp, a tiny mummy wrapped in swaddling. Ashes to ashes, into the ground. Bonne's daily devotional draws her deep into the red-lipped darkness. Daily death and resurrection. Each day emptying herself into God. Again and again, her virginity restored in that "glorious slit."[33]

1349. Maubuisson, France. Thirty-four years old, Bonne is dying. Plague prowls the region,

But one of the soldiers with a spear pierced his side, and forthwith came there out blood and water.[153]

A common trope of medieval mysticism is to caress, kiss, drink from, bathe in, enter Christ's glorious slit.

Married to God, mystics are virgins. Their love-making is not about sex.

Virginity is the "restoration of an original relation": an experience of the "flesh" that transforms individuals into conduits for God.[154]

impervious to rank, wealth, or age. As a noblewoman, Bonne has done her part to keep the line going. Ten deliveries in ten years. Her first-born, Charles, will one day be king, succeeding his father, John II. Every labor agony. Each contraction a knife in the gut. In the unbearable times, she enters the wound. Daily prayer has taught her to do this. *Imitatio Christi*.

Now blood and pus seep from her bubos: groin, neck, armpit. Vomit rises to her throat. Dry heaves. No more deliveries. Nothing left to expel. Her body shivers, sweats. Hours of this. As night falls, her soul enters the "fathomless wound."³⁴ She will not return from this union. When Bonne exhales for the last time, there is ecstasy. At last. Respite.

Irigaray knows that "ecstasy is there in that glorious slit where she curls up in her nest, where she rests as if she had found her home."³⁵

8.

A philosopher writes: "One of Irigaray's most disconcerting characteristics is her conceptual imprecision, the absence of definitions, the appropriation and conflation of concepts from a range of quite different conceptual systems."³⁶ A religion scholar defends these limitations

The plague hit Western Europe in 1347. By 1350 it had killed nearly a third of the population.

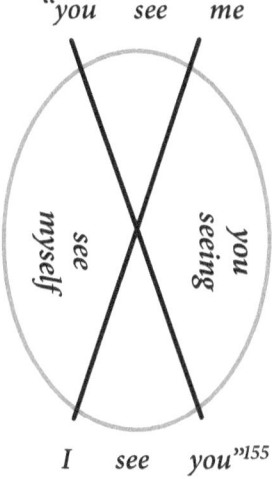

"you see me / see myself / you seeing / I see you"¹⁵⁵

*"Snipping the wires, cutting the current, breaking the circuits, switching the connections" of the "teleological order."*¹⁵⁶

*"Teresa of Avila ... hoped for and allowed 'nuevas palabras' to come forth."*¹⁵⁷

"in the face of mystical experience."[37] Irigaray's "fragmented sentences, the confusion of pronouns, and her almost ejaculatory and incantatory style mirror the dispersal of the subject."[38] Another philosopher agrees: "Irigaray writes . . . *as* a mystic, making language twist and turn until it begins to stammer in a voice that defies the logic of the subject."[39]

"Reading can be freefall."[158]

Foucault makes a new arrangement of these Irigaray fragments. Together they float in the murmur. Thought's activity crisscrossing a sea. We look for a self but cannot find her.

What we find is a verb, reflexive, without a subject:

"m'hystère."[40]

9.

In the sea of unreason are sentences, words, images, brackets. They crisscross one another, then drift apart. This crisscross—chiasmus—is the movement of enjambment, from the French *enjamber*, to straddle.

"Enjambment . . . would momentarily wedge apart with sense the hammering iteration of rhythm."[159]

Irigaray enjambs Foucault

Foucault enjambs Irigaray

This is not

The cut is the necessary condition for enjambment. To cut is to slash and bind. It is "the poetic gesture of straddling lines together syntactically, but also a pushing apart of lines."[41]

to straddle is to cut

a vagina

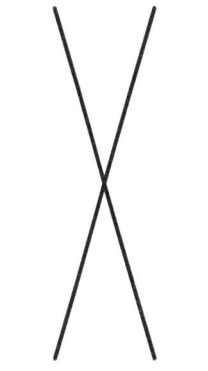

to cut is to straddle

La mystérique performs poetic enjambment. A gesture repeated in different forms, in different times, in different places. Here she performs a Foucault wire snipped, spliced with Irigaray. A chiasmus.

10.

This chiastic collage is an arrangement of fragments in the play of déraison. Take away unreason and you have no reason. This is dé-raison's collage.

Cutting and pasting déraison does *not* make an assemblage. Collaging performs Deleuzian *agencement* (usually translated into English as assemblage, causing confusion). *Agencement* lays out numbers to track-think a shifting called mysterics.

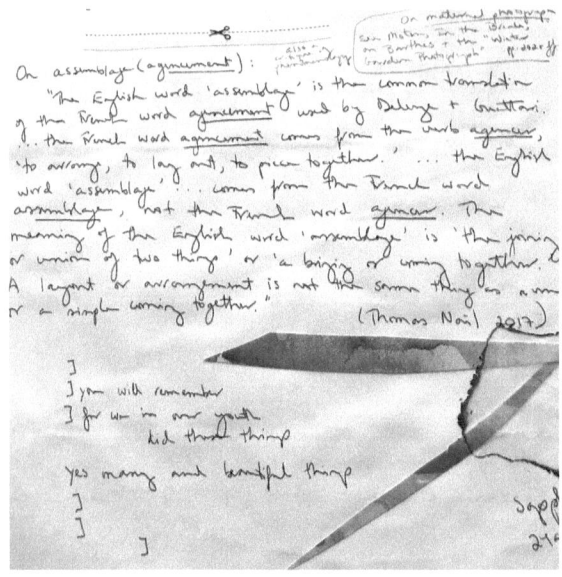

"*the French word* agencement *comes from the verb* agencer, *'to arrange, to lay out, to piece together.'* . . . *A layout or arrangement is not the same thing as a union or a simple coming together.*"[160]

11.

Like the opening image of what is *not* a vagina monologue, mysterical discourse is apophatic. La mystérique points to the transcendent but "denies that the transcendent can be named or given attributes."[42] For

> to say "X is beyond names," if it is true, entails that it cannot then be called by the name "X." In turn, the statement "it cannot then be called X" becomes suspect, since the "it," as a pronoun, substitutes for a name, but the transcendent is beyond all names.[43]

This mysterical "linguistic regress" is apophasis: unsaying or speaking away.

> Any saying (even a negative saying) demands a correcting proposition, an unsaying. But that correcting proposition which unsays the previous

Lacan says "elle n'est pas toute."[161] *But the statement "elle n'est pas toute" becomes suspect, since* elle *substitutes for a name-that-is-not one (*la femme*), but* elle *is beyond all names.*

Lacan demands a correcting proposition: an unsaying. Irigaray's mystérique is that unsaying. But she is herself proposition is in itself a "saying" that must be "unsaid" in turn.⁴⁴

a saying that must be unsaid in turn.

Mysterical discourse says and unsays. This is not a theory of the ineffable but a practice of unsaying: "unnameability is not only asserted but performed."⁴⁵

Irigaray and Foucault are mysterical: they write apophatically. The "performative intensity" of their apophatic practice tends to be "at the high end of the scale."⁴⁶ Their mysterical discourse "turns back relentlessly upon its own propositions and generates distinctive paradoxes that include within themselves a large number of radical transformations."⁴⁷

*"All constructs are empty.
The construct that all constructs are empty is empty.
The construct that the construct that all constructs are empty is empty is empty."*¹⁶²

What's at stake in this apophasis? Mysterics is not a theory of transcendence, the ineffable, or the French sublime. Apophatic mysterics is a practice: a performance of emptying. Empty is a verb.

Not a noun, not nothing.

12.

This mysterical apophasis think-tracks emptying to describe the disjointed relation between the sayable and the seeable that is a treachery of images. The image of a vagina that is not one is apophatic in this sense. Like Magritte's pipe painting, the opening mimetic fragment, *Mystérique I*, uses words—*Ceci n'est pas une*—to unsay an image. This phrase "performs rhetorically as apophasis, meaning that it pretends to deny what the very form of the painted [slit] juxtaposed with it already affirms."⁴⁸ This rhetorical arrangement of image with words

*"Seeing is thinking, and speaking is thinking, but thinking occurs in the interstice, or the disjunction between seeing and speaking."*¹⁶³

mirrors the disjunctive relation between the seeable and the sayable. By unsaying what is seen, apophatic saying unsees the image.

13.

"Brackets are exciting,"[49] Anne Carson says. Carson's translations of Sappho's fragments think by tracking. As traces of lacunary tracking, brackets mark an activity of thought: to track emptying by simultaneously filling and unfilling it with marks.

Ancient papyri were burned, lice-eaten, riddled with holes. In the place of missing matter a cut appears: a bracket as a trace of thinking.

14.

The Foucault-Irigaray mystérique thinks extinction by tracking the emptying that is earth's finitude: silences, murmurs, line breaks in the archive of life on a planet. The gaps in these archives gape. But where exactly the archive gapes is impossible to say. To say anything about it is to float in unreason: to unsay it. To invite reading as freefall. To straddle the gap with syntax is to stutter, howl, babble. To cut the circuits of grammar. To hollow out forms of thought-as-usual.

"this wide, wild, unwary space that she is (on) earth."[164]

This is why the bracket lacks precision: it is not the trace of every disappearance, of every emptying. To attempt such precision would turn a translation of Sappho, an accounting of the Middle Passage, a history of madness into an illegible "blizzard of marks."[50]

"I am fully aware that I have never written anything other than fictions. For all that,

Thinking as the tracking of disappearance is imprecise. This does not make it untrue. The bracket, mark of emptying, is a fiction. It fictions something "starting from a . . . reality that renders it true."[51]

15.

This thought collage fictions Anthropocene emptying. Species fall behind the horizon. We only "know" this verb, this disappearing act, from the noun that lingers, the shadow cast after it's gone. That shadow looms: a bracket.

A cut's shadow, the bracket enjambs the shadows of other cuts. They proliferate, crisscrossing each other in agencements of cutting and pasting. The mysterical collage fictions something that can't be seen starting from a reality that renders it true.

16.

These word-image fragments perform the apophatic play of self-emptying graphics. To read them is to engage that mysterical play. Mysterics practices the mysteria it explores. To encounter la mystérique in forms of thought-as-usual—sentences and paragraphs with logical conclusions—would be to betray her.

These experiments in form invite a self-emptying experience of reading.

17.

Mysterical emptying tracks both a figure and a field, forming and dissolving itself, never quite

I would not say that they were outside the truth. It seems plausible to me to make fictions work within truth . . . to make discourse arouse, 'fabricate' something which does not yet exist, and thus to fiction something." [165]

becoming a substance. We tend to imagine the figure as an individual or a type: a swooning statue, a heretical body burning on a scaffold. But she also tracks the ordering of knowledge: an assemblage, a science, a field like "la physique" or "la mathématique"—physics or mathematics—that takes its name "from an adjectival forerunner."[52] As a self-unsaying fable, the thought collage fictions a figure-as-field: an experiment that "passes from place to place and age to age."[53] La mystérique as mysterics.

"Hundreds of brilliant fragments remain."[166]

18.

Mysterics practices the poetics and science of the face as *facies*. Bernini's iconic mystic, the Saint Teresa statue in Rome, becomes a field as series: iconic photographs of hysterics in the nineteenth-century Salpêtrière in Paris. Photographs form a grid, a quadrillage, the squared-off cells of a scientific tableau. The tableau is brutal, a pressure cooker. It condenses "the Type . . . in a unique image, or in a univocal series of images—the *facies*."[54] As the condensation of singularities, the facies generalizes the case, creates a species. "*Facies* simultaneously signifies the singular *air* of a face, . . . as well as the *genre* or *species* under which this aspect should be subsumed."[55] The mysterical face-tableau documents the rise of the Darwinian species body.

Charles Darwin, *The Expression of the Emotions in Man and Animals (1871)*

"Why the face?"[56] Its "*surface* makes visible something of the movements of the soul, ideally."[57] Duchenne de Boulogne, nineteenth-century physician at the Salpêtrière, looked to the face in all its muscular, expressive detail for signs of emotion. The facies is a composite, a layering of surfaces "always seeking depth."[58]

"Visibility is a trap."[167]

The photographic tableau—a gridded collage, a condensation of figures— brings the soul into visibility in the ordering of fragments. Together the *facies* perform the invention of life and the death hidden in its depths.

"*a perpetual devouring of life by life.*"[168]

:)

Today our smart phones proliferate the progeny of these Darwinian fragments across multiple screens: emoticons and emojis everywhere!

19.

For a long time, the story goes, the mysterical face signaled the ecstatic mutism of sexual pleasure. That ghost of sexuality still lingers on our screens. The "uneasy doubling"[59] of mystic with hysteric, spiritual with terrestrial ecstasy, has been central to the modern constitution of sex as the problem of truth. Foucault relentlessly problematized this sex-truth relation over four volumes of the *History of Sexuality*.[60] But the 19th-century assemblage of sex as science and Christian pastoral began to dematerialize even as it formed.[61] Sexology—as much an *ars erotica* as a *scientia sexualis*—would proliferate its perverts through the "reversed and somber escutcheon"[62] of a self-hollowing bourgeoisie.

In one of his journals (1893), André Gide used the device of heraldry to illustrate mise en abyme's lacunary structure. [169] *Bourgeois sexuality's "defamatory quarters" invert this aristocratic emblem.*

Degeneration and subsequent generations of biopolitical thought would arrange themselves as sexology's mise en abyme of its own fictions. The more sexual knowledge tried to add to its store of knowledge, the more it hollowed itself out. La mystérique is the archive of that hollowing. With its stuttering, stammering, short-circuited speech, the sexual assemblage she appears to represent is pocked with holes. Her Sapphic skin charred and crisscrossed with cuts.

"*A's acceptance of the ability to be reproduced produces a lacuna within the identity of A. [T]he addition of B to A in fact subtracts from it. . . . [Each shield] can only take on the form the previous shield prescribes for it by incorporating a new shield, which, in turn, makes a hole in it.*" [170]

20.

The royal escutcheon beneath Christ's side wound in Bonne's gold-leaf miniature celebrates the union of her Luxembourg family—the double-tailed lion against a red background—with the Valois dynasty of her husband, John II—gold fleurs-de-lis in a royal blue field. Formal elements of the miniature—repetition of the color scheme and details of the *arma Christi*—connect the royal family to God. Divinely ordained sovereign power secures the family line.

Bonne de Luxembourg's family crest beneath Christ's side wound in her daily psalter.

"On 1 June 1310 in Paris at the Place de Grèves a beguine, referred to as a 'pseudo-mulier,' was burned at the stake as a relapsed heretic, having written a book 'filled with errors and heresies.' . . . Her name was Marguerite Porete."

In Bonne de Luxembourg's time, the unruly who opposed the king and could not be brought to God were exiled, confined in asylums, or burned at the stake as heretical. The beheading of the king is the symbolic moment of the death of God. In 1795, as the crown was falling, Philippe Pinel freed mystics from their chains into a new secular science, *psyche-logos*. Long after Pinel's death, Tony Robert-Fleury's state-commissioned painting, "Pinel Freeing the Insane" (1878), mythologized this event at the Salpêtrière as a "decisive chiasmus."[63] In the painting's final version, Robert-Fleury "added a woman writhing on the ground with an arched back in the archetypical hysterical posture (arc-de-cercle)."[64]

"*Seizure duration is 25–35 seconds and they cluster mainly during sleep.*

Seizure frequency is 10–15 seizures per day."[171]

MYSTERICS

Philosophically, the arc-de-cercle was a "turning point." [65] Hegel absorbed historical time into the dialectic. The mysterical chiasmus-as-freedom formed the dialectical pivot in this Hegelian conception of progressive chronology that finds its victory in us, in the present. In the play of déraison, mysterical unreason belongs to a past superseded by reason: a guilty, sexual nature sublated by science into reason's order. But the mystérique enters modernity as a "caged freedom."[66]

That cage is psyche-logos, documented in the archives of the Salpêtrière. In the modern hospital, the new science of neurology recreates the hysteric in the image of the early modern mystic's ecstatic swoon: la mystérique. In the late nineteenth century, Charcot's photographers, Paul Régnard and Albert Londe, proliferate Bernini's Teresa statue, posing actual bodies, then reproducing their image in albums, *Iconographie photographique de la Salpêtrière* (3 volumes, 1876–77, 1878, and 1879–80) and *Nouvelle Iconographie de la Salpêtrière* (1888–1918).

The nineteenth-century Salpêtrière invented a panoptical technology whose product was a photographic mysterical science. With Régnard and Londe, Charcot turned photography into a "hospital service" whose glass-walled studio was well equipped with props (backdrops, screens, beds, platforms), lenses, and artificial lighting. This service also included archiving: "a whole itinerary of the image, from the 'observation' all the way to the filing cabinet."[67] Shaped by the baton-marks of a postsovereign power, mysterics would take its place in the archives of the infamous.[68]

Foucault describes Hegel's evil genius in part three of the Encyclopedia, *where Hegel introduces an evil nature that inserts "guilt in the form of a sexual fault."*[172]

21.

Liberated again by Freud into psychoanalysis at the end of the 19th century, the mystérique would reinvent herself in another form of capture: the specular, spectacular apparatus of sexuality. No need to put anyone in the panopticon's central tower, which plays the role of what used to be God. The phallic tower would be the Irigarayan complement—Other of the Same—to the nothing to see: vagina, womb, anus, unconscious, death, crypt, cavern, tain, mother-matter. Half a century later, Lacan, the faithful Freudian son, would project the sexy starlet onto a psycholinguistic screen.

La mystérique would become the stuff of wet dreams and mediatized fantasies of ecstatic departure: sex and death alone in the dark.

22.

Father Lacan says the obvious in Seminar XX: *Encore! Encore!*[69] "As for Saint Theresa—you only have to go and look at Bernini's statue in Rome. . . ."[70] Wink wink. It sure looks like she's coming but she's stiff as a board. Once you see it, it's undeniable.

"In Rome? So far away? To look? At a statue?"[173]

The mysteric is the will-have-been of living: a corpse.

Speculum mundi. Cupped in these hands, you're a sexy starlet. A crimson planet tilting off its axis. Lithic *jouissance*.

"Place one in my looking-glass hands."[174]

23.

The lips convulse. Stuttering, spasmic, fiery. Mystics and hysterics for centuries now. Lacan's Saint Teresa has become a star. You go to Rome and you "understand immediately that she's coming, there is no doubt about it."[71] *Encore*!

Lynne Huffer, *La Mystérique II*, collage, 2021

Seminar XX only pretends to be X-rated. To attract an audience.

XX isn't about sex but an
ex-istential double X:
X-istence
and
X-tinction.

But, as usual, Father Lacan is toying with us. "What was tried at the end of the last century, at the time of Freud, . . . was an attempt to reduce the mystical to questions of fucking . . . that is not what it is all about."[72] He knows it's not about fucking. It's about "that which puts us on the path of ex-istence."[73] Which is also the path of non-existence. No more breath, no more swooning. Just absence and silence. *La* crossed out. ~~La~~ femme.

God may be dead, but Lacan still preaches the holy word, in graduate seminars, philosophy

"God is dead. God remains dead. And we have killed [her]. Yet [her] shadow

lectures, psychoanalytic sessions, and some versions of Afropessimism. He is abundantly useful for thinking about nothingness.

La mystérique is the figure who makes possible this contemporary Lacanian speech about nothingness. Centuries of unreason confined or heretics burned at the stake produce a blank where God once was. God disappears over the horizon, leaving a silhouette, a trace darkened by the shadow of God's fall. Covered in blood, God's murderers crave transcendence. "The language of sexuality has lifted us into the night where God is absent," Foucault writes.[74] Into the blank where God governed rushes the carceral speech of a swooning *scientia sexualis*.

"Obey, keep quiet, your body will speak," Foucault barks, mimicking Charcot.[75] The hysteric acquiesces not only with convulsions, but also with "stigmata": "contraction of the visual field, simple or double hemianaesthesia, pharyngal anesthesia, contracture caused by a circular bond around a joint."[76] Another Christian mystical borrowing, "all these wonderful stigmata were clearly responses to instructions."[77]

The hysteric's obedient body leaves open another gap: the mutism of her stigmatic wound. "Into the breach"—into that silent slit—comes the sexual speech, invented by science, now ventriloquized as medical evidence in the hysteric's recounting of her "sexual life."[78] Such speech proliferates to this day, from scandalous accounts of sex trafficking politicians to the tangled word webs we call queer theory to Facebook's ever-burgeoning gender identities (seventy-one and counting).[79]

still looms. How shall we comfort ourselves, the murderers of all murderers? What was holiest and mightiest of all that the world has yet owned has bled to death under our knives: who will wipe this blood off us?"[175]

"Now, Facebook offers dozens of options. It's easy to edit your current gender option or add a new one if you never set it. Here's how."[176]

24.

The mysteric collapses centuries of European history (fragments 19–23): Christianity's mystics and sexuality's hysterics flipped vertically, condensed into an absent-present figure-field of rupture. The mysteric is a breach, break, slit, fissure, crack. She looks like nothing and "know[s] nothing."[80] But she is not nothing. She empties.

To empty is to ask to be filled. Into the emptying come those priestly intonations, from Lacan in the lecture hall to subreddit porn channels. Multitudes memorize these mysterical liturgies. But the mysteric we praise—look, she's coming!—was always already a corpse.

As collapsed time, the mysteric is a ghost: both digital pootang and the glorious slit in Bonne de Luxembourg's psalter. Irigaray calls her "mother-matter,"[81] the maternal ground as hole. Civilization is the repeated thrusting of spears into mother-matter's side. The wounds are wars, slavery, colonization, indentured labor, genocide, devastated landscapes, acidic oceans, toxic air, white mob rule, forest and bodies and crosses burning. Each new stabbing "repeating a murder that has probably already taken place."[82] "God is dead. God remains dead and we have killed [her]."[83] But this God-the-mysteric, mother earth, was "already-dead: the poor present of an effigied copula."[84]

"the depths of a gulf where now everything is burning."[177]

25.

Encore! You are ill. Your coastal seas are rising, heaving into skyscrapers and subway tunnels. Your breath is hot, even in the valleys of your highest mountains. Your torrid air and boiling oceans keep giving birth to monster storms. With your poles melting, your axis of rotation is tilted. You're fainting eastward into space. You're burning, convulsive and weakened. Time-lapse maps show this rash spreading from coast to coast. Your skin getting redder and redder.

It's afternoon. The wind is howling, hissing through leaves. Tornado warnings throughout the South. Rings of color swallow the blue dot where I live on my iPhone screen. I look up from my psychedelic storm tracker app, beyond the window to the gyrating trees. Every gust feels apocalyptic. Alarms ring in my brain, algorithmic, faster than the speed of consciousness. Every thunderclap means impending disaster. Earthquakes, volcanoes, tornados, plague, hurricanes, fires, Floridification. Do we have extra candles? Bottled water? Canned goods? In the storm's aftermath, invasive species will take over. Burmese pythons will slither from the Everglades to invade our home in Atlanta. Another plague, much worse than AIDS or COVID, will descend on us. It will enter our lungs. We will die in agony, gasping for breath, our bodies oozing with bubos.

These mental spasms in Technicolor incited by computer code more powerful than divine kings or Charcot's baton.

26.

La mystérique is a cryptogram of the present as vertical time. The present is the switch point Foucault predicted, where we no longer know what sexuality was. We cling to sex as the site of our intelligibility, but sexuality was already breaking apart the moment it began to take shape.

"Perhaps one day people will wonder at this. They will not be able to understand."[178]

Treachery of images: la mystérique is not about sex. She could be anyone, or no one: the masses. She is a cipher, an enigma, a "logogriph"[85] without language, a spectacle of emptying.

She is geontological—

"bone, mummy, ash, soil"[179]

Welcome to the Anthropocene.

It's about "that which puts us on the path of existence"[86] and nonexistence. We cannot see the disappearance of species. We only notice extinction as something that happened between recognition of endangerment and the last sighting of a species. This disappearance is lacunary: an event that did not take place. To think extinction is to track an emptying that "appears at sunset to announce a day it will not see."[87]

Extinction requires a mysterical rendering: syntax short-circuited, data transverberated to follow in unreason's wake. To think the Anthropocene is to track that emptying of meaning. "The end of a world is postulated in all of the spiritual poetics."[88]

Knowledge cannot know the Anthropocene. "Knowing it too much, [knowledge] passes it over."[89] This makes geontology an experience of unreason. The mysteric's cryptographic conversions are unknowable, in part, because sexuality is giving way to AI. What was once a Freud problem is now algorithmic. That "other scene, off-stage,"

To use the admittedly rebarbative term—Anthropocene—is to take a mental shortcut. Yes, it's annoying. The word is everywhere, drained of meaning. Why use it again, spreading the contagion? Apophasis with an edge: wield it like a blade. A word-as-cut into the present, to unsay it. Not as knowledge, scientific or otherwise, but as a poetic cut. A chiastic catachresis for the mess we've made. The mess we're still making.

"Perhaps we will be led, by its confused murmurings, toward the city become sea."[180]

the place consciousness "finds *cryptic*,"⁹⁰ has been en-crypted, "like a corpse."⁹¹

This everyday Anthropocene "un-knowledge" is also a problem of scale. We can't see extinction, its encryption of corpses, even as it's happening all around us. We can only feel its **arrhythmia** as the sirens wail.

*"A certain arrhythmia/the sonic irruption of the outside"*¹⁸¹

Encore.

27.

There is a tight geography at work in this vertical cryptogram of the present: a spatial constriction in this temporal stacking of la mystérique that distorts the unthinkable geological scale. Mystic and hysteric convulse in the same spot, along with those who come before and after: the medieval witch, the convulsing nun, the early modern mystic, Charcot's Augustine in the Salpêtrière. A century later, in the place where Augustine swooned, Foucault will die from complications of AIDS. After his death, unreason's recursions will send him back to his writerly beginnings in *History of Madness*. The ghost of the stigmatized "*sidaïque*"—a French fascist's leper—will inhabit the emptied leprosaria "at the edges of the community,"⁹² "conjured up" as "a new incarnation of evil, another grinning mask of fear."⁹³ The mystérique—AIDS patient, leper, and plague victim—will evolve into the same species as the famous homosexual who died in a bed not far from the ashes of an earlier sodomite, Etienne Deschauffours who, burned on the scaffold at the Place de Grèves, mingled with the ashes of Marguerite Porete. Genealogy is gray.

*"Le sidaïque est une espèce de lépreux"*¹⁸²

*"lowly lives reduced to ashes . . . those flash existences, those poem- lives"*¹⁸³

28.

"Knowledge . . . is made for cutting":[94] mysterics cuts into our geological present. At stake in the Anthropocene is massive death, the extinguishment of populations and species. Mysterical fragments sink and bob, marking a current extinction rate whose projections rival the five previous die-offs in the earth's prehuman past. Our number is up: six.

"Making a documentary film means cutting. You'll have to cut the shot—and my words with it—at some point. Knowledge is knowing how to cut. Writing is knowing how to cut. And the high point is poetry, since we cut at the end of every line."[184]

We "know" extinction mathematically after we cut into the earth for fossils. But we cannot know it as experience. Such disjunctions are the stuff of genealogy, in the sense Foucault borrowed from Nietzsche. These genealogical fragments? A historical ontology of a convulsing planet, fixed and frozen like a statue in a mirror.

The earth is an archive. La mystérique is its poem. Foucault's paleontology is a historical ontology: a vertical cut into the sedimented layers of mysterical time.

This mystical poetics performs the cut of ex-istence as the threatened life of a planet. A somber prospect. *Mysterica poetica* cuts the currents of rational discourse, unsaying the present in a secular world where religion murmurs. Apophasis without redemption.

29.

And yet something fortuitous, even joyful, happens: thinking as surrender, "abiding in emptiness."[95] This is not at all the same as sexuality's swoon.

30.

If *la mystérique* were to enter the pages of *History of Sexuality, Volume 1*, she would signal the *beyond* of sexuality: a catachresis for the will-have-been of sex and species-life. As an open bracket, she would be "empty and peopled,"[96] hollowed out and inhabited, not only by self-emptying medieval mystics, but also by the four disappearing strategic unities that structure modern biopower's chiastic conversions from individual to population: hysterical woman, Malthusian couple, masturbating child, perverse adult. La mystérique "is" this disappearance. Her soul is fiery, the sexual-species body's self-immolating prison. Her concave, self-mirroring, chiastic conversions will continue to translate this sexuality—individual and populations—into the Neuralinked soul of cyborgs.

]

[[[

"Your phone is already an extension of you. You're already a cyborg. If your biological self dies, you can upload into a new unit. Literally."[185]

Who cares if the poles are melting?

[

]

31.

All these crisscrosses unsaying themselves. Apophatic, like star-cross'd lovers, Romeos and Juliets X-ing themselves out even they profess their love to each other. Foucault with Irigaray, saying something only to unsay it.

"One who is missing moves it to be written."⁹⁷

A former Emory student, Alexa Cucopulos, wrote her undergraduate honors thesis about chiasmus in Foucault. Her poem life of the species body invited its readers into something fleeting. Nobody knew then what it was: a very personal writing of the will-have-been. The echo of a future silence. Alexa keeping watch over her own shadow falling.

If I had known then what I know now. That four years later she would disappear beneath the horizon. Would I have encouraged her to write in this tense of the will-have-been?

Even now, she remains unflinching. I find joy in surrendering to her writing. "Reading begins in me an elaborate abandonment."⁹⁸ The effect is apophatic: "perception retreats or rather turns towards this dark interiority that isn't my own."⁹⁹

Since Alexa's passing, this elaborate self-abandonment has taken an obsessional form: chiasmus. "Here is form. The reader loves without knowing."¹⁰⁰ This X. Wherever there is reading, it is there. Yes, wherever

        there is reading

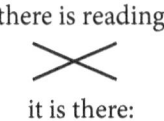

        it is there:

this self-hollowing turn towards

    an inside that is outside me

or, perhaps,

    an outside that is inside me,

or. perhaps. neither.

"The experience of one's own epistemic limits forces a subject to split from oneself or, more aptly, within oneself, and look back on oneself as strange, while still being unable to cross over to an outside. There is no outside, just an asymptotical tending toward the limits of one's own life."¹⁸⁶

Alexa said there's "no outside, just an asymptotical tending."[101] Asymptotical curve of
                            tenderness,
                tending in grief
"towards this dark interiority that isn't my own."[102]

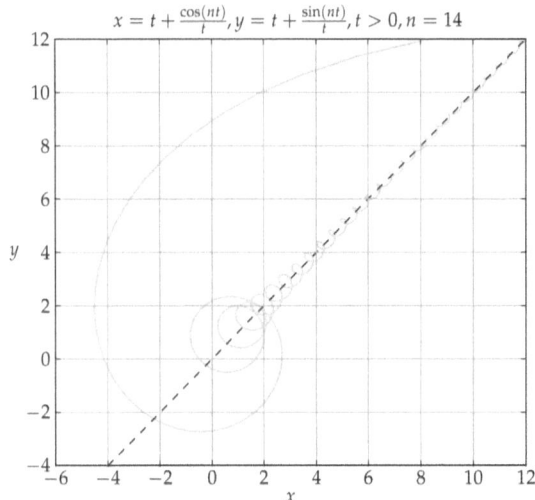

Alexa knew that there's more to this star-cross'd love affair than gridding or rhetoric. In her apophatic writing, the history of sexuality is coming undone. Undoing itself into something much darker than sexuality's "grumble of death."[103]

History of Sexuality, Volume 1, ends in the future anterior tense. Alexa's time, the temporality of the will-have-been. "Perhaps one day people will wonder at this."[104] But the future the book holds out is here, now. We inhabit the ending in the future anterior as the pressure of a thought—*no future*—in our present. Alexa was able to see, feel, hear this pressure. She was able to bend down, bend down further toward this speech without a subject, this "charred root of meaning," this "lump in the throat."[105] Able to see the shadow cast by extinguished fireflies, able to hear Foucault as an elegy for the extinction of species. Able to write her own thesis-elegy, writing over the corpses of others in a will-have-been without her.

32.

Irigaray holds up a *speculum mundi*. The world's mirror is *Speculum*'s fiery empty soul.

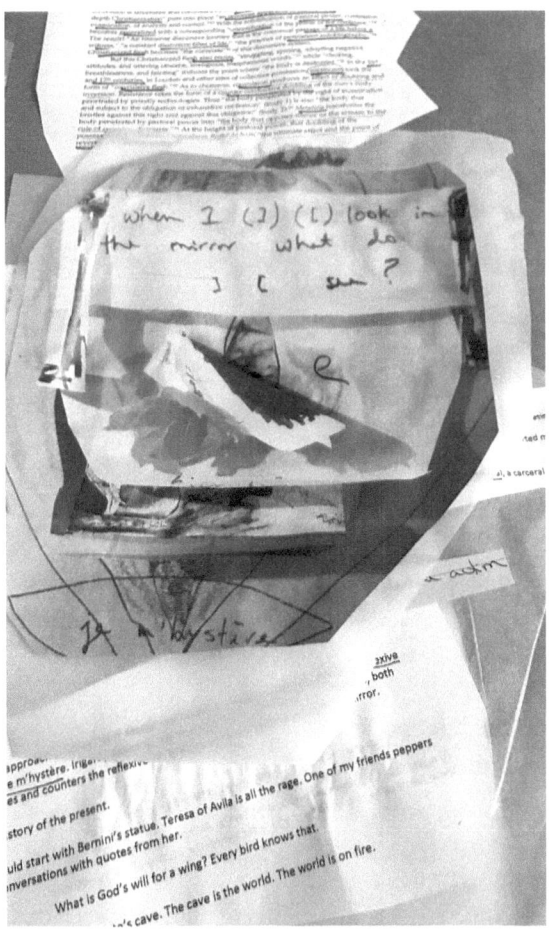

33.

Welcome to the Anthropocene. Extinction of species, planet burning: the *speculum mundi* says.

The Anthropocene welcome is a return to Hieronymous Bosch, Michel de Certeau's gateway to the mystic fable.[106] Bosch is the mystical painter of a medieval *mappa mundi*: "the map of the world, or of a world."[107] His landscapes are peopled with "species" and their hybrid "variants," fragments of "a lacunary system."[108] This "strange picture" becomes the untimely, "endless account of missing elements,"[109] a witness to extinction.

"Bosch has been called a raving lunatic: quite to the contrary, he makes others rave.*"*[187]

The Anthropocene's twenty-first-century hybrids are human and nonhuman, religious and secular, medieval and modern. In Foucault, Goya's *Monk*, *Witches' Sabbath*, and *Gran Disparate* transport Bosch's *gryllos* into modern voids without foundation. La mystérique is one such figure: a Boschian monster transported, à la Goya, into a "bottomless" landscape, where "even the faces themselves begin to decompose."[110] A mental shortcut, a "lump in the throat,"[111] a poetic cut at the end of the line, she is a species without a landscape: "utterly real" and "utterly unreal."[112] A heterotopian mirror, a labial catachresis.

"The desert of Bosch's Saint Anthony was infinitely peopled.... Goya's forms are born of nothing."[188]

34.

When "I" looks in the mirror, when the lips speak: out comes a reflexive verb without a subject: "m'hystère."[113]

Brilliant scholars have identified la mystérique with historical names: Angela of Foligno, Marguerite Porete, Teresa of Avila, Charcot's

"We, the surrealists want to celebrate the fiftieth

Augustine, Freud's Dora, surrealism's Augustine (again, "the poor starlet"),[114] Lacan's Teresa (Bernini turned her into stone). The same figure, the same face, over and over. "Snapshots of ecstasy."[115] Head thrown back, lips parted, eyes closed. "Prostrate, pale, like a dead woman,"[116] but burning with love. Her rapturous pain bright like a star.

anniversary of hysteria, the greatest poetic discovery of the nineteenth century."[189]

35.

A Boschian hybrid, she makes love with God in a timeless temporality that Nietzsche described as the experience of eternal recurrence. Her *jouissance* an eternal recurrence, the "untimely within the world,"[117] the time of unreason. She is past present: before and after the death of God. She "makes love with nothing"[118] in an always-deferred future. An incitement of emptying, she calls to the will-have-been. Again and again, we binge-watch her, "gorgonized"[119] by her *jouissance*. Encore!

"Your whole life, like a sandglass, will always be reversed, and will ever run out again."[190]

Mystic-hysteric: a "superposition," a "composite type,"[120] a collage of lovemaking with a self-emptying God. Anthropocene fragments, she swoons and stutters toward the will-have-been of species.

36.

"La Mystérique" is alterity split between the truth of emptying—Irigaray's Other's Other—and her capture as Man's mirror—the Other of the Same. The fact that we still see his looking glass *everywhere* means anthropos has not yet ceased its specula(riz)ing work. We live in the meantime of brackets closing.

[Lars von Trier's *Nymphomaniac* is an obvious twenty-first-century example of this *everywhere*.]

We still cling to this I, Man with his Other of the Same, his complement, his specular reflection.

The specula(riza)tion that is Western culture's Other of the Same requires the fantasy of a plane mirror: Man1 and Man2 infinitely reflected back to himself through successive acts of autoaffection. The Other in the mirror's names proliferate—BIPOC, Woman, Queer—as she is repeatedly captured, pinned down as saying, as Man's reflection. Even the planet and the incomprehensible other-than-human blank that is geological time reinvents itself in the image of Man: a neat succession of temporal strata, divided and subdivided into eons, eras, periods, and epochs. Culminating, of course, in the present-as-Man: the Anthropocene.

Sylvia Wynter

[1

] 2 /

37.

The Anthropocene's flat *speculum mundi* is the big white mirror of *anthropos*, from the depths of the Pacific to the top of the Himalayas. So many dark-skinned divers and sherpas hauling his oxygen tanks, giving him air. His extractive needs are infinite and elemental. He kills as he feeds.

Introducing curvature into this flat specula(riza)tion, *Speculum* exposes what Man tries to mask: the speculum mundi is not flat. The elemental planet is a *built* concavity whose algorithms conceal its parametric design.

Irigaray's elements books include Amante marine *(water),* L'Oubli de l'air *(wind), and* Passions élémentaires *(earth). Where's the fire?*

38.

Man's flat mirror collapses curvature, fluidity, resonance, vibration, unpredictability into reason's abstractions. The historical present it conceals is horrific, passages flattened by mathematical equations that obscure and cover over the leaking, bleeding, en-crypted violence, the ship's movement from there to here. Hortense Spillers exposes this concealment with an "American Grammar Book" whose violence begins with names: "Peaches," "Brown Sugar," "Sapphire," and so forth. One of those names is "Earth Mother."[121]

This elemental mother was forged and brutalized over centuries of extractive labor. Her invention materializes the building of a world: the theft of beings, their transport as commodities in a fragmenting, floating Western *hystera*. Frozen effigies. Horizontal narratives tell this founding New World history as a Middle Passage. But like the flat mirror, the narrative conceals by papering over the gaps between fragments. The "rhetorical wealth"[122] accumulated in the linear syntax of a story's forward movement in space and time flattens the curve of the oceanic suspension and

                    the

                         vestibular,

      dark,

                    "female flesh 'ungendered'"[123]

                    it created.

Grammar's equations tidy up the déraison of cut flesh—its "seared, divided, ripped-apartness."[124] Still bleeding, it is recaptured by grammar as a frozen Platonic Form.

> *"I murder the text, literally cut it into pieces."*[191]

> *"Modern logistics is founded with the first great movement of commodities. . . . Logistics could not contain what it had relegated to the hold."*[192]

> *"The not-telling of this particular story is in fragmentation and mutilation of the text, forcing the eye to track across the page in an attempt to wrest meaning from words gone astray."*[193]

39.

But the planet's Forms are melting. Earth's
leprosaria—"large, barren, uninhabitable areas"[125]
where species once lived—
force a reckoning with these once-frozen axes
of symmetry that collapsed the passage from
Old World to New.

Now the world is burning. "*Miroir ardent.*"[126]   "*a dark night that is also*
"An embrace of fire."[127]   *fire and flames.*"[194]

40.

La mystérique is *Speculum* ungendered.

This lesson comes after Foucault, after Irigaray, in
Spillers's grammar for thinking the movement that
is empty. A verb. "Female flesh ungendered." [128]
Sexuality's before is also its after. Speculum mundi   **Speculum** *is Irigaray's*
of the Anthropocene, la mystérique performs,   *"missing 'fire' book."*[195]
after Spillers, the vestibular mirror of a future   *Missing for decades, until*
anterior world on fire.   *Sharing the Fire.*[196]

When sunrays hit the tain of a concave mirror,
they bounce back, chiastic, as flame.

41.

No one asks to be born.   "*the viscous glandular*
To be born is to begin to die.   *embryo opens the cycle*
To exist is to become an endangered species.   *that ends in the rotting of*
To go extinct.   *death.*"[197]
Man blames Woman for this. She's the one who
birthed him.
"Many legends have the hero falling and forever
lost in maternal darkness: a cave, an abyss, hell."[129]

42.

La Mystérique is the field and figure of this despised maternal finitude. Her solar anus births us into death.
She is dark, a hole: the Other's Other.
The sodomitical mother.

Geontology rescales this harsh biological truth in a "degodded"[130] world. "Geology, it is said, wrested earth away from God."[131] Without God, the planet's 4.5 billion years shrink anthropos into a single bioluminescent pulsation: flicker of a minor species in the long dark corridor of deep time.

"The terrestrial globe is covered with volcanoes, which serve as its anus."[198]

"Death will do you too."[199]

"the new genre of being human, in its now purely degodded conception."[200]

43.

I

II

fragments

]   [

\

/

]

/

\

/

Firefly
(Coleoptera: Lampyridae)
"The flashy synchronous shows of Malaysia; the summertime magic of Japanese hotaru; *the rippling sparks of the Great Smoky Mountains: More than 2,000 different firefly species flit, flicker, and glimmer around the globe. But a recent paper in the journal* Bioscience *warns that their lights could go out for good—and human activity is to blame."*[201]

44.

It's simply not possible to force the jigsaw pieces of la mystérique into anything like coherence. Her form is light and shadow against the walls of philosophy's underland, the hold of a ship, the amniotic sewers where fluids flow and prisoners are shackled.

The art of the fragment rearranges the mysteric's gridded face. Degridded and unruly, she opens up another path, another passage. That passage is a different middle.

The different middle is the space-time of endings: convulsions in the middle, in the passage between the time of the end and the end of time. In the meantime, without a closing bracket. The Anthropocene is this chiasmus. Time suspended between birth and death, existence and extinction. Wounded and gasping for breath, la mystérique planet is an "empty and peopled"[132] poem life whose language is broken, disjointed, unsaid. A heterotopian mirror that "destroy[s] 'syntax,'" "stop[s] words in their tracks," and "contest[s] the very possibility of grammar at its source."[133]

A stutter.

The space-time of the middle is the mystical meantime of Anthropocene species life. In the early twenty-first century, this middle feels more dangerous than ever. The stakes of this middle are geontological: specula(riza)tion boomeranging back on itself, destroying its own habitat, becoming suicidal. Nilling.

]

]

"Fire flares up in the inexhaustible abundance of her underground source."[202]

the Anthropocene is this chiasmus

time of the end
✕
end of time [203]

[

]

[

45.

Rearranged as juxtaposed fragments, the mysteric's face exposes collapsed time. Mystic with hysteric, old with new, a theistic cosmology in a degodded world. Horizontal European time—from third- and fourth-century virgins to sixteenth- and seventeenth-century mystics to Charcot's hysterics to nymphomaniacs everywhere (this is the West's image of freedom).

Her face is historically white: figure of the feminine as fragile, bourgeois, pale, and fainting. Over time she has darkened, proliferating in different shades throughout the social body.

The iconic Billie is the mysteric of our time, an American grammar emptying itself. La mystérique condenses history into a single act of apparent transcendence: "mystery—mysteric myself—": "mystère—m'hystère—"[134] Yes, something trembles. Something is trying to free itself in that subjectless reflexivity. But transcendence drops beneath the horizon: unsays itself, over and over. Apophasis, caught in a circle without God, sadly repetitive. Trapped in the history that invented her. The sayable and the seeable in apophatic relation to each other.

Mysterics is the practice of enjambment across the cut between then and now. This mysterics is a history of the present. It tracks the contingencies of spectacle and speech by exposing the conditions of the seeable and the sayable. A pornographic mystical poetics, she straddles the lips of the cut between fragments.

Lynne Huffer, *La Mystérique III*, collage, 2021

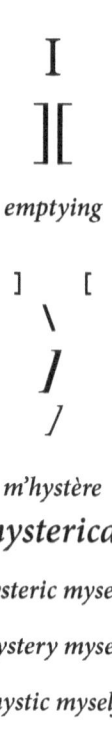

emptying

m'hystère
mysterical
hysteric myself
mystery myself
mystic myself

Through retroaction and condensation, fragments turn the mysterical archive against itself. The mysterical archive-fragment—Marguerite Porete, Augustine, Billie—turns in revolt against the ensemble that contains it. This is fragment as mise en abyme. A *contre*-move, fragmentation breaks up the ground, the conditions of the sayable and the seeable. Mysterical fragmentation as archival counterconduct.

Like the ship of fools, like heterotopias, like mirrors everywhere, these counterconductive fragments are real and imaginary, temporal hybrids, composites of sovereign and biopolitical subjection.

There will be no formula for this degridding. Counterconduction happens in the gaps, the murmuring backdrop of fragments. In the empty space where events didn't happen. That space invites the movement of enjambment. That straddled space, the place of the cut that separates fragment from fragment, is also the space-time where something new can happen. That something new can be oh so tiny, just the sliver of a split second. A flicker of movement unnamed. Light emptying from what will have been a firefly.

46.

"Mystery—mysteric myself—": "mystère—m'hystère—"[135]
The mysterical fragment is apophatic. A reflexive verb without a subject, it says a self only to unsay it, ad infinitum. In the earth archive, subjectless beings rest in soil, disappear in strata. This is the time of the will-have-been: the fossil record, breath preserved as CO_2 in ice.[136] Geontological, apophasis turns to relic. Extinct worlds without a mirror to see them.

I   emptying   ][   ]

m'hystère

One day perhaps there will be no one here to wonder at this. No self as grammar's shadow, a silhouette of a disappearance over the horizon. Without return.

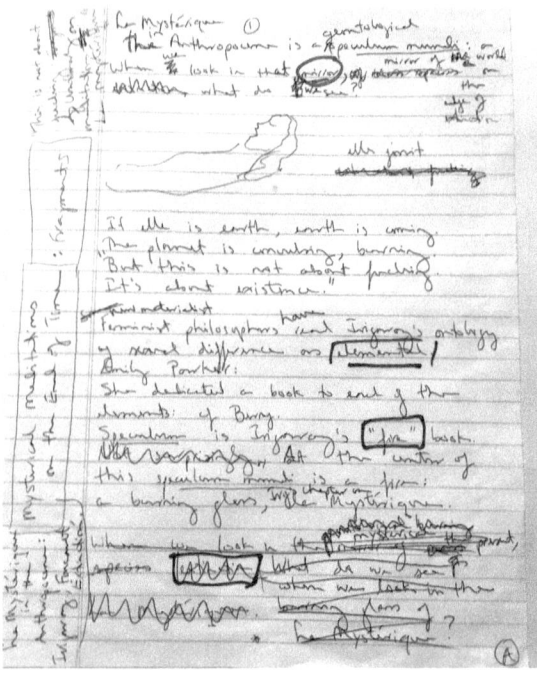

47.

There are so many guides through this thicket, apophatic unthreading of a tangled sexuality's no future. Writing as thinking as tracking a not-self: *anatta*. "You go out at night and, if it's a clear night and the stars are out, most people can recognize the constellation of the Big Dipper . . . Big Dipper is a concept . . . but there's no Big Dipper. So, self is like Big Dipper."[137] Just a concept we overlay on points of light in the dark. Seeing the self only to unsay it, over and over.

The Buddha

In the meantime, in this middle, the world is burning. "Can life go on in such violence, however sweet it may be? Does one not die from dying, or die from not dying?" [138]

Irigaray, Teresa, Bataille

How to receive these questions in a degodded world? How to go on?

48.

You see how strong love is;
life, do not hinder me,
you see, all I need do to gain you
is to lose you.
Come on already sweet death
come quickly death
that I die because I do not die.

Teresa

To gain is to lose

To die is to not die

The chiastic poem is a mise en abyme: to gain is to lose, like Gide's shields. And the reverse: to lose is to gain, to die is to not die. Mysterics turns back on itself, generating a minefield of "paradoxes, aporia, and coincidences of opposites."[139] This retroaction of mise en abyme is the mirror to infinity where "I" hears her own death, her mother's death, earth's death, the death of species.

"Come quickly" then, she says to death.

It will come quickly enough. She knows not when. She lives in the meantime. Practicing this emptiness, this self-undoing.

Vivo sin vivir en mí.
No subject here. *Anatta.* Just living.

Teresa otra vez

49.

Beginning again. Always a beginner. Mystérique, Other's Other, you are invited here, into this, whatever this is. In this time of the end that is not quite yet the end of time.

To write is to enter grammar's shadow, *inachevé*

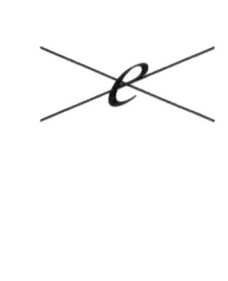

"Perec, a holocaust orphan, had in 1968 finished writing a novel without E's. Sans eux. *Without them. Mother, Father, parents.*"[204]

"Without ever finding a way to utter this absence

Where the Big Dipger becomes points of light without a shape. Where the "I" illusion begins to die. Just a flicker. "That 'I' die because 'I' do not die." Straddling that gap, the mystérique flares. She speaks silence: burning heart of apophatic speech. At the center of the X—the place of a relentless dedialectizing turning of the dialectic—light rays converge. The retroaction of light bounced back from the concave speculum. When you add paper at that focal point—retroaction with condensation—writing will burst into flame. Mysterical flame: the X of the meantime. Living as flash, bioluminescent, this is geontology on extinction's edges, between the time of the end and the end of time.

other than by using it as a mould."[205]

"The 'I' is empty still."[206]

To rest in that home is a fissured experience: this moment as a cut in time. Our planetary present is that "glorious slit."[140] Like Angela of Foligno, whom Irigaray mimics,[141] curl up inside the crack that once was God. It is now degodded: the gaping hole of she-knows-not-what. With devotion straddling "the lips of that slit."[142] Another enjambment, counterconductive, in the middle of this burning speculum.

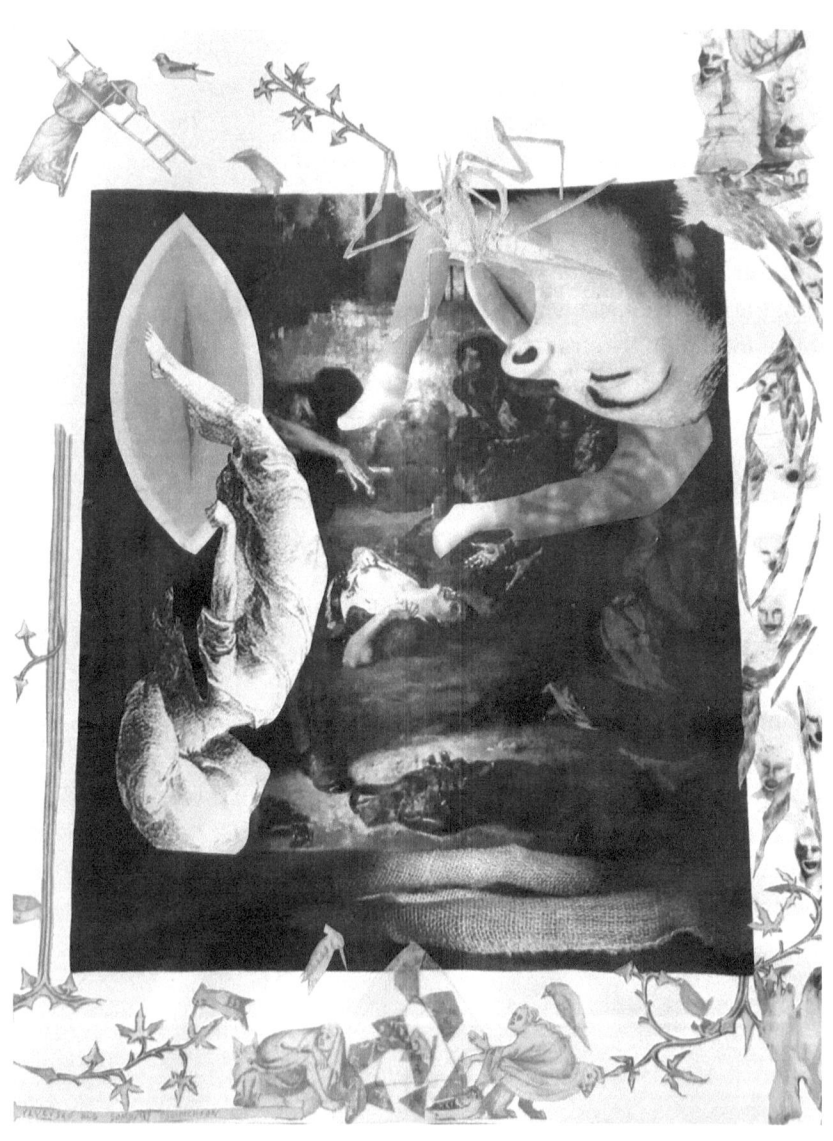

Lynne Huffer, *La Mystérique IV*, collage, 2021

BIBLIOGRAPHY

Alvis, Jason. "Transcendence of the Negative: Günther Anders' Apocalyptic Phenomenology." *Religions* 8, no. 4 (2017). https://doi.org/19.3390/re18040059.
Anders, Günther. "Theses for an Atomic Age." *Massachusetts Review* 3, no. 3 (1962): 493–505.
Armstrong, Guy. *Emptiness: A Practical Guide for Meditators*. Somerville, MA: Wisdom, 2017.
Bataille, Georges. *L'Anus solaire*. Paris: Editions de la Galerie Simon, 1931.
———. "Solar Anus." https://theanarchistlibrary.org/library/georges-bataille-the-solar-anus.
Beauvoir, Simone de. *The Second Sex*. Trans. Constance Borde and Sheila Malovany-Chevallier. New York: Knopf, 2010.
Berry, Philippa. "The Burning Glass: Paradoxes of Feminist Revelation in *Speculum*." In *Engaging with Irigaray*, 229–247. Ed. Carolyn Burke, Naomi Schor, and Margaret Whitford. New York: Columbia University Press, 1994.
Bynum, Caroline. *Christian Materiality: An Essay on Religion in Late Medieval Europe*. New York: Zone, 2011.
Carson, Anne. *Float*. New York: Knopf, 2016.
———. *If Not, Winter: Fragments of Sappho*. New York: Random House, 2002.
Certeau, Michel de. *The Mystic Fable*, vol. 1: *The Sixteenth and Seventeenth Centuries*. Trans. Michael B. Smith. 2 vols. Chicago: University of Chicago Press, 1992.
Cucopulos, Alexa. "Poiesis and Death: Foucault's Chiastic Undoing of Life in *History of Sexuality Volume One*." Honors Thesis, Emory University, 2016.
Dällenbach, Lucien. *The Mirror in the Text*. Trans. Jeremy Whiteleley with Emma Hughes. Cambridge: Polity, 1989.
Damdul, Geshe Dorji. "Ontological Reality: Quantum Theory and Emptiness in Buddhist Philosophy." In *Quantum Reality and Theory of Sūnya*, 345–349. Ed. Siddheshwar Rameshwar Bhatt. Singapore: Springer, 2019.
Deleuze, Gilles. *Foucault*. Trans. Séan Hand. Minneapolis: University of Minnesota Press, 1988.
Didi-Huberman, Georges. *Invention of Hysteria: Charcot and the Photographic Iconography of the Salpêtrière*. Trans. Alisa Hartz. Cambridge, MA: MIT Press, 2003.
———. "Knowing When to Cut." In *Foucault Against Himself*, 77–109. Ed. François Caillat. Trans. David Homel. Vancouver: Arsenal Pulp, 2015.
Eschner, Kat. "Humans Are Putting Fireflies at Risk of Extinction." *Popular Science*. February 3, 2020. https://www.popsci.com/story/environment/firefly-extinction/.
Foucault, Michel. "A Preface to Transgression." In *Essential Works of Foucault, 1954–1984*, 2:69–88. Ed. Paul Rabinow. 3 vols. New York: New Press, 1998.
———. "Different Spaces." In *Essential Works of Foucault, 1954–1984*, 2:175–186. Ed. Paul Rabinow. 3 vols. New York: New Press, 1998.
———. *Discipline and Punish: The Birth of the Prison*. Trans. Alan Sheridan. New York: Random House, 1977.
———. *History of Madness*. Trans. Jonathan Murphy and Jean Khalfa. London: Routledge, 2006.
———. "Lives of Infamous Men." In *Essential Works of Foucault, 1954–1984*, 3:157–175. Ed. Paul Rabinow. 3 vols. New York: New Press, 2000.

——. "Nietzsche, Genealogy, History." In *Essential Works of Foucault, 1954–1984*, 2:369–392. Ed. Paul Rabinow. 3 vols. New York: New Press, 1998.

——. *Psychiatric Power: Lectures at the Collège de France, 1973–1974*. Trans. Graham Burchell. New York: Palgrave Macmillan, 2006.

——. "The History of Sexuality: Interview with Lucette Finas" (1977). In *Power/Knowledge: Selected Interviews and Other Writings, 1972–1977*, 194–228. Ed. Colin Gordon. New York: Pantheon, 1980.

——. *The History of Sexuality*, vol. 1: *An Introduction*. Trans. Robert Hurley. 4 vols. New York: Vintage, 1978.

——. *The History of Sexuality*, vol. 4: *Confessions of the Flesh*. Ed. Frédéric Gros. Trans. Robert Hurley. 4 vols. New York: Pantheon, 2021.

——. *The Order of Things: An Archeology of the Human Sciences*. New York: Random House, 1970.

Goldstein, Joseph. "The Theory and Practice of Not-Self." Interview with Robert Wright. January 18, 2020. https://nonzero.org/post/self-joseph-goldstein.

Goul, Pauline. "1610 Wood/Cut: The Anthropocene, Uprooted." In *Critical Zones: The Science and Politics of Landing on Earth*, 188–189. Ed. Bruno Latour and Peter Weibel. Cambridge, MA: MIT Press, 2020.

Harney, Stefano, and Fred Moten. *The Undercommons: Fugitive Planning and Black Study*. New York: Minor Compositions, 2013.

Hollywood, Amy. *Sensible Ecstasy: Mysticism, Sexual Difference, and the Demands of History*. Chicago: University of Chicago Press, 2002.

——. "'That Glorious Slit': Irigaray and the Medieval Devotion to Christ's Side Wound." In *Acute Melancholia and Other Essays: Mysticism, History, and the Study of Religion*, 171–188. New York: Columbia University Press, 2016.

Howe, Susan. *Spontaneous Particulars: The Telepathy of Archives*. New York: New Directions, 2014.

Huffer, Lynne. "Respite: 12 Anthropocene Fragments." Special issue: Autotheory Theory, ed. Robyn Wiegman. *Arizona Quarterly: A Journal of American Literature, Culture, and Theory* 76, no. 1 (2020): 167–196.

Jagose, Anne-Marie. *Orgasmology*. Durham: Duke University Press, 2013.

Jones, Rachel. *Irigaray: Towards a Sexuate Philosophy*. Cambridge: Polity, 2011.

Lacan, Jacques. "God and the Jouissance of T̶h̶e̶ Woman." In *Feminine Sexuality: Jacques Lacan and the école freudienne*, 149–161. Ed. Juliet Mitchell and Jacqueline Rose. Trans. Jacqueline Rose. New York: Norton, 1982.

——. *Le Séminaire, livre XX: Encore, 1972–73*. Paris: Editions du Seuil, 1975.

Le Pen, Jean-Marie. "L'heure de vérité." *Antenne* 2. May 6, 1987. https://www.ina.fr/video/I09203636.

Lewis, Simon L., and Mark A. Maslin. "Defining the Anthropocene." *Nature* 519 (2015): 171–180.

Lochrie, Karma. "Mystical Acts, Queer Tendencies." In *Constructing Medieval Sexuality*, 180–200. Ed. Karma Lochrie, Peggy McCracken, and James A. Schultz. Minneapolis: University of Minnesota Press, 1997.

Luciano, Dana. "Sacred Theories of Earth: Matters of Spirit in *The Soul of Things*." *American Literature* 86, no. 4 (2014): 713–736.

Moten, Fred. *Black and Blur*. Durham: Duke University Press, 2017.

Musk, Elon on "The Joe Rogan Experience" no. 1169. *YouTube*. September 7, 2018. https://www.youtube.com/watch?v=ycPr5-27vSI.

Nail, Thomas. "What Is an Assemblage?" *Substance* 46, no. 1 (2017): 21–37.

Nelson, Maggie. *The Argonauts*. Minneapolis: Graywolf, 2015.

New Oxford Annotated Bible with the Apocrypha: New Revised Standard Version. Ed. Michael D. Coogan, MarcZ. Brettler, and Carol A Newsom. Oxford: Oxford University Press, 2001.

Nietzsche, Friedrich. "Eternal Recurrence." In *The Complete Works of Friedrich Nietzsche*, 16:148–161. Ed. Oscar Levy. Trans. Anthony M. Ludovici. 18 vols. Edinburgh: Foulis, 1911.

———. *The Gay Science*. Trans. Walter Kaufman. New York: Random House, 1974.

O'Grady, Lorraine. "Interview with Malik Gaines." *Frieze: Contemporary Art and Culture* no. 2018 (2021): 74–81.

Parker, Emily Anne. *Elemental Difference and the Climate of the Body*. New York: Oxford University Press, 2021.

Pestaña Knight, Elia et al. "*Arc de cercle* as a Manifestation of Focal Epileptic Seizures." *Neurology Clinical Practice* 8, no. 4 (2018): 354–356. https://www.ncbi.nlm.nih.gov/pmc/articles/PMC6105072/.

Philip, M. NourbeSe. *Zong!* Middletown, CT: Wesleyan University Press, 2008.

Povinelli, Elizabeth A. *Geontologies: A Requiem to Late Liberalism*. Durham: Duke University Press, 2016.

Rawlinson, Mary C. *The Betrayal of Substance: Death, Literature, and Sexual Difference in Hegel's* Phenomenology of Spirit. New York: Columbia University Press, 2021.

Robertson, Lisa. *Nilling*. Toronto: BookThug, 2012.

Ruíz-Gomez, Natasha. "The Painter, the Psychiatrist, and a Fashion for Hysteria," *Wellcome Collection*, March 4, 2020. https://wellcomecollection.org/articles/X144UhIAACEANhux.

Schmidt, Michael S., Katie Benner, and Nicholas Fandos. "Matt Gaetz Is Said to Face Justice Dept. Inquiry Over Sex With an Underage Girl." *New York Times*, March 30, 2021. https://www.nytimes.com/2021/03/30/us/politics/matt-gaetz-sex-trafficking-investigation.html.

Sedgwick, Eve Kosofsky. "A Poem Is Being Written." In *Tendencies*, 177–214. Durham: Duke University Press, 1993.

Sells, Michael A. *Mystical Languages of Unsaying*. Chicago: University of Chicago Press, 1994.

Sharpe, Christina. *In the Wake: On Blackness and Being*. Durham: Duke University Press, 2016.

Soussloff, Catherine M. *Foucault on Painting*. Minneapolis: University of Minnesota Press, 2017.

Spillers, Hortense J. "Mama's Baby, Papa's Maybe." In *Black, White, and in Color: Essays on American Literature and Culture*. Chicago: University of Chicago Press, 2003.

Stockton, Katherine Bond. *God Between Their Lips: Desire Between Women in Irigaray, Brontë, and Eliot*. Stanford: Stanford University Press, 1994.

Walker, Leslie. "How to Edit Your Gender Identity on Facebook." *Lifewire: Tech for Humans*, October 20, 2021. https://www.lifewire.com/edit-gender-identity-status-on-facebook-2654421.

Whitford, Margaret. *Luce Irigaray: Philosophy in the Feminine*. London: Routledge, 1991.
Wynter, Sylvia. "Unsettling the Coloniality of Being/Power/Truth/Freedom: Towards the Human, After Man, Its Overrepresentation—an Argument," *CR: The New Centennial Review* 3. no. 3 (2003): 257–337.

NOTES

1. Kathryn Bond Stockton, *God Between Their Lips: Desire Between Women in Irigaray, Brontë, and Eliot* (Stanford: Stanford University Press, 1994), 50.
2. Irigaray, S, 200.
3. Hannah Arendt in Lisa Robertson, *Nilling* (Toronto: BookThug, 2012), 13n2.
4. Michel Foucault, "Nietzsche, Genealogy, History," in *Essential Works of Foucault, 1954–1984*, 3 vols., ed. Paul Rabinow (New York: New Press, 1998), 2:369, translation modified.
5. Michel Foucault, *History of Madness*, trans. Jonathan Murphy and Jean Khalfa (London: Routledge, 2006), 174.
6. Foucault, xxxi.
7. Foucault, 547.
8. Many thanks to Kent Brintnall for this formulation.
9. Foucault, *History of Madness*, 12.
10. Foucault, 12.
11. Robertson, *Nilling*, 27.
12. Foucault, *History of Madness*, 174.
13. Foucault, 11.
14. Foucault, 12.
15. Foucault, 26.
16. Christopher Columbus's flagship.
17. A British slave ship that arrived in North America in 1619.
18. A British slave ship whose crew massacred 132 enslaved Africans by throwing them overboard in late November 1781, leading to a legal controversy over insurance claims made by the ship's owners *in Gregson v. Gilbert* (1783). See M. NourbeSe Philip, *Zong!* (Middletown, CT: Wesleyan University Press, 2008).
19. The first ships of Indian indenture to arrive in the Caribbean (British Guiana) in 1838.
20. Foucault, *History of Madness*, 41.
21. Stefano Harney and Fred Moten, *The Undercommons: Fugitive Planning and Black Study* (New York: Minor Compositions, 2013), 93.
22. Harney and Moten, 26.
23. Philip, *Zong*, 203.
24. Philip, 206.
25. Christina Sharpe, *In the Wake: On Blackness and Being* (Durham, NC: Duke University Press, 2016), 5.
26. Sharpe, 3.
27. Foucault, *History of Madness*, 11.
28. Foucault, 11.
29. Sharpe, *In the Wake*, 5.

30. Amy Hollywood, "'That Glorious Slit': Irigaray and the Medieval Devotion to Christ's Side Wound," in *Acute Melancholia, and Other Essays: Mysticism, History, and the Study of Religion* (New York: Columbia University Press, 2016), 171.
31. Carolyn Bynum, *Christian Materiality: An Essay on Religion in Late Medieval Europe* (New York: Zone, 2011), 197. See also Karma Lochrie, "Mystical Acts, Queer Tendencies," in *Constructing Medieval Sexuality*, ed. Karma Lochrie, Peggy McCracken, and James A. Schultz (Minneapolis: University of Minnesota Press, 1997), 180–200.
32. Bynum, *Christian Materiality*, 197.
33. Irigaray, S, 200. For an indispensable reading of this "glorious slit," see Hollywood, "'That Glorious Slit.'"
34. Irigaray, S, 200.
35. Irigaray, 200.
36. Margaret Whitford, *Luce Irigaray: Philosophy in the Feminine* (London: Routledge, 1991), 36.
37. Amy Hollywood, *Sensible Ecstasy: Mysticism, Sexual Difference, and the Demands of History* (Chicago: University of Chicago Press, 2002), 196.
38. Hollywood, 197.
39. Rachel Jones, *Irigaray: Towards a Sexuate Philosophy* (Cambridge: Polity, 2011), 155.
40. Irigaray, *Speculum de l'autre femme* (Paris: Editions de Minuit, 1974), 250. The published English translation (S, 200) turns Irigaray's reflexive verb ("*m'hystère*") into a noun ("me-hysteria").
41. Eve Kosofsky Sedgwick, "A Poem Is Being Written," in *Tendencies* (Durham, NC: Duke University Press, 1993), 185.
42. Michael A. Sells, *Mystical Languages of Unsaying* (Chicago: University of Chicago Press, 1994), 2.
43. Sells, 2.
44. Sells, 3.
45. Sells, 3.
46. Sells, 3.
47. Sells, 3.
48. Catherine M. Soussloff, *Foucault on Painting* (Minneapolis: University of Minnesota Press, 2017), 74.
49. Anne Carson, "Introduction," in *If Not, Winter: Fragments of Sappho* (New York: Random House, 2002), xi.
50. Carson, xi.
51. Michel Foucault, "The History of Sexuality: Interview with Lucette Finas" (1977), in *Power/Knowledge: Selected Interviews and Other Writings, 1972–1977*, ed. Colin Gordon (New York: Pantheon, 1980), 193.
52. Michael B. Smith, "Translator's Note," in *The Mystic Fable*, by Michel de Certeau, vol. 1, *The Sixteenth and Seventeenth Centuries*, trans. Michael B. Smith, 2 vols. (Chicago: University of Chicago Press, 1992), x.
53. de Certeau, *The Mystic Fable*, 1:298.
54. Georges Didi-Huberman, *Invention of Hysteria: Charcot and the Photographic Iconography of the Salpêtrière*, trans. Alisa Hartz (Cambridge, MA: MIT Press, 2003), 48.

55. Didi-Huberman, 49.
56. Didi-Huberman, 49, original emphasis.
57. Didi-Huberman, 49, original emphasis.
58. Didi-Huberman, 49.
59. Anne-Marie Jagose, *Orgasmology* (Durham, NC: Duke University Press, 2013), 141.
60. Michel Foucault, *The History of Sexuality*, vol. 1, *An Introduction*, trans. Robert Hurley, 4 vols. (New York: Vintage, 1978), 156.
61. Foucault, 1:63.
62. Foucault, 1:124.
63. Didi-Huberman, *Invention of Hysteria*, 4.
64. Natasha Ruíz-Gomez, "The Painter, the Psychiatrist, and a Fashion for Hysteria," *Wellcome Collection*, March 4, 2020, https://wellcomecollection.org/articles/Xl44UhIAACEANhux.
65. Didi-Huberman, *Invention of Hysteria*, 4.
66. Foucault, *History of Madness*, 436.
67. Didi-Huberman, *Invention of Hysteria*, 45.
68. See Michel Foucault, "Lives of Infamous Men," in Rabinow, *Essential Works of Foucault*, 3:157–175.
69. Jacques Lacan, *Le Séminaire, livre XX: Encore, 1972–73* (Paris: Editions du Seuil, 1975).
70. Jacques Lacan, "God and the Jouissance of T̶h̶e̶ Woman," in *Feminine Sexuality: Jacques Lacan and the école freudienne*, ed. Juliet Mitchell and Jacqueline Rose, trans. Jacqueline Rose (New York: Norton, 1982), 147.
71. Lacan, 147.
72. Lacan, 147.
73. Lacan, 147.
74. Michel Foucault, "A Preface to Transgression," in Rabinow, *Essential Works of Foucault*, 2:70.
75. Michel Foucault, *Psychiatric Power: Lectures at the Collège de France, 1973–1974*, trans. Graham Burchell (New York: Palgrave Macmillan, 2006), 305.
76. Foucault, 309.
77. Foucault, 309.
78. Foucault, 318.
79. See, for example, allegations against a Florida senator in Michael S. Schmidt, Katie Benner, and Nicholas Fandos, "Matt Gaetz Is Said to Face Justice Dept. Inquiry Over Sex With an Underage Girl," *New York Times*, March 30, 2021, www.nytimes.com/2021/03/30/us/politics/matt-gaetz-sex-trafficking-investigation.html.
80. Lacan, "God and the Jouissance of T̶h̶e̶ Woman," 147.
81. Irigaray, S, 195.
82. Irigaray, "Plato's Hystera," in S, 364.
83. Friedrich Nietzsche, *The Gay Science*, trans. Walter Kaufman (New York: Random House, 1974), section 125.
84. Irigaray, S, 364.
85. Irigaray, 13.
86. Lacan, "God and the Jouissance of T̶h̶e̶ Woman," 147.
87. de Certeau, *Mystic Fable*, 1:14.

88. de Certeau, 1:14.
89. Foucault, *History of Madness*, xxxiv.
90. Irigaray, S, 191, original emphasis.
91. Didi-Huberman, *Invention of Hysteria*, 148.
92. Foucault, *History of Madness*, 3.
93. Foucault, 3.
94. Foucault, "Nietzsche, Genealogy, History," 380.
95. Guy Armstrong, *Emptiness: A Practical Guide for Meditators* (Somerville, MA: Wisdom, 2017), 3.
96. Foucault, *History of Madness*, xxxi.
97. de Certeau, *Mystic Fable*, 1:1.
98. Robertson, *Nilling*, 14.
99. Robertson, 14.
100. Robertson, 14.
101. Alexa Cucopulos, "Poiesis and Death: Foucault's Chiastic Undoing of Life in *History of Sexuality Volume One*," Honors Thesis, Emory University (2016), 11.
102. Robertson, *Nilling*, 14.
103. Foucault, *Sexuality*, 1:156.
104. Foucault, 1:157.
105. Foucault, *History of Madness*, xxxi–xxxii.
106. See de Certeau, *The Mystic Fable*, 1:49–72, chapter 2, "The Garden: Delirium and Delights of Hieronymous Bosch."
107. de Certeau, *Mystic Fable*, 1:55.
108. de Certeau, 1:56.
109. de Certeau, 1:57.
110. Foucault, *History of Madness*, 531.
111. Foucault, xxxi–xxxii.
112. Michel Foucault, "Different Spaces," in Rabinow, *Essential Works of Foucault*, 2:175–186.
113. Irigaray, *Speculum de l'autre femme*, 250.
114. Didi-Huberman, *Invention of Hysteria*, 148.
115. Didi-Huberman, 148.
116. Irigaray, S, 198–199.
117. Foucault, *History of Madness*, 363.
118. Didi-Huberman, *Invention of Hysteria*, 148.
119. Didi-Huberman, 148.
120. Didi-Huberman, 50.
121. Hortense J. Spillers, "Mama's Baby, Papa's Maybe," in *Black, White, and in Color: Essays on American Literature and Culture* (Chicago: University of Chicago Press, 2003), 203.
122. Spillers, 203.
123. Spillers, 207.
124. Spillers, 206.
125. Foucault, *History of Madness*, 3.
126. Irigaray, *Speculum de l'autre femme*, 238.
127. Irigaray, S, 191.
128. Spillers, "Mama's Baby," 207.

129. Simone de Beauvoir, *The Second Sex*, trans. Constance Borde and Sheila Malovany-Chevallier (New York: Knopf, 2010), 166.
130. Sylvia Wynter, "Unsettling the Coloniality of Being/Power/Truth/Freedom: Towards the Human, After Man, Its Overrepresentation—an Argument," *CR: The New Centennial Review* 3, no. 3 (2003): 322.
131. Dana Luciano, "Sacred Theories of Earth: Matters of Spirit in *The Soul of Things*," *American Literature* 86, no. 4 (2014): 713.
132. Foucault, *History of Madness*, xxxi.
133. Foucault, *The Order of Things: An Archeology of the Human Sciences* (New York: Random House, 1970), xviii.
134. Irigaray, S, 201, translation modified; Irigaray, *Speculum de l'autre femme*, 250.
135. Irigaray, S, 201, translation modified; Irigaray, *Speculum de l'autre femme*, 250. The published English translation turns Irigaray's reflexive verb ("*m'hystère*") into a noun ("me-hysteria") and changes the surrounding hyphens ("mystère—*m'hystère*—") into a comma ("Mystery, me-hysteria").
136. See Simon L. Lewis and Mark A. Maslin, "Defining the Anthropocene," *Nature* 519 (2015): 171–180. Lewis and Maslin introduce the "Orbis hypothesis" for a new Anthropocene golden spike: a drop of CO_2 in an Antarctic ice core registering the genocidal effects of the Columbian exchange on the indigenous peoples of the Americas. For reflections on the Orbis hypothesis as a "cut" in time, see Pauline Goul, "1610 Wood/Cut: The Anthropocene, Uprooted," in *Critical Zones: The Science and Politics of Landing on Earth*, ed. Bruno Latour and Peter Weibel (Cambridge, MA: MIT Press, 2020), 188–189.
137. Joseph Goldstein, "The Theory and Practice of Not-Self," interview with Robert Wright, January 18, 2020, https://nonzero.org/post/self-joseph-goldstein.
138. Irigaray, S, 196.
139. Sells, *Mystical Languages*, 3.
140. Irigaray, S, 200.
141. See especially Hollywood, "'That Glorious Slit.'"
142. Irigaray, S, 200.
143. Sappho, fragment 16, in *If Not, Winter*, 27.
144. Lorraine O'Grady, "Interview with Malik Gaines," *Frieze: Contemporary Art and Culture*, no. 2018 (2021): 81.
145. Irigaray, S, 142.
146. Geshe Dorji Damdul, "Ontological Reality: Quantum Theory and Emptiness in Buddhist Philosophy," in *Quantum Reality and Theory of Sūnya*, ed. Siddheshwar Rameshwar Bhatt (Singapore: Springer, 2019), 348.
147. Philip, *Zong*, 196.
148. Foucault, *History of Madness*, 13.
149. Robertson, *Nilling*, 27.
150. Philip, *Zong*, 193.
151. Philip, 207.
152. Sharpe, *In the Wake*, 18.
153. John 19:34 in *New Oxford Annotated Bible with the Apocrypha: New Revised Standard Version*, ed. Michael D. Coogan, Marc Z. Brettler, and Carol A. Newsom (Oxford: Oxford University Press, 2001), 156 NT.
154. Foucault, *The History of Sexuality*, vol. 4, *Confessions of the Flesh*, ed. Frédéric

Gros, trans. Robert Hurley (New York: Pantheon, 2021), 127.
155. Irigaray, S, 200.
156. Irigaray, 142.
157. de Certeau, *Mystic Fable*, 1:112.
158. Anne Carson, *Float* (New York: Knopf, 2016), frontispiece.
159. Sedgwick, "A Poem Is Being Written," 185–186.
160. Thomas Nail, "What Is an Assemblage?," *Substance* 46, no. 1 (2017): 22.
161. Lacan, *Séminaire XX*, 68.
162. *Vimalakirti Sutra*, in Sells, *Mystical Languages*, 4.
163. Gilles Deleuze, *Foucault*, trans. Séan Hand (Minneapolis: University of Minnesota Press, 1988), 87.
164. Irigaray, S, 198.
165. Foucault, "The History of Sexuality: Interview with Lucette Finas" (1977), 193.
166. de Certeau, *Mystic Fable*, 1:7.
167. Michel Foucault, *Discipline and Punish: The Birth of the Prison*, trans. Alan Sheridan (New York: Random House, 1977), 200.
168. Foucault, *The Order of Things*, 277.
169. Lucien Dällenbach, *The Mirror in the Text*, trans. Jeremy Whiteleley with Emma Hughes (Cambridge: Polity, 1989), 111.
170. Dällenbach, 111.
171. Elia Pestaña Knight et al., "*Arc de cercle* as a Manifestation of Focal Epileptic Seizures," *Neurology Clinical Practice* 8, no. 4 (2018): 354–356, www.ncbi.nlm.nih.gov/pmc/articles/PMC6105072/.
172. Foucault, *History of Madness*, 522.
173. Luce Irigaray, "Così Fan Tutti," in TS, 91.
174. Susan Howe, *Spontaneous Particulars: The Telepathy of Archives* (New York: New Directions, 2014), 41.
175. Nietzsche, *The Gay Science*, section 125.
176. Leslie Walker, "How to Edit Your Gender Identity on Facebook," *Lifewire: Tech for Humans*, October 20, 2021, www.lifewire.com/edit-gender-identity-status-on-facebook-2654421.
177. Irigaray, S, 195.
178. Foucault, *Sexuality*, 1:157.
179. Elizabeth A. Povinelli, *Geontologies: A Requiem to Late Liberalism* (Durham, NC: Duke University Press, 2016), 28.
180. de Certeau, *Mystic Fable*, 1:17.
181. Fred Moten, *Black and Blur* (Durham, NC: Duke University Press, 2017), 10–11.
182. Jean-Marie Le Pen, "L'heure de vérité," *Antenne* 2 (May 6, 1987), www.ina.fr/video/I09203636.
183. Foucault, "Lives of Infamous Men," 158–159.
184. Georges Didi-Huberman, "Knowing When to Cut," in *Foucault Against Himself*, ed. François Caillat, trans. David Homel (Vancouver: Arsenal Pulp, 2015), 84–85.
185. Elon Musk on *The Joe Rogan Experience*, no. 1169, *YouTube*, September 7, 2018, www.youtube.com/watch?v=ycPr5-27vSI.
186. Cucopulos, "Poiesis and Death," 11.
187. de Certeau, *Mystic Fable*, 1:52.
188. Foucault, *History of Madness*, 531.

189. Didi-Huberman, *Invention of Hysteria*, 148.
190. Friedrich Nietzsche, "Eternal Recurrence," in *The Complete Works of Friedrich Nietzsche*, ed. Oscar Levy, trans. Anthony M. Ludovici, 18 vols. (Edinburgh: Foulis, 1911), 16:156.
191. Philip, *Zong*, 193.
192. Harney and Moten, *Undercommons*, 92.
193. Philip, *Zong*, 198.
194. Irigaray, S, 191.
195. Philippa Berry, "The Burning Glass: Paradoxes of Feminist Revelation in *Speculum*," in *Engaging with Irigaray*, ed. Carolyn Burke, Naomi Schor, and Margaret Whitford (New York: Columbia University Press, 1994), 231.
196. Irigaray published *Sharing the Fire* in 2019, forty-five years after the publication of *Speculum* and twenty-five years after Philippa Berry's essay about the "missing fire" (Berry, "Burning Glass," 231). In an email correspondence Mary Rawlinson interprets this elemental "fire" as a development of Irigaray's concept of transcendence: a sharing of Hegelian "spirit." On this view, *Sharing the Fire* returns the reader to the mysterical fire that fuels *Speculum*. For a fuller consideration of sexual difference, transcendence, and spirit in Hegel, see Mary C. Rawlinson, *The Betrayal of Substance: Death, Literature, and Sexual Difference in Hegel's* Phenomenology of Spirit (New York: Columbia University Press, 2021), chapter 4, "Spirit." For a brilliant meditation on an Irigarayan elemental difference, or a "collaboration *of* elementalities" beyond sexual difference, see Emily Anne Parker, *Elemental Difference and the Climate of the Body* (New York: Oxford University Press, 2021), 94.
197. de Beauvoir, *The Second Sex*, 165.
198. Georges Bataille, "Solar Anus," https://theanarchistlibrary.org/library/georges-bataille-the-solar-anus. For French original with drawings by André Masson, see Georges Bataille, *L'Anus solaire* (Paris: Editions de la Galerie Simon, 1931).
199. Maggie Nelson, *The Argonauts* (Minneapolis: Graywolf, 2015), 134.
200. Sylvia Wynter, "Unsettling the Coloniality of Being," 322.
201. Kat Eschner, "Humans Are Putting Fireflies at Risk of Extinction," *Popular Science*, February 3, 2020, www.popsci.com/story/environment/firefly-extinction/.
202. Irigaray, S, 195.
203. Günther Anders, "Theses for an Atomic Age," *Massachusetts Review* 3, no. 3 (1962): 493. See also Jason Alvis, "Transcendence of the Negative: Günther Anders' Apocalyptic Phenomenology," *Religions* 8, no. 4 (2017), https://doi.org/10.3390/rel8040059. For reflections on Anders in the Anthropocene, see Lynne Huffer, "Respite: 12 Anthropocene Fragments," in *Arizona Quarterly: A Journal of American Literature, Culture, and Theory* 76, no. 1 (2020): 167–196; this appears in the special issue "Autotheory Theory."
204. Robertson, *Nilling*, 45.
205. Robertson, 45.
206. Irigaray, S, 195.

CONTRIBUTORS

EDITORS

Mary C. Rawlinson is Senior Research Fellow at the Institute for Advanced Studies, University College London, and Professor Emerita of Philosophy, Stony Brook University. Her books include *The Betrayal of Substance: Death, Literature, and Sexual Difference in Hegel's* Phenomenology of Spirit (Columbia University Press, 2021) and *Just Life: Bioethics and the Future of Sexual Difference* (Columbia University Press, 2016), as well as the edited volume *Engaging the World: Thinking After Irigaray* (SUNY Press, 2016). She is the cofounder of the Irigaray Circle.

James Sares is Affiliated Faculty in Philosophy at Emerson College. He recently completed his PhD in Philosophy from Stony Brook University, defending a dissertation titled "The Irresolvable Dialectic of Existence and the Antinomies of Time: A Hegelian Argument." He specializes in modern philosophy and phenomenology and has published several articles and book chapters on Irigaray and sexual difference, as well as articles on sexual difference in *Transgender Studies Quarterly* and *philoSOPHIA: A Journal of transContinental Feminism*. He is the recipient of the 2018 Karen Burke Memorial Prize awarded by the Irigaray Circle.

CONTRIBUTORS

Ovidiu Anemțoaicei is Lecturer at the Faculty of Journalism and Communication Studies, University of Bucharest, Romania. He is the author of *Male Bodies and Sexual Difference: A Proposal for a Feminist Corporeoethics* (Cambridge Scholars, 2018) and coauthor of articles in journals including *International Journal of Philosophical Studies*, *AnaLize—Journal of Gender and Feminist Studies*, and *Critical Legal Thinking*.

Emanuela Bianchi is Associate Professor of Comparative Literature at New York University with affiliations in Classics and Gender and Sexuality Studies. She is the author of *The Feminine Symptom: Aleatory Matter in the Aristotelian Cosmos* (Fordham University Press, 2014), *La naturaleza en disputa: Physis y eros en el pensamiento antiguo* (Hueders/Philosophica, 2022) (in Spanish), as well as the editor of *Is Feminist Philosophy Philosophy?* (Northwestern University Press, 1999), and coeditor of *Antiquities Beyond Humanism* (Oxford University Press, 2019). She is book review editor for *philoSOPHIA: A Journal of transContinental Feminism*.

Jennifer Carter is a Lecturer in Philosophy at Stony Brook University. Her research focuses on continental philosophy and phenomenology, especially the philosophy of Luce Irigaray, philosophy of touch, feminist philosophy, phenomenology and philosophy of science, and the intersections of ethics and political philosophy. Her recent publications include "On Peaceful Political Relations Between Two in Luce Irigaray's Work" in *Sophia* (2022), "How to Lead a Child to Flower: Luce Irigaray's Philosophy of the Growth of Children" in *Towards a New Human Being* (Irigaray et al., eds., 2019), and *Touch and Caress in the Work of Luce Irigaray* (2018).

Ruthanne Crapo Kim is a faculty member in the Department of Philosophy at Minneapolis College and Affiliate Faculty at the Pennsylvania State University. Her research queries feminist philosophy, critical philosophy of race, Caribbean philosophy, environmental philosophy, and decolonial studies. Her interests include decolonizing pedagogy and ontological labor in the academy. She is a coeditor of *Horizons of Difference: Rethinking Space, Place, and Identity with Irigaray* (SUNY Press, 2022).

CONTRIBUTORS

Penelope Deutscher is the Joan and Sarepta Harrison Professor of Philosophy at Northwestern University. Her many books include *Foucault's Futures: A Critique of Reproductive Reason* (Columbia University Press, 2017), *The Philosophy of Simone de Beauvoir: Ambiguity, Conversion, Resistance* (Cambridge University Press, 2008), *How to Read Derrida* (Granta/Norton 2006), and *A Politics of Impossible Difference: The Later Work of Luce Irigaray* (Cornell University Press, 2002).

Belinda Eslick is a Casual Academic at the University of Queensland, where she lectures in Gender Studies, and a Casual Senior Research Fellow at the Griffith Asia Institute, Griffith University. Her engagement with the philosophy of Luce Irigaray primarily addresses questions of sexual difference and "essence" in feminist thought as well as feminist perspectives on the home and reproductive labor, work, and care.

Elizabeth Grosz has taught in Philosophy, Gender, and/or Literature programs at Duke, Rutgers, SUNY Buffalo, and SUNY Stony Brook in the United States, as well as at the University of Sydney and Monash University in Australia. She is, most recently, the author of *The Incorporeal: Ontology, Ethics and the Limits of Materialism* (Columbia University Press, 2017), *Becoming Undone: Darwinian Reflections on Life, Politics and Art* (Duke University Press, 2012), and *Chaos, Territory, Art: Deleuze and the Framing of the Earth* (Columbia University Press, 2008). She has worked on Irigaray's writings for over forty years.

Rebecca Hill is Senior Lecturer in the School of Media and Communication at RMIT University in Narrm/Melbourne. She is author of *The Interval: Relation and Becoming in Irigaray, Aristotle, and Bergson* (Fordham University Press, 2012) and has published articles on the ontology of sexual difference in journals including *Hypatia*, the *Australian Feminist Law Journal*, *Philosophy Compass*, and *Deleuze Studies*.

Iván Hofman is a doctoral candidate in the Department of Comparative Literature at New York University, working on literature and philosophy in Spanish, German, and French. He is currently translating Severo Sarduy's *Barroco* into English.

Sabrina L. Hom is Associate Professor of Philosophy and Coordinator of the Women's and Gender Studies Program at Georgia College in Milledgeville, Georgia. She earned her doctorate at Stony Brook University. With Mary C. Rawlinson and Serene Khader, she cofounded the Luce Irigaray Circle, and currently serves as codirector. She has published work on feminist philosophy and race theory in venues such as *Hypatia*, *Philosophy Today*, and *Critical Philosophy of Race*. She lives in Macon, Georgia, with her family.

Lynne Huffer is the Samuel Candler Dobbs Professor of Philosophy at Emory University. Her books include *Foucault's Strange Eros* (Columbia University Press, 2020), *Are the Lips a Grave?* (Columbia University Press, 2013), *Mad for Foucault* (Columbia University Press, 2010), *Maternal Pasts, Feminist Futures* (Stanford University Press, 1998), and *Another Colette* (University of Michigan Press, 1992).

Rachel Jones is Associate Professor in the Department of Philosophy at George Mason University. She is author of *Luce Irigaray: Towards a Sexuate Philosophy* (Polity, 2011) and has published articles on Irigaray's philosophy in journals including *Hypatia* and the *Journal of the British Society for Phenomenology*.

Mitchell Damian Murtagh is Visiting Assistant Professor in Women's, Gender, and Sexuality Studies at Emory University. He holds a PhD from Duke University's Literature Program with certificates in Feminist Studies and the History and Philosophy of Science, Technology, and Medicine. He completed his BA at Rutgers University, New Brunswick, in English and Philosophy. His research spans feminist philosophy, trans studies, continental philosophy, and philosophy of physics. He is a recipient of the Irigaray Circle's Karen Burke Memorial Prize and has been published in *philoSOPHIA: A Journal of Transcontinental Feminism* and *Horizons of Difference: Rethinking Space, Place, and Identity with Irigaray* (SUNY Press, 2022).

Laura Roberts is Lecturer in Women's and Gender at Flinders University and received her PhD in Philosophy from the University of Queensland. She is author of *Irigaray and Politics: A Critical Introduction* (Edinburgh

CONTRIBUTORS

University Press, 2019), is coeditor of *Irigaray and Politics* (Sophia, 2022), and has published articles in edited collections and journals including *Hypatia*, *Feminist Review*, and *Australian Feminist Studies*.

Yvette Russell is Associate Professor of Law and Feminist Theory at the University of Bristol Law School. Her work examines the interfaces between law and contemporary feminist philosophy, especially the philosophy of Irigaray. She is the author of articles in journals including *Feminist Legal Studies*, *Australian Feminist Law Journal*, and *Signs*, and of the monograph *Sexual History Evidence and the Rape Trial* (with Joanne Conaghan), forthcoming with Bristol University Press.

Stephen D. Seely is a Newcastle University Academic Track (NUAcT) Fellow in the School of Geography, Politics, and Sociology. His essays on queer theory, sexual difference, and political theory have appeared in several anthologies and such journals as *Signs*, *philoSOPHIA*, *Sexualities*, and *Australian Feminist Law Journal*.

Oli Stephano lives on Wabanaki land in coastal Maine, where his research and teaching interests span feminist and queer theory, environmental ethics, and continental philosophy, with special attention to questions of materiality, normativity, and becoming. His essays on sexual difference, Spinoza, and ecological ethics appear in journals including *Hypatia*, *SubStance*, and *Environmental Philosophy*.

INDEX

Aboriginal people, 314–315, 318–320, 328*n*12, 330*n*41
absolute knowing: Hegel and, 40, 42–46, 52, 56*n*5, 56*nn*15–16, 344; metaphysics of, 57*n*19; nihilism and, 53, 54; with time and space, 40, 47; transcendence and, 50
abuse: of Earth, 58*n*37, 298, 318, 319, 325, 330*n*41; sexual, 309*n*3; violence and, 280, 291*n*23
actualization, 63–64, 72, 73
Adorno, Theodor W., 357, 369*n*5
ageism, 111
AIDS, 200, 394, 396
"Ain't I a Woman?" (Truth), 261
alienation, 132, 253, 312, 315, 326
"American Grammar Book." *See* "Mama's Baby, Papa's Maybe"
American Society for the Prevention of Cruelty to Animals, 291*n*23
"Am I That Name?" (Riley), 77*n*28
anabasis (upward motion), 338, 348
anachrony, 346
anal: birth and cloacal theory, 197, 199–200; eroticism, 197, 198–199, 200; Irigaray and ontology of, 196–201; male bodily reimaginings and, 201–206

analepsis, 346
Anarcha (enslaved person), 262, 263
Angela of Foligno, 354*n*30, 402, 415
"Animal Compassion" (Irigaray), 323–324
animals, 96*n*3, 231, 291*n*23, 320, 323–324
Anthropocene, 385, 395–397, 402–404, 406, 408, 424*n*136
anti-Blackness, 157–159, 161, 164*n*2, 254–259, 267
antiessentialism, 124–128, 134–138
Antigone (mythological figure), 280–281, 303–306
antisocial queer theory, 123*n*43
"Any Theory of the Subject . . ." (Irigaray), 344
apophasis, 382, 383, 395, 397, 409, 411
Aquinas, Thomas, 76*n*7, 76*n*11
Archimedes, 339–340, 353*n*16
Arendt, Hannah, 58*n*35, 373, 374
Are the Lips a Grave (Huffer), 123*n*43
Aristotle, 55*n*4, 76*n*5, 131, 151, 344, 346–348; with "at least two" sexes, 225*n*2; Irigaray and, 329*n*23, 338; menstrual fluid and, 359; theory of place and, 316; *tokos* and, 356; universals and, 60
Assuming a Body (Salamon), 149–150, 238

asylum seekers, immigration, 278, 288
"At Least Two" (Hill), 244–245
Augustine (saint), 347, 396, 403, 410
Australia, 314–315, 318–320, 324–325, 328n12, 328n15, 330n41
auto-affection, 212, 213, 217–219
autodifferentiating, 150, 167n44
autological circle, 39–41, 42, 43, 46, 47
Avicenna, 76n11
Aydemir, Murat, 209n42

Bacchanalian revel, 44, 55n3
Bachelard, Gaston, 207n1
bacteria, xin1, 25, 231
Bal, Mieke, 344
Beauvoir, Simone de, 6, 165n19
becoming: infinite, 40–47, 55n4; trans, 327n8; "the/a woman" as model of, 211–212, 214, 219–220. *See also* sexual difference, as qualitative becoming; sexuation, as frame for human becoming
Becoming Human (Jackson, Z. I.), 157, 160, 161, 274n36
Becoming Undone (Grosz), 120n3, 235
being: beings and, 274n41; indebtedness and gift of, 357; "neuter," 38n37; sexuation and, 211; trans, 228, 242, 243, 247; *Through Vegetal Being*, 125, 132, 140n5, 324; white masculine, 120n4
beings: being and, 274n41; finitude of, 17, 18; sexuate with sexed, 36n1. *See also* human beings
"Belly of the World, The" (Hartman), 254, 277nn106–107
Bennett, Jane, 156
Bergson, Henri, 212–215, 244, 245
Bernini, Gian Lorenzo, 352n6, 386, 389, 390
Berry, Philippa, 337, 426n196
Bersani, Leo, 123n43, 200, 201
Betsey (enslaved person), 262, 263
Bettcher, Talia Mae, 226n38
Between East and West (*Entre Orient et Occident*) (Irigaray), 59, 74, 90, 140n5

beyond-binary grammar, of sexual difference, 227–232
Bianchi, Emanuela, 254–255
bimodal, human sexes as, 68, 73, 228, 232, 245
binary logic, 229, 232
bio (life), 106
biological: body, 10, 108, 144, 156–157; classification, 26; determinism, 127, 138, 148; essentialism, 4, 82–84, 89, 96n3, 107; Irigaray and, 264
biology, 153, 155, 166n28, 176, 262
bio-morphological, 110–111
birth, 132, 140n9, 197, 199–200, 202, 205, 257–258
Black, Anna, 294–295, 299–303, 305
Black, C. F., 319
Black Atlantic. *See* sexuate difference, in Black Atlantic
Black bodies, 150, 160, 161, 262–265
Black embodiment, slavery and, 161
Black(ened) *mater*(nal), 262, 270, 275n55
Black feminism, 269, 270
Black health, in U.S., 160
Black Lives Matter movement, 120n4
Black maternal bodies, 160
Black maternity, 257–258, 259, 266, 269, 270
Blackness, 256, 260, 274n30. *See also* anti-Blackness
Black on Both Sides (Snorton), 274n36
Black women, 158, 254–255, 259, 261–263, 267–269, 275n47
"Blind Spot of an Old Dream of Symmetry, The" (Irigaray), 333, 353n11
blood: in Irigaray and Spillers, 280–285, 286; law and, 280–282; menstrual fluid, 359; parental rights and, 282, 285–286, 287; placental, 288. *See also* kinship
Bloodchild (Butler, O.), 170n94
Blumenberg, Hans, 367
bodies: anatomical, 83, 84; *Assuming a Body*, 149–150, 238; biological, 10, 108, 144, 156–157; Black, 150, 160, 161, 262–265; consciousness and, 187; with

INDEX

corporeal undecidability and sexual difference, 149–152; culture and, 38n36; *Elemental Difference and the Climate of the Body*, 241; female, 7, 81, 84, 106, 118, 127, 144, 147, 153, 156, 183, 196–197, 199, 202, 209n43, 212–213, 234; maternal, 89, 92–93, 132, 160, 266, 268–269; medical experiments on Black, 262, 263, 264; of mothers and reproductive power, 202; nonbinary, 209n43; of nonwhite women, 121n10, 283, 285; sexuate identity and, 4; slavery as "theft of," 272n3; spiritual exchange with breath and, 205; with surgery and chemical intervention, 233, 235, 236, 237, 245, 249n12; trans embodiment, 122n22, 225n3, 241; trans exceptionalism and, 237; transformed and opposite sex, 235, 249n12; *Volatile Bodies*, 233–234, 235. See also lips; male bodies; sexuate body

"Bodies of Philosophy" (Wolfe, E.), 249n12

bodies of water: masculine, 91; maternal feminine and, 90; onto-logic of amniotics and, 91–92, 93, 94; *poétique du corps*, 144, 145, 156, 164n11; sexuate difference and, 82, 87–89

Bodies of Water (Neimanis), 87, 93, 100n103

bodily: composition and individuation, 189, 191; form, 106, 175–177, 180, 184, 189; lips as both figuratively and, 175–177; morphology, 173, 179, 185, 335, 336; semantic and, 175–180

Boethius, 60–61, 76n7

bondage dialectic, slavery and, 253

Bonne de Luxembourg, 378–379, 388, *388*, 393

Bosch, Hieronymous, 402, 403

Braidotti, Rosi, 94, 98n26

breath: birth and, 132; mothers with gift of air, 363; sexuation and, 133; spiritual exchange with body and, 205

Buffon, Georges, 353n16

Bunitj clan, Australia, 314–315, 318

Burke, Carolyn, 121n10

Burke, Karen, 116

burning glass (*miroir ardent*), 335, 337–339, 341–342, 345, 353n16, 353n22, 354n24, 406

Butler, Judith, 38n38, 77n28, 109, 145, 157, 164n11, 238, 240; gender performativity and, 230–231, 241; Grosz and, 169n79, 242–243; on Irigaray, 147, 153; on nature/culture, 146, 165n14, 165n17

Butler, Octavia, 170n94

Carby, Hazel, 257, 274n36

Caribbean, 420n19

carnal knowledge, 203, 204, 205

Carson, Anne, 373, 384

Castoriadis, Cornelius, 207n1

castration anxiety, 199–200, 202, 209n42, 361

Categories (Aristotle), 60

Catherine of Siena, 354n30

Cavarero, Adriana, 266

cave metaphor, 333, 338, 342–343, 347, 367, 406

Certeau, Michel de, 402

Changing Difference (Malabou), 124, 135, 148

Chanter, Tina, 121n5, 256

Charcot, Jean-Martin, 389, 392, 394, 396, 402–403, 409

Charles V (King of France), 379

Cheah, Pheng, 296, 302

children, 132–133, 178, 257, 288; abuse of, 280, 291n23, 309n3; Black girls, 254, 255; daughters, 185, 208n12, 292n30; family separation, 278–279, 283, 285, 287; forced removal of Native American, 278, 286, 291n23; mothers and, 50–51, 52, 58n40, 197, 202, 280, 284, 363; rights and, 282, 285–287; sons, 198–199, 284; white families and kinship to black, 283, 285

Christ, 378, 388, *388*

INDEX

"Cisgenderism" (Lennon and Mistler), 226*n*38
cissexism, 11, 82, 86, 211–212, 223–224, 226*n*38, 241
cissexual difference, 223
Cixous, Hélène, 144, 352*n*6, 365
climate crisis, 298, 319
cloacal theory of birth, 197, 199–200
Colman, Athena V., 122*n*22
colonialism: with erasure of sexual difference, 284; kinship with slavery and, 283; maternal bodies and technologized, 92; modern gender system and, 261; race and, xi, 45, 117, 256–257; racism and, 57*n*24, 57*nn*18–19; violence of settler, 259–260, 316; white supremacy and, 57*n*24, 279
colonization, 54, 186, 196, 279, 284, 314, 393
"Commodities Among Themselves" (Irigaray), 365
common nature (*natura communis*), 60–68, 74, 76*n*11, 76*n*14, 76*n*16
conjugated mirrors, 341, 341–342, 343
consciousness, 115, 243, 296, 365, 394; body and, 187; phenomenology of, 39, 41, 42; self-, 43, 44, 46
Cornell, Drucilla, 295
corporeal: incorporeal, 243, 247, 317; plasticity and slavery, 161; undecidability and sexual difference, 149–152. *See also* bodies
corporeality, female, 127, 147, 156, 213
cosmos, 298, 299, 313, 314, 317–321, 325, 412, 415
Cover, Robert, 293, 296
Creative Evolution (Bergson), 244
Creon (mythological figure), 281, 304
criminal justice system: "second rape" by, 293–295, 298–303, 306, 307; trial transcripts, 309*n*7. *See also* law
Cucopulos, Alexa, 399–401
"cultivation of nature, the" ("la culture de la nature"), 116
culture, 38*n*36, 190; language and, 166*n*31; nature with time and, 112–118; *A New Culture of Energy*, 132; patriarchy, 112, 127, 185, 191; Western, 35, 84, 131–134, 141*n*52, 312, 315, 404. *See also* nature/culture
"culture de la nature, la" ("the cultivation of nature"), 116

Darwin, Charles, 84, 120*n*3, 149, 244, 260, 386
daughters, mothers and, 185, 208*n*12, 292*n*30
debt. *See* indebtedness
decolonization, 314
"Defining the Anthropocene" (Lewis and Maslin), 424*n*136
Del Gatto, Lucia, 116
democracy, 74, 97*n*15
Democracy Begins Between Two (Irigaray), 59, 74
Derrida, Jacques, 55*n*4, 56*n*16, 143, 148, 295, 297, 369*n*3
Descartes, Rene, 32, 353*n*16, 354*n*24; Eighth Discourse, 339–341, *340*; self-reflection and, 359–360; in *Speculum of the Other Woman*, 338, 342–343, 344, 347, 353*n*18, 366, 377
Deschauffours, Etienne, 396
desire, 53, 57*n*30, 186, 353*n*20
Deutscher, Penelope, 114
difference: *Changing Difference*, 124, 135, 148; cissexual, 223; *Elemental Difference and the Climate of the Body*, 241; feminine sexuate subjectivity and, 186–188; genital, 175; identity and, 46; interval of, 221; Malabou and, 169*n*68; positive, 211, 216, 223; qualitative multiplicity and, 213–214, 215, 220; quantitative multiplicity and, 214; racial, 8–9, 259, 262; sexed, 25; sexuate subjectivity and, 10. *See also* ontological difference; sexual difference; sexuate difference
differentiation, 63–64. *See also* sexual differentiation; sexuate differentiation
Dioptrique (*Optics*) (Descartes), 339–341, *340*
Diotima, 48–49, 68

INDEX

discourse, 55*n*5, 227, 333–334, 335, 358; Descartes and Eighth Discourse, 339–341, *340*; *Narrative Discourse*, 345–346; sex/gender, 105, 108, 110
"divine law" of blood, 281, 282
Djang, 318–321, 325
Donne, John, 339, 353*n*23
Douzinas, Costas, 304
downgoing (*katabasis*), 337–338, 347, 348, 349
Duchenne de Boulogne, Guillaume, 386
Duras, Marguerite, 352*n*6

Earth, 44, 56*n*15, 317, 320, 324, 397; alienation from, 312, 326; Orbis hypothesis, 424*n*136; violations of, 58*n*37, 298, 318, 319, 325, 330*n*41. *See also* nature
economy, 358, 359, 367; financialization, 362, 364–366; placental, 258, 259, 267–270. *See also* indebtedness
Eighth Discourse, *Optics*, 339–341, *340*
elemental, 103, 104, 118; contiguities with, 89–95; gendered belonging and, 110, 111
Elemental Difference and the Climate of the Body (Parker), 241
Elemental Passions (Irigaray), 321–322, 365, 404
ellipses, 118, 151, 337, 339–343
elsewhere, 253–255, 268, 335
embodiment, trans, 122*n*22, 225*n*3, 241
emotion, qualitative multiplicity and, 214–215
Engaging with Irigaray (Burke, C., Schor and Whitford), 121*n*10
enjambment, 380–381, 409, 411, 415
Enneads (Plotinus), 353*n*21
Entre Orient et Occident (*Between East and West*) (Irigaray), 59, 74, 90, 140*n*5
"epidermal racial schema," 256, 260
erasure, 259–260, 283–284, 302, 306, 363–365
eroticism, anal and male, 197, 198–199, 200
essentialism, 113, 118, 120*n*2, 246; antiessentialism, 124–128, 134–138; biological, 4, 82–84, 89, 96*n*3, 107;

Irigaray and, 125, 128–131; realist, 122*n*38, 129, 130; strategic, 129, 130, 148
Essere Due (*To Be Two*) (Irigaray), 59
"Eternal Irony of the Community, The" (Irigaray), 280–281
Ethics of Dissensus (Ziarek), 167*n*41
Ethics of Eros (Chanter), 121*n*5
Ethics of Sexual Difference, An (Irigaray), 48, 85, 113, 157, 227; anality in, 197; indebtedness in, 362; interval in, 220–221, 329*n*28; place in, 167*n*37
everyday temporality, 349
"Evil Deceivers and Make-Believers" (Bettcher), 226*n*38
evolution, 132, 244–245, 260
extinction, 23, 384, 395–397, 401–402, 408, 415

Facebook, 392
families, 280, 282, 286; separation, 278–279, 283, 285, 287; trees as, 320, 321, 324. *See also* children; fathers; kinship; mothers
Fanon, Frantz, 253, 256
fathers, 198–199, 236, 254, 280–287, 359–361
feeling: as knowledge, 320–321; listening to, 315, 318–321, 325; of love, 321–324; place thinking and, 325; "story about," 314–316, 318, 328*n*15
"Female Gender, The" (Irigaray), 347–348
femaleness, 6, 130, 245, 259
females, 235, 283; biology, 153, 155; bodies, 7, 81, 84, 106, 118, 127, 144, 147, 153, 156, 183, 196–197, 199, 202, 209*n*43, 212–213, 234; morphology, 13*n*20, 89, 90, 147; mystics, 334–335, 338, 344, 352*n*6, 366, 403
feminine, 6, 59, 115, 219, 254, 333–335; generic, 71–72; *jouissance*, 338, 349, 352*n*6; justice, 305, 306; masculine and, 7–8, 127; masculinity reproduced with, 147; maternal, 80–82, 84–85, 89, 90, 92, 196, 208*n*30; self-affection, 4, 178–179, 183, 189–190; as term, 225*n*13; transcendence, 358, 365–366; transformational, 168*n*62; writing, 144, 176, 352*n*6, 365

feminine sexuate subjectivity, 11, 195, 201; bodily and semantic, 175–180; bodily morphology and, 173, 179, 185; difference and, 186–188; lips, tactility and, 174, 180–186; with newly subjective, 188–191
"feminine silhouette," law with, 297
feminine subjectivity, 7, 127, 173, 293, 365; lips and, 178, 181–182; masculine and, 187, 190
femininity, x, 105; Freud and, 333, 353n11; lippedness and, 178, 180; masculinity and, 150, 154, 155, 158, 179, 183, 276n75
feminism, 83, 117, 140n12, 327n8; Black, 269, 270; French, 144, 255, 257, 352n6; sex/gender and, 104, 121n6
feminists, 100n103, 121n6, 238, 249n8, 279–280; new materialism, 97n23, 227; perspectives, 124–128, 135; phenomenology, 100n103, 206
fiction, mimesis and, 346
financialization, 362, 364–366
finitude, 38n36, 314, 384, 407; limit and, 17–18, 19; sexual difference and, 20–23, 30, 35
First Nations people, 316, 328n12
Flannigan-Saint-Aubin, Arthur, 209n38
flesh loathing (somatophobia), 105, 116
Floyd, George, 120n4
fluids, 182–184, 193n11, 217, 281, 344; male bodily, 198, 202–203, 206, 209n42, 359, 361; "the/a woman" and, 219–220. *See also* blood
Forgetting of Air in Martin Heidegger, The (Irigaray), 131, 317, 353n20, 363, 404
Foucault, Michel, 146, 148, 284, 374, 387, 394, 396, 399–401; on God, 392; Hegel and, 389; Irigaray and, 380–381, 383, 384, 398; Nietzsche and, 397
frame (*Gestell*), 28, 37n26, 107
Frank, Adam, 166n27
French feminism, 144, 255, 257, 352n6
Freud, Sigmund, 148, 151, 197, 199, 274n30, 345, 347, 352n4, 403; femininity and, 333, 353n11; imaginary and, 207n1; influence of, 390; neutral sexual identity and, 208n12; Plato and, 343
fugitive resistance, 254–255, 258, 259, 267–270
Fukushima disaster, 319
fungi, xin2, 26

Gallagher, Cormac, 352n5
Gallop, Jane, 115, 145, 164n6, 164n11, 176
Ganot, Adolphe, *341*
Garner, Eric, 120n4
Gatens, Moira, 122n32
Gay Science, The (Nietzsche), 245–246
gender, 5, 115, 118, 239, 347–348; division of labor, 55n2, 57n24; dysphoria, 235; identity and, 55n2, 70, 392; injustice, 57n18; Irigaray and, 59, 67–68; neutrality, 105, 109; nominalism, 69, 77n28; nonbinary, 57n24, 73, 105, 110, 150, 209n43, 223, 226n38, 247, 313; performativity, 228, 230–231, 237, 241–244, 246; pronouns, 32, 38n40, 110, 248, 320; race and, 261–262; sex and, 7, 67–68, 168n55; sexual difference, the two and, 59, 60, 66–75; sexuate, sex and, 103, 104–108, 139n1; as social construction, 106, 121n11, 146, 148, 241; transformational feminine and, 168n62; ungendered, 262, 263, 283, 405, 406. *See also* sex/gender; transgender people
gender-affirming care, 287
gender-affirming interventions, 236
gender-as-malleable, 241
gender-confirmation surgery, 236
gendered belonging, 10, 105, 109–112
gender nonconforming people, 6, 86, 104, 179, 191, 238, 277n101
Gender Trouble (Butler, J.), 77n28, 145, 146, 153, 230–231
genealogy, 23, 106, 111, 147, 201–202, 208n12, 377, 396
genera (*genres*), 67–68
Genette, Gérard, 344, 345–346
genitals, 177, 250n13, 353n11; difference, 175; vulva, 154, 168n61, 186, 336, 343. *See also* anal; phallus

INDEX

genocide, 259, 324–325, 393, 424*n*136
genre humain (humankind), 110, 179, 276*n*87
genres (*genera*), 67–68
gestational, sexuate difference as, 91
gestational rhythms, labors of care and, 268
Gestell (frame), 28, 37*n*26, 107
Gide, André, 387
gift, 154, 198, 205, 357, 361, 363, 369*n*3
Gill, Gillian C., 193*n*11
Gill-Peterson, Jules, 327*n*8
God, 392, 393, 403, 407, 415
Goodrich, Peter, 297, 305
Goya, Francisco, 402
Graeber, David, 357
grammar, 227–232, 263, 405
Gran Disparate, 402
Gregson v. Gilbert, 420*n*18
Grosz, Elizabeth, 120*n*3, 126, 128, 149, 203, 227, 249*n*12; J. Butler and, 169*n*79, 242–243; criticism of, 238–241; on ethics of Stoicism, 246–247; on Irigaray, 80–81; on law and violence, 296, 302; limits of sexedness and, 234–237; with nature/culture, 122*n*32; on phallocentrism, 97*n*10; sexual difference and, 84–86, 98*n*44, 98*nn*35–36; with transphobia, 232–235, 237–238, 242
Grosz Paradox, 228–229, 237–244

haecceity (*haecceitas*), 62–64, 68, 70–71, 76*n*10, 76*n*16, 77*n*32
Halley, Janet, 148, 166*n*24
Haraway, Donna, 261
Harrison, Hubert, 275*n*47
Hartman, Saidiya, 259, 261, 263, 277*nn*106–107; on Black women and labors of care, 267–268, 269; "dream of an elsewhere" and, 253–254, 255; on men and women, 276*n*87
Harwood, Tristen, 320
Hegel, Georg Wilhelm Friedrich, 55*n*2, 59, 151, 304, 357; absolute knowing and, 40, 42–46, 52, 56*n*5, 56*nn*15–16, 344; autological circle and, 39, 40–41,

42; Bacchanalian revel and, 44, 55*n*3; bondage dialectic and, 253; finitude and, 17–18; Foucault and, 389; Irigaray on transcendence and, 57*n*30; with spirit as language, 55*n*5; time and, 39, 43, 44; with time and space, 36*n*5
Heidegger, Martin, 55*nn*4–5, 98*n*26, 204; on Being and beings, 274*n*41; *The Forgetting of Air in Martin Heidegger*, 131, 317, 353*n*20, 363, 404; *Gestell* and, 37*n*26, 107; Irigaray and, 298; Malabou on, 357; nature and, 77*n*21; ontological difference and, 362; temporality and, 347
hetero-affection, 174, 183, 186, 187, 189, 190, 203–204
heterogeneity, x, 109, 347
heteronormativity, 82, 148, 150, 166*n*25
heteros, 27
heterosexuality, 109, 146, 200–201, 209*n*43, 231, 242
Hill, Rebecca, 93, 127, 139*n*1, 222, 244–245
Hird, Myra J., 231
historicity, 117, 123*n*40
History of Madness (Foucault), 396
History of Sexuality (Foucault), 387, 398, 400
Hom, Sabrina L., 121*n*10, 255
"homme-osexuality," 148, 198, 201
homosexuality, 148, 166*n*25, 166*n*32, 168*n*51, 198–201
horizontal transcendence, 111, 196, 304–305
hormonal alterations, 235, 236, 237, 245, 249*n*12
"house of Being," language as, 55*n*5
Huffer, Lynne, 114–115, 123*n*43, 372, 377, 383, 391, 410, 416
human beings, 3, 55*n*2, 231; *Becoming Human*, 157, 160, 161, 274*n*36; kinship between Earth and, 320, 324; law and, 296; medical experiments on, 262, 263, 264; rights, 57*n*24; as sexuate being, 9–10; Whiteness as "unraced" sign of, 260–261. *See also* sexuation, as frame for human becoming

humankind (*genre humain*), 110, 179, 276n87
humors, theory of, 274n30
Husserl, Edmund, 38n38, 55n4, 130, 369n5
hylomorphism, sex/gender, 276n75
hystera (womb), 338, 405
hysteria, 403

Iconographie photographique de la Salpêtrière, 389
idealism, realism and, 30, 32–33
Idea of sex, 264–265
identity, 6, 8, 20, 126, 137, 261; difference and, 46; gender and, 55n2, 70, 392; self-, 184, 217; trans, 237, 240–241. *See also* sexual identity; sexuate identity
identity/subjectivity, Imaginary/Symbolic, and, 207n1
If Not, Winter (Sappho), 373
I Love To You (*J'aime à toi*) (Irigaray), 22, 59, 73–74, 116, 150, 201–202; speech act in, 322–323; transphobia in, 232
Images of Bliss (Aydemir), 209n42
Imaginary/Symbolic, identity/subjectivity and, 207n1
immigration, asylum seekers, 278, 288
incarceration, 278, 279
Ince, Kate, 96n3
"*incontournable volume, L'*" ("Volume-Fluidity" or "Volume Without Contours") (Irigaray), 182–184, 193n11, 193n14, 217, 344
incorporeal, 243, 247, 317
Incorporeal, The (Ruyer), 243
indebtedness: Adorno and, 369n5; gift of being and, 357; to mothers, 359, 363–364; patriarchy and, 359, 360–361; reversing reversal of, 362–368; sexual difference and, 356–358, 369n13; structure of ontological, 358–362; Western philosophy and, 356–357, 362–363
Indigenous peoples: Aboriginal people, 314–315, 318–320, 328n12, 330n41; cosmos and, 314, 318; erasure of, 259, 260; First Nations, 316, 328n12; forced removal of Native American children, 278, 286, 291n23; genocide of, 259, 393, 424n136; non-, 318, 321, 325; as the other, 260; settler colonialism and, 316; with "story about feeling," 314–316, 318, 328n15; violence against, 260, 278
"individual," Scotus with, 76n10
individuation, 73, 204, 211, 212, 243; bodily composition and, 189, 191; common nature and, 65, 67, 68; defined, 61–62; haecceity and, 62, 68; process of, 63
Inessential Woman (Spelman), 77n28
infinite becoming, 40–47, 55n4
insects, sexes of, xin2
instantiation, 63, 112, 243
intelligibility, of sex, 146, 165n18, 394
interest (offspring, *tokos*), 356, 357
interruptivity, 349
intersex, 6, 28, 37n24, 73, 244; human species and, 245; in plants and animals, 231; TIGNC people, 179, 191, 238–239
intervals (sensible transcendental), 193n8, 267, 348; defined, 212, 220; Irigaray on, 93, 220–221, 316–317, 329n28; love as, 322; between matter and form, 215; place thinking, 315–317; self-affection and, 47–52; of sexual difference, 220–224, 228; of sexuate difference, 313–314, 317
In the Beginning, She Was (Irigaray), 178–179, 364
In the Wake (Sharpe), 274n36
intimate-partner abuse, 280
intuition, 39, 49, 57n30, 313, 316, 317
invisibility, 176, 256
Irigaray (Jones, R.), 120n1
Irigaray, Luce, 37n33, 121n10, 149, 207n1; "Animal Compassion," 323–324; "Any Theory of the Subject . . . ," 344; with "at least two" sexes, xin2, 27, 117, 225n2, 266, 327n8; *Between East and West*, 59, 74, 90, 140n5; "The Blind Spot of an Old Dream of Symmetry,"

333, 353n11; "Commodities Among Themselves," 365; criticism of, 106, 125, 127, 238–239, 379; *Democracy Begins Between Two*, 59, 74; Descartes, Lacan and, 342; *Elemental Passions*, 321–322, 365, 404; *Essere Due*, 59; "The Eternal Irony of the Community," 280–281; "The Female Gender," 347–348; *The Forgetting of Air in Martin Heidegger*, 131, 317, 353n20, 363, 404; *In the Beginning, She Was*, 178–179, 364; *Key Writings*, 139n1; with Lacan at University of Paris, 352n5; *Marine Lover of Friedrich Nietzsche*, 90–91, 99n74, 131, 315, 317, 353n20, 404; "La Mystérique," 338, 342–344, 347, 353n18, 366–367, 377; *A New Culture of Energy*, 132; "Perhaps Cultivating Touch Can Still Save Us," 204; "Plato's *Hystera*," 333, 342, 343; "The Power of Discourse and the Subordination of the Feminine" interview and, 333–334, 335; *Sexes and Genealogies*, 106, 201–202, 208n12; *Sharing the World*, 37n17, 39–41, 45, 47, 49, 51, 53, 56n10; *This Sex Which Is Not One*, 106, 184–185, 192nn2–3, 333–334, 336–337, 351n3; *To Be Born*, 20, 124, 125, 132–133, 323; with transphobia, 232, 237, 242, 327n8, 354n35; *Through Vegetal Being*, 125, 132, 140n5, 324; "Volume Without Contours," 182–184, 193n11, 193n14, 217, 344; *The Way of Love*, 110; "Women, the sacred and money," 371n54. *See also Ethics of Sexual Difference, An*; *I Love To You*; *Sharing the Fire*; *Speculum of the Other Woman*; *specific subjects*

"Irigaray and the Ontology of Sexual Difference" (Grosz), 98n35

"Irigaray and the 'Priority' of Sexual Difference" (Sares), 85

"Irreducibility and (Trans) Sexual Difference" (Stephano), 239–240

"Is the Rectum a Grave?" (Bersani), 200

Jackson, Zakiyyah Iman, 157–162, 170n93, 262, 270, 274n36

J'aime à toi. *See I Love To You*

JanMohamed, Abdul, 284–285

John II (King of France), 379, 388

Johnston, Tim, 238–239, 240

Jones, Emma, 36n1, 98n26

Jones, Ernest, 97n10

Jones, Rachel, 96n3, 120n1, 130, 139n1, 230, 343

jouissance (sexual ecstasy), 345, 347, 390; of female mystic, 334–335, 344, 366, 403; feminine, 338, 349, 352n6; Lacan and, 366, 370n31; "penis-envy" and, 361; Teresa of Avila, 352n6, 403; with women as mirror, 336–337, 342–343

Kaminski, Phyllis H., 369n13

katabasis (downgoing), 337–338, 347, 348, 349

katholou (universal), 347

Kennedy, David, 294, 299–303

Kepler, Johannes, 341

Key Writings (Irigaray), 139n1

Khader, Serene J., 282

Kim, Ruthanne Crápo, 274n30

King, Peter, 63, 64, 77n17

King, Tiffany Lethabo, 259, 260

King Brown Snake Dreaming, 318

kinship (blood): "bleaching" and breaching of, 282–283; with colonialism and slavery, 283; between Earth and people, 320, 324; family separation, 278–279, 283, 285, 287; in Irigaray and Spillers, 280–285, 286; maternal, 281, 283, 284; politics and, 281; unkinning, 283–284, 285; violence, 282–283, 285–288; with white supremacy and patriarchy, 284

Kirby, Vicki, 143–146, 156–157, 162, 164n6, 164n8, 164n11, 176

Kircher, Athanasius, 353n16

Kristeva, Julia, 123n40, 349

Kuppers, Petra, 262

INDEX

labor: of care, 267–268, 270, 281; gender division of, 55n2, 57n24

Lacan, Jacques, 12n2, 115, 148, 335, 345, 352n4, 374, 382, 403; imaginary and, 207n1; Irigaray, Descartes and, 342; with Irigaray at University of Paris, 352n5; *jouissance* and, 366, 370n31; Seminar XXII and, 352nn5–6, 390, 391–392; on subjectivity, 187–188

Lacquer, Thomas, 241

language: of Aboriginal people, 315, 318, 320; culture and, 166n31; discourse and, 227; erasure of women and, 363–365; of family values as oppressive, 280; female power and, 202; feminine bodily morphology and, 185; grammar, 227–232, 263, 405; as "house of Being," 55n5; Irigaray on, 57n23; of law, 295, 296, 298; lippedness and, 176; love and speech act, 322–323; morphology and, 166n34; "mother tongue," 363; mystic, 380; mystic speech, 365–366; natural, 106–107; of polarity with sexual difference, 226n14; of political economy, 359, 367; representation and, 166n27; for self-affection, 187; as sexed, 108; sexuate body and, 106–107; spirit as, 55n5

lateral transcendence, 46–47, 49–50

law: blood and "divine," 281, 282; Bunitj, 315; Creon with arbitrary, 304; *Djang*, 318–321, 325; of the father, 254, 280–281, 361; "feminine justice" and, 305, 306; with "feminine silhouette," 297; human beings and, 296; language of, 295, 296, 298; of property, 52, 57n18; rape victim and perpetrator in court, 299–303; with "second rape" by criminal justice system, 293–295, 298–303, 306, 307; sexual violence, ontology and, 293, 297–299; sexuate identity and, 297–298, 306; sexuate jurisprudence and, 294, 303–307; state, 281; technicity and, 307; violence with force of, 293–297, 302

Lee, Stephen, 278

Leeuwen, Anne van, 98n26, 342

Lehtinen, Virpi, 128–129, 130–131

Lennon, Erica, 226n38

Lévi-Strauss, Claude, 148

Lewis, Simon L., 424n136

life (*bio*), 106; birth, 132, 140n9, 197, 199–200, 202, 205, 257–258; "Mathematics Black Life," 274n36; *poeisis* of, 317. *See also* sexual difference, life and

limits: finitude and, 17–18, 19; interval as, 220, 221; "knowing one's," 44; male bodies and imaginary projection of, 203; of nature, 67; negative self-reference and, 17; negativity of, 18, 21; ontological negativity, 34; self-, 112, 115; of sexedness, 234–237; sexuation and determinate, 29

lippedness: as bodily expression, 177, 184; femininity and, 178, 180; as human experience, 184; language and, 176; literary textuality and, 192n2; masculine, 178; self-affection and, 178; tactility and, 180

lips, 337, 353n11; *Are the Lips a Grave*, 123n43; bodily and figuratively, 175–177; feminine sexuate subjectivity with tactility and, 174, 180–186; feminine subjectivity and, 178, 181–182; open-closed nature of, 174; self-affection and, 178, 181, 182, 183; two, 78n36, 144, 151, 153–154, 157, 177–178, 189, 336, 343, 353n23; vulva, 154, 168n61, 186, 336, 343

listening: to feeling, 315, 318–321, 325; to story with spirit, 318–321

"Litany for Survival, A" (Lorde), 267, 277n106

literary textuality, lippedness and, 192n2

livable future, 40, 47, 54, 288

logos (words, rationality), 106

Londe, Albert, 389

Lorde, Audre, 160, 267, 277n106

Lorraine, Tamsin, 225n13

Lose Your Mother (Hartman), 253

love: eros, 204; feeling of, 321–324; *Marine Lover of Friedrich Nietzsche*,

INDEX

90–91, 99*n*74, 131, 315, 317, 353*n*20, 404; maternal, 50–51, 58*n*38; nonhuman animals and, 323–324; philosophy and, 48–49; of sameness, 196–197; two forms of, 321–322; *The Way of Love*, 110. *See also I Love To You*
Luce Irigaray (Whitford), 207*n*1
Luce Irigaray and the Philosophy of Sexual Difference (Stone), 37*n*33, 149
Lucy (enslaved person), 262, 263
Lugones, Maria, 261, 266

Macey, David, 193*n*11
Magritte, René, 373, 383
Making Sex (Lacquer), 241
Malabou, Catherine, 124, 143, 149, 162, 167*n*40, 168*n*56, 357; difference and, 169*n*68; on multiplicity of genders, 148; on ontology and biology, 166*n*28; with plasticity and texts, 170*n*96; with plasticity and violence of antiessentialism, 126, 134–138; with plasticity of sexual difference, 152–155; sexual difference and, 167*n*44; on transformational feminine and gender, 168*n*62
male bodies, 173, 196–197, 207*n*1, 207*n*7, 208*n*30, 234, 264; with body of mother, 202; castration anxiety and, 199–200, 202, 209*n*42, 361; female bodies and production of, 199; fluids, 198, 202–203, 206, 209*n*42, 359, 361; heterosexual, 200, 201, 209*n*43; with imaginary projection of limits on other bodies, 203; reimaginings and anality, 201–206
male eroticism, 197, 198–199, 200
maleness, 6, 130, 245, 259, 363
male re-imaginings: anality with body and, 201–206; Irigaray, ontology of anal and, 196–201
males: females and, 235; homosexuality, 166*n*25; imaginary, 195, 201–202, 203; Middle Passage and space for prisoners, 283; self-replicating species, 231
"Mama's Baby, Papa's Maybe" (Spillers), 405

Marcellus (Roman general), 353*n*16
Marder, Michael, 323
Margarula, Yvonne, 319
Marine Lover of Friedrich Nietzsche (Irigaray), 90–91, 99*n*74, 131, 315, 317, 353*n*20, 404
masculine, 120*n*4, 225*n*13; feminine and, 7–8, 127; feminine subjectivity and, 187, 190; lippedness, 178; morphology, 297; self-affection, 4, 178–179, 183, 187, 189–190, 195, 203, 204, 205; sexuate subjectivity, 11; subjectivity, 7, 10, 185, 187, 189–190, 196, 201, 203, 207*n*7; watery bodies, 91
masculinity, 6, 207*n*1; anal eroticism and, 200; feminine and reproduction of, 147; femininity and, 150, 154, 155, 158, 179, 183, 276*n*75; mothers and, 202–203, 363; phallocentrism and, 97*n*10, 200; technicity and, 299; Western metaphysics and, 72
Maslin, Mark A., 424*n*136
materialism. *See* new materialism; radical materialism
maternal: bodies, 89, 92–93, 132, 160, 266, 268–269; Christ as, 378; feminine, 80–82, 84–85, 89, 90, 92, 196, 208*n*30; kinship, 281, 283, 284; love, 50–51, 58*n*38; touch, 52
maternity, Black, 256, 257–258, 259, 266, 269, 270
"Mathematics Black Life" (McKittrick), 274*n*36
matricide, 32, 84, 253, 255, 297
Mbembe, Achille, 284
McKittrick, Katherine, 269, 270, 274*n*36
medical experiments, human, 262, 263, 264
melancholia, theory of humors, 274*n*30
melanin, politics of, 256
memory, 202, 296, 347
men: fathers, 198–199, 236, 254, 280–287, 359–361; with partial transcendence, 45; white, 121*n*10, 260, 283, 285; women and, 114, 124, 150, 157, 195–196, 233, 276*n*87, 313, 363–365
menstrual fluid, 359

mental internalization, 324
Merleau-Ponty, Maurice, 51, 100*n*103, 130, 151
metamorphosis, 135, 152, 218, 219–220
metaphysical conceit, 339, 342, 351*n*2
metaphysics: of absolute knowing, 57*n*19; Aristotelian-Husserlian idea of, 55*n*4; defined, 77*n*21; discourse and, 55*n*5; doubled, 114–115; new, 125; physics and, 45; of sameness, 264; with sight over touch, 51, 52; time and space and, 55*n*4. *See also* sexual difference, Irigaray and metaphysics of; Western metaphysics
Metaphysics (Aristotle), 76*n*5, 344
Metz, Christian, 345
Middle Passage, 258, 283, 384, 405
Mills, Charles, 256, 279, 286
Milroy, Gladys Idjirrimoonya, 324–325
Milroy, Jean, 324–325
mimesis, 129, 334–338, 345–348
miroir ardent (burning glass), 335, 337–339, 341–342, 345, 353*n*16, 353*n*22, 354*n*24, 406
Mirrar clan lands, Australia, 318, 319, 330*n*41
mirrors: baroque nature of, 364, 371*n*46; burning glass, 335, 337–339, 341–342, 345, 353*n*16, 353*n*22, 354*n*24; conjugated, *341*, 341–342, 343; *jouissance* and women as, 336–337, 342–343; of the other, 404; self-reflection and, 359–360
miscegenation, 121*n*10
Mistler, Brian J., 226*n*38
Moi, Toril, 127, 338
Monk, 402
monosexuality, 112, 232
Moore, G. E., 32
Morega, Cherríe, 255
Moreton-Robinson, Aileen, 328*n*12
Morgan, Jennifer, 257
morphological: bio-, 110–111; defined, 264; elemental and, 104; sexual difference, 118
morphology: biology and, 176; bodily, 173, 179, 185, 335, 336; female, 13*n*20, 89, 90, 147; language and, 166*n*34; masculine, 297; touch and sexual, 181; two lips, 144, 153
Morrissey, Philip, 318, 321
Mortenson, Ellen, 98*n*26
mothering persons, 288, 292*n*30
mothers: as autonomous subject denied, 197–198; Black Atlantic and condition of, 259, 267; Black maternity and, 256, 257–258, 259, 266, 269, 270; children and, 50–51, 52, 58*n*40, 197, 202, 280, 284, 363; daughters and, 185, 208*n*12, 292*n*30; with gift of air to child, 363; indebtedness to, 359, 363–364; *Lose Your Mother*, 253; male body with body of, 202; masculinity and, 202–203, 363; matricide, 32, 84, 253, 255, 297; parental rights, 282, 285–287; pregnancy of trans, 236; reproduction with, 360; reproductive power and body of, 202; slave code and Black, 259; slavery and myth of, 253, 257, 269
"mother tongue," 363
multiplicity: defined, 213; qualitative, 212–215, 220, 223–224; quantitative, 213–214
mushrooms, sexes of, xi*n*2
"Mystérique, La" (Irigaray), 338, 342–344, 347, 353*n*18, 366–367, 377
Mystérique I, La (collage), *372*, 377, 383
Mystérique II, La (collage), *391*
Mystérique III, La (collage), *410*
Mystérique IV, La (collage), *416*
mysticism, 366, 371*n*51, 378
mystics, 337, 339, 342, 349, 354*n*30, 393; female, 334–335, 338, 344, 352*n*6, 366, 403; Lacan and, 352*n*6; language, 380; speech, 365–366; as virgins, 378

narrative: role of, 345–346; in *Speculum of the Other Woman*, 333–334; story and, 346; *Time and Narrative*, 346; trans, 233
Narrative Discourse (Genette), 345–346
"natality," 58*n*35
Native Americans, forced removal of children, 278, 286, 291*n*23

INDEX

natura communis. See common nature
natural language, 106–107
natural living universe, 112
nature: cosmos, 298, 299, 313, 314, 317–321, 325, 412, 415; "the cultivation of nature," 116; with culture and time, 112–118; Earth and, 44, 56*n*15, 58*n*37, 298, 312, 317–320, 324–326, 330*n*41, 397, 424*n*136; Heidegger and, 77*n*21; human, 66–68; limits of, 67; novelty and, 57*n*18; place thinking and, 314–315; plants, 25, 37*n*19, 67, 96*n*3, 125, 132, 140*n*5, 156, 231, 320, 324–326; quasi-transcendental notion of, 113; rhythm of, 122*n*38; as spirit, 44; temporality of, 348; trees, 320, 321, 324–326. *See also* common nature
nature/culture, 103, 153, 264; alienation and, 132; J. Butler and, 146, 165*n*14, 165*n*17; sex/gender and, 105, 112, 145, 149; sexuate subjectivity and, 86; women and, 112–113, 122*n*32, 138
navel, umbilical cord and, 202
negative self-reference, 17, 21, 23, 25, 26
negativity: generational, 17, 19, 20–21, 23–24; with identity and otherness, 20; of limit, 18, 21; of sexual difference, 22–23, 169*n*79; sexual differentiation and, 17; sexuate, 18–24; Stone and, 167*n*44; technology and ontological, 36*n*13. *See also* sexual difference, ontological negativity of
Neidjie, Bill: *Djang* and, 318–321, 325; place thinking and, 318, 325, 326; with "story about feeling," 314–316, 318, 328*n*15
Neimanis, Astrida, 82, 87–93, 99*n*74, 100*n*103
Nelson, Maggie, 259
neuroscience, 134, 135
"neuter" being, 38*n*37
New Culture of Energy, A (Irigaray), 132
new materialism: anti-Blackness and, 157–158; feminist, 97*n*23, 227; Irigaray and, 146–149; Kirby and pinch, 143–146, 164*n*8; plasticity, sexual difference and, 152–155, 157–162;

Salamon on Irigaray, 149–152; scope of plasticity, 155–157
Nietzsche, Friedrich, 55*n*4, 111, 227, 296, 397, 403; indebtedness and, 360, 362; *Marine Lover of Friedrich Nietzsche*, 90–91, 99*n*74, 131, 315, 317, 353*n*20, 404; onto-ethics, 229, 245–248; on philosophy as art of transfiguration, 245–246
nihilism, 53, 54, 323
Noir, Jean le, 378
nominalism, 29, 60, 61, 65, 69–71, 76*n*6, 77*n*28
nonbinarism, 109, 111
nonbinary: bodies, 209*n*43; people, 57*n*24, 73, 105, 110, 150, 223, 226*n*38, 313; sexual difference and, 247
non-numerical unities, 60–66, 72, 78*n*36
nothing in common (*rien en commun*), 65, 69, 71, 76*n*12
not-One, 115, 217
Nouvelle Iconographie de la Salpêtrière, 389
numerical unity: less-than-, 62, 65; nominalists on, 61; non-, 60–66, 72, 78*n*36; Scotus and, 62–63, 76*n*11
nursing/breastfeeding, rethinking masculinity and, 202

Oele, Marjolein, 269
offspring (interest, *tokos*), 356, 357
"Only a God Can Save Us" (Heidegger), 204
onto-ethics, of transsexual difference: beyond-binary grammar of sexual difference, 227–232; Grosz Paradox, 228–229, 237–244; Nietzschean or Stoic, 229, 245–248; primary and secondary sexual difference, 242–245; sexual difference as transphobic?, 232–237
ontological dependence, 357
ontological difference: Heidegger and, 362; Irigaray with, 104, 211, 274*n*41; sexuate difference as, 86, 258, 263, 265–266, 270, 274*n*41
ontological privilege, 359

INDEX

Ontological Terror (Warren), 157, 158
onto-logic of amniotics, 91–92, 93, 94
ontology: of anal and Irigaray, 196–201; biology and, 166n28; indebtedness, 358–362; Irigaray and, 98n26; "Irigaray and the Ontology of Sexual Difference," 98n35; racialized, 258; sexual, 18, 24–26, 31, 33; sexual difference, ix, 21–22, 79, 84–86, 230, 249n8; sexual violence, law and, 293, 297–299; sexuate, 86; of sexuate difference, 79, 81–82; sexuate identity and, 107; woman as "ontological amputation," 124, 137. *See also* sexual difference, ontological negativity of
Ontology of the Accident (Malabou), 135
Operation Yewtree, 294, 309n3
opposite sex, bodies transformed and, 235, 249n12
optics, 334, 335, 337, 339, 342, 344
Optics (Dioptrique) (Descartes), 339–341, 340
Orbis hypothesis, 424n136
Ordinatio (Scotus), 61
other, the: building with, 53–54; human beings as self-reproducing with, 55n2; Indigenous people as, 260; Irigaray on, 58n32, 58n49; mirror of, 404; as other, 115; overcoming nihilism and, 54; placental economy and, 267; racialization and non-homogeneity of, 260; silence cultivated to hear, 205; time and space with transcendence and relation with, 39–40, 47, 108; truth and, 53, 54
otherness: feminine subjectivity and, 365; negativity with identity and, 20

panoptical technology, 389
parental rights, blood and, 282, 285–286, 287
Parisi, Luciana, 231
Parker, Emily Anne, 175, 241
Partus Sequitur Ventrem, slave code and, 259

Patanjali, 324
patriarchy: culture, 112, 127, 185, 191; identity of women and, 126, 137; indebtedness and, 359, 360–361; kinship with white supremacy and, 284; "law of the father," 254, 280–281, 361; racialization and, 285; sons and fathers with, 198–199, 284; violence, 279
"penis-envy," 361
"Perhaps Cultivating Touch Can Still Save Us" (Irigaray), 204
phallic gesture, colonization as, 284
phallocentric economy, 358
phallocentrism, x, 11, 59, 196, 201, 239; masculinity and, 97n10, 200; Western metaphysics and, 312; Western philosophy and, 124
phallogocentrism, 88, 109, 120n3, 254
"phallomorphism," 264
phallus: "penis-envy," 361; power and, 362, 369n9; with steel fig leaf removed, 209n38; as umbilical cord, 202
phenomenology: of consciousness, 39, 41, 42; feminist, 100n103, 206; imaginary and, 207n1; of male bodily experience, 203
Phenomenology of Spirit (Hegel), 39, 40–41, 43, 344
philosophy: absolute knowing and, 44–45, 46; as art of transfiguration, 245–246; "Bodies of Philosophy," 249n12; Irigaray on, 47–48, 167n39; with livable future, 47; love and, 48–49; *Luce Irigaray and the Philosophy of Sexual Difference*, 37n33, 149; medieval, 60, 61, 76n5; sexual difference and, 50, 246. *See also* Western philosophy
Physics IV (Aristotle), 316
pinch, Kirby and, 143–146, 164n8
Pinel, Philippe, 388
"Pinel Freeing the Insane," 388
place: defined, 314–315; elsewhere, 253–255, 268, 335; in *An Ethics of Sexual Difference*, 167n37; as interval,

316–317; rhythms of, 315; sexual difference and, 216; tactility and, 222; touching, sexuality and, 215; women and, 217
placental blood, 288
placental economy, 258, 259, 267–270
place thinking: defined, 317–318, 325; feeling and, 325; intervals, 315–317; listening to story with spirit, 318–321; love and living becoming, 321–324; nature and, 314–315; with trees, 324–326; writers and, 317–318
plants, 67, 96n3, 156, 231; as nonsexuate, 25, 37n19; trees, 320, 321, 324–326; *Through Vegetal Being*, 125, 132, 140n5, 324. *See also* nature
plasticity: anti-Black racialization and, 161; defined, 134–135, 151; destructive, 135, 137; Malabou with violence of antiessentialism and, 126, 134–138; new materialism, sexual difference and, 152–155, 157–162; scope of, 155–157; sexuate frame as plastic essence, 126, 138; slavery and corporeal, 161; texts and, 170n96
Plato, 55n4, 62–63, 68, 131, 151, 317, 347, 367; Freud and, 343; Irigaray and, 333, 336, 338, 339, 342, 343; realism, universals and, 76n7; with sun and truth, 45; *tokos* and, 356; with vertical transcendence, 48
"Plato's *Hystera*" (Irigaray), 333, 342, 343
Plotinus, 338–339, 344, 353nn21–22
Poetics (Aristotle), 346, 347
poétique du corps, 144, 145, 156, 164n11
politics, 97n15, 108, 120n4, 256, 281, 359, 367
Porete, Marguerite, 354n30, 388, 396, 402, 410
pornography, 336, 383, 409
"posthuman feminist phenomenology," 100n103
Pottage, Alain, 296
power, 281, 287, 362, 369n9; *Djang* with sacred, 318, 319; language and female, 202; sexuality as, 200; with slavery and racism, 284–285

"Power of Discourse and the Subordination of the Feminine, The" interview, 333–334, 335
pregnancy, 160, 231, 236, 267, 268, 277n101
"Primacy of Perception, The" (Merleau-Ponty), 51
primary sexual difference, secondary and, 242–245
privilege, 140n12, 261, 285–286, 359
prolepsis, 346
Pronger, Brian, 200, 201
pronouns, 32, 38n40, 110, 233, 248, 320, 380, 382
property: children as, 257, 283; law of, 52, 57n18; rights, 112, 286
Puar, Jasbir, 237

qualitative multiplicity, 212–215, 220, 223–224
Quandamooka Nation, Australia, 328n12
quantitative multiplicity, 213–214
quasi-transcendental, 113
queerness, 111, 115, 123n43, 267, 277n101
queer theory, 115, 123n43, 135, 244, 392
"Questioning the Threshold of Sexual Difference" (Johnston), 238–239

race: ability and, 180; with Blackness as subhuman, 260; colonialism and, xi, 45, 117, 256–257; colonization with racial contract, 279; "epidermal racial schema," 256, 260; gender and, 261–262; racialization and, 255; sex/gender as racialized forgetting of sexuate difference, 259–266, 276n75, 285; transatlantic slave trade and, 255; with Whiteness as "unraced" sign of human, 260–261
racial difference, 8–9, 259, 262
racialization, 111, 255; of biology, 262; with non-homogeneity of the other, 260; ontology, 258; patriarchy and, 285; plasticity and anti-Black, 161; of rights, 286; sex/gender as racialized forgetting of sexuate difference, 259–266, 276n75, 285; sexual differentiation and, 158–159

racialized harassment, violence and, 120n4
racial privilege, 261, 285–286
racism: anti-Black, 255; colonialism and, 57n24, 57nn18–19; human medical experiments and, 262, 263, 264; power with slavery and, 284–285; white supremacy, 57n24, 279, 284
radical materialism: biological essentialism and, 82–84; contiguities with elemental and, 89–95; development of, 82–86; ontology of sexuate difference and, 81; sexual difference and, 93; sexuate difference and bodies of water, 82, 87–89
rape: with colonization as phallic gesture, 284; criminal justice system with "second," 293–295, 298–303, 306, 307; victim and perpetrator in court, 299–303. See also sexual violence
Rawlinson, Mary, 286, 426n196
realism: common nature, non-numerical unities and, 60–66; idealism and, 30, 32–33; Plato, universals and, 76n7; sexual difference and, 30
Reconstructing Womanhood (Carby), 274n36
Régnard, Paul, 389
relational autonomy, 279
"reproducible kinlessness," 257
reproduction: in animals and plants, 231; exploitation of wombs of women, 257; fathers and, 359–361; generational, 20, 22–25, 28–29, 236; injustice, 257; with mother, 360; power of, 202; sexually differentiated, 20; subjectivity and, 173; unfreedom, 257
reproductive justice, transgender people and, 236
"A Requiem to Sexual Difference" (Weinstein), 237–238, 249n8
retouch, self-affection and, 178, 183–184
Reunion Island, 257
Ricoeur, Paul, 344, 346, 347, 348
rien en commun (nothing in common), 65, 69, 71, 76n12

rights, 57n24, 112, 282, 285–288, 292n25, 303–304, 306
Riley, Denise, 77n28
Robert-Fleury, Tony, 388
Roberts, Dorothy, 160, 278, 288
Ronell, Avital, 297
Rosario, Vernon, 245
Rouch, Hélène, 267
Ruddick, Sara, 292n30
Ruyer, Raymond, 243
Ruysbroeck the Admirable, 342

Salamon, Gayle, 149–153, 162, 166n34, 166nn31–32, 167n40, 238, 241
Sappho, 68, 373, 384
"Sappho to Philaenis" (Donne), 353n23
Sares, James, 85–86, 249n6
Savile, Jimmy, 309n3
Schelling, Friedrich, 149
Schiller, Britt-Marie, 202
Schor, Naomi, 81, 83–84, 86, 87, 121n10, 165n23
Schwab, Gail, 292n25
Scotus, John Duns (c. 1265–1308): with common nature, 60–66, 76n14, 76n16; gender and, 68; with "individual," 76n10; individuation and, 61–62, 63; as "moderate" realist, 76n7; numerical unity and, 62–63, 76n11; with universals and universality, 61
secondary sexual difference, primary and, 242–245
Sedgwick, Eve Kosofsky, 143, 144, 148–149, 166n25, 166n27
Seely, Stephen, 298
self-affection, 3, 115; feminine, 4, 178–179, 183, 189–190; hetero-affection and, 174, 183, 187, 189, 190, 203–204; language for, 187; lippedness and, 178; lips and, 178, 181, 182, 183; masculine, 4, 178–179, 183, 187, 189–190, 195, 203, 204, 205; retouch and, 178, 183–184; sensible transcendental to, 47–52; touch and, 185
self-limitation, 112, 115
self-recognition, with touch, 187–188

INDEX

self-reflection, Descartes and, 359–360
self-replicating, plants and animals as, 231
self-sensing, touch and, 181, 184
semantic, bodily and, 175–180
semen, 209*n*42
Seminar XXII, Lacan and, 352*nn*5–6, 390, 391–392
sensible transcendental, 47–52, 93, 193*n*8, 267, 317, 348. *See also* intervals
sensuous immediacy, 19, 36*n*6, 41
settler colonialism, violence of, 259–260, 316
sex: biological essentialism and, 107; bodies transformed and opposite, 235, 249*n*12; essentialism, 120*n*2; gender, sexuate and, 103, 104–108, 139*n*1; gender and, 7, 67–68, 168*n*55; genitals and, 250*n*13; in human beings versus animal and plants, 231; Idea of, 264–265; intelligibility of, 146, 165*n*18, 394; *Making Sex*, 241; as primary ontological difference, 211; sexual identity and, 105. *See also This Sex Which Is Not One*
sexedness, limits of, 234–237
sexed rights, 285, 288, 292*n*25
sexes: "at least two," x, xi*n*2, 27, 117, 225*n*2, 244–245, 266, 327*n*8; bimodality of human, 68, 73, 232, 245; of fungi, xi*n*2; of insects, xi*n*2; rhythm of, 113
Sexes and Genealogies (Irigaray), 106, 201–202, 208*n*12
sex/gender, 3, 4, 103, 115, 258; binary, 10, 228, 230, 232; defined, 276*n*75; discourse, 105, 108, 110; distinction, 6, 67, 121*n*5, 146, 152, 263–264; erasure of, 283; feminism and, 104, 121*n*6; hylomorphism, 276*n*75; map, 104, 105, 106, 107; nature/culture and, 105, 112, 145, 149; as racialized forgetting of sexuate difference, 259–266, 276*n*75, 285
sexual, sexuate and, 12*n*4
sexual abuse, 309*n*3. *See also* sexual violence

sexual difference: arguments against, 228, 230, 239; as autodifferentiating, 167*n*44; Beauvoir and failure of, 165*n*19; beyond-binary grammar of, 227–232; colonialism with erasure of, 284; corporeal undecidability and, 149–152; defined, 98*n*36, 232, 273*n*24; feminine, 254; finitude and, 20–23, 30, 35; gender stereotypes and, 5; genealogy of, 147; generational negativity and, 17; Grosz and, 84–86, 98*n*44, 98*nn*35–36; heterogeneity and, x; homosexuality as choice versus, 166*n*32; indebtedness and, 356–358, 369*n*13; Irigaray and, x, xi, 1–12, 79–81, 104, 146–148; "Irigaray and the Ontology of Sexual Difference," 98*n*35; "Irigaray and the 'Priority' of Sexual Difference," 85; "Irreducibility and (Trans) Sexual Difference," 239–240; as irreducible in three senses, 55*n*2; with language of polarity, 226*n*14; *Luce Irigaray and the Philosophy of Sexual Difference*, 37*n*33, 149; morphological, 118; negativity of, 22–23, 169*n*79; nonbinary and, 247; ontology, ix, 21–22, 79, 84–86, 230, 249*n*8; openness or indeterminacy of, x; philosophy and, 50, 246; place and, 216; plasticity, new materialism and, 152–155, 157–162; primary and secondary, 242–245; "Questioning the Threshold of Sexual Difference," 238–239; question of, 1–12; radical materialism and, 93; realism and, 30; "A Requiem to Sexual Difference," 237–238, 249*n*8; sexual identity and, 234; sexuate and, 230; sexuate difference and, 3, 120*n*1, 220; sexuate difference in Black Atlantic and, 255–259, 265, 273*n*24, 274*n*41; technology and, 21, 23, 28, 36*n*13; temporality and, 118, 334, 345; time and space and, 20, 25; trans embodiment and, 122*n*22; transphobia and, 228–230, 232–238,

sexual difference (*continued*)
240, 243; universality and, 46, 57*n*19, 59–60, 69, 73; universals and, 59–75; Whiteness and, 256. *See also Ethics of Sexual Difference, An*; onto-ethics, of transsexual difference

sexual difference, as qualitative becoming: with Bergson and qualitative multiplicity, 212–215; cissexual two and, 223–224; intervals of, 220–224, 228; "the/a woman" and, 211–220

sexual difference, Irigaray and metaphysics of: autological circle and, 39–41, 42, 43, 46, 47; building with the other, 53–54; sensible transcendental to self-affection, 47–52; time and space, 40–47, 55*n*4

sexual difference, life and: gendered belonging and, 105, 109–112; with nature, culture and time, 112–118; with sex, gender and sexuate, 103, 104–108

sexual difference, ontological negativity of: reality of, 29–35; referents of, 24–29; two forms of sexuate negativity, 18–24. *See also* ontology

sexual difference, problem of universals and: with genders and the (non-numerical) two, 59, 60, 66–75; realism, common nature, non-numerical unities and, 60–66

sexual differentiation: evolution and, 244–245; negativity and, 17; racialization and, 158–159; tendencies and, 245

sexual ecstasy. *See jouissance*

sexual identity: anatomical body and, 83, 84; biological essentialism and, 83; blurring of, 96*n*3; children with neutral, 208*n*12; sex and, 105; sexual difference and, 234

sexuality: *History of Sexuality*, 387, 398, 400; place, touching and, 215; as power, 200

sexual ontology, 18, 24–26, 31, 33

sexual selection, 84, 244

sexual violence: abuse and, 309*n*3; law, ontology and, 293, 297–299; Malabou and, 168*n*56; nature of harm, 305, 306; rape, 284, 293–295, 298–303, 306, 307; reform with response to, 294; sexuate subjectivity and, 297

sexuate: alternative economy, 367; being, 9–10; elemental and, 104; frame as plastic essence, 126, 138; human nature as, 67–68; ontology, 86; rights, 303–304, 306; sex, gender and, 103, 104–108, 139*n*1; sexed being and, 36*n*1; sexual and, 12*n*4; sexual difference and, 230; temporality, 103, 349; universal, 68–69, 111

sexuate body, 4, 12*n*2; annihilation of, 299, 307; with entry into presence, 138; feminine subjectivity and, 127; Irigaray and, 27; language and, 106–107; with matter and form, 107; subjectivity and, 6, 38*n*36

sexuate difference: bodies of water and, 82, 87–89; as gestational, 91; human beings and, 3; interval of, 313–314, 317; Irigaray and, 3, 315; as ontological difference, 86, 258, 263, 265–266, 270, 274*n*41; ontology of, 79, 81–82; politics and, 97*n*15; sexual difference and, 3, 120*n*1, 220

sexuate difference, in Black Atlantic: anti-Blackness and, 254, 255–259; condition of mother, 259, 267; feminine sexual difference and, 254; placental economies of fugitive resistance and, 258, 259, 267–270; with race and gender, 261–262; with sex/gender as racialized forgetting, 259–266, 276*n*75, 285; sexual difference and, 255–259, 263, 265, 273*n*24, 274*n*41; slavery and myth of mother, 253, 257, 269

sexuate differentiation, 111, 179, 304–305

sexuate identity, 5, 6, 38*n*36, 84, 208*n*12; Antigone and, 303; body and, 4; Irigaray and, 106, 118, 190; law and, 297–298, 306; ontology and, 107

INDEX

sexuate jurisprudence, law and, 294, 303–307
sexuate negativity, two forms of, 18–24
sexuate subjectivity, 89, 95, 103, 107, 138, 211, 223; difference and, 10; masculine, 11; nature/culture and, 86; sexual violence and, 297. *See also* feminine sexuate subjectivity
sexuation, 4, 29, 131–134, 211
sexuation, as frame for human becoming: with birth and breath, 132; essentialism, Irigaray and, 125, 128–131; feminist perspectives, 124–128, 135; Malabou, plasticity and violence of antiessentialism, 126, 134–138; originary structure and, 125, 126, 140n9; plastic essence and, 126, 138; style and, 131; Western culture and, 132, 133–134; in works of Irigaray, 131–134
sexué, with plants and animals, 96n3
Sharing the Fire (Irigaray), 39, 41, 125, 406, 426n196; desire in, 53, 353n20; evolution in, 132; lips in, 174; philosophy in, 47–48
Sharing the World (Irigaray), 37n17, 39–41, 45, 47, 49, 51, 53, 56n10
Sharpe, Christina, 258, 268, 274n36
sight, metaphysics with touch over, 51, 52
silence: Blackness with invisibility and, 256; double, 261, 262; hearing the other by cultivating, 205; imposed on women, 364–365
Sims, James, 262, 264
sizeism, 111, 117
slave code (1662), 259
slavery: anti-Blackness and, 159; Black women in, 262, 263, 267; bondage dialectic and, 253; with children as property, 257, 283; corporeal plasticity and, 161; with erasure of kinship and maternal lines, 283; with fugitive resistance, 254–255, 258, 259, 267–270; *Gregson v. Gilbert*, 420n18; kinship with colonialism and, 283; medical experiments, 262, 263, 264; Middle Passage, 258, 283; myth of mother, 253, 257, 269; power with racism and,

284–285; as theft of body, 272n3; transatlantic slave trade, 159, 253–255, 261, 270, 272n3, 284; unkinning of, 283, 285
Snorton, C. Riley, 262–263, 264, 265, 274n36
social construction, 106, 121n11, 146, 149, 241
social constructionism, 156, 167n44, 238
social constructivism, 4, 38n38, 227, 230, 249n6
Socrates, 48, 61, 62, 342
Söderbäck, Fanny, 123n40
somatophobia (flesh loathing), 105, 116
sons, fathers and, 198–199, 284
Sophocles, 303
space, absolute knowing and, 43. *See also* time and space
Spade, Paul, 61
species, gender and, 110
speculum: as elliptical lens, 335, 336; as medical instrument, 335–336; as military weapon, 339–340, 353n16, 354n24; *miroir ardent*, 335, 337–339, 342, 345, 353n16, 353n22, 354n24, 406. *See also* mirrors
Speculum of the Other Woman (Irigaray), 11, 20, 39, 72, 139n1, 351n3, 406; anality in, 197; "Any Theory of the Subject . . ." in, 344; "The Blind Spot of an Old Dream of Symmetry" in, 333, 353n11; "The Female Gender" in, 347–348; lips in, 174, 337; "*La Mystérique*" in, 338, 342–344, 347, 353n18, 366–367, 377; narrative in, 333–334; ontological indebtedness and rereading, 358–362; "Plato's *Hystera*" in, 333, 342, 343; reversing reversals and debt beyond, 362–368; "Speculum" essays in, 333–334, 336–338; theory of humors, 274n30; "Volume Without Contours" in, 182–184, 193n11, 193n14, 217, 344; Western philosophy, indebtedness and, 356–357
Spelman, Elizabeth, 77n28
sperm, 198, 209n42, 359, 361

Spillers, Hortense, 269, 405; kinship with blood in Irigaray and, 280–285, 286; with plasticity and sexual difference, 158–159; sex/gender as racialized forgetting and, 262–263, 264; with sexuate difference and anti-Blackness, 256, 258–259; slavery and, 283; on slavery as theft of body, 272n3

spirit: breath and body with exchange of, 205; cognition and, 40; as language, 55n5; listening to story with, 318–321; nature as, 44; *Phenomenology of Spirit*, 39, 40–41, 43; self-conscious, 41; in time, 42

state violence, 278, 288

Stephano, Oli, 238, 239–241

Stockton, Kathryn Bond, 372

Stoic onto-ethics, 229, 245–248

Stone, Alison, 30, 37n33, 98n26, 128–130, 137, 162; negativity and, 167n44; on sexual difference, 149; on women and nature/culture, 112–113, 122n32

story: narrative and, 346; "story about feeling," 314–316, 318, 328n15

Story About Feeling (Neidjie), 314–316, 318, 328n15

style, sexuation and, 131

subjectivity: Irigaray on, 56n10; Lacan on, 187–188; language of law and, 296; masculine, 7, 10, 185, 187, 189–190, 196, 201, 203, 207n7; relationships and, 279; reproduction and, 173; sexuate body and, 6, 38n36; transcendental, 193n8, 317; "the/a woman" and human, 186–187. *See also* feminine sexuate subjectivity; feminine subjectivity; sexuate subjectivity

subject-subject relations, women and, 4, 208n12

Supiot, Alain, 306–307

surgery, with chemical intervention, 233, 235, 236, 237, 245, 249n12

Symposium (Plato), 48

tactility: feminine sexuate subjectivity with lips and, 174, 180–186; of fluids, 219; lippedness and, 180; place and, 222. *See also* touch

Taylor, Keith, 318

technicity, 11, 298–299, 303, 305, 307

technology: ontological negativity and, 36n13; panoptical, 389; sexual difference and, 21, 23, 28, 36n13

temporality, 51, 258, 313, 342, 400, 403; Antigone and, 305; Bergson on, 214; with doubled sense of time, 117; everyday and feminine, 349; of experience, 34; interruptive, 349; of nature, 348; with nature/culture, 103; paradox and analysis of, 104, 113; with "renewal" and "return," 114; Ricoeur, Heidegger and, 347; sexual difference and, 118, 334, 345; sexuate, 103, 349; with story and narrative, 346

Teresa of Avila, 352n6, 354n30, 379, 386, 389–391, 402–403

testicularity, 202, 209n38

texts, plasticity and, 170n96

theory fatigue, 143, 148

"This Essentialism Which Is Not One" (Schor), 83–84

This Sex Which Is Not One (Irigaray), 106, 184–185, 192nn2–3, 333–334, 336–337, 351n3

Thomas, Calvin, 199–200, 201

Through Vegetal Being (Irigaray), 125, 132, 140n5, 324

TIGNC (transgender, intersex, and gender-nonconforming) people, 179, 191, 238–239

Timaeus (Plato), 339

time: absolute knowing as outside, 42–43; consciousness and, 39; cyclical, 113–114; doubled sense of, 117; Hegel and, 39, 43, 44; historicity and, 123n40; linear, 113; nature with culture and, 112–118; place and, 316; spirit in, 42. *See also* temporality

Time and Narrative (Ricoeur), 346

time and space, 19, 36n7, 113, 348, 405, 408; absolute knowing with, 40, 47; Hegel with, 36n5; infinite becoming and rethinking, 40–47, 55n4; with

INDEX

maternal touch, 52; metaphysics and, 55*n*4; nonhuman animals with, 324; sexual difference and, 20, 25; with transcendence and relation with other, 39–40, 47, 108

To Be Born (Irigaray), 20, 124, 125, 132–133, 323

To Be Two (*Essere Due*) (Irigaray), 59

tokos (offspring, interest), 356, 357

Tomkins, Silvan, 166*n*27

touch: feminine sexuate subjectivity with tactility and lips, 174, 180–186; maternal, 52; metaphysics with sight over, 51, 52; "Perhaps Cultivating Touch Can Still Save Us," 204; self-, 154, 157, 181, 184, 188–190, 212–213, 217–219, 222; self-affection and, 185; self-recognition with, 187–188; self-sensing and, 181, 184; sexuality, place and, 215; sexual morphology and, 181

trans: affirming, 242; becoming, 327*n*8; being, 228, 242, 243, 247; critiques, 227, 234; embodiment, 122*n*22, 225*n*3, 241; exceptionalism, 237; feminism, 327*n*8; identification, 237, 240–241; "Irreducibility and (Trans) Sexual Difference," 239–240; narratives, 233; studies scholars, 229. *See also* transgender people

transatlantic slave trade, 159, 253–255, 261, 270, 272*n*3, 284

transcendence: absolute knowing and, 50; counterconcept of, 40; feminine, 358, 365–366; horizontal, 111, 196, 304–305; Irigaray on Hegel and, 57*n*30; lateral, 46–47, 49–50; men with partial, 45; quasi-transcendental, 113; with time and space and relation with other, 39–40, 47, 108; vertical, 46, 48

transcendental subjectivity, 193*n*8, 317

transfiguration, philosophy as art of, 245–246

transgender people, 28, 223, 226*n*38, 313; reproductive justice and, 236; TIGNC, 179, 191, 238–239; trans, 122*n*22, 225*n*3, 227–229, 233–234, 237, 239–243, 247, 327*n*8

transphobia, 117, 248; Grosz with, 232–235, 237–238, 242; Irigaray with, 232, 237, 242, 327*n*8, 354*n*35; sexual difference and, 228–230, 232–238, 240, 243

transsexuality, 168*n*56, 233–237, 246. *See also* onto-ethics, of transsexual difference

trauma: intergenerational, 279; of "second rape" by criminal justice system, 294–295, 298

Treachery of Images, The, 373, 383

trees, 320, 321, 324–326

trial transcripts, in England and Wales, 309*n*7

Trier, Lars von, 404

truth, 45, 53, 54, 297

Truth, Sojourner, 261

two, the: human nature as, 66–67; sexual difference, gender and, 59, 60, 66–75

umbilical cord, male imaginary and, 202

UN Convention on the Rights of the Child, 285–286

unfreedom, reproductive, 257

ungendered, 262, 263, 283, 405, 406

United Kingdom, 294, 309*n*3, 309*n*7

United States (U.S.): Black health in, 160; Black Lives Matter movement, 120*n*4; child rights in, 285–286; forced removal of Native American children, 278, 286, 291*n*23; illegal immigration, 278; parental rights, 282

universality, 30, 61, 151, 256, 259; gender and, 69, 75; sexual difference and, 46, 57*n*19, 59–60, 69, 73; Western metaphysics and, 66, 67

universals: defined, 60–61, 65–66, 74–75; gendered identity and, 70; incomplete, 71; instantiation and, 63; *katholou* and, 347; medieval philosophy and, 60, 61; nominalism and, 76*n*6; Plato, realism and, 76*n*7; Scotus and, 61; sexual difference and

universals: defined (*continued*)
problem of, 59–75; sexuate, 68–69, 111; of white men as human species, 260
University of Paris, 352*n*5
unkinning, 283–284, 285
upward motion (*anabasis*), 338, 348
uranium mines, on Aboriginal lands, 318, 319, 330*n*41
U.S. *See* United States

Vergès, Françoise, 255, 257
vertical transcendence, 46, 48
Vibrant Matter (Bennett), 156
violence: abuse, 280, 291*n*23; anti-Blackness and, 267; of antiessentialism, Malabou and plasticity, 126, 134–138; of family separation, 278; with force of law, 293–297, 302; of human medical experiments, 262, 263, 264; against Indigenous peoples, 260, 278; institutionalized, 279; kinship, 282–283, 285–288; patriarchal, 279; racialized harassment and, 120*n*4; of settler colonialism, 259–260, 316; state, 278, 288; systemic, 109; against TIGNC people, 238–239; truth and, 297; women and, 124, 136, 137. *See also* sexual violence; slavery
Virno, Paolo, 65, 66, 74
viruses, xi*n*1, 157, 231
Volatile Bodies (Grosz), 233–234, 235
"Volume Without Contours" ("Volume-Fluidity" or "*L'incontournable volume*") (Irigaray), 182–184, 193*n*11, 193*n*14, 217, 344
vulva, 154, 168*n*61, 186, 336, 343

Waldby, Catherine, 200, 201
Warren, Calvin, 147, 157, 158, 159, 268
Warrington, Ronnie, 304
Way of Love, The (Irigaray), 110
Wayward Lives (Hartman), 253–254, 255
Weinstein, Jami, 231, 237–238, 239, 249*n*8
welfare system, children, 278, 288
Western culture, 35, 84, 131–134, 141*n*52, 312, 315, 404

Western metaphysics, 59, 60, 69, 307, 313, 316; masculinity and, 72; pathology of, 293; as phallocentric, 312; technicity and, 298–299; universality and, 66, 67
Western philosophy, 66, 112, 279; indebtedness and, 356–357, 362–363; Irigaray and, 117, 124, 125, 140*n*5, 183, 312–314; phallocentrism and, 124; sameness with, 103; women and, 358, 359
Weston, Kath, 280
white children, removal of, 291*n*23
White gaze, 254, 256
white masculine Being, 120*n*4
white men, 121*n*10, 260, 283, 285
whiteness, 11, 158–159, 161, 256, 260–262
Whiteness, as "unraced" sign of human, 260–261
white supremacy, 57*n*24, 279, 284
white women, 121*n*10, 140*n*12, 261
Whitford, Margaret, 5, 121*n*10, 193*n*11, 203, 207*n*1, 317; on Irigaray, 335; on men and women, 195–196; radical materialism and, 82, 83, 84, 86
William of Ockham, 77*n*17
Williams, Linda, 336
Wilson, Elizabeth, 144–145
Witches' Sabbath, 402
Wolfe, Esther, 234, 249*n*12
Wolfe, Patrick, 316
"woman, the/a": fluids and, 219–220; human subjectivity and, 186–187; Irigaray and, 211–220; as model of becoming, 211–212, 214, 219–220; qualitative multiplicity and, 213, 214, 220; self-identity and, 184, 217; self-touching, 218
womb, 188, 202, 343, 347, 363; bodies of water and, 87, 90–91; as cave, 367; gestation and, 90; *hystera*, 338, 405; reproduction of exploitation of, 257
women: "Ain't I a Woman?," 261; Black, 158, 254–255, 259, 261–263, 267–269, 275*n*47; bodies of nonwhite, 121*n*10, 283, 285; category of, 127–128; of

color, 121n10, 255, 257, 261, 283, 285; definition, 70–71; as "ethically good," 166n24; exploitation of wombs of, 257; feminine generic and, 71–72; genealogy of, 111; Hegel with, 55n2; heterogeneity of, 109; with identity claimed and deconstructed, 261; *Inessential Woman*, 77n28; liberation of, 70–71, 109; men and, 114, 124, 150, 157, 195–196, 233, 313, 363–365; as mirrors, 336; nature/culture and, 112–113, 122n32, 138; as not-One, 217; as "ontological amputation," 124, 137; patriarchy and identity of, 126, 137; place and, 217; *Reconstructing Womanhood*, 274n36; self-affection and, 4; silence imposed on, 364–365; as social construction, 106; subject-subject relations and, 4, 208n12; violence and, 124, 136, 137; Western philosophy and, 358, 359; white, 121n10, 140n12, 261. *See also* mothers; *Speculum of the Other Woman*

"Women, the sacred and money" (Irigaray), 371n54

words, rationality (*logos*), 106

writers, place thinking and, 317–318

writing, feminine, 144, 176, 352n6, 365

Wynter, Sylvia, 260–261, 270

Yoga Sutras (Patanjali), 324

yogic practice, 132, 140n5

Ziarek, Ewa, 149, 151–153, 162, 167n40, 167n44, 167nn40–41

GPSR Authorized Representative: Easy Access System Europe, Mustamäe tee
50, 10621 Tallinn, Estonia, gpsr.requests@easproject.com

www.ingramcontent.com/pod-product-compliance
Lightning Source LLC
Chambersburg PA
CBHW031228290426
44109CB00012B/197